Bridges to Understanding

Other Scarecrow Press Books Sponsored by the United States Board on Books for Young People

Children's Books from Other Countries, edited by Carl M. Thomlinson, 1998

The World through Children's Books, edited by Susan Stan, 2002

Crossing Boundaries with Children's Books, edited by Doris Gebel, 2006

Bridges to Understanding

Envisioning the World through Children's Books

Edited by
Linda M. Pavonetti

THE SCARECROW PRESS, INC.
Lanham • Toronto • Plymouth, UK
2011

Published by Scarecrow Press, Inc.
A wholly owned subsidary of The Rowman & Littlefield Publishing Group, Inc.
4501 Forbes Boulevard, Suite 200, Lanham, Maryland 20706
http://www.scarecrowpress.com

Estover Road, Plymouth PL6 7PY, United Kingdom

Illustrations from Clausen, G., et al. (1885). *Children of All Nations: Their Homes, Their Schools, Their Playgrounds.* New York: Cassell.

British Library Cataloguing in Publication Information Available

Library of Congress Cataloging-in-Publication Data

Bridges to understanding : envisioning the world through children's books / edited by Linda M. Pavonetti.
   p. cm.
  Includes bibliographical references and index.
  ISBN 978-0-8108-8106-8 (pbk. : alk. paper) — ISBN 978-0-8108-8107-5 (ebook)
  1. Children's literature—History and criticism. 2. Children's literature—Appreciation. 3. Children—Books and reading. I. Pavonetti, Linda M.
  PN1009.A1B766 2011
  809'.89282—dc22
                                    2011011715

Printed in the United States of America

Contents

Preface

I was recently asked how I became interested in international books. That took me aback. "It was the art and Uncle Bill," I finally responded.

My background is unmitigated middle America. My father's family came from Germany and my mother's from Ireland, all arriving in the United States at least a century before I was born. By that time, the relatives had lost all of their foreignness in the "great" melting pot of early twentieth-century American society.

But Uncle Bill was different. He joined the army and reenlisted to serve in Korea. He sent me a kimono when he lived in Japan, a music box from Germany, and he called me on my birthday—from a ship crossing the international dateline somewhere on the Pacific Ocean. He vacationed in Italy and Ireland (he was from that side of the family) and played golf in Korea and Japan. He was unique—and he made me the envy of my midwestern friends. I studied the globe more carefully because of him. I learned about islands and nations that I wanted to visit some day. Uncle Bill opened the door to the world for me.

The art came later as I read and studied and lived my life. It was gradual: I recall a field trip with my first graders to the Houston Art Museum. I allowed the docent to dismissively explain about "Seurat's dots." After she left us, I urged the children to move close to the painting—then slowly walk backward to observe what happened. They were fascinated. Gradually, this revelation translated into my obsession with illustrated literature for children.

A third strand is entwined in this mixture: the United States Board on Books for Young People. Because of USBBY, my appreciation for the art of international children's books suffused my teaching. Jella Lepman, founder of the International Board on Books for Young People (IBBY), worked to heal the damage from Hitler's book-burning and censorship policies in post–World War II Germany. In her autobiography, *A Bridge of Children's Books* (1964/2002), Lepman wrote, "If one is to believe in peaceful coexistence, the first messengers of that peace will be these children's books" (34). When Lepman requested books for the first International Exhibition of Children's Books, she noted that picture books "help overcome the language barrier" and that "pictures will speak an international language and cheer children everywhere" (36).

This book confronts a similar challenge: to introduce books from around the world that will act as messengers of peace to twenty-first-century readers. We hope that through picture books, poetry, informational texts, and longer novels—fantasies and fictions both historical and contemporary—English-speaking librarians, teachers, and parents will explore recent international books with young people in their communities. Perhaps in this way, children will learn that different need not be alien and foreign need not exclude friendship.

Reference

Lepman, Jella. *A Bridge of Children's Books: The Inspiring Autobiography of a Remarkable Woman.* Trans. by Edith McCormick. Dublin: O'Brien Press in association with IBBY Ireland and USBBY, 1964/2002. Originally published as *Die Kinderbuchbrücke* in German by S. Fischer Verlag in 1964.

Acknowledgments

This book began in the fall of 2003 at the IBBY Regional Conference at Chautauqua, New York. Sitting on the porch of the Athenaeum Hotel, Susan Stan encouraged me to apply for a fellowship at the International Youth Library in Munich. She had just returned from there, and her anecdotes were intriguing. I wrote a research proposal and filled out an application.

That weekend also introduced me to this book. Doris Gebel was in the process of editing the third edition, and she needed reviewers. I volunteered.

I will forever be grateful to these two scholars of international children's literature. I have learned so much through them and from them.

Another good friend was at Chautauqua that weekend, Ashley Bryan. He went on to be the United States' nominee for the Hans Christian Andersen Illustrator Award in 2006 and generously agreed to create the cover for this volume. Ashley Bryan is a person who walks the walk, softly and humbly. He has done a multitude of good works in Kiboya, Kenya, by providing support for a permanent library, trees, and water. "Ashley . . . gave the money for a library to be built at Kiboya. This is the first stone building, a large, lovely, light-filled building, at a school basically made of sticks" ("Traveling Companions," ¶21). Thank you, Ashley, for the beauty you have brought into so many lives.

To the welcoming staff at the Internationale Jugendbibliothek (IJB)—Barbara Scharioth, who was director in 2005; Petra Woersching, chef extraordinaire, tour expeditor, and "mother hen" to all the stipendiaten; Jochen Weber, linguist and friend—thank you for making so much of this possible. The other stipi and I shared literature and lunches, castles, Oktoberfest, and the Frankfurt Book Fair with you. Mehdi Hedjvani (Tehran, Iran), Mónica Domínguez Pérez (Santiago de Compostela and now Nigeria), André Moura (Rio de Janeiro), Justyna Deszcz-Tryhubczak (Wroclaw, Poland), and many more friends have enriched my life and understanding of the world and children's literature because of our work at the IJB. Danke!

To the publishers who so generously provided review copies—mere words cannot convey my gratitude. Thank you!

I send a giant hug to everyone at Oakland University who made this monumental project possible: Sigrid and Paula, the ERL staff, Mary Otto and Jim C. Finally, to the doctoral students who opened boxes, tagged, shelved, scanned and categorized books, proofed URLs, and even gave up space in their offices to shelve books—thanks for all you have done to keep this book moving forward.

Since that weekend at Chautauqua, I have profited from the opportunities afforded to me by my association with USBBY and now IBBY. I hope that these experiences will be passed on to you through this book.

One note of explanation is in order: The illustrations at the beginning of each bibliographic chapter are taken from a book published in 1885 entitled *Children of All Nations: Their Homes, Their Schools, Their Playgrounds*. It was published as part of the *Home Chat Series*, with original illustrations by numerous artists. At best, these drawings are quaint. Most of them I found quite offensive—and those were not included. However, as a student of children's literature through the ages, I find the shifts in knowledge, understanding, and, in this case, *depiction* of the peoples of the world informative. The colleagues who wrote reviews for this book read more than seven hundred books from ninety-six countries and territories and would agree that what we read in no way resembled what this *one* book from the distant past portrays. These illustrations demonstrate how American illustrators represented the world for children at the end of the nineteenth century. I believe the world of international children's books has progressed exponentially since 1885, and I hope that the books we have reviewed will continue to bring readers to a better understanding of their world and the other young people who inhabit it.

References

Clausen, G., N. De Dmitrieff, C. Gregory, W. Hatherell, W. C. Horsley, H. Johnson et al., illus. *Children of All Nations: Their Homes, Their Schools, Their Playgrounds*. London: Cassell, 1885.

"Traveling Companions." Notes on a presentation by Kemie Nix, Charity Mwangi, and Ashley Bryan in Kenya (circa 2004). Introduction by Ann Lazim, British IBBY. Downloaded on February 2, 2011, from www.sacbf.org.za/2004%20papers/Ashley%20Bryan%20%20Kemie%20Nix%20%20Charity%20Mwangi.rtf.

PART I

INTERNATIONAL CHILDREN'S LITERATURE

CHAPTER ONE

Introduction: Where Books Begin

Andrea Cheng

I first learned about the International Board on Books for Young People (IBBY) when I spoke in Budapest at an International Reading Association (IRA) World Congress. I was seated with a Hungarian children's book author, and we spoke a kind of Hungarian-English pidgin. It turned out, as we got to talking, that we were the same age and there were many similarities in our backgrounds, except that my parents left Hungary and his didn't. He wrote children's books in Hungarian, and I wrote children's books in English.

He said to me, "You don't know how lucky you are because you could be like me, writing in Hungarian."

Somewhat defensively, I said, "Well, what's wrong with that? It's a cool language. I speak Hungarian and I enjoy speaking Hungarian."

He replied, "Oh, yeah, it's a cool language, but think about it as a children's book author. The number of people who read Hungarian is very small."

He gave me one of his books that day, and I read it in Hungarian. It was a fantastic children's book. I thought, "How can I get this book published . . . translated and published in the United States?" I thought it was a really, really good book. My Hungarian is not good enough to translate, and even though I have tried, I'm not a professional translator. I found someone who translated the first few chapters, and I sent them to my editor.

"Isn't this great?" I said. "This guy's just amazing."

She read it and responded, "I don't know why you think that way. I don't see what you like about this book."

She didn't *get* it. One huge problem to overcome in translation is word play. The numerous puns and other forms of word play were one feature of this Hungarian book that just didn't come through in translation. Unfortunately, I could never get this book published in English.

So my new friend remained a Hungarian author. As far as I know, none of his books were translated and published in other languages to any great extent. Certainly not in English.

I recently heard that my friend, Békés Pál, has died. He was a long-time member of IBBY Hungary, serving as its president and attending IBBY World Congresses, including 2005 in Macau (where he was photographed with the USBBY delegation) and 2009 in Copenhagen.

I was crushed. I felt like I failed him because, when he gave me that book, it was almost as if he was saying, "See if you can do something. We're almost the same—except you're American and I'm Hungarian."

Never, ever, had I thought, "I write in English. Isn't that amazingly lucky?" Now, when I write books that take place in Hungary, I think in Hungarian and I've sometimes had trouble writing things in English, especially dialogue. If the people in the scene are speaking Hungarian and I write it in English, it seems weird. When I write stories that take place in China—because I do speak some Chinese besides Hungarian—I experience this unsettled feeling of "How should I write it?"

I have another problem when I'm writing books that are set in other countries. I think of my mother-in-law, who speaks English with a Chinese accent. She often omits articles such as *a*, *an*, or *the*, and she sometimes confuses verb tense. But she speaks perfect Chinese. So if I'm writing a conversation that's supposed to be in Chinese but I'm writing it in English, I think I should write it in perfect English because her Chinese is perfect. Why would I make it not perfect? But in order to give the flavor of how she speaks, I would have to write it differently.

These are some of the conflicts that come with writing about other cultures. If I write a conversation that's spoken in Hungarian, the word order would be different from what it is in English. But if I write it in an ungrammatical *English* word order, it seems as if the characters are uneducated and don't speak properly. But of course they speak *Hungarian* well! I run into these problems frequently in my writing because I draw heavily from my multilinguistic background.

What I'd like to try to communicate here is how my background comes through in my work. So even though I was not born in Hungary, that culture comes through in my books. And even though I am not Chinese, through my experiences living and sharing with my husband's family, that culture comes through in my books. And it is through exposure to other cultures—often through reading and other artistic activities—that we and our students (or patrons) learn curiosity, tolerance, and eventually understanding of other customs, traditions, religions, races, and lifestyles.

What are the roots of my writing, my philosophy of life?

My parents were refugees who, after World War II, emigrated from Budapest to Switzerland to Australia, where they lived for a number of years before coming to America. My father always valued writing and music and visual arts.

By far the biggest influence on my writing is my own childhood. I went to the neighborhood school, and I still live in that part of Cincinnati. Sometimes I think I wouldn't be able to write if I ever left the neighborhood where I grew up, where my mom and my sister live, and where my home is. I feel very, very lucky for the way I grew up—so diverse in so many ways. I lived in a predominantly African American neighborhood with African American dialect spoken on the street, Hungarian in the house, and so-called proper English at school. So I got used to a lot of ways of talking, and I became very facile—able to switch from one place to another without much trouble. I think that's really an asset in a person's life. You can't always be multilingual, but you can learn different ways of speaking, and everybody does, to some degree. I saw this in my own kids. They could switch, especially the youngest one, who can switch from English to Spanish to African American dialect. When we walk the streets of Boston where she lives, people often say "Hola" because they think she is from Guatemala.

How do these influences become my books? *Marika* (2002) is a Holocaust novel based on my mother's life from 1935 to 1945. My mother is a Holocaust survivor. Both my parents and my grandparents were. My mother's background, and consequently mine, always surprised people: a Jewish white kid in an African American neighborhood with a Christmas tree. I wrote *Marika* to explain that it's just my mom's life. My mother was raised Catholic, even though she was ethnically Jewish, in an effort to save her life.

I have a document that proves the papers my mother carried—the ones that stated she was Roman Catholic—were forged. And I have papers documenting my grandmother's release from Auschwitz. I remember touching the number that was on her arm and saying, "What is that?" She never told me. My mom would only say it was a tattoo, which I didn't understand. Eventually, I fit the pieces together to write *Marika*.

Marika was translated into Hungarian—another disconnect between writing for children in America and writing for children in Hungary.

When the book was released, my mother was mortified because they put her picture on the cover and classified it as nonfiction. It *is* based on my mom's life, but it's fictionalized because it's full of dialogue. The translator's note says that every word in the book is true even though she did not consult me to confirm this. The back of the book also surprised me. When my grandfather died in Budapest, my aunt had his photos, letters, and other memorabilia. When they published *Marika* in Hungarian, they asked my aunt for photos and she gave my grandfather's to them to look at, she thought, and they printed photos of my family in the back of the book. Even with all that, the translation from English to Hungarian is very good as far as I can tell.

Most of my writing depends on family history. *The Lace Dowry* (2005a) was my Hungarian aunt's story. Can today's young people understand cultures that continue customs like arranged marriages and dowries? Books provide an entrée, time to consider—to make sense of traditions so different from their own.

The girl in *The Shanghai Messenger* (2005b) travels to Shanghai by herself. My daughters didn't travel alone to Shanghai, but when I was eleven, I went to Budapest by myself. Think about 1968, behind the Iron Curtain. My parents put me on a plane, and I flew there by myself. The feelings that the girl has about going to Shanghai are my feelings that I had about going to Budapest, some thirty years earlier. My books are a pastiche of my life.

My husband, born and raised in St. Louis, doesn't speak Chinese. His parents were immigrants from China but they made a concerted effort not to teach him Chinese. In the early and mid-twentieth century everything was assimilate, assimilate, assimilate. Fit in. Being an Asian in suburban St. Louis, there was no way my husband and his sisters could ever blend in, but his parents thought their best chance would be if they were as Americanized as possible. They speak English perfectly, but so does *anyone* born here. As adults, they all are very sorry that they don't speak Chinese, and his sisters have all studied Chinese. Recently I realized how many gaps there are between my husband and his parents because he never spoke their first language. Can you imagine not being able to communicate with your parents in their first language? It means there must be things that were never communicated because the language barrier could not be completely overcome.

I was the one who wanted to go to China to meet my husband's extended family. He had never met any of his aunts and uncles and cousins. They were all in China. It was more difficult than I anticipated. My daughter got sick from eating food that was different. We experienced Shanghai's worst flood in 120 years. All the kids went out and played—in the standing water with fish heads and other refuse floating in it. Can you see this in your mind? What are the differences between this scene in Shanghai and the images of New Orleans after Katrina?

There was a good side to that flood, also. My husband's uncle came one day during the flood to insist that we move into his apartment. His apartment was two rooms. We were four people (my husband had returned to the States)—me and the three kids. I objected: we would crowd them terribly. He told me to look out the window. He asked his son-in-law who had a motorbike to help move us because they were worried about us. We lived in their rooms the rest of the time we were in Shanghai. How different is family from one side of the world to the other?

Many of the memories in *Shanghai Messenger* are from that time in Shanghai—the warmth we felt even though we didn't speak the same language. The amazing warmth and the way they took care of us—I'll always be grateful.

I have a picture of my husband, Jim, and me with our three kids. It's the most amazing thing: Nick lives in Beijing and speaks fluent Chinese; Ann, the youngest one, spent some time in Guatemala and is fluent in Spanish. Jane lives in London but will attend graduate school in Switzerland—in Lausanne, the same town where my parents lived, the same place where I worked. Jane is fluent in German and French. Her boyfriend is German. I never would have thought, with my family's background, that my daughter would speak German, that my daughter might love a German man. Another piece of the sometimes baffling cultural puzzle that I piece together in my books.

I earned a master's degree in teaching English as a Second Language because I love languages and linguistics. I studied Chinese and French. I lived in a French-speaking country for several years and became fluent in French. Now I am studying Spanish. Knowing a country's language provides a peephole into another culture.

The librarian and the instructional assistant at my children's school were amazing: they had such sensitivity for stories. My children went to the Academy of World Languages, an inner-city school that was predominantly African American but also offered ESL, Russian, Chinese, Arabic, and Japanese. All the immigrant children from the area attended. The librarian and the assistant realized that my stories resonated with those kids. They did not understand why they couldn't find stories like the ones I was writing—long before I was ever published—in the library. Why did these children like my stories more than the other books in the library?

Grandfather Counts (2000) is based on real people. My daughter, my father-in-law; it's a book about communication. My father-in-law didn't speak English very well, and my kids didn't speak Chinese. There was a barrier to communication, but somehow they managed. Many children understand that there are different ways to interact. When I talk to kids, I ask them, "If you couldn't talk to your grandfather because you didn't share the same language, what would you do? How would you communicate?" And they always respond, "I'd write." They don't understand that if they don't *speak* English, they probably couldn't read it. But it's often a first response.

Goldfish and Chrysanthemums (2004) is based on a story my mother-in-law told me. My mother-in-law was really sad one day because she found out from her brother that her grandfather's house in Suzhou was being torn down. In China there's a huge building boom, so many of the old houses are being torn down. It is difficult for children to understand why someone who is so old would be sad about losing her childhood home. But as she told us about her house in Suzhou I could visualize the effect this story could have on young readers. Another step in understanding culture and heritage.

Everybody in my family, my husband's family in China, has been an influence on me and on my worldview.

I'm hoping that, as you read and share the books in this volume, you will find similarities in your own background or in your students' experiences that might help you to connect to the universal in books that are translated or imported from other countries.

One more thing: I recently learned that one of my books, *Where the Steps Were* (2008), is on the 2009 White Ravens List.

This introduction is for all those authors whose books have not been translated and for all those young people who have never explored other cultures through translated books.

References

Cheng, Andrea. *Goldfish and Chrysanthemums*. Illus. by Michelle Chang. New York: Lee & Low Books, 2004.

Cheng, Andrea. *Grandfather Counts*. Illus. by Ange Zhang. New York: Lee & Low Books, 2000.

Cheng, Andrea. *The Lace Dowry*. Asheville, NC: Front Street, 2005a.

Cheng, Andrea. *Marika*. Asheville, NC: Front Street, 2002.

Cheng, Andrea. *Shanghai Messenger*. Illus. by Ed Young. New York: Lee & Low Books, 2005b.

Cheng, Andrea. *Where the Steps Were*. Honesdale, PA: Wordsong, 2008.

Andrea Cheng is an author, poet, teacher, and accomplished illustrator. Her woodblock prints adorn one of her books of poetry, *Where the Steps Were* (Wordsong, 2008). Her latest book *Where Do You Stay?*—number 17—was published by Boyds Mills Press (2011).

CHAPTER TWO

Reading Globally: The Reader's Responsibility in Literary Transactions

Barbara A. Lehman

One of IBBY's primary goals has always been to promote global diversity and tolerance through children's books. However, in literary transactions, readers also have a major responsibility to *read globally*, which my colleagues and I describe in our work elsewhere (Lehman, Freeman, and Scharer 2010). This chapter addresses two aspects of that term. One meaning for reading globally is to read *widely*—that is, to read books from outside our own cultural contexts, indeed from around the whole world. A second way of reading globally is to read *critically*—that is, to become informed readers who assess the authenticity of global books.

In the first case—that is, reading widely—I have found in my work with U.S. teachers and students that reading globally often is facilitated by pairing books from abroad with American texts that have similar themes, characters, or plots. These kinds of pairs help readers to see connections more easily between the familiar and the foreign. Based upon my experience as an American who has lived and researched children's literature in South Africa, I will demonstrate this type of reading globally through a pair of picture books—*The Day Gogo Went to Vote,* by Elinor Batezat Sisulu (1996) from South Africa, and *Papa's Mark,* by Gwendolyn Battle-Lavert (2003) from the United States.

The primary theme of these two stories concerns first voting experiences for previously disenfranchised groups of people. In *Gogo,* young Thembi's one-hundred-year-old great-grandmother is determined to vote in the first democratic election in South Africa in 1994 in spite of her family's doubts about Gogo's physical stamina to wait in a long line at the polls. Thembi proudly accompanies Gogo to the polling booth in a rich neighbor's fancy car and watches Gogo show her identity book, have her hand swabbed with ultraviolet ink, and cast her secret ballot for Nelson Mandela. As the oldest voter in the township, Gogo has her picture taken with Thembi for the newspaper, and the whole extended family later celebrates the election at home with feasting, singing, and dancing. Helpfully for non–South African readers, unfamiliar terms are explained in a glossary and pronunciation guide.

Papa's Mark, which is set in a southern state after the end of the U.S. Civil War, portrays an African American community's excitement leading up to the first election day in which they will be permitted to vote. A boy named Simms is determined to teach his papa how to write his name so he will be able to sign his name properly to get his ballot. The "mark" in the title refers to the X that illiterate persons used as their signature. With daily practice, Papa's "chicken scratch" becomes legible, and he proudly leads a group of African American men to the courthouse to cast their votes. An author's note adds historical context regarding the rights of black people to vote in spite of southern whites' repeated attempts to disenfranchise them. Legal milestones during the century from 1870, when the Fifteenth Amendment to the U.S. Constitution guaranteed black men's right to vote, until 1965, when the landmark Voting Rights Act passed Congress, are described.

Both books also depict intergenerational relationships, as two children accompany and/or assist their elders with voting. Gogo insists, despite Thembi's parents' objections, that she needs Thembi's help at the polling place to hold her blue bag while Gogo votes. The experience makes a huge impression on Thembi, which her great-grandmother certainly intends. Gogo wants the child to witness Gogo's first—and possibly last—time to exercise the right for which black South Africans had struggled for so many years. Likewise, Simms, who attends school and writes signs urging black Americans to vote, wants to help his papa be spared the shame of only being able to mark an X for his name. When Papa at first resists Simms's offer to teach him how to write his name, Simms persists until Papa gets it right. Thus, both children are educated by their families in the significance of the vote to their hard-won freedom and equality and the importance of voting to a better future for them. Both children also feel part of the democratic process and make an important contribution to it. Thembi and Simms share personal and political commonalities, ones with which many other child readers may identify and empathize.

The second aspect of reading globally—that is, reading critically—involves becoming educated about the authenticity of books to the cultures they represent. This can be particularly problematic for readers who are outside those cultures. To demonstrate this type of reading globally, I present two novels with many parallels for older readers, *Song of Be,* by South African author Lesley Beake (1993), and *Julie of the Wolves,* by American writer Jean Craighead George (1972). These two books, which feature indigenous cultures and young female protagonists coming to terms with modern realities, offer many benefits for broadening readers' perspectives. Both books have received wide literary critical acclaim and have been translated into multiple languages in addition to English.

Song of Be is a novella set in Namibia at the time of its independence from South Africa. The protagonist, Be, is a Bushmen girl who has gone with her mother from their tribal home to live with her grandfather, who works on a white farmer's land. When they arrive at the farm, Be is befriended and educated by the boss's wife Min, but slowly Be loses her childhood innocence as she discovers secrets about the boss, his deeply troubled wife, and Be's own mother, Aia. As Be learns these things, she becomes very disillusioned—a classic coming-of-age theme, when the realization of parental faults dashes childhood images of perfection.

Another clear theme in this novel is the clash between indigenous cultures and dominant outside colonizers whose modernity threatens a traditional way of life. The current lives of people like the Bushmen have become degraded by the removal from their land to "locations" established by white settlers, by a lack of meaningful employment, and by alcohol abuse. Although this former way of life, in a sense, is dying and must change, we later learn that some Bushmen—far from becoming extinct, as in the popular perception voiced by both Min and a visiting journalist—were actively involved in the independence movement and politically and socially reinvented their place in the new country. Thus, as Be matures, she must come to terms with both positive and negative realities of life and decide what she wants for her future.

In comparison, *Julie of the Wolves* portrays how Julie/Miyax, a thirteen-year-old Alaskan native, flees an intolerable home and arranged marriage situation in Barrow on the North Slope and becomes lost on the tundra. She is saved by a wolf pack and, in the end, finds her father but must come to terms with his new life. This classic realistic novel also depicts the clash between a traditional way of life and modern civilization, as symbolized by her very name, Miyax/Julie. Her culture, like many other Native American cultures, has been degraded by Western civilization in ways similar to those that the Bushmen have suffered. In addition, Miyax, too, is disillusioned when she discovers that her idealized father, Kapugen, is implicated in the changes she so resists. He has married a gussack (a white woman), and in order to make a living, he has acquired a small airplane that he uses to carry sportsmen on hunts from the air, endangering the very wolves that had saved her life. A theme similar to the one in *Song of Be* is echoed in the last lines of the novel: "*That the hour of the wolf and the Eskimo is over* (italics in original). Julie pointed her boots toward Kapugen" (170), meaning that she decides to stay with her father. Julie's way of making peace with these realities seems to be resignation. However, this resolution, which is less hopeful than in *Song of Be*, is mitigated in the novel's sequels, *Julie* (1994) and *Julie's Wolf Pack* (1997). Julie becomes an activist for saving the wolves in the second book, and in the third novel, Kapu, the wolf pup in *Julie of the Wolves*, is the central character. Julie, now an adult, returns to study him and his wolf pack on the Alaskan tundra, thus demonstrating a more positive and proactive response by Julie about her future.

Both *Song of Be* and *Julie of the Wolves* present the thoughts and emotions of early adolescents who are emerging from the innocence of childhood into the disconcerting and sometimes even disillusioning realities that accompany maturity. In spite of their geographical separation, these girls share many of the same concerns. They also share significant social and political similarities that affect both their personal future and the fate of their cultures' ways of life. These broader issues can provide opportunities for students at this age to make comparisons between the two indigenous cultures depicted in the novels and with their own lives, wherever they live in the world. In the process, they may gain empathy from the broader perspectives afforded by reading them as a pair.

However, both books also have been criticized for their depictions (by outside writers) of the cultures represented, and it would be dishonest to ignore these critiques. Beginning with *Song of Be*, I learned from Lesley Beake's website (2010) about her work with an anthropologist, begun prior to Namibian independence, as founders of the Village Schools Project in Nyae Nyae, Namibia, the setting for *Song of Be*. Recently, she initiated a new project with the people of Nyae Nyae to develop a website, with the stated goal to provide

a virtual space for networking and exchange of information among contemporary Kalahari communities and individuals throughout Southern Africa. On it, the San and other indigenous Kalahari dwellers speak in their own voices to each other and to interested people outside their communities. (Kalahari Peoples Network 2010)

On this website, I learned more about Be's people, and a page on the site, called "Primary School," includes information particularly addressed to students. From this research, I can tell that Beake is a knowledgeable outsider dedicated to the culture about which she writes.

Similarly, Jean Craighead George's website (2010) tells me about her background in a family of naturalists; her dual science-literature bachelor's degree; her summer at the Naval Arctic Research Laboratory in Barrow, Alaska, among wolf researchers; her two sequels to this book; and the nearly one hundred books she has written, virtually all on environmental and nature topics. I am impressed with her credentials, and I believe both authors have credible expertise about the subjects of their books.

Still, I realize that both women are white and not true insiders of the cultures they portray in these books. Both have been questioned about their status and authority to write about the cultures, and George has been criticized for inaccuracies and stereotypes in her portrayal of the Iñupiat culture. For example, see Martha Stackhouse's (2006) review of the book on the Alaska Native Knowledge Network website. Critics also charge that George presents the culture as becoming extinct (similar to the perception of Bushmen). Both authors have defended the terminology they call the people. In *Julie's Wolf Pack*, George explains why she refers to Miyax's people as "Eskimos," a term sometimes viewed as inaccurate or demeaning. In an author's note, she writes, "Currently the name *Eskimo* is being replaced by *Inuit* to identify the circumpolar Eskimo people living in North America, Greenland, and Siberia." However, "The native people of Alaska's North Slope call themselves Eskimos or Iñupiat Eskimos" (unpaged). Likewise, Beake defends her use of "Bushmen," explaining in her author's note, "Much has been written about [the Ju/'hoan] people, who are sometimes called the San, but who prefer to be known as the Bushmen" (unpaged). At least both authors acknowledge the controversy and explain their rationales for the language they use, citing the native people's own preferences. Readers must balance the evidence in their own evaluation of these books.

In the end, as important as it is for authors to bear responsibility for the authenticity of what they write—particularly when they are not insiders to the cultures they are depicting—readers must educate themselves to be thoughtfully critical in responses to books, especially when those books are outside our own realm of experience and knowledge. Teachers and librarians who are committed to the ideals of IBBY will want to provide young readers with the kind of wide reading material that encircles the globe. At the same time, we should teach young people to read critically and become informed rather than to accept such texts unquestioningly. In the end, reading globally is as much the reader's responsibility in the literary transaction as it is the author's to strive for authenticity. The rewards and values of reading widely will be enhanced with reading critically.

References

Battle-Lavert, Gwendolyn. *Papa's Mark*. New York: Holiday House, 2003.

Beake, Lesley. *Song of Be*. New York: Puffin, 1993.

Beake, Lesley. "Lesley Beake" [online]. Accessed June 2010, from www.lesleybeake.co.za/.

George, Jean Craighead. *Julie of the Wolves*. New York: HarperCollins, 1972.

George, Jean Craighead. *Julie*. New York: HarperCollins, 1994.

George, Jean Craighead. *Julie's Wolf Pack*. New York: HarperCollins, 1997.

George, Jean Craighead. "Jean Craighead George" [online]. Accessed June 2010, from www.jeancraigheadgeorge.com.

Kalahari Peoples Network. "About the Site" [online]. Accessed June 2010, from www.kalaharipeoples.net/about.php.

Lehman, Barbara A., Evelyn B. Freeman, and Patricia L. Scharer. *Reading Globally, K–8: Connecting Students to the World through Literature*. Thousand Oaks, CA: Corwin, 2010.

Sisulu, Elinor Batezat. *The Day Gogo Went to Vote: South Africa, April 1994*. Boston: Little, Brown, 1996.

Stackhouse, Martha. "Honoring Alaska's Indigenous Literature" [online]. Alaska Native Knowledge Network. Accessed June 2010, from ankn.uaf.edu/IKS/HAIL/JulieWolves.html.

Barbara A. Lehman is a professor of teaching and learning at Ohio State University, where she teaches graduate courses in children's literature and literacy at the Mansfield Campus. Her scholarly interests focus on multicultural and global children's literature and child-centered literary criticism. She coedited *Teaching with Children's Books: Paths to Literature-Based Instruction* (National Council of Teachers of English [NCTE], 1995) and coauthored with Evelyn Freeman *Global Perspectives in Children's Literature* (Allyn & Bacon, 2001). Her third title, *Children's Literature and Learning: Literary Study across the Curriculum*, was published by Teachers College Press (2007). She has had articles published in *ChLA Quarterly*, *Children's Literature in Education*, and the *Journal of Children's Literature*, among others. She has coedited the *Journal of Children's Literature* (Children's Literature Assembly of NCTE) and *Bookbird: A Journal of International Children's Literature* for the International Board on Books for Young People. She has served on the USBBY board and was president in 2011. Dr. Lehman has chaired book- and author-award committees, such as the Hans Christian Andersen Award U.S. nominating committee, the USBBY's Astrid Lindgren Memorial Award nominating committee, and the International Reading Association's Notable Books for a Global Society Committee. She was a Fulbright Scholar in South Africa during 2004 to 2005 and the 2009 recipient of the Arbuthnot Award from the International Reading Association. This chapter is adapted from Dr. Lehman's latest book, *Reading Globally, K–8: Connecting Students to the World through Literature,* by Barbara A. Lehman, Evelyn B. Freeman, and Patricia L. Scharer (Corwin Press, 2010).

PART II

BIBLIOGRAPHY

About the Bibliography

International literature. What an amorphous term. Ask the next hundred people you meet to define it, and you will have a hundred different definitions, or at least different connotations. Carl Tomlinson, in his *Children's Books from Other Countries* (1998)—the first volume in this series—defined international literature as books published for children outside the United States and later published in the United States. Susan Stan's addition to the series, *The World through Children's Books* (2002), expanded the definition of international literature to include not only books published in other countries but also books published in the United States that are set in other lands. Doris Gebel, editor of the third volume, *Crossing Boundaries with Children's Books* (2006), explained why she adhered to the same definition. "For some countries listed here, the only books available were those written by American authors . . . In the same way, you will find books by international authors, setting their stories in countries other than their own" (21).

In the five years since *Crossing Boundaries with Children's Books* was published, the definition of *international literature* has morphed again, and this time it is because of business trends. Many of the small-to-medium-sized publishing houses have been bought by larger publishers and international conglomerates. The first impact has been to effectively decrease the number of children's publishers, but the second, and more germane to this discussion, has been to internationalize publishing.

Tomlinson points to the Harry Potter series as a bellwether that opened Americans' eyes to the international nature of literature. It is also true that the success of this series changed the face of publishing for children—worldwide. In 1997, Bloomsbury (London) published *Harry Potter and the Philosopher's Stone* (Rowling). The following summer, Arthur A. Levine issued an Americanized version—to much derision and consternation—called *Harry Potter and the Sorcerer's Stone* (Rowling 1998). Fairly rapidly, as *Publishers Weekly* notes, Harry reinvented the way books are published.

> Territorial rights used to mean something. Publishers released books in a country on their own terms, in their own time. But as American sales of the second Potter, *The Chamber of Secrets*, leeched away to Amazon's British site, which had the book first, publishers had to do something. And so a new concept was born: the global publication. Forget sovereignty; all English-language publishers now would agree on the best single date that provided the greatest good to the greatest number of houses. Today the global one-day laydown is standard for big books, from Bill Clinton on down. (Zeitchik 2005, 12)

Consequently, one of the changes in this volume is that a number of the books we have reviewed have been copublished or concurrently released in a number of countries.

The most important change from previous editions is the list of Outstanding International Books (OIB) that USBBY published for the first time in 2006. The popularity of this list has grown exponentially since the idea was first suggested early in the decade. We have included a listing of all the books, their country of publication, and suggested age groups at the end of chapter 11, "Children's Book Awards." We have also attempted to include reviews for every book on the five OIB lists in appropriate chapters. Bibliographic information and URLs for the *School Library Journal* articles about each of the five OIB lists conclude the chapter.

Bridges to Understanding: Envisioning the World through Children's Books includes books published from 2005 to 2010 that have been translated into English, published in English in other nations, or published in the United States but set in another country. Many of the books originally released in the United States have been written by authors or illustrated by artists who currently live in or have moved to the United States from other nations. We have sought out books that provide an insider's view of a culture whenever possible, especially when the books originated in the United States. In all cases, we have tried to add notes about the authors' or illustrators' country of origin or current residency.

Some reissued older books have been included, especially if the book is a classic or if the edition adds significantly to the book's readability. However, as a rule, these types of books were put aside for newly issued books. There are relatively few folktales included for the simple reason that there are enough variants and parodies published each year to create a separate book. Consequently, we have left those to other bibliographies.

Each bibliographic entry follows the same general format: author or editor, followed by translator, then title—capitalized and bolded. The illustrator's name is next, then the publisher and the date of publication. If the book was previously published, that information includes the original title if it varies from the American edition, the publisher, and the date of the original publication. Finally, the publishing data concludes with the thirteen- and ten-digit ISBN, the number of pages, approximate reading level, and the genre. Major awards conclude the critical commentary, followed by initials indicating who wrote the annotation. There are two final lines: information about the author or illustrator and awards received by the book, the author, or in some cases, the illustrator.

One of the most formidable challenges in editing a book like this is assigning each book to a country. Our choices included 1) the land or culture the book described, 2) the author's home country, 3) the country in which the book was originally published. To the extent possible, we followed the advice of the annotators and the direction set by previous editions and used the author's native country. When confronted by different origins—for the author, illustrator, or the publisher—or settings for the plot, we cross-referenced countries. *Wildwood Dancing* by Juliet Marillier is set in Hungary and Transylvania, but the author is a native New Zealander who lives in Australia. We listed it in Transylvania with reference to it in Hungary. In most cases, we have attempted to explain how the book is culturally relevant, which might help in those cases where multiple countries have been represented. It is important to understand, as Susan Stan (2002) so elegantly wrote, "National borders are arbitrary distinctions and . . . it is our cultures—customs, traditions, beliefs, behaviors—that distinguish communities of people from one another" (41).

In general, we have used the genre categories from the previous three volumes: novel (fiction), picture book, nonfiction, poetry, fantasy, and historical fiction. Ages are also noted, but we hope you realize that assigning an age category is always uncertain at best. We tried to take into consideration interest levels and maturity of the reader as well as ability. But you are the final judge of the suitability of any book for the reader standing in front of you. Please use our annotations only as a guide.

Following each country and at the end of each chapter, we have included information relevant to that part of the world. Details about the International Board on Books for Young People (IBBY) national sections are another constant here. IBBY's website and the national sections' websites are provided whenever possible. Additionally, national awards, book fairs, and other relevant details have been noted.

Bridges to Understanding: Envisioning the World through Children's Books is the fourth bibliography collaboratively published by Scarecrow Press and the United States Board on Books for Young People (USBBY). If we had realized that this would grow into a series when Carl Tomlinson published the first volume in 1998, we would have done at least one thing differently—given the series a name. I hope I have corrected that oversight with this volume; *Bridges to Understanding* is now the series name and the subtitle, *Envisioning the World through Children's Books*, is the actual title of this book. We hope you find this edition as useful for selecting literature for your library, classroom, home, or gift-giving as you have the previous three volumes. We hope to continue this series as long as there is a need for learning about other cultures.

Annotators

Carolyn Angus (ca)
George G. Stone Center for
   Children's Books, Claremont
   Graduate University
Claremont, CA

Margaret A. Chang (mac)
Massachusetts College of Liberal Arts
North Adams, MA

Jim Cipielewski (jfc)
Oakland University
Rochester, MI

Peg Ciszek (pwc)
Northbrook Public Library
Northbrook, IL

Susan Corapi (sc)
University of Arizona
Tucson, AZ

Hilary S. Crew (hc)
Kean University, retired
Union, NJ

Danielle L. DeFauw (dld)
Davison Community Schools
Davison, MI

Andrea Erickson (ae)
Prince George's County Memorial
   Library System
Laurel, MD

Bindy E. Fleischman (bef)
Harvard University Art Museums
Boston, MA

Evelyn B. Freeman (ebf)
Ohio State University, Mansfield
Mansfield, OH

Doris Gebel (*dlg*)
Northport-East Northport Public
   Library
Northport, NY

Nancy L. Hadaway (*nlh*)
University of Texas, Arlington
Arlington, TX

Sandra Imdieke (*si*)
Northern Michigan University
Marquette, MI

Kathleen T. Isaacs (*kti*)
Towson University
Towson, MD

Andrea Karlin (*ak*)
Lamar University
Beaumont, TX

Barbara A. Lehman (*bal*)
Ohio State University, Mansfield
Mansfield, OH

Miriam Martinez (*mm*)
University of Texas, San Antonio
San Antonio, TX

Janelle B. Mathis (*jm*)
University of North Texas
Denton, TX

Mary Lois Nicholls (*mln*)
Smithtown Library, retired
Smithtown, NY

Linda M. Pavonetti (*lmp*)
Oakland University
Rochester, MI

Nancy L. Roser (*nlr*)
University of Texas
Austin, TX

Nancy Ryan (*nrr*)
Bethel College
Mishawaka, IN

Carol Hanson Sibley (*chs*)
Minnesota State University,
   Moorhead
Moorhead, MN

Susan Stan (*ss*)
Central Michigan University
Mount Pleasant, MI

Leah van Belle (*lvb*)
Madonna University
Livonia, MI

Sylvia Vardell (*smv*)
Texas Women's University
Arlington, TX

Marilyn J. Ward (*mjw*)
Carthage College
Kenosha, WI

Domonique Gene White (*dgw*)
University of Phoenix
Southfield, MI

Natalie Ziarnik (*nrz*)
Ela Area Public Library
Lake Zurich, IL

References

Gebel, Doris, ed. *Crossing Boundaries with Children's Books*. Lanham, MD: Scarecrow Press, 2006.

Rowling, J. K. *Harry Potter and the Philosopher's Stone*. London: Bloomsbury, 1997.

Rowling, J. K. *Harry Potter and the Sorcerer's Stone*. New York: Scholastic/Arthur A. Levine Books, 1998.

Stan, Susan, ed. *The World through Children's Books*. Lanham, MD: Scarecrow Press, 2002.

Tomlinson, Carl M., ed. *Children's Books from Other Countries*. Lanham, MD: Scarecrow Press, 1998.

Zeitchik, Steven. "The Potter Effect." *Publishers Weekly* 252, no. 27 (July 11, 2005): 12–13.

CHAPTER THREE

Latin America and the Caribbean

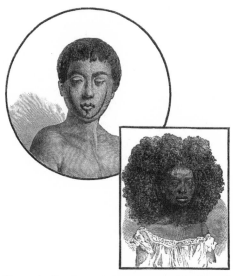

Young Indian from the Amazon / Girl of Brazil
(see p. xii for more information on illustrations)

ANTIGUA

Carling, Amelia Lau. **Sawdust Carpets**. Illustrated by the author. Toronto, Groundwood Books/Douglas & McEntyre, 2005. ISBN 978-0-888-99625-1, 0-888-99625-X. 30 p. (4–8). Picture book.

Each year during Lent the people of Antigua create ornate carpets of dyed sawdust and fresh-cut flowers to line the streets for the Good Friday procession. The narrator, a Chinese girl raised in Guatemala, tells of her family's visit to relatives in Antigua to attend the baptism of her baby cousin on Easter Sunday and to observe Holy Week with them. A neighbor invites the children to create their own sawdust carpet from his leftover materials. Soft illustrations beautifully depict the weeklong celebrations for the families that blend both religious and cultural traditions. A glossary is included. *ca*

Author/illustrator was born and raised in Guatemala and now lives in the United States.

EASTER, ANTIGUA, CHINESE GUATEMALA, FICTION

ARGENTINA

Bernasconi, Pablo. **Captain Arsenio: Inventions and (Mis)Adventures in Flight**. Illustrated by the author. Boston, Houghton Mifflin, 2005. ISBN 978-0-618-50749-8, 0-618-50749-3. 32 p. (5–10). Picture book.

In this creative spoof, Bernasconi imagines the discovery of an important diary that documents the attempts of Captain Arsenio in the eighteenth century to invent a flying machine. Excerpts from the diary are produced along with detailed diagrams, formulas, and illustrated pages for six failed projects that include, for example, an "Aerial Submarine," whose "miraculous" but flammable gas and wooden "flight vessel" leads to disaster, and the uncontrollable "Illusion Burner"—a prototype of the turbine engine. Untutored in the sciences but with an unflagging optimism, Captain Arsenio survives one disaster after another, refusing to let physical pain and the destruction of his machines deter him from yet another attempt. *hc*

Author/illustrator lives in Patagonia, Argentina.

FLYING MACHINES, DIARIES, HUMOROUS STORIES, FANTASY PICTURE STORYBOOKS

Colombo, Natalia. Translated by Esther Sarfatti. **So Close**. Illustrated by the author. Toronto, Tundra Books, 2010. Originally published as *Cerca* in Spanish by Kalandraka Editora Spain, in 2008. ISBN 978-1-77049-207-3, 1-77049-207-0. 24 p. (4–7). Picture book.

Mr. Rabbit and Mr. Duck are neighbors who pass each other every day—on their way to and from work, walking, driving their cars, riding their bikes, in the rain and snow. Yet, they never speak. Each goes his way, navigating his daily life with a half-awake automaticity, until at last they notice one another. The book ends with them walking arm-in-arm under an umbrella, playing on a teeter-totter, sipping steamy mugs of cocoa—friends who are no longer lonely. A sweet book, beautifully illustrated. *First International Compostela Prize for Picture Books, 2008. lvb*

Author/illustrator lives in Buenos Aires, Argentina.
DUCKS, RABBITS, SALUTATIONS, FRIENDSHIP, FICTION

Isol. Translated by Elisa Amado. **Petit, the Monster**. Illustrated by the author. Toronto, Groundwood Books, 2010. Originally published as *Petit, el Monstruo* in Spanish by Océano-SEP-Comisión Nacional de Libros de Texto Gratuitos México, in 2006. ISBN 978-0-88899-947-4, 0-88899-947-X. 32 p. (4–8). Picture book.

Petit is a sweet boy when he plays fetch with his dog or shares a loving moment with Grandfather, but Petit also terrorizes pigeons with his slingshot and yanks the pigtails of little girls. Isol, a finalist for the Hans Christian Andersen Award, artfully weaves Petit's two sides into the illustrations. When Petit is good, the line drawing of his body suggests the subtle shape of a shining sun, a bunny rabbit, or an angel with wings. But when he is engaged in the naughtiness that only he can do, the shape becomes a wolf, a devil with horns, or a bat. *lvb*

Author/illustrator lives in Buenos Aires, Argentina.
BEHAVIOR, MOTHERS AND SONS, PARADOX, FICTION

RELATED INFORMATION

Book Fairs

Buenos Aires Book Fair–Argentina
www.el-libro.org.ar/
Usually held in April

Buenos Aires International Book Fair
Buenos Aires, Argentina
www.el-libro.org.ar/
Usually held in April–May

Online Resources

Imaginaria. This is a monthly electronic journal from the Argentina Association of Children's Literature and is available in Spanish.
www.imaginaria.com.ar/

Organizations

IBBY Argentina

www.alija.org.ar/

The Argentinian IBBY National Section was founded in March 1985 and is represented by the Argentine Association of Children and Young Adult Literature (ALIJA). ALIJA is a nonprofit, private organization engaged in promoting research and assessment of quality children's and young adult books. Since its inception, it has offered writers, illustrators, storytellers, publishers, librarians, teachers, experts, and enthusiasts of children's literature a forum for the exchange of ideas and projects. Every year ALIJA appoints a jury of experts to select the *Destacados de ALIJA*. These *Destacados* are the outstanding books, writers, illustrators, and publishing houses that merit the ALIJA awards, presented once a year at the National Book Fair. Other regular ALIJA IBBY activities include nominating Argentine candidates for the IBBY Hans Christian Andersen Awards and for the International IBBY-Asahi Award, organizing the International Meeting of Storytellers with the *Fundación del Libro and Summa Institute*, publishing a Latin American catalog of recommended book titles for children and young people in cooperation with CERLALC (Centro Regional para el Fomento del Libro en América Latina y el Caribe), and all national IBBY Latin-American sections and Fundación Sánchez Ruipérez, Spain, ALIJA. In 2004, under the auspices of the Cámara Argentina del Libro, ALIJA published *A través del espejo: Libros, lectura y escritura literaria en los libros infantiles y juveniles*, and *Cómo Incentivar la lectura en nuestros hijos* [*Through the Mirror: Books, Reading and Literary Writing in Infantile and Youthful Books*, and *How to Stimulate Reading in our Children*].

BOLIVIA

Ellis, Deborah. **I Am a Taxi**. Toronto, Groundwood Books/House of Anansi Press, 2006. ISBN 978-0-88899-735-7, 0-88899-735-3. 205 p. (10–14). Novel.

Twelve-year-old Diego is a "taxi" who earns money by running errands while living with his mamá and young sister in a Bolivian prison. Although intelligent and diligent, Diego becomes entangled in the rapacious cocaine trade. Trying to atone for a costly momentary lapse, Diego ends up in a forced-labor camp carrying kilos of coca leaves, then treading endlessly in chemical soups, which later become cocaine. He finally escapes into the jungle—unmindful of his fate. Ellis parts the curtain, allowing us to see how a gift of the gods becomes the raw material of a destructive drug trade. *2007 White Ravens, 2008 OLA Golden Oak Award Nominee, 2008 Shortlisted—Alberta Children's Choice Book Award, 2008 Shortlisted—Manitoba Young Reader's Choice Award, 2007 SSLI Honor Book Award, 2007 YALSA Best Books for Young Adults, 2007 CLA Book of the Year Honour Book, 2007 CCBC Our Choice, 2007 Winner Ruth and Sylvia Schwartz Children's Book Award, 2007 SYRCA Snow Willow Award, 2007 CCBC Choice. jfc*

Author lives in Canada.

Coca Industry–Bolivia, Jungles, Bolivia, Fiction

Ellis, Deborah. **Sacred Leaf**. Toronto, Groundwood Books/House of Anansi Press, 2007. ISBN 978-0-88899-751-7, 0-88899-751-5. 206 p. (10 up). Novel.

In this sequel to *I Am a Taxi* (reviewed here), twelve-year-old Diego lives in the mountains with the Ricardo family, cocalero farmers who nursed him back to health after he escaped from illegal cocaine traffickers. Diego begins to glimpse the meaning of family only to lose that security when the army destroys the Ricardo family's crops. He joins the farmers' blockade of Bolivia's major highways in an emotional effort to remain with his adopted family. The action-packed narrative opens a window on the coca plant's centrality to the Latin American economy, legal or illegal, that is little understood in the United States. *2008 USBBY Outstanding International Books, 2008 CCBC Best Books for Kids & Teens, 2008 Américas Award Commended Titles, 2008 Horace Mann Upstanders Honor Book, 2008 CCBC Choices, 2007 CLA Book of the Year for Children Award. lmp*

Author lives in Canada.

Farmers, Coca Industry–Bolivia, Bolivia Social Conditions 1982–present, Fiction

RELATED INFORMATION

Organizations

IBBY Bolivia
   www.librarythuruchapitas.org/web/home/index.php
   www.ibby.org/index.php?id=408

BRAZIL

Harrison, David L. **Sounds of Rain: Poems of the Amazon**. Illustrated with photographs by Doug Duncan. Honesdale, PA, Wordsong/Boyds Mills Press, 2006. ISBN 978-1-59078-442-6, 1-59078-442-1. 32 p. (10 up). Poetry, Picture book.

This collection of poems celebrates the verdant lushness and vibrant life of the Amazon River and surrounding rain forests. Through the use of richly descriptive language and visual imagery, the poems explore the interconnectedness of plants, animals, and humans in the ecosystem. Poems range from serious and insightful, such as considering the commonalities of humans in "Face of the Amazon," to playfully humorous in "Lost in Translation," in which the poet decides that he simply can't muster the courage to swim amid piranhas. *lvb*

Author and illustrator live in the United States.

AMAZON RIVER, RAIN FOREST, NATURE, SOUTH AMERICA, POETRY

Hussey, Charmian. **The Valley of Secrets**. Illustrated by Christopher Crump. New York, Simon & Schuster Books, 2005. First published by Saint Piran Press Great Britain, in 2003. ISBN 978-0-689-87862-6, 0-689-87862-1. 382 p. (12 up). Novel.

Orphan Stephen Lansbury has always been without family, so he is shocked when he inherits an English estate from his late uncle. The surprises multiply as he sets out to discover something about himself and the family he never knew. The adventure that unfolds is part fantasy, part ecological mystery. *2006 USBBY-CBC Outstanding International Books List.*

Author lives in Great Britain.

INHERITANCE AND SUCCESSION, ORPHANS, ADVENTURE AND ADVENTURERS, FAMILY, AMAZON RIVER REGION, CORNWALL, ENGLAND, FICTION

Machado, Ana Maria. Translated by Elisa Amado. **Wolf Wanted**. Illustrated by Laurent Cardon. Toronto, Groundwood Books/House of Anansi Press, 2010. Originally published as *Procura-se Lobo* in Portuguese by Editora Ática Brazil, in 2005. ISBN 978-0-88899-880-4, 0-88899-880-5. 40 p. (4–7). Picture book.

It all starts with a small ad in the newspaper—wolf wanted. Manny is human, but he's unemployed and his last name is Wolf, so he decides to apply for the job anyway. The company hires him to work in their human resources department, sorting through the letters from wolves that have applied for the position. Reading the letters, Manny quickly figures out which wolves aren't right for the job and writes reply letters that redirect them to more fitting jobs, such as the Big Bad Wolf in the story of the "Three Little Pigs" or the wolf in sheep's clothing in *Aesop's Fables*. *Ana Maria Machado has received the most significant Brazilian awards and international honors. In 2000, she was awarded the Hans Christian Andersen Award for her life's work. lvb*
   Author and illustrator live in Brazil.
   WOLVES, CHARACTERS IN LITERATURE, FAIRY TALES, HUMOROUS STORIES, ADVERTISING–CLASSIFIED, FICTION

Taylor, Sean. **The Great Snake: Stories from the Amazon**. Illustrated by Fernando Vilela. Simultaneously published by Frances Lincoln Great Britain and by Frances Lincoln United States, in 2008. ISBN 978-1-84507-529-3, 1-84507-529-3. 61 p. (8–12). Folklore.
   Taylor describes rivers, forests, and villages as he travels along the Amazon and shares tales of tricksters, myths, and magic he has read or heard from storytellers during his travels in Brazil. Diary entries serve as a frame story and add an element of adventure. Vilela's woodcuts are bold and dramatic. *The Great Snake* also introduces readers to the importance of collecting traditional tales. Taylor links the preservation of stories with the need for sustainable development of the rain forests, if both are not going to vanish. Includes source notes on the stories, a glossary, and notes on the Amazon rain forest. *2009 USBBY Outstanding International Books List. ca*
   Author lives in England and in Brazil; the illustrator lives in Brazil.
   AMAZON RIVER, AMAZON RAIN FOREST, FOLKLORE, BRAZIL, DIARIES

RELATED INFORMATION

Organizations

IBBY Brazil
   www.fnlij.org.br/
   www.ibby.org/index.php?id=409

CHILE

Bondoux, Anne-Laure. Translated by Y. Maudet. **The Killer's Tears**. New York, Random House/Delacorte Press, 2006. Originally published as *Les Larmes de l'Assassin* in French by Bayard Editions Jeunesse France, in 2003. ISBN 978-0-385-73293-2, 0-385-73293-7. 162 p. (14 up). Novel.

Angel Allegria is an escaped thief and murderer. He appears at the Poloverdo's farm, isolated at the tip of Chile, and slits the parents' throats but spares Paolo, their child. Angel's motivation is simply his need for shelter and a hideout, and Paolo's presence doesn't threaten his safety. If anything about this book were humorous, we could attribute the parents' murder in the opening scenes to the classical orphan trope. However, Bondoux has not written a comedy, and the murder is only the tip of an iceberg that chills readers' sensibilities and leaves them asking questions for which there are no answers. *2007 USBBY Outstanding International Books List, 2007 Batchelder Honor Book, winner of the French Prix Sorcières.* lmp

Author lives in France.

FATHERS AND SONS, METAMORPHOSIS, INTERPERSONAL RELATIONS, OUTLAWS, THIEVES, ROBBERS AND OUTLAWS, CHILE, FICTION

Délano, Poli. Translated by Sean Higgins. **When I Was a Boy Neruda Called Me Policarpo**. Illustrated by Manuel Monroy. Toronto, Groundwood Books, 2006. Originally published as *Policarpo y el Tío Pablo: Historias de una Tierna Amistad con Pablo Neruda* in Spanish by Sudamericana Chile, in 2004. ISBN 978-0-88899-726-5, 0-88899-726-4. 84 p. (10 up). Autobiography, Memoir, Poetry.

Poli Delano spent his early years growing up in the company of Pablo Neruda, the Nobel Prize–winning poet from Chile. Some childhood memories of the adventures with Pablo include a carnivorous pet badger that attacks Poli, a fighting competition between a pampered pet tarantula and a walking stick insect, and Pablo's fondness for exotic dishes such as iguana, worms, and snakes. Following each chapter is a poem by Neruda. At the end of the book is a six-page biographical note on the poet. pwc

Author lives in Chile.

PABLO NERUDA (1904–1973), POLI DÉLANO (1936–), CHILDHOOD AND YOUTH, 20TH CENTURY CHILEAN POETS, 20TH CENTURY CHILEAN AUTHORS, BIOGRAPHY, CHILE

Foreman, Michael. **Mia's Story: A Sketchbook of Hopes and Dreams**. Illustrated by the author. Cambridge, MA, Candlewick Press, 2006. Originally published by Walker Books Great Britain, in 2006. ISBN 978-0-7636-3063-8, 0-7636-3063-2. 32 p. (6–10). Picture book.

Mia lives in a house by a dump near Santiago, Chile. Each day her father sells scrap in the city. One day as Mia searches in the nearby Andes Mountains for her lost dog, she makes an unexpected discovery in the snow—a field of beautiful white flowers. Mia digs up clumps of the flowers and replants them near her house. The wind spreads the seeds, and the next spring the village and dump are covered with beautiful flowers, which Mia and Papa take to the city to sell. Foreman's sketchbook drawings and soft watercolors add lovely detailing without overwhelming Mia's story. *2007 USBBY Outstanding International Books List. ca*

Author/illustrator lives in England.

FAMILY LIFE–CHILE, VILLAGES, FLOWERS, CHILE, FICTION

Ray, Deborah Kogan. **To Go Singing through the World: The Childhood of Pablo Neruda**. Illustrated by the author. New York, Farrar, Straus and Giroux/ Frances Foster Books, 2006. ISBN 978-0-374-37627-7, 0-374-37627-1. 32 p. (9–12). Picture book.

This Pablo Neruda biography focuses on the famous poet's childhood in Temuco, a southern Chilean frontier town. Ray's lyrical prose captures the curious and quiet—almost reclusive—child's feelings and emotions while simultaneously revealing influences that shaped him—the rain forest and volcanoes that surrounded his isolated town and the Mapuche stories told by his stepmother. Poet Gabriela Mistral's books and encouragement may have been his greatest inspiration, however. When Neruda finally left Temuco, he "took with him the songs of his childhood . . . to go singing through the world." Excerpts from Pablo Neruda's poems and notebooks bring to life the voice of this renowned poet. *mm*

Author lives in the United States.

PABLO NERUDA (1904–1973), CHILDHOOD AND YOUTH, 20TH CENTURY CHILEAN POETS, CHILE, BIOGRAPHY

RELATED INFORMATION

Book Fairs

Feria Internacional del Libro de Santiago
Santiago, Chile
Phone: 52 8328 4323
E-mail: filmty@filmty.itesm.mx
Website: www.camlibro.cl/
October–November

Organizations

IBBY Chile
   www.ibbychile.cl/
   www.ibby.org/index.php?id=411

COLOMBIA

Winter, Jeanette. **Biblioburro: A True Story from Colombia**. Illustrated by
the author. New York, Simon & Schuster/Beach Lane Books, 2010. ISBN
978-1-4169-9778-8, 1-4169-9778-4. 32 p. (6–9). Biography.

Based on the program started in 2000, Winter describes and celebrates the
efforts of Luis Soriano to reach children in a remote northern Colombian region and to share his passion for reading with them. By transporting books via
donkey, children are able to read, return, and exchange books via a makeshift
mobile library. Illustrations done in pen and ink and acrylic produce a feltlike
effect that suggests bright and lush surroundings as well as demonstrates the
way in which stories and books can color and enrich their young recipients. *bef*
   Author/illustrator lives in the United States.

   Luis Soriano, Teachers, Librarians, Traveling Libraries, Books
and Reading, Colombia Biography, Nonfiction

RELATED INFORMATION

Organizations

IBBY Columbia
   www.fundalectura.org/

CUBA

Cárdenas, Teresa. Translated by David Unger. **Old Dog**. Toronto, Ground-wood Books/House of Anansi Press, 2007. Originally published as *Perro Viejo* in Spanish by Casa de las Américas, in 2006. ISBN 978-0-88899-757-9, 0-88899-757-4. 104 p. (12 up). Novel.

The Old Dog, Perro Viejo in Spanish, can't remember when he was ever called anything else. The old master gave him the name when he was just a child. Perro Viejo sniffed everything—searching for his mother's aroma—as if he were one of the old bloodhounds who hunted escaped slaves. Perro Viejo closed off his heart after awhile, but he continued sniffing. In this slim novella, the Old Dog is worn out by years of hard labor on his master's sugar plantation. He has never lived anywhere else, nor has he ever ventured beyond the gate he is charged with opening. He is lame, hard of hearing, and almost blind, but he bears the most painful scars in his heart. *Casa de las Américas Prize (Cuba's highest literary honor)*. lmp

Author lives in Havana, Cuba.

SLAVES, BLACKS, CUBAN HISTORY (1810–1899), SUGAR INDUSTRY, CUBA, HISTORICAL FICTION

Deedy, Carmen Agra. **Martina, the Beautiful Cockroach: A Cuban Folk-tale**. Illustrated by Michael Austin. Atlanta, GA, Peachtree, 2007. ISBN 978-1-56145-399-3, 1-56145-399-4. 32 p. (8–12). Picture book.

Martina the cockroach is ready to marry, so her grandmother tells Martina to spill coffee on her suitors' shoes. This will make them angry and show how they might react in the future. Martina tries the "coffee test" with a rooster, a pig, and a lizard, and all fail miserably. She is ready to give up when her grandmother encourages her to meet the tiny, brown mouse in the garden. When Martina attempts the coffee test, he turns the tables, spilling coffee on her instead. After all, he has a Cuban grandmother, too, and he knows about the coffee test. *2008 Pura Belpré Honor Book for Narrative, 2008 NCSS/CBC Notable Trade Books for Young People in the Field of Social Studies*. nlh

Author was born in Cuba.

COCKROACHES, FOLKLORE, CUBA

Engle, Margarita. **The Poet Slave of Cuba: A Biography of Juan Francisco Manzano**. Illustrated by Sean Qualls. New York, Henry Holt, 2006. ISBN 978-0-8050-7706-3, 0-8050-7706-5. 192 p. (10 up). Novel in Poems.

Engle presents a powerful biography of Juan Francisco Manzano, exposing the physical and psychological horrors of slavery. Manzano, a child prodigy, earns manumission for his parents, but his own is to be delayed until the death of his first owner. After his owner's death, Manzano remains enslaved by a new owner, La Marquesa de Prado Ameno, who disregards his manumission. She engages him in a horrific battle for control of his actions, thoughts, and dispositions. Her punishments are maniacal; his endurance approaches superhuman. Engle merges poems from multiple perspectives, including Manzano's, his parents, and owners to form a compelling narrative. *2008 Pura Belpré Author Award, ALA Best Books for Young Adults, ALA Notable Children's Books; Winner of the Américas Award for Children's and Young Adult Literature, IRA Children's Book Award, IRA Teachers' Choices, NCTE Notable Children's Books in the Language Arts, Bank Street Best Children's Book of the Year, NYPL Books for the Teen Age, CCBC Choice. jfc*

Author and illustrator live in the United States.

JUAN FRANCISCO MANZANO (1797–1854), SLAVES, POETS, CHILDREN'S POETRY, CUBA, POETRY

RELATED INFORMATION

Organizations

IBBY Cuba
www.ibby.org/index.php?id=414

Conferences

IBBY Cuba Biennial Congress is convened during the fall of odd-numbered years.
www.lectura2009.org/congreso

EL SALVADOR

Argueta, Jorge. **Talking with Mother Earth: Poems**. Illustrated by Lucia Angela Perez. Toronto, Groundwood Books/Libros Tigrillo, 2006. ISBN 978-0-88899-626-8, 0-88899-626-8. 32 p. (9–12). Poetry, Picture book.

This collection of bilingual poems about a young Nahuatl boy explores the bitter effect of blatant racism and the healing power of Mother Earth. A loving Nahuatl grandmother has taught Tetl—also called Jorge—to seek spiritual sustenance from Mother Earth. These poems delve into the pain of bigotry while simultaneously celebrating the healing power found in ancient stones, the song of birds, the gift of corn, the warmth of the sun, the playful spirit of the wind, and the life-giving water. mm

A native Salvadoran and Pipil Nahua Indian, the author now lives in San Francisco.

RACISM, PIPIL INDIANS, BILINGUAL SPANISH LANGUAGE MATERIALS, EL SALVADOR, POETRY

Argueta, Jorge. Translated by the author. **Sopa De Frijoles: Bean Soup**. Illustrated by Rafael Yockteng. Toronto, Groundwood Books/Libros Tigrillo/ House of Anansi Press, 2009. ISBN 978-0-88899-881-1, 0-88899-881-3. 30 p. (4–8). Poetry, Picture book.

You can almost smell and taste the bean soup as you read this "recipe" poem full of vivid metaphors and similes. It's a long, segmented poem spread out across fourteen pages of text (always on the left) accompanied by rectangular paintings framed in white (always on the right). This pleasing, predictable format makes it easy to read either the Spanish or English poems—or both. The paper is thick and creamy, and the little boy pictured in every scene is an engaging "everyboy." Argueta wrote both the Spanish and English versions, capturing the music of the poem in both languages. 2010 USBBY Outstanding International Books List, 2010 Cooperative Children's Book Center (CCBC) Choices. smv

Author was born in El Salvador but currently lives in the United States.

SOUPS, BEANS, COOKERY, BILINGUAL ENGLISH-SPANISH LANGUAGE MATERIALS, LATIN AMERICA, SAN SALVADOR, POETRY

GUATEMALA

Amado, Elisa. **Tricycle**. Illustrated by Alfonso Ruano. Toronto, Groundwood Books, 2007. Simultaneously published as *El Triciclo* in Spanish by Groundwood/Libro Tigrillo Canada. Additional simultaneous publications as *El Triciclo* in Spanish by SM de Ediciones México, D. F., and as *Triciclo* in

Portugese by Comboio de Corda Brazil. ISBN 978-0-88899-614-5, 0-88899-614-4. 32 p. (4–8). Picture book.

From her perch high in a favorite tree, Margarita has a view of both sides of a green hedge: her wealthy family's garden on one side and the poor shanty home where her friend Rosario and her family live on the other side. When she sees her young neighbors taking her tricycle, which she has left out, Margarita must choose between disclosing what she has witnessed and protecting her friend's family. The realistic illustrations that accompany the spare text offer clues to the Latin American setting and give readers a sense of the great socioeconomic differences among the characters. *2008 USBBY Outstanding International Books List, 2008 Américas Award Commended Titles. Illustrator Alfonso Ruano is the recipient of the Américas Award and the Jane Addams Award for* The Composition. *ca*

Author is a Guatemalan writer and translator who lives in Toronto, Canada. Illustrator lives in Madrid.

SOCIAL RESPONSIBILITY, POVERTY, LATIN AMERICA, COMPASSION, TRUTH-FULNESS AND FALSEHOOD, FRIENDSHIP, HONESTY, FICTION, GUATEMALA, PICTURE BOOKS

Pellegrino, Marge. **Journey of Dreams**. Simultaneously published by Frances Lincoln in Great Britain and in the United States, in 2009. ISBN 978-1-84780-061-9, 1-84780-061-0. 250 p. (10 up). Novel.

A thirteen-year-old Mayan girl recounts the harrowing story of her family's escape from their Guatemalan mountain village in the face of civil war in 1984. Details of village life, the journey across national borders, the power of storytelling, and the resilience of the human spirit are all vividly portrayed. *2010 USBBY Outstanding International Books List, 2009 Judy Goddard Award for Young Adult Literature, Independent Children's Booksellers 2009 "ABC Best Books for Children," Kirkus Magazine's "Best Books of 2009," 2009 Southwest Books of the Year, 2009 Smithsonian Notable Books for Children, 2010 CCBC Choices, 2010 Chicago Public Library: One Book, One Chicago, 2010 Americas Award Commended List.*

Author lives in the United States.

MAYAS, REFUGEES, IMMIGRANTS–UNITED STATES, VOYAGES AND TRAVELS, GUATEMALA–HISTORY–CIVIL WAR (1960–1996), FICTION

Resau, Laura. **Red Glass**. New York, Random House/Delacorte Press, 2007. ISBN 978-0-385-73466-0, 0-385-73466-2. 275 p. (10 up). Novel.

Sophie the frightened becomes Sophie La Fuerte, a strong and brave teenage girl who comes of age in this eloquently written novel. Her family takes in Pablo, a five-year-old orphan who almost died of dehydration when his family attempted to illegally cross the border. Sophie embarks on a journey to Mexico with Pablo to meet his extended family, who force a difficult decision upon him. Propelled into dangerous situations she's unable to control, Sophie learns to accept her own fear for the sake of those she loves. *Américas Award Winner, IRA Young Adult Fiction Award Winner, 2008 CCBC Choice List, 2007 School Library Journal Best Book, ALA-YALSA Best Book for Young Adults, Colorado Book Award Winner, Cybil Award Finalist.* dld

Author lives in Colorado. She previously lived in the Mixtec region of Oxaxa, Mexico.

MEXICO, GUATEMALA, SELF-CONFIDENCE, AUTOMOBILE TRAVEL, ORPHANS, FAMILY LIFE, ILLEGAL ALIENS, FICTION

HAITI

Elvgren, Jennifer Riesmeyer. **Josias, Hold the Book**. Illustrated by Nicole Tadgell. Honesdale, PA, Boyds Mills Press, 2006. ISBN 978-1-59078-318-4, 1-59078-318-2. 32 p. (6–10). Picture book.

Josias's friends call to him on their way to school, asking when he will "hold the book"—join them at school. Josias has no use for reading and writing; he must tend the beans so his family has enough food. However, his garden is not faring well despite his best efforts. At this point, Josias realizes that books might hold the key to his gardening problems and he convinces his family to allow him to attend school. Author's notes provide helpful information about rural Haiti and the difficulty of acquiring an education for children living in the countryside. *2007 America's Award from the Center for Latin American & Caribbean Studies.* nlh

Author lives in the United States.

GARDENING, EDUCATION, FAMILY LIFE, HAITI, FICTION

RELATED INFORMATION

Organizations

AYIBBY, the IBBY National Section of Haiti
(No website available)

🪷

JAMAICA

Mordecai, Martin. **Blue Mountain Trouble**. New York, Scholastic/Arthur A. Levine Books, 2009. ISBN 978-0-545-04156-0, 0-545-04156-2. 353 p. (8–12). Novel.

Filled with Jamaican dialect, sensory descriptions of the countryside, and adventures of eleven-year-old twins, Pollyread and Jackson Gilmore, this book offers insight to the Jamaican culture that is not easily found. The twins are finishing sixth grade and waiting for the test results that determine their future. The adventures and dreams of these young twins living in a village high in the mountains provide personal connections for all readers through the lyrical voice of the author, who is from Jamaica. Readers of all ages will appreciate the zest and richness of life showcased here despite, or because of, the twins living in a somewhat impoverished area. *2010 USBBY Outstanding International Books List, 2009 Kirkus Reviews Best Children's Books. jm*

Author was born and raised in Kingston, Jamaica, and now lives in Toronto, Canada.

TWINS, BROTHERS AND SISTERS, MOUNTAIN LIFE, JAMAICA, FICTION, NOVEL

Winter, Jeanette. **Angelina's Island**. Illustrated by the author. New York, Farrar, Straus and Giroux/Frances Foster Books, 2007. ISBN 978-0-374-30349-5, 0-374-30349-5. 32 p. (4–8). Picture book.

"Every day," Angelina tells her mother that she wants "to go home." Her mother always answers that Angelina "is home now" (n.p.). But Angelina is homesick for her former West Indian home. She dreams of the food she used to enjoy and misses the sea, her school, the rainbow-colored birds, and her grandmother. Then, her mother reads about the Carnival. When Angelina dances in her beautiful costume, she finally accepts New York as her home. Glowing full-color illustrations in flat perspective highlight the contrast between Angelina's homes. They are framed, like pages, in rectangular panels against solid colored backgrounds. *2008 Américas Award Commended Title. Jeanette Winter's awards include the 2005 Flora Stieglitz Award for* The Librarian of Basra: A True Story from Iraq. *hc, nrz*

Author is from the United States.

HOMESICKNESS, JAMAICAN AMERICANS, PARADES, NEW YORK (NY), FICTION

MÉXICO

Bernier-Grand, Carmen T. **Frida: Viva La Vida! Long Live Life!** Tarrytown, NY, Marshall Cavendish, 2007. ISBN 978-0-7614-5336-9, 0-7614-5336-9. 64 p. (12 up). Biography, Poetry.

Through powerful poems, Carmen Bernier-Grand paints a biographical portrait of the artist Frida Kahlo. The poems depict her parents, her battle with polio as a child, the tragic bus accident that resulted in numerous operations, and her two turbulent marriages to Diego Rivera. The poems are interspersed with Kahlo's own artwork. Author's notes at the end, a chronology of the artist's life, and a glossary provide more detailed information. *2008 Notable Social Studies Trade Book for Young People NCSS-CBC, 2008 Pura Belpré Honor Book, 2008 ALA Notable Book.* nlh

Author grew up in Puerto Rico and now lives in the United States.

Frida Kahlo, Painters, Mexico, Biography, Poetry

Dorros, Alex & Arthur Dorros. **Número Uno.** Illustrated by Susan Guevara. New York, Harry N. Abrams Books, 2007. ISBN 978-0-8109-5764-0, 0-8109-5764-7. n.p. (4–8). Picture book.

Which is more important? Brains or brawn? Socrates insists that with his brains he contributes the most to the village, while Hercules argues that with his strength he is the more valuable member of this Mexican community. A young boy suggests a competition to settle the argument—the outcome of which surprises these archrivals. Spanish phrases are skillfully woven throughout the text. Done in a folk art style, Guevara's illustrations are filled with bright colors and details of a Michoacán landscape. mm

Author Alex Dorros created a first draft of the story when he was twelve. He and his father, Arthur Dorros, collaborated on this version of the story. They live in Seattle, Washington.

Competition, Jealousy, Humorous Stories, Mexico, Fiction

Gusti. **Half of an Elephant.** Illustrated by the author. La Jolla, CA, Kane/Miller Books, 2006. Originally published in Spanish by Ediciones Serres Mexico, in 2004. ISBN 978-1-933605-09-8, 1-933605-09-X. 32 p. (6 up). Picture book.

An elephant loses his back half when the world suddenly splits in two. He finds he is not alone, and he and other creatures search the world for their missing halves. After unsuccessful matching attempts, the elephant decides that living as a half might not be so bad. When the world magically becomes one again, the halves are reunited, but not quite in the same way as before. The imaginative animals are digital images constructed of corrugated cardboard, springs, paintbrushes, broken dishes, nuts, bolts, and other discarded objects. A modern love story told with humorous text, this book is a rare gem that speaks on many levels to the power of belonging and love. *Gusti received an IBBY Honor List diploma for illustrations; Parenting Magazine Best Books of the Year. mjw, lvb*

Author/illustrator was born in Argentina.

FRIENDSHIP, BELONGING, ANIMALS, LOVE, FANTASY

Luján, Jorge. Translated by Elisa Amado. **Tarde De Invierno/Winter Afternoon**. Illustrated by Mandana Sadat. Toronto, Groundwood Books/Libros Tigrillo, 2006. Originally published as *Tarde de Invierno* in Spanish by SM México, in 2005. ISBN 978-0-88899-718-0, 0-88899-718-3. 28 p. (4–6 up). Picture book.

Inside her home on a frigid day, a young girl clears a crescent moon shape on a frosty window. Peering through the moon, the girl sees her mother returning home. As her mother nears, the girl enlarges the moon so that she can always see her mother. On the final pages, the hugging mother and child are framed inside the moon. *pwc*

Author was born in Argentina and lives in Mexico.

WINTER, MOTHER AND CHILD, SPANISH LANGUAGE MATERIALS, MEXICO, BILINGUAL PICTURE BOOKS, POETRY

Luján, Jorge. Translated by Elisa Amado. **Sky Blue Accident/Accidente Celeste**. Illustrated by Piet Grobler. Toronto, Groundwood Books/House of Anansi Press/Libros Tigrillo, 2007. Originally published as *Accidente Celeste* in Spanish by Fondo de Cultura Económica México, in 2006. ISBN 978-0-88899-805-7, 0-88899-805-8. 25 p. (4–8). Poetry, Picture book.

Written in parallel English and Spanish text, this book takes readers on a flight of imagination as a little boy and his classmates discover the magic they can have with a few bits of sky blue that have broken off the sky. The sparse text is accompanied by quirky and delightful gouache and pastel illustrations. Together, these create a magical world where teachers grow wings, clouds get lost, the moon directs traffic, and children work together to create a new sky. Utterly and unforgettably charming. *Jorge Luján was awarded the Premio de Poesia parap Niños de ALIJA (IBBY Argentina). Piet Grobler has received awards in Bratislava and in Japan and France as well as his native South Africa. lvb, lmp*

Author lives in México, and the illustrator lives in South Africa.
Sky, Accidents, Bicycles, Bilingual Spanish Language Materials, Poetry

Montejo, Victor. Translated by Chloe Catan. **White Flower: A Maya Princess**. Illustrated by Rafael Yockteng. Toronto, Groundwood Books, 2005. Originally published as *Blanca Flor: Una Princess Maya* in Spanish by Groundwood Books/House of Anansi Press Canada, in 2005. ISBN 978-0-88899-599-5, 0-88899-599-7. 36 p. (8–10). Picture book.

There once was a poor boy who was so traumatized he forgot his name. He fell in love with Lord Witz Ak'al's daughter and was subjected to formidable trials before he was allowed to marry her. Mayan anthropologist Victor Montejo weaves together motifs that introduce readers to a folktale "White Flower" or "Blanca Flor" that originated in Spain and evolved into several variants when it migrated to Latin America. This version reflects Mayan beliefs, culture, and traditions. The earth-tone watercolor illustrations integrate Mayan animals—snakes, jaguars, monkeys, and lizards—with ruins similar to Yucatan temples. *lmp*
Author and illustrator live in Guatemala.
Mayan People, Quests, Princesses, Kings and Rulers, Indians of Central America, Picture Book, Folklore Central America

Ó Flatharta, Antoine. **Hurry and the Monarch**. Illustrated by Meilo So. New York, Random House/Alfred A. Knopf, 2005. ISBN 978-0-375-83003-7, 0-375-83003-0. 32 p. (5–9). Picture book.

On her migration south to Mexico, Monarch stops to rest in Wichita Falls, Texas, and befriends an old tortoise named Hurry. As the two friends converse, they reveal how biology has beautifully dictated their different perspectives on life: Monarch's quick-moving and busy life strongly contrasts the slow, long life of the tortoise, which patiently awaits the changes of the seasons. Yet both lives intertwine and are filled with the magic of transformation. After winter ends and Monarch flies north from Mexico, she again stops in Texas to visit Hurry. She lays her eggs in his garden, leaving him to be the first to greet her offspring. This excellent addition to literature on butterflies takes the concept of metamorphosis a step future by placing it in a larger context. *nrz*
Author lives in Ireland; illustrator was born in Hong Kong but now lives in Scotland.
Turtles, Monarch Butterfly, Butterflies, Wichita Falls, TX, Fantasy, Ireland, Mexico

Ramírez, Antonio. Translated by Elisa Amado. **Napí Goes to the Mountain**. Illustrated by Domi. Toronto, Groundwood Books/House of Anansi Press, 2006. Simultaneously published in Spanish as *Napí va a la Moñtana* by Groundwood Books/House of Anansi Press Toronto. ISBN 978-0-88899-713-5, 0-88899-713-2. 48 p. (6–10). Picture book.

When her father is taken away for fighting for his land, Napí and her brother, Mazateca Indians from Mexico, go into the mountains to find him. Magically transformed into fawns, they are befriended in their search by the animals of the jungle. Finally, it is a mother armadillo that tells the children their beloved father can be found at home. The illustrations contain splashes of bright colors often used in Mexican folk art. A glossary defines Mazateca terms used in the book. *Napí* was the first publication (Groundwood, 2004), and *Napí Funda un Pueblo/Napí Makes a Village* (Groundwood, 2010) was released as a bilingual book. mm

Author and illustrator live in Tlaquepaque, Mexico. They are husband and wife.

MAZATEC INDIANS, ANIMALS, QUESTS (EXPEDITIONS), MEXICO, FATHERS, MAGICAL REALISM, FANTASY FICTION

Ramírez, Antonio. Translated by Elisa Amado. **Napí Funda un Pueblo/ Napí Makes a Village**. Illustrated by Domi. Toronto, Groundwood Books/ House of Anansi Press, 2010. ISBN 978-0-88899-965-8, 0-88899-965-8. 48 p. (6–10). Picture book.

Napí and her little brother, Niclé, move with their family as the Mexican government relocates their Mazateca community in order to build a new dam. In the new village everyone works hard to clear the rain forest, plant crops, and build a new town: "We were giving birth to Nuevo Ixcatlán, and that meant we had to make sacrifices." And yet, amid the sacrifice, there is also beauty in the forest spring, the silent jaguar in a tree, and family who love each other deeply. Parallel texts feature Spanish on the left of every double-page spread and the English translation on the right. *lvb*

Author and illustrator live in Tlaquepaque, Mexico.

MAZATEC INDIANS, RELOCATION, INDIANS OF MEXICO, VILLAGES, FATHERS AND DAUGHTERS, BILINGUAL SPANISH LANGUAGE MATERIALS, NATIVE AMERICANS, MEXICO, FICTION

Resau, Laura. **Red Glass**. New York, Random House/Delacorte Press, 2007. ISBN 978-0-385-73466-0, 0-385-73466-2. 275 p. (10 up). Novel.

See Guatamala for description.

Serrano, Francisco. Translated by Trudy Balch (biography) & Jo Anne Engelbert (poetry). **The Poet King of Tezcoco: A Great Leader of Ancient Mexico**. Illustrated by Pablo Serrano. Toronto, Groundwood Books, 2007. Originally published as *El Rey Poeta: Biografía de Nezahualcoyotl* in Spanish by CIDCLI Mexico, in 2006. ISBN 978-0-88899-787-6, 0-88899-787-6. 34 p. (10 up). Poetry, Biography.

Along with the Aztec empire in the valley of Mexico, there were numerous city-states. One of those, Texcoco, was ruled by Nezahualcoyotl, a great leader as well as a poet. During his rule, he brought many advances to the people, including a new legal system, architectural splendors, and a university. Rich illustrations highlight the biographical information along with some of this ruler's original poems. A chronology of Nezahualcoyotl's life and a glossary at the end of the book provide helpful information. Endpapers have a map of the valley of Mexico in the 1400s with key points labeled. *2007 New York Public Library: Children's Books Titles for Reading and Sharing.* nlh

Author lives in Mexico.

NEZAHUALCÓYOTL, KING OF TEXCOCO (1402–1472), TEZCUCAN INDIANS KINGS AND RULERS BIOGRAPHY, MEXICAN INDIAN POETRY, MEXICO HISTORY TO 1519

Stanton, Karen. **Papi's Gift**. Illustrated by Rene King Moreno. Honesdale, PA, Boyds Mills Press, 2007. ISBN 978-1-59078-422-8, 1-59078-422-7. n.p. (4–8). Picture book.

Graciela's father travels to California to find work because of the drought in their Latin American village. Papi promised Graciela a special birthday gift, but it is lost in the mail. Graciela is angry and fears that, like the box, her father will also be lost to her. To console her daughter, Graciela's mother lovingly fashions a doll from cornhusks and old clothing scraps. This simple gift becomes a symbol of hope for Graciela's eventual reunion with her father. Spanish phrases are intermingled, and illustrations feature Latino cultural scenes. However, the Latin American setting is never identified. mm, nlh

Author lives in San Francisco, and the illustrator lives in Chicago.

FATHERS AND DAUGHTERS, BIRTHDAYS, DROUGHTS, LATIN AMERICA, FICTION

Wu, Liz. **Rosa Farm: A Barnyard Tale**. Illustrated by Matt Phelan. New York, Random House/Alfred A. Knopf, 2006. ISBN 978-0-375-83681-7, 0-375-83681-0. 134 p. (8–12). Novel.

Young rooster Gallileon takes his crowing responsibilities seriously in his father's absence. Although this is a story of ducks, geese, and chickens, it is also a story about brothers and sisters, bullies, and teenage coming-of-age experiences. Delicate illustrations add to the gentle humor and tone. *si*
Author lives in Mexico.
ROOSTERS, CHICKENS, GEESE, DOMESTIC ANIMALS, FARM LIFE, FICTION

RELATED INFORMATION

Book Fairs

Guadalajara International Book Fair—Mexico
Guadalajara, Mexico
www.fil.com.mx/
November–December

Organizations

IBBY Mexico
www.ibbymexico.org.mx/

PERU

Krebs, Laurie. **Up and Down the Andes: A Peruvian Festival Tale.** Illustrated by Aurélia Fronty. Cambridge, MA, Barefoot Books, 2008. ISBN 978-1-84686-203-8, 1-84686-203-5. n.p. (4–8). Picture book.

Children travel from near and far to Cusco's central square to offer thanks and praise in honor of the Sun God. They bring their traditional hats, capes, and costumes along with multicolored corn to celebrate the Incan festival of Inti Raymi with laughter, song, and dancing to the lively beat of the music. Bold acrylic paintings illustrate this simple tale. Several pages of additional information are appended about the holiday, other Peruvian festivals, the history and people of Peru, and the famous site of Machu Picchu. *Chosen for the 2009 Children's Catalog. djg*
Author lives in the United States.

INTI RAYMI FESTIVAL, INDIANS OF SOUTH AMERICA, ANDES REGION SOCIAL LIFE AND CUSTOMS, FESTIVALS–ANDES REGION, NONFICTION BOOK

RELATED INFORMATION

Organizations

IBBY Peru—Centro de Documentación e Información de Literatura Infantil (CEDILI)
www.atrapandoelmundoenpalabras.blogspot.com/

ANDES REGION

Buxton, Jane. **The Littlest Llama**. Illustrated by Jenny Cooper. New York, Sterling, 2008. Originally published by Mallinson Rendel New Zealand, in 2005. ISBN 978-1-4027-5277-3, 1-4027-5277-6. 32 p. (3–6). Picture book.

A young llama looks for someone to play with high in the mountains of what could be a South American landscape. The text is related in rhyming couplets, and the plants and animals typical of that region are found in the detailed illustrations. *djg*

Author and illustrator live in New Zealand.

LLAMAS, PLAY, STORIES IN RHYME, ANDES MOUNTAINS, FICTION

TRINIDAD

Brand, Dionne. **Earth Magic**. Illustrated by Eugenie Fernandes. Toronto, Kids Can Press, 2006. Originally published by Kids Can Press Canada, in 1979. ISBN 978-1-55337-706-1, 1-55337-706-0. 32 p. (8 up). Poetry, Picture book.

An accomplished author of poetry for adults, Brand debuts her poems for children in this homage to her beloved homeland of Trinidad. She has a gift for finding beauty and wonder in the small everyday events: watching the fishermen pull in their nets, shopping in the open-air market, washing clothes in the river, delighting in hummingbirds. While most of the poems are lighthearted, Brand also writes thoughtfully about serious topics, such as the devastation a hurricane brings to the island and the horrors of the slave trade. *Brand is the winner of the Governor General's Award for Poetry, one of Canada's most prestigious awards for literature; additionally, she is the recipient of the Trillium Award and the Pat Lowther Award. lvb*

Author born in Trinidad, lives in Canada; illustrator lives in Canada.
CARIBBEAN, NATURE, POETRY

VENEZUELA

Cottin, Menena. Translated by Elisa Amado. **The Black Book of Colors.** Illustrated by Rosana Faría. Toronto, Groundwood Books, 2008. Originally published as *El Libro Negro de los Colores* in Spanish by Ediciones Tecolote Mexico, in 2006. ISBN 978-0-88899-873-6, 0-88899-873-2. n.p. (6–10). Picture book.

Picture storybooks depend on illustrations for much of their meaning, but blind children miss out on the visual part of the storytelling. *The Black Book of Colors* meets the demands of a concept book for visually challenged youngsters on multiple levels: Braille text empowers those who can read it with independence, but alphabetic print is included for the sighted. Descriptions infused with sensory impressions provide mental images for any reader, while embossed illustrations supply an additional means of perception for blind and sighted readers. Menena Cottin's Braille text is complemented by Rosana Faría's bas-relief, glossy black images on flat, black paper. The descriptive white alphabetic print is the only part that is immediately visible for sighted readers. *2007 Bologna New Horizons Prize, New York Times Best Illustrated Children's Book Awards. lmp*

Author and illustrator live in Caracas, Venezuela.
COLORS, TOUCH, BRAILLE BOOKS, BLIND BOOKS AND READING, LATIN AMERICA

RELATED INFORMATION

Organizations

IBBY Venezuela—Banco del Libro
www.bancodellibro.org.ve/portal/

WEST INDIES

Lawrence, Iain. **The Castaways**. New York, Delacorte Press, 2007. ISBN 978-0-385-73090-7, 0-385-73090-X. 243 p. (12–14). Novel.

Sinking at sea, Tom Tin and his companions board an apparently deserted "East Indiaman," but they soon pick up the captain ("Beastly") and first mate, Mr. Moyle, from an iceberg. The boys learn to sail under the cruel "Beastly," but they also discover the ship's dreadful cargo. Once they reach the Caribbean, the boys narrowly escape being sold as slaves. Tom grows in courage and moral fiber in this swashbuckling tale as he foils villains, saves his friend from the dreadful Moyle, and sets sail from England to search for his father. The history of England's slave trade is explained in a note. *The Castaways* is book 3 in the *Curse of the Jolly Stone Trilogy* and a sequel to *The Convicts* and *The Cannibals*. hc *Author lives in Canada.*

ADVENTURE STORIES, SEAFARING LIFE, SLAVE TRADE, SURVIVAL AFTER SHIPWRECKS, FATE AND FATALISM, WEST INDIES HISTORY–19TH CENTURY, HISTORICAL FICTION

RELATED INFORMATION

Awards

Américas Award for Children's and Young Adult Literature

Sponsored by the National Consortium of Latin American Studies Programs at the University of Wisconsin, Milwaukee, this award is given in recognition of U.S. works of fiction, poetry, folklore, or nonfiction published in the previous year in English or Spanish that authentically and engagingly portray Latin Americans, Caribbean people, or Latinos in the United States. Visit the website for additional information: www4.uwm.edu/clacs/aa/index.cfm.

Norma-Fundalectura Latin American Children's Literature Award

Beginning on November 15, 2010, the Norma Publication Group assumed sole responsibility for the award, which will be called the **Premio Norma de Literatura Infantil y Juvenil**. Because of the fifteen-year alliance between Norma and Fundalectura, magnificent works were published for the Latin American market, many regional writers were first published, and thus numerous promising literary works were discovered. The winner of the Premio Norma de Literatura Infantil y Juvenil will be announced before the 2011 Bogota Book Fair, where a celebration for the introduction of the award will occur.

Established in 1996 to promote better books for children and young people in Latin America, this award is given to an unpublished work that has not already received another prize and is open to any author who is a citizen of a Latin American country. It carries a cash award and ensures publication by Grupo Editorial Norma.

www.fundalectura.org/

Pura Belpré Award

The Pura Belpré Award, established in 1996, is presented to a Latino/Latina writer and illustrator in the United States whose work best portrays, affirms, and celebrates the Latino cultural experience in an outstanding work of literature for children and youth. It is cosponsored by the Association for Library Service to Children (ALSC), a division of the American Library Association (ALA), and the National Association to Promote Library and Information Services to Latinos and the Spanish-speaking (REFORMA), an ALA affiliate. Visit the website for a listing of award winners: www.ala.org/ala/mgrps/divs/alsc/awardsgrants/bookmedia/belpremedal/index.cfm

The Tomás Rivera Mexican American Children's Book Award

Texas State University College of Education developed the Tomás Rivera Mexican American Children's Book Award to honor authors and illustrators who create literature that depicts the Mexican American experience. The award was established in 1995 and was named in honor of Dr. Tomás Rivera, a distinguished alumnus of Texas State University. Visit the website for additional information: www.education.txstate.edu/departments/Tomas-Rivera-Book-Award-Project-Link.html.

Online Resources

La Biblioteca de Catalunya, Barcelona

This institution maintains a significant collection of children's literature in Catalonia.

www.gencat.net/be/

Centro de Estudios de Promoción de la Lectura y Literatura Infantil (CEPLI), University of Castille de la Mancha, Spain

This website offers links and information on a wide variety of publications, libraries, activities, schools, and other connections to Catalan children's literature.

www.uclm.es/cepli/

The Isabel Schon International Center for Spanish Books for Youth
The Isabel Schon Collection has relocated to the San Diego Public Library. It provides information about high-quality books in Spanish for children and adolescents published around the world as well as noteworthy books in English about Latinos.
www.isabelschoncenter.org

WorldReaders—South America
WorldReaders is an online social network site for exploring students' independent reading interests while providing them with an opportunity for communicating with readers in other countries.
http://worldreaders.org/continent-resources/south-america/

Organizations

Banco del Libro
The Banco del Libro (Book Bank) is a private, Venezuelan nonprofit civil association dedicated to investigating, experimenting, innovating, and imparting activities dedicated to children and young people for the promotion of reading habits. To this end, the Banco del Libro studies, evaluates, recommends, and distributes books and other reading material in Spanish, destined to children and young people. Furthermore, it compiles and disseminates useful information on reading and books for the formation of adult promoters of reading habits, such as parents, teachers, librarians, specialists, editors, book collectors, and others. The goal is to guide parents, teachers, and library personnel in the different ways of creating good reading habits in homes, schools, and libraries.
www.bancodellibro.org.ve/portal/

ADDITIONAL IBBY NATIONAL SECTIONS IN LATIN AMERICA

Ecuadorian Section of IBBY
www.ibby.org/index.php?id=497

Guatemalan National Section of IBBY
www.ibby.org/index.php?id=777

IBBY Uruguay
www.ibby.org/index.php?id=464

Print Resources

Schon, Isabel. *Recommended Books in Spanish for Children and Young Adults, 2004–2008.* Lanham, MD: Scarecrow Press, 2009.

This book is an outstanding reference tool that includes annotated entries for more than 1,200 books in Spanish published between 2004 and 2008 in the United States, Spain, Mexico, Venezuela, and Argentina. Each entry includes an extensive critical annotation, the title in Spanish as well as English, the tentative grade level, and the approximate price. The books have been selected because of their quality of art and writing, the presentation of material and appeal to the intended audience, and the support of the informational, educational, recreational, and personal needs of Spanish speakers from preschool through the twelfth grade.

Publishers

Arte Público Press
This is the nation's largest and most established publisher of literature by U.S. Hispanic authors.

Its imprint for children and young adults, Piñata Books, is dedicated to the realistic and authentic portrayal of the themes, languages, characters, and customs of Hispanic culture in the United States. Based at the University of Houston, Arte Público Press, Piñata Books, and the U.S. Hispanic Literary Heritage project provide the most widely recognized and extensive showcase for Hispanic literary arts, history, and politics.

www.latinoteca.com/

Cinco Puntos Press
Cinco Puntos Press was founded in 1985 as a small, very independent publishing company in El Paso, Texas, just north of the U.S.-Mexican border. In recognition of their importance as a regional voice and their commitment to literature, they have received the American Book Award for excellence in publishing and have been inducted into the Latino Literary Hall of Fame.

www.cincopuntos.com/

Ediciones Ekaré
Ediciones Ekaré is a small, independent Latin American publisher that was founded in 1978. It was one of the first children's book publishers in Latin

America, specializing in picture books and illustrated books. The publisher now has its offices in Caracas, Venezuela; Santiago, Chile; and Barcelona, Spain. Ediciones Ekaré's mission is to produce meaningful books—books that children and adults can read with interest and that will stay in their memories and their hearts.

www.ekare.com.ve/index.html

Celebrations

El Día de los Niños/El Día de los Libros

Children's Day/Book Day, also known as El día de los Niños/El día de los Libros (Día), is a celebration of children, families, and reading held annually on April 30. The celebration emphasizes the importance of literacy for children of all linguistic and cultural backgrounds. Visit the website for additional information: www.ala.org/ala/mgrps/divs/alsc/initiatives/diadelosninos/aboutdia/aboutdia.cfm.

CHAPTER FOUR

Canada and the Far North

Eskimo Encampment

CANADA

Andrekson, Judy. **Little Squire: The Jumping Pony**. Illustrated by David Parkins. Toronto, Tundra Books, 2007. ISBN 978-0-88776-770-8, 0-88776-770-2. 67 p. (8–11). Chapter book.

See Ireland for description.

Asch, Frank. **Time Twister: Journal #3 of a Cardboard Genius**. Toronto, Kids Can Press, 2008. ISBN 978-1-55453-230-8, 1-55453-231-5. 144 p. (7–10). Novel.

Once again, Alex flexes his scientific imagination in the third volume of this series. Alex works reluctantly with Jonathan, his pesky little brother, to develop a time travel machine. Good friend Zoe joins in the fun and danger as the trio discovers an unseen world of time travelers. Alex's ambition gets the best of him when he steals a device from one of the travelers. This puts the trio in jeopardy, and they must flee in the Star Jumper. Although the spacecraft is designed for two, Alex finds an ingenious way to include both Jonathan and Zoe. *dgw*

Author lives in the United States.

Science Fiction, Time Travel, Boy Inventors, Humorous Stories, Space Vehicles, Science Fiction

Bailey, Linda. **Stanley at Sea**. Illustrated by Bill Slavin. Toronto, Kids Can Press, 2008. ISBN 978-1-55453-193-6, 1-55453-193-4. 32 p. (2–5). Picture book.

Rejected by his human family while they enjoy a picnic meal, Stanley wanders away and forges an alliance with his hungry dog friends. Their hunt for food leads them to a ham sandwich on a boat, but it is only a one-dog meal. While the dogs quarrel over the food, the boat breaks free, and they are soon surrounded by the sea. Their surprise rescue includes an enormous meal of steaks and sausages and a safe trip back home. *dgw*

Author lives in British Columbia.

Dogs, Pets, Ships, Voyages and Travels, Fiction

Baker, Deirdre F. **Becca at Sea**. Toronto, Groundwood Books, 2007. ISBN 978-0-88899-737-1, 0-88899-737-X. 165 p. (9–12). Novel.

Beginning in February and ending in late summer, this episodic story chronicles young Becca's visits to her grandmother's home on a remote island off the coast of British Columbia. While Becca's parents remain on the mainland preparing for a new baby, Becca copes with her eccentric, adventurous grandmother and helps host a stream of wildly diverse visiting relatives and friends. She gardens, learns to handle various kinds of boats, minds a baby seal, and eventually finds a friend all her own. The sharply drawn characters and vividly realized setting evoke a place where life follows the change of seasons and rhythms of the sea. *CCBC Best Books for Kids & Teens 2008 Starred Selection; Horn Book Mind the Gap 2008 Winner. mac*

Author lives in Canada.

Grandmothers, Family Life, Islands, Maturation (Psychology), Canada, British Columbia, Fiction

Bell, Joanne. **Breaking Trail**. Toronto, Groundwood Books/House of Anansi, 2005. ISBN 978-0-88899-630-5, 0-88899-630-6. 135 p. (11–14). Novel.

Becky is determined to train Ginger, Pepper, and Salt to be her first dog team even though she has been told that "they will never pull for her" (9). Her chance to prove herself as a handler comes when her mother and father return to their isolated cabin in an attempt to help Becky's depressed father. Their journey is not made easier when her father's lead dog dies and when Ginger gives birth to pups. There are vivid, detailed descriptions of the Yukon and wildlife as the family hurries to beat the melting of the ice as spring approaches. hc

Author was born in England and lives in Yukon Territory, Canada.

SLED DOGS, CHILDREN OF DEPRESSED PERSONS, DETERMINATION (PERSONALITY TRAIT), ADVENTURE

Bell, William. **The Blue Helmet: A Novel**. Toronto, Random House/Doubleday Canada, 2006. ISBN 978-0-385-66246-8, 0-385-66246-7. 167 p. (12 up). Novel.

Lee Mercer is angry with life and is on a fast track to trouble. When a cop intervenes and has Lee sent to live with his Aunt Reena outside of Toronto, Lee realizes he had better cooperate or else he will spend his best years behind bars. He helps out in his aunt's café and gradually builds a new self-image as well as a delivery business on his bike. He befriends some of the local residents, among them Cutter, a depressed genius who feels the government is out to get him. When Cutter dies and leaves his property to Lee, his only friend, Lee has to clean out Cutter's house and files of research. As he reads Cutter's journals of being a Blue Helmet Peacekeeper, he realizes there are multiple ways to respond to violence and hurt. CLA *Young Adult Book Award (2007)*. sc

Author lives in Ontario, Canada.

CHOICES, UN PEACEKEEPING, VIOLENCE, GANGS, PROBLEM YOUTH, FICTION

Bennett, Holly. **The Bonemender**. Victoria, BC, Orca Books, 2005. ISBN 978-1-55143-336-3, 1-55143-336-2. 203 p. (12 up). Novel.

Gabrielle is a renowned bonemender, or healer, in the kingdom of Verdeau. When a stranger, the elf Féolan, brings his injured friend, Danaïs, to her for help, Gabrielle's world suddenly expands. She learns about the elves' lives and peaceful community. As Danaïs heals, Féolan and Gabrielle fall in love and despair that their life spans (one a long elf life and the other a shorter human one) are not comparable. The relationship gets placed on hold while the elves and humans engage in a battle to defeat the Greffaires. The intersection of cultures permits Gabrielle to learn more about her past, and she soon discovers that she is, in fact, half elf, leading to a wonderfully touching romance at the end. *nrz*

Author lives in Canada.

HEALERS, FANTASY, ELVES, BATTLES, ROMANCE, FANTASY

Brooks, Martha. **Mistik Lake**. New York, Farrar, Straus and Giroux, 2007. Originally published by Groundwood Books Canada, in 2007. ISBN 978-0-374-34985-1, 0-374-34985-1. 207 p. (14 up). Novel.

In this melancholy and pensive, yet ultimately hopeful novel, Odella struggles to piece together the secrets of her mother's past and to uncover the truth surrounding three generations of women in her family. It is the story of first love set amid family difficulties and takes place mainly in the small town of Mistik Lake, Manitoba. This beautifully and sparely written narrative alternates among three narrators' points of view of events past and present. As the revelations about the past come to light and Odella's life is changed in unexpected ways, she begins to realize how complicated love really can be. *2008 USBBY Outstanding International Books List, ALA Best Books for Young Adults, NYPL Books for the Teen Age, CCBC Choice, Kirkus Reviews Editor's Choice, Publishers Weekly Best Children's Books of the Year, Capitol Choices Noteworthy Titles for Children and Teens. ae*

Author lives in Winnipeg, Canada.

SECRETS, INTERPERSONAL RELATIONS, MOTHERS, ICELANDERS, MANITOBA, CANADA, FICTION

Campbell, Nicola I. **Shi-Shi-Etko**. Illustrated by Kim LaFave. Toronto, Groundwood Books, 2005. ISBN 978-0-88899-659-6, 0-88899-659-4. 30 p. (4–8). Picture book.

One of the travesties of recent history is the forced removal of indigenous children from their homes to be educated at Eurocentric boarding schools. Without judgment, Campbell relates the fictional story of the four days before Shi-shi-etko must leave her family. Each day, the young girl is taken on outings meant to imprint memories of home. The relatives come for a feast, but still Shi-shi-etko must climb into the pickup truck and leave her family for almost a year. LaFave's digital illustrations evoke a peaceful and unspoiled natural setting. Introductory material provides background on Canadian residential schools. Prequel to *Shin-chi's Canoe* (reviewed here). *lmp*

Author and illustrator live in British Columbia.

INDIGENOUS CHILDREN–CANADA, NATIVE CHILDREN–CANADA, INDIANS OF NORTH AMERICA–EDUCATION, OFF-RESERVATION BOARDING SCHOOLS–CANADA, RESIDENTIAL SCHOOLS, HOME, MEMORY, CANADA, FICTION

Campbell, Nicola I. **Shin-Chi's Canoe**. Illustrated by Kim LaFave. Toronto, Groundwood Books, 2008. ISBN 978-0-88899-857-6, 0-88899-857-0. 40 p. (7–10). Picture book.

Shin-chi and his older sister, Shi-shi-etko, spend long months away from their family and village at an Indian residential school, where they endure many injustices. A toy canoe made by his father helps keep Shin-chi's spirit alive. Warm, brown tones are used in the illustrations, which are based on archival photographs. Introductory notes provide information about the period of history beginning around 1860 and lasting more than one hundred years, during which tens of thousands of children were removed from their homes and required to attend Indian boarding, mission, and industrial schools in the United States and Canada. Sequel to *Shi-shi-etko* (2005). *2009 USBBY Outstanding International Books List. ca*
Author and illustrator live in British Columbia.
FIRST NATIONS, NATIVE PEOPLES OF NORTH AMERICA, RESIDENTIAL SCHOOLS, CANADA, HISTORICAL FICTION

Collins, Yvonne & Sandy Rideout. **The Black Sheep**. New York, Hyperion Books for Children, 2007. ISBN 978-1-4231-0156-7, 1-4231-0156-1. 348 p. (12 up). Novel.

Kendra is frustrated by her rigid and conservative parents, so she does what many fifteen-year-olds only dream about doing. Kendra trades them for a new set of parents with the help of the producer of a popular TV show, *Black Sheep*. Kendra's new family comes with hippie parents, six children, and a ferret. During Kendra's stay, she gets arrested, falls for her new older "brother," and is horribly misunderstood. But Kendra is eventually transformed into a mature and compassionate person. *dgw*
Authors live in Canada.
REALITY TELEVISION PROGRAMS, PARENT AND TEENAGER, FAMILY LIFE, OTTERS, WILDLIFE RESCUE, MONTEREY, CALIFORNIA, FICTION

Croza, Laurel. **I Know Here**. Illustrated by Matt James. Toronto, Groundwood Books, 2010. ISBN 978-0-88899-923-8, 0-88899-923-2. 29 p. (4–7). Picture book.

The little girl who narrates Croza's memoir is worried about leaving the familiarity of her family's mobile home at the edge of the forest for the big city of Toronto. To help her remember all that she loves and so that she can share it with new friends in the city, she draws a giant picture of everything she loves about Saskatchewan and carries it with her to the big city. Children around the world will relate to the love for places they've left behind. *2010 Winner of the Boston Globe-Horn Book Award for Excellence in Children's Literature (Picture Book). lvb*

Author lives in Markham, Ontario; illustrator lives in Toronto.

SASKATCHEWAN, CANADA, FICTION

Curtis, Christopher Paul. **Elijah of Buxton**. New York, Scholastic Press, 2007. ISBN 978-0-439-02344-3, 0-439-02344-0. 341 p. (10 up). Novel.

Elijah is the only child of former slaves, but more importantly, he was the first freeborn child of the historic Buxton settlement in Ontario, Canada. Understandably, Elijah is carefully protected from the harsh realities his parents experienced before escaping to freedom. Curtis uses Elijah's eleven-year-old voice and perspective to masterfully tell the story of the young boy's maturation as he helps a friend try to recover the stolen money that was set aside to buy a family's freedom. Elijah makes his way to Michigan, a place ripe with free slaves, runaway slaves, and paddy-rollers seeking to catch and return to the South those who sought what Elijah comes to appreciate more and more, freedom. *2007 Governor General's Literary Award (Honor Book), 2008 Geoffrey Bilson Award for Historical Fiction for Young People, 2008 CLA Book of the Year for Children Award, 2008 Ruth and Sylvia Schwartz Children's Book Award (Honor Book), 2008 Newbery Honor Book, 2007 Coretta Scott King Award, 2008 Scott O'Dell Award for Historical Fiction (Honor Book), 2008 Jane Addams Children's Book Award (Honor Book). sc*

Author lives in the United States.

SLAVERY, COMING OF AGE, BLACKS–CANADA, NORTH BUXTON (ONTARIO) HISTORY 19TH CENTURY, CANADA HISTORY 1763–1867, HISTORICAL FICTION

De Lint, Charles. **The Blue Girl**. New York, Penguin/Viking, 2004. ISBN 978-0-670-05924-9, 0-670-05924-2. 368 p. (14 up). Short Stories.

In this urban fantasy, Imogene is trying to lead a normal life at Redding High, Newford, after being a gang member at her previous school. She becomes best friends with Maxine, but there are still bullies to deal with—and others—because Imogene "walks at the edges of how the world's supposed to be . . ." (165). Imogene's childhood companion, "Pelly," thought to be imaginary, reappears; and Imogene and Maxine meet the school ghost, Adrian, who is mixed up with malevolent fairies. Imogene, Maxine, and Adrian take turns in narrating as they make plans, with Pelly, to defeat the "anamithin" who would eat their souls. *2006 White Pine Award Ontario Library Association Best Canadian Young Adult Fiction, 2005 YALSA Best Books for Young Adults. hc*

Author was born in the Netherlands and lives in Canada.

FAIRIES, GHOSTS, IMAGINARY PLAYMATES, DREAMS, CONDUCT OF LIFE, HIGH SCHOOLS, FANTASY FICTION

Debon, Nicolas. **The Strongest Man in the World: Louis Cyr**. Illustrated by the author. Toronto, Groundwood Books, 2007. ISBN 978-0-88899-731-9, 0-88899-731-0. 27 p. (8–10). Picture book.

Beginning with endpapers that show turn-of-the-century circus legends in feats of amazing human strength and agility, this graphic novel is a lively piece of biographical writing. On the eve of his retirement from performing as the strongest man in the world, Louis Cyr recounts to his young daughter the story of how he came to hold his weightlifting title and to create his own circus. The graphic format of the text highlights the enormity of Cyr's feats and moves the reader through extensive nonfiction text. The afterward includes additional biographical information as well as photos of Cyr and his family. *2008 USBBY Outstanding International Books List. Two of Debon's previous books,* Four Pictures by Emily Carr *and* Dawn Watch, *have been short-listed for Canada's prestigious Governor General's Award. lvb*

Author was originally from Canada but now lives in France.

CYR, LOUIS, 1863–1912, STRONGMEN, QUÉBEC, BIOGRAPHY, WEIGHT LIFTERS, CIRCUS

Ellis, Deborah. **Off to War: Voices of Soldiers' Children**. Toronto, Groundwood Books, 2008. ISBN 978-0-88899-894-1, 0-88899-894-5. 175 p. (10 up). Nonfiction.

As the subtitle suggests, *Off to War* is told in the voices of soldiers' children. When this book was written, the Boys and Girls Clubs of America estimated that "1.2 million young people in the United States have at least one parent in the armed forces" (11). These young voices remind us that for every soldier sent away from home, others remain behind. In their own words, these youngsters tell Ellis their problems, fears, and how they cope while their parents are thousands of miles away, fighting wars in Afghanistan and Iraq. *2009 Winner Society of School Librarians International Honor Book Award, 2009 Canadian Children's Book Centre–Best Books for Kids and Teens, 2008 Library Media Connection Editor's Choice Awards–Social Studies. lmp*

Author lives in Canada.
CHILDREN AND WAR, CHILDREN OF MILITARY PERSONNEL INTERVIEWS, CANADA, UNITED STATES, NONFICTION

Fagan, Cary. **Ten Old Men and a Mouse**. Illustrated by Gary Clement. Toronto, Tundra Books, 2007. ISBN 978-0-88776-716-6, 0-88776-716-8. 32 p. (6 up). Picture book.

Ten Old Men and a Mouse is a charming story about the unlikely friendship that develops between ten old men whose lives revolve around their daily prayer sessions, the care of an old synagogue, and a mouse that decides to take up residency there. The humor in the whimsical illustrations that accompany the text will put a smile on readers' and listeners' faces regardless of age. *The author has won the Sydney Taylor Honor Book Award, a Mr. Christie Silver Medal, and a Silver Birch Honor Book Award. The illustrator has won the Governor General's Award for Illustration (Canada). ak*

Author and illustrator live in Canada.
MICE, JEWS, SYNAGOGUES, PROBLEM SOLVING, FICTION

Frost, Helen. **The Braid**. New York, Farrar, Straus and Giroux/Frances Foster Books, 2006. ISBN 978-0-374-30962-6, 0-374-30962-0. 95 p. (12 up). Novel in Verse.

"You / me / sisters / always" (7). In 1850, Sarah and Jeannie's family are evicted from their home in the Outer Hebrides and are forced to emigrate to Canada. But Sarah decides to stay behind with their grandmother on Mingulay and makes a braid of Jennie's hair and her own so that each will carry with them a symbol of their love. Similarly, Frost masterfully braids together the sisters' stories of their different lives heard in alternating narrative poems interspersed with short "praise poems." The settings of Mingulay and Cape Breton together with historical details, relevant to each context, are beautifully rendered in this novel in verse. *2007 YALSA Best Books for Young Adults, The Lion and Unicorn Award for Excellence in North American Poetry, 2007 NCSS-CSC Notable Trade Book in the Field of Social Studies, 2007 Notable Book in Historical Fiction, 2007 Notable Children's Book in the Language Arts List. hc*

Author lives in the United States.
SISTERS, FAMILY, ISLANDS, EMIGRATION AND IMMIGRATION, MINGULAY (SCOTLAND), CAPE BRETON ISLAND (N.S.), SCOTLAND, CANADA, HISTORICAL FICTION 1841–1867

Gay, Marie-Louise. **Caramba!** Illustrated by the author. Toronto, Groundwood Books/House of Anansi Press, 2005. ISBN 978-0-88899-667-1, 0-88899-667-5. 32 p. (3–7). Picture book.

Caramba is a cat with a disability. Unlike all other cats, Caramba cannot fly. As hard as he tries, and in spite of the help of his friends, he remains firmly on the ground. One glorious day his friends take him for a ride in the air; however, the day almost ends in tragedy as they drop Caramba into the sea . . . and he discovers that he can swim! The adventure ends when the nautical cat rows off with Portia the pig, ready for new adventures and much more accepting of himself. *2006 Ruth and Sylvia Schwartz Children's Book Award. sc*
   Author is French-Canadian and lives in Montreal.
   CATS, FLIGHT, DETERMINATION, SELF-ACCEPTANCE, FICTION

Gay, Marie-Louise. Translated by the author. **When Stella Was Very, Very Small**. Illustrated by the author. Toronto, Groundwood Books, 2009. Simultaneously published as *Quand Stella était Toute Petite* in French by Dominique et Compagnie Québec. ISBN 978-0-88899-906-1, 0-88899-906-2. 32 p. (4–8). Picture book.
   Stella has always been captivating, sporting halos of tangerine corkscrews and unconventional perspectives. *When Stella Was Very, Very Small* reminisces on her early life—when the world was so large and "cups jumped off the table, just like that!" Gentle watercolors, with appropriate crayon wall drawings, provide a very, very small person's perspective—and unwitting humor. New readers will identify with Stella remembering when ". . . words looked like ants running off the pages," but all ages will enjoy reminiscing about "when I was very, very small." Meanwhile, everyone can revel in Gay's extraordinary language. *Marie-Louise Gay has been nominated for the Astrid Lindgren and Hans Christian Andersen Awards. lmp*
   Author lives in Montreal.
   BROTHERS AND SISTERS, CANADA, FICTION

Gay, Marie-Louise & David Homel. **Travels with My Family**. Illustrated by Marie-Louise Gay. Toronto, Groundwood Books/House of Anansi Press, 2006. ISBN 970-88899-688-6, 0-88899-688-8. 119 p. (7–10). Novel.
   Their parents like to spend family vacations in "out-of-the-way" places, narrates their elder son (13). In each short chapter he recounts the family's adventures: a hurricane in Maine, a sandstorm in the Arizona desert, and how he saves his younger brother from a dangerous wave on a beach in California. Other adventures include a visit to an unusual farm in British Columbia, experiencing Christmas and New Years in Mexico, and a narrow escape on a beach holiday at Tybee Island, Georgia. Interesting information about different locales is integrated with the narrator's humorous observations. *Among her many awards, Marie-Louise Gay has won The*

Canada Council Children's Literature Prize for Illustration, the Governor General's Literary Award for Illustrations, and the Amelia Frances Howard-Gibbon Illustrator's Award. hc

Marie-Louise Gay is from Canada; David Hormel lives in Canada and was born in Chicago.

Voyages and Travels, Brothers and Sisters, Parent and Child, Adventure Stories, Automobile Travel, Fiction

Ghent, Natale. **No Small Thing**. Cambridge, MA, Candlewick Press, 2005. Originally published by HarperCollins Canada, in 2003. ISBN 978-0-7636-2422-4, 0-7636-24225. 245 p. (10–14). Novel.

The family has little money since their father left, but Nathaniel and his sisters are determined to keep the beautiful white pony that was given away to anyone who can offer him a "good home" (1). In this warm family story set in Ontario in 1977, Nat, who uses his paper-route money to hire a stall in a broken-down barn, tells about the joys and difficulties of owning Smokey as he and his sisters struggle with poverty. When a fire threatens Smokey's life, Nat knows he must sell him, but after one last desperate ride, there is hope after all. *hc*

Author lives in Canada.

Brothers and Sisters, Horses, Single-parent Families, Poverty, Ontario History–20th Century, Canada Fiction

Gilkerson, William. **Pirate's Passage**. Illustrated by the author. Boston, Trumpeter Books/Shambhala, 2006. ISBN 978-1-59030-247-7, 1-59030-247-8. 364 p. (10 up). Novel.

In memoir style, a contemporary adult narrator (who takes the name "Jim Hawkins") recounts a tale of his twelfth year of life when an ancient sailboat bearing a mysterious old sea captain is blown off course into his Nova Scotia bay. Captain Charles Johnson, a lover of rum and a teller of tales, not only becomes a guest at the inn run by Jim's widowed mother but also Jim's tutor on pirate history. Throughout, the Captain's origin, motives, and even his integrity remain uncertain. Noted marine artist Gilkerson produced amazingly detailed illustrations as well as vignettes of ships, cannons, and maps to illuminate chapter openers. *2006 Canadian Governor General's Award, 2006 New York Library Association "Book of the Season" Award. nlr*

Author is from Nova Scotia, and he is a journalist, historian, sailor, and maritime artist.

Pirates, Sailing, Nova Scotia, Historical Fiction

Gingras, Charlotte. Translated by Susan Ouriou. **Pieces of Me**. Toronto, Kids Can Press, 2009. Originally published as *La Liberté? Connais pas* in French by La Courte Échelle Canada in 2005. ISBN 978-1-55453-242-1, 1-55453-242-6. 144 p. (14 up). Novel.

Mirabelle, like many teens, is an unreliable narrator when she assesses relationships. Her father is bigger than life—in her memory—while her mother, with whom she lives, is portrayed as a total wacko. To escape, Mira has always turned to books and art, particularly if the natural world is involved. Her second-year art teacher, whom everyone calls "the Birdman," encourages her to take risks but also to get counseling. It is through Mira's newfound ability to accept life and friendship as tentative but worthwhile that she is finally able to pick up the pieces. *2010 USBBY Outstanding International Books List, 2010 ALA/YALSA Best Books for Young Adults, 2009 winner of the Governor General's Literary Award (translation)*. lmp

Author lives in Montreal, Canada.

MOTHER-DAUGHTER RELATIONSHIP, TEENAGE GIRLS, SELF-ACTUALIZATION, SEX, GRIEF, TEACHER-STUDENT RELATIONSHIPS, ARTISTS, CANADA, FICTION

Gregory, Nan. **I'll Sing You One-O**. New York, Clarion Books, 2006. ISBN 978-0-618-60708-2, 0-618-60708-0. 220 p. (9–14). Novel.

Gemma wants to return to her foster family rather than live with relatives she has never known. After reading a book about saints, she begins to look for an angel to save her from her problems. Unique writing reveals Gemma's inner thoughts and perspectives, sometimes unrealistic and confused, which still strongly communicate her individual character. *si*

Author lives in Canada.

ORPHANS, FOSTER HOMES, SIBLINGS, REALISTIC FICTION

Harley, Avis. **Sea Stars: Saltwater Poems**. Illustrated by Margaret Butschler. Honesdale, PA, Boyds Mills Press/Wordsong, 2006. ISBN 978-1-59078-429-7, 1-59078-429-4. 35 p. (6–11). Poetry.

Using a variety of poetic forms, including rhyming couplets, haiku, and acrostic, Avis Harley has crafted twenty-seven short poems inspired by Margaret Butschler's extraordinary close-up color photographs of marine plants and animals. An appended "Looking Deeper" double-page spread identifies the subject of each poem, with common name and brief notes. The design of the book, with the framing of the photographs by thin, white borders and varying placement of the poems and photographs on flat-colored backgrounds that suggest an ocean setting, invites readers to explore the beauty of underwater life. *ca*

Author and illustrator live in British Columbia.

Poetry, Marine Plants and Animals

Haworth-Attard, Barbara. **Theories of Relativity**. New York, Henry Holt, 2005. Originally published by HarperCollins Canada, in 2003. ISBN 978-0-8050-7790-2, 0-8050-7790-1. 231 p. (14 up). Novel.

Banished from the house by his mother so her new man won't know about his existence, sixteen-year-old Dylan tries surviving on the streets with teen runaways and those who prey on them. With no family to turn to, some do-gooders offer a hand if he wants to accept it. *2006 USBBY-CBC Outstanding International Books List, nominated for a Governor General's Award (Canada).*

Author lives in Canada.

Teenage Boys, Homeless Teenagers, Street Life, Fiction

Hodge, Deborah. **Lily and the Mixed-up Letters**. Illustrated by France Brassard. Toronto, Tundra Books, 2007. ISBN 978-0-88776-757-9, 0-88776-757-5. 32 p. (6–10). Picture book.

Lily loves to paint. She also loves school until she experiences difficulty reading. She tries to come up with excuses for why she should stay home or shouldn't have to read at school. She finally confides to her mother that she will not be able to read her assigned page on Parent Day. Her mother then explains that she, too, had difficulty learning to read when she was young. With the help and support of her mother, teacher, and a reading buddy at school, Lily overcomes her difficulties and gains the confidence to succeed. Colorful, expressive illustrations by France Brassard beautifully enhance the story. *ak*

The award-winning author lives in Burnaby, British Columbia.

Dyslexia, Self-acceptance, Determination

Horvath, Polly. **The Corps of the Bare-Boned Plane**. New York, Farrar, Straus and Giroux, 2007. Simultaneously published by Groundwood Books Canada. ISBN 978-0-374-31553-5, 0-374-31553-1. 261 p. (12 up). Novel.

The death of both their parents catapults cousins Meline and Jocelyn into the household of their eccentric Uncle Marten, an independently wealthy hermit who, in earlier years, played the stock market so that he could now be alone and think about what interests him. Alone no longer, the arrival of the girls means adding a housekeeper, a butler, a zany helicopter pilot, and a

romantic doctor into the household mix. The characters have one thing in common: they are each in their own unique ways learning to deal with the death of loved ones and the resulting loneliness. Set on an isolated island off the Vancouver coast with events narrated by alternating characters, the mystery surrounding Meline and Jocelyn's family is solved only as the teenagers begin to learn that running away from pain does not help start life again. *2008 Sheila A. Egoff Children's Literature Prize, 2008 CLA Young Adult Book Award finalist. Polly Horvath has won the National Book Award, the Newbery Honor, the Boston Globe-Horn Book Honor, the Mr. Christie Award, the Young Adult Canadian Book of the Year, and has been listed on the White Raven's list. sc*
Author lives in Victoria, British Columbia.
DEATH, GRIEF, UNCLES, COUSINS, AIRPLANES, BRITISH COLUMBIA, FICTION

Ibbitson, John. **The Landing: A Novel**. Toronto, Kids Can Press, 2008. ISBN 978-1-55453-234-6, 1-55453-234-5. 160 p. (10 up). Novel.
Fifteen-year-old Ben longs to play the violin instead of working alongside his Uncle Henry, scraping a living from selling gasoline and doing odd jobs for "cottagers" on Lake Muskoka. There is no money in Ben's Depression-strapped world for violin lessons. When a wealthy widow hires him to repair her home, then encourages his interest in music, Ben struggles with this newfound opportunity. The resolution is sudden when a freak squall sinks his uncle's boat, and Ben is unable to save him. Ben and his mother leave the Landing, resolved to do what it takes for Ben to study music. *2009 USBBY Outstanding International Books List, 2008 Governor General's Literary Award–Canada. sc*
Author lives in Canada.
MUSIC, COMING OF AGE, BOYS, UNCLES, VIOLINISTS, MUSKOKA–ONTARIO LAKE DISTRICT, SOCIAL CONDITIONS (1918–1945), HISTORICAL FICTION

Jenkins, Emily. **Skunkdog**. Illustrated by Pierre Pratt. New York, Farrar, Straus and Giroux/Frances Foster Books, 2008. ISBN 978-0-374-37009-1, 0-374-37009-5. n.p. (4–8). Picture book.
"Dumpling was a dog of enormous enthusiasm, excellent obedience skills—and very little nose" (n.p.). Since she could not sense smell, Dumpling could not differentiate between dogs and cats or garbage and flowers. So even though "she went into paroxysms of joy over people coming home" (n.p.), she had no animal friends. This combination becomes a significant problem when Dumpling and her human family move to the country and Dumpling discovers an animal in her yard. Lovely language and humorously expressive illustrations enrich this subtle tale of friendship. *Pierre Pratt is the*

recipient of the Governor General's Literary Award for Illustration, Canada's most prestigious award for children's books, and he was a finalist for the Hans Christian Andersen Award in 2008. lmp

Author lives in New York, and the illustrator lives in Montreal.

FRIENDSHIP, DOGS, SKUNKS, FANTASY, U.S.

Jocelyn, Marthe. **Would You**. New York, Random House/Wendy Lamb Books, 2008. ISBN 978-0-375-83703-6, 0-375-83703-5. 165 p. (12 up). Novel.

Would you rather lose all your hair or all your teeth? Those are the kinds of questions Natalie and her friends pose when they are together. But when her beloved sister, Claire, steps in front of a car and winds up in a coma, their thoughts turn to more serious subjects, like would you rather die or have those around you die? Her anticipated summer of working, hanging around with friends, and seeing Claire off to college is transformed into a nightmare of doctors, hospitals, and well-meaning neighbors. A realistic and moving account of a family dealing with grief and loss. *2009 USBBY Outstanding International Books List, 2009 Young Adult Book Award Honour Book–Canada, 2009 Best Books for Kids and Teens, Canadian Children's Book Centre*. djg

Author lives in New York City and Stratford, Ontario.

SISTERS, FAMILY LIFE, TRAFFIC ACCIDENTS, MEDICAL CARE, COMA, FICTION

Larsen, Andrew. **The Imaginary Garden**. Illustrated by Irene Luxbacher. Toronto, Kids Can Press, 2009. ISBN 978-1-55453-279-7, 1-55453-279-5. 30 p. (4–8). Picture book.

When Poppa, who loves gardening, moves into an apartment, his grand-daughter Theo helps him create a colorful imaginary garden full of flowers for his balcony—on a huge canvas. When Poppa goes on a holiday leaving Theo to take care of the garden, she is uncertain how to proceed alone, but she dons her gardening hat, picks up a brush, paints a garden full of colorful blossoms—and completes the garden by painting in two comfy lawn chairs. *The Imaginary Garden* is a cheery, colorful celebration of the imagination, the possibilities of art, and the special relationship between a grandparent and grandchild. *2010 USBBY Outstanding International Books List*. ca

Author and illustrator both live in Toronto, Ontario.

GARDENS, IMAGINATION, PAINTING, GRANDFATHERS, FICTION

Lawrence, Iain. **Gemini Summer**. New York, Delacorte Press, 2006. ISBN 978-0-385-73089-1, 0-385-73089-6. 261 p. (10 up). Novel.

Set in the mid-1960s in a valley called Hog's Hollow in Toronto, this tale features the River family, each with a secret dream (or nightmare). Danny wants a dog; his older brother, Beau, hopes to become an astronaut; their mother fancies herself an author of antebellum southern fiction; and their father, Old Man River, fears a nuclear disaster as the Vietnam War heats up. When tragedy befalls the family, a stray dog—named Rocket by Danny—comes into the picture, and Danny sets off with Rocket to Cape Canaveral to meet astronaut Gus Grissom and to try to fulfill Beau's dream. *2007 Canadian Governor General's Literary Award. bal, sc*
Author lives in the Gulf Islands of Canada.
VIRGIL I. GRISSOM, PROJECT GEMINI (U.S.), BROTHERS, DOGS, DEATH, FAMILY LIFE, HISTORICAL FICTION

Lawson, JonArno. **Black Stars in a White Night Sky**. Illustrated by Sherwin Tjia. Honesdale, PA, Wordsong/Boyds Mills Press, 2008. Originally published by Pedlar Press Canada, in 2006. ISBN 978-1-59078-521-8, 1-59078-521-5. 118 p. (10 up). Poetry.

Short poems on diverse, offbeat, and sometimes surprising topics are supported by imaginative black-and-white illustrations in this interesting collection. Alliteration, assonance, rhythm, and comical sound play introduce characters, such as an eloquent elephant, "Winsome Billy Willoughby," and "Merciful Percival." Some selections are thought provoking. "Why do days and months have names but not weeks?" "How, without arms / did the sun / climb over the trees?" Endnotes provide information about the sources for the poems. *mjw*
Author lives in Canada.
CHILDREN'S POETRY, CANADA, POETRY

Leavitt, Martine. **Keturah and Lord Death**. Asheville, NC, Front Street, 2006. ISBN 978-1-932425-29-1, 1-932425-29-2. 216 p. (14 up). Fiction.

Sixteen-year-old Keturah is known for her storytelling in the medieval village of Tide-by-Rood, but when she is lost in the forest, she begins to tell the most important story she has ever told—to Lord Death—in order to bargain for her life. The handsome lord, taken by Keturah's beauty, also agrees to let her live if she can find her "true love." Although she wins the heart of Lord Temsland's son because of her role in saving the villagers from the plague, Keturah realizes that she wishes to be the bride of the lord she really loves, Lord Death. *2006 U.S. National Book Award Finalist, 2008 Young People's Literature, Ontario Library Association's White Pine Award. Martine*

Leavitt's awards include YALSA Best Books for Young Adults, 2005 for Heck: Superhero *(also a finalist for the Governor General's Literary Award, 2004) and for* The Dollmage, *2003, and a Mr. Christie Award for* Tom Finder, *2003. hc*
Author lives in Canada.
DEATH, INTERPERSONAL RELATIONS, LOVE STORIES, GRANDMOTHERS

Leck, James. **The Adventures of Jack Lime**. Toronto, Kids Can Press, 2010. ISBN 978-1-55453-364-0, 1-55453-364-3. 126 p. (10–14). Novel.

The "hard-boiled" detective story has a colorful history in literature and film. Although most of the genre's archetypes involve tough guys living in Los Angeles, Jack Lime's home turf is Iona High School, Nova Scotia. Jack nurses a root beer float, carries no weapons, collects no retainers; he usually ends up at the wrong end of a fist, but he always solves his cases, bringing the culprits to justice. Jack Lime introduces himself and the three short stories in this collection, saying, "I'm a detective, a private investigator, a gumshoe. What I do is fix problems" (7). What he'll do is provide mysteries to challenge his readers. *lmp*

Author grew up in Nova Scotia but has lived in Canada and Japan. He currently resides in Kuwait.
HIGH SCHOOL STUDENTS, ORPHANS, NARCOLEPSY, CANADA, FICTION, MYSTERY

Lee, Ingrid. **Dog Lost**. New York, Scholastic/Chicken House, 2008. Originally published by Chicken House Great Britain, in 2008. ISBN 978-0-545-08578-6, 0-545-08578-0. 197 p. (10–14). Novel.

Boy-and-dog stories undeniably should have happy endings. However, from the first chapter of *Dog Lost*, readers will steel themselves for the inevitable tragedy that awaits Mackenzie and the stray pit bull puppy his drunken father unceremoniously dumps on Mack's bed. Consequently, when Cash—still a puppy—inadvertently trips Mack's dad and shatters his bottle of whiskey, we are prepared for the worst. What keeps us ardently reading are the parallel stories of the bedraggled dog missing his boy, the depressed boy lonely for his dog, the cop, two dying strangers, and a community seething to exterminate every pit bull they find. *2009 USBBY Outstanding International Books List. lmp*

Author lives in Canada.
PIT BULL TERRIERS, DOGS, FICTION

Love, Ann & Jane Drake. **Sweet! The Delicious Story of Candy**. Illustrated by Claudia Dávila. Toronto, Tundra Books, 2007. ISBN 978-0-88776-752-4, 0-88776-752-4. 64 p. (8 up). Picture book.

Beginning their history of sweets in 6000 BC—when primitive cave dwellers drew pictures of people scooping honey from trees—to the present day, authors Ann Love and Jane Drake explore the universal fascination and love of sweets, particularly candy. The book is chock full of "sweet" facts that will give readers insight into the who, what, where, when, and how of candy. Claudia Dávila's humorous illustrations, informative maps, and time lines are the "eye candy" for the book. *2009 Hackmatack Children's Choice Book Award (English Nonfiction Winner)*. ak

Authors live in Toronto, Canada. Illustrator Claudia Dávila was born in Chile.

CANDY, HISTORY, NONFICTION

Luxbacher, Irene. **Mattoo, Let's Play!** Illustrated by the author. Toronto, Kids Can Press, 2010. ISBN 978-1-55453-424-1, 1-55453-424-0. 32 p. (4–8). Picture book.

A little girl and her best pal spend the day pretending to fly a rocket ship and to go camping on safari. As much fun as they're having, it would be so much more fun with Mattoo, the kitten. Alas, Mattoo wants no part of the loud adventures and hides. The bedroom is transformed into a blend of tropical forest and savannah, with zebras, giraffes, monkeys, and snakes taking over the pages of the book and camouflaging Mattoo. The thing about cats, though, is that when it gets quiet, they come out of their hiding places, and Mattoo finally decides to join the fun as a jungle cat that loves tuna snacks. lvb

Author lives in Canada.

CATS, HUMAN-ANIMAL RELATIONSHIPS, IMAGINATION, FANTASY

Major, Kevin. **Aunt Olga's Christmas Postcards**. Illustrated by Bruce Roberts. Toronto, Groundwood Books/House of Anansi Press, 2005. ISBN 978-0-88899-593-3, 0-88899-593-8. 32 p. (5–12). Picture book.

Just before Christmas, Anna visits her ninety-five-year-old great-great-aunt Olga for tea. Aunt Olga shows Anna her beloved collection of historic Christmas postcards and talks about the time when she had a job writing the poems that appeared on several of the cards. Aunt Olga blurs the distinction between reality and fantasy, leaving Anna to guess which stories are true and which are fantasy. Aunt Olga and Anna snack on gingerbread and, with much merriment, write new Christmas verses inspired by the postcards. This book includes postcard images from around the world, with holiday greetings in many languages. *Kevin Major has won the Vicky Metcalf Award for his body of work.* nrz

Author lives in St. John's, Newfoundland, Canada.

CHRISTMAS STORIES, AUNTS, INTERGENERATIONAL STORIES, POSTCARDS, CANADA, FICTION

Melanson, Luc. **Topsy-Turvy Town**. Illustrated by the author. Toronto, Tundra Books, 2010. Originally published as *Ma Drôle de Ville* in French by Dominique et Compagnie/Les Editions Héritage Canada, in 2004. ISBN 978-0-88776-920-7, 0-88776-920-9. 32 p. (2–5). Picture book.

Luc Melanson, winner of Canada's Governor General's Literary Award for outstanding fiction writing, allows readers to peek into the outrageous imagination of a little boy whose topsy-turvy world is filled with cars made of chocolate, postmen who travel by cloud, and a unicycle-riding moon. No one believes in his topsy-turvy town, except his mother, who rides off with him in an origami boat—piloted by an elephant sea captain, of course. This book is sure to resonate with every child who has imagined her own land of wild things or his own land beyond the wardrobe closet. *lvb*

Author lives in Montreal, Quebec.

IMAGINATION, FICTION, FANTASY

Napier, Matt. **Hat Tricks Count: A Hockey Number Book**. Illustrated by Melanie Rose. Chelsea, MI, Sleeping Bear Press, 2005. ISBN 978-1-58536-163-2, 1-58536-163-1. n.p. (6–12). Concept book.

Canada's proud sporting tradition is reflected in this hockey number book, a companion volume to *Z is for Zamboni* (2002). Son of a Montreal Canadiens player, Napier offers four-line rhymes for each number from 1 to 20 (then takes readers to 100 by tens). Numbers are used to convey hockey essentials as well as ephemera, such as the number of goals one player must make to ensure that fans' hats are tossed onto the ice (3) and the record number of Stanley Cup wins (11 by Henri Richard). Players, equipment, and rules are explained through sidebars and are amplified by Rose's perspectives in oils. *nlr*

Author and illustrator live in Canada.

SPORTS, HOCKEY, NUMBER CONCEPTS, COUNTING, NONFICTION

Nitto, Tomio. **The Red Rock: A Graphic Fable**. Illustrated by the author. Toronto, Groundwood Books, 2006. ISBN 978-0-88899-669-5, 0-88899-669-1. 28 p. (6–10). Picture book.

Old Beaver loves to look over the valley to the strange red rock across the way. Unbeknownst to him, developers plan to build a dam, hotel, and casino there. Eventually, the animals become aware of the plan as trees are cleared for the construction. The animals organize to protest and to try to stop the development, but they are unsuccessful. In a dream, Old Beaver realizes what he must do. The author inserts a wordless, graphic section in which Old Beaver demonstrates what will eventually happen if the project continues. This innovative combination of formats offers a strong message about the environment. *nlh*

Author is an award-winning graphic artist who moved to Canada from Japan.

NATURE, ENVIRONMENTAL PROTECTION, FOREST ANIMALS, FICTION

Oberman, Sheldon. **Solomon and the Ant: And Other Jewish Folktales**. Honesdale, PA, Boyds Mills Press, 2006. ISBN 978-1-59078-307-8, 1-59078-307-7. 165 p. (10 up). Folktale Anthology.

Master storyteller Oberman retells forty-three traditional Jewish folktales, including legends of King Solomon, religious tales, medieval fables, wisdom tales, tricksters tales, Chelm "fool" stories, and riddle stories, with gentle humor. Each tale is given an informative introduction and ends with notes, commentary, and notations of sources and variants. Folklorist Peninnah Schram provides an introduction to the book, epilogue, glossary, and bibliography, all of which add to the value of this outstanding collection of Jewish folktales. *ca*

Sheldon Oberman lived in Canada; Peninnah Schram lives in New York.

JEWS, FOLKLORE

Oldland, Nicholas. **Big Bear Hug**. Illustrated by the author. Toronto, Kids Can Press, 2009. ISBN 978-1-55453-464-7, 1-55453-464-X. 30 p. (4–8). Picture book.

Tree-huggers rejoice! Here is an environmental allegory that relies on humor—in illustrations as well as text—rather than heavy-handed didacticism. Big Bear was "so filled with love and happiness" that he hugged every living thing in the forest—even "creatures that bears have been known to eat." However, when a man with an axe attacks one of the forest's most magnificent specimens, Bear no longer feels like hugging. The story is perfectly paced so that page turns provide opportunities for prediction and surprise. Oldland's subdued palette of greens and blues, accented by bear and his red-bird companion, focuses readers' eyes on facial expressions that add to the comical layer to this tale. *lmp*

Author lives in New Brunswick, Canada.

HUGGING, BEARS, PICTURE STORYBOOKS, CANADA, FICTION

Oppel, Kenneth. **Skybreaker**. New York, HarperCollins/Eos, 2006. ISBN 978-0-06-053229-1, 0-06-053229-7. 544 p. (9 up). Novel.

The second in the *Airborn* trilogy, *Skybreaker* continues the adventures of Matt and Kate aboard the massive airships developed around the 1900s and used for cargo and passenger transportation around the world. Matt is an aviation student at the Airship Academy in Paris, and Kate is pursuing her interest in biology and unusual creatures. Together they embark on a voyage to find the gold-laden lost ship *Hyperion* that has been floating at high altitudes for forty years. Oppel delivers more nail-biting adventure as Matt and Kate battle air pirates, high altitude, prejudices, lethal life-forms, and eccentric scientists. The trilogy includes *Airborn* (2004), *Skybreaker* (2005), and *Starclimber* (2009). *2006 Ruth and Sylvia Schwartz Children's Book Award, 2006 CLA Young Adult Canadian Book Award (Shortlist), 2005 London Times Children's Novel of the Year. sc*

Author lives in Toronto.

Dirigibles, Airships, Pirates, Inventions, Mythical Animals, Fantasy

Oppel, Kenneth. **Darkwing**. Illustrated by Keith Thompson. New York, HarperCollins/Eos, 2007. ISBN 978-0-06-085054-8, 0-06-085054-X. 422 p. (10 up). Novel.

Set in the Paleocene period when dinosaurs were dying out, Oppel chronicles the early life of Dusk, a chiropter who, unlike the others in his colony, is missing a digit and fur on his sails. Over time, Dusk realizes how different he is as he tries to fit in with his gliding relatives, suppressing his strong impulse to fly like birds. When the colony is threatened by carnivores, Dusk's ability to echolocate and fly becomes important as the chiropters evade predators on their migration to a new and safer home. Oppel ably drops the reader into the fascinating and evolving world as it could have been sixty-five million years ago. Prequel to Oppel's bat trilogy *Silverwing, Sunwing,* and *Firewing*. *2008 Ruth and Sylvia Schwartz Children's Book Award, 2008 CLA Book of the Year Award for Children (Shortlist). sc*

Author lives in Toronto.

Bats, Evolution, Paleocene Period, Prehistoric Creatures, Fantasy Fiction

Porter, Pamela Paige. **The Crazy Man**. Toronto, Groundwood Books/House of Anansi Press, 2005. ISBN 978-0-88899-694-7, 0-88899-694-2. 214 p. (11–13). Novel.

In this free-verse novel set in the Saskatchewan prairie of the 1960s, twelve-year-old Emaline faces personal and family trauma. After her father

accidentally runs over her leg in a tractor accident, leaving her permanently disabled, he shoots her beloved dog, whom he blames for the accident. He then leaves Emaline and her mother to deal with the challenges of farming. Emaline's mother hires Angus, a patient at a nearby mental hospital, to plant and take care of the crops. While the townspeople fear and persecute Angus, Emaline befriends him, and through their friendship she slowly begins to heal, physically and psychologically. *2005 Governor General's, Literary Award for Children's Literature, 2006 TD Canadian Book Award, 2006 Geoffrey Bilson Award for Historical Fiction, 2006 Jane Addams Children's Honor Book. chs*
   Author lives in British Columbia.
   ABSENTEE FATHERS, GRIEF, FARM LIFE, PEOPLE WITH DISABILITIES, SAS-KATCHEWAN

Quan, Elizabeth. **Once Upon a Full Moon**. Illustrated by the author. Toronto, Tundra Books, 2007. ISBN 978-0-88776-813-2, 0-88776-813-X. 48 p. (8–12). Picture book.
   In the 1920s the Lee family journeyed across Canada and the Pacific Ocean to return to their father's homeland, mainland China. They travelled for days before boarding a ship for Japan under the watchful eye of the pale moon, and they continue their adventures by train, double-decker bus, cable car, rickshaw, ferry, and foot before arriving under the new full moon. The story is rich with observations about all the exciting things the Lee family sees and experiences on their journey. Quan, a former protégée of Jackson Pollack and an artist with an international reputation in her own right, has a bachelor of arts degree in East Asian studies and has previously published an illustrated collection of Chinese puppet plays, *The Immortal Poet of the Milo. lvb*
   Author/illustrator lives in Canada.
   CHINESE SOCIAL LIFE AND CUSTOMS 1912–1949, CHINA, EMIGRATION, JOURNEY, 1920S, BIOGRAPHY

Rivera, Raquel. **Arctic Adventures: Tales from the Lives of Inuit Artists**. Illustrated by Jirina Marton. Toronto, Groundwood Books/House of Anansi Press, 2007. ISBN 978-0-88899-714-2, 0-88899-714-0. 47 p. (9 up). Illustrated Nonfiction book.
   In a unique cultural snapshot, Rivera has crafted stories related by four Inuit artists as well as their biographical information, photographs, and a reproduction of one of their prints, paintings, or sculptures. The artists' stories as well as their artwork underscore the weather, activities, danger, and beauty of the far north. The author's multifaceted approach offers a personal

as well as an informative look inside Inuit culture. Author's notes, a glossary, and further reading suggestions provide additional information. *2008 USBBY Outstanding International Books List. nlh*

Author lives in Montreal, Quebec.

INUIT ARTISTS, LEGENDS, CANADA, BIOGRAPHY

Roberts, Ken. **Thumb and the Bad Guys**. Illustrated by Leanne Franson. Toronto, Groundwood Books/House of Anansi Press, 2009. ISBN 978-0-88899-916-0, 0-88899-916-X. 119 p. (8–12). Novel.

Something suspicious is happening in the fishing village of New Auckland in this third adventure of Leon, aka Thumb. He and his friend Susan set out to solve the mystery and instead uncover an archaeological conundrum that may change their small community forever. Other titles include *The Thumb in the Box* (2002) and *Thumb on a Diamond* (2007). *2010 USBBY Outstanding International Books List, 2010 CCBC Choice. djg*

Author lives near Brantford, Ontario.

ARCHAEOLOGY, DETECTIVE AND MYSTERY STORIES, BEST FRIENDS, FISHING VILLAGES, CANADA, NOVEL, FICTION

Shoveller, Herb. **Ryan and Jimmy: And the Well in Africa That Brought Them Together**. Toronto, Kids Can Press, 2006. ISBN 978-1-55337-967-6, 1-55337-967-5. 55 p. (8 up). Picture book.

Ryan and Jimmy: And the Well in Africa That Brought Them Together is the inspiring true story of how determination and tenacity can bring about progress that is life changing. At age six, Canadian first-grader Ryan Hreljac learned that there were people in the world that did not have safe water to drink. From that moment on, he became determined to do something that would bring clean water to others. This book takes readers on Ryan's journey, literally and figuratively, to secure clean drinking water for a group of people in Agweo village, Uganda, Africa. Photographs, copies of letters, and drawings accompany the text. *2007–2008 Great Lakes Great Books Awards–Fourth and Fifth Grade Honor. ak*

Author lives in Canada.

RYAN'S WELL FOUNDATION, INTERNATIONAL COOPERATION, WATER WELLS, AFRICA

Slade, Arthur G. **Jolted: Newton Starker's Rules for Survival**. Illustrated by Antonio Javier Caparo. New York, Random House/Wendy Lamb Books, 2009. ISBN 978-0-385-74700-4, 0-385-74700-4. 227 p. (10–14). Novel.

Newton Starker is a student at a Saskatchewan boarding school dedicated to survival skills. As part of the broader experience at school, he learns that getting along with others is as much a part of surviving as avoiding the light-ning that seeks out his family members. Canadian author Arthur Slade uses an unusual and humorous premise to deliver a strong message. *2010 USBBY Outstanding International Books List, 2008 Saskatoon Book of the Year Saskatch-ewan Book Award, 2008 Fiction Book of the Year Saskatchewan Book Award, 2008 Children's Book of the Year Saskatchewan Book Award.* nlh

Author lives in Saskatchewan, Canada.

Lɪɢʜᴛɴɪɴɢ, Bᴏᴀʀᴅɪɴɢ Sᴄʜᴏᴏʟs, Fɪᴄᴛɪᴏɴ

Spearman, Andy. **Barry, Boyhound**. New York, Random House/Alfred A. Knopf, 2005. ISBN 978-0-375-83264-2, 0-375-83264-2. 230 p. (8–12). Novel.

Barry wakes up and discovers that he is a boyhound—a boy in outward appearance but with a mind of a dog—which leads him to abandon boy be-havior for dog behavior, including chasing cats and biting friends. Spearman incorporates a wealth of sidebars, charts, footnotes, illustrations, and other features, all of which will amuse some readers but distract others. The wacky, and at times gross, humor will appeal particularly to boys. ca

Author lives in Canada.

Dᴏɢs, Fʟᴇᴀs, Hᴜᴍᴏʀᴏᴜs Sᴛᴏʀɪᴇs, Fɪᴄᴛɪᴏɴ

Swanson, Bruce. **Gray Wolf's Search**. Illustrated by Gary Peterson. Toronto, Second Story Press, 2007. ISBN 978-0-9777918-3-5, 0-9777918-3-1. 24 p. (4–8). Picture book.

In his quest to seek guidance for his future, young Gray Wolf is told by the medicine man that his future in the clan depends upon his success in finding and becoming acquainted with an important person. This task sends Gray Wolf on a yearlong journey along the northwest coast inquiring among the various animals he encounters, but they are unable to help him. Finally, in a vision, Gray Wolf learns he is already acquainted with many important people. Each person in his clan is of equal importance. dgw

Author lives in the United States.

Iɴᴅɪᴀɴs ᴏꜰ Nᴏʀᴛʜᴡᴇsᴛ Cᴏᴀsᴛ ᴏꜰ Nᴏʀᴛʜ Aᴍᴇʀɪᴄᴀ, Sʜᴀᴍᴀɴs, Hᴜᴍᴀɴ-Aɴɪᴍᴀʟ Cᴏᴍᴍᴜɴɪᴄᴀᴛɪᴏɴ, Sᴇʟꜰ-ᴀᴄᴛᴜᴀʟɪᴢᴀᴛɪᴏɴ, Aɴɪᴍᴀʟs, Fɪᴄᴛɪᴏɴ

Teevee, Ningeokuluk. Translated by Nina Manning-Toonoo. **Alego**. Il-lustrated by the author. Toronto, Groundwood Books, 2009. ISBN 978-0-88899-943-6, 0-88899-943-7. 21 p. (3–6). Picture book.

For the first time Alego, a young Inuit girl, goes digging for clams with her grandmother at low tide. Alego searches for clams buried in the sand and also discovers the various animals that inhabit the tide pools of the Canadian Arctic. The text is written in both Inuktitut and English. The realistic illustrations are done in graphite and colored pencil. The book includes an illustrated glossary of sea animals labeled with both their Inuit and English names and a map of Baffin Island. *2010 USBBY Outstanding International Books List. ca*

Author lives in Kinngait (Cape Dorset), Nunavut, Canada.

INUIT, MARINE ANIMALS, TIDE POOLS, BAFFIN ISLAND, CANADA, FICTION

Thomson, Sarah L. **Imagine a Day**. Illustrated by Rob Gonsalves. New York, Simon & Schuster/Atheneum Books, 2005. ISBN 978-0-689-85219-0, 0-689-85219-3. 32 p. (4–12). Picture book.

Reminiscent of M. C. Escher, Gonsalves illustrates flights of imagination where reality escapes the confines of time and gravity and meets youthful dreams. Adding words to Gonsalves's paintings, Thomson calls readers to dive into their imaginations and go on adventures while jumping on castle-like rocks in a lake, playing with a dollhouse, ice skating on the path to the moon, or surfing on foam-covered waves that flow into snowcapped mountains. The series includes *Imagine a Night* (2003), *Imagine a Day* (2005), and *Imagine a Place* (2008). *2005 Governor General's Literary Award. sc*

Author lives in the United States; illustrator lives in Ontario, Canada.

IMAGINATION, TROMPE L'OEIL, FICTION

Uegaki, Chieri. **Rosie and Buttercup**. Illustrated by Stéphane Jorisch. Toronto, Kids Can Press, 2008. ISBN 978-1-55337-997-3, 1-55337-997-7. n.p. (3–7). Picture book.

Rosie's enthusiasm over her baby sister, Buttercup, wanes as the toddler grows older and becomes a nuisance. When Buttercup attempts to take possession of Rosie's highly prized pet crickets, Rosie can no longer tolerate her little sister's self-centeredness. Subsequently, Rosie devises a near-perfect plan to remedy the situation by giving Buttercup away to a neighbor. But Rosie's tranquility is short-lived when her heart pines for the companionship of her little sister. She then prepares to make the ultimate sacrifice to get Buttercup back. *Illustrator is a three-time winner of the Governor General's Award for Illustration. dgw, mjw*

Author is a Canadian of Japanese heritage who lives in British Columbia; illustrator lives in Canada.

SISTERS, SIBLING RIVALRY, NEW BABY IN THE FAMILY, TODDLERS, FAMILY RELATIONSHIPS, BABYSITTERS, FANTASY FICTION

Ulmer, Michael. **Loonies and Toonies: A Canadian Number Book**. Illustrated by Melanie Rose. Chelsea, MI, Sleeping Bear Press, 2006. ISBN 978-1-58536-239-4, 1-58536-239-5. n.p. (8 up). Concept book.

One of several concept books issued by Sleeping Bear Press that highlight the geography, history, and culture of Canada, *Loonies and Toonies* refer to natives' names for Canadian one- and two-dollar coins. Written on two levels, each spread presents both a simple rhyme for numerals 1 through 20 (skipping to 50 and 100), as well as sidebars with denser text to extend background information. Topics range from the numbers of kinds of salmon (5), time zones (6), and provinces (13) to the number of barrel riders attempting Niagara Falls (15). Lush oil paintings amplify the text.

Other books in the Canadian nonfiction series include: *A Is for Algonquin: An Ontario Alphabet* (by Lovenia Gorman, illustrated by Melanie Rose); *P Is for Puffin: A Newfoundland and Labrador Alphabet* (by Janet Skirving, illustrated by Odell Archibald); and *S Is for Spirit Bear: A British Columbia Alphabet* (by G. Gregory Roberts, illustrated by Bob Doucet). *nlr*

Author and illustrator live in Canada.

Counting, Canada, Nonfiction

Upjohn, Rebecca. **Lily and the Paper Man**. Illustrated by Renné Benoit. Toronto, Second Story Press, 2007. ISBN 978-1-897187-19-7, 1-897187-19-X. n.p. (4–8). Picture book.

Lily enjoys a friendly walk in the rain with her mother, but she becomes frightened when she sees the Paper Man. His frazzled appearance stands in stark contrast to the well-ordered world of this young girl. On subsequent days, Lily avoids the Paper Man by requesting that she and her mother ride on the bus instead of walking. When winter arrives, Lily's encounter with the Paper Man awakens compassion within her as she realizes his inadequate attire and hapless demeanor is no match for the frigid winter season. Then, Lily makes special plans to help keep the Paper Man warm. *dgw*

Author lives in Canada.

Homeless Persons, Compassion, Helpfulness, Consolation, Fiction

Villeneuve, Anne. **The Red Scarf**. Illustrated by the author. Toronto, Tundra Books, 2010. Originally published as *L'Escharpe Rouge* in French by Les 400 Coups Canada, in 1999. ISBN 978-0-88776-989-4, 0-88776-989-6. 36 p. (5–8). Fiction.

Turpin the taxi-driving mouse picks up his first fare of the day and begins his wordless adventure. Driving the lady with the red beret goes smoothly, but the mysterious man in the black cap and top hat leaves his red scarf in the backseat, and Turpin tries to follow him into a circus tent to return it. Once inside, Turpin barely escapes being done in by the lion-taming act, the fire juggler, and other circus performances rife with danger for small mice. *Governor General's Literary Award–Children's Illustration, TD Canadian Children's Literature Award. lvb*

Author lives in Canada.

SCARVES, LOST ARTICLES, CIRCUS, MAGICIANS, FICTION

Watt, Mélanie. **Scaredy Squirrel**. Illustrated by the author. Toronto, Kids Can Press, 2006. ISBN 978-1-55337-959-1, 1-55337-959-4. 36 p. (5–8). Picture book.

Scaredy Squirrel never leaves his safe tree so he will not have to bump into dangers like tarantulas, green Martians, killer bees, sharks, germs, and poison ivy. His life is routinely the same. He is prepared for any crises with his emergency kit, which contains items that will help him deal with the above list of foes. However, one day a real killer bee approaches, and panicked, Scaredy Squirrel knocks his emergency kit out of the tree and has to jump into the unknown to retrieve it. Incredibly, on his way down he discovers he is a flying squirrel and that his list of dangers will not bother him any time soon. He alters his safe routine to include flying into the unknown adventure of each day. Other books in the series include *Scaredy Squirrel Makes a Friend* (2007), *Scaredy Squirrel at the Beach* (2008), and *Scaredy Squirrel at Night* (2009). *2006 Cybils Award winner, 2007 NCBLA List, 2007 Amelia Frances Howard-Gibbon Illustrator's Award. sc*

Author lives in Montreal, Quebec.

SQUIRRELS, FEAR, COURAGE, FANTASY

Watt, Mélanie. **Augustine**. Illustrated by the author. Toronto, Kids Can Press, 2006. ISBN 978-1-55337-885-3, 1-55337-885-7. 32 p. (4–8). Picture book.

Augustine is a young penguin whose Dad is being transferred to the North Pole. The move precipitates all kinds of feelings as Augustine packs up her room, says goodbye to her friends and extended family, and makes the trip North on Penguin Air. After finding a new house, a very nervous Augustine goes to her new class, where she discovers that her drawings are a wonderful "ice breaker" and a way to help her make new friends. A gentle story about dealing with new situations, *Augustine* is also full of layered ice and cold/North Pole humor wrapped up in Augustine's versions of classic paintings, such as da Vinci's *Mona Lisa*, Wood's *American Gothic*, and Warhol's *Campbell Soup Can. sc*

Author lives in Montreal, Quebec.
MOVING, ART, PENGUINS, NORTH & SOUTH POLES

Watt, Mélanie. **Chester**. Illustrated by the author. Toronto, Kids Can Press, 2007. ISBN 978-1-55453-140-0, 1-55453-140-3. 32 p. (5–9). Picture book.

Chester is Mélanie Watt's cat, and he definitely has an attitude. The two "authors" of the book have a tug-of-war over the story line as Mélanie tries to begin writing about a small mouse. Chester stops the action and insists it is HIS story, and she better just admit it. The two go back and forth as a very egotistical Chester takes over the narrative and drawings until Mélanie performs the ultimate "coup" and puts Chester in a pink tutu. Chester is not defeated . . . just take a look at the back flap biography on the author (or authors). This series continues with *Chester's Back* (2008) and *Chester's Masterpiece* (2010). *2008 Amelia Frances Howard-Gibbon Illustrator's Award. sc*
Author lives in Montreal, Quebec.
CATS, MICE, AUTHORSHIP, FANTASY FICTION

Watts, Leslie Elizabeth. **The Baabaasheep Quartet**. Illustrated by the author. Markham, Ontario, Fitzhenry & Whiteside, 2005. ISBN 978-1-55041-890-3, 1-55041-890-4. 32 p. (4–7). Picture book.

When four sheep retire from the farm and move to the city, they look forward to adapting to a metropolitan lifestyle. They soon realize they just do not fit in. However, when they find a ripped playbill advertising what they think says "baabaasheep quartet," they practice in earnest for the contest, again hoping to fit in. Arriving at the competition, they discover it is for barbershop quartets, not for talented sheep. Some quick thinking and action helps them adapt to the requisite costumes, and the Baabaasheep quartet are winners. *2006 Amelia Frances Howard-Gibbon Illustrator's Award. sc*
Author lives in Ontario.
SHEEP, BARBERSHOP QUARTETS, HUMAN-ANIMAL RELATIONSHIPS, CITY AND TOWN LIFE, IDENTITY, FITTING IN/ADAPTATION, FICTION

Wynne-Jones, Tim. **Rex Zero and the End of the World**. New York, Farrar, Straus and Giroux/Melanie Kroupa Books, 2007. Originally published by Groundwood Books Canada, in 2006. ISBN 978-0-374-33467-3, 0-374-33467-6. 186 p. (8–12). Novel.

At almost eleven, Rex has moved from Vancouver to Ottawa, can't speak French—required in his new school—and has no friends. Until he meets Buster and James. When he introduces himself—Rex Norton-Norton—and explains the hyphen, Buster states, "Like a minus sign." Norton minus Norton equals zero: Rex Zero—the best nickname in the universe (44). The historical setting, replete with the language, food, "modern" conveniences, and icons of the 1960s will be unfamiliar to most readers, and the Cold War images will need explanation. But this small slice of the good ol' days proves to be an engaging mystery-adventure for reading alone or aloud. *2008 USBBY Outstanding International Books List, ALA Notable Children's Books, Boston Book Review–Winner, Bank Street Best Children's Book of the Year, CCBC Choice. lmp*

Author lives in Canada.

MOVING, FAMILIES, FAMILY LIFE, FRIENDSHIP, COLD WAR, CANADA, HISTORICAL FICTION

Wynne-Jones, Tim. **Rex Zero, King of Nothing**. New York, Farrar, Straus and Giroux/Melanie Kroupa Books, 2008. Originally published by Groundwood Books Canada, in 2007. ISBN 978-0-374-36259-1, 0-374-36259-9. 217 p. (8–12). Novel.

Rex has matriculated to sixth grade, where he encounters complex situations that challenge him to examine his shortcomings. At home, he struggles to live up to his father's expectations. In his Rex Zero, Private Eye, persona, he stumbles across a maiden in distress who triggers questions about his values: bullying, truthfulness, and friendship. The most terrifying quandary Rex faces, however, is admitting his actions have repercussions that extend beyond his expectations. *Rex Zero, King of Nothing* is a well-drawn dynamic character who faces situations that will be uncomfortably familiar to many readers. *2009 USBBY Outstanding International Books List. lmp*

Author lives in Canada.

COMING OF AGE, FAMILY LIFE, INTERPERSONAL RELATIONS, SCHOOLS, OTTAWA HISTORY, CANADA SOCIAL CONDITIONS 1945–1971, HISTORICAL FICTION

Yerxa, Leo. **Ancient Thunder**. Illustrated by the author. Toronto, Groundwood Books/House of Anansi Press, 2006. ISBN 978-0-88899-746-3, 0-88899-746-9. 32 p. (4–10). Picture book, Poetry.

At the time of the Strawberry Moon (June), Leo Yerxa celebrates the horse, galloping across the prairie and living among buffalo, eagles, fellow horses, and man. Yerxa's beautifully illustrated poem evokes the sounds and the life of a herd of horses on the plains. Done with paper collages but looking like leather clothing, the illustrations move quickly across the page as the reader follows the horses as they spend a day on the plains. *2006 Governor General's Literary Award. sc*

Author lives in Ottawa, Ontario.

Wild Horses, Indians of North America—Great Plains Native Americans/First Nations, Poetry

RELATED INFORMATION

Organizations

The Canadian Children's Book Centre (CCBC)
www.bookcentre.ca
Suite 101, 40 Orchard View Blvd., Toronto, ON M4R 1B9; telephone: 416-975-0010, fax: 416-975-8970

Founded in 1976, this national, nonprofit organization promotes and encourages the reading, writing, and illustrating of Canadian children's books through such activities as Children's Book Week and the publications *Children's Book News* and *Best Books for Kids & Teens* (formerly *Our Choice*). The website has links to pages that provide names and addresses of Canadian publishers, bookstores, and related organizations as well as author web pages and an explanation of the Canadian children's books awards.

Programs and publications of the Canadian Children's Book Center:

- TD Canadian Children's Book Week (first week of May), www.book-week.ca/
- *Canadian Children's Book News* (quarterly magazine), http://main.book-centre.ca/publications/canadian_childrens_book_news
- *Best Books for Kids & Teens* (formerly *Our Choice*), www.bookcentre.ca/publications/best_books_for_kids_and_teens

Canadian Society of Children's Authors, Illustrators, and Performers (CANSCAIP)
40 Orchard View Blvd., Suite 104, Toronto, ON M4R 1B9; telephone: 416-515-1559; fax: 416-515-7022
www.canscaip.org/content/about-canscaip

The Canadian Society of Children's Authors, Illustrators, and Performers (CANSCAIP) is a group of professionals in the field of children's culture with members from all parts of Canada. For over twenty years, CANSCAIP has been instrumental in the support and promotion of children's literature through newsletters, workshops, meetings, and other information programs for authors, parents, teachers, librarians, publishers, and others. CANSCAIP also has over five hundred friends—teachers, librarians, parents, and others—who are also interested in aspects of children's books, illustrations, and performances.

IBBY Canada
www.ibby-canada.org/

Awards

More information about Canadian children's and young adult book awards can be found at www.bookcentre.ca/awards/canadian_awards_index.

The Amelia Frances Howard-Gibbon Illustrator's Award
www.bookcentre.ca/awards/amelia_frances_howard_gibbon_illustrators_award

Given by the Canadian Association of Children's Librarians (CACL), this annual award is presented to the illustrator of an outstanding children's book published during the previous calendar year in Canada. The illustrator must be a Canadian citizen or permanent resident of Canada, and the book must be suitable for children up to age fourteen.

Canadian Library Association Book of the Year for Children Award
www.bookcentre.ca/awards/canadian_library_association_book_year_children_award

Given by the Canadian Association of Children's Librarians (CACL), this annual award is presented to the author of an outstanding children's book published during the previous calendar year in Canada. The author must be a Canadian citizen or permanent resident of Canada. The book must be suitable for children up to age fourteen.

Canadian Library Association Young Adult Canadian Book Award
www.bookcentre.ca/awards/canadian_library_association_young_adult_canadian_book_award

This award was established in 1980 by the Young Adult Caucus of the Saskatchewan Library Association and is administered by the Young Adult Services Group (YASIG). This prize is awarded to the author of an outstanding English language book for young adults (ages thirteen to eighteen) published in the preceding calendar year. The winning book must be a work of fiction (novel or collection of short stories) written by a Canadian citizen or landed immigrant published in Canada.

Elizabeth Mrazik-Cleaver Award
www.bookcentre.ca/awards/elizabeth_mrazikcleaver_canadian_picture_book_award

This award is administered by the Canadian section of the International Board on Books for Young People (IBBY) and presented to a Canadian illustrator of a picture book published in Canada in English or in French during the previous calendar year.

Geoffrey Bilson Award for Historical Fiction for Young People

www.bookcentre.ca/awards/geoffrey_bilson_award_historical_fiction_young_people

This annual prize is awarded to the author of an outstanding work of historical fiction for young readers, by a Canadian author, published in the previous calendar year.

Governor General's Literary Awards

www.bookcentre.ca/awards/governor_generals_literary_awards

Up to four annual awards (one each to an English-language writer, a French-language writer, an illustrator of an English-language book, and an illustrator of a French-language book) can be given each year by the Canada Council. All books for young people written or illustrated by a Canadian citizen in the previous year are eligible, whether published in Canada or abroad.

IBBY Honour List

www.ibby-canada.org

Each national section of IBBY is invited to nominate titles every two years that are representative of the best in children's literature from each country. All books must be considered suitable for publication throughout the world. IBBY-Canada may nominate one book for illustration (in either English or French) and one or two books for text (in English and/or French). Text may be fiction or nonfiction. IBBY-Canada also nominates one or two titles in the translation category (English to French and/or French to English).

Information Book Award

www.bookcentre.ca/awards/information_book_award

Sponsored by the Children's Literature Roundtables of Canada, the Information Book Award is given to recognize an outstanding information book for children and young people five to fifteen years of age written in English by a Canadian citizen.

Mr. Christie's Book Award

Presented from 1989 until the 2003 awards were announced, this award no longer exists.

Norma Fleck Award for Canadian Children's Non-Fiction

www.bookcentre.ca/awards/norma_fleck_award_canadian_childrens_nonfiction

The Norma Fleck Award for Canadian Children's Non-Fiction was established by the Fleck Family Foundation and the Canadian Children's Book Centre in May 1999 to recognize and raise the profile of nonfiction books. The $10,000 annual award honors exceptional quality in content and production in children's nonfiction by a Canadian author. It is considered to be one of Canada's most prestigious literary prizes.

Reader's Choice Awards

There are many reader's choice awards, often known as the "tree" awards, which include the Ontario Library Association's Blue Spruce, Hackmatack (Maritimes), Silver Birch, Red Maple, White Pine, Red Cedar (BC), Willow (Saskatchewan), and the Manitoba Young Reader's Choice. For more information, see the CCBC website at www.bookcentre.ca/awards/canadian_awards_index.

Ruth and Sylvia Schwartz Children's Book Award

www.bookcentre.ca/awards/ruth_and_sylvia_schwartz_children%E2%80%99s_book_award

This prize recognizes authors and illustrators who demonstrate artistic excellence in Canadian children's literature. It is judged by juries of children from public schools in Ontario and is administered by the Ontario Arts Council Foundation, the Ontario Arts Council, and the Canadian Booksellers' Association.

Sheila A. Egoff Children's Literature Prize

www.bookcentre.ca/awards/sheila_a_egoff_childrens_literature_prize

The Sheila A. Egoff Children's Literature Prize is awarded annually as part of the British Columbia Book Prize program to what is judged to be the best children's book published anywhere in the world in the previous year by a writer who has been a resident of British Columbia (or the Yukon) for three of the previous five years.

TD Canadian Children's Literature Award

www.bookcentre.ca/awards/td_canadian_childrens_literature_award

In October 2004 the Canadian Children's Book Centre and the TD Bank Financial Group announced the establishment of a new children's book award for the most distinguished book of the year. All books, in any genre, written by a Canadian and for children ages one through twelve, are eligible.

In the case of a picture book, both the author and the illustrator must be Canadian. Only books first published in Canada are eligible for submission.

Vicky Metcalf Award for Children's Literature
www.bookcentre.ca/awards/vicky_metcalf_award_childrens_literature
This annual award is presented by the Writer's Trust of Canada to a Canadian writer (citizen or landed immigrant) who has produced a body of work (at least four books) that, in the opinion of the judges, demonstrates the highest literary standards.

Websites

Canadian Children's Book Centre
www.bookcentre.ca
The website of the Canadian Children's Book Centre has links to Canadian children's book publishers, author and illustrator home pages, and a comprehensive listing of all of the Canadian children's book awards.

Canadian Children's Illustrated Books in English
http://ccib.arts.ubc.ca/CCIB/Welcome.html
This website provides information about research on the historical context and current state of Canadian children's illustrated books in English and the history of publishing for children in Canada from an interdisciplinary perspective. It provides hundreds of annotated resources on aspects of Canadian children's books, international illustration, and children's publishing in Canada, as well as links to electronic resources and a searchable database of award-winning Canadian children's illustrated books.

Children's Literature Web Guide
http://people.ucalgary.ca/~dkbrown/index.html
Created and maintained by David K. Brown of the University of Calgary, this comprehensive site is international in scope and is used by people all around the world. Some lists may be out of date.

Festivals

Canadian Children's Book Week
www.bookweek.ca/
Across Canada from the end of April through the first week of May
Organized by the Canadian Children's Book Centre
E-mail: info@bookweek.ca

Festival of the Written Arts
www.writersfestival.ca/
Sechelt, BC, Canada
E-mail: info@writersfestival.ca

Journals

CM: Canadian Review of Materials

www.umanitoba.ca/cm/
CM—an electronic reviewing journal published by the Manitoba Library Association—features book reviews, media reviews, news, and author profiles of interest to teachers, librarians, parents, and kids. CM reviews include publications produced in Canada or published elsewhere but of special interest or significance to Canada, such as those having a Canadian writer, illustrator, or subject.

Canadian Children's Book News

www.bookcentre.ca/publications/canadian_childrens_book_news
Published since 1977 by the Canadian Children's Book Centre, *Canadian Children's Book News* has helped parents, teachers, librarians, and booksellers discover new Canadian children's books and keep up with industry issues and ideas. Each issue is packed with news, book reviews, author and illustrator interviews, profiles of publishers and bookstores, and information about the world of children's books in Canada. Published quarterly in an attractive full-color format and distributed nationwide, *Canadian Children's Book News* is the source for adults who select books for young readers. Available through membership or by subscription.

Jeunesse: Young People, Texts, Cultures
(formerly *Canadian Children's Literature / Littérature canadienne pour la jeunesse*)

http://jeunessejournal.ca/
Jeunesse is an interdisciplinary, refereed academic journal whose mandate is to publish research on, and to provide a forum for discussion about, cultural productions for, by, and about young people. Although the journal has been renamed and has redefined its mission, it remains housed at the Centre for Research in Young People's Texts and Cultures (http://crytc.uwinnipeg.ca/). *Jeunesse*'s scope has expanded to become international; the journal continues to have a special interest in Canada, and it publishes manuscripts about all areas and cultures. *Jeunesse*'s focus is on the cultural functions and representations of "the child."

The Looking Glass: New Perspective on Children's Books
www.lib.latrobe.edu.au/ojs/index.php/tlg/index
The Looking Glass: New Perspectives on Children's Books is a peer-reviewed electronic journal about children's literature that is published three times per year. As the name suggests, the journal combines an interest in the traditional with an eye to the modern. Most readers and contributors are academics, librarians, teachers, parents, and anyone else fascinated by the world of children's literature.

Print Resources

Baker, Deirdre & Ken Setterington. **A Guide to Canadian Children's Books in English**. Illustrated by Kady MacDonald Denton. Toronto, Canada: McClelland & Stewart, 2003. ISBN 978-0-7710-1064-4, 0-7710-1064-8. 350 p.
    Two experts offer guidance in the selection and sharing of the best Canadian children's books. Features over five hundred recommended titles organized by age and genre.

Edwards, Gail & Judith Saltman. **Picturing Canada: A History of Canadian Children's Illustrated Books and Publishing**. Toronto, Canada, University of Toronto Press, 2010. ISBN 978-0-8020-37596, 0-8020-3759-3. 381 p.
    The study of children's illustrated books is located within the broad histories of print culture, publishing, the book trade, and concepts of childhood. Over 130 interviews with Canadian authors, illustrators, editors, librarians, booksellers, critics, and other contributors to Canadian children's book publishing document the experiences of those who worked in the industry.

Jones, Raymond E. & Jon C. Stott. **Canadian Children's Books: A Critical Guide to Authors and Illustrators**. Ontario, Canada: Oxford University Press, 2000. ISBN 978-0-19-541222-2, 0-19-541222-2. 538 p.
    A thorough introduction to the history of Canadian children's literature is followed by author entries for all of Canada's major children's book writers. An appendix of major English-language Canadian Book Awards and a bibliography conclude this useful reference work.

Weber, Jochen (with selection, texts, and translation by Claudia Söffner & Elena Kilian). **Children's Books from Canada / Livres du Jeunesse du Canada**. München, Germany, Internationale Jugendbibliothek, 2002. 55 p.
    This catalogue of the travelling exhibition, *Children's Books from Canada*, includes bibliographical references and an index.

CHAPTER FIVE

Asia

Chinese Flying Their Kites

AFGHANISTAN

Khan, Rukhsana. **Wanting Mor**. Toronto, Groundwood Books, 2009. ISBN 978-0-88899-858-3, 0-88899-858-9. 190 p. (10–14). Novel.

Life in a war zone is a grim story. Jameela's tale opens with her mother's death. Mor provided the glue that held the family together, so it is not surprising that after her death everything deteriorates. Baba abandons Jameela on a street in Kabul, but this becomes her salvation when a caring shopkeeper takes her to an orphanage. Jameela is a resilient girl whose Muslim faith intensifies as her life deteriorates. Readers are reassured by her decisions and strength, so they close the book hopeful. Like Patricia McCormick's *Sold* (2006), *Wanting Mor* is a fictionalized view of many girls' reality rooted in their families' extreme poverty. *lmp*

Author was born in Pakistan but now lives in Toronto.

AFGHAN WAR, 2001, GIRLS, ORPHANAGES AFGHANISTAN, FICTION

O'Brien, Tony & Mike Sullivan. **Afghan Dreams: Young Voices of Afghanistan**. Illustrated by Tony O'Brien's photographs. New York, Bloomsbury, 2008. ISBN 978-1-59990-287-6, 1-59990-287-7. 80 p. (8–14). Nonfiction.

Photojournalist O'Brien and Sullivan travelled to Afghanistan to interview children between the ages of eight and fifteen, asking standard questions about their past, their families, and their everyday lives. They also inquired about their dreams and hopes for the future. Dreams and reality rarely coincided—as with education. "We walk two hours each way to school. We are very tired afterward, and it is hard to do our studies" (Kamilad, age fourteen, p. 61). Afghanistan is a land of beauty and horrific scars—in its land and its citizens. *Afghan Dreams: Young Voices of Afghanistan* brings the beauty, scars, and voices to life. ALA *Notable Children's Book, Bank Street Children's Books of the Year, CCBC Choices, Notable Social Studies Trade Books for Young People* (NCSS/CBC). *lmp*

Authors live in the United States.

TEENAGERS, AFGHANISTAN, BIOGRAPHY

Winter, Jeanette. **Nasreen's Secret School: A True Story from Afghanistan**. Illustrated by the author. New York, Simon & Schuster/Beach Lane Books, 2009. ISBN 978-1-4169-9437-4, 1-4169-9437-8. 40 p. (6–9). Picture book.

Nasreen lives in Herat, an ancient city of Afghanistan during the time of the Taliban takeover. After her father disappears and her mother leaves to go in search of him, Nasreen withdraws into a silent world. In despair, her grandmother risks everything to enroll her in a secret school for girls. The story is told in the first-person voice of her grandmother. An author's note includes information about the Global Fund for Children, a nonprofit organization committed to helping children around the world. The author also addresses the tragic circumstances of girls during the 1996–2001 reign of the Taliban in that country. *CCBC Choices, CBC/NCSS Notable Social Studies Trade Book, Jane Addams Children's Book Award. djg*

Author lives in the United States.

TALIBAN, GIRLS' SCHOOLS–AFGHANISTAN, GIRLS EDUCATION–AFGHANISTAN, PARENT-SEPARATED CHILDREN, AFGHANISTAN SOCIAL CONDITIONS 21ST CENTURY, NONFICTION, "A GLOBAL FUND FOR CHILDREN" BOOK

BALI ISLAND

Reynolds, Jan. **Cycle of Rice, Cycle of Life**. Illustrated by the author's photographs. New York, Lee & Low Books, 2009. ISBN 978-1-60060-254-2, 1-60060-254-1. (8–13). Nonfiction.

See Indonesia for description.

BURMA

Smith, Roland. **Elephant Run**. New York, Hyperion Books for Children, 2007. ISBN 978-1-4231-0402-5, 1-4231-0402-1. 318 p. (10 up). Novel.

World War II London is a dangerous place, with daily air raids and bombings. When fourteen-year-old Nick Freestone's flat is destroyed, his mother sends him to Burma to his father's teak plantation. Nick is thrilled, not just because he longs to spend time with his father but also because he can learn to handle the massive elephants that are integral to the teak plantation's daily routine. Rumors of a Japanese invasion prove true, endangering Nick, his father, and the elephants they respect and love. This fast-paced historical fiction sheds light on a little-known aspect of the Pacific theater. *2009 William Allen White Award (Kansas), and ten other state awards or nominations, 2009 ALA BBYA List. lmp*

Author lives in the United States.

WORLD WAR (1939–1945) BURMA, PRISONERS OF WAR, ELEPHANTS, BURMA HISTORY, JAPANESE OCCUPATION (1942–1945), HISTORICAL FICTION

CAMBODIA

Lord, Michelle. **Little Sap and Monsieur Rodin**. Illustrated by Felicia Hoshino. New York, Lee & Low Books, 2006. ISBN 978-1-58430-248-3, 1-58430-248-8. n.p. (8–14). Picture book.

The lives of a young Cambodian dancer and the artist Auguste Rodin merge when the Cambodian dance troupe performs in France. Inspired by the grace and beauty of the dancers, the artist chooses Little Sap as a subject for his drawings. A foreword and back matter offer additional information about the history of Cambodia, Khmer dance, and Auguste Rodin. *si*

This Texas author's inspiration for her story stems from her visit to Cambodia.

Auguste Rodin (1840–1917), Dance, Cambodia History (1863–1953), Historical Fiction

Lord, Michelle. **A Song for Cambodia**. Illustrated by Shino Arihara. New York, Lee & Low Books, 2008. ISBN 978-1-60060-139-2, 1-60060-139-1. n.p. (6–10). Biography, Picture book.

Arn Chorn-Pond remembered the haunting sounds of his grandfather's music and his mother's melodies from before the Khmer Rouge stormed his village. Arn was wrenched from his family and taken to a children's camp, where he slaved planting and harvesting rice. Vietnam attacked the Khmer Rouge four years later, allowing Arn to escape to Thailand, then America. The musical talent he developed during Pol Pot's regime helped him survive the labor camp and assuaged his mind and spirit. Today, he assists Cambodians to heal from the violence. Background on Cambodia and extensive author's sources—books, films, interviews, and Internet sites—substantiate this informative biography. *lmp*

Author lives in the United States; illustrator grew up in Japan but now lives in the United States.

Arn Chorn-Pond (1966–), Musicians, Cambodia, Biography

CHINA

Cheng, Andrea. **Shanghai Messenger**. Illustrated by Ed Young. New York, Lee & Low Books, 2005. ISBN 978-1-58430-238-4, 1-58430-238-0. n.p. (9–12). Free-verse novel.

Eleven-year-old Xiao Mei has been invited to visit Shanghai by her Chinese relatives. She is afraid because she must travel alone and meet people she's never seen before. And worst of all, she speaks little Chinese. Her mother and grandmother have ignored that part of her heritage. "In America / everyone thinks I'm Chinese even though my dad's not, / and people here stare at me / in the street. . . . [I am] half and half / everywhere / in the world" ("Braids," n.p.). Ed Young's pastel and colored-pencil illustrations highlight the differences—and the similarities—between the cultures that Andrea Cheng's free-verse novel explores. *2005 Junior Library Guild Selection, Original Art Show–Society of Illustrators, Children's Books of the Year–Bank Street College Children's Book Committee, A Parent's Choice Recommended Award Winner, Starred Review–Kirkus Reviews. Illustrator Ed Young received the Caldecott Medal in 1990 and Caldecott Honors in 1993 and 1989.* lmp

Author lives in the United States with her Chinese American husband; illustrator was born in China but today lives in the United States.

CHINESE AMERICANS, VOYAGES AND TRAVELS, FAMILIES, RACIALLY MIXED PEOPLE, CHINA, FICTION, POETRY

Compestine, Ying Chang. **Revolution Is Not a Dinner Party: A Novel**. New York, Henry Holt, 2007. ISBN 978-0-8050-8207-4, 0-8050-8207-7. 248 p. (9–14). Novel.

Taking Chairman Mao's aphorism as its title, Compestine's novel springs from her childhood in Wuhan, China, from 1972 (when she is nine years old) to 1976, at the end of the Cultural Revolution. Ling, the privileged child of doctors, suffers escalating humiliation at the hands of her Red Guard classmates as well as privation brought on by political chaos. After her father is arrested, her rebellious spirit both endangers and sustains her. When Mao's death brings an end to the turbulent years, Ling's tormenters lose their power and her family is happily reunited. mac, mm

Author was born in China but now lives in the United States.

PERSECUTION, CHINESE FAMILY LIFE, COMMUNISM, CHINA, HISTORICAL FICTION, CULTURAL REVOLUTION, 1966–1976

Crane, Carol. **D Is for Dancing Dragon: A China Alphabet**. Illustrated by Zong-Zhou Wang. Chelsea, MI, Sleeping Bear Press, 2006. ISBN 978-1-58536-273-8, 1-58536-273-5. 48 p. (5–9). Nonfiction.

Art and text combine in generous double-page spreads to elucidate diverse elements of Chinese culture, one for each letter of the Western alphabet. Four-line verses identify the subject of each illustration, while sidebars offer longer nonfiction entries on subjects as diverse as the Great Wall, chopsticks, Chinese inventions, and Chinese food. The result is an encyclopedic gathering of information about China's land, people, history, and customs, illuminated by richly colored, realistic, and enticing oil paintings. *mac*

Author lives in the United States; illustrator was born in China but now lives in the United States.

CHINA, CIVILIZATION, NONFICTION ALPHABET BOOK

Jimi. (English text adapted by Sarah L. Thompson). **The Blue Stone**. Illustrated by the author. New York, Little, Brown, 2008. Originally published as *Lan Shi Tou* in Chinese by Locus Publishing China, in 2006. ISBN 978-0-316-11383-0, 0-316-11383-2. 78 p. (8 up). Picture book.

A beautiful blue stone is split in two, and one half of it is taken by artists, who marvel at its beauty. It then undergoes many transformations, but no matter its shape or form, it remains the same blue stone that longs to return home to its other half that still lies deep in the forest. This story is a fable about the effects of time, the inevitability of change, about homesickness and longing, yet it is also about hope and love, about beauty and creativity, possibilities, and ultimately about the circle of life. *Author is the winner of twelve awards, including the 2006 Most Recommendable Book of the Year from Taiwan's Council of Cultural Affairs. ae*

Jimi (pseudonym for Jimmy Liao) lives near Taipei, Taiwan.

ROCKS, HOMESICKNESS, CHINA, FICTION

Li, Moying. **Snow Falling in Spring: Coming of Age in China during the Cultural Revolution**. New York, Farrar, Straus and Giroux/Melanie Kroupa Books, 2008. ISBN 978-0-374-39922-1, 0-374-39922-0. 176 p. (11 up). Nonfiction, Autobiography.

Moying Li's coming-of-age memoir follows the fortunes of her Beijing family as they live through terrible times. The story begins in her courtyard home in the summer of 1958, when the heady enthusiasm of the Great Leap Forward gripped her family, and continues through the tyranny and persecution of the Cultural Revolution, which Moying experiences both at home and school. The death of Chairman Mao and the arrest of the Gang of Four in 1977 open a door that allows Moying to leave her country and study in America. *mac*

Author was born in China but now lives in the United States.

MOYING LI-MARCUS (1954–), CHINA, HISTORY, CULTURAL REVOLUTION, 1966–1976, AUTOBIOGRAPHY

Lin, Grace. **Where the Mountain Meets the Moon**. New York, Little, Brown, 2009. ISBN 978-0-316-11427-1, 0-316-11427-8. 278 p. (8–12). Novel.

Minli's family ekes out a meager subsistence from the rice fields in Fruit-less Mountain's shadow where the Jade River, whose color in reality dispar-ages its name, meanders past the village. The only real joys in the young girl's life are her father's fantastic tales of Fruitless Mountain, Jade Dragon, and the Old Man of the Moon. Minli sets out on a marvelous journey to bring prosperity to her family and their village, guided only by her father's mythol-ogy, a goldfish, and the magic that prevails in hearts pure enough to believe. Grace Lin embellishes this original fairy tale with striking, gold spot art and evocative full-page, color illustrations. *2010 Newbery Honor.* lmp

Author lives in the United States.

DRAGONS, MOON, CHINA, FAIRY TALES, FANTASY FICTION

Louis, Catherine. Translated by MaryChris Bradley. **My Little Book of Chinese Words**. Illustrated by Shi Bo (calligraphy). New York, NorthSouth Books, 2008. Originally published as *Mon Imagier Chinois* in French by Edi-tions Philippe Picquier France, in 2004. ISBN 978-0-7358-2174-3, 0-7358-2174-7. (6 up). Picture book.

In this small, square paperback, Chinese characters are presented opposite pictures of the words they represent. The arrangement of words demonstrates how the characters build on one another; for instance, the character for mouth is presented, followed by that for speak, call, and teeth, all of which are visually related. Louis's color-saturated illustrations combine silkscreen and collage in simple designs with appeal for all ages. ss

Author lives in Switzerland.

CALLIGRAPHY, CHINESE LANGUAGE MATERIALS, BILINGUAL BOOKS, CHI-NESE LANGUAGE GLOSSARIES, VOCABULARIES, NONFICTION

Ma, Yan (introduced and edited by Pierre Haski). Translated by Lisa Appig-nanesi from the French (the diaries were originally translated from the Man-darin by He Yanping). **The Diary of Ma Yan: The Struggles and Hopes of a Chinese Schoolgirl**. New York, HarperCollins, 2005. Originally published as *Le Journal de Ma Yan* in French by Editions Ramsay France, in 2002. ISBN 978-0-06-076496-8, 0-06-076496-1. 166 p. (10 up). Nonfiction, Diary.

Amid the extreme poverty and harsh climate of her remote Chinese vil-lage, thirteen-year-old Ma Yan registers her overwhelming desire to be edu-cated through her diary entries. These diaries, handed to a French journalist by her mother, were originally published in France. Although the entries reveal she is frequently berated for her academic performance and is often hungry, cold, and exhausted by the long walk to her boarding school, she remains steadfastly determined to continue her schooling so as to make her family proud and to give back to her community. *2006 USBBY-CBC Outstanding International Books List. nlr*

Author was a teenager from Ningxia, China—only thirteen and fourteen—when she wrote these diary entries.

MA, YAN (1987–), GIRLS, CUSTOMS, CHINA, DIARIES, NONFICTION

Quan, Elizabeth. **Once Upon a Full Moon**. Illustrated by the author. Toronto, Tundra Books, 2007. ISBN 978-0-88776-813-2, 0-88776-813-X. 48 p. (8–12). Picture book.

See Canada for description.

Sellier, Marie. Translated by Sibylle Kazeroid. **Legend of the Chinese Dragon**. Illustrated by Catherine Louis. Calligraphy and chop marks by Wang Fei. New York, NorthSouth Books, 2007. Originally published as *La Naissance du Dragon* in French by Editions Philippe Picquier France, in 2006. ISBN 978-0-7358-2152-1, 0-7358-2152-6. 30 p. (5–8). Picture book.

Long ago in China, people in various areas lived under the protection of different animal spirits. When the tribes became envious of each other, war broke out. The children's solution to war was to create a protective spirit with bits of all the animal spirits. Thus the dragon became a sign of peace for China. The tale is told in English and Chinese with colorful linocut illustrations. *2008 USBBY Outstanding International Books List. pwc*

Author lives in France, and illustrator lives in Switzerland.

DRAGONS, CHINA HISTORY TO 221 BC, FICTION

Sellier, Marie. **What the Rat Told Me: A Legend of the Chinese Zodiac**. Illustrated by Catherine Louis. Calligraphy and chop marks by Wang Fei. New York, NorthSouth Books, 2009. Originally published as *Le Rat m'a Dit: La Vraie Histoire de l'Horoscope Chinois* in French by Editions Picquier Jeunesse France, in 2008. ISBN 978-0-7358-2220-7, 0-7358-2220-4. 32 p. (7–10). Folklore, Picture book.

The story of how the Great Emperor of Heaven chose the twelve animals of the Chinese zodiac—and why rats and cats are enemies even to this day—is told in this beautifully designed book. Two colors, black and red, on creamy white paper are used to create the stunning artwork of linoleum prints and chop marks. The back matter includes a "Which sign are you?" section, in which readers can learn which sign they were born under. There is also a chart of the animals of the zodiac, their chop marks, and their names in Chinese calligraphy. *2010 USBBY Outstanding International Books List, 2010 CCBC Choices. ca*

Author lives in France; illustrator lives in Switzerland.
ANIMALS, ZODIAC, ASTROLOGY, CHINA, LEGENDS, FOLKLORE

Shannon, George. **Rabbit's Gift: A Fable from China**. Illustrated by Laura Dronzek. Orlando, FL, Harcourt, 2007. ISBN 978-0-15-206073-2, 0-15-206073-1. 32 p. (5–9). Picture book.

Cooperation and generosity are the themes of this Chinese fable. As winter snow approaches, Rabbit searches for food and finds two turnips. He thinks about his neighbor, Donkey, and decides to share one of his turnips. Donkey isn't home, so Rabbit leaves the turnip by the door. Thus begins a chain reaction as Donkey shares with goat, who in turn shares with Deer. Deer completes the circle of generosity by returning the turnip to Rabbit, who divides the turnip and shares it with his friends to make a "cozy" meal. The author's note discusses this tale's origin. *CCBC Choices*. nlh
Author and illustrator live in the United States.
FABLES, FOLKLORE, FRIENDSHIP, CHINA

Wilkinson, Carole. **Garden of the Purple Dragon**. New York, Hyperion Books for Children, 2007. Originally published by Black Dog Books, Australia, in 2005. ISBN 978-1-4231-0338-7, 1-4231-0338-6. 354 p. (10 up). Novel.

Ping, the girl who saved the last Chinese dragon in *The Dragon Keeper*, now protects his son, the appealing baby dragon Kai. Trying to escape her old enemy, an evil necromancer who wants to kill Kai for his magical body parts, Ping and her trusty sidekick, the rat Hua, lie low in an Imperial Lodge, where she hopes her old friend, the boy emperor, will protect her. But the necromancer's power extends farther than she thought, and she needs all her courage and second sight to keep Kai alive. The author's research into Chinese culture during the Han dynasty informs this fantasy adventure. *2006 West Australian Young Book Readers Awards*. mac
Author lives in Australia.
DRAGONS, SELF-CONFIDENCE, FATE AND FATALISM, CHINA HAN DYNASTY, 202 BC–AD 220, FANTASY FICTION

Xiong, Kim. Illustrated by the author. **The Little Stone Lion**. Alhambra, CA, Heryin Books, 2005. Originally published in Chinese by Tomorrow Publishing House and by China Times Publishing House China, in 2005. ISBN 978-0-9762056-1-6, 0-9762056-1-0. 32 p. (4–7). Picture book.

The little stone lion is the guardian spirit of the village. Although the lion is small, he is older than any villager. Everyone loves him. When children are walking at night they feel safe because of the stone lion. The lion thinks that when the children grow up and leave the village, they might forget him. He always remembers them and misses them. *The Little Stone Lion* is by two brothers, Xiong Lei and Xiong Liang, who have published in the United States under the name Xiong Kim. *The China Times "Reading" Best Children's Book Award. pwc*

Authors live in Beijing.
STATUES, LIONS, CHINA, FICTION

Yang, Belle. **Always Come Home to Me**. Illustrated by the author. Cambridge, MA, Candlewick Press, 2007. ISBN 978-0-7636-2899-4, 0-7636-2899-9. 32 p. (4–8). Picture book.

During the Ching Ming Spring Festival, Mei-Mei and Di-Di receive a pair of young doves. They lovingly care for the doves through the summer, but when Uncle Baldy helps with the harvest, the twin's father thanks Baldy for his help by giving him the doves. The twins are devastated and sneak away to their uncle's farm. On arriving, their aunt explains that the doves have disappeared. The twins return home to face their parents' disapproval for running away. Instead, they are surprised to learn their doves have returned. Beautiful gouache illustrations reveal the joy of the reunion. *Best Children's Book of 2008 awarded by the Chinese American Librarians Association. nlh*

Author was born in Taiwan and now lives in the United States.
TWINS, BROTHERS AND SISTERS, PIGEONS, CHINA

RELATED INFORMATION

Awards

Feng Zikai Chinese Children's Picture Book Award

The Feng Zikai Chinese Children's Picture Book Award was established in 2008 to recognize, promote, and encourage the creation of Chinese-language illustrated children's literature. The first award was announced in 2009. The Feng Zikai Award is the first international Chinese children's picture book award.

www.fengzikaibookaward.org/

Organizations

IBBY China
www.ibby.org/index.php?id=412

The Chinese Board on Books for Young People (CBBY) was established in 1986. It participates in reading promotion activities that include distributing books to disadvantaged areas of China and sponsoring seminars on literature and reading. CBBY hosted the IBBY World Congress in 2006 in Macau.

HONG KONG

Mochizuki, Ken. **Be Water, My Friend: The Early Years of Bruce Lee**. Illustrated by Dom Lee. New York, Lee & Low Books, 2006. ISBN 978-1-58430-265-0, 1-58430-265-8. n.p. (8–14). Picture book.

Young Bruce Lee's nickname of Mo Si Tung means "never sits still" in English. Yet he sits still to read about heroes and warriors to the point of needing glasses. As a young martial arts student, Bruce learns how to balance the strength of his training with the need to be gentle in its application. His teachers and parents instill in him the need to discover his own inner calm. *si*

Author lives in Seattle.

BRUCE LEE (1940–1973), BIOGRAPHY, MARTIAL ARTISTS

RELATED INFORMATION

Book Fairs

Hong Kong Book Fair
www.hkbookfair.com/en/index.aspx

INDIA

Banerjee, Anjali. **Looking for Bapu**. New York, Random House/Wendy Lamb Books, 2006. ISBN 978-0-385-74657-1, 0-385-74657-1. 162 p. (9–12). Novel.

Not quite nine-year-old Anu lives with his parents in Seattle and spends a lot of time with his grandfather, Bapu. He is devastated when his beloved Bapu has a stroke and dies. Anu tries everything to bring him back to life. He shaves his head, fasts, and adapts mystical ways, such as somersaulting to school, thus copying the sadhu (holy man) who rolled thousands of miles. A visit to the island of the Mystery Museum brings this touching and sometimes humorous first-person narrative to a satisfying conclusion. Hindu gods and goddesses that Bapu worshipped and Indian traditions and customs are smoothly woven into the story of a young boy coping with death. *mjw*

Author was born in India and grew up in Canada and the United States.

GRANDFATHERS, DEATH, HINDUS, EAST INDIAN AMERICANS, SCHOOLS, NORTHWEST, PACIFIC, FICTION

Charles, Veronika Martenova. **The Birdman**. Illustrated by Annouchka Gravel Galouchko & Stéphan Daigle. Toronto, Tundra Books, 2006. ISBN 978-0-88776-740-1, 0-88776-740-0. 32 p. (5–8). Nonfiction.

Based on an article that appeared in a Toronto newspaper, *The Birdman* explores the life of Noor Nobi, a man from Calcutta, India, who, numb after the tragic death of his three children, begins to buy and care for sick, caged birds. As he nurses the birds back to health, he begins to regain his own strength. When the birds have been rehabilitated, he frees them and eventually frees himself from his painful past. This inspiring story, with richly colored illustrations that invite the reader into Noor's world, is a book for young and old alike. *2006 Canadian Governor General's Literary Award nominee. ak*

Author lives in Toronto, and illustrators live in Quebec.

NOOR NOBI (PERSON), BIRDS, GRIEF, CALCUTTA, INDIA, NONFICTION

Divakaruni, Chitra Banerjee. **The Mirror of Fire and Dreaming: A Novel**. New Milford, CT, Roaring Brook Press/A Neal Porter Book, 2005. ISBN 978-1-59643-067-9, 1-59643-067-2. 329 p. (10–14). Novel.

Anand, hero of *The Conch Bearer* (2003), is now an apprentice to the Brotherhood of Healers, developing magical skills he will use for the good of mankind. Trying to save his master Abhaydatta from the clutches of an evil sorcerer, Anand discovers a mirror that sends him and his companions back to the time when the Moguls ruled India, where they engage the sorcerer and his malevolent jinn in a battle to the death. Drawing on Indian mythology and philosophy, this fantasy adventure is distinguished by appealing characters and grounded in specific, sensory descriptions of Indian food, clothing, customs, and language. *mac*

Author lives in the United States but was born in India.

HEALERS, TIME TRAVEL, MAGIC, INDIA 1526–1765, HISTORICAL FICTION, FANTASY

Gavin, Jamila. **The Blood Stone**. New York, Farrar, Straus and Giroux, 2005. Originally published by Egmont Great Britain, in 2003. ISBN 978-0-374-30846-9, 0-374-30846-2. 340 p. (11 up). Novel.

Early in the seventeenth century, Filippo Veroneo encounters adventure, intrigue, danger, and relentless enemies as well as unexpected friends when he journeys from Venice to free his father, Geronimo, a hostage in Afghanistan. Filippo plans to raise his father's ransom in Hindustan at the court of the Mogul emperor Shah Jahan by using a magnificent diamond Geronimo cut and set years ago—a diamond men would spill blood for. A visionary from birth, Filippo finds his second sight enhanced after the diamond is embedded in his skull. A believable setting, strong characters, and a compelling plot rich in adventure, intrigue, and danger distinguishes this fine historical novel. *mac*

Author lives in England but was born in India. Author won the 2000 Whitbread Award for Coram Boy.

VOYAGES AND TRAVELS, FATHERS AND SONS, EXTRASENSORY PERCEPTION, TAJ MAHAL (AGRA, INDIA), INDIA HISTORY 1526–1765, HISTORICAL FICTION, VENICE (ITALY) HISTORY 1508–1797, HISTORICAL FICTION

Heydlauff, Lisa. **Going to School in India**. Illustrated by Nitin Upadyhe's photographs. Watertown, MA, Charlesbridge, 2005. Originally published in English by Penguin Books India, in 2003. ISBN 978-1-57091-666-3, 1-57091-666-7. 97 p. (9 up). Nonfiction.

Across bamboo and rope bridges, by bicycle, rickshaw, and small boats called vallam, aboard army trucks, camel carts, and school buses, children in India make the trek to school in many different ways. Just as diverse as the means of reaching school are the many different places that school is held—in a bus, under a mango tree, on a mountaintop, and in the desert. This photo-rich text offers a fascinating glimpse of schooling in India. A glossary at the end provides definitions for some key terms. *2006 USBBY-CBC Outstanding International Books List, National Council for the Social Studies and CBC Notable Social Studies Trade Books for Young People. nlh*

Author grew up in England, Canada, and the United States and now calls India her home.

EDUCATION, SCHOOLS, HISTORY, INDIA, NONFICTION

McCormick, Patricia. **Sold**. New York, Hyperion Books for Children, 2006. ISBN 978-0-7868-5171-3, 0-7868-5171-6. 263 p. (12 up). Novel.

Lakshmi lives in abject poverty in a remote Nepalese village—until the monsoons destroy what few crops her family produces. When this happens,

her stepfather announces Lakshmi must earn money to help support her family. Unbeknownst to Lakshmi or her mother, she has actually been sold into prostitution. Her mother's words, "simply to endure . . . is to triumph" (16), sustain her. This book is brutally graphic in places, so a mature audience is recommended. *Sold* pairs well with *Wanting Mor* (Khan 2009) and *The Shepherd's Granddaughter* (Carter 2008) because of the girls' ability to survive despite extreme adversity. An author's note details McCormick's research into sexual slavery in Nepal and India. *2006 National Book Award finalist. lmp*
Author lives in the United States.
Teenage Girls, Families, Friendship, Child Prostitution, Human Trafficking, Slavery, India, Nepal, Fiction

Michaelis, Antonia. Translated by Anthea Bell. **Tiger Moon**. New York, Harry N. Abrams Books/Amulet Books, 2008. Originally published as *Tigermond* in German by Loewe Verlag Germany, in 2006. ISBN 978-0-8109-9481-2, 0-8109-9481-X. 453 p. (12 up). Novel.
Street urchin and clever thief, Farhad spies a trinket sparkling in a lotus pond. As soon as he retrieves the bauble, a bolt of lightning bearing Lord Krishna blocks Farhad's escape. The silver locket has thrust him between Krishna and the Demon King, Ravana. Proclaiming the amulet identifies Farhad as his designated hero, Krishna discloses that Farhad is destined to save his daughter before the next full moon, when the Demon King plans to marry her. The only obstacles? Traversing the length of India, finding and defeating Ravana, and battling the Demon King and his minions all the way. Farhad's helper? A magnificent white tiger. *2009 USBBY Outstanding International Books List, 2009 Batchelder Honor. lmp*
Author lives in Germany.
Arranged Marriage, Storytellers, Robbers and Outlaws, Tigers, Princesses, India, Young Adult Fiction, Fantasy

Nayar, Nandini. **What Should I Make?** Illustrated by Proiti Roy. Berkeley, CA, Tricycle Press, 2009. Simultaneously published as *What Shall I Make?* in English and Hindi by Tulika Publishers India, in 2007. ISBN 978-1-58246-294-3, 1-58246-294-1. 20 p. (3–6). Picture book.
While Neeraj's mother kneads dough for chapatis, she gives her young son a lump of dough to play with. Neeraj molds the dough into a snake, imagines it might bite him, and quickly rolls the dough back into a ball. He then makes a mouse that he fears will run through the house and then a cat that he fears will grow into a lion. Finally he rolls out a big round chapati, which his mother bakes for him. The illustrations show Neeraj shaping the

dough and the fearsome animals he imagines he has created. Step-by-step directions for making chapatis are included. *2010 USBBY Outstanding International Books List. ca*

Author and illustrator live in India.

MOTHERS AND SONS, INDIAN COOKERY, DOUGH, IMAGINATION, INDIA, FICTION

Rao, Sandhya. **My Mother's Sari.** Illustrated by Nina Sabnani. New York, NorthSouth Books, 2006. Originally published by Tulika India, in 2006. ISBN 978-0-73582-101-9, 0-73582-101-1. n.p. (4–8). Picture book.

This vibrantly colored and beautifully illustrated picture book, combining photographs of real sari fabric with simple drawings of children, captures the sweet warmth and tenderness of a child's playful imagination. Each double-page illustration shows a young child's attachment to and delight in the saris and the many ways they can be seen and used, from a child's sailing down a river of blue to her being wrapped to sleep in the fabric's warmth and softness. The endpapers show step-by-step instructions for how to wear this traditional Indian garment. *2007 USBBY Outstanding International Books List. ae*

Author lives in India.

SARIS, MOTHERS AND DAUGHTERS, INDIA, FICTION

Ravishankar, Anushka. **Elephants Never Forget!** Illustrated by Christiane Pieper. Boston, Houghton Mifflin, 2008. Originally published by Tara Publishing India, in 2007. ISBN 978-0-618-99784-8, 0-618-99784-9. 40 p. (3–6). Picture book.

During a storm in the jungle, a little elephant is separated from his mother. After fleeing from monkeys who pester him, he is welcomed by some buffaloes and grows up as a useful member of the herd. When he finally encounters elephants and is faced with an important choice, he decides to remain with his buffalo family. Pieper illustrates this story in rhyme with digitally created illustrations that resemble woodcuts. The use of pattern, line, and color is stunning; the integration of the text and illustrations adds interest. *2009 USBBY Outstanding International Books List. ca*

Author and illustrator live in India.

ELEPHANTS, BUFFALOES, IDENTITY, STORIES IN RHYME, INDIA, FANTASY FICTION

Sheth, Kashmira. **Monsoon Afternoon.** Illustrated by Yoshiko Jaeggi. Atlanta, GA, Peachtree, 2008. ISBN 978-1-56145-455-6, 1-56145-455-9. n.p. (4–8). Picture book.

A small boy expresses his excitement as the monsoon rains begin, signaling the end of the hot, dry summer. But no one in his extended family wants to play in the rain except Dadaji, his grandfather. They sail boats and swing from the banyan tree, watch ants and peacocks, and pick the last mangoes, just as Dadaji did as a child. Sheth emphasizes the cyclical nature of India's weather and the unpredictability of monsoons. She also includes—without comment—cultural markers such as cows wandering the streets. There is an author's note about her childhood in India. *2009 Notable Social Studies Trade Books for Young People.* lmp

Author was born in India; illustrator was born in Japan. Both currently live in the United States.

Rain and Rainfall, Monsoons, Grandfathers, India, Fiction

Singh, Vandana. **Younguncle Comes to Town**. Illustrated by B. M. Kamath. New York, Penguin/Viking, 2006. Originally published as *Young Zubaan* in India, in 2004. ISBN 978-0-670-06051-1, 0-670-06051-8. 152 p. (8–10). Chapter book.

After two years of adventures, Younguncle comes to live with his nephew and nieces and to "settle down" to a more routine life. Yet the children soon discover that Younguncle's unconventional personality will never settle into any type of routine. This uncle finds every job he takes to be "too interesting" and quickly changes from one position to the next. As a type of Indian Robin Hood, he also mischievously takes from the rich and gives to those more unfortunate. In each humorous episode, Younguncle makes a fool of himself and others in order to help those in need, such as rescuing his sister from an upcoming marriage to a man she does not love. This collection of Younguncle's eccentric adventures provides a fresh and often irreverent perspective of contemporary India. The stories will bring joy and laughter to readers of all ages. *2007 USBBY Outstanding International Books List.* nrz

Author grew up in New Delhi, India, where she heard myths, legends, and village lore from her mother and paternal grandmother. She now lives in Boston and New Delhi.

Uncles, Eccentrics and Eccentricities, India, Fiction

Venkatraman, Padma. **Climbing the Stairs**. New York, Penguin Group/ G. P. Putnam's Sons, 2008. ISBN 978-0-399-24746-0, 0-399-24746-7. 247 p. (12 up). Novel.

The plot is familiar: an adolescent battles the constraints of her culture and ultimately succeeds. Yet fifteen-year-old Vidya's story is eminently compelling, set as it is in 1941 India amid nonviolent protests by Gandhi's adherents and the brutal British response. Vidya's comfortable world and future plans for college crumble when her father's skull is crushed by a British soldier. Compelled to live with her father's family, Vidya dreads the customary arranged marriage relatives threaten for her instead of attending a university as she wishes. Venkatraman gives readers a window into World War II–era India, rich in day-to-day detail and rooted in tradition. *jfc*

Author was born in India but currently lives in the United States.

Prejudices, Brain Damage, Family Life, India History–British Occupation (1765–1947) India, Historical Fiction

Whitaker, Zai. **Kali and the Rat Snake**. Illustrated by Srividya Natarajan. La Jolla, CA, Kane/Miller Books, 2006. Originally published by Tulika Books India, in 2000. ISBN 978-1-933605-10-4, 1-933605-10-3. 32 p. (8–10). Picture book.

Kali is an Indian boy who had been proud of his family's heritage as Irulas, or tribal snake catchers, until he starts school and worries that the other children will laugh at his traditional ways, his family's work, or his fried termites for lunch (actually his favorite treat). Even though Kali is the best student in the class, he still can't seem to make friends . . . until the fateful day a menacing rat snake finds its way into the classroom and it's up to Kali to use everything he knows about snake catching to rescue the class. Includes a glossary of words in the Indian language of Tamil. *lvb*

Author lives in India; illustrator was born in India and now lives in Canada.

Courage, School, Making Friends, Diversity, Fiction

RELATED INFORMATION

Organizations

Children's Book Trust

www.childrensbooktrust.com/index.htm

The Children's Book Trust was founded in 1957 by Keshav Shankar Pillai, popularly known as SHANKAR, who was India's most celebrated cartoonist before and after India's independence. Housed in Nehru House since 1965, CBT is the pioneer publisher of children's books in India whose goal is to promote the production of well-written, well-illustrated, and well-designed books for children.

IBBY India

Works in conjunction with the Association of Writers and Illustrators for Children (AWIC), Nehru House, 4 Bahadur Shah Zafar Marg, IN-New Delhi 110 002

www.awic.in/

www.ibby.org/index.php?id=427

Awards

Competition for Writers of Children's Books

The Competition for Writers of Children's Books includes eight categories of books for children of all ages in all genres. Sponsored by Children's Book Trust.

www.childrensbooktrust.com/writing.htm

Book Fairs

Mumbai International Book Fair

http://internationalbookfair.com/

India is one of the ten biggest book-publishing centers in the world and is only third, after the United States and the United Kingdom, for the number of English titles published. Mumbai is India's biggest market for all kinds of books.

Publishers in India

Tara Publishing

Tara Books is an independent publisher of picture books for adults and children based in Chennai, South India, that strives for a union of fine form with rich content.

www.tarabooks.com/

Tulika Publishers

Tulika is an independent publishing house producing quality books for children. Their focus is to give children images of India that go on to show how all parts of this world come together to make it a diverse and dynamic whole, a changing yet changeless continuum.

www.tulikabooks.com/

Publications

Khorana, Meena. **The Indian Subcontinent in Literature for Children and Young Adults: An Annotated Bibliography of English-Language Books**. New York, Greenwood Press, 1991. ISBN 978-0-313-25489-5, 0-313-25489-3. 350 p.

This bibliography examines literature for young people concerning the Indian subcontinent and associated areas: Bangladesh, the Himalayan kingdoms of Bhutan, Nepal, Sikkim, Tibet, India, Pakistan, and Sri Lanka. Over nine hundred entries are organized by country or subregion. Each chapter is divided by genre.

Writer and Illustrator: The quarterly journal of AWIC—Association of Writers and Illustrators for Children. Nehru House, 4 Bahadur Shah Zafar Marg, New Delhi 110 002 India, www.awic.in/.

This publication of IBBY India focuses on children's books in India; research-based articles; profiles of Indian writers, illustrators, and storytellers; and their works. Stories may be written in Hindi or English, and there are reviews of books in sixteen Indian languages and English.

INDONESIA

Reynolds, Jan. **Cycle of Rice, Cycle of Life**. Illustrated by the author's photographs. New York, Lee & Low Books, 2009. ISBN 978-1-60060-254-2, 1-60060-254-1. (8–13). Nonfiction.

Cycle of Rice, Cycle of Life is a spectacular photo essay that traces rainfall from the highest peaks on Bali Island, Indonesia, to the rice fields below. The book is divided into chapters, first about the most necessary component for the cycle of rice—water. Ancient farmers constructed an intricate system of streams that carry water through a series of water temples. The second chapter introduces the way rice is grown and then questions if the system is sustainable. The final chapter, "Saving the Cycle," pits tradition against technology. Author's note, maps, websites, and a glossary constitute the end matter. *Bank Street College of Education Best Children's Books of the Year, Smithsonian Magazine Notable Children's Books, Honor Book—Grade K–6 Social Studies (Society of School Librarians International)*, *IRA Notable Books for a Global Society*, *John Burroughs Young Readers Award*. lmp

Author lives in the United States.

SUSTAINABLE AGRICULTURE, RICE, INDONESIA, BALI ISLAND, NONFICTION

Organizations

Indonesian Section of IBBY—INABBY

ITC Permata Hijau, Rukan Diamond No. 22 & 23, Jl. Arteri Permata Hijau, Jakarta 12210.

www.ibby.org/index.php?id=538

www.kpba-murti.org

INABBY has been actively involved in relief efforts in north Sumatra in the Aceh region, bringing relief to the victims of the Tsunami disaster that struck the Indian Ocean in December 2004. IBBY has also sponsored work in the region through the IBBY-Tsunami Fund. Reports about this work can be found at www.ibby.org/index.php?id=491.

JAPAN

Gershator, Phillis. **Sky Sweeper**. Illustrated by Holly Meade. New York, Farrar, Straus and Giroux, 2007. ISBN 978-0-37437-007-7, 0-374-37007-9. 32 p. (6–10). Picture book.

As a young boy, Takeboki finds work as the temple Flower Keeper, sweeping the paths of the Japanese garden clean of fallen cherry blossoms and leaves. But this is considered to be child's work, and as Takeboki grows older, his family encourages him to find more suitable grown-up work—work that will pay more money. Takeboki will not leave his beloved garden because he delights in knowing that he makes the garden a beautiful and serene retreat for the monks. Takeboki knows that he is rich beyond words because the charms of the garden and a job well done are riches greater than gold to him. lvb

Author lives in the U.S. Virgin Islands; illustrator lives in the United States.

JAPAN, MONKS, BUDDHISM, PRIDE IN WORK, SELF-ACTUALIZATION, HISTORICAL FICTION

Hale, Christy. **The East-West House: Noguchi's Childhood in Japan**. Illustrated by the author. New York, Lee & Low Books, 2009. ISBN 978-1-60060-363-1, 1-60060-363-7. n.p. (8–10). Biography, Picture book.

A young poet came to the United States from Japan to improve his English. He fell in love, and shortly after he returned to his homeland, his son Isamu was born. Mother and son moved to Japan and lived there until 1918, when the boy returned to the United States. During his time in Japan, Isamu immersed himself in learning Japanese arts. He continued his artistic studies during college and for the rest of his life. Isamu Noguchi may not be a well-known name, but his work has influenced contemporary art here and in Japan. Extensive background information is included. *2009 Kirkus Reviews Best Books*. lmp

Author lives in the United States.

ISAMU NOGUCHI (1904–1988), CHILDHOOD AND YOUTH, JAPANESE-AMERICAN SCULPTORS, BIOGRAPHY

Kitamura, Satoshi. **Igor: The Bird Who Couldn't Sing**. Illustrated by the author. New York, Farrar, Straus and Giroux, 2005. Originally published by Andersen Press Great Britain, in 2005. ISBN 978-0-374-33558-8, 0-374-33558-3. n.p. (4–8). Picture book.

It's spring, and Igor desperately wants to join in with the Dawn Chorus for the first time in his life. But his voice spoils the chorus, and even music lessons don't help. Igor seeks out a quiet place on top of a rock and builds a nest. In this peaceful place, he tries to sing once more. His singing awakens the rock that is really a bird, and someone finally appreciates Igor's discordant sounds. Humorous illustrations of a canine rock band and alligators with bongo drums elucidate the text. si

Author was born in Tokyo and now lives in England.

BIRDS, DETERMINATION, SELF-ACTUALIZATION, FANTASY, FICTION

Kiyuduki, Satoko. Translated by Satsuki Yamashita & Alexis Ekerman. **Shoulder-a-Coffin Kuro, Volume 1**. Illustrated by the author. New York, Hatchett/Yen Press, 2008. Originally published as *Hitsugi Katsugi no Kuro Kaichu Tabinowa Vol. 1* in Japanese by Houbunsha Japan, in 2006. ISBN 978-0-7595-2897-0, 0-7595-2897-7. 119 p. (13 up). Graphic Novel.

An inscrutable traveler on a mission to find a witch journeys the countryside with bats and twin catlike children she rescued from an abandoned mansion. Known as Kuro, the traveler incites controversy wherever she goes, with her black attire and a coffin strapped to her back. Although Kuro is misunderstood by her many acquaintances, she remains good natured, but she never divulges the secrets of her mysterious bandages, nor does she disclose the details of her mission. *dgw*

Author lives in Japan.

TEENAGE GIRLS, COMIC BOOKS, QUESTS (EXPEDITIONS), JAPANESE TRANSLATIONS INTO ENGLISH, GRAPHIC NOVELS, YOUNG ADULT FICTION

Kojima, Naomi. **Singing Shijimi Clams**. Illustrated by the author. La Jolla, CA, Kane/Miller Books, 2006. Originally published as *Utau Shijimi* in Japanese by Kaisei-Sha Publishing Japan, in 2005. ISBN 978-1-933605-12-8, 1-933605-12-X. 32 p. (5–9). Picture book.

An old witch, who used to be mean and feisty, buys some clams to put in her miso soup. Yet, surprisingly and much to the disappointment of her cat, she becomes attached to the cute clams and is unable to eat them. Instead, she raises money so that she can take the train to deliver the clams to the sea. Placing them on the beach, she says, "The waves will soon come and take you home." At the end, the witch and her cat are also happy as clams and decide to live at the beach where they can hear their new friends sing every day. This unusual yet delicate tale of friendship will resonate with those children who perceive the spirit of all living creatures. *nrz*

Author lives in Japan.

FRIENDSHIP, CLAMS, JOURNEY HOME, FANTASY, JAPAN

Meehan, Kierin. **Hannah's Winter**. La Jolla, CA, Kane/Miller Books, 2009. Originally published by Penguin Group Australia, in 2001. ISBN 978-1-933605-98-2, 1-933605-98-7. 212 p. (9 up). Novel.

An exciting mystery is always a winner, and *Hannah's Winter* blends an exotic location, ghosts, floating objects, and enough intrigue to lure the most jaded sleuths. All disbelief in supernatural elements is willingly suspended because of the author's superb setup: Hannah rationally and disgustedly details her mother's crazed, over-the-top behavior before they ever arrive in Japan. The strange events begin soon after: Hannah and Miki—the Japanese daughter of her mother's friends—discover a puzzling riddle stuck to a box of antique books. Suddenly, as the bizarre events accumulate, it is obvious that the enigmatic riddle must be solved. *2010 USBBY Outstanding International Books List. lmp*

Author lives in Brisbane, Australia.

RIDDLES, AUSTRALIANS IN JAPAN, JAPAN CIVILIZATION, FICTION

Messager, Alexandre. Translated by Christopher Pitts. **We Live in Japan: Kids around the World**. Illustrated by Sophie Duffet. New York, Harry N. Abrams Books, 2007. Originally published as *Aoki, Hayo et Kenji vivent au Japon* in French by Editions de la Martiniere France, in 2006. ISBN 978-0-8109-1283-0, 0-8109-1283-X. 47 p. (all ages). Nonfiction.

The geography, history, and culture of Japan are depicted through the lives of three children, Aoki of Tokyo, Hayo of Kyoto, and Kenji of Hiroshima. The trio explores the topography of Japan, volcanic mountaintops that peek out above the ocean, along with the earthquakes, tsunamis, and typhoons that have plagued it. Japan's rich history of emperors, samurai, shogun, and the influence of Chinese culture are probed. Through the experiences of Aoki, Hayo, and Kenji, the traditions of flower arranging, tea ceremonies, Japanese writing, and sumo wrestling are vividly described. *dgw*
   Author lives in France.
   CHILDREN, JAPAN, NONFICTION BOOKS

Miyabe, Miyuki. Translated by Alexander O. Smith. **Brave Story**. Illustrated by Yoichiro Ono. San Francisco, CA, VIZ Media, 2007. Originally published as *Bureibu sutori* in Japanese by Kadokawa Shoten Publishing Japan, in 2003. ISBN 978-1-4215-1196-2, 1-4215-1196-7. 816 p. (12 up). Novel.

In Miyuki Miyabe's fourth translated book, ten-year-old Wataru is appalled that his father plans to divorce his mother and marry another woman. When his mother attempts suicide, Wataru enters the fantastic land of Vision, where he struggles against internal and external monsters to reach the Tower of Destiny. His journey pits good against evil, friendship against personal goals, and leads him through animelike adventures. Although the 816-page text is intimidating, gamers will readily identify with this book. In Japan, it was serialized, published as manga, as video games, and as an animated movie. Introduce readers who crave similar fantasy worlds to Michael Ende's *The Neverending Story* (1979/1983). *2008 Batchelder Award. lmp*
   Author lives in Japan.
   ADVENTURE, JAPAN SOCIAL LIFE AND CUSTOMS, FANTASY FICTION

Nakagawa, Chihiro. Translated by the author. **Who Made This Cake?** Illustrated by Junji Koyose. Asheville, NC, Front Street, 2008. Originally published as *Otasuke Kobito* in Japanese by Tokuma Shoten Japan, in 2007. ISBN 978-1-59078-595-9, 1-59078-595-9. 32 p. (4–8). Picture book.

An entertaining play on perspective and on cake construction, the black ink and brightly colored illustrations in this minimally worded picture book show us the workday of a hard-working crew of tiny construction workers and their vehicles on the building site. Each stage of cake construction, from egg breaking to the final icing, is shown in careful detail, culminating in the final presentation of the whipped-cream-and-strawberry-topped cake to a young boy as part of his birthday celebration. *2009 USBBY Outstanding International Books List, 2008 National Parenting Publications Awards Honor Book, 2008 Horn Book Magazine Best Books for Preschoolers. ae*

Author lives in Japan.

CONSTRUCTION EQUIPMENT, CAKE, BAKING, JAPAN, FICTION

Nara, Yoshitomo. Translated by Tomoko Fujii. **The Lonesome Puppy**. Illustrated by the author. San Francisco, CA, Chronicle Books, 2008. Originally published as *Tomodachi Ga Hoshi Katta Koinu* in Japanese by Magajin Hausu Japan, in 1999. ISBN 978-0-8118-5640-9, 0-8118-5640-2. n.p. (4–8). Picture book.

Lonesome puppy's silhouette, tears dripping freely from assumed eyes and foregrounded on a field of teardrops, introduces this Japanese import. He is all alone because "I am . . . this BIG!" The puppy dwarfs the earth's sphere with paws positioned in Japan and Russia, California, and the Pacific Ocean. He is so big no one ever notices him. Until one day a small but determined girl climbs his legs, back, head, and tumbles down his nose. When she sings to him they become fast friends. The illustrations are charmingly simple, incorporating crayon; thick, black outlining; and collage with additional printing and painting techniques. *lmp*

Author is one of Japan's most popular contemporary artists. He lives in Tochigi, Japan.

DOGS, FRIENDSHIP, FANTASY, JAPAN

Nishimura, Kae. **Bunny Lune**. Illustrated by the author. New York, Clarion Books, 2007. ISBN 978-0-618-71606-7, 0-618-71606-8. 31 p. (6–9). Picture book.

After receiving a letter from a friend in Japan that describes the Japanese full moon celebration, Bunny Lune becomes preoccupied with going to the moon. He checks on moon tours, but they are too expensive. Bunny Lune meets an old man who teaches him that he can visit the moon any time by simply looking up and imagining he is there. Nishimura's watercolor illustrations add a touch of humor and wistfulness to the playful text. Author's notes discuss the traditions of the Japanese Moon Festival. *nlh*

Author was born and raised in Japan and now lives in the United States.

RABBITS, MOON FESTIVAL, JAPAN, FICTION

Onishi, Satoru. **Who's Hiding?** Illustrated by the author. La Jolla, CA, Kane/ Miller Books, 2007. Originally published in Japanese by Poplar Publishing, in 1993. ISBN 978-1-933605-24-1, 1-933605-24-3. 31 p. (3–5). Concept Picture book.

Eighteen colorful animals appear on the first double-page spread. The next illustration is identical to the first, except one animal is missing. It is up to the reader to remember what animal occupied that space. Frequently the question at the top of the following pages is "who's hiding?," but occasionally the reader is asked to identify the animal that is sleeping or angry or backwards. An answer key is provided. *pwc*

Author lives in Japan.

QUESTIONS AND ANSWERS, VISUAL PERCEPTION, ANIMALS, PICTURE PUZZLES, HIDDEN PICTURES, JAPAN

Sakai, Komako. **The Snow Day**. Illustrated by the author. New York, Scholastic/Arthur A. Levine Books, 2009. Originally published as *Yuki Ga Yandara* in Japanese by Gakken Ltd. Japan, in 2005. ISBN 978-0-545-01321-5, 0-545-01321-6. n.p. (2–8). Picture book.

What's more enjoyable than a snow day? Anthropomorphic little rabbit is no different from any five-year-old. "I jumped out of bed and ran for my boots." Disappointed that he must remain indoors until the snow stops, little rabbit sneaks onto the balcony and makes a little snow dumpling. Along with little rabbit, readers watch the silent snowfall, play quiet card games, and, when the snow finally stops, make monsters and footprints in the pristine whiteness. Soft as the snow blanketing little rabbit's world, the phrasing and illustrations will generate conversation as children share their "snow day" experiences. *2009 New York Times Best Illustrated Children's Books, BCCB Blue Ribbon Book, Booklist Editors' Choices for 2009. lmp*

Author lives in Japan.

SNOW, RABBITS, MOTHER AND CHILD, FICTION

Uehashi, Nahoko. Translated by Cathy Hirano. **Moribito: Guardian of the Spirit**. Illustrated by Yuko Shimizu. New York, Scholastic/Arthur A. Levine Books, 2008. Originally published as *Seirei no Moribito* in Japanese by Kaisei-Sha Publishing Japan, in 1996. ISBN 978-0-545-00542-5, 0-545-00542-6. 260 p. (10–14). Novel.

Reflexively, Balsa dives into the raging river to save Chagum, second son of New Yogo's Mikado. The second queen, Chagum's mother, beseeches Balsa to conceal her son and protect him from the evil forces attempting to kill him. Somewhat reluctantly Balsa agrees, and she and the prince begin their journey. It is not until the final chapter that the secret of the Moribito's quest—protecting the magical egg called Nyunga Ro Im, which provides rain for the nation's life-giving crops—is disclosed. The intervening chapters provide adventures so heart-stopping few will be able to stop reading until the conclusion. *2009 Outstanding International Books List, 2009 Mildred L. Batchelder Award Winner*. lmp

Author is an associate professor of anthropology at Kawamura Gakuen Women's University. She lives in Tokyo.

Water Spirits, Princes, Monsters, Fathers, Fantasy, Japan

Uehashi, Nahoko. Translated by Cathy Hirano. **Moribito II: Guardian of the Darkness**. Illustrated by Yuko Shimizu. New York, Scholastic/Arthur A. Levine Books, 2009. Originally published as *Yami no Moribito* in Japanese by Kaisei-Sha Publishing Japan, in 1999. ISBN 978-0-545-10295-7, 0-545-10295-2. 245 p. (10–14). Novel.

In order to protect Balsa and himself, Jiguro Balsa's stepfather had been forced to kill eight former friends sent by the nefarious King Rogsam. So when Balsa returns to her native Kanbal, she is on a pilgrimage of reparation for Jiguro's misdeeds. The longer Balsa remains in Kanbal, however, the more dangers she faces. Yuguro, her stepfather's younger brother, and King Radalle, Rogsam's son, have conspired to kill the Mountain King and steal the mountain's precious luisha. Balsa must protect the young message carrier Kassa, but Balsa herself is predestined to perform the Spear Dance with the hyohlu, spirit guardians of the Mountain King. *2010 USBBY Outstanding International Books List*. lmp

Author is an associate professor of anthropology at Kawamura Gakuen Women's University. She earned a PhD, focusing on Australian Aborigines. She lives in Tokyo.

Swordplay, Orphans, Fantasy, Japan

Yamada, Utako. **The Story of Cherry the Pig**. La Jolla, CA, Kane/Miller Books, 2007. Originally published in Japanese by Kaisei-Sha Japan, in 2002. ISBN 978-1-933605-25-8, 1-933605-25-1. n.p. (4–6). Picture book.

In a style reminiscent of Roger Duvoisin's carefree lines, pastel palette, and benign faces, Cherry the Pig, who loves to eat—"She was, after all, a pig" (n.p.)—parlays her talent into a bake-off entry for the Harvest Festival. Although her sweet apple cake seems the perfect competitor, Cherry's confidence is eroded when she overhears a mouse family making disparaging comments. Even so, the judges award her the golden whisk, and Cherry Pig learns a bit about different "tastes." The labels on canisters, signs, and wall plaques are in English; only Cherry's conciliatory note to the mice family is in Japanese. *nlr*

Author/illustrator lives in Tokyo.

FRIENDSHIP, COOKING, SELF-ESTEEM, JAPAN, FANTASY FICTION

Yamamura, Anji. **Hannah Duck**. La Jolla, CA, Kane/Miller, 2008. Originally published as *Ahiru No Hannah* in Japanese by Singpoosha Publishing Japan, in 2005. ISBN 978-1-933605-74-6, 1-933605-74-X. 25 p. (3–5). Picture book.

Hannah Duck lives peacefully in a house with a parakeet and a turtle. Every Sunday Hannah goes for a walk to the park. One day she admits to her friends that the walks scare her. The parakeet offers to join her. With the companionship of a friend, the park is not as frightening and Hannah discovers what a beautiful place it is. *pwc*

Author lives in Japan.

ANIMALS, DUCKS, PARKS, FEAR, FANTASY FICTION

RELATED INFORMATION

Awards

Children's Storybook and Picture Book Grand Prix

The Nissan Children's Storybook and Picture Book Grand Prix contest aims to provide children with inspiring and imaginative storybooks and picture books.

www.nissan-global.com/EN/NEWS/2010/_STORY/100305-01-e.html

Japanese Association of Writers for Children Prize 2006

Japanese Association of Writers for Children first granted this prize in 1961. The award is selected from among the works published during the previous year and is announced in the association's magazine, *Nihon Jido Bungaku [Japanese Literature for Children]*.

www.jbby.org/en/books/pop_Japanese.html

Kodansha Publication Culture Award for Children's Picture Books

The Kodansha Culture Prize was founded in 1970 to exploit new fields, elevate quality, and ameliorate the culture of publishing. The awards are granted in May every year in different fields, such as illustration, photographs, book design, and picture books.

Nihon Ehon Award/Japan Picture Book Award

The original award, the Japan Picture Book Award, was founded in 1978 by the Yomiuri Shimbun, one of the Japanese national newspaper companies, and the Japan School Library Association, but it was suspended in 1992. It then resumed as the Japan Picture Book Award in 1995 to disseminate picture book arts, to promote reading, and to contribute to the development of children's books.

Noma Prize for Juvenile Literature

Noma Cultural Foundation was established to carry out the wishes of Mr. Seiji Noma. He was the first president of Kodansha Ltd., a Japanese publishing company. The foundation began to grant the Noma Prize for Literature in 1942 and separately the Noma Prize for Juvenile Literature in 1963 to encourage children's literature that plays a part in human fundamental development. The awards are presented in November every year.

Shogakukan Children's Publication—Culture Award

This award was established in 1952 to promote the culture of children. The award is open to all children's publications, including books and magazines.

Other Book Awards

Akaitori Award for Children's Literature
Iwaya Sazanami Award
Sankei Award for Children's Books and Publications
Tsubota Joji Literary Prize

More information about all of Japan's children's book awards is available online at the JBBY website, www.jbby.org/.

Organizations

IBBY Japan

The goal of Japan IBBY (JBBY), founded in 1974, is to provide children with access to books of high literary and artistic merit and to encourage the publication and distribution of quality children's books.

www.ibby.org/index.php?id=432
www.jbby.org/

Museums and Research in Children's Literature

Chihiro Art Museum Tokyo

4-7-2, Shimo-Shakujii, Nerima-ku, Toyko 177-0042, Japan
Telephone: 81-3-3995-0612
Exhibitions featuring selections from the Chihiro Iwasaki Collection and International Collection are organized according to various themes and are rotated every two months for visitors' enjoyment and to protect and conserve the delicate artwork.

www.chihiro.jp/global/en/tokyo/index.html

The Foundation for Child Well-Being National Children's Castle

Jingumae, Shibuya ward, Tokyo
The International Institute for Children's Literature, Osaka, which opened in 1984, is Japan's first comprehensive center for international children's literature.

www.kodomono-shiro.or.jp [Japanese only]
www.nissan-global.com/EN/NEWS/2010/_STORY/100305-01-e.html [English]

International Institute for Children's Literature, Osaka

10-6 Banpaku-Koen, Senri Suita-Shi, 565-0826 Japan
This institute houses a research collection of children's books and offers reference services and seminars; it publishes an annual bulletin and a newsletter, which is available online, in English, at its website. You can also review samples of one hundred children's books at this site.

www.iiclo.or.jp/index.html

International Library of Children's Literature

12-49 Ueno Park, Taito-ku, Tokyo, 110-0007 Japan
Opened in 2000, The ILCL provides internationally linked library services for children's literature and related materials published in Japan and in other countries. The ILCL is the first national library of its kind in Japan.

www.kodomo.go.jp/english/index.html

Karuizawa Museum of Picture Books

Based on the idea "conversation with nature," this museum consists of a collection of picture books of fairy tales from the woods, many of which were written by the Brothers Grimm. Original illustrations from these picture books are also on display. Additional picture books and toys, especially from

other wooded terrains in Europe and the United States, give visitors a feeling of the three-hundred-year history of the world of picture books.
www.museen.org/english/index.html

Kawasaki City Museum

The Kawasaki City Museum opened in November 1988 and provides space for community-based learning activities.
www.kawasaki-museum.jp/english/

National Olympics Memorial Youth Center

An educational institution established to promote the healthy development of young people and youth education in Japan and to promote cooperation among institutions and groups connected to youth education.
http://nyc.niye.go.jp/e/

Oshima Museum of Picture Books

This facility houses more than ten thousand Japanese and foreign picture books along with book art. There are studios and storytelling facilities as well.
www.ehonkan.or.jp/english/index.html

Setagaya Art Museum

Features a variety of exhibitions, not only visual art but also music and film. This museum features art from the surrounding district and caters to adult patrons.
www.setagayaartmuseum.or.jp/

Society of Children's Book Writers and Illustrators—Japan

The Tokyo chapter of this international writers' group offers members throughout Japan support, information, and community.
www.scbwi.jp/home.htm

Yokohama Museum of Art

The Yokohama Museum of Art was founded in 1989 to foster the development of a rich civic culture in Yokohama. This museum features fine art and caters to adult patrons.
www.yaf.or.jp/yma/english/030exhibitions/

Book Fairs

Nissan Joyful Storybook and Picture Book Exposition

In addition to displaying many outstanding storybook and picture books, creative workshops for children are also held. This exhibition is now a popular spring vacation event, attracting some thirty thousand children and parents a year.

www.nissan-global.com/GCC/PHILANTHROPY/ACTIVITY/2000/english/2_2.html

Tokyo International Book Fair (TIBF)
www.bookfair.jp/

Online Resources

Japanese Children's Books
This website is a bilingual magazine on children's books published by the Yamaneko Honyaku Club.

www.yamaneko.org/einfo/mgzn/index.htm

Publications

Hasegawa, Ushio. **Jidou Bungaku No Naka No Shogaisha [People with Disabilities in Children's Literature]**. Illustrated by Makiko Futaki. Tokyo, Budousha, 2005. ISBN 978-4-89240-181-7. 216 p.

There are many children's books with disability themes. This is the first professional reference to examine these kinds of published books, beginning with the late nineteenth century until today. *Japanese Association of Writers for Children Prize 2006.*

Author was born in Tokyo. He is a children's literature critic and researcher.

PEOPLE WITH DISABILITIES, LITERATURE HISTORY, DISABILITY ISSUES

Tinker Bell. **Journal of JSCLE: The Japan Society for Children's Literature in English**. Annual covering literature and culture of English-speaking countries. Essays in Japanese and English.

www.irscl.ac.uk/journals.htm#japanese

Publishers Related to Picture Books and Children's Books:

Froebel-kan Co., Ltd.: www.froebel-kan.co.jp/ [English and Japanese]
Fukuinkan Shoten, Publishers, Inc.: www.fukuinkan.com/ [English and Japanese]
Holp Shuppan, Publishers: www.holp-pub.co.jp [Japanese only]
Iwasaki Publishing Company: www.iwasakishoten.co.jp/ [Japanese only]
Japanese Association of Children's Book Publishers: www.kodomo.gr.jp [Japanese only]

Kaisei-sha Co. Ltd.: www.kaiseisha.co.jp/ [Japanese only]
Kawade Shobo Shinsha, Publishers: www.kawade.co.jp/ [English and Japanese]
Kodansha, Ltd.: www.bookclub.Kodansha.co.jp/ [Japanese only]
Poplar Publishing Co., Ltd.: www.poplar.co.jp [Japanese only]
Shiko-sha, Co., Ltd.: www.ehon-artbook.com/ [English and Japanese]
Shogakukan, Inc.: www.shogakukan.co.jp/ [Japanese only]

KOREA

Bae, Hyun-Joo. **New Clothes for New Year's Day**. Illustrated by the author. La Jolla, CA, Kane/Miller Books, 2007. Originally published as *The New Year's Best Clothes* in Korean by Sakyejul Publishing Korea, in 2006. ISBN 978-1-933605-29-6, 1-933605-29-4. 32 p. (5–9). Picture book.

It's New Year's Day, and a young Korean girl celebrates by donning the new clothes her mother has made for her. Vivid illustrations and simple text lead readers through the process as the young girl puts on each item of clothing. Endnotes provide information about the Lunar New Year and the customs of dressing up on New Year's Day. In addition, there is a diagram of the young girl with each of the clothing items labeled. *2008 USBBY Outstanding International Books List, CCBC Choices, and Notable Books for a Global Society. nlh, mjw*

Author studied in Korea.

LUNAR NEW YEAR, CUSTOMS, TRADITIONAL CLOTHING, KOREA, FICTION

Choi, Yangsook. **Behind the Mask**. Illustrated by the author. New York, Farrar, Straus and Giroux/Frances Foster Books, 2006. Originally published in Korean as *Haraboji ui t`al* by K`ureyong Hausu Seoul, in 2007. ISBN 978-0-374-30522-2, 0-374-30522-6. 40 p. (4–8). Picture book.

Korean theater traditions meet American Halloween customs in this story about Kimin's discovery of the perfect trick-or-treat costume. Searching through his grandfather's boxes, he finds a frightening white-eyebrowed, white-bearded mask and family photos of his grandfather, who was a famous mask dancer in Korea. By dressing as a Talchum dancer, Kimin connects to his grandfather and his Korean heritage and informs his friends about it. Whimsical illustrations, masks on the endpapers, and a note on traditional Korean mask dance illuminate the descriptive text. *Bank Street Best Chil-*

dren's Book of the Year, 2007 NCSS-CBC Notable Trade Book in the Field of Social Studies. mjw
   Author grew up in Korea and lives in New York.
   HALLOWEEN, MASKS, GRANDFATHERS, KOREAN AMERICANS, FICTION

Choung, Eun-hee. **Minji's Salon**. La Jolla, CA, Kane Miller Books, 2007. Originally published in Korean by Sang Publishing Korea, in 2007. ISBN 978-1-933605-67-8, 1-933605-67-7. 36 p. (3–5). Picture book.
   Minji peeks through the window of the salon where her mom is having her hair styled. She decides to create a home salon with her dog as her client. As we watch the hairdresser fashion mom's hair, we see Minji on the opposite page trying to replicate the actions of the stylist. When Mom returns home, she is surprised by the mess but quickly smiles when Minji asks her if she would like an appointment. *pwc*
   Author lives in South Korea.
   GIRLS, PLAY, BEAUTY SHOPS, KOREA, FICTION

Kwon, Yoon-duck. **My Cat Copies Me**. Illustrated by the author. La Jolla, CA, Kane/Miller Books, 2007. Originally published in Korean as *My Cat Copies Only Me* by Changbi Publishers Korea, in 2005. ISBN 978-1-933605-26-5, 1-933605-26-X. 40 p. (4–8). Picture book.
   The special friendship between a cat and a timid young girl is beautifully illustrated in this charming book. Initially, readers see the cat playfully following the young girl and copying her in all her actions around the house. Her cat's fearlessness inspires her to go outside and make new friends together. Brilliant Korean genre paintings become more complex and detailed as the story unfolds. *2008 USBBY Outstanding International Books List, Children's Book Sense Pick. nlh, mjw*
   Author lives in South Korea.
   CATS, PETS, FRIENDSHIP, IMAGINARY PLAY, KOREA, FICTION

Lee, Suzy. **The Zoo**. Illustrated by the author. La Jolla, CA, Kane/Miller Books, 2007. Originally published in Korean as *The Zoo* by BIR Seoul Korea, in 2004. ISBN 978-1-933605-28-9, 1-933605-28-6. 32 p. (4–8). Picture book.
   Beautiful illustrations capture the joy of a visit to the zoo. The author/illustrator weaves the playful story of a young girl's imaginary experiences with her parents' actual adventures. Double-page spreads with grisaille illustrations and limited text describe the visit to the zoo. Alternating wordless pages with color illustrations show the child's imaginative play as she wanders away from her parents, falls asleep on a bench, and dreams of real

encounters among the animals. CCBC *Choices, Notable Children's Books in the Language Arts. nlh*

    Author was born in Korea and now lives in the United States.

Zoos, Missing Children, Korea, Contemporary Realistic Fiction

Lee, Tae-Jun. Translated by Eun Hee Chun. **Waiting for Mama**. Illustrated by Kim Dong-Seong. New York, NorthSouth Books, 2007. Originally published as *Omma Majung* in Korean by Sonyon Hangil South Korea, in 2004. ISBN 978-0-7358-2143-9, 0-7358-2143-7. 35 p. (3–5). Picture book.

    On a cold day, a small Korean boy waits for his mother at the streetcar station. Several streetcars come and go without Mama appearing. Finally Mama arrives and the two set off for home, hand in hand, through the snow. This is a beautifully designed bilingual picture book. The text is simple, and the illustrations are striking in composition and color choice. Endnotes about the Hangeul writing and information about the illustrator's depiction of Korea in 1938 are valuable additions. *ca*

    Author lived in North Korea until his death in 1956; illustrator lives in South Korea.

Mother and Child, Korea History 20th Century, Korea, Historical Fiction, Bilingual Stories

Park, Janie Jaehyun. **The Love of Two Stars: A Korean Legend**. Illustrated by the author. Toronto, Groundwood Books, 2005. ISBN 978-0-88899-672-5, 0-88899-672-1. 32 p. (5–8). Picture book.

    A retelling of a Korean legend in which Kyonu, who raises cattle, and Jingnyo, a talented weaver, fall in love. Punished by the king of the sky kingdom for neglecting their duties, they are sent to opposite ends of the sky and are allowed to meet only once a year. When they find the Milky Way too difficult to cross, "magpies and crows" devise a way to help them (n.p.). Double-spread full-page paintings of deep blues and whirling patterns evoke the vastness of the sky kingdom. Park includes a note about the legend. *hc*

    Author lives in Canada and was born in Seoul, South Korea.

Stars, Mythology, Love, Legends, Korea

Park, Linda Sue. **Bee-Bim Bop!** Illustrated by Ho Baek Lee. New York, Clarion Books, 2005. ISBN 978-0-618-26511-4, 0-618-26511-2. 31 p. (4–8). Picture book.

    Lively illustrations portray a young girl working with her mother to create a favorite meal for the family—bee-bim bop. As they shop, prepare food, and set the table, the child chants "Hungry, hungry, hungry, for some BEE-BIM BOP." The story culminates as the other family members join the child and her mother to enjoy a meal of bee-bim bop. The children and parents are dressed in Western clothing, while the grandmother wears traditional Korean clothes. An author's note includes a recipe for bee-bim bop as well as an explanation of how this popular Korean dish is served. *mm*

Author lives in the United States. She is a first-generation Korean American.
KOREAN COOKING, STORIES IN RHYME, KOREA, FICTION

RELATED INFORMATION

Book Fairs

Nami Island Children's Book Festival
The Nami Island Children's Book Festival was first held in 2005 in honor of the two-hundredth anniversary of the birth of Hans Christian Andersen and aimed "to create on this island a fairytale world in nature through books."
www.nambook.org/Web/main/index.php

Seoul International Book Fair
www.sibf.or.kr/eng/

Organizations

Korean Board on Books for Young People—KBBY
www.kbby.org
In 2009 Woo-hyon Kang, former president of KBBY and founder of the Nami Island Children's Book Festival, pledged the support of Nami Island, Inc., as sponsors of the Hans Christian Andersen Awards for the next ten years.
www.ibby.org/index.php?id=434

LAOS

Gerdner, Linda & Sarah Langford. **Grandfather's Story Cloth / Yawg Daim Paj Ntaub Dab Neeg**. Illustrated by Stuart Loughridge. Walnut Creek, CA,

Shen's Books, 2008. ISBN 978-1-88500834-3, 1-88500834-1. 31 p. (5–10). Picture book.

Life is slowly changing for a Hmong family as Grandfather succumbs to the effects of Alzheimer's disease. Ten-year-old Chersheng is given the responsibility of helping to care for the story cloth that Grandfather so skillfully embroidered in the refugee camp. After listening to Grandfather relate the story of his escape from Laos as stitched in the cloth, he is inspired to create his own colorful collage of their new life in America to help Grandfather remember. The bilingual story is sympathetically told from the point of view of Chersheng and illustrated with impressionistic watercolor paintings. An afterward provides more information about story cloths and Alzheimer's disease. *2009 CCBC Choices, Moonbeam Children's Book Awards, 2008 Silver Health Issues United States. djg*

Author is from the United States and has visited Hmong villages in northern Laos.

GRANDFATHERS, ALZHEIMER'S DISEASE, MEMORY, QUILTS, LAOTIAN AMERICANS, FAMILY LIFE, HMONG LANGUAGE MATERIALS–BILINGUAL, FICTION

MALAYSIA

Buchmann, Stephen L. & Diana Cohn. **The Bee Tree**. Illustrated by Paul Mirocha. El Paso, TX, Cinco Puntos Press, 2007. ISBN 978-0-938317-98-2, 0-938317-98-9. 40 p. (8–12). Picture book.

The Bee Tree is a wonderful collaboration among entomologist Stephen Buchmann, award-winning children's book author Diana Cohn, and illustrator Paul Mirocha. Through their words and lush illustrations, readers are transported to the rain forests of Malaysia for the annual honey hunt with the young fictional narrator Nizam and his grandfather. Nizam's coming-of-age story is steeped with cultural richness as readers ". . . enter the forest as if visiting a neighbor's home." As an added bonus, readers will find eight pages of nonfiction information pertaining to Malaysia, including a map, detailed drawings, and photographs. *ak*

Authors and illustrator live in the United States.

BEES, HONEY, COURAGE, COMING OF AGE, MALAYSIA, FICTION

Lat. **Kampung Boy**. Illustrated by the author. New York, First Second, 2006. Originally published as *The Kampung Boy* by Berita Publishing Malaysia, in 1979. ISBN 978-1-59643-121-8, 1-59643-121-0. 141 p. (10 up). Graphic Novel.

Kampung Boy is a thinly veiled graphic autobiography of Malaysia's most revered cartoonist. Published when he was only thirteen, it relates "Mat's" life from birth until he leaves for boarding school. The author depicts Muslim ceremonies, family life, school, and recreation through his personal recollections. He also includes observations about the transformation of his kampung, or village, from a family-oriented, agricultural economy to an industrialized corporate system. Lat's wry—and occasionally acerbic—humor is revealed through his black-and-white line illustrations more than through the narrative. However, the two levels combine to create a seamless exploration of a Malaysian childhood. *2007 USBBY Outstanding International Books List, 2006 Booklist Editor's Choice, 2006 BCCB Blue Ribbon Book. Lat received the Malaysian honorific title Datuk in 1994 and the Malaysian Press Institute's Special Jury Award. lmp*

   Author lives in Malaysia.

FAMILY, MUSLIMS, COUNTRY LIFE, MALAYSIA, GRAPHIC NOVELS, BIO-GRAPHICAL FICTION

Lat. **Town Boy**. Illustrated by the author. New York, First Second, 2007. Originally published as *Town Boy* by Berita Publishing Malaysia, in 1980. ISBN 978-1-59643-331-1, 1-59643-331-0. 191 p. (10 up). Graphic Novel.

   Town Boy continues where *Kampung Boy* ends: Mat's move to boarding school at the age of ten. Mat's interest in music eventually secures him his first friend, who introduces him to the joys and challenges of puberty. Mat and Frankie explore the cultural and religious differences between Chinese and Muslim Malaysians, as when Frankie asks, "How come you cannot eat pork . . . if I may ask" (51). Their ever-expanding circle of friends explore rock and roll, breaking rules, dating—even peep shows. This second volume in Lat's graphic autobiography ends when Mat chooses art over higher education. *lmp*

   Author lives in Malaysia.

MUSLIMS, TEENAGE BOYS, CITY AND TOWN LIFE, MALAYSIA, GRAPHIC NOVELS, BIOGRAPHICAL FICTION

RELATED INFORMATION

IBBY Malaysia

   Malaysian Board on Books for Young Children (MBBY) [Majlis Buku Kanak-kanak dan Remaja Malaysia]
   www.ibby.org/index.php?id=439
   www.mbby.net/

Ahmad Redza Ahmad Khairuddin (Kuala Lumpur, Malaysia) was elected to serve as IBBY president at the Thirty-second IBBY General Assembly in Santiago de Compostela, Spain. He served as vice president from 2008 to 2010 and as a member of the IBBY EC from 2006 to 2008.

MONGOLIA

Baasansuren, Bolormaa (adapted by Helen Mixter). **My Little Round House.** Illustrated by the author. Toronto, Groundwood Books/House of Anansi Press, 2006. Original text in Mongolian; adapted from the Japanese translation *Boku No Uchi Wa Gel.* ISBN 978-0-88899-934-4, 0-88899-934-8. 32 p. (2–5). Picture book.

Little Jilu is a baby recounting his first year in a Mongolian community. He describes their nomadic lifestyle from his birth in a ger, the traditional round dwelling in which the family lives, to their seasonal moves by camels to different camps and the celebration of Tsagaan Sar to commemorate the arrival of spring. The gentle narrative is complemented by the author's gouache folk art illustrations that capture the cycle of seasons. The author received the Noma Concours Grand Prize for this book, which was first published in Japan. *2010 USBBY Outstanding International Books List. bal*

Author/illustrator lives in Ulaanbaatar, Mongolia.

Dwellings, Mongolia

Lewin, Ted & Betsy Lewin. **Horse Song: The Naadam of Mongolia.** Illustrated by the authors. New York, Lee & Low Books, 2008. ISBN 978-1-58430-277-3, 1-58430-277-1. 56 p. (7–10). Picture book.

Ted and Betsy Lewin traveled to Bulgan, eight hundred unpaved miles from the Ulaanbaatar airport, to experience the Naadam festival firsthand. Mongolians have held Naadam festivals, which include archery and wrestling in addition to horse racing, for almost one thousand years. Many Mongolians are nomads, so Naadam is also an opportunity for socializing with friends and relatives. Betsy's cartoon sketches are a playful counterbalance to her husband's full- and double-page watercolor spreads, which provide a detailed, realistic impression of the people and terrain. This is an informative explanation of a cultural event that has taken place longer than the United States has existed. *ALA Notable Children's Book, Best Children's Books of the*

*Year–Bank Street College of Education, Parents' Choice Recommended Winner,
Editor's Choice–Booklist. The Lewins separately won Caldecott Honor awards for
their illustrations.* lmp

Author/illustrators live in the United States.

SUMMER FESTIVALS, MONGOLIA–SOCIAL LIFE AND CUSTOMS, ANIMALS,
ASIAN CULTURAL DIVERSITY, FAMILY TRADITIONS, HOLIDAYS & CELEBRA-
TIONS, SPORTS, MONGOLIA, NONFICTION

RELATED INFORMATION

IBBY Mongolia

After struggling for many years to introduce IBBY to Mongolia, Dashdondog Jamba and Sunjidmaa Jamba finally succeeded in forming the national section in 2005. MBBY has published 108 picture books—Mongolian
national fairy tales and stories written by modern authors. These books,
together with other children's books, have been read by hundreds of children
in rural as well as urban areas of Mongolia, thanks to the mobile library that
was initiated and is run by Mr. Dashdondog. The Mobile Library received the
IBBY-Asahi Reading Promotion Award in 2006.

www.ibby.org/index.php?id=485

NEPAL

Kerr, P. B. **The Cobra King of Kathmandu: Children of the Lamp, Book
Three.** New York, Scholastic/Orchard Books, 2007. Originally published by
Scholastic Great Britain, in 2006. ISBN 978-0-439-67023-4, 0-439-67023-3.
ix, 373 p. (14 up). Novel.

When Dybbuk uses his djinn powers to steal a baton that once belonged
to Hermann Goering, his life is in danger, for hidden in the baton is a picture
with a secret code. This leads Dybbuk and his twin djinn friends, Philippa
and John, to Lucknow, India, where they find the valuable "Cobra King" that
had once belonged to a snake cult. Here, they are captured by the guru who
has already kidnapped the twin's uncle and best friend, but the guru's plan
to use the children's blood to become a djinn backfires in a spectacular way.
Sequel to *The Blue Djinn of Babylon.* hc

Author is from England.

GENIES, MAGIC, TWINS, BROTHERS AND SISTERS, KATHMANDU (NEPAL), FANTASY FICTION

Stryer, Andrea Stenn. **Kami and the Yaks**. Illustrated by Bert Dodson. Palo Alto, CA, Bay Otter Press, 2007. ISBN 978-0-9778961-0-3, 0-9778961-0-2. (4–8). Picture book.

Sherpa guides depend on yaks when they lead climbers into the Himalayas. Knowing that his father and brother were leading an expedition that morning, Kami was surprised to find them searching for their yaks. Even though he could not hear the sound—Kami was deaf—he knew Curly Horn always responded when he blew his whistle. This story of a fictionalized Nepalese Sherpa family and their young son's courage in the face of a sudden mountain storm provides readers with a window into a culture most people never encounter. Dodson's watercolor illustrations are evocative of the frigid Himalayan landscape and isolation. *2008 Schneider Family Book Award (Young Children)*. lmp

Author and illustrator live in the United States.

DEAF CHILDREN, PEOPLE WITH DISABILITIES, SHERPA (NEPALESE PEOPLE), YAKS, HIMALAYA MOUNTAINS, FATHERS AND SONS, NEPAL, FICTION

RELATED INFORMATION

IBBY Nepal

Nepalese Section of IBBY—NBBY functions in conjunction with the Nepalese Society for Children's Literature (NESCHIL)

www.ibby.org/index.php?id=527

www.neschil.org.np/

OCEANIA

Pratchett, Terry. **Nation**. New York, HarperCollins, 2008. ISBN 978-0-06-143301-6, 0-06-143301-2. 367 p. (12 up). Novel.

When the world has gone awry, send a disaster to eradicate the past and allow pristine youth to reform civilization. This is the core thesis of *Nation*, and the tsunami that wipes out Mau's nation effectively traps him between childhood and manhood. Daphne is rescued from society's clutches by the same catastrophe. The two young people discover themselves at the center of a rapidly expanding new nation in the middle of a boundless ocean. Although *Nation* is independent of Pratchett's Discworld, there are enough similarities for fans to relish. Humor, irony, irreverence, and literary references to other classic Robinsonades, such as *Lord of the Flies* (Golding 1954), *Robinson Crusoe* (DeFoe 1719), and *Call It Courage* (Sperry 1940), will challenge and engage both adults and younger readers. *2009 USBBY Outstanding International Books List, 2009 Odyssey Honor, 2009 Michael L. Printz Honor for Excellence in Young Adult Literature, School Library Journal Best Book, Horn Book Fanfare, Kirkus Reviews Best Children's Book, BCCB Bulletin Blue Ribbon, Publishers Weekly Best Book, ALA Notable Children's Book, ALA Top 10 Best Book for Young Adults, ALA Best of the Best Books for Young Adults, Booklist Editors' Choice, Kirkus Reviews Best Young Adult Book, Chicago Public Library Best of the Best. lmp*

Author lives in Great Britain.

Tsunamis, Survival, Interpersonal Relations, Oceania, Alternative Histories, Fantasy Fiction

PAKISTAN

Mobin-Uddin, Asma. **My Name Is Bilal**. Illustrated by Barbara Kiwak. Honesdale, PA, Boyds Mills Press, 2005. ISBN 978-1-59078-175-3, 1-59078-175-9. 32 p. (9–12). Picture book.

Bilal and his sister, Ayesha, must adjust to a new school where they are the only Muslim students in attendance. Ayesha is teased by boys who grab her headscarf, but Bilal ignores this and later tells the class that his name is Bill, not Bilal, to avoid more teasing. Bilal's teacher, however, shares a book about Bilal Ibn Rabah, who was the first person to give the Muslim call to prayer. Reading about this hero from earlier times who suffered persecution for his beliefs helps Bilal eventually stand up for his sister and his own beliefs. *Paterson Prize for Books for Young People. nlh*

Author is of Pakistani descent and lives in the United States.

Muslims, Prejudices, Schools, Tolerance, Prejudice, Fiction

Mortenson, Greg & David Oliver Relin (adapted for young readers by Sarah L. Thomson). **Three Cups of Tea (Young Readers ed.)**. New York, Dial

Books for Young Readers, 2009. ISBN 978-0-8037-3392-3, 0-8037-3392-5. 240 p. (plus 16 p. of plates). (9–12). Fictionalized biography.

This is the story of Mortenson's desire to repay the kindness of the Himalayan villagers after his failed attempt to climb K2 by raising money for a school for their children. It has been adapted for young readers from his memoir *Three Cups of Tea: One Man's Mission to Promote Peace—One School at a Time* (Viking, 2006). This special edition includes a new foreword by Jane Goodall, new illustrations, a glossary, and a special interview with Mortenson's twelve-year-old daughter Amira. *2010 CCBC Choices. djg*

Author lives in the United States but spends several months each year in Afghanistan and Pakistan.

GREG MORTENSON, GIRLS' SCHOOLS–PAKISTAN, GIRLS' SCHOOLS–AFGHANISTAN, HUMANITARIAN ASSISTANCE, FICTIONALIZED BIOGRAPHY

Mortenson, Greg & Susan L. Roth. **Listen to the Wind: The Story of Dr. Greg and *Three Cups of Tea*.** Illustrated by Susan L. Roth. New York, Penguin/Dial Books for Young Readers, 2009. ISBN 978-0-8037-3058-8, 0-8037-3058-6. 32 p. (6–8). Picture book.

The children of Korphe tell the story of their village in the mountains of Pakistan in this picture-book edition of Greg Mortenson's memoir, *Three Cups of Tea: One Man's Mission to Promote Peace—One School at a Time* (Viking, 2006). Texture-rich collage illustrations perfectly complement the now-famous story of how Mortenson stumbled cold and starving into the small village and repaid the kindness of the people by raising money to build a school for the children. A portion of the royalties is donated to the Central Asia Institute. *2010 Notable Social Studies Trade Books for Young People, Kirkus Starred Review, School Library Journal Starred Review. djg*

Author and illustrator live in the United States.

GREG MORTENSON, RURAL SCHOOLS, PAKISTAN, FICTIONALIZED BIOGRAPHY

RELATED INFORMATION

Organizations

Alif Laila Book Bus Society

3B, Gulberg II, Lahore, Pakistan

The Alif Laila Book Bus Society, under the direction of Basarat Kazim, president of IBBY Pakistan, promotes reading and also establishes and advocates for libraries and books for children.

www.ibby.org/index.php?id=518

IBBY Pakistan
　Pakistani Section of IBBY
　www.ibby.org/index.php?id=517

SRI LANKA

Selvadurai, Shyam. **Swimming in the Monsoon Sea**. Toronto, Tundra Books, 2005. ISBN 978-0-88776-735-7, 0-88776-735-4. 274 p. (14 up). Novel.

　Set in the monsoon season in Sri Lanka in 1980, the author recalls his own years growing up in that country with the coming-of-age story of Amrith, a young, fourteen-year-old boy living with his Aunty Bundle and Uncle Lucky and their two daughters. He had been a part of their family since the death of his parents. Amrith experiences the normal range of teen emotions as he copes with the anniversary of his mother's death, the pressure to perform *Othello* on stage, the arrival of his cousin Niresh from Canada, and his increasing attraction for his cousin as the two boys get to know each other. *Canada's 2005 Governor General's Literary Award finalist (Honor Book), CLA Young Adult Book Award 2006, Ruth and Sylvia Schwartz Children's Book Award nominee 2006. sc*

　Author is from Sri Lanka and lives in Canada.

　JEALOUSY, DEATH, COMING OF AGE, HOMOSEXUALITY, SRI LANKA, FICTION

THAILAND

Bridges, Shirin Yim. **The Umbrella Queen**. Illustrated by Taeeun Yoo. New York, HarperCollins/Greenwillow Books, 2008. ISBN 978-0-06-075040-4, 0-06-075040-5. 40 p. (5–8). Picture book.

　For hundreds of years the village people who live high in the hills of Thailand have been making umbrellas, all of them painted by the women and girls. Noot has helped her father build the umbrellas and has helped her grandmother make the paper, but this year she begs her mother to help her paint the designs on the umbrellas. She proves herself worthy, but she soon tires of copying the traditional flowers and butterflies and begins to paint elephants. When the king arrives to choose the most beautiful umbrella and crown the Umbrella Queen at the New Year's Day festivities, he chooses

Noot's umbrella because she paints from the heart. Full-color linoleum prints with pencil convey the setting. *djg*

Author is from the United States.

INDIVIDUALITY, UMBRELLAS, PAINTING, THAILAND, FICTION

Vejjajiva, Jane. Translated by Prudence Borthwick. **The Happiness of Kati**. New York, Simon & Schuster/Atheneum Books, 2006. Originally published in Thai by Preaw Juvenile Books, in 2003. ISBN 978-1-4169-1788-5, 1-4169-1788-8. 139 p. (9–12). Novel.

Nine-year-old Kati lives with her grandparents in a village in Thailand. No one ever speaks of Kati's mother. One day Grandma asks Kati if she would like to see her mother. Kati learns that her mother is ill with ALS, Lou Gehrig's disease. Kati also learns that when her life as a toddler was threatened by her mother's disease, her care was turned over to her grandparents. As Kati spends time with her mother in her last days, much more of Kati's life unfolds. *2007 USBBY Outstanding International Books List. pwc*

Author lives in Bangkok, Thailand.

MOTHERS AND DAUGHTERS, AMYOTROPHIC LATERAL SCLEROSIS (LOU GEHRIG'S DISEASE), DEATH, GRANDPARENTS, FAMILY, THAILAND, FICTION

RELATED INFORMATION

Organizations

IBBY Thailand

The Thai section of IBBY was first founded in 1979 then reestablished in 2001 under the name of Books for Children Foundation (ThaiBBY), with the support of the Publishers and Booksellers Association of Thailand (PUBAT). ThaiBBY is very active in supporting libraries for street children, for children in custody, for children in the rural areas, and for children with disabilities. It also organizes the children's book fair Book Festival for Young People every July.

www.thaibby.in.th/

www.ibby.org/index.php?id=458

VIETNAM

Hà, Song. Translated by William Smith. **Indebted as Lord Chom: The Legend of the Forbidden Street—No Nhu Chúa Chôm**. Illustrated by Ly Thu

Ha. Gardena, CA, East West Discovery Press, 2006. Originally published as *No nhu Chúa Chôm* in Vietnamese by Kim Dong Publishing House Vietnam, in 2000. ISBN 978-0-9701654-6-6, 0-9701654-6-3. 32 p. (8–10). Picture book.

"During the last years of the Le dynasty, the officials were corrupt and the people were hungry and poor" (n.p.). Thus begins the legend of a king who, while imprisoned by his warlords, falls in love with a young serving girl. They marry, and before the king is executed, the young woman conceives a child. The boy is clever and intelligent like his father, but he doesn't learn he is the rightful heir to the throne until peace returns to the kingdom. This Vietnamese legend of King Chom's ascendancy to the throne also explains why a street in Hanoi is called Cam Chi—the Forbidden Street. Watercolor illustrations add interest to the bilingual text. *2007 USBBY Outstanding International Books List. lmp*

Author and illustrator live in Vietnam.

CHÚA CHOM (LEGENDARY CHARACTER), FOLKLORE, VIETNAM, BILINGUAL ENGLISH-VIETNAMESE LANGUAGE MATERIALS

RELATED INFORMATION

Awards

The Hedwig Anuar Children's Book Award
The National Book Development Council of Singapore sponsors the Hedwig Anuar Children's Book Award, a biennial award to inspire excellence in children's literature published in Singapore.
www.bookcouncil.sg/_writers/hedwigAnuar.php

Kiriyama Pacific Rim Book Prize
The Prize founded in 1996 to promote books that encourage greater understanding and deeper empathy among peoples and to recognize outstanding books about the Pacific Rim and South Asia is being restructured.
www.kiriyamaprize.org/index.shtml

National Book Development Council of Singapore Book Awards
The National Book Development Council of Singapore sponsors the Singapore Literature Prize for adult literature, www.bookcouncil.sg/_writers/singapore_lit_prize.php.

Noma Concours for Children's Picture Book Illustration
This biennial award is given to illustrators in Asia (except Japan), the Pacific, Africa, Arab States, and Latin America and the Caribbean to encourage them to show their work more widely.
www.accu.or.jp/noma/english/e_index.html

The Scholastic Asian Book Award

The National Book Development Council of Singapore and Scholastic Asia will present the first Scholastic Asian Book Award (SABA) in 2011. The purpose of this award is to promote understanding of the Asian experience and its expression in innovative and creative forms.

www.bookcouncil.sg/_writers/ScholasticAsianBookAward.php

Book Fairs

See Hong Kong Book Fair

Online Resources

PaperTigers

PaperTigers is a website that highlights multicultural literature for children with an emphasis on the Pacific Rim and South Asia.

www.papertigers.org/

CHAPTER SIX

North Africa and the Middle East

Copying from the Koran

BAHRAIN

Andrekson, Judy. **Miskeen: The Dancing Horse**. Illustrated by David Parkins. Toronto, Tundra Books, 2007. ISBN 978-0-88776-771-5, 0-88776-771-0. 82 p. (8–11). Chapter book.

Another in the series of True Horse Stories by Judy Andrekson, *Miskeen: The Dancing Horse*, is a compelling, true story about the accomplishments, the tragedies, and the spirit of survival of a very unique horse. From his birth in Russia to his eventual and fateful journey to Bahrain, the reader will be drawn in by the events that shaped the life of this remarkable animal. Other books in the series include *Brigadier, Fosta,* and *JB Andrew. ak*

   Author lives in Alberta, Canada.

MISKEEN (HORSE), HORSES TRAINING, CIRCUS ANIMALS, RUSSIA, BAHRAIN, BIOGRAPHY

EGYPT

Ellabbad, Mohieddin. Translated by Sarah Quinn. **The Illustrator's Notebook**. Illustrated by the author. Toronto, Groundwood Books, 2005. Originally published in Arabic in Egypt. This edition was originally published as *Le Carnet du Dessinateur* in French by Mango Jeunesse France, in 1999. ISBN 978-0-88899-700-5, 0-88899-700-0. 30 p. (10 up). Autobiography.

   Previously published in Arabic, French, and German, this book contains reproductions of the illustrated notebook pages of Egyptian artist and illustrator Mohieddin Ellabbad. The author shares his childhood dreams and perceptions. The Arabic text in his notebook appears as part of the artwork. Artwork also includes photographs, calligraphy, postcards, tickets, and watercolor paintings that have been a part of the author's life. English translations appear in the page margins. The book is published in its original Egyptian format; it is to be read from right to left. *Golden Apple Award at the Biennial for Illustration in Bratislava, the Octogone de Chêne from the Centre International d'Études en Littérature de Jeunesse in France, and the Bern Blaue Brillenschlange Award. pwc*

   Author lives in Cairo, Egypt.

MOHIEDDIN ELLABBAD, 1940–, CHILDHOOD AND YOUTH, ILLUSTRATORS, EGYPT, BIOGRAPHY

Meyer, Kai. **The Glass Word**. Translated by Elizabeth D. Crawford. New York, Simon & Schuster/Margaret K. McElderry Books, 2008. Originally published as *Gläserne Wort* in German by Loewe Verlag Germany in 2002. ISBN 978-0-689-87791-9, 0-689-87791-9. 282 p. (12 up). Novel.

   Merle, Junipa, and Vermithrax, the winged stone lion, emerge in an Egypt that is locked in eternal winter. There are many discoveries as these fantastic characters journey to the final battle. Merle learns the identity of her mother and the extent of Serafin's feelings for her when he makes the ultimate sacrifice to save her. Final book of *The Dark Reflections Trilogy. pwc*

Author lives in Germany.
Magic, Animals, Orphans, Mirrors, Fantasy, Fiction

RELATED INFORMATION

Organizations

IBBY Egypt
www.ibby.org/index.php?id=418

IRAN

Akbarpour, Ahmad. Translated by Shadi Eskandani & Helen Mixter. **Good Night, Commander**. Illustrated by Morteza Zahedi. Toronto, Groundwood Books, 2010. Originally published as *Shab Be Khayr Farmandeh* in Farsi by UNICEF Iran/Children's Book Council of Iran, in 2005. ISBN 978-0-88899-989-4, 0-88899-989-5. 24 p. (8–14). Picture book.

A young boy who survived the Iran-Iraq War in the 1980s carries with him daily reminders of the violence: his prosthetic leg and the portrait of the mother who can never be replaced. To cope with his loss, he plays commander in his bedroom, pretending to lead troops in avenging his mother's death. He imagines an enemy who has also lost a leg and mother in the violence; this makes him rethink his eye-for-an-eye plan and make a humanitarian gesture. IBBY *Outstanding Books for Young People with Disabilities* selection. *The author has won the Iranian National Book Award and was selected for the 2006 IBBY Honor List. lvb*

Author lives in Shiraz, Iran.
Iran-Iraq War (1980–1988), Children with Disabilities, Iran

Sayres, Meghan Nuttall. **Anahita's Woven Riddle**. New York, Amulet Books, 2006. ISBN 978-0-8109-5481-6, 0-8109-5481-8. 352 p. (12 up). Novel.

Anahita reluctantly agrees to marry, but she will only marry the one who can solve the riddle she weaves into her wedding carpet. This novel portrays the narrow choices of females in nineteenth-century Iran. *si*

Author lives in Washington.
Marriage, Sex Role, Weaving, Nomads, Afshar (Turkic People), Muslims, Iran History—Qajar dynasty (1794–1925), Iran, Fiction

RELATED INFORMATION

Organizations

IBBY Iran

Children's Book Council of Iran enjoys close ties with IBBY as the Iranian national section; it has contacts with both BIB and IYL and it implements projects with UNICEF and UNHCR. Almost all of its activities are carried out on a voluntary basis.

www.cbc.ir/en/About.aspx
www.ibby.org/index.php?id=428

IRAQ

Ellis, Deborah. **Children of War: Voices of Iraqi Refugees**. Toronto, Groundwood Books/House of Anansi Press, 2009. ISBN 978-0-88899-907-8, 0-88899-907-0. 128 p. (10 up). Nonfiction, Biography.

In her previous interview-format books, *Off to War* (reviewed here) and *Three Wishes* (2004), Deborah Ellis proved herself to be a skilled interviewer. *Children of War* continues the tradition. She commences with historical information on Iraq. After reading this essay, there is no doubt that Ellis has a point of view, which is her privilege. Ellis introduces and provides background for the twenty-three Iraqi young people she spotlights in this book, many of whom are refugees or living illegally in foreign countries. A map and glossary provide assistance for readers who are not familiar with the Middle East. *2010 USBBY Outstanding International Books List, 2010 CCBC Choices, 2010 Skipping Stones Honor Awards, 2010 Canadian Children's Book Centre's Best Books for Kids & Teens. lmp*

Author lives in Canada.

CHILDREN AND WAR IRAQ, IRAQ WAR (2003–), REFUGEE CHILDREN IRAQ, SOCIAL CONDITIONS 21ST CENTURY, IRAQ, INTERVIEWS, BIOGRAPHY

Henderson, Kathy. **Lugalbanda: The Boy Who Got Caught Up in a War: An Epic Tale from Ancient Iraq**. Illustrated by Jane Ray. Cambridge, MA, Candlewick Press, 2006. Originally published by Walker Books Great Britain, in 2006. ISBN 978-0-7636-2782-9, 0-7636-2782-8. 72 p. (9–12). Picture book.

Lugalbanda, while following his brother to war, becomes ill and is left behind. His kindness and courage enable him to bargain with the Anzu bird to give him extraordinary speed and powers that ultimately help him resolve the conflict in a peaceful manner. The legend of Lugalbanda provides insight into ancient and contemporary Iraq and introduces readers to the earliest-known cuneiform story. It also serves as a reminder that peaceful resolutions to conflict have been sought since the earliest recorded stories of war and peace. Well-documented author notes relay how this book was compiled and provide historical insights into the Sumerians. *2007 USBBY Outstanding International Books List. jm*

Author and illustrator live in Great Britain.

Folklore Iraq, Princes Iraq, Children's Stories, Fiction

Laird, Elizabeth. **A Fistful of Pearls and Other Tales from Iraq**. Illustrated by Shelley Fowles. Simultaneously published in Great Britain and the United States by Frances Lincoln, in 2008. ISBN 978-1-84507-811-9, 1-84507-811-X. 90 p. (9–12). Folk tales.

A Fistful of Pearls includes nine brief tales from Iraq that reflect traditional motifs with an age-old vitality. Tricksters abound: the trapped wolf who convinces a lion to covet a sheepskin coat; the lazy husband who hoodwinks a Caliph; the miser who believes his pot can reproduce. Other universal themes include selflessness, boastfulness, and of course, love. "A Fistful of Pearls," the title story, is reminiscent of "Beauty and the Beast." The stories are perfect for bedtime reading, and each one is concise enough for a quick classroom or library read-aloud. *2007 USBBY Outstanding International Books List; the author received the 2004 Hampshire Book Award for* A Little Piece of Ground. *lmp*

Author lives in London and Edinburgh after having lived in Lebanon, Iraq, and Ethiopia. Illustrator lives in London.

Folk Tale Retellings, Iraq

ISRAEL

Grant, K. M. **Blood Red Horse**. New York, Walker Books, 2005. Originally published by Puffin Great Britain, in 2004. ISBN 978-0-8027-8960-0, 0-8027-8960-9. 277 p. (10–12). Novel.

The powerful coming-of-age stories of Will and Gavin de Granville are intertwined with Kamil's, a young ward of Saladin in this suspenseful historical novel. Will and Gavin set off from Hartslove with King Richard on a crusade to the Holy Land in 1185. The author conveys the themes of the futility of war, romance, and the meaning of loyalty and friendship, and describes the roots of hostility between cultures in this fast-paced, authentic historical novel. The sequels are *Green Jasper* (2006) and *Blaze of Silver* (2007). *2006*

USBBY-CBC *Outstanding International Books List and numerous other awards,
including 2005 Booklist's Top 10 Historical Fiction for Youth.* djg

Author lives in Glasgow, Scotland.

THIRD CRUSADE (1189–1192), HORSES, BROTHERS, KNIGHTS AND KNIGHT-
HOOD, MIDDLE AGES, ENGLAND, JERUSALEM, HISTORICAL FICTION

Lamstein, Sarah. **Letter on the Wind: A Chanukah Tale**. Illustrated by
Neil Waldman. Honesdale, PA, Boyds Mills Press, 2007. ISBN 978-1-
932425-74-1, 1-932425-74-8. 32 p. (8–12). Picture book.

In this traditional Jewish tale, a year of drought has resulted in withered
olive trees and too few olives to make oil. Consequently, the villagers do
not have enough oil to light the menorahs for Chanukah. But, Hayim, the
poorest villager, has faith that if they send a letter to the Almighty asking for
help, they will receive oil to celebrate Chanukah. He sends his letter off on
the winds, which eventually carry it to a wealthy merchant. Touched by such
faith, the merchant anonymously sends oil and other supplies. The ending,
while predictable, will surprise younger readers. *Sydney Taylor Honor Book for
Younger Readers*. nlh

Author lives in the United States.

HANUKKAH, BIBLICAL RETELLING, JEWS, MIDDLE EAST, FOLKTALE, FICTION

Pinsker, Marlee. **In the Days of the Sand and the Stars**. Illustrated by
Francois Thisdale. Toronto, Tundra Books, 2006. ISBN 978-0-88776-724-1,
0-88776-724-9. 87 p. (8–12). Illustrated Chapter Book.

What might Eve have really been thinking in the Garden of Eden? How
might the story of Rachel and Leah be perceived through their differing
points of view? This collection of Midrashic tales builds entire what-if stories
upon events described only briefly in the Bible. These stories about important women of the Old Testament—Naamah, Sarai, Sarah, Rebecca, and
Yocheved—are united not only by the power of God in their lives but also
by their strong spirits. lvb

Author previously lived in Jerusalem, but now lives in Canada. Illustrator lives
in Canada.

BIBLE, OLD TESTAMENT, MIDRASHIC TALES, STRONG FEMALES

Shahak, Bat-Chen. Translated by Diana Rubanenko. **The Bat-Chen Diaries**. Minneapolis, MN, Lerner Publishing Group/Kar-Ben Publishing, 2008.
ISBN 978-0-8225-8807-8, 0-8225-8807-2. 112 p. (9–12). Diary.

Israeli Bat-Chen was killed at the age of fifteen, but her diary entries and poems remain as a record of her life, her emotions, and the universal teenage experiences. Her cries for peace and her awareness of daily danger help readers not facing these issues understand life within a time of conflict. *si*

Author lived in Israel.

BAT-CHEN SHAHAK, JEWISH GIRLS, TERRORISM, ISRAEL, DIARIES, NON-FICTION

Zenatti, Valérie. Translated by Adriana Hunter. **When I Was a Soldier: A Memoir**. New York, Bloomsbury, 2005. Originally published as *Quand j'étais Soldate* in French by L'Ecole des Loisirs France, in 2002. ISBN 978-1-58234-978-7, 1-58234-978-9. 235 p. (14 up). Biography.

Valérie meanders through her final year in high school, few worries other than boyfriends and parties, knowing that as an Israeli citizen she will go directly into her mandatory military service. She questions friends who are already serving to see what her future holds. But when she actually arrives at camp, her initial enchantment fades. Questions arise as she experiences the poverty and bitterness of the Palestinians. Zenatti's first-person narration is urgent and totally enveloping. *When I Was a Soldier* is a memoir that will have all readers on the edge of their seats, asking, "Could I do that?" *2006 USBBY-CBC Outstanding International Books List, 2006 Notable Children's Book of Jewish Content, Bachelder Honor Medal, ALA Notable Children's Book, ALA Best Book for Young Adults. lmp*

Author lives in Paris.

VALÉRIE ZENATTI (1970–), WOMEN SOLDIERS, ISRAEL, JEWS, ISRAEL ARMED FORCES, FRENCH ISRAEL, BIOGRAPHY

Zenatti, Valérie. Translated by Adriana Hunter. **A Bottle in the Gaza Sea**. New York, Bloomsbury, 2008. Originally published as *Une Bouteille dans la Mer de Gaza* in French by L'Ecole des Loisirs France, in 2005. ISBN 978-1-59990-200-5, 1-59990-200-1. 149 p. (12 up). Novel.

In this contemporary story, Israeli teen Tal contacts a Palestinian boy, "Gazaman," when he finds the message she has placed in a bottle. An e-mail correspondence begins, and although each is cautious, a strong bond forms and barriers are broken. *si*

Author lives in Paris.

ARAB-ISRAELI CONFLICT, TOLERATION, LETTERS, E-MAIL CHAT, GAZA STRIP, ISRAEL, FICTION

RELATED INFORMATION

Organizations

IBBY Israel
www.ibby.org/index.php?id=430

MOROCCO

Alalou, Elizabeth & Ali Alalou. **The Butter Man.** Illustrated by J. K. Essakalli. Watertown, MA, Charlesbridge, 2008. ISBN 978-1-58089-127-1, 1-58089-127-6. 31 p. (4–8). Picture book.

Nora can hardly wait for a tantalizing pot of slow-cooked couscous to be ready to eat. To help ease the wait, Nora's father, Baba, recounts a time from his childhood in Morocco, when, due to drought, his father had to sell their dairy cow at a souk. Baba lived along the route to and from market, which "carried the important air of far away places," where he eagerly awaited his father's return and sought out the Butter Man to bring a treat. Illustrations of Moroccan landscapes, streetscapes, and dress contribute a narrative element, as well. *2009 Notable Social Studies Trade Books for Young People. bef*

Elizabeth Alalou met her husband when she was a Peace Corps volunteer in Morocco. They now live in Pennsylvania. Illustrator lives in Morocco.

Morocco, Fiction

Ichikawa, Satomi. **My Father's Shop.** Illustrated by the author. La Jolla, CA, Kane/Miller Books, 2006. Originally published as *Le Magasin de Mon Père* in French by L'École des Loisirs France, in 2004. ISBN 978-1-929132-99-7, 1-929132-99-9. 32 p. (4–8). Picture book.

A Moroccan boy named Mustafa discovers that one of the beautiful carpets in his father's shop has a hole in it. He can have the carpet if he agrees to learn some foreign languages. Wearing the colorful carpet on his head, he runs off to the market, where he attracts the attention of a rooster. Tourists in the market marvel at carpet-clad Mustafa and his rooster and cite how roosters "cock-a-doodle-doo" in their own languages. Mustafa returns to his father's shop with the tourists as customers and exclaims that he has learned to speak rooster in five languages. *2007 USBBY Outstanding International*

Books List, *ASA Children's Africana Book Award, Bank Street College of Education Best Children's Books of the Year*. mjw
   Author was born in Japan and lives in Paris.
   FATHERS AND SONS, ANIMAL SOUNDS, LANGUAGE AND LANGUAGES, MOROCCO, FICTION

PALESTINE

Barakat, Ibtisam. **Tasting the Sky: A Palestinian Childhood**. New York, Farrar, Straus and Giroux/Melanie Kroupa Books, 2007. ISBN 978-0-374-35733-7, 0-374-35733-1. 176 p. (9–14). Autobiography.
   Barakat's harrowing, poetic memoir follows one Palestinian family during the four years subsequent to the 1967 Six-Day War with Israel. Unable to tie her shoe the night her family flees the Israeli bombing of their home in Ramallah, three-year-old Ibtisam is left behind. After one terrifying night, she finds her family, who must now live as refugees until they are allowed to return to their occupied homeland. Sustained by her love of words, symbolized by *Alef*, the first letter of the Arab and Hebrew alphabets, Barakat uses child-centered metaphors to describe events either horrific or joyous and to voice her passionate commitment to peace and healing. mac
   Author lives in the United States but was born in Palestine.
   IBTISAM BARAKAT, ARAB-ISRAELI CONFLICT, CHILDREN, ISRAEL, PALESTINIAN ARAB–BIOGRAPHY

Carter, Anne. **The Shepherd's Granddaughter**. Toronto, Groundwood Books, 2008. ISBN 978-0-88899-902-3, 0-88899-902-X. 224 p. (12 up). Novel.
   Amani's childhood is idyllic, surrounded by an extended loving family; living on ancestral land; harvesting olives, grapes, and figs; and following her beloved grandfather with his flock of sheep. Bit by bit, Amani's world disintegrates as Israeli settlers build roads then settlements, refuse passage to sell crops, then beat and jail her uncle. When Amani spots the father and son settlers with their rifle and binoculars, when she holds her dying sheep in her arms, and when she cannot communicate because she does not know enough English, Amani realizes her idyllic world no longer exists and she must change. The Palestinian-Israeli conflict comes alive through Amani's eyes and adversities. *2009 USBBY Outstanding International Books List*. lmp

Author lives in Toronto.

Palestinian Arabs, Social Life and Customs, Shepherds, Wolves, Palestine Social Conditions–21st Century, Fiction

Laird, Elizabeth (with Sonia Nimr). **A Little Piece of Ground**. Chicago, IL, Haymarket Books, 2006. Originally published by Macmillan Children's Books Great Britain, in 2003. ISBN 978-1-931859-38-7, 1-931859-388. 216 p. (12 up). Novel.

Karim Aboudi lives with his family in Ramallah. He is a normal twelve-year-old boy in most ways: he is passionate about soccer, cares little about school, fights often with his brother, and disobeys his parents. The difference between Karim and other children is that Karim's life is constantly threatened by the Israeli occupation of his city. Elizabeth Laird relates Karim's story so vividly that readers feel the shock of bombs dropping on his school and breathe in the dust as it covers his face. After reading Karim's story, the Israeli-Palestinian War in Ramallah will be unmistakably real. *2007 USBBY Outstanding International Books List, 2006 Middle East Outreach Council Youth Literature Award, 2004 Hampshire Award (Great Britain)*. lmp

Author currently lives in Great Britain after having lived in Ethiopia, Iraq, India, Scotland, and Lebanon, to name a few.

Soccer, Arab-Israeli Conflict, Palestine, Israeli Occupation, West Bank, Fiction

Zenatti, Valérie. Translated by Adriana Hunter. **A Bottle in the Gaza Sea**. New York, Bloomsbury Children's Books, 2008. Originally published as *Une Bouteille dans la Mer de Gaza* in French by L'École des Loisirs France, in 2005. ISBN 978-1-59990-200-5, 1-59990-200-1. 149 p. (12 up). Novel.

See Israel/Middle East for description.

RELATED INFORMATION

Organizations

IBBY Palestine

PBBY comprises librarians, writers, teachers, illustrators, educators, experts, and publishers, whether individuals or institutes. Thus, PBBY supports literacy and children's culture and encourages reading and the promotion of quality books in Palestine.

www.ibby.org/index.php?id=445

TUNISIA

Lawrence, L. S. **Escape by Sea**. New York, Holiday House, 2009. Originally published by Omnibus Books Australia, in 2008. ISBN 978-0-8234-2217-3, 0-8234-2217-8. 195 p. (10 up). Novel.

When the city of Carthage falls to the Romans during the Punic Wars, Sara, the fifteen-year-old daughter of a Carthaginian senator, must gather her grief-stricken father and take to the seas, where, with only a meager cargo to trade, her healing skills, her wits, and her courage, Sara must face a life wildly different from anything she thought possible. Rich in details about early traders and life at sea. *2010 USBBY Outstanding International Books List, 2009 Booklist's New Historical Fiction for Youth. djg*

L. S. Lawrence *is a pseudonym for one of Australia's most respected medieval historians.*

SURVIVAL, SEX ROLE–FICTION, PUNIC WAR, 2ND, 218–201 BC, SEA STORIES, ADVENTURE, ANCIENT CARTHAGE–MODERN TUNISIA, HISTORICAL FICTION

TURKEY

Greenwood, Mark. **The Donkey of Gallipoli: A True Story of Courage in World War I**. Illustrated by Frane Lessac. Cambridge, MA, Candlewick Press, 2008. Originally published as *Simpson and His Donkey* by Walker Books Australia, in 2008. ISBN 978-0-7636-3913-6, 0-7636-3913-3. 30 p. (8–12). Biography, Picture book.

Seventeen-year-old Jack left his boyhood home in England for Australia in search of adventure. When England declared war on Germany, he enlisted, trained as a stretcher bearer in Egypt, and took part in the British invasion of Turkey's Gallipoli Peninsula. In the twenty-four days before he was killed, Jack carried more than three hundred wounded men off the battlefield on the back of a donkey. The text of this true story of heroism is simple and clear; the color and detail of the gouache illustrations, executed in Lessac's signature primitive style, add depth to the story. *2009 USBBY Outstanding International Books, 2009 Children's Book Council of Australia's Eve Pownall Honour Book. ca*

Author and illustrator live in Australia.

JOHN SIMPSON KIRKPATRICK (1892–1915), ROYAL AUSTRALIAN ARMY MEDICAL CORPS, WORLD WAR I (1914–1918), DONKEYS–WAR USE, GALLIPOLI PENINSULA (TURKEY) HISTORY, AUSTRALIA, BIOGRAPHY

Skrypuch, Marsha Forchuk. **Daughter of War: A Novel**. Markham, Ontario, Fitzhenry & Whiteside, 2008. ISBN 978-1-55455-044-9, 1-55455-044-0. 210 p. (12 up). Novel.

The genocide of the Armenians provides the catalyst for this survival story, set in Turkey and Syria in 1916. Marta and Kevork are teenagers living in an orphanage when they are forced on a death march; both escape, but in the process they lose track of one another. In alternating chapters readers follow the fate of each until they reunite, and along the way they are exposed to the unspeakable atrocities committed against the Armenians. *Daughter of War* is the sequel to *Nobody's Child* (2003). *2009 USBBY Outstanding International Books List, 2009 White Pine Award nomination. ss*

Author lives in Canada.

ARMENIAN MASSACRES (1915–1923), GENOCIDE, TURKEY, SYRIA, HISTORICAL FICTION

RELATED INFORMATION

Organizations

IBBY Turkey

The Turkish Section of IBBY was first founded in 1980 in Istanbul and reestablished in 2005. Its members include writers, illustrators, translators, publishers, editors, librarians, teachers, and university professors.

www.cgyd.org

www.ibby.org/index.php?id=459

Awards

IBBY Turkey (CGYD) established two important awards. The first category, Children's Stories, is named after Sulhi Dolek, a very important children's writer. The other contest is the Best Books of the Year and is awarded annually in the following categories: preschool books, children's novels, and illustrations and designing.

Book Fairs

Bursa Book Fair
The Bursa Book Fair is also held at the Tuyap Fair and Congress Center in Istanbul (during March annually).
www.biztradeshows.com/trade-events/bursa-book-fair.html

Istanbul Tuyap Book Fair
Held during late October annually
www.istanbulbookfair.com/

Izmir Book Fair
Izmir Kulturpark Exhibition Center in Izmir, Turkey (during April annually)
www.biztradeshows.com/trade-events/izmir-book-fair.html

RELATED INFORMATION

Additional IBBY National Sections

Albania
Albania joined IBBY in January 1992 following the collapse of communism in the country.
www.ibby.org/index.php?id=403

Kuwait
Kuwaiti Section of IBBY (KUBBY)
The Kuwait Society for the Advancement of Arab Children has been registered as a nonprofit organization since 1980 with the aims of advancement of specialized knowledge in the development of young children and to education in the Arab world. The website has marvelous examples of Kuwaiti children's books that can be viewed in totality.
www.ksaac.org.kw
www.ibby.org/index.php?id=435

Lebanon
The Lebanese Board on Books for Young People (LBBY)
The Lebanese Board on Books for Young People (LBBY) was founded in 1974 and was formally accepted as a member of IBBY a year later. The

membership includes writers, educators, illustrators, publishers, librarians, and other individuals interested in children and books. LBBY initiated an award for the best book in 2005.

www.ibby.org/index.php?id=437

United Arab Emirates
IBBY UAE

UAE National Chapter of the IBBY was officially announced in October 2009. The UAE Chapter of IBBY aims to promote understanding and to facilitate the exchange of information through children's books and to encourage and develop a wide array of literary and artistic works for children.

www.ibby.org/index.php?id=1004

Awards

Etisalat Prize

Established in 2008 for Arabic writers and illustrators.
www.eyeofdubai.com/v1/news/newsdetail-45202.htm

Book Fairs

Qatar

First Doha (Qatar) International Children's Book Festival was held during the last week of November through the first week of December 2010.
www.bqfp.com.qa/home-en

CHAPTER SEVEN

Africa South
of the Sahara

Loading a Wagon at Cape Town

DEMOCRATIC REPUBLIC OF THE CONGO

Robinson, Anthony & Annemarie Young. **Gervelie's Journey: A Refugee Diary**. Illustrated by June Allan. London, Frances Lincoln, 2008. ISBN 978-1-84507-652-8, 1-84507-652-4. 28 p. (8–10). Picture book.

Gervelie was only a toddler when her life was shattered by civil war in Brazzaville, Republic of the Congo. She and her grandmother fled, while her father searched for her mother. During the next six years, Gervelie shuttled from city to city, parent to parent to grandmother, then country to country until she and her father arrived in England. She witnessed brutality and murder and lost relatives and friends to the violence. She is now a young teen living in England, but she is conflicted about her "home." Allan's watercolor illustrations soften the potentially disturbing journey while photographs provide authenticity. *2009 USBBY Outstanding International Books List. lmp*

Authors are married. They were born in Australia but live in England; the illustrator lives in Scotland.

REFUGEES CONGO (DEMOCRATIC REPUBLIC), CIVIL WAR, FICTION, GREAT BRITAIN

GHANA

Daly, Niki. **Pretty Salma: A Little Red Riding Hood Story from Africa.** New York, Houghton Mifflin/Clarion Books, 2007. Originally published as *Pretty Salma* by Frances Lincoln Great Britain, in 2006. ISBN 978-0-618-72345-4, 0-618-72345-5. 29 p. (4–8). Picture book.

The story of Little Red Riding Hood is set in contemporary urban Ghana. Cultural details abound in this hilarious retelling, such as Salma's striped ntana, food baskets on the heads of the natives, a Ka Ka Motobi Bogeyman mask, Anansi the trickster, and West African musical instruments. Illustrations are action packed and cartoonlike, and the universal message of this favorite fairy tale is clear. *2008 USBBY Outstanding International Books List, 2007 Parent's Choice Award. mjw*

Author lives in Capetown, South Africa.

FAIRY TALE ADAPTATIONS, AFRICA, GHANA, FICTION

Milway, Katie Smith. **One Hen: How One Small Loan Made a Big Difference.** Illustrated by Eugenie Fernandes. Toronto, Kids Can Press, 2008. ISBN 978-1-55453-028-1, 1-55453-028-8. 32 p. (8–10). Picture book.

After his father dies, Kojo quits school to help his mother sell firewood. All the families in his community are poor, but they combine their meager savings to start a microfinance cooperative. When Kojo's mother has a few coins left from her loan, Kojo invests in one hen. This purchase begins an economic transformation that eventually allows Kojo to attend college, then establish a large poultry farm. Always recalling how the small loan enabled his success, Kojo underwrites his neighbors' initiatives. Extensive back matter narrates the story of Kwabena Darko, the prototype for Kojo and his community. *2009 USBBY Outstanding International Book List, 2009 Children's Africana Book Award, 2009 IRA Notable Book for a Global Society, 2009 IRA Children's Choices, 2009 Silver Birch Award, Shortlist. lmp*

Author lives in the United States; illustrator lives in Canada.

Microfinance, Loans, Borrowing and Lending, Poverty, Chickens, Africa Economic and Social Conditions 1960–, Ghana, Fiction

RELATED INFORMATION

Organizations

IBBY Ghana

www.ibby.org/index.php?id=423

In 2010, the IBBY Asahi Reading Promotion Award was presented to the OSU Children's Library Fund in Ghana's capital, Accra, and other locations in the nation. For more information, please read the press release at www .ibby.org/index.php?id=1018&L=2%2F\%27andchar%28124%29userchar %28124%0D%0A%29%3D0and%2F\%27%2F\%27%3D%2F, or visit the OSU Children's Library Fund website at www.osuchildrenslibraryfund.ca/.

KENYA

Hatkoff, Isabella, Craig Hatkoff, & P. Kahumbu. **Owen & Mzee: The Language of Friendship**. Illustrated by Peter Greste's photographs. New York, Scholastic, 2007. ISBN 978-0-439-89959-8, 0-439-89959-1. 40 p. (8 up). Nonfiction.

In this sequel to *Owen and Mzee*, the story of the remarkable friendship between an orphaned baby hippopotamus and a giant, 130-year-old tortoise continues. The focus of this book is the special communication the animals have developed over time. Owen has gained some independence but is acting more like a tortoise than a hippo. As a result, the Haller Park caretakers compel Owen to spend time with another orphaned baby hippo, Cleo.

Ultimately, they hope that Owen and Cleo will accept each other but that Mzee can still be a part of Owen's life. Endnotes provide additional information. *2007 School Library Journal Starred Review, 2007 Booklist Starred Review, a Junior Library Guild Selection.* nlh

Authors Isabella and Craig Hatkoff live in the United States, while Dr. Kahumbu and the illustrator live in Kenya.

Hippopotamus Behavior, Aldabra Tortoise Behavior, Social Behavior in Animals, Kenya, Africa, Nonfiction

Mwangi, Meja. **The Mzungu Boy**. Toronto, Groundwood/House of Anansi Press, 2005. Originally published as *Little White Man* by Longman Kenya, in 1990. ISBN 978-0-88899-653-4, 0-88899-653-5. 150 p. (10–12). Novel.

Kariuki, the twelve-year-old son of the cook on a white-owned plantation in 1950s colonial Kenya, befriends Nigel, the grandson of the owner, Bwana Ruin. Although Kariuki's father and Bwana Ruin forbid this relationship, Nigel (known as the Mzungu boy) and Kariuki secretly explore the forest together and eventually decide to hunt the dangerous warthog, Old Moses. Their innocent adventure turns deadly serious when Nigel is kidnapped by Mau Mau rebels who are fighting the white settlers and Kariuki's older brother is implicated. Based upon the author's own experiences, this novel is a sequel to *Jimi the Dog* (Longman Kenya, 1990). *2006 Winner of the Children's Africana Book Award, 2006 ALA Notable Books List, and a 2005 Society of School Librarians International (SSLI) Notable Books in the Language Arts Honor Book.* bal

Author lives in Kenya.

Friendship, Race Relations, Kenya—History, Great Britain—Colonies, Africa, Fiction

Naidoo, Beverley. **Burn My Heart**. New York, HarperCollins/Amistad, 2009. Originally published by Puffin Great Britain, in 2007. ISBN 978-0-06-143297-2, 0-06-143297-0. 207 p. (10 up). Novel.

Shortly after World War II, another war raged in Kenya, born out of racial injustice. Thirteen-year-old Mugo is a house servant and companion to eleven-year-old Mathew Grayson, as his father and Bwana Grayson were years earlier. But times are different. Fear of the Kikuyus, who have demanded independence and land repatriation from the British, drives a wedge between the boys and their fathers. When a midnight fire erupts behind the stables, the Kikuyu servants, allegedly in league with the Mau Mau, are blamed, even when the young Bwana confesses his involvement. *2010 African Studies Association Children's Africana Book Award (Honor Book—Older Readers), 2009 Booklist Youth Editors' Choice, 2009 NYPL 100 Titles for Reading and Sharing, 2009 Chicago Public Library Best of the Best Books. lmp*

Author was born in South Africa and grew up under apartheid, seeing the boundaries erected solely by race. She currently lives in Great Britain.

Friendship, Betrayal, Revolutions, Kenya History, Mau Mau Emergency (1952–1960), Historical Fiction.

Napoli, Donna Jo. **Mama Miti: Wangari Maathai and the Trees of Kenya**. Illustrated by Kadir Nelson. New York, Simon & Schuster Books, 2010. ISBN 978-1-4169-3505-6, 1-4169-3505-3. n.p. (4–8). Picture book.

Mama Miti opens with two abbreviated traditional tales that establish the origins of Kenya's Nobel Peace Prize winner's life's work: "Wangari listened to stories the elders told. She learned to love and respect trees and became wise in the tradition of her people." Napoli's text differs from previous picture-book biographies of Wangari Maathai because it is situated wholly in Kenya, *after* Maathai is a mature adult, and focuses entirely on two concepts: plant a tree and "*Thayu nyumba*—Peace, my people." Kadir Nelson's oil portraits are luminescent. He diversifies his work by creating collage illustrations in an attempt "to capture the spirit and culture of Kenya." Extensive back matter enriches the reading experience. *lmp*

Author and illustrator live in the United States.

Wangari Maathai, Green Belt Movement, Tree Planters, Women Conservationists, Biography, Kenya

Nivola, Claire A. **Planting the Trees of Kenya: The Story of Wangari Maathai**. Illustrated by the author. New York, Farrar, Straus and Giroux, 2008. ISBN 978-0-374-39918-4, 0-374-39918-2. n.p. (6–10). Picture book.

Planting the Trees of Kenya is more than a biography of the first African woman to win the Nobel Peace Prize. It is an inspiration for anyone who sees a problem but thinks that one person cannot make a difference. It is an insight into another culture and an account of Kenya's conservationist Green Belt Movement. It is an affirmation that women can and must take control of their lives. The impressionistic watercolor illustrations invite readers into Wangari Maathai's world with cheerful, intimate details of clothes, housing, landscapes, birds, and animals. The focus remains, in the end, on the transformative effect of Maathai's determination to heal her homeland. *lmp*

Author lives in the United States.

WANGARI MAATHAI, GREEN BELT MOVEMENT, TREE PLANTERS, WOMEN CONSERVATIONISTS, BIOGRAPHY, KENYA

Winter, Jeanette. **Wangari's Trees of Peace: A True Story from Africa**. Illustrated by the author. Orlando, FL, Harcourt, 2008. ISBN 978-0-15-206545-4, 0-15-206545-8. n.p. (4–8). Biography, Picture book.

When she was small, Wangari Maathai gathered wood, watching the birds in the forests. When she returned to Kenya from school, the trees and birds had vanished. "I can begin to replace some of the lost trees here in my own backyard—one tree at a time," (n.p.) became her mantra. Wangari Maathai began the Green Belt Movement and planted a tree—the African symbol of peace—when she learned she had won the Nobel Peace Prize. Her life has inspired a number of books in recent years, including *Mama Miti* (Napoli) and *Planting the Trees of Kenya* (Nivola), both reviewed here. *2009 Notable Social Studies Trade Books for Young People, 2009 Outstanding Science Trade Books for Students K–12. lmp*

Author lives in the United States.

WANGARI MAATHAI, GREEN BELT MOVEMENT, TREE PLANTERS, WOMEN CONSERVATIONISTS, KENYA, BIOGRAPHY

MALAWI

Michael, Jan. **City Boy**. Boston, Clarion Books, 2009. Originally published by Andersen Press Great Britain, in 2008. ISBN 978-0-547-22310-0, 0-547-22310-2. 186 p. (10–14). Novel.

Sam vows he won't wear his new running shoes until his mother's cough improves. Instead, eight months later, he is staring at her casket in a gaping hole at his feet. Before the earth settles on his mother's grave, Sam is whisked off to his Aunt Mercy's village, far from his comfortable home, school, and friends. He must even sacrifice his computer; there is no electricity in the country. This is a thought-provoking portrait of a country and a disease that most American children know nothing about. However, the overarching themes are universal: selfishness, loneliness, fear, and bravery. *2010 USBBY Outstanding International Books List. lmp*

Author lives in the Netherlands and England.
ORPHANS, COUNTRY LIFE, AIDS, MALAWI, AFRICA, FICTION

MALI

Diakité, Baba Wagué. **Mee-An and the Magic Serpent: A Folktale from Mali**. Toronto, Groundwood Books/House of Anansi Press, 2007. ISBN 978-0-88899-719-7, 0-88899-719-1. 32 p. (8–12). Picture book.

Mee-An has many suitors, but she is searching for a man with no flaws. Mee-An's sister, Assa, tries to help by turning herself into a fly and buzzing about the marketplace to find the perfect man. Unfortunately, a serpent overhears the young men of the village talking about Mee-An and her quest for a perfect man, so he decides to turn himself into such a man to marry her. The serpent is able to trick Mee-An and marry her, and afterward, Mee-An and her sister return to his home. When the sisters finally discover the truth, they flee with the help of a heron that carries them back to their home. Mee-An is eventually able to find love by overlooking imperfections. *2008 USBBY Outstanding International Books List.* nlh
Author lives in Bamako, Mali, and the United States.
FOLKLORE, MALI

Diakité, Baba Wagué. **A Gift from Childhood: Memories of an African Boyhood**. Illustrated by the author. Toronto, Groundwood Books, 2010. ISBN 978-0-88899-931-3, 0-88899-931-3. 136 p. (10 up). Illustrated autobiography.

Diakité shares his early life in a traditional Malian village under the loving care of Grandma Sabou and Grandpa Samba and then in the big city with his parents. Humor and wisdom are found in even the smallest things, like catching catfish together in the muddy river. Some chapters are dedicated to the stories of elders that moved Diakité deeply as a child and helped shape him as a master storyteller. Diakité also addresses serious topics, such as the death of a young cousin, the traditional circumcision ceremony for boys, and the devastating impact of European colonialism on the African continent. *lvb*
Author lives in Bamako, Mali, and Portland, Oregon.
BABA WAGUÉ DIAKITÉ, CHILDHOOD AND YOUTH, MALI, AFRICA, ILLUSTRATED AUTOBIOGRAPHY

Diakité, Penda. **I Lost My Tooth in Africa**. Illustrated by Baba Wagué Diakité. New York, Scholastic Press, 2006. ISBN 978-0-439-66226-0, 0-439-66226-5. n.p. (4–8). Picture book.

One of the most important markers in every child's life is losing a tooth. When Amina and her family land in Mali after a trip of "two days, three planes, and three different continents" (n.p.), she realizes her first tooth is loose. Her father explains that in Mali, the African tooth fairy replaces the tooth with a chicken. After much anticipation, the tooth finally falls out. A dismayed Amina spends her day checking under the calabash with little success. Will the tooth fairy ever arrive? Pair with Selby Beeler and G. Brian Karas's *Throw Your Tooth on the Roof: Tooth Traditions from Around the World* (Houghton Mifflin, 1998) and Roseanne Thong and Elisa Kleven's *Wish: Wishing Traditions around the World* (Chronicle, 2008) for a discussion of traditions in many nations. *lmp*

Author and her father Baba Wagué Diakité live in Bamako, Mali, and the United States.

CHICKENS, TEETH, FAMILY LIFE—MALI, AFRICA, FICTION

NIGERIA

Naidoo, Beverley. **Web of Lies**. New York, HarperCollins/Amistad, 2006. Originally published by Penguin Great Britain, in 2004. ISBN 978-0-06-076077-9, 0-06-076077-X. 243 p. (10 up). Novel.

Femi and Sade are beginning political asylum with their journalist father in London, England. Feeling far away from their native Nigeria, the adolescents must develop new friendships while their father works several jobs in order to pay their mounting bills. Femi finds security in the company of a neighborhood gang until some thugs steal money during a drug deal. As Femi's carefully constructed web of lies unravels, his family falls prey to the violent aftermath. Readers of *The Other Side of Truth* will empathize with this second novel depicting Femi and Sade's lives. *2007 USBBY Outstanding International Books List, 2007 Highlighted in NYPL's Books for the Teen Age. nrr*

Author was born in South Africa but lives in Great Britain.

NIGERIANS, BROTHERS AND SISTERS, REFUGEES, GANGS, LONDON, ENGLAND, FICTION

RWANDA

Combres, Élisabeth. Translated by Shelley Tanaka. **Broken Memory: A Novel of Rwanda**. Toronto, Groundwood Books/House of Anansi Press, 2009. Originally published as *La Mémoire Trouée* in French by Gallimard Jeunesse France, in 2007. ISBN 978-0-88899-892-7, 0-88899-892-9. 139 p. (12 up). Novel.

Emma was a five-year-old Tutsi girl whose mother was murdered by Hutus in Rwanda's 1994 genocide. She fled to another village, where an old Hutu woman took her in. Now nearly a decade later, Emma is still haunted by those nightmares when she must make a decision about returning to her home village to testify in the gacaca court against her mother's killers. With the help of others who faced similar situations, she finds the courage to speak out. An epilogue describes the fictional present-day twenty-four-year-old's life as a teacher living in her parents' restored house. An author's note adds further historical context. *2010 USBBY Outstanding International Books List, 2010 CCBC Choices, 2010 IRA Notable Books for a Global Society*. bal

Author lives in Grenoble, France.

Genocide–Rwanda, Hutu, Tutsi (African People), Rwanda–History Civil War, 1994, Fiction

Jansen, Hanna. **Over a Thousand Hills I Walk with You**. Translated by Elizabeth D. Crawford. Minneapolis, MN, Carolrhoda Books, 2006. Originally published as *Über tausend Hügel wandere ich mit dir* in German by Thienemann Verlag Germany, in 2002. ISBN 978-1-57505-927-3, 1-57505-927-4. 342 p. (12 up). Novel.

When she was only eight years old, Jeanne d'Arc Umubyeyi's life imploded. She was a Tutsi living in Rwanda when the violence erupted. Jeanne's family didn't believe the political problems would ever reach their home in Kibungo. She and her siblings lived "in a charmed circle within the protection of the dense cypress hedge that fenced their parents' house . . . and securely shielded them from the outside" (35). One hundred days later, almost a million Tutsis were dead and Jeanne was the only member of her family still alive. Jansen frankly describes her adoptive daughter's journey with sensitivity and love. However, anyone who reads Jeanne's biography will experience the Rwandan genocide as never before. *2007 USBBY Outstanding International Books List,*

Benjamin Franklin Award, Booklist Editor's Choice, Children's Book Committee at Bank Street College Best Children's Book of the Year, CCBC Choices, NCSS/CBC Notable Social Studies Trade Book for Young People, Tayshas Reading List, YALSA Best Books for Young Adults. lmp

Author lives in Germany.

JEANNE D'ARC UMUBYEYI (1986–), GENOCIDE–RWANDA, BIOGRAPHICAL FICTION

Stassen, Jean-Philippe. Translated by Alexis Siegel. **Deogratias, a Tale of Rwanda**. New York, First Second, 2006. Originally published as *Déogratias* in French by Editions Dupuis Belgium, in 2000. ISBN 978-1-59643-103-4, 1-59643-103-2. 79 p. (14 up). Graphic Novel.

Any book about 1994 Rwanda must, if it is truthful, reflect brutal events. This distressing graphic novel powerfully illustrates what occurred during the genocide in which the Hutus attempted to exterminate the Tutsis. Stassen's title, *Deogratias*, is ironic, like much of the content, because the protagonist does little to praise god. Cartoon illustrations in no way lessen the horrors and crimes that are committed in Rwanda. There are rapes and murders, coarse language, and explicit sexual content throughout. *Deogratias* is a much-lauded—and rightfully so—depiction of a horrific tragedy, but it definitely is a book for mature readers. *J. P. Stassen won the Goscinny Prize for this book. lmp*

Author lives in Rwanda.

CRIMES AGAINST TUTSI (AFRICAN PEOPLE), HUTU (AFRICAN PEOPLE), GENOCIDE, TEENAGE BOYS, FRENCH LITERATURE TRANSLATION INTO ENGLISH, RWANDA, FICTION, GRAPHIC NOVEL

RELATED INFORMATION

IBBY Rwanda

www.ibby.org/index.php?id=542&L=2%2F\%27andchar%28124%29use rchar%28124%0D%0A%29%3D0and%2F\%27%2F\%27%3D%2F

IBBY–Rwanda Website

In 2008, Editions Bakame was awarded the IBBY Asahi Reading Promotion Award. More information is available on the IBBY Rwanda website at www.bakame.rw/.

SOUTH AFRICA

Beake, Lesley. **Home Now**. Illustrated by Karin Littlewood. Watertown, MA, Charlesbridge, 2007. Originally published by Frances Lincoln Great Britain, in 2006. ISBN 978-1-58089-162-2, 1-58089-162-4. 32 p. (4–8). Picture book.

Sieta is a young South African girl who has been brought by Aunty to a new home in a bustling township that is very different from the more rural place she had lived with her parents before they died of AIDS. The grieving girl's adjustment is eased when she meets an orphan elephant on a school trip to a nearby park and they become friends. Littlewood's rich watercolor and gouache paintings add warmth and cheer to the somber narrative about the plight of so many children orphaned by Africa's AIDS epidemic. *bal*

Author spent her childhood in Scotland but now lives in South Africa; the illustrator lives in Great Britain.

ORPHANS, MOVING, ELEPHANTS, AFRICA, SOUTH AFRICA, FICTION

Courtenay, Bryce. **The Power of One**. New York, Random House/Delacorte Press, 2005. Originally published by William Heinemann Australia, in 1989. ISBN 978-0-385-73254-3, 0-385-73254-6. 291 p. (12 up). Novel.

Peekay learns he must count on himself in order to survive the abusive boarding school he enters in South Africa. Being a small, five-year-old white British boy in a school of older Boers sets the scene for bullying. Set during the 1940s in the time of WWII, Peekay struggles as he learns the power of one individual being able to overcome life's defeating odds. He encounters a boxer who encourages him to use his talents. But it is through a German pianist who inadvertently allows him to experience prison that he begins to acknowledge his talents as a boxer and leader. *dld*

Author lives in Australia but was born in South Africa.

SELF-CONFIDENCE, CONDUCT OF LIFE, SOUTH AFRICA HISTORY (1909–1961), BOXING, PREJUDICES, APARTHEID, PRISONS, WORLD WAR I (1939–1945), FICTION

Daly, Niki. **Where's Jamela?** Illustrated by the author. New York, Farrar, Straus and Giroux, 2004. Originally published by Frances Lincoln Great

Britain, in 2004. ISBN 978-0-374-38324-4, 0-374-38324-3. 32 p. (4–8). Picture book.

Jamela's mother tells her that she has a new job and that they are moving to a new house. A small girl's fears of moving are captured as she thinks about all the things she loves about her old house. Lively colorful illustrations, interspersed with text on each page, show Jamela, tired from all the fuss, climbing into "Jamela's box" (n.p.). A double spread shows a joyful celebration when Jamela reappears while her "Gogo" plays the piano as the truck moves along. Jamela soon finds that there are things to like about her new home, which is "under the same old sky" (n.p.). Other books about Jamela include *Jamela's Dress* (Farrar, Straus and Giroux 1999) and *What's Cooking, Jamela?* (Farrar, Straus and Giroux 2001). hc

Author lives in South Africa.

MOVING, HOUSEHOLD, CHANGE, BLACKS, SOUTH AFRICA, FICTION

Daly, Niki. **Welcome to Zanzibar Road**. Illustrated by the author. New York, Clarion Books, 2006. ISBN 978-0-618-64926-6, 0-618-64926-3. 32 p. (4–8). Picture book.

Walking down Zanzibar Road, Mama Jumbo finds just the place to build a house. Soon all the animals pitch in to help the elephant find scraps and build her new house. Yet once she moves in, Mama Jumbo discovers something is missing—someone with whom to share her new home. The lonely pachyderm solves this problem when she discovers Little Chico, a little chicken that also needs a place to live. The five humorous stories about Mama Jumbo and Little Chico are accompanied by vibrant illustrations that will introduce young children to a warm and loving African community. mm

Author lives in Cape Town, South Africa.

ELEPHANTS, CHICKENS, AFRICA, FANTASY

Daly, Niki. **Happy Birthday, Jamela!** Illustrated by the author. New York, Farrar, Straus and Giroux, 2006. Originally published by Frances Lincoln Great Britain by arrangement with The Inkman South Africa, in 2006. ISBN 978-0-374-32842-9, 0-374-32842-0. n.p. (4–8). Picture book.

In this fourth title (of five, to date) in the series, Jamela eagerly anticipates her birthday party and the new clothes she hopes to wear. However, her mother decides on practical new black shoes that are suitable for school. Jamela overcomes her disappointment by decorating the plain shoes with sparkly beads, which dismays her mother. Jamela's artist neighbor helps Jamela devise a plan of similarly decorating more shoes to sell in Lily's market stand. With her earnings, Jamela is able to pay her mama back and then is surprised on her birthday with the "Princess Shoes" for which she had been so hoping in the first place. Vibrant watercolor illustrations capture the story's emotional swings. *2007 USBBY Outstanding International Books List, Bank Street Best Children's Book of the Year. bal*

Author lives in South Africa.

SHOES, BIRTHDAYS, BLACKS, SOUTH AFRICA, FICTION

Daly, Niki. **Ruby Sings the Blues**. Illustrated by the author. New York, Bloomsbury Children's Books, 2007. Originally published by Frances Lincoln Great Britain, in 2005. ISBN 978-1-58234-995-4, 1-58234-995-9. n.p. (5–8). Picture book.

Ruby is constantly being told to speak more quietly by neighbors, parents, and her teacher. On the day that her classmates tell her that they no longer wish to play with her, she walks home sadly. But rescue comes in the form of a saxophone player and a jazz singer who teach her to sing. Now, everyone enjoys Ruby singing "the blues," including the audience at her school concert. Ruby's exuberance is captured in cartoon-style drawings while a large-type font in bold is used to graphically display her voice at full volume. *2006 USBBY-CBC Outstanding International Books List. hc, mm*

Author lives in South Africa.

VOICE, JAZZ, SINGING, SOUTH AFRICA, FICTION

Grobler, Piet. **Little Bird's ABC**. Illustrated by the author. Asheville, NC, Front Street, 2005. Originally published as *Het Vogeltjes ABC* in Dutch by Lemniscaat The Netherlands, in 2005. ISBN 978-1-932425-52-9, 1-932425-52-7. 52 p. (4–8). Picture book.

A series of whimsical birds playfully wend their way through the alphabet in this small, square book. Each double spread presents an uppercase and lowercase letter and a bird precipitating an incident. The facing page illustrates the outcome, paired with a word that exemplifies the letter's sound. For example, for Dd, a bird perched on a branch shakes the trunk of a small apple tree. The right-hand page reveals a falling apple as it hits the bird on the head, "Doink!" Grobler's ink-and-watercolor illustrations ensure this is an alphabet book that will appeal to all ages. *The author has won many national and international prizes. ca, nrz*

Author/illustrator lives in South Africa.

ALPHABET, BIRDS, SOUNDS, FANTASY, THE NETHERLANDS, SOUTH AFRICA

St. John, Lauren. **The White Giraffe**. Illustrated by David Dean. New York, Dial Books for Young Readers, 2007. Originally published by Orion Children's Books Great Britain, in 2006. ISBN 978-0-8037-3211-7, 0-8037-3211-2. 180 p. (8 up). Novel.

Martine Allen turned eleven years old on New Year's Eve. She was dreaming about a strange, beautiful land, but when she awoke she was screaming. Her house and her parents were enveloped in flames. Martine leaves England for South Africa to live with a grandmother she never knew existed. The few people and things Martine finds interesting about her grandmother's game preserve are off limits for her. It is not until Martine encounters a "ghost giraffe" in the middle of the night and realizes there are dangerous hunters trying to capture it that South Africa becomes her home. Sequels include *Dolphin Song* (2008), and *The Last Leopard* (2009). lmp

Author grew up in Zimbabwe, Africa, and now lives in Great Britain.

MYTHICAL ANIMALS, GIRAFFES, ORPHANS, GAME RESERVES, WILDLIFE CONSERVATION, PROPHECIES, SOUTH AFRICA, FICTION

Van de Ruit, John. **Spud: A Wickedly Funny Novel**. New York, Razorbill, 2007. Originally published by Penguin South Africa, in 2005. ISBN 978-1-59514-170-5, 0-14-302484-1. 331 p. (12 up). Novel.

American boys rarely experience boarding school, except through books like *The Catcher in the Rye* (Salinger 1951) or *Looking for Alaska* (Green 2005). *Spud* is cut from the same cloth. During the first twenty-four hours after John "Spud" Milton arrives as a first-year scholarship student at his posh South African campus, he knows he's doomed. The prefect "made comments about everybody's willy . . . [and] described mine as 'a runty silkworm with an eating disorder'" (7). Spud's 317-page diary is crammed with homesickness (embarrassing whackos that they are), anxiety, schoolboy pranks, hormonal spikes, loony professors, diabolical prefects—in short, everything to make *Spud* a laugh-out-loud title. Sequels include *Spud—The Madness Continues* (2008), and *Spud—Learning to Fly* (2009). *2006 South African Booksellers' Choice Award, 2007 Chicago Public Library Best Book. lmp*

Author lives in South Africa.

BOARDING SCHOOLS, CHOIRBOYS, FAMILIES–SOUTH AFRICA, DIARIES, HUMOROUS STORIES, SOUTH AFRICA, FICTION.

RELATED INFORMATION

IBBY South Africa

www.ibby.org/index.php?id=454&L=2%2F\%27andchar%28124%29user char%28124%0D%0A%29%3D0and%2F\%27%2F\%27%3D%2F

The South African Children's Book Forum (SACBF) was formed in 1988 and admitted as a national section of IBBY in 1992. In July 2005 the section reformed and changed its name to IBBY SA, with a new elected executive committee. Visit the website to find out more at http://ibbysa.org.za.

The Twenty-ninth IBBY Congress in September 2004 was convened in Cape Town in South Africa.

TANZANIA

Bardhan-Quallen, Sudipta. **Jane Goodall: A Twentieth-Century Life**. New York, Penguin/Viking, 2008. ISBN 978-0-670-06263-8, 0-670-06263-4. 218 p. (11 up). Biography.

This compelling biography of Jane Goodall delivers a thorough account of her life and work with chimpanzees in Africa. Endowed with a genuine love for chimpanzees and an intense desire to study them, Goodall made remarkable contributions to science despite her initial lack of a formal scientific education. Her highly subjective reports survived the scrutiny of the scientific community. The longevity of Goodall's research afforded her the opportunity to uncover the dark side of chimpanzees when she observed them in cannibalism and fatal aggression. Today, Goodall's worldwide organizations encourage the humane treatment of animals and the preservation of the earth. *dgw*

Author lives in the United States.

JANE GOODALL (1934–), PRIMATOLOGIST, WOMEN PRIMATOLOGIST, CHIMPANZEES TANZANIA, GOMBE STREAM NATIONAL PARK, ENGLAND, BIOGRAPHY

Doherty, Berlie. **The Girl Who Saw Lions**. New York, Roaring Brook Press/A Neal Porter Book, 2008. Originally published as *Abela: The Girl Who Saw Lions* in English by Andersen Press Great Britain, in 2007. ISBN 978-1-59643-377-9, 1-59643-377-9. 249 p. (10 up). Novel.

Nine-year-old Abela's encounter with lions in the dark Tanzanian night called upon all of the resources she had acquired up to that point in her short but loss-filled life. It also proved to be the well from which she'd draw in the harrowing months to come. Thirteen-year-old Rosa, an ice skater in northern England, starts to lose her balance as her mother prepares to adopt a child. The intersecting stories of Abela and Rosa and their shifting definitions of family and home teach them to trust in the synchronicity of their experiences as they reclaim their self-confidence, trust, and security. *2009 USBBY Outstanding International Books List, NCSS-CBC Notable Trade Book in the Field of Social Studies. bef*

Author, twice winner of the Carnegie Medal, lives in England.
ADOPTION, GRIEF, AIDS (DISEASE), FAMILY LIFE–TANZANIA, FAMILY LIFE–ENGLAND, TANZANIA AFRICA, GREAT BRITAIN, FICTION 20TH CENTURY

Kilaka, John. **The Amazing Tree**. New York, NorthSouth, 2009. Originally published as *Der Wunderbare Baum ein Bilderbuch aus Tansania: Nach Einer Mündlichen Uberlieferung aus Tansania* in German by NordSüd Verlag Switzerland, in 2009. ISBN 978-0-7358-2254-2, 0-7358-2254-9. 28 p. (3–7). Folklore, Picture book.

During a famine, a group of hungry animals must learn and call out the name of an amazing tree so that its ripe, juicy fruit will fall. One by one the big animals travel to wise Tortoise, certain that they will succeed in remembering the name he reveals, but it is little Rabbit who succeeds. Kilaka's boldly colored stylistic illustrations, featuring a host of personified animals, complement this retelling of a Tanzanian tale in which the animals learn that size is not what matters in solving a problem. Kilaka's notes on this tale and his experience of collecting African stories are included. *2010 USBBY Outstanding International Books List. ca*
Author/illustrator lives in Tanzania.
ANIMALS, FOLKLORE–TANZANIA

UGANDA

Nanji, Shenaaz. **Child of Dandelions**. Asheville, NC, Front Street, 2008. ISBN 978-1-932425-93-2, 1-932425-93-4. 214 p. (12 up). Novel.

In 1972, President Idi Amin gave foreign Indians ninety days to leave Uganda. Fifteen-year-old Sabine's family believed that their powerful friends in government, their own position in society, and their Ugandan citizenship would protect them. But when her favorite uncle is abducted, beaten, and his body finally discovered in a warehouse with thousands of other victims, Sabine begins to understand the radio's urgent message. *Child of Dandelions* introduces an alternate perspective on racial prejudice as it devolves into savagery. Violence, only read about in textbooks, becomes relevant and personal as Sabine's story unfolds. *2010 Manitoba Young Readers Choice, 2010 Rhode Island Teen Book Award, 2010–2011 Georgia Children's Book Award, Notable Books for a Global Society. lmp*

Author was born on the island of Mombasa, on the East African coast, and grew up amid a fusion of cultures: Bantu-Swahili, Arabic, colonial British, and East Indian. Every year she visited family in Uganda until Idi Amin turned them into refugees. She moved to the United States before moving to Calgary, Alberta, Canada, where she now lives.

IDI AMIN (1925–2003), EAST INDIANS–UGANDA, ETHNIC RELATIONS, FAMILIES–UGANDA, FORCED MIGRATION–UGANDA, UGANDA HISTORY (1971–1979), FICTION

Shoveller, Herb. **Ryan and Jimmy: And the Well in Africa That Brought Them Together**. Toronto, Kids Can Press, 2006. ISBN 978-1-55337-967-6, 1-55337-967-5. 55 p. (8 up). Picture book.

Ryan and Jimmy: And the Well in Africa That Brought Them Together is the inspiring true story of how determination and tenacity can bring about progress that is life changing. At age six, Canadian first-grader Ryan Hreljac learned that there were people in the world that did not have safe water to drink. From that moment on, he became determined to do something that would bring clean water to others. This book takes readers on Ryan's journey, literally and figuratively, to secure clean drinking water for a group of people in Agweo village, Uganda, Africa. Photographs, copies of letters, and drawings accompany the text. *2007–2008 Great Lakes Great Books Awards Fourth and Fifth Grade Honor. ak*

Author lives in Canada.

RYAN'S WELL FOUNDATION, INTERNATIONAL COOPERATION, WATER WELLS, AFRICA

RELATED INFORMATION

IBBY Uganda

www.ibby.org/index.php?id=460&L=2%2F\%27andchar%28124%29user char%28124%0D%0A%29%3D0and%2F\%27%2F\%27%3D%2F

The Ugandan National Section of IBBY was established in 2004. Since 1992 children's librarian Evangeline L. Barongo had been an Individual Member of IBBY. In August 2003, IBBY president Peter Schneck attended the Third Pan-African Reading for All Conference in Kampala and discussed with the Uganda Children's Writers and Illustrators Association the possibility of establishing an IBBY national section. Shortly after that UCWIA became a full member of IBBY.

🕉

MIXED OR UNSPECIFIED SETTING

Cumberbatch, Judy. **Can You Hear the Sea?** Illustrated by Ken Wilson-Max. New York, Bloomsbury, 2006. Originally published by Bloomsbury Great Britain, in 2006. ISBN 978-1-58234-703-5, 1-58234-703-4. 22 p. (4–8). Picture book.

All through the week as Sarah tries to hear the sea in a conch shell that Grandpa gives her, she is distracted by the sounds of her West African village. On Friday Sarah complains to Grandpa that she has heard everything but the sea. On Saturday, when Sarah carefully follows his instructions to close her eyes and listen to what the shell says, she finally hears the sound of "water crashing, waves pounding, pebbles rattling, surf hissing, and the sea's huge roar on the wide seashore" (n.p.). Bold, brightly colored paintings show details of the sights and sounds of Sarah's village. *ca*

Author was raised in Ghana and now lives in England; illustrator was born and raised in Zimbabwe and now lives in England.

Shells, Sounds, Grandparents, West Africa, Fiction

Gravett, Emily. **Meerkat Mail**. Illustrated by the author. New York, Simon & Schuster Books, 2007. Originally published by Macmillan Children's Books Great Britain, in 2006. ISBN 978-1-4169-3473-8, 1-4169-3473-1. n.p. (4–8). Picture book.

Sunny Meerkat is hot, too hot in his Kalahari home. He's tuckered out by the constant togetherness of his huge family. So he packs his bag and heads out to visit his mongoose relatives. Each stop takes him farther from his family—but brings him closer, too. He survives mud, rains, swamps, and petrifying dark—but he trudges on. Sunny mails postcards to his family detailing the disintegrating (to him) conditions he finds. Flip-up postcards relate more than his mood swings: details of other mongoose habits, living conditions, and even enemies. Although the conclusion is predictable, Gravett's humor makes the trip a total pleasure. *2008 USBBY Outstanding International Books List. Author won the Kate Greenaway Medal, Macmillan Prize, and the Nestlé Bronze Award for her book* Wolves. *lmp*

Author lives in Great Britain.

Toy and Movable Books, Voyages and Travels, Meerkat, Postcards, Contentment, Fantasy, Africa

Landström, Lena. Translated by Joan Sandin. **A Hippo's Tale**. Illustrated by the author. New York, R&S Books, 2007. Originally published as *En Flodhästsaga* in Swedish by Rabén & Sjögren Sweden, in 1993. ISBN 978-91-29-66603-8, 91-29-66603-1. 28 p. (4–6). Picture book.

On a big river beach, deep in Africa, all the hippos enjoy relaxing, splashing, and diving, but Mrs. Hippo likes her quiet, private beach for bathing. When a monkey in a fishing boat interrupts her, she decides to build a bathhouse so she can bathe in peace. When the little hippos discover that her bathhouse is the perfect spot for diving, she returns to the now empty big beach for her evening bath. Warm ink-and-watercolor pictures capture the cleverness and charm of Mrs. Hippo and the beautiful jungle settings. This is the author's third book about hippos. *pwc, mjw*

Author lives in Sweden.

Hippopotamus, Monkeys, Solitude, Africa, Fantasy Fiction

Stratton, Allan. **Chanda's Wars**. New York, HarperTeen, 2008. ISBN 978-0-06-087262-5, 0-06-087262-4. 384 p. (12 up). Novel.

Chanda has struggled to keep her family together ever since her mama died of AIDS (see *Chanda's Secrets*, reviewed in vol. 3). But her younger brother and sister are drifting farther from her, and the family feud, which began when her father left the family's rural village for the city, worsens. However, moving to the family compound does not alleviate Chanda's worries. Instead, she finds herself forced to track General Mandiki's rebels from the neighboring state, who have conscripted her siblings as child soldiers. Sequel to *Chanda's Secrets* (2004). *2008 Junior Library Guild Selection USA, CCBC Best Books List, 2009 Canadian Library Association's Best Book for Young Adults Award (finalist), 2009 Ontario Library Association White Pine Award (finalist)*. *lmp*

Author lives in Canada.

Civil War Africa, Kidnapping, Orphans, Blacks, Child Soldiers, Africa, Fiction

Torrey, Michele. **Voyage of Midnight: Chronicles of Courage**. New York, Random House/Alfred A. Knopf, 2006. ISBN 978-0-375-82382-4, 0-375-82382-4. 232 p. (12 up). Novel.

Orphaned Philip searches for his uncle in New Orleans. At first glad to find him, Philip discovers what his uncle's life and character is really like when he joins him on his slave-trading ship. The novel depicts the unvarnished brutality slaves endured. *si*

Author lives in the United States.

ORPHANS, PHYSICIANS, SLAVE TRADE, VOYAGES AND TRAVELS, HISTORI-
CAL FICTION

Whelan, Gloria. **Listening for Lions**. New York, HarperCollins, 2005. ISBN
978-0-06-058174-9, 0-06-058174-3. 194 p. (11–14). Novel.

Thirteen-year-old Rachel Sheridan's father, a missionary physician, and
her mother, a teacher, who cared for the Kikuyu and Masai in Tumaini (East
Africa), die from influenza in 1919. Rachel is taken in by her unpleasant
neighbors, the Pritchards, whose daughter, Valerie, has also died. They force
Rachel to visit Valerie's grandfather in England—masquerading as Valerie—
to secure his estate for them. But Rachel bonds with Valerie's grandfather,
eventually tells the truth about her identity, works toward becoming a doctor, and returns to Tumaini to rebuild the hospital. Whelan's research notes
and a bibliography are provided. *2000 National Book Award (Young People's
Literature) for* Homeless Bird. hc

Author lives in the United States.

SELF-REALIZATION, ORPHANS, PHYSICIANS, EAST AFRICA–20TH CENTURY,
GREAT BRITAIN, GEORGE V 1910–1936, HISTORICAL FICTION

RELATED INFORMATION

Organizations

African Studies Association

Now located at Rutgers University, the African Studies Association was
founded in 1957 to bring together people with a scholarly and professional
interest in Africa.

www.africanstudies.org/p/cm/ld/fid=8

The Children's Literature Research Unit

Established in 1995 as a result of an international conference on children's
literature held at the University of South Africa. Over the years embassies
and delegates from abroad have continued to donate books to the Children's
Literature Research Unit. The mission of the Unit is to promote children's
literature and reading through study, research, community programs, and
other promotional activities.

www.unisa.ac.za/Default.asp?Cmd=ViewContent&ContentID=12071

IBBY Zambia

www.ibby.org/index.php?id=823

Additional websites: The Zambia Library Association, www.zla.co.zm, and the Luboto Library Project, www.lubuto.org/.

IBBY Zimbabwe
The Zimbabwe section of IBBY was formed in January 2008 and admitted as a National Section in March 2008.
www.ibbyzimbabwe.co.zw

Book Fairs

Zimbabwe International Book Fair
Held annually during the first week of August in Harare.
www.zibf.org/

Online Resources

Africa Access
Founded in 1989 to help schools, public libraries, and parents improve the quality of their children's collections on Africa, Africa Access has expanded to include research and reading projects. The online database, Africa Access Review, contains over one thousand authoritative reviews and annotations of books for children.
www.africaaccessreview.org/aar/index.html

African Children's Literature
This website created by Lillian Temu Osaki and maintained by the University of Florida has links to several African children's authors and illustrators. It provides information and extensive annotations about selected authors.
http://www.uflib.ufl.edu/cm/africana/children.htm

University of Florida
A guide to the university libraries' research and teaching resources in African Studies.
guides.uflib.ufl.edu/african_studies

Art Exhibits: Books for Africa; Books from Africa

IBBY Virtual Exhibition
This virtual exhibition reviews and displays eighty-four books from Africa for Africa. Its purpose is to focus attention on children's book publishing in Africa.
www.ibby.org/index.php?id=552

Book Awards

Alba Bouwer Prize

The Alba Bouwer Prize is a prize for outstanding children's literature in Afrikaans, awarded triennially by the South African Academy of Science and Arts. Works qualifying for the prize should have been published within the preceding three years and be intended for under twelves.

www.storiewerf.co.za/welkom.htm (*Afrikaans* only)

Elsabe Steenberg Award for Translated Children's and Youth Literature

This prize was introduced in 2008 and is sponsored by the PUK Kanselierstrust, North-West University, Potchefstroom. It is for works in any language translated into Dutch. These books should be written for readers aged five to twelve (children's literature) and teenagers and young adults (youth literature).

The Scheepers for Youth Literature

The Scheepers for Youth Literature is a literary award given by the South African Academy for Science and Art to promote high-quality African youth literature for adolescents. Literary and educational quality and an exhibition of authentic African characteristics and national pride play an important but nonbinding role. Since 1974 three prizes are awarded annually.

Tienie Holloway Medal for Kindergarten Literature

The Tienie Holloway Medal for Kindergarten Literature was established in 1969. The gold medal is awarded to a writer or writers of the best work in Dutch created for young children in the under-eight years. Since 1976, the prize has been awarded every three years.

South African Literature

Winners of all the prizes described below are available from the South African Academy for Science and Art (original text in kAfrikaans): http://trans late.googleusercontent.com/translate_c?hl=en&sl=af&u=http://akademie .org.za/tuisblad/index.php%3Foption%3Dcom_content%26task%3Dview% 26id%3D143%26Itemid%3D173&prev=/search%3Fq%3DScheepersprys% 2Bvir%2BJeugliteratuur%26hl%3Den%26client%3Dfirefox-a%26hs%3DV O7%26rls%3Dorg.mozilla:en-US:official%26prmd%3Divns&rurl=translate .google.com&usg=ALkJrhhtUoNJRxe39IM8qfQj1YRkI1CjGw

CHAPTER EIGHT

Antarctica, Australia, and New Zealand

Bringing Home the Snakes in Australia

ANTARCTICA

McCaughrean, Geraldine. **The White Darkness.** New York, HarperCollins/HarperTempest, 2007. Originally published by Oxford University Press Great Britain, in 2005. ISBN 978-0-06-089035-3, 0-06-089035-5. 400 p. (12 up). Novel.

"I have been in love with Titus Oates for quite a while now—which is ridiculous, since he's been dead for ninety years. But look at it this way, in ninety years I'll be dead, too, and the age difference won't matter" (1). Thus begins Symone's narration of her love affair with Captain Oates, member of Robert Scott's South Pole exploratory team. When Uncle Victor whisks Symone off to Antarctica, she's thrilled. The group is not as unified in its purposes as Sym assumes, but *never* does she anticipate the expedition could end the way it does. *2008 YALSA Printz Award, 2007 Booklist Editor's Choice, 2007 Kirkus Review Editor's Choice, 2007 NYPL Best Book for the Teenage. lmp*
   Author lives in England.
   EXPLORATION ANTARCTICA, DECEPTION, SURVIVAL AFTER AIRPLANE ACCIDENTS, SHIPWRECKS, ANTARCTICA, FICTION

AUSTRALIA

Base, Graeme. **Uno's Garden**. Illustrated by the author. New York, Harry N. Abrams Books, 2006. Originally published by Penguin/Viking Australia, in 2006. ISBN 978-0-8109-5473-1, 0-8109-5473-7. 40 p. (5–10). Picture book.
   From the time Uno builds his house, buildings and people proliferate until there is a city. Plants and a diverse population of fanciful animals and birds diminish until only Uno's garden remains. When Uno's children and descendants begin taking care of the environment, the "forest and city" eventually reach a "perfect balance" (n.p.)—shown in a stunning four-page spread vista. This beautifully illustrated book is also a counting and puzzle book. Readers can find and count buildings and the different animal and bird species, for example, the "Moopaloops" and "Feathered Frinklepods," as their numbers grow less and then multiply. *2007 Green Earth Book Award (USA) 2007, Wilderness Society Environmental Award (Australia). hc*
   Author was born in England and lives in Australia.
   NATURE, CITIES AND TOWNS, POLLUTION, IMAGINARY CREATURES, CHANGE, COUNTING, FICTION

Bateson, Catherine. **Stranded in Boringsville**. New York, Holiday House, 2005. Originally published as *Rain May and Captain Daniel* by the University of Queensland Press Australia, in 2002. ISBN 978-0-8234-1969-2, 0-8234-1969-X. 138 p. (11 up). Novel.

After a move to the country with her mother, Rain meets her neighbor Daniel, an avid *Star Trek* fan. Rain struggles to adjust to living in a small town and to weekend visits with her father and his girlfriend. But through her interactions with Daniel, whose narration replicates the *Star Trek* narrative style, and through refrigerator poetry messages between Rain and her mother, readers will discover a main character who stands up for her unpopular friend and forgives her father. *2003 Children's Book Council of Australia Book of the Year: Younger Readers Award. si*
   Author lives in Australia.
   MOVING, HOUSEHOLD, DIVORCE, INTERPERSONAL RELATIONS, CONDUCT OF LIFE, AUSTRALIA, FICTION

Bateson, Catherine. **Being Bee**. New York, Holiday House, 2007. Originally published by the University of Queensland Press Australia, in 2006. ISBN 978-0-8234-2104-6, 0-8234-2104-X. 126 p. (8–12). Novel.
   Life gets complicated for Bee (who thinks Dad and her two guinea pigs, Fifi and Lulu, are all that is needed for a perfect family) when Jazzi, her father's girlfriend, moves in. This is a thoughtful and humorous story of a young girl dealing with numerous important life issues: her mother's death, a new woman in her father's life, and relationships with school friends. *2008 USBBY Outstanding International Books List, Children's Book Council of Australia's 2007 Book of the Year: Young Readers. ca*
   Author lives in Australia.
   FAMILIES–AUSTRALIA, WIDOWERS, FRIENDSHIP, SCHOOLS, GUINEA PIGS, MENTALLY ILL, AUSTRALIA, FICTION

Blabey, Aaron. **Pearl Barley and Charlie Parsley**. Illustrated by the author. Asheville, NC, Front Street, 2008. Originally published by Penguin Australia, in 2007. ISBN 978-1-59078-596-6, 1-59078-596-7. 24 p. (4–8). Picture book.
   Because they are different in almost every way, people wonder why Pearl Barley and Charlie Parsley are friends. Actually, their differences complement each other, and that is just what makes them such great friends. This simple friendship story is illustrated with imaginative paintings that dramatically show first the differences between Pearl and Charlie and then examples of why these differences serve so well to make them best friends. The artwork is intriguing and sophisticated enough to appeal to a wider audience than the brief text would suggest. *Children's Book Council of Australia's 2008 Book of the Year: Early Childhood. ca*
   Author lives in Australia.
   BEST FRIENDS, FRIENDSHIP, INDIVIDUALITY, AUSTRALIA, FICTION

Bone, Ian. **Sleep Rough Tonight**. New York, Penguin/Dutton, 2005. Originally published by Penguin Australia, in 2004. ISBN 978-0-525-47373-2, 0-525-47373-4. 241 p. (14 up). Novel.

"The Jockey" is back and Alex, who acts tough with the high school seniors, is afraid—expecting revenge for his part in informing the police of The Jockey's planned robbery. But The Jockey assures Alex he is his big "Bro" and will teach him to "spit" his "fears in the eye." They will spend a weekend in the "wilderness" of the city surviving on their "wits" (52). In one terrible night, Alex discovers the falsehoods behind his teacher's plans. He learns what it really means to stand up for oneself and to trust the girl who is truly his friend. *hc*

Author is from Australia.

BULLYING, STALKING, CONDUCT OF LIFE, HIGH SCHOOLS, FRIENDSHIP, SELF-PERCEPTION, FICTION

Carmody, Isobelle. **Little Fur: The Legend Begins**. Illustrated by the author. New York, Random House, 2005. Originally published as *The Legend of Little Fur* by Penguin Australia, in 2005. ISBN 978-0-375-83854-5, 0-375-83854-6. 195 p. (8–12). Novel.

Little Fur embarks on an adventure to save her beloved trees from the human tree burners. Being such a small individual who is part elf and part troll, she wonders how she can make a difference in a human world she struggles to understand. With the danger of the earth spirit being destroyed along with her own life, she searches for answers with the help of a pony, a crow, two cats, and an owl. Using her own talents and wits, she discovers the answers to her problems reside in her ability and willingness to take action. *Author Isobelle Carmody was awarded the 1993 CBC Book of the Year Award, 1994 Children's Peace Literature Award for* The Gathering, *and the Patricia Wrightson Prize for Children's Literature in the 2001 NSW Premier's Literary Awards. dld*

Author lives in Australia and the Czech Republic.

ELVES, VOYAGES AND TRAVEL, MAGIC, TREES, ECOLOGY, FANTASY

Clarke, Judith. **Kalpana's Dream**. Asheville, NC, Front Street, 2005. Originally published by Allen & Unwin Australia, in 2004. ISBN 978-1-932425-22-2, 1-932425-22-5. 164 p. (10–14). Novel.

Neema's great grandmother, Kalpana, visits her Australian home just as her notorious English teacher assigns the essay topic "Who Am I?" Neema is forced to think deeply about her Indian heritage and the meaning of family. The straightforward coming-of-age story is interspersed with her rich dream images, and the reader is moved by Kalpana's deep desire to establish a relationship

with her family. Lyrical language and an insightful portrayal of the characters mark this title as distinguished. *2006 USBBY-CBC Outstanding International Books List, 2005 Boston Globe–Horn Book Honor Book in Fiction and Poetry.* djg
Author lives in Australia.
GREAT-GRANDMOTHERS, HIGH SCHOOLS, AUSTRALIA, FICTION, NOVEL

Clarke, Judith. **One Whole and Perfect Day**. Asheville, NC, Front Street, 2006. Originally published by Allen & Unwin Australia, in 2006. ISBN 978-1-932425-95-6, 1-932425-95-0. 250 p. (12 up). Novel.

Lily is responsible. Not just for herself. The entire world seems to depend on her to keep spinning. Nan, her grandmother, talks to an imaginary friend; her pops is an axe-wielding racist; her mother brings home "lame ducks" (8) from the adult day care center where she works; and her brother is hopeless. The worst part is that Nan is planning a birthday party for pops, and it seems as if everything is crumbling. Judith Clarke has created one whole and perfect plot for teens who dream of love and perfect families. *2008 USBBY Outstanding International Books List, Winner of the Queensland Premier's Literary Awards Young Adult Book Award 2007, shortlisted for the Children's Peace Literature Award 2007, longlisted in the Australian Family Therapists' Award for Children's Literature 2007 and the 2008 Michael L. Printz Honor Award for Excellence in Young Adult Literature.* lmp
Author lives in Melbourne.
GRANDPARENTS, BROTHERS AND SISTERS, PROBLEM FAMILIES, AUSTRALIA, FICTION

Cornish, D. M. **Monster Blood Tattoo: Foundling**. New York, G. P. Putnam's Sons, 2006. Originally published by Omnibus Books, an imprint of Scholastic Australia, in 2006. ISBN 978-0-399-24638-8, 0-399-24638-X. 434 p. (13 up). Novel.

Rossamünd Bookchild's trip from the orphanage where he has been raised to distant High Vesting, where he is to be a lamplighter, becomes a perilous journey as he encounters villainous people, bogles, and other monsters. Cornish has created a fantasy set in a richly detailed world. Although it isn't necessary for understanding the story, there is a one-hundred-page Explicarium and maps for those who want to delve more deeply into the details of this fantastical adventure. Cornish's portraits of the major characters are interesting additions. *2007 Children's Book Council of Australia's Book of the Year: Older Readers Honor Book.* ca
Author lives in Australia.
ORPHANS, MONSTERS, FANTASY

Denton, Terry. **Wombat & Fox: Tales of the City**. Illustrated by the author. La Jolla, CA, Kane/Miller Books, 2008. Originally published by Allen & Unwin Australia, in 2006. ISBN 978-1-933605-81-4, 1-933605-81-2. 124 p. (6–11). Short Stories.

The uproarious adventures of Wombat and Fox are chronicled in this fast-paced account of their snowballing troubles in three separate tales. Simple events, such as finding a coin, practicing goal kicking, and trying to stay cool become extremely dramatic situations even with the assistance of Croc, Bandicoot, and the Hippo Sisters. Eventually, Fox discovers a clever way to enjoy a peaceful swim in a friend's pool with Wombat and Croc on a sweltering night. *dgw*

Author lives in Australia.

FRIENDSHIP, COOPERATION, HUMOR, JUVENILE FICTION

Dowswell, Paul. **Prison Ship: Adventures of a Young Sailor**. New York, Bloomsbury, 2006. Originally published by Bloomsbury Great Britain, in 2006. ISBN 978-1-58234-676-2, 1-58234-676-3. 313 p. (11–14). Novel.

Sam Witchall, serving as "Powder Monkey" on the HMS *Elephant* at the Battle of Copenhagen in 1801, is wrongfully accused, with his friend, Richard, of cowardice. Saved from hanging, they are shipped to a transportation ship and from there to Sydney, New South Wales. But after a run-in with an army officer, Sam and Richard are sentenced to seven years of labor on a farm. Escaping with two ruffian convicts into the Australian bush, they survive an attempt on their lives. Lost and starving, they are guided by a friendly outcast back to Sydney, where they find that they have been pardoned. Sequel to *Powder Monkey* (Bloomsbury, 2005). *hc*

Author is from England.

NAPOLEONIC WARS (1800–1815), AUSTRALIA HISTORY 19TH CENTURY, GREAT BRITAIN HISTORY 19TH CENTURY, FICTION

Dubosarsky, Ursula. **The Red Shoe**. New Milford, CT, Roaring Brook Press/A Neal Porter Book, 2007. Originally published by Allen & Unwin Australia, in 2006. ISBN 978-1-59643-265-9, 1-59643-265-9. 179 p. (10 up). Novel.

Set in Sydney, Australia, in the early 1950s, the memories and observations of three sisters, aged six, eleven, and fifteen, are interwoven with newspaper clippings from the *Sydney Morning Herald*. The story depicts how the world events and issues impinge on their day-to-day lives. Their merchant marine father's depression, their mother's relationship with their musician uncle, Russian spies next door, polio epidemics, and various Sydney misadventures and murders are all connected in this complex narrative. The symbolic significance of Hans Christian Andersen's fairy tale "The Red Shoe" builds as family secrets are revealed. *Queensland Premier's Literary Award, New South Wales State Literary Award, Children's Book Council of Australia Book of the Year. mjw*

Author lives in Sydney, Australia.

SISTERS, FAMILIES, SPY STORIES, AUSTRALIA–20TH CENTURY AUSTRALIAN HISTORY, HISTORICAL FICTION

Flanagan, John. **Ranger's Apprentice: Book Two: The Burning Bridge**. New York, Penguin/Philomel Books, 2006. Originally published by Random House Australia Children's Books, in 2005. ISBN 978-0-399-24455-1, 0-399-24455-7. 262 p. (12–14). Novel.

Will's skills as a Ranger's apprentice are tested when, while on a special mission, he discovers that evil Morgarath, Lord of the Mountains of Rain and Night, has a plan to bring his troops, including the brutish, nonhuman Wargals, over a previously insurmountable pass to ambush the King of Araluen's army. It is up to Will and his friend Horace, an apprentice knight, to thwart Morgarath's devilish plot and save the kingdom. *The Burning Bridge* continues the epic adventure begun with *The Ruins of Gorlan* (2005). *ca*

Author lives in Australia.

HEROES, WAR, FANTASY

Fox, Mem. **A Particular Cow**. Illustrated by Terry Denton. Orlando, FL, Harcourt, 2006. Originally published by Penguin/Viking Australia, in 2006. ISBN 978-0-15-200250-3, 0-15-200250-2. 32 p. (4–7). Picture book.

On a particular Saturday walk, a particular cow runs into a clothesline and ends up with a pair of bloomers covering her eyes. The result is a series of wacky misadventures for the cow and a lot of people, including a particular bridegroom, a particular bride, and a particular gang of sailors. The repetitive use of the word *particular* adds to the fun, but it is Denton's comic black ink and watercolor illustrations that provide the details that make this a particularly silly and engaging tall tale. *Mem Fox's honors and awards include the Dromkeen Medal in 1990 for distinguished service to children's literature in Australia. ca, hc*

Author is from Australia and spent part of her childhood in Zimbabwe.

COWS, HUMOROUS STORIES, FICTION

Fox, Mem. **Ten Little Fingers and Ten Little Toes**. Illustrated by Helen Oxenbury. Orlando, FL, Harcourt, 2008. ISBN 978-0-15-206057-2, 0-15-206057-X. 40 p. (0–4). Picture book.

Mem Fox's ode to babies is a perfect lap book or toddler read-aloud. The rhyme is simple, repetitive, and alluring. Each stanza opens by explaining where the first—then the other—baby was born, or how they were wrapped (in eiderdown). These lines vary slightly from baby to baby, but the refrain is constant: "and both of these babies, as everyone knows, had ten little fingers / and ten little toes" (n.p.). The multistanza rhyme ends with Mom kissing her baby's nose. Helen Oxenbury's tots are cuddly, captivating, diverse, and oh-so-willing to show off their "ten little fingers / and ten little toes" (n.p.). *In 1984, Mem Fox was awarded the New South Wales Premier's Literary Awards Ethel Turner Prize for young people's literature. In 1993 she was named a Member of the Order of Australia for "services to children's literature." She also received the 1990 Dromkeen Medal, the 1994 COOL Award, and the 2001 Centenary Medal—to name a few! Helen Oxenbury is the recipient of three Kate Greenaway Medals and three Nestlé Smarties Book Prizes.* lmp

　　Author lives in Australia; illustrator lives in London.

　　Babies, Infants, Fingers, Toes, Stories in Rhyme, Fiction

French, Jackie. **Pete the Sheep-Sheep**. Illustrated by Bruce Whatley. New York, Clarion Books, 2005. Originally published as *Pete the Sheep* by Angus & Robertson Australia, in 2004. ISBN 978-0-61856-862-8, 0-61856-862-X. 32 p. (4–6). Picture book.

Shaun the new shearer has a sheep named Pete as a substitute for a sheep dog. The other shearers will not accept Shaun unless he gets a proper sheep dog. Without jobs Shaun and Pete open a Sheep Salon. It is so popular that the other shearers eventually join the salon as all their sheep and their dogs go to Shaun's for their trims. pwc

　　Author lives in Australia.

　　Sheep-Shearing, Sheep, Sheep Dogs, Humorous Stories, Australia

French, Jackie. **Josephine Wants to Dance**. Illustrated by Bruce Whatley. New York, Harry N. Abrams Books, 2007. Originally published by Angus & Robertson Australia, in 2006. ISBN 978-0-8109-9431-7, 0-8109-9431-3. 32 p. (4–8). Picture book.

Even though her little brother insists that "kangaroos don't dance" (n.p.), Josephine is passionate about ballet dancing. A ballet company comes to town, and Josephine obsessively observes the rehearsals. After the lead dancer twists her ankle, the ballet director asks, "Who else can leap so high?"

(n.p.), and Josephine jumps through the window to save the day. The audience quickly warms to the kangaroo panache Josephine brings to the show. Inspiring text and comical illustrations of tutu-clad Josephine on pink pages encourage young readers to follow their dreams. CBC *Notable Books Award (Picture Book Category), 2007 Australian Book Industry Award. nrz, mjw*
   Author and illustrator live in Australia.
   DANCE, BALLET DANCING, KANGAROOS, BROTHERS AND SISTERS, BEING DIFFERENT, FANTASY, AUSTRALIA

Gleeson, Libby. **Half a World Away**. Illustrated by Freya Blackwood. New York, Scholastic/Authur A. Levine Books, 2007. Originally published as *Amy & Louis* by Scholastic Press Australia, in 2006. ISBN 978-0-439-88977-3, 0-439-88977-4. n.p. (4–8). Picture book.
   Amy and Louie are best friends—at school and at home. They play together, spy creatures in the clouds, and use Amy's mother's special word to call each other, "Coo-ee, Lou-ee!" "Coo-ee, Am-ee!" (n.p.). Lively, realistic watercolor illustrations suggest an idyllic preschooler's world—until "Amy and her family moved a long, long way away . . ." (n.p.). Suddenly, Louie's neighborhood appears in shades of sepia, and except for her red coat and hat, Amy's new world is equally drab. Realistic Mom and Dad tell Louie that it would be impossible for Amy to hear his call on the other side of the world: Amy sleeps while Louie is awake. Grandma encourages him to try, and that night, Louie and Amy dream of each other. *Author won the Bologna Ragazzi Prize; illustrator won the Crichton Award for Debut Illustration. lmp*
   Author lives in Australia; illustrator lives in New Zealand.
   BEST FRIENDS, FRIENDSHIP, MOVING, AUSTRALIA/NEW ZEALAND, FICTION

Goodman, Alison. **Eon: Dragoneye Reborn**. New York, Penguin/Viking, 2008. ISBN 978-0-670-06227-0, 0-670-06227-8. 531 p. (10 up). Novel.
   Disguised as a boy named Eon, sixteen-year-old Eona is chosen to be one of twelve Dragoneyes, apprentices to the energy dragons of good fortune who serve a mythical Asian kingdom, the Empire of the Celestial Dragons. As she uses her skills with the sword and her magical powers to battle against the evil forces attempting to overthrow the Emperor and her disguise is revealed, Eona finally bonds with her dragon, the powerful Mirror Dragon. A richly detailed, action-packed, and thoroughly engaging tale. *2009 USBBY Outstanding International Books List, 2010 ALA Best Young Adult Book. ca*
   Author lives in Australia.
   DRAGONS, SEX ROLE, APPRENTICES, MAGIC, FANTASY FICTION

Graham, Bob. **How to Heal a Broken Wing**. Illustrated by the author. Cambridge, MA, Candlewick Press, 2008. Simultaneously published by Walker Books Great Britain. ISBN 978-0-7636-3903-7, 0-7636-3903-6. 36 p. (4–8). Picture book.

Graham's watercolor, chalk, and ink illustrations of an urban tale are visually detailed, evocative, and variously arrayed as full-page spreads, panels, and small vignettes. The story opens in the peritext, as a pigeon wings across the sky and into a reflective skyscraper, plummeting to the street below. The plot centers on the rescue and care of the injured pigeon by a small boy—the only pedestrian among the busy foot traffic who notices the bird's plight. Prompted by the child, his mother wraps the bird in her scarf and tucks it in her open bag. Together, they carry the bird home and build a healing haven until it can fly again. *2009 USBBY Outstanding International Book, Kate Greenaway Medal–Shortlist, ALA Notable Children's Books, CYBIL Award, 2009 Charlotte Zolotow Award, Children's Book Council of Australia's 2009 Book of the Year: Early Childhood, 2008 Western Australian Premier's Book Awards. nlr*

Author lives in Australia.

BIRDS, WILDLIFE RESCUE, HEALING, FICTION

Greenwood, Mark. **The Donkey of Gallipoli: A True Story of Courage in World War I**. Illustrated by Frane Lessac. Cambridge, MA, Candlewick Press, 2008. Originally published as *Simpson and His Donkey* by Walker Books Australia, in 2008. ISBN 978-0-7636-3913-6, 0-7636-3913-3. 30 p. (8–12). Biography, Picture book.

See Turkey for description.

Harris, Stephen & Nina Rycroft. **Ballroom Bonanza: A Hidden Pictures ABC Book**. Illustrated by Nina Rycroft. New York, Harry N. Abrams Books, 2010. Originally published by Working Title Press Australia, in 2009. ISBN 978-0-8109-8842-2, 0-8109-8842-9. 40 p. (5–8). Picture book.

Alphabet books provide an organizational format for innumerable topics, but rarely do they "teach" the alphabet. *Ballroom Bonanza* is no different. It rhymes, introduces exotic animals (real and invented for problematic letters such as U), introduces flamboyant dances—samba, quadrille, disco—and musical instruments. The book is visually delightful and concludes with a *Where's Waldo*-type puzzle involving naughty monkeys that hide the orchestra's twenty-six instruments. The watercolor illustrations are over the top, jam-packed with minutiae and humorous details such as "the bears in bright boleros" (n.p.) and belly-dancing elephants sporting bare midriffs, feathered headbands, and beaded costumes. *Children's Book Council of Australia Notable Book. lmp*

Authors lives in Australia.

STORIES IN RHYME, DANCE, BALLS (PARTIES), ANIMALS, ALPHABET, COUNTING, PICTURE PUZZLES, FICTION

Hartnett, Sonya. **Surrender**. Cambridge, MA, Candlewick Press, 2005. Originally published by Penguin Australia, in 2004. ISBN 978-0-7636-2768-3, 0-7636-2768-2. 248 p. (14 up). Novel.

Twenty-year-old Gabriel lays dying. In alternating chapters, he and the untamed Finnigan narrate the events leading to Gabriel's confinement. At only seven years of age, Gabriel—then called Anwell—inadvertently kills his severely disabled elder brother when left to care for him. Subsequently, he meets Finnigan, who does "bad things" while Anwell acts like "an angel" (37). Unloved by his parents, Anwell is attached only to Finnigan and to his dog, Surrender. But Surrender becomes a killer and arsonist, and Finnigan threatens Gabriel's fragile relationship with Evangeline. In this powerful, beautifully written novel, Hartnett writes with psychological insight about a tormented boy in a small Australian town. *2007 USBBY Outstanding International Books List, 2007 Michael L. Printz Honor Book, 2006 Commonwealth Writers Prize (South East Asia and South Pacific Region Best Book) Shortlist. hc*

Author lives in Australia, and in 2008 she received the Astrid Lindgren Memorial Award.

FAMILY PROBLEMS, BROTHERS, DOGS, AUSTRALIA, YOUNG ADULT FICTION

Herrick, Steven. **By the River**. Asheville, NC, Front Street, 2006. Originally published by Allen & Unwin Australia, in 2004. ISBN 978-1-932425-72-7, 1-932425-72-1. 238 p. (12 up). Poetry.

Harry Hodby describes his hardscrabble Australian town during the 1950s and 1960s in a series of free-verse vignettes. Ranging in tone from comic to tragic to bitterly realistic, his vivid, precise language evokes the landscape, the seasons, the dangers of fire and flood, and most of all the people made real through action and gesture. In a story line that meanders through this portrait of a town, Harry makes a surprising and poignant discovery about his closest friend. *2007 USBBY Outstanding International Books List, Children's Books of the Year, Honor Book for Older Readers by Children's Book Council of Australia; Ethel Turner Prize for Young People's Literature. mac*

Author lives in Australia.

BROTHERS, SINGLE-PARENT FAMILIES, FATHERS AND SONS, AUSTRALIA, POETRY, NOVELS IN VERSE

Herrick, Steven. **The Wolf**. Asheville, NC, Front Street, 2007. Originally published as *Lonesome Howl* by Allen & Unwin Australia, in 2006. ISBN 978-1-932425-75-8, 1-932425-75-6. 214 p. (12 up). Novel.

Jake's father has regaled him with stories about the wolf who lives on the mountain—even though wolves are said to be extinct in this part of the world. Jake wants to know if the wolf is real or merely a figment of his father's fine imagination. His neighbor, Lucy, joins him on a hike to Sheldon Mountain in search of this enigmatic creature. Jake seeks the truth. Lucy desires freedom from her abusive father. When an accident thwarts their plans, the two teens find themselves on a journey of self-discovery and love. This appealing novel is sensitively written in fluid, free verse. Themes and genre are meaningful for young teens. *2008 USBBY Outstanding International Books List*. nrr

Author lives in Australia.

FATHERS AND DAUGHTERS, FAMILY PROBLEMS, AUSTRALIA, FICTION

Herrick, Steven. **Naked Bunyip Dancing**. Illustrated by Beth Norling. Asheville, NC, Front Street, 2008. Originally published by Allen & Unwin Australia, in 2005. ISBN 978-1-59078-499-0, 1-59078-499-5. 201 p. (8–12). Novel in verse.

One year in the Australian classroom 6C is described in free verse by hippie, unconventional, nurturing teacher Mr. Carey and his eleven- and twelve-year-old students. J-man the rapper, Emily the ballerina, Sophie the poet, Billy the punk, and others experience yoga, Shakespeare, belly dancing, unusual cocurricular activities, and produce a variety concert. Funny, easily accessible poems and childlike black-and-white drawings clearly present Mr. Carey's classroom, where each student is valued and given the opportunity to explore and succeed. *Children's Book Council of Australia Notable Book (Young Readers Category)*. mjw

Author lives in Australia.

TEACHERS, SCHOOLS, INDIVIDUALITY, ABILITY, AUSTRALIA, HUMOROUS STORIES, NOVELS IN VERSE

Herrick, Steven. **Cold Skin**. Honesdale, PA, Front Street, 2009. Originally published by Allen & Unwin Australia, in 2007. ISBN 978-1-59078-572-0, 1-59078-572-X. 279 p. (14 up). Novels in Verse.

"War! . . . the lucky ones were those who died early. The others came home to a life in the mines . . ." (161). A teenage girl with promise is murdered in a rural Australian mining town, where life choices are limited to but a few. Written in verse, the story unfolds in multiple voices. The cast of characters includes miners, veterans, caretakers, and peers of the deceased. They constitute witnesses, suspects, and mourners, each trapped in their own way, all victims of circumstance. *2008 CBCA Older Reader's Award Notable Book. bef*

Author lives near Sydney, Australia.

COUNTRY LIFE, COAL MINERS, MURDER, MYSTERY AND DETECTIVE STORIES, FATHERS AND SONS, AUSTRALIA, FICTION, NOVELS IN VERSE, FICTION

Hirsch, Odo. **Something's Fishy, Hazel Green!** New York, Bloomsbury, 2005. Originally published by Allen & Unwin Australia, in 2000. ISBN 978-1-58234-928-2, 1-58234-928-2. 207 p. (8–12). Novel.

Hazel Green frequently visits Mr. Petrusca, the fishmonger, to see the two large lobsters he has bought for Mr. Trimbel's annual lobster dinner. When someone steals them and leaves a note in code, addressed to Mr. Trimbel, on the tank, Hazel enlists the help of her friend, the "Yak," a mathematical genius, who breaks the code. Together, they solve the mystery of the stolen lobsters. Hazel, then, works out how she can help Mr. Petrusca with his biggest secret—he has not ever learned to read. Hazel is a delightful character in a story that is rich in descriptive language. Other books in the Hazel Green series include *Hazel Green* (2003) and *Have Courage, Hazel Green* (2006). *2001 Children's Book Council of Australia Book of the Year, Younger Readers Shortlist, 2001 Children's Peace Literature Awards Shortlist. hc*

Author was born in England and lives in Australia.

SECRETS, READING, LOBSTERS, INTERPERSONAL RELATIONS, CITY AND TOWN LIFE, MYSTERY AND DETECTIVE STORIES, AUSTRALIA, FICTION

Hume, Lachie. **Clancy the Courageous Cow**. Illustrated by the author. New York, HarperCollins/Greenwillow Books, 2007. Originally published by Scholastic Australia, in 2006. ISBN 978-0-06-117249-6, 0-06-117249-9. 30 p. (4–8). Picture book.

Because he lacks the Belted Galloway breed's characteristic white belt around his middle, Clancy is an outcast until he defeats a Hereford in the annual Cow Wrestling Contest and wins his herd grazing rights to the richest field. Clancy then goes on to convince everyone that they should tear down fences and all be cows together. The clever text and cartoonlike illustrations gently—and with humor—offer the message that being different is sometimes a very good thing and that we are all more alike than we are different. *ca*

Author/illustrator lives in Victoria, Australia.

COWS, INDIVIDUALITY, PREJUDICES, FICTION

Kelleher, Victor. **Dogboy**. Asheville, NC, Front Street, 2006. Originally published by Penguin Group Australia, in 2005. ISBN 978-1-932425-76-5, 1-932425-76-4. 214 p. (14 up). Novel.

The Boy, raised by a dog and shunned by people, lives in two worlds and embarks on a quest to discover who he really is. His gift of divining water sources offers moral choices and insight into the value of friendship and loyalty over riches and fame. *2007 USBBY Outstanding International Books List.*

Author lives in Australia but was born in London and lived in Africa and New Zealand.

Villages, Feral Children, Self-esteem, Dogs, Droughts, Rain and Rainfall, Australia, Fiction

Laguna, Sofie. **Surviving Aunt Marsha**. New York, Scholastic, 2005. Originally published by Scholastic/Omnibus Books Australia, in 2003. ISBN 978-0-439644-85-3, 0-439644-85-2. 202 p. (9–12). Novel.

Eleven-year-old Bettina and her two younger brothers are left with their dreaded Aunt Marsha while their parents take a three-week vacation to Paris. Aunt Marsha doesn't allow Sunday morning television, comic books, or the dog in the house. She even makes them eat kidney pie. When Aunt Marsha gets stuck in the children's tree house, her rescue brings them closer than anyone could have imagined. *2006 USBBY-CBC Outstanding International Books List.* hc, mjw

Author lives in Melbourne, Australia

Aunts, Brothers and Sisters, Australia, Realistic Fiction

Lanagan, Margo. **Black Juice**. New York, HarperCollins/Eos, 2005. Originally published by Allen & Unwin Australia, in 2004. ISBN 978-0-060743-90-1, 0-060743-90-5. 201 p. (14 up). Short Stories.

Black Juice is disconcerting. Although the author's writing is brilliant, the ten short stories are not pleasant, nor are they immediately accessible. They are the stuff of contemplation. "Singing My Sister Down," (3–16) opens the volume and sets the tone. A young woman has been sentenced to death for killing her husband. The twist is *how* she dies. Lanagan perfectly describes her stories' affect: "Those angels . . . was like crushed mint to my brain, breathing open huge new spaces there that I'd not the faintest notion how to fill" (128). *Black Juice* will jostle not only your brain but also your emotions. *2006 USBBY-CBC Outstanding International Books List, Michael L. Printz Honor Book, World Fantasy Award for Best Collection, ALA Best of the Best Books for Young Adults.* lmp

Author lives in Australia.

INTERPERSONAL RELATIONS, CONDUCT OF LIFE, AUSTRALIA, FICTION, SHORT STORIES

Lanagan, Margo. **White Time**. New York, HarperCollins/Eos, 2006. Originally published by Allen & Unwin Australia, in 2000. ISBN 978-0-060743-93-2, 0-060743-93-X. 216 p. (14 up). Short Stories.

Ten provocative and surreal short stories explore a variety of other worlds, dimensions, and states of being. A range of emotions and experiences are deftly woven into the themes of each story. Glorious, compelling prose proves challenging yet unforgettable. *2007 USBBY Outstanding International Books List, ALA Best Book for Young Adults, NYPL Books for the Teen Age.*
Author lives in Australia.
INTERPERSONAL RELATIONS, CONDUCT OF LIFE, AUSTRALIA, FICTION, SHORT STORIES

Lofthouse, Liz. **Ziba Came on a Boat**. Illustrated by Robert R. Ingpen. La Jolla, CA, Kane/Miller Books, 2007. Originally published in English by Penguin/Viking Australia, in 2007. ISBN 978-1-933605-52-4, 1-933605-52-9. 32 p. (6–9). Picture book.

Softly muted illustrations frame this hauntingly simple story of immigration. Ziba makes her journey to a new life on a soggy, old fishing boat. Along the way, she remembers the life she has left behind—the laughter and play with her cousins, the rich aromas of family meals, her mother weaving rugs on the loom, and her father's storytelling. She also recalls the night she and her mother had to flee from their village amid gunfire and angry voices. At the end of their journey, she and her mother hope for freedom and a chance to learn and laugh again. *2008 USBBY Outstanding International Books List. nlh*
Author and illustrator live in Australia.
IMMIGRATION, REFUGEES, DIVERSITY, GLOBAL AWARENESS, AUSTRALIA

Marsden, John. **While I Live: The Ellie Chronicles**. New York, Scholastic, 2007. Originally published by Pan Macmillan Australia, in 2003. ISBN 978-0-439783-18-7, 0-439783-18-6. 299 p. (14 up). Novel.

The war between Australia and New Zealand is over. Ellie, one of many child soldiers from Marsden's *Tomorrow* series, is trying to resume a normal life when a border raid and ambush leave her parents and neighbor dead. Struggling to survive, the teen must fight old enemies and new ones. *2008 USBBY Outstanding International Books List.*
Author lives in Australia.

War–Psychological Aspects, War–Moral and Ethical Aspects, Grief, Self-reliance, Interpersonal Relations, Coming of Age, War, Australia Fiction

Millard, Glenda. **The Naming of Tishkin Silk**. Illustrated by Patrice Barton. New York, Farrar, Straus and Giroux, 2009. Originally published by ABC Books Australia, in 2003. ISBN 978-0-374354-81-7, 0-374354-81-2. 101 p. (9–12). Novel.

Griffin Silk is the youngest boy in an unusual family, and that makes it extraordinarily difficult to blend into his new school. He is teased and tormented, but that is not the only burden he bears. He is only just coming to love his new baby sister, the baby girl without a name, when his mother goes away, taking the baby. It is only when his new friend Layla suggests that he invite his mother home to a naming party that the family begins to heal from their sadness and Griffin realizes that he has uncommon courage and the heart of a lion. *2010 USBBY Outstanding International Books List, New South Wales Premier's Literary Awards (Shortlist), Children's Book Council of Australia Book of the Year Awards Honor Book. djg*
Author lives in Victoria, Australia.
Names, Families, Death, Friendship, Self-acceptance, Australia, Novel, Fiction

Murray, Martine. **Henrietta, There's No One Better**. Illustrated by the author. New York, Scholastic/Arthur A. Levine Books, 2006. Originally published by Allen & Unwin Australia, in 2004. ISBN 978-0-439807-47-0, 0-439807-47-6. 88 p. (7–10). Novel.

Meet breezy, free spirit Henrietta P. Hoppenbeck, who describes herself as "half a hen and half a Rietta" (26). In this imaginative and unusual chapter book, Henrietta tells, in a free-flowing, informal style, about her brother, Albert; her mom and dad; her dog and two pet mice; her best friend, Olive; and the imaginary "Rietta" from the "Island of Rietta," which she, and only she, has visited. The innovative graphic design, with its many black, white, and red cartoon-style illustrations and frequently changing fonts adds to the zaniness of Henrietta's warm, funny narrative about herself and her family life. *Henrietta (the Great Go-Getter)* was published in 2007. *hc*
Author is from Australia.
Individuality, Family Life, Pets, Imagination, Fiction

Niland, Deborah. **Annie's Chair**. Illustrated by the author. New York, Walker Books, 2006. Originally published by Viking/Penguin Australia, in 2005. ISBN 978-0-802780-82-9, 0-80278-082-2. n.p. (2–5). Picture book.

Annie loves her chair. It is her special place, and absolutely no one is allowed in it. When Annie discovers Benny, the family's dog, napping there, she tries everything to get him out. Finally, she resorts to tears. "W-A-A-A-A-A-AAAH!" (n.p.). Benny cries too, then leaps from the chair to give Annie a big cheer-up lick. Annie gives Benny a scolding about never sitting on her chair again, but she softens it by adding ". . . without me" (n.p.). The bold, brightly colored gouache and digital illustrations, featuring the round-headed Annie and her plump, roly-poly pooch, are expressive and toddler pleasing. *2006 Winner of the Children's Book Council of Australia's Children's Book of the Year: Early Childhood. ca*
Author/illustrator lives in Australia.
CHAIRS, DOGS, FICTION

Odgers, Darrel & Sally Odgers. **Jack Russell, Dog Detective Book 3: The Mugged Pug**. Illustrated by Janine Dawson. La Jolla, CA, Kane/Miller Books, 2007. Originally published by Scholastic Australia, in 2005. ISBN 978-1-933605-32-6, 1-933605-32-4. 76 p. (7–9). Novel.

Like *Hank the Cow Dog*, Jack Russell makes great bad jokes en route to solving crimes. Fortunately, Jack offers a glossary to help readers through his more elusive usages (often pawful puns). For example, a "jack-attack" is a full throttle bite on trouser legs: "Very loud. Quite harmless" (6). In his third adventure, Jack is determined to discover the perpetrator of a rash of dog collar thefts. Aided by the flea-prone Foxy the Terrier and the not-so-bright Lord Red the Setter (with support from their human "landlords"), Jack makes short work of crime in a jocular series for transitioning chapter-book readers. The series, which now numbers 11—or more—is titled *Jack Russell: Dog Detective. nlr*
Authors live in Tasmania, Australia.
DOGS, MYSTERY, MYSTERY AND DETECTIVE STORIES, AUSTRALIA, FANTASY

Oliver, Narelle. **Mermaids Most Amazing**. Illustrated by the author. New York, G. P. Putnam's Sons, 2005. Originally published by Onmibus Books/Scholastic Australia, in 2001. ISBN 978-0-399242-88-5, 0-399242-88-0. 32 p. (8–12). Picture book.

The first three chapters provide background information on mermaids and mermen: Where did they come from? Did they ever exist? What mermaid sightings have been recorded? What frauds and tricks have been used to create fakes? Five folktales from around the world provide a sampling of mermaid and mermen lore. The book closes with a list of sources and additional information. Appealing illustrations in hand-colored linocuts and collage enhance the text. *2002 Australian Children's Book Council Notable Book. chs*

Author is from Brisbane, Australia.
MERMAIDS

Ormerod, Jan. **Lizzie Nonsense: A Story of Pioneer Days**. Illustrated by the author. New York, Clarion Books, 2005. Originally published by Little Hare Books Australia, in 2004. ISBN 978-0-618574-93-3, 0-618574-93-X. 32 p. (5–8). Picture book.

While Papa is away for a long time taking the sandalwood he has cut into town, Lizzie, Mama, and the baby are left alone in their little house in the Australian bush. Young Lizzie uses her imagination—what Mama calls her nonsense—to brighten the days of hard work and loneliness until Papa returns. Ormerod's watercolor illustrations for this story, based upon events in her own family's history, beautifully portray the hardships the family faces in the bush and the warmth of the loving relationship that sustains them. *2006 USBBY-CBC Outstanding International Books List, 2006 IBBY Honor List, 2005 BCCB Blue Ribbon Picture Book Award, shortlisted for the Children's Book Council of Australia's 2005 Picture Book of the Year Award. ca, hc*

Author/illustrator grew up in Western Australia and now lives in England.
IMAGINATION, AUSTRALIA, HISTORICAL FICTION

Tan, Shaun. **The Arrival**. Illustrated by the author. New York, Scholastic/ Arthur A. Levine Books, 2007. Originally published by Lothian Books Australia, in 2006. ISBN 978-0-439895-29-3, 0-439895-29-4. n.p. (10 up). Graphic novel.

Each year, authors publish books about one of life's most difficult experiences: moving to a new place. Libby Gleeson's *Half a World Away* (reviewed in this volume) is such a story. In *The Arrival*, however, Shaun Tan extends this painful experience and plunges readers into a world so strange it outstrips imagination. Wordless except for nonlinguistic characters sparsely employed, *The Arrival's* sepia-toned illustrations communicate the story of a man who leaves his family behind when he emigrates to a foreign land. Every facet of the book appears aged; even the cover seems worn and battered. The graphic-novel format and futuristic surrealism will appeal to older audiences and science fiction or fantasy fans. *2008 USBBY Outstanding International Books List, New South Wales Premier's Literary Award, Bologna Ragazzi Award–Special Mention, World Fantasy Artist of the Year, A Publishers Weekly Best Book of 2007, A New York Times Best Illustrated Book of 2007, Booklist Editors' Choice 2007, A School Library Journal Best Book of 2007, Bulletin of the Center for Children's Books Blue Ribbon for Fiction, ALA Notable Children's Book–2008, ALA Top Ten Best Books for Young Adults–2008, ALA Top Ten*

Great Graphic Novels for Teens–2008, Horn Book Fanfare Book 2007, An IRA Notable Book for a Global Society, 2008, 2008 Locus Award, Best Art Book, 2008 Boston Globe–Horn Book Award, special citation for excellence in graphic storytelling, CCBC Choices 2008. lmp

Author lives in Australia.

WORDLESS GRAPHIC NOVELS, EMIGRATION AND IMMIGRATION, FICTION

Tan, Shaun. **Tales from Outer Suburbia**. New York, Scholastic/Arthur A. Levine Books, 2009. Originally published by Allen & Unwin Australia, in 2008. ISBN 978-0-545055-87-1, 0-545055-87-3. 92 p. (12 up). Short Stories.

Shaun Tan's *Tales from Outer Suburbia* forces readers to go beyond normal literary conventions as they read and scrutinize this book. Bewilderment is normal until a second or third conversation with the text—when an extraordinary view of possible worlds unfolds. The fifteen short stories, humorous or haunting but always stimulating, combine Tan's surrealistic art with his ingenious wordsmithing. "Our Expedition" (84–91), told in the first person, offers a modern-day Columbian dilemma: Do the suburbs end where the map ends? The boys' trek through Tan's exaggerated suburban landscapes seems unremarkable until the precipitous final page turn. These stories challenge conventional thinking. *2010 USBBY Outstanding International Books List, Spring 2009 Kid's Indie Next List, 2009 Best Artist–World Fantasy Awards, 2009 CBCA Book of the Year, Publishers Weekly Best Books of 2009, 2009 New York Times Best Illustrated Children's Books, 2009 BCCB Blue Ribbon Book, Washington Post Best Kids' Books of the Year, Booklist Editors' Choices for 2009, 2010 YALSA Best Book for Young Adults, 2010 ALA Notable Book for Children, LA Times Book Prize–Finalist.* jfc, lmp

Author lives in Australia.

AUSTRALIAN CHILDREN'S STORIES, SUBURBAN LIFE, AUSTRALIA, FICTION, SHORT STORIES

Wild, Margaret. **Bobbie Dazzler**. Illustrated by Janine Dawson. La Jolla, CA, Kane/Miller Books, 2007. Originally published by Working Title Press Australia, in 2006. ISBN 978-1-933605-46-3, 1-933605-46-4. 32 p. (3–6). Picture book.

Bobbie, a wallaby, can jump, bounce, skip, and hop, but she cannot do the splits. Although her friends Koala, Wombat, and Possum tell her not to mind, she minds a lot. Bobbie keeps practicing until she succeeds—although initially there is a problem of getting up again. Soon she can do the splits perfectly and, with lots and lots of practice, her friends can, too. This story conveys gentle lessons on the importance of practice in achieving one's goals and the value of friendship. The inclusion of native Australian plants adds to the setting. *ca*

Author and illustrator both live in Australia.

WALLABIES, FRIENDSHIP, AUSTRALIA, FICTION

Wild, Margaret. **Woolvs in the Sitee**. Illustrated by Anne Spudvilas. Asheville, NC, Front Street, 2007. Originally published by Penguin Group Australia, in 2006. ISBN 978-1-590785-00-3, 1-590785-00-2. n.p. (10 up). Picture book.

Black-on-black endpapers establish the mood: childish, unsophisticated sketches of oversized wolves appear only if the light is perfect. The slapdash font and invented spelling challenge readers and hinder their progress. A secondary effect is to slow the page turns so that eyes linger longer on each page—linger to question the perspective from the anonymous narrator's basement window or roof of a building. The text describes a world without water or heat, food, or safety. The expressionistic—verging on surrealistic—illustrations evoke alarm and foreboding. *Woolvs in the Sitee* is a picture book to introduce dystopia to older students. *Children's Book Council of Australia shortlisted book. lmp*

Author and illustrator live in Australia.

DYSTOPIAS, CITY AND TOWN LIFE, ORPHANS, HORROR STORIES, NEIGHBORS, SENIOR WOMEN, MISSING PERSONS, INTERGENERATIONAL RELATIONS, FEAR IN BOYS, COURAGE IN BOYS, FICTION

Zusak, Markus. **I Am the Messenger**. New York, Random House/Alfred A. Knopf, 2005. First published as *The Messenger* by Pan Macmillan Australia, in 2002. ISBN 978-0-375830-99-0, 0-375830-99-5. 357 p. (14 up). Novel.

Nineteen-year-old Ed Kennedy is a loser, and he knows it. As a cabbie, he's nobody. He gambles and drinks with other washouts. His reeking dog is the only thing that distinguishes Ed from the pack. He has no goals, no ambition. One day, he accidentally stops a bank robbery, which changes his life. Then the mystery unfolds: Ed receives a playing card with a scribbled message he instinctively understands is a heroic task only he can fulfill. The cards and messages continue; Ed continues to succeed. In following the clues, Ed discovers fortitude, moral fiber, and realizes he actually cares about life. *2006 USBBY-CBC Outstanding International Books List, 2006 Michael L. Printz Award Honor Book, 2006–Texas TAYSHAS High School Reading List, 2006–ALA Best Books for Young Adults, 2006–Kentucky Bluegrass Master List. lmp*

Author lives in Australia.
SELF-ESTEEM, HEROES, TAXICAB DRIVERS, FICTION

RELATED INFORMATION

Organizations

Australia Centre for Youth Literature

The State Library of Victoria has put together a list of young adult books that "explore the lives and experiences of young people from many cultures and countries."

Woolcott Research, Australia Council, State Library of Victoria, Australian Centre for Youth Literature & Australia Council—Audience and Market Development Division. **Young Australians Reading: From Keen to Reluctant Readers**. Melbourne, Australian Centre for Youth Literature, 2001. 44 p.

A national research report on the reading experience of ten- to eighteen-year-olds: www.slv.vic.gov.au/.

The Children's Book Council of Australia

The Children's Book Council of Australia (CBCA) is a volunteer-run, not-for-profit organization that was established in 1945 and is comprised of branches of individual members who are passionate about children's and young adult literature.

http://cbca.org.au/

IBBY Australia

IBBY Australia has a newly independent status. Australia's national section of IBBY was founded more than forty years ago and has been part of ALIA (Australian Library and Information Association) ever since. IBBY national sections are encouraged to have a representative membership from all areas of children's literature, including librarians and teacher-librarians, writers and illustrators, editors and publishers, booksellers, storytellers, teachers, academics and critics, parents and grandparents, and other enthusiasts. Consequently, IBBY Australia has become an independent organization in order to represent all constituents.

www.ibby.org/index.php?id=405
http://ibbyaustralia.wordpress.com/

Society of Children's Book Writers and Illustrators

SCBWI Australia provides information, support, and encouragement to writers and illustrators of children's books. Founded in 1971, the Society of Children's Book Writers and Illustrators is an international organization with over twenty thousand members and chapters in seventeen countries.

http://scbwi.ampl.com.au

Festivals

The Norman Lindsay Festival of Children's Literature

The Eleventh Annual Norman Lindsay Festival of Children's Literature is held within the grounds of the home of *The Magic Pudding*, the Norman Lindsay Gallery in Faulconbridge. Speakers discuss writing and illustrating for children via workshops and talks.

www.normanlindsay.com.au/events/festival-childrens-literature.php

Australian Children's Book Awards

The Children's Book Council of Australia—Children's Book of the Year Awards

The Children's Book Council of Australia—Notable Books

The Children's Peace Literature Award

The Children's Peace Literature Award encourages the dissemination of information related to peaceful means of resolving conflict and promoting peace at the global, local, and interpersonal level. It is administered by the Australian Group of Psychologists for Peace.

www.psychology.org.au/about/awards/childrens/#s1

The Crichton Award

The Crichton Award aims to recognize and encourage new talent in the field of Australian children's book illustration.

Categories

CBCA Book of the Year: Early Childhood Notables (twenty-one titles) website: http://cbca.org.au/EarlyChildhood_Notables_2010.htm

CBCA Book of the Year: The Eve Pownall Award for Information Books Notables (twenty titles) website: http://cbca.org.au/EvePownall_Notables_2010.htm

CBCA Book of the Year: Older Readers Notables (twenty-two titles) website: http://cbca.org.au/OlderReaders_Notables_2010.htm
CBCA Book of the Year: Picture Book of the Year Notables (thirty titles) website: http://cbca.org.au/PictureBook_Notables_2010.htm
CBCA Book of the Year: Younger Readers Notables (twenty-eight titles) website: http://cbca.org.au/YoungerReaders_Notables_2010.htm

Western Australian Premier's Book Awards

Children's Book Award
For a work of prose and/or poetry written for children. In the case of a book containing original illustrations, the judging panel may determine that the award and prize money be shared between the writer and the illustrator.
Young Adults Award
For a work of prose and/or poetry written for young adults.
www.slwa.wa.gov.au/about_us/premiers_book_awards

Additional Australian Children's Book Awards can be found at www.det .wa.edu.au/education/cmis/eval/fiction/awards/index.htm

Book Supplier

Austral Ed Book Supplier
www.australed.iinet.net.au/
Austral Ed is an Australian book supplier from Adelaide, Australia, specializing in the supply of books to overseas international schools and universities, especially in Asia, the Middle East, and Europe with an emphasis on international and multicultural children's books.

NEW ZEALAND

Knox, Elizabeth. **Dreamhunter: Book One of the Dreamhunter Duet**. New York, Farrar, Straus and Giroux/Frances Foster Books, 2005. Originally published as *The Rainbow Opera: The Dreamhunter Duet* by Faber and Faber Great Britain, in 2005. ISBN 978-0-374318-53-6, 0-374318-53-0. 365 p. (13 up). Novel.

As fifteen-year-old Laura becomes a dreamhunter, one of a special few individuals who can enter the Place to catch dreams and broadcast them to others, her father's disappearance leads her also into a world of intrigue and political corruption. The idea of selling dreams is thought provoking, as is the moral dilemma of the possibility of using a special gift for good or for evil. Knox builds a fascinating fantasy world with all-too-believable and disturbing aspects. *ca*

Author lives in New Zealand.

Teenage Girls, Dreams, Family Life, Fathers and Daughters, Missing Persons, Young Adult Fiction, Fantasy

Mahy, Margaret. **Down the Back of the Chair**. Illustrated by Polly Dunbar. New York, Clarion Books, 2006. Originally published by Frances Lincoln Great Britain, in 2006. ISBN 978-0-618693-95-5, 0-618693-95-5. 29 p. (3–7). Picture book.

When Dad loses his keys and is in danger of missing work, two-year-old Mary suggests he look "down the back of the chair" (n.p.). But as is revealed, there are more things hidden in the chair than can be dreamed of, including a long-lost will and a treasure trove so that a poor family will be poor no more. Lively watercolor and "cut paper" drawings reinforce the surprise and joy experienced over each startling new discovery in this lighthearted rhyming story. *2007 USBBY Outstanding International Books List. Margaret Mahy's honors and awards include the 2006 Hans Christian Andersen Award, the Carnegie Medal awarded in 1982 for* The Haunting *and in 1984 for* The Changeover, *and the Phoenix Award for* The Catalogue of the Universe *in 2005 and for* Memory *in 2007. hc*

Author is from New Zealand, and illustrator is from Great Britain.

Chairs, Lost and Found Possessions, Stories in Rhyme

Mahy, Margaret. **Bubble Trouble**. Illustrated by Polly Dunbar. New York, Houghton Mifflin/Clarion Books, 2009. Originally published by Frances Lincoln Great Britain, in 2008. ISBN 978-0547074-21-4, 0-547074-21-2. 37 p. (2–8). Poetry, Picture book.

In rhyming text that is as bubbly as the story it tells, "Little Mabel blew a bubble, and it caused a lot of trouble . . ." (n.p.). Mabel's bubble bobs and bobbles and wafts Baby away. Baby's bubbly, bobbling adventure as he travels inside the bubble continues until a pebble from a slingshot bursts the bubble. Not to worry, Mabel and her friends save Baby with a "calculated catch" (n.p.). Dunbar's humorous illustrations and the rollicking rhythm of the text

make this a great read-aloud choice. *2010 USBBY Outstanding International Books List 2010, Boston Globe–Horn Book Award Book. Margaret Mahy received the Hans Christian Andersen Award and the Order of New Zealand, the highest honor a citizen can receive. ca*
    Author lives in New Zealand, and illustrator lives in Brighton, England.
    BUBBLES, STORIES IN RHYME, HUMOROUS STORIES, FICTION

Mahy, Margaret. **The Magician of Hoad**. New York, Simon & Schuster/ Margaret K. McElderry Books, 2009. Originally published by HarperCollins New Zealand, in 2008. ISBN 978-1-416978-07-7, 1-416978-07-0. 432 p. (12 up). Novel.
    Three children meet—by chance—on the battlefield where the kingdom of Hoad's peaceful future is being negotiated. The king's third son, the "mad" prince; the princess-heir of a minor province; and an aboriginal boy who's "not right" gradually mature into their predestined roles of royal successors and court magician. Hans Christian Andersen–award winner Margaret Mahy explores the mysteries and complexities of freedom, friendship, fate, treachery, and love in this complex fantasy set in an imaginary kingdom—much like the real world—where peace is not always desired by all. *2010 USBBY Outstanding International Books List. Mahy was awarded the Order of New Zealand and in 2006 won the Hans Christian Andersen Award. She has also twice won the Carnegie Medal, been honored by New Zealand as a Living Icon, and received the Prime Minister's Award for Literary Achievement in Fiction. lmp*
    Author lives in New Zealand.
    MAGICIANS, VISIONS, IDENTITY, BOYS, ROYAL HOUSES, FANTASY FICTION

Markle, Sandra. **Little Lost Bat**. Illustrated by Alan Marks. Watertown, MA, Charlesbridge, 2006. ISBN 978-1-570916-56-4, 1-570916-56-X. 32 p. (6–10). Nonfiction.
    In Bracken Cave, Texas, a female free-tailed bat gives birth and "folds up her tail membrane to keep" her baby "from falling" to the cave floor (n.p.). She nurses him and keeps him safe. But one night, when she is out hunting for food, an owl swoops down, and he is left alone for three days until adopted by another mother bat. Scientific information is embedded in the story, with additional information on the last page. The beautiful illustrations of the bats stand out from the washes of blue-tinted watercolors used for the settings of the cave and night sky. *hc*
    Author is from the United States but now lives in New Zealand.
    TADARIDA BRASILIENSIS, INFANCY, MEXICAN FREE-TAILED BAT

RELATED INFORMATION

Organizations

IBBY New Zealand

The IBBY national section consists of a small committee working within an organization known as Storylines: Children's Literature Trust of New Zealand. Storylines was formed in 2000 following a merger of the Children's Book Foundation (established in 1991) and the Auckland-based Children's Literature Association (established in 1968).

www.ibby.org/index.php?id=443
www.storylines.org.nz/

New Zealand Children's Book Council

The council promotes books and reading by bringing readers, writers, publishers, editors, and schools together. The Book Council also welcomes international visitors to literary New Zealand and presents a literary map of New Zealand.

www.bookcouncil.org.nz/index.html

Special Collections

National Library of New Zealand

www.natlib.govt.nz/collections
77 Thorndon Quay, Pipitea, Wellington, New Zealand
Phone: +64 4 474 3000

The Library has three collections specifically of children's books and a number of other collections that contain children's books or related resources. You can find most items in these collections by searching the National Library Catalogue.

Awards

New Zealand Children's Internet Gateway

This website provides links to New Zealand authors, illustrators, publishers, and other media of interest to young people.

http://christchurchcitylibraries.com/Resources/Kids/StoriesBooks Authors/

New Zealand Children's Literary Prizes and Awards

For a complete listing and links, visit http://christchurchcitylibraries.com/kids/literaryprizes/.

New Zealand Post Children's Book Awards

(AIM Children's Book Awards are now the New Zealand Post Book Awards for Children and Young Adults.)

http://christchurchcitylibraries.com/Kids/LiteraryPrizes/NZPost/

Categories

Best First Book: http://christchurchcitylibraries.com/Kids/Literary Prizes/NZPost/FirstBook/

Book of the Year: http://christchurchcitylibraries.com/Kids/LiteraryPrizes/NZPost/BookoftheYear/

Children's Choice: http://christchurchcitylibraries.com/Kids/Literary Prizes/NZPost/Choice/

Junior Fiction: http://christchurchcitylibraries.com/Kids/Literary Prizes/NZPost/JuniorFiction/

Nonfiction: http://christchurchcitylibraries.com/Kids/LiteraryPrizes/NZ Post/Non-Fiction/

Picture Book: http://christchurchcitylibraries.com/Kids/LiteraryPrizes/NZPost/PictureBook/

Young Adult Fiction: http://christchurchcitylibraries.com/Kids/Literary Prizes/NZPost/SeniorFiction/

Prime Minister's Awards for Literary Achievement

Initiated in 2002, the annual Prime Minister's Awards for Literary Achievement recognize writers who have made a significant contribution to New Zealand literature. The nominated writers should have written a body of work that has received national acclaim and/or international recognition. They may also be working in other genres. The Fiction category includes novels, short stories, plays, children's fiction, and scriptwriting.

http://christchurchcitylibraries.com/Literature/Prizes/PrimeMinister/

Storylines Children's Literature Charitable Trust Awards

www.storylines.org.nz/Awards/Other+awards.html

Awards

Betty Gilderdale Award

Awarded each year to a supporter of children's literature. Prior to 2000, the award was known as the Children's Literature Association's Award for Services to Children's Literature.

www.storylines.org.nz/Awards/Betty+Gilderdale+Award.html

Gaelyn Gordon Award

The award is made annually for a work of fiction seen by Storylines as one that has stood the test of time and that is generally recognized as a successful, enduring children's book. It is for a book by a living author; it must be still in print and have been in print for at least five years. Or, if the book has been reissued after a period of time out of print, then it must have been available for at least two years. The book must not have won a major New Zealand award, but it may have been shortlisted and it may have won an award overseas.

www.storylines.org.nz/Awards/Gaelyn+Gordon+Award.html

Gavin Bishop Award

The Storylines Gavin Bishop Award was established in 2009. The award aims to encourage the publication of new and exciting high-quality picture books from New Zealand illustrators.

www.storylines.org.nz/Awards/Gavin+Bishop+Award.html

Joy Cowley Award

The aim of the award is to foster the publication of excellent picture books by writers permanently resident in New Zealand. The award is open to both published and new writers.

www.storylines.org.nz/Awards/Joy+Cowley+Award.html

Margaret Mahy Award

The award is presented annually to a person who has made a significant contribution to the broad field of children's literature and literacy. This includes writing, illustration, publishing, and academic fields.

www.storylines.org.nz/Awards/Margaret+Mahy+Award.html

Tessa Duder Award

This award is made annually, when merited, to the author of a work of fiction for young adults aged thirteen and above. The writer, who must be a New Zealand resident, must not have had a trade book for children or young adults previously published, nor have one in the process of publication.

www.storylines.org.nz/Awards/Tessa+Duder+Award.html

Tom Fitzgibbon Award

This award is made annually, when merited, to the author of a work of fiction for children between seven and thirteen years of age. The writer, who

must be a New Zealand resident, must not have had a trade book for children previously published, nor have one in the process of publication.
www.storylines.org.nz/Awards/Tom+Fitzgibbon+Award.html

Notable Books List
www.storylines.org.nz/Awards/Notable+Books+List.html

Other Awards
An expanded list of winners and shortlists for these awards is included in *The Inside Story*, the Storylines yearbook, each year.
www.storylines.org.nz/Awards/Other+awards.html

Books

Cowley, Joy & Storylines Children's Literature Trust of New Zealand. **Writing from the Heart: How to Write for Children**. Auckland, NZ, Storylines Children's Literature Trust of New Zealand, 2010. ISBN 978-0-473175-15-3, 0-473175-15-0. 80 p.

Chapters include: Introduction; Plot; Dialogue; Discipline; Humour; Writing for the New Reader; Novels for Children and Young Adults; Picture Books; Plays; Poetry; Putting on Your Editor's Hat; Presentation
CHILDREN'S LITERATURE AUTHORSHIP, TECHNIQUE

CHAPTER NINE

Europe

Poland—Minstral

AUSTRIA

Glatshteyn, Yankev. Translated by Jeffrey Shandler. **Emil and Karl**. New Milford, CT, Roaring Brook Press/A Neal Porter Book, 2006. Originally published as *Emil un Karl* in Yiddish by Farlag M. S. Shklarski New York, in 1940. ISBN 978-1-596431-19-5, 1-596431-19-9. 194 p. (10 up). Novel.

This book, originally written in Yiddish for children who attended Yiddish-speaking schools in the United States, makes a distinct contribution to Holocaust fiction for middle school readers. Set in Vienna in 1940 prior to the U.S. entry into World War II, the story revolves around the friendship of two young boys, one Jewish and one non-Jewish. Separated from their families, the boys must survive alone amid the terrifying events that are occurring. This book presents a balanced perspective, with the victims including both Jews and non-Jews and several Austrian characters assisting the two boys. *ebf*

Author, who was born in Poland and died in 1971, was one of the leading figures in Yiddish literature in New York City.

WORLD WAR II (1939–1945), AUSTRIA, BEST FRIENDS, JEWS, RIGHTEOUS GENTILES IN THE HOLOCAUST, HISTORICAL FICTION

Winter, Jonah. **The 39 Apartments of Ludwig van Beethoven.** Illustrated by Barry Blitt. New York, Random House/Schwartz & Wade Books, 2006. ISBN 978-0-375836-02-2, 0-375836-02-0. 40 p. (6–10). Picture book.

This quirky look at Beethoven's frequent moves from apartment to apartment emphasizes the humorous side of the composer's chaotic life. No concrete historical evidence explains how Beethoven's heavy, legless pianos were moved, so the author creates some fantastical yet sometimes believable methods. Young readers will enjoy the logistical fun, and, at the same time, they will be introduced to the tumultuous elements of this composer's stressful life. The pen and ink drawings depict the composer with wild, frazzled hair and a scowling mouth. The author's note at the end attempts to clarify which elements in the story are true and which are fictional, but some readers may still be left confused. *nrz*

Author lives in Pittsburgh, Pennsylvania.

BEETHOVEN, LUDWIG VAN, 1770–1827, PIANOS, APARTMENTS, MOVING, AUSTRIA, HISTORICAL FICTION

RELATED INFORMATION

Organizations

IBBY Austria

www.ibby.org/index.php?id=406

Jella Lepman's cofounder of IBBY, Richard Bamberger, was responsible for helping to establish the Austrian section of IBBY in 1953. IBBY Austria is an amalgam of children's book-related organizations:

- The International Institute for Children's Literature and Reading Research: www.jugendliteratur.net
- Interest Group of the Authors of Children's and Juvenile Literature
- Association of Children's Book Publishers: www.buecher.at
- Austrian Federation of Public Libraries: www.bvoe.at/en/
- Buch.Zeit Wels (a center on books and reading promotion in the Upper Austrian province): www.buchzeit.at/
- Graphic Design Austria (GDA): www.designaustria.at/
- Austrian Research Society on Children's and Juvenile Literature: http://biblio.at/oegkjlf
- Austrian Children's Book Club: www.buchklub.at/. The purpose: "the furthering of good juvenile literature and the elimination of poor reading materials." Approximately 90 percent of all Austrian school children were enrolled in 1972, only twenty-five years after the organization was founded (http://muse.jhu.edu/journals/chl/summary/v003/3.lederer.html).
- Austrian Library Service: www.obvsg.at/
- Study and Information Centre on Children's Literature and the Association of Translators: www.jugendliteratur.net/

Other Organizations

STUBE
A function of the Archdiocese of Vienna for studying and discussing kinder-und jugendliteratur.
www.stube.at

Awards

DIXI Children's Literature Prize
www.kinderliteraturpreis.at (German only)

Österreichischer Kinder- und Jugendbuchpreis/Austrian Children's and Youth Book Prize
www.buchklub.at/Buchklub/Service/Oesterreichischer-Kinder-und -Jugendbuchpreis.html (German only)

Book Festivals

Buch Wien: Vienna International Book Fair and Reading Festival
Occurs in November, originated in 2008
www.buch-messe.at/en/index.html

Publications

Tausend und ein Buch (*A Thousand and One Books*) is published four times a year in German by IBBY Austria. It offers professional articles on children's literature.

Print and Online Resources

"History of Austrian Children's Literature from 1800 to the Present." *Book-bird*, summer 1998 issue.

The twenty-three prominent contributors represented in this volume consider the themes, genres, authors, and artists that have made Austrian children's literature one of the world's most interesting and diverse traditions. A wealth of illustrations, many in color, and extensive bibliographic references enhance the value of this first-ever history of Austrian children's books. The essays are based on papers presented at a conference that took place at Schloss Rauischholzhausen, October 8–11, 1995.

BELARUS

Manushkin, Fran. **How Mama Brought the Spring**. Illustrated by Holly Berry. New York, Penguin/Dutton Children's Books, 2008. Originally published as *Grandma Beatrice Brings Spring to Minsk* by Hyperion, in 2005. ISBN 978-0-525420-27-9, 0-525420-27-4. 32 p. (5–8). Picture book.

Rosie is sick of winter and doesn't want to get out of bed. But she perks right up when Mama begins to tell her a story about when her grandmother was a little girl in Minsk. How did Grandma Beatrice lure her mother out of bed? First with song: "We have the eggs and the milk and the cheese . . ."; next some mixing; then some cooking. And as the kitchen warms and the toasty bundles come out of the pan, they enjoy a delicious blintz. The recipe is included in this cozy tale of a delightful family tradition, and the book is illustrated with folk-style pictures. *Kirkus Starred Review, 2009 CCBC Choices. djg*

Author and illustrator are from the United States.

Blintzes, Winter, Grandmothers, Family Life, Belarus, Fiction

BELGIUM

Moeyaert, Bart. Translated by Wanda Boeke. **Brothers: The Oldest, the Quietest, the Realest, the Farthest, the Nicest, the Fastest, and I.** Illustrated by Gerda Dendooven. Asheville, NC, Front Street, 2005. Originally published as *Broere: De Oudste, de Stilste, de Echtste, de Verste, de Liefste, de Snelste, en Ik* in Flemish by Querido The Netherlands, in 2000. ISBN 978-1-932425-18-5, 1-932425-18-7. 163 p. (12 up). Autobiography.

Moeyaert's *Brothers* contains forty-two brief stories about growing up in Belgium in the late 1960s and early 1970s as the youngest of seven brothers. Day-to-day family events as well as the adventures and misadventures of the siblings are viewed through the eyes of the youngest. The personalities of the seven brothers, as suggested in the subtitle, are revealed in the stories, which were originally published in a Belgian magazine on literature and culture. Family photographs are included in the endpapers. *Brothers* will be appreciated most by fans of this award-winning author. *Awarded the Woutertje Pieterse Prijs in 2001. ca*

Author and illustrator live in Belgium. Illustrator was nominated for the Hans Christian Andersen award in 1996.

Family Life–Belgium, Brothers, Fiction

Moeyaert, Bart. Translated by Wanda Boeke. **Dani Bennoni: Long May He Live.** Asheville, NC, Front Street, 2008. Originally published as *Dani Bennoni, Lang Zal Hij Leven* in Flemish by E. M. Querido's Uitgeverij B.V. The Netherlands, in 2004. ISBN 978-1-932425-97-0, 1-932425-97-7. 93 p. (14 up). Novel.

Bing wants to learn soccer from the great local player, Dani, so that he can impress his older brother, Mone, when he returns from war. Dani refuses, so Bing creates a dangerous game between Dani and the local girls in an attempt to have them pressure Dani to be his teacher. When Dani is drafted into military service, it is considered a just punishment for his cruel treatment of Bing. Homosexual innuendos suggest this is a book for older audiences. *Author is the youngest nominee for the Hans Christian Andersen Medal. He has been nominated four times for the Hans Christian Andersen Medal and three times for the Astrid Lindgren Memorial Medal. pwc*

Author lives in Belgium.

INTERPERSONAL RELATIONS, REVENGE, SOCCER, WAR, BELGIUM, HISTORI-
CAL FICTION

Norac, Carl. **My Daddy Is a Giant**. Illustrated by Ingrid Godon. New York,
Clarion Books, 2005. Originally published by Macmillan Children's Books
Great Britain, in 2004. ISBN 978-0-618443-99-4, 0-618443-99-1. 29 p.
(0–5). Picture book.

A little boy describes how his father seems to be "a giant" who towers
above him. Larger than life, his father is tall enough for clouds to "sleep"
on his "shoulders" (11) and for "birds" to nest "in his hair" (17). But as
strong and invincible as his father appears, the boy can "beat" his father at
"marbles" (21) and experiences him as a gentle protector. Their relative sizes
are depicted in large format paintings in "paint and pastels," in which the
figure of the father, viewed from below, fills much of the page in comparison
to his small son. *hc*

Author was born in Belgium but now lives in France; illustrator lives in Belgium.
FATHERS AND SONS, SIZE PERCEPTION, FICTION

Norac, Carl. Translated by Elisa Amado. **Monster, Don't Eat Me!** Illustrated
by Carll Cneut. Toronto, Groundwood Books/House of Anansi Press, 2006.
Originally published as *O Monster, Eet Me Niet Op!* in Dutch by Uitgeverij
De Eenhoorn Belgium, in 2006. ISBN 978-0-888998-00-2, 0-888998-00-7.
32 p. (4–8). Picture book.

Alex the pig's mother scolds him for eating between meals and orders him
to take a bath. On his way to the river, Alex meets his match at the raspberry
bushes: a monster that eats everything in his path. Alex cries, "Monster,
don't eat me!" and tricks the beast until eventually, the monster's patience
runs out and its hunger increases. Just as it opens its mouth to swallow Alex,
the monster's mother appears, scolds the monster for eating between meals,
and orders it to take a bath. This amusing story reminds us that all mothers
and sons share common struggles, despite their size or species. *nrz*

Author lives in Belgium.
ANIMALS, MOTHERS AND SONS, GREED, FANTASY, BELGIUM

Robberecht, Thierry. **Sam Is Never Scared**. Illustrated by Philippe Goos-
sens. New York, Clarion Books, 2006. Originally published as *Benno is Nooit
Bang* in Dutch by Clavis Uitgeverij The Netherlands, in 2005. ISBN 978-0-
618732-78-4, 0-618732-78-0. 29 p. (3–5). Picture book.

In contrast to his friend, Max, who is afraid of lots of things, dog-child Sam
appears to be fearless. Sam, however, does get scared at night, although he

would never tell his friends about this. One day Sam is scared to tears when a spider lands on his hand, and it is Max who bravely removes it. Now Sam has a new fear. Will Max tell everyone? Dad reassures Sam that everyone is afraid of something, Max doesn't tell about Sam's crying, and Sam has learned important lessons about owning up to one's fears and about friendship. *ca*

Author and illustrator live in Belgium.

FEAR, FRIENDSHIP, FICTION

Spillebeen, Geert. Translated by Terese Edelstein. **Kipling's Choice**. Boston, Houghton Mifflin, 2005. Originally published as *Kiplings Keuze* in Dutch by Averbode Belgium, in 2002. ISBN 978-0-618431-24-3, 0-618431-24-1. 147 p. (12 up). Novel.

In 1915 as he lies dying in Loos, France, on the field of his first battle, Rudyard Kipling's eighteen-year-old son, John, remembers his childhood preparation for service to his country and the carefree days before the Great Picnic turned out to be something quite different. *2006 USBBY-CBC Outstanding International Books List, 2006 ALA Best Book for Young Adults, 2005 Bulletin Blue Ribbon Book.*

Author lives in Izegem, Belgium.

FATHERS AND SONS, JOHN KIPLING (1897–1915), RUDYARD KIPLING (1865–1936), DEATH, BATTLE OF LOOS-EN-GOHELLE FRANCE–1915, WORLD WAR I (1914–1918), FRANCE, WAR FICTION

RELATED INFORMATION

Organizations

Foundation for Flemish Literature: This organization develops and implements literary policy. www.fondsvoordeletteren.be

IBBY Belgium (French Branch)
www.ibbyfrancophone.be

IBBY Belgium—IBBY Flanders (Flemish Branch)
www.stichtinglezen.be
The Flemish Branch of IBBY–Belgium is located in Antwerp.

Organization for the Support of French-speaking Students: Québec/Wallonie-Bruxelles www.oqwbj.org/

Stichting Lezen / Focuspunt Jeugdliteratuur (the Reading Association/ Center for Children's Literature)

www.stichtinglezen.be

The Center has a complete collection of children's books by Flemish authors, illustrators, and translators published after 1976. In addition, the Center has a fine collection of specialized literature in the field of children's books and reading promotion, ranging from reference works and monographs, periodicals, congress reports, exhibition catalogues, and cuttings collections.

Awards

La Petite Fureur de Lire

www.fureurdelire.cfwb.be/

Prix Ado-Lisant

www.librarything.com/bookaward/Prix+Ado-Lisant

Prix Bernard Versele

www.prix-litteraires.net/prix/480,prix-bernard-versele.html

Prix "Et-lisez-moi"

www.et-lisez-moi.be/

Prix Farniente

www.prixfarniente.be/

Prix LIBBYLIT

www.ricochet-jeunes.org/les-prix/pays/belgique/prix/207-prix-libbylit

Les prix en littérature jeunesse: Lire à deux c'est mieux! (Read Two Is Better)

www.ricochet-jeunes.org/les-prix/pays/belgique/prix/136-lire-agrave -deux-c-est-mieux

Prix Lydia Chagoll

www.kbs-frb.be/call.aspx?id=209662&LangType=2060

Prix Tactus

www.ricochet-jeunes.org/les-prix/pays/france/prix/43-prix-tactus

Online Resources

Book Quest site for children
www.boekenzoeker.org

Villa Kakel Bont: A website that provides news about children's books, authors, illustrators, and translators.
www.villakakelbont.be

Places to Visit

Le Wolf: La Maison de la Littérature de Jeunesse
www.lewolf.be/en/page/1.aspx

BULGARIA

Kyuchukov, Hristo & Ian F. Hancock. **A History of the Romani People**. Honesdale, PA, Boyds Mills Press, 2005. ISBN 978-1-563979-62-0, 1-563979-62-4. 32 p. (7–12). Picture book.
See "Global" for description.

CZECH REPUBLIC

Pacovská, Květa. Translated by Anthea Bell. **The Little Flower King**. Illustrated by the author. New York, Penguin Young Readers Group/Minedition, 2007. Originally published as *Der Kleine Blumenkönig* in German by Van Holkema & Warendorf The Netherlands, in 1992. ISBN 978-0-698400-54-2, 0-698400-54-2. 40 p. (4–8). Picture book.
The Little Flower King was lonely. He planted tulips, but still "his heart was empty and full of longing" (n.p.). After an exhaustive search, the king found a princess and they were married the same day. Now the Little Flower King is "as happy as the day is long" (n.p.). Andersen Award–winner Pacovská's Picasso-like illustrations transform this simple fairy tale into an amazingly complex visual delight. Using layers of primary colors, mirrors, alphanumeric cutouts, and textured papers, she creates art that is both

surrealistic and naïve. The die cut windows—front and back—invite readers into a fairy-tale world of imagination. *Květa Pacovská is the 1992 recipient of the Hans Christian Andersen Award for Illustration.* lmp

Author/illustrator lives in Prague, Czechoslovakia.

FAIRY TALES, KINGS, QUEENS, RULERS, FICTION WITH DIE CUTS

Sís, Peter. **The Wall: Growing Up behind the Iron Curtain**. Illustrated by the author. New York, Farrar, Straus and Giroux/Frances Foster Books, 2007. ISBN 978-0-374347-01-7, 0-374347-01-8. 56 p. (9 up). Autobiography.

Between Sís's one-page introduction and his afterword, the author/illustrator paints a personal and poignant portrait of his birthplace, Czechoslovakia, under the control of the Soviet Union until the Iron Curtain fell. Interspersed with his illustrations and brief captions are a sampling of his own journal entries from 1954 to 1977. Most of the illustrations are black-and-white and are punctuated by the symbolic red of Communism and the Soviet regime. Endpapers offer a map of the world with an inset of Czechoslovakia. *2008 ALA Caldecott Honor Book, 2008 ALA Robert F. Sibert Nonfiction Book Medal, ALA Best Books for Young Adults, ALA Notable Children's Books, IRA Notable Books for a Global Society, NCTE Orbis Pictus Recommended List.* nlh

Author grew up in Czechoslovakia and now lives in the United States.

PETER SÍS, AUTHOR AND ILLUSTRATOR (1949–), CHILDHOOD AND YOUTH, CZECH AMERICANS, CZECHOSLOVAKIA HISTORY AND SOCIAL CONDITIONS (1945–1992), AUTOBIOGRAPHY

RELATED INFORMATION

Organizations

IBBY Czech Republic (Czech only)
www.ibby.cz/

Awards

Zlatá stuha/Gold Ribbon Award
The Gold Ribbon Award is given to books for children and youth released in the previous year. The award is a joint activity of the Czech section of IBBY, the Writers Guild, and the Organization of Children's Book Illustrators.

Book Fair

International Book Fair and Literacy Festival: Bookworld Prague (held in the Spring each year)
Prague, Czech Republic
http://bookworld.cz

DENMARK

Bredsdorff, Bodil. **Eidi.** New York, Farrar, Straus and Giroux, 2009. Originally published as *Eidi: Børnene i Kragevigin 2* in Danish by Høst & Son Denmark, in 1993. ISBN 978-0-374312-67-1, 0-374312-67-2. 138 p. (8–12). Novel.

Eidi has made enormous adjustments in her short life, but this latest seems impossible to accept. Her mother Foula has given birth to a baby boy. Not wanting to share her mother, Eidi departs, wearing her "better-luck-next-time" (11) shawl, to help Rossan weave his sheep's wool. Instead, Rossan takes her to market on the far side of the peninsula. Fate intervenes so that Eidi and Rossan must stay in Eastern Harbor longer than expected. Reluctantly, Eidi accepts the surprises she encounters and absconds with an abused orphan, eventually arriving home at Crow Cove. Bodil Bredsdorff has penned an engrossing companion to her 2005 Batchelder Honor Book, *The Crow-Girl. 2010 USBBY Outstanding International Books List, 2010 Mildred L. Batchelder Honor Book. lmp*
Author lives in Denmark.
ORPHANS, DENMARK, FICTION

Rasmussen, Halfdan Wedel. Translated by Marilyn Nelson. **The Ladder.** Illustrated by Pierre Pratt (original illustrations by Kai Matthiessen). Cambridge, MA, Candlewick Press, 2006. Originally published as *Stigen* in Danish by Det Schønbergske Forlag Denmark, in 1969. ISBN 978-0-763622-82-4, 0-763622-82-6. n.p. (4–8). Picture book.

A red ladder roams the countryside looking for companionship. It inadvertently raises the characters it meets up to heaven, and it is sad when they don't come back down. During a storm, though, using a bolt of lightning that "looked exactly like a stair" (n.p.), all the people and animals that climbed the ladder along the way are able to return. Acrylic illustrations provide bold color, directive angles, and sweeping brushstrokes, and fold-out pages emphasize the reach of the ladder. Celebrated American poet Marilyn Nelson gives astounding treatment to this story in verse, maintaining rhyme and style in translation. *2007 USBBY Outstanding International Books List. bef*

Author's poetry is a fundamental part of the children's literary canon in Denmark. He passed away in 2002. Translator lives in the United States and is, herself, a Newbery Honor and Coretta Scott King Award winner; illustrator lives and works in Montreal and Lisbon.

LADDERS, STORIES IN RHYME, FICTION

Toksvig, Sandi. **Hitler's Canary**. New Milford, CT, Roaring Brook Press/A Deborah Brodie Book, 2007. Originally published by Random House/Doubleday Great Britain, in 2005. ISBN 978-1-596432-47-5, 1-596432-47-0. 191 p. (8–12). Novel.

When Germany quietly invades Denmark, Bamse's theatrical parents continue life as if nothing has happened. Mother wows the soldiers on stage, while his father paints sets and creates cartoons. But Bamse and his siblings have other ideas. Orlando and Bamse support the Resistance. Masha, however, falls in love with a German soldier. In the end, the entire family orchestrates an unorthodox plot to save their Jewish neighbors. They follow Mother's suggestion to foil Hitler's armies by doing what they do best. *Hitler's Canary* is based on the author's family stories. *2008 USBBY Outstanding International Books List, National Jewish Book Award Finalist, NYPL Book for Reading and Sharing. nrr*

Author was born in Copenhagen but lives in Great Britain.

WORLD WAR II (1939–1945), JEWS RESCUE, DENMARK HISTORY–GERMAN OCCUPATION (1940–1945), DENMARK, HISTORICAL FICTION

RELATED INFORMATION

Organizations

IBBY Denmark

IBBY Denmark works under the name Selskabet for børnelitteratur (Society for Children's Books). It was founded in 1964. In 2008, The IBBY World Congress was convened in Copenhagen, Denmark. Speeches and papers are available at www.ibby.org/index.php?id=712.

IBBY Denmark publishes the quarterly magazine *Klods Hans* (*Simple Simon*).

www.ibby.dk/

Collections

Centre for Children's Literature (Center for Bornelitteratur)

The Centre for Children's Literature opened in Autumn 1998. It is situated at the Royal Danish School of Educational Studies in connection with the National Library of Education. It is the task of the Centre to create the most favorable conditions for the production and dissemination of and research on literature for children and young people.

www.dpu.dk/site.aspx?p=15970

Danish Agency for Libraries and Media

Danish Agency for Libraries and Media is an agency under the Ministry of Culture and the central government organ for libraries and media.

The National Library of Education

This is one of the largest collections of children's literature in Europe. Librarian Vibeke Stybe started the collection in 1954, and today it consists of approximately eighty thousand volumes: Danish children's literature, a certain amount of non-Danish (especially Nordic) children's literature, cartoons and children's magazines, Danish and non-Danish scholarly literature, and other literature about children's books and Danish and non-Danish journals.

www.cfb.dk

Awards

Klods Hans Award

IBBY Denmark presents the Klods Hans Award, named after Simple Simon. It is the only prize in Denmark that is given to a person who spreads the message about children's books.

Book Awards

Danish Children's Book Prize
Danish School Library Association's Children's Book Award
The Orla Prize

Programs That Promote Books and Reading

The Danish Bookstart Program

The Danish Bookstart Program is the national program that encourages all parents in Denmark to share books with children from as early an age as possible. It offers Bookstart packs of free books and guidance materials. Librarians deliver the packages to families in their homes and explain the benefits of book sharing.

The Bookstart goal is for every child in the program to develop a lifelong love of books.

www.bibliotekogmedier.dk/english/bookstart-program/

FRANCE

Alcantara, Pedro de. **Befiddled**. New York, Random House/Delacorte Press, 2005. ISBN 978-0-385732-65-9, 0-385732-65-1. 179 p. (9–12). Novel.

Becky Cohen, age thirteen, is obsessed with playing the violin, but her widowed mother cannot afford private lessons. At the Y's group lessons, Becky struggles to perform in front of her fellow students and impatient teacher. Her clever younger brother writes and publishes his own newspaper, *The Splinter*, in which he provides hilarious, but sympathetic, commentary on Becky's life. She finally gets help in achieving her goal of obtaining a music scholarship from Mr. Freeman, the handyman at her apartment building. He teaches her to believe in herself when others don't and to discover the music within herself. *bal*

Author lives in France.

Violin, Schools, Music Competitions, African Americans, Fiction

Babin, Claire. Translated by Claudia Zoe Bedrick. **Gus Is a Fish**. Illustrated by Olivier Tallec. New York, Enchanted Lion Books, 2008. Originally published as *Gustave est un Poisson* in French by Adam Biro Jeunesse France, in 2004. ISBN 978-1-592701-01-8, 1-592701-01-9. 26 p. (3–5). Picture book.

As Gus splashes around in the bathtub, his mother compares him to a little fish. Gus's imagination takes over, and he swims out of the tub into a pond with plants, animals, and even a predator fish. A dozen nature words in the story are highlighted. A glossary at the end of the book illustrates the words and provides a short description. *pwc*

Author lives in Paris.
BATHS, FISHES, PONDS, IMAGINATION, FRANCE

Bachelet, Gilles. **My Cat, the Silliest Cat in the World**. New York, Harry N. Abrams Books, 2006. Originally published as *Mon Chat le plus Bête du Monde* in French by Éditions du Seuil France, in 2004. ISBN 978-0-810949-13-3, 0-810949-13-X. n.p. (4–8). Picture book.

The artist's "cat is very fat, very sweet, and very, very silly" (n.p.). He certainly acts like a cat in the way he sleeps, eats, and plays. He is a very clean "cat" but leaves prints all over the artist's work. But is he a cat? He lands on his back rather than on his feet when he falls, and the artist cannot identify his breed. A sense of the absurd is produced by the incongruity between the word *cat* in the text and the humorous illustrations of the artist's pet elephant. *2007 ALSC Notable Book*. hc
Author is from France.
CATS, ARTISTS, ELEPHANTS, HUMOROUS STORIES

Bachelet, Gilles. Translated by Nicholas Elliott. **When the Silliest Cat Was Small**. Illustrated by the author. New York, Harry N. Abrams Books, 2007. Originally published in French by Éditiones du Seuil et Crapule France, in 2006. ISBN 978-0-810994-15-7, 0-810994-15-1. 25 p. (3–6). Picture book.

The narrator, who says he knew nothing about cats before adopting a pet, tells about selecting a kitten from a litter and his silly kitten's adjustment to his new home. It is only from the illustrations that readers know the kitten is actually a baby elephant. Children love it when they think they know something the storyteller seemingly doesn't know, so this book is a read-aloud hit. The clever illustrations will induce giggles from the very first page, which shows a basket of baby elephants with the color markings of cats. Prequel to *My Cat, the Silliest Cat in the World* (2006). ca
Author/illustrator lives in France.
ELEPHANTS, CATS, PETS, FICTION, HUMOROUS STORIES

Banks, Kate. **The Great Blue House**. Illustrated by Georg Hallensleben. New York, Farrar, Straus and Giroux/Frances Foster Books, 2005. ISBN 978-0-374327-69-9, 0-374327-69-6. 32 p. (0–5). Picture book.

The "great blue house" in the countryside is imagined through all the seasons from summer, when children's voices fill the air, to when the family leaves through winter, spring, and to the next summer when they return. The house, however, is neither quiet nor empty when the family is absent, as one is invited to listen to the sounds made, for example, by the "buckle and crack" of the frost and by those who inhabit the house: a mouse, a cat, and a bird. The poetic narrative is accompanied by Impressionist-style paintings of the house and surroundings in predominantly blue and green hues. Still-life paintings depict the interior of the house in glowing colors. *hc*

Author was born in the United States but now lives in the south of France; the illustrator lives in Paris.

DWELLINGS, SEASONS, FICTION

Banks, Kate. **Max's Words**. Illustrated by Boris Kulikov. New York, Farrar, Straus and Giroux/Frances Foster Books, 2006. ISBN 978-0-374399-49-8, 0-374399-49-2. n.p. (8–10). Picture book.

Inspired by his brothers' collections of stamps and coins, Max searches for familiar, favorite, or exciting words from magazines and newspapers. His word collection, contrary to his brothers' collections, is exciting. "When Max put his words together, he had a thought" (n.p.). Max rebuffs his brothers' refusal to trade. "When I have a few more words, I'll have a story" (n.p.). Eventually, his brothers abandon their collections to compose an adventure with Max. Boris Kulikov extends this tale of wish fulfillment through whimsical children observed from unusual perspectives. Sprinkled throughout are words—*exotic, glorious, curious, colorful*—illustrated to signify their meaning. *lmp*

Author lives in the south of France.

LANGUAGE AND LANGUAGES, COLLECTORS AND COLLECTING, STORYTELL-
ING, FICTION, FRANCE

Banks, Kate. **Lenny's Space**. New York, Farrar, Straus and Giroux/Fran-
ces Foster Books, 2007. ISBN 978-0-374345-75-4, 0-374345-75-9. 151 p. (8–11). Novel.

Lenny Brewster is more intelligent than other students in his fourth-grade class. He's also more disruptive—until he meets Muriel, the school counselor. Additionally, he makes a friend, his first real friend, who isn't overwhelmed by his encyclopedic knowledge and curiosity. The problem is that Van, Lenny's new friend, has leukemia and dies during a bone marrow transplant. The angry energy Lenny experiences is redirected when he creates a tower in Van's memory. Muriel tells him, "People continue to live on in . . . things we've done with them and for them" (150). Banks doesn't dwell on Van's death but allows readers to feel the family's pain and Lenny's loss. *Kate Banks has received the Boston Globe-Horn Book Award and the Charlotte Zolotow Award. lmp*

Author lives in the south of France.

SINGLE-PARENT FAMILIES, COUNSELORS, FRIENDSHIP, SCHOOLS, CHILDREN
WITH LEUKEMIA, FICTION

Banks, Kate. **Fox**. Illustrated by Georg Hallensleben. New York, Farrar,
Straus and Giroux/Frances Foster Books, 2007. ISBN 978-0-374399-67-2,
0-374399-67-0. 40 p. (1–5). Picture book.

Art by a talented German-born illustrator distinguishes this lyrical story.
Born in the spring, baby fox grows through the ripening summer, learning
from his mother and father to forage, hunt, and protect himself, until at last
he is ready to live on his own. Impressionistic paintings in lush, harmonious
colors portray the loving fox family and the changing moods of the countryside, from moonlit forest to sun-drenched fields. Little Fox's repeated question, "Am I ready yet?" resonates with children longing for competence. *mac*
Author lives in the south of France; illustrator lives in Paris.
FOXES, ANIMALS, INFANCY, FICTION

Banks, Kate. **Max's Dragon**. Illustrated by Boris Kulikov. New York, Farrar,
Straus and Giroux/Frances Foster Books, 2008. ISBN 978-0-374399-21-4,
0-374399-21-2. n.p. (4–8). Picture book.

Max is the youngest brother and as usual, the brunt of all jokes. When he
shows up in the middle of his brothers' croquet game, trailing an imaginary
cloud dragon and rhyming his words to produce a rainstorm, his brothers
hoot. But Max has the last laugh when everyone takes shelter from the
dragon's storm—under his umbrella. Kulikov's children are real kids, messy
hair, dirty fingernails, Crocs and all. Mix in dragons, dinosaurs, cloud figures,
and silly rhymes, and what do you get? *Max's Dragon* combines all these elements to create a satisfying portion of imaginative play and a healthy dose
of wish fulfillment. *lmp*
Author lives in the south of France.
DRAGONS, IMAGINATION, IMAGINARY PLAYMATES, PLAY, FICTION, FRANCE

Bataille, Marion. **ABC3D**. Illustrated by the author. New York, Roaring
Brook Press/A Neal Porter Book, 2008. Originally published by Jeunesse
Albin Michel France, in 2008. ISBN 978-1-596434-25-7, 1-596434-25-2. 40
p. (6–9). Toy book, Picture book.

Alphabet books are a tricky genre. "Who is the audience?" is a prime
question. *ABC3D* crosses borders well from country to country—there's
no text, and younger to older viewers (even adults) will enjoy it—and the
construction and concept beg for additional viewings. The artistry is in the

simplicity: red, black, or white three-dimensional letters appear or disappear when pages open. One particular flaw—all the letters are uppercase except for two: i and j. In order to spread across the verso and recto, these two letters share the large dot that pops up from the gutter. This won't teach the alphabet but may inspire creativity. *lmp*

Author lives in Paris.

ENGLISH-LANGUAGE ALPHABET BOOKS, TOY AND MOVABLE BOOKS, POP-UP OR MOVABLE ILLUSTRATIONS, FRANCE

Blexbolex. Translated by Claudia Zoe Bedrick. **Seasons**. Illustrated by the author. New York, Enchanted Lion Books, 2010. Originally published as *Saisons* in French by Jeunesse Albin Michel France, in 2009. ISBN 978-1-592700-95-0, 1-592700-95-0. 180 p. (4–8). Picture book.

Readers of all ages will be engaged by the artful design and evocative, nostalgic feelings in the writing and illustrations. Blexbolex's gorgeous artwork and minimal text are distilled to a symbiotic poetry—almost like a form of multimedia haiku. While small children will have fun with the color-saturated art and talking about what is happening in the illustrations, the adult reader is left with a sense of "Yes! Here is someone who sees, really sees, the wonder in the everyday." *Blexbolex received the prestigious Golden Letter Award in 2009 for the world's best book design. lvb*

Author lives in France.

SEASONS, FICTION, CONCEPT BOOK

Bondoux, Anne-Laure. Translated by Anthea Bell. **The Princetta**. New York, Bloomsbury, 2006. Originally published as *La Princetta et le Capitaine* in French by Hachette Jeunesse France, in 2004. ISBN 978-1-582349-24-4, 1-582349-24-X. 430 p. (12 up). Novel.

Princetta Malva of Galnicia is fifteen years old when she escapes from an unwelcome arranged marriage. However, the ship on which she and her maid take passage is not altogether what it seems. Back in Galnicia, Orpheus McBott, who has never captained a ship, convinces the king to name him leader of the marine quest for Malva. Their eventual meeting is less than satisfying because Malva refuses to be rescued. The ensuing adventures send Malva and Orpheus past the veil of reality into unknown worlds. Wisps of classic adventure sagas permeate Bondoux's tale of *The Princetta. lmp*

Author lives in Paris.

PRINCESSES, ADVENTURES, VOYAGES AND TRAVELS, COMING OF AGE, FRENCH TRANSLATED STORIES, FANTASY

Bondoux, Anne-Laure. Translated by Y. Maudet. **Vasco, Leader of the Tribe**. New York, Random House/Delacorte Press, 2007. Originally published as *La Tribu* in French by Bayard Editions Jeunesse France, in 2004. ISBN 978-0-385733-63-2, 0-385733-63-1. 336 p. (9–12). Novel.

Life on the wharf is easy for the young rat Vasco until the day he discovers that most of his tribe has been killed. To escape the humans who are exterminating them, Vasco journeys with a few rodents on a freighter in search of a peaceful place to live. The journey aboard the ship is fraught with danger, as is life in their final destination. After many challenges Vasco is able to establish a safe refuge for his new tribe. *Anne-Laure Bondoux has received France's Prix Sorcières Award. pwc*

Author lives in France.

SURVIVAL, RATS, VOYAGES AND TRAVELS, TOLERATION, SHIPS, QUESTS, ADVENTURE, FRIENDSHIP, ESCAPES, ENEMIES, FRANCE, FANTASY FICTION

Brun-Cosme, Nadine. Translated by Claudia Zoe Bedrick. **Big Wolf & Little Wolf**. Illustrated by Olivier Tallec. New York, Enchanted Lion Books, 2009. Originally published as *Grand Loup & Petit Loup* in French by Père Castor Éditions Flammarion France, in 2005. ISBN 978-1-592700-84-4, 1-592700-84-5. 32 p. (4–8). Picture book.

Big Wolf always lived alone until the day Little Wolf climbs the hill and sits—uninvited—under Big Wolf's tree. Like a shadow, Little Wolf emulates Big Wolf's every move. But it is not until Little Wolf disappears that Big Wolf realizes that, "Without you . . . I was lonely." As the book closes, Little Wolf admits his loneliness too, and we recognize our hope that the friends' adventures will continue. *Big Wolf & Little Wolf* received a Batchelder Honor award for its spare, but evocative, translated text. However, it may be the expressionistic mixed-media illustrations that captivate younger audiences because illustrator Olivier Tallec captures each mood so perfectly. *2010 Batchelder Honor Book. lmp*

Author lives in France; illustrator lives in Brittany.

WOLVES, LONELINESS, PICTURE STORYBOOK, FRANCE

Brun-Cosme, Nadine. Translated by Claudia Zoe Bedrick. **Big Wolf & Little Wolf: The Little Leaf That Wouldn't Fall**. Illustrated by Olivier Tallec. Brooklyn, NY, Enchanted Lion Books, 2009. Originally published as *Grand Loup & Petit Loup: La Petite Feuille qui ne Tombait pas* in French by Père Castor Éditions Flammarion France, in 2007. ISBN 978-1-592700-88-2, 1-592700-88-8. 32 p. (4–8). Picture book.

Little Wolf is fascinated by a small leaf, quite far up in the tree. Big Wolf counsels him to wait—through spring, summer, and fall. But the leaf that looks good enough to taste, shiny enough to be a mirror, and soft enough for his cheek to rest on never falls. As his friend climbs to retrieve the leaf, Little Wolf worries that having it is not worth risking his friend's safety. As he looks up (and Big Wolf stares down) on the crumbling flakes of red and gold—a "rain of gentle stars" (n.p.)—both wolves realize that true friendship often requires taking risks. lmp

Author lives in France; illustrator lives in Brittany.

WOLVES, LEAVES, FRIENDSHIP, FRANCE, TRANSLATED BOOKS, SEQUEL/COMPANION TO BIG WOLF & LITTLE WOLF

Cali, Davide. **The Enemy: A Book about Peace**. Illustrated by Serge Bloch. New York, Random House/Schwartz & Wade Books, 2009. Originally published as *L'Ennemi* in French by Éditions Sarbacane France, in 2007. ISBN 978-0-375-84500-0, 0-375-84500-3. n.p. (all ages). Picture book.

Enemy soldiers shoot at each other from their foxholes while recalling how their "manuals" describe the enemy—a monster who will kill them and their families. Eventually, hunger and cold drive the soldiers from their hiding places, and as one soldier approaches the foxhole of another, each is surprised to find many common items—family pictures and a manual sharing lies about the enemy. The concept of common life experiences and dreams invariably leads to discussions about the origins of peace—and war. Simple sketches on a barren, white battlefield illustrate this tale of the senselessness of war. *2010 USBBY Outstanding International Books List, 2010 NCSS/CBC Notable Children's Trade Books in the Field of Social Studies*. jm

Author lives in Genoa, Italy; illustrator lives in New York.

SOLDIERS, WAR, ENEMIES, FICTION

Donnio, Sylviane. Translated by Leslie Martin. **I'd Really Like to Eat a Child**. Illustrated by Dorothée De Monfreid. New York, Random House, 2007. Originally published as *Je Mangerais Bien un Enfant* in French by l'École des Loisirs France, in 2004. ISBN 978-0-375-83761-6, 0-375-83761-2. n.p. (4–8). Picture book.

Achilles, a teeny-tiny crocodile, tired of eating bananas for breakfast, wants to eat a child instead. His parents offer more bananas, sausage, and even chocolate cake, but Achilles is determined. He heads for the river where he finds a little girl, bares his teeth, and attacks. The girl finds him scrawny, tickles him, and tosses him into the river. Hungrier than ever, Achilles runs home to eat more bananas so he will grow big enough to eat a child. Simple comic drawings bring the story to life. *mjw*

Author and illustrator live in France.

FOOD HABITS, CROCODILES, SIZE, FANTASY FICTION

Faller, Régis. **The Adventures of Polo**. Illustrated by the author. New Milford, CT, Roaring Brook, 2006. Originally published as *Voyage de Polo* in French by Bayard Éditions Jeunesse France, in 2002. ISBN 978-1-59643-160-7, 1-59643-160-1. 75 p. (4–8). Picture book.

Polo, an adventurous little dog, straps on a small backpack filled with useful supplies and leaves his island tree house to see the world. Polo travels from sea to land to air, and even to the moon. When Polo gets in a tight spot (and he gets into a lot of them), he reaches into his backpack and finds just the right thing to allow him to continue safely on his adventure. Faller uses different-sized, brightly colored cartoon panels to tell this imaginative story without words. Other books in the series are *Polo and the Magic Flute*, *Polo and Lily*, *Polo and the Magician!*, *Polo and the Dragon*, *Polo: The Runaway Book*. *2007 USBBY Outstanding International Books List. ca*

Author lives in Paris.

DOGS, ADVENTURE AND ADVENTURERS, FICTION, STORIES WITHOUT WORDS

Fombelle, Timothée de. Translated by Sarah Ardizzone. **Toby Alone**. Illustrated by François Place. Somerville, MA, Candlewick Press, 2009. Originally published as *Tobie Lolness* in French by Gallimard Jeunesse France, in 2006. ISBN 978-0-7636-4181-8, 0-7636-4181-2. 384 p. (9 up). Novel.

Toby Lolness used to live happily and peacefully with his mother and father, a brilliant scientist. But Professor Lolness's greatest and most recent discovery disrupts Toby's universe. He has announced to the world that the tree they call home is alive. You see, Toby, his family, and the other people in his world are measured in millimeters and literally live in a tree. *Toby Alone* is chockablock with action, intrigue, and marvelous—if tiny—characters who live in an allegorical world with environmental hazards and villains that threaten to destroy the very life that sustains them. *The book won the Marsh Award (Great Britain) for children's literature in translation, France's Prix Sorcières, and Italy's Premio Andersen Prize. lmp*

Author lives in France.

TREES, FATHER AND CHILD, ENVIRONMENT, FANTASY, FICTION

Fromental, Jean-Luc. **365 Penguins**. Illustrated by Joëlle Jolivet. New York, Harry N. Abrams Books, 2006. ISBN 978-0-8109-4460-2, 0-8109-4460-X. 44 p. (4–8). Picture book.

In this idiosyncratic story about global warming, a family is surprised when a penguin is delivered anonymously. By year's end, 365 penguins have arrived. The blue, orange, black, and white illustrations on oversized pages show the family coping as the uninvited guests take over their home and everyday lives. The text includes the arithmetic used in working out the food required and how best to store the penguins. When Uncle Victor, an ecologist, arrives, he explains that it was his way of sending the endangered penguins from their diminishing territory in the South Pole to the North Pole. *Boston Globe-Horn Book Picture Book Honor Award, 2007.* hc

Author and illustrator are from France.

PENGUINS, GIFTS, ARITHMETIC, FICTION

Fromental, Jean-Luc. Translated by Thomas Connors. **Oops!** Illustrated by Joëlle Jolivet. New York, Abrams Books for Young Readers, 2010. Originally published as *Oups!* in French by Hélium France, in 2009. ISBN 978-0-8109-8749-4, 0-8109-8749-X. 32 p. (4–8). Picture book.

The Parisian family in *Oops!* is trying to get to Djerba for their summer vacation. Given the title, it is clearly not going to be a smooth trip to the airport, and all manner of madness ensues—runaway Ferris wheels, swarms of angry bees, a police helicopter chase, and friendly aliens who return a bar of soap. Jolivet's vibrant illustrations spill off the pages and invite readers to try to find silly details everywhere and predict what will happen next. Another winner from the team that created *365 Penguins*. lvb

Author lives in France; illustrator lives and works in Ivry-sur-Seine, France.

VACATIONS, VOYAGES AND TRAVELS, HUMOROUS STORIES, PARIS, FRANCE, FICTION

Gay, Marie-Louise & David Homel. **On the Road Again! More Travels with My Family**. Toronto, Groundwood Books/House of Anansi Press, 2008. ISBN 978-0-88899-846-0, 0-88899-846-5. 141 p. (9–12). Novel.

This hilarious sequel to *Travels with My Family* is narrated by Charlie, a young boy whose adventuresome parents decide to move the family to a small French village for the year. Through Charlie's eyes, we see the differences between his big-city life in Montreal and the rural life he experiences, right down to the annual bull run through the village streets. Initially reluctant to leave Montreal, Charlie makes fast friends and comes to love his new home; before he knows it, it's time to return to Montreal. *ss*

Authors live in Montreal.

VILLAGES, FAMILIES, BROTHERS, PARENT AND CHILD, FRANCE, FICTION

Goscinny, Rene. Translated by Anthea Bell. **Nicholas**. Illustrated by Jean-Jacques Sempe. New York, Phaidon Press, 2005. Originally published as *Le Petit Nicolas* in French by Éditions Denoël France, in 1960. ISBN 97-8-071484-529-6, 0-714845-29-9. 126 p. (9–12). Novel.

For decades children in France have enjoyed the antics of Nicholas and his pals. Nineteen small adventures written by the author made famous by his *Asterix* series distinguish this introduction to the hapless school friends. Nicholas narrates his misadventures, and they are made all the more humorous by Jean-Jacques Sempe's many line drawings. Other books in the series include *Nicholas Again* (2006), *Nicholas on Holiday* (2006), *Nicholas on Vacation* (2006), *Nicholas and the Gang* (2007). *2006 Batchelder Honor Book. djg*

Author (1926–1977) was born in Paris and lived in Buenos Aires and New York before returning to France.

HUMOROUS STORIES, BEHAVIOR, SCHOOL STORIES, FRANCE, FRENCH TRANSLATIONS INTO ENGLISH, SHORT STORIES, FICTION

Goscinny, Rene. Translated by Anthea Bell. **Nicholas and the Gang**. Illustrated by Jean-Jacques Sempe. New York, Phaidon Press, 2007. Originally published as *Le Petit Nicolas et les Copains* in French by Éditions Denoël France, in 1960. ISBN 978-0-714847-88-7, 0-714847-88-7. 112 p. (9–12). Novel.

Nicholas and the Gang is a continuation of the beloved French series about Nicholas and his friends. The sixteen episodic chapters, each a self-contained story, are wonderful for reading aloud. The topics are universal and will appeal to most readers. Chapters include: "Matthew Has Glasses," "Going Camping," "Collecting Stamps," "A Rainy Day," "Playing Chess," "The New Bookstore," "Rufus Is Sick," and "Athletics." *2008 Batchelder Honor Book. djg*

Author (1926–1977) was born in Paris and lived in Buenos Aires and New York before returning to France.

HUMOROUS STORIES, BEHAVIOR, BIRTHDAY PARTIES, SCHOOL STORIES, FRIENDSHIP, FRANCE, FRENCH TRANSLATIONS INTO ENGLISH, SHORT STORIES, FICTION

Greif, Jean-Jacques. Translated by the author. **The Fighter**. New York, Bloomsbury Children's Books, 2006. Originally published as *Le Ring de la Mort* in French by l'Ecole des Loisirs France, in 1998. ISBN 978-1-58234-891-9, 1-58234-891-X. 211 p. (12 up). Novel.

    See Poland for description.

Herbauts, Anne. Translated by Claudia Zoe Bedrick. **Monday**. Illustrated by the author. New York, Enchanted Lion Books, 2006. Originally published as *Lundi* in French by Casterman France, in 2004. ISBN 978-1-59270-057-8, 1-59270-057-8. 36 p. (4–8). Picture book.

    Monday is joined by his friends Lester Day and Tom Morrow. They drink tea and play the piano. Each of the seasons arrives with a poem describing the season. When winter arrives, Monday is slowly, over several pages, covered with snow until he completely disappears. When Monday returns, he is just a little different. The book cover has a cutout in the shape of a house. There are several pages in the story that are embossed in various designs. *pwc*

    Author divides her time between Belgium and France.

    TIME, FRIENDSHIP, FANTASY FICTION, FRANCE

Hoestlandt, Jo. Translated by Y. Maudet. **Gran, You've Got Mail!** Illustrated by Aurélie Abolivier. New York, Delacorte Press, 2008. Originally published as *Mémé t'as du Courrier!* in French by Editions Nathan France, in 1999. ISBN 978-0-385-73565-0, 0-385-73565-0. 112 p. (9–12). Novel.

    Annabelle reluctantly begins writing letters to her great-grandmother as a means to improve her keyboard skills, but she must send hard copies since her great-grandmother does not use e-mail. Through a series of their letters, readers see how their relationship grows, how her great-grandmother becomes someone Annabelle can confide in, and even though they may not be the same age, just like all of us, they share similar emotions and experiences. *si*

    Author lives in France.

    GREAT-GRANDMOTHERS, LETTERS, FRANCE, FICTION

Jesset, Aurore. Translated by Katja Alves. **Loopy**. Illustrated by Barbara Korthues. New York, NorthSouth Books, 2008. Originally published as *Komm zurück, Schnuffel* in German by NordSüd Verlag Switzerland, in 2008. ISBN 978-0-7358-2175-0, 0-7358-2175-5. 28 p. (3–6). Picture book.

    Loopy is a long-eared stuffed toy that the child narrator simply must have at bedtime. When she discovers Loopy has been left behind at the doctor's office and her mother says it is too late to retrieve him, the narrator imagines all kinds of frightening situations that could happen to Loopy and to herself—should she be daring enough to rescue him. Fortunately, the doctor comes by about then to deliver her Loopy home. Pairing this book with Mo Willem's *Knuffle Bunny Free* (2010) offers opportunities to highlight similarities in children's feelings along with differences in the cultural contexts. *ss*

    Author lives in Paris; illustrator lives in Germany.

    Soft Toys, Fiction

Lacombe, Benjamin. **Cherry and Olive**. Illustrated by the author. New York, Walker Books, 2007. Originally published as *Cerise Griotte* in French by Seuil Jeunesse France, in 2006. ISBN 978-0-8027-9707-0, 0-8027-9707-5. 32 p. (4–8). Picture book.

    Shy, plump, and lonely, Cherry longs to have a friend. She finds a very good one when she discovers that the owner of Olive, the shy, plump, wrinkly, and lost puppy she has been caring for at her father's animal shelter, is Angelo, a popular classmate. Lacombe's use of perspective, color, and detailing in his stylized illustrations for this beautifully designed book is intriguing; he deftly shows the special relationship that develops between Cherry and Olive. *2008 USBBY Outstanding International Books List, a Book Sense Pick. ca*

    Author lives in Paris.

    Bashfulness, Dogs, Animal Shelters, Teasing, Friendship, France, Translated Books, Fiction

Lord, Michelle. **Little Sap and Monsieur Rodin**. Illustrated by Felicia Hoshino. New York, Lee & Low Books, 2006. ISBN 978-1-58430-248-3, 1-58430-248-8. n.p. (8–14). Picture book.

    See Asia/Cambodia for description.

Louis, Catherine. Translated by MaryChris Bradley. **My Little Book of Chinese Words**. Illustrated by Shi Bo (calligraphy). New York, North-South Books, 2008. Originally published as *Mon Imagier Chinois* in French by Editions Philippe Picquier France, in 2004. ISBN 978-0-7358-2174-3, 0-735821-74-7. (6 up). Picture book.

    See Asia/China for description.

Luciani, Brigitte. Translated by Carol Klio Burrell. **Mr. Badger and Mrs. Fox #1, the Meeting**. Illustrated by Eve Tharlet. Minneapolis, MN, Lerner/ Graphic Universe, 2010. Originally published as *La Rencontre (Monsieur Blaireau et Madame Renard: 1)* in French by Dargaud France, in 2006. ISBN 978-0-7613-5625-7, 0-7613-5625-8. 32 p. (4–8). Graphic Novel.

Mr. Badger and Mrs. Fox are single parents who decide to combine their two families, despite the protests of their children who think that "badgers and foxes are not meant to live together" (23) because they're different animals. Ultimately, plotting and attempting to break their parents up is what brings the little badgers and their new fox sister together. Although the stepsiblings in this graphic novel for developing readers are woodland animals, their new sibling rivalry and resistance to changes in family structure will resonate with children from blended families. *lvb*

Author was born in Hanover, Germany, and now lives in France; illustrator lives in France.

SINGLE-PARENT FAMILIES, BROTHERS AND SISTERS, BADGERS, FOXES, TOLERATION, GRAPHIC NOVELS, BEGINNING READERS, FICTION

Mandine, Selma. Translated by Michelle Williams. **Kiss Kiss**. Illustrated by the author. New York, Golden Books, 2009. Originally published as *Bisous, Bisous* in French by Editions Philippe Auzou France, in 2008. ISBN 978-0-375-86431-5, 0-375-86431-8. n.p. (0–5). Picture book.

What is a kiss? Can anyone explain? A tiny tot attempts to describe the variety of kisses he has experienced: mother's—"supersoft, like cuddly wool," (n.p.) and father's—"sometimes, just like a cactus, it prickles . . . it tickles!" (n.p.). Metaphors and similes classify, clarify, and compare every imaginable kiss to chocolate, lollipops, cotton candy, and more. All of a toddler's significant friends and family are included in this lecture—appropriately presented to his menagerie of stuffed animals. The illustrations exude love and dreams—the perfect ambience for a lap book. *lmp*

Author was born and educated in Hong Kong but now lives in France.

KISSING, FICTION

McCaughrean, Geraldine. **Cyrano**. Orlando, FL, Harcourt, 2006. Originally published as *Cyrano: From the Play by Edmond Rostand: For Anyone Who's Ever Been Hopelessly in Love* by Oxford University Press Great Britain, in 2006. ISBN 978-0-15-205805-0, 0-15-205805-2. 114 p. (14 up). Novel.

In seventeenth-century France, long-nosed Cyrano de Bergerac, poet and master swordsman, secretly loves his beautiful cousin Roxane. Cyrano writes passionate love letters to her but, knowing that he is too ugly to win her, he gives them to Christian, a handsome rival, so that he may woo her. McCaughrean's retelling of Edmond Rostand's play is superb. The setting of the story and the major players, Cyrano, Roxane, Christian, and the Comte de Guice, are clearly delineated. This is a classic love story that will appeal to today's young adults because it is so beautifully crafted. *ca*

Author lives in Great Britain.

CYRANO DE BERGERAC (1619–1655), EDMOND ROSTAND (1868–1918), FRANCE–HISTORY 17TH CENTURY, LOVE, POETS, SOLDIERS, FICTION

McCaughrean, Geraldine. **The Death-Defying Pepper Roux**. New York, HarperCollins, 2010. Originally published by Oxford University Press Great Britain, in 2009. ISBN 978-0-06-183665-7, 0-06-183665-6. 336 p. (10 up). Novel.

It began with a dream—devout Aunt Mireille's to be precise. The baby boy will be dead by his fourteenth birthday, declared St. Constance. Consequently, instead of calling him by his given name, Paul, the boy's family referred to him as le pauvre—poor one. On the playground—when Paul achieved the appropriate age to attend school—and with children's language being vagrant, Pauvre transmogrified into Poivre: Pepper. Hence, on his fourteenth birthday, hoping to spare his parents and devout aunt's sensibilities, Pepper Roux dauntlessly departs to meet his irrevocable fate. The humor of Pepper's madcap adventures is reminiscent of McCaughrean's *Stop the Train!* (HarperCollins, 2003). *Geraldine McCaughrean has been awarded the Carnegie Medal, the Guardian Prize, the Whitbread Children's Book Award, and the Michael L. Printz Award.* lmp

Author lives in Great Britain.

ADVENTURE AND ADVENTURERS, DISGUISE, SURVIVAL, FATE AND FATALISM, FRANCE–HISTORY 20TH CENTURY, FICTION

McClintock, Barbara. **Adèle & Simon**. Illustrated by the author. New York, Farrar, Straus and Giroux/Frances Foster Books, 2006. ISBN 978-0-374-38044-1, 0-374-38044-9. 33 p. (3–8). Picture book.

The bustling streets of early twentieth-century Paris are an integral part of the story as Adèle accompanies her younger brother Simon home from school. Their route, laid out on a 1907 Baedeker map printed on the endpapers, takes them to well-known sites. At each stop, Simon loses something—a drawing, a hat, a glove, his crayons. McClintock invites children to pore over her lovingly detailed illustrations, laden with visual references, to discover the lost article shown in each spread. A happy ending, coupled with the close relationship between feckless Simon and responsible, exasperated Adèle, adds human warmth to this celebration of a remarkable city. *American Library Association Notable Children's Books, New York Times Best Illustrated Books of the Year.* mac

Author lives in the United States.

LOST AND FOUND POSSESSIONS, BROTHERS AND SISTERS, PARIS, FRANCE, HISTORICAL FICTION PICTURE BOOK

Morgenstern, Susie Hoch. Translated by Gillian Rosner. **It Happened at School: Two Tales**. Illustrated by Serge Bloch. New York, Penguin/Viking, 2005. Originally published separately as *Le Fiancé de la Maitresse* in French by l'École des Loisirs France, in 1997, and *L'autographe* by l'École des Loisirs France, in 2003. ISBN 978-0-670-06022-1, 0-670-06022-4. 82 p. (9–12). Short Stories.

Morgenstern's second translated book humorously highlights differences between a tiny village school in France and schools in America. "The Autograph" chronicles teachers' creativity. When an assignment has unpleasant repercussions for a sensitive student, the teacher transforms it into an historical search for personal heroes. "Our Teacher's Boyfriend" demonstrates technology's progression as well as differences between cultures. A two-classroom village school has a telephone and fax machine installed, but the incessant ringing and avalanche of faxes from Maurice cause an extended disruption in teaching. With a theme of love lightheartedly present, this book is a good choice as a February read-aloud. *2006 USBBY-CBC Outstanding International Books List. Author wrote the 2002 Batchelder Award–winning* A Book of Coupons. *lmp*

Author, illustrator, and translator all live in France.

SCHOOLS, TEACHERS, HUMOROUS STORIES, FRENCH TRANSLATIONS INTO ENGLISH, FRANCE, FICTION, SHORT STORIES

Mourlevat, Jean-Claude. Translated by Y. Maudet. **The Pull of the Ocean**. New York, Random House/Delacorte Press, 2006. Originally published as *L'enfant Océan* in French by Pocket Jeunesse France, in 1999. ISBN 978-0-385-73348-9, 0-385-73348-8. 190 p. (10 up). Novel.

Yann Doutreleau is the youngest of seven brothers—all twins but him. He is undersized—only about two feet tall—and electively mute. His parents believe Yann to be slow-witted, but this is far from the truth. Yann leads his brothers westward across France, evading authorities, until they reach the sea. The narrative voices, individual as each brother, parent, and stranger who encounters Yann, create a distinctive storytelling style that positions readers in the center of a gaggle of eyewitnesses, all vying to be heard. Mourlevat's tale is a loosely based modern adaptation of Charles Perrault's "Hop o' My Thumb" (c.f., Andrew Lang's *The Blue Fairy Book*, 1965, pp. 231–41). *2007 Batchelder Award, winner of France's prestigious Prix Sorcières. lmp*

Author lives in France.

SIZE, TWINS, BROTHERS, SELECTIVE MUTISM, FRANCE, FICTION

Mourlevat, Jean-Claude. Translated by Anthea Bell. **Winter's End**. Somerville, MA, Candlewick Press, 2009. Originally published as *Le Combat d'Hiver* in French by Gallimard Jeunesse France, in 2006. ISBN 978-0-7636-4450-5, 0-7636-4450-1. 415 p. (12 up). Novel.

In a dystopian world, Milena and Helen use a pass from their prisonlike boarding school to travel into town. They meet Bartolomeo and Milos, who attend a similar boys school, traveling in the opposite direction. When Milena and Bartolomeo decide not to return to their schools, the other teens also decide to escape. Although not traveling together, the four are hunted by fierce dog-men intent upon killing the teens. The discovery that their deceased parents were members of a resistance movement pushes the students to become involved in overthrowing their oppressive and cruel government. Believable characters compel readers to consider themes of repression and courage. *2010 USBBY Outstanding International Books List, Booklist, Publishers Weekly, Kirkus Starred Reviews. pwc, djg*

Author lives in France.

DESPOTISM, ADVENTURE AND ADVENTURERS, ORPHANS, FANTASY FICTION

Pieńkowski, Jan. Translated by David Walser. **The Fairy Tales**. Illustrated by the author. New York, Penguin/Viking, 2006. Originally published in this form by Puffin Great Britain, in 2005; "Sleeping Beauty," "Snow White," "Hansel and Gretel," and "Cinderella" first published by William Heinemann and Gallery Five Great Britain, in 1977. ISBN 978-0-670-06189-1, 0-670-06189-1. 185 p. (4–8). Short Stories.

See Germany for description.

Prévost, Guillaume. Translated by William Rodarmor. **The Book of Time**. New York, Scholastic/Arthur A. Levine Books, 2007. Originally published as *La Pierre Sculptée* in French by Gallimard Jeunesse France, in 2006. ISBN 978-0-439-88375-7, 0-439-88375-X. 213 p. (10–12). Novel.

When Sam's mother dies, his distraught father sells their home and purchases an antique bookstore. Sam's father now seems to have disappeared. As Sam investigates the bookstore for a clue into his father's disappearance, he discovers a secret room. Inside the room is a coin that when placed in a stone sculpture sends Sam on time travel adventures. When Sam returns home, clues suggest that his father has been imprisoned in another time—in Dracula's castle! This is the first in the *The Book of Time* trilogy. Sequels are *The Gate of Days* (Arthur A. Levine Books, 2008) and *The Circle of Gold* (Arthur A. Levine Books, 2007). *pwc*

Author lives in France.
TIME TRAVEL, MISSING PERSONS, FRANCE, FANTASY FICTION

Rodriguez, Béatrice. **The Chicken Thief**. Illustrated by the author. New York, Enchanted Lion Books, 2010. Originally published as *Le Voleur de Poule* in French by les Editions Autrement France, in 2005. ISBN 978-1-59270-092-9, 1-59270-092-6. 32 p. (4–8). Picture book.

Foxes are so very maligned in children's literature—always cunning, never cuddly. And Rodriguez's chicken-thieving fox follows in the villainous footsteps of his literary predecessors, snatching Chicken away as Bear, Rabbit, and Rooster sit down to an al fresco picnic. Cue the heroic music, though; the animals will save the day, pursuing the fox and his captive through the woods, over the mountain, and across the sea. The drama of the chase in this wordless picture book is a lively one, and Rodriguez captures the range of emotions effortlessly and clearly on the animals' faces. *lvb*

Author lives in France.
ANIMALS, FOXES, CHICKENS, FICTION, STORIES WITHOUT WORDS

Ruelle, Karen Gray. **The Grand Mosque of Paris: A Story of How Muslims Rescued Jews during the Holocaust**. Illustrated by Deborah Durland DeSaix. New York, Holiday House, 2009. ISBN 978-0-8234-2159-6, 0-8234-2159-7. 40 p. (10–12). Picture book.

Little has been written about the French Resistance during World War II until recently. *The Grand Mosque of Paris* reveals Parisians' efforts during this time period. Built in 1926 by Muslims from North Africa whose homelands were under French control, the Grand Mosque is an expansive labyrinth of buildings, gardens, apartments, offices, even a restaurant and a clinic. The author weaves together facts and anecdotes, letters and suppositions to widen the lens on life in France under the Nazis and their puppet Vichy government. The back matter is extensive and includes an index and glossary. DeSaix's oil canvases convey the era's desperate mood while expanding readers' vision of the Grand Mosque's splendor. *lmp*

Author and illustrator live in the United States.
WORLD WAR II (1939–1945), JEWS, RESCUE, PARIS FRANCE, HOLOCAUST, RIGHTEOUS GENTILES IN THE HOLOCAUST, JEWISH-ARAB RELATIONS, FRANCE

Schneider, Christine. **I'm Bored!** Illustrated by Hervé Pinel. New York, Clarion Books, 2006. Originally published as *Je m'ennuie* in French by Albin Michel Jeunesse France, in 2004. ISBN 978-0-618-65760-5, 0-618-65760-6. 36 p. (3–5). Picture book.

Charlie is bored until he discovers that his toys, Teddy, Robot, and Donkey, can talk and that they, too, are bored because he doesn't play with them anymore. Together they transform Charlie's desk into the Monster Who Eats Boredom and do battle against boredom. The illustrations for this story about the power of imaginative play change from gray tones during Charlie's period of boredom to more and more colorful ones as the toys in his bedroom join in with Charlie's play, effectively highlighting the dramatic transformation of a boring Sunday to a fun-filled one. *ca*

Author and illustrator live in France.

BOREDOM, TOYS, FICTION

Sellier, Marie. Translated by Sibylle Kazeroid. **Legend of the Chinese Dragon**. Illustrated by Catherine Louis (Calligraphy and chop marks by Wang Fei). New York, NorthSouth Books, 2007. Originally published as *La Naissance du Dragon* in French by Editions Philippe Picquier France, in 2006. ISBN 978-0-7358-2152-1, 0-7358-2152-6. 30 p. (5–8). Picture book.

See China for description.

Sfar, Joann. Translated by Alexis Siegel & Edward Gauvin. **Little Vampire**. Illustrated by Mark Siegel & colors by Walter Siegel. New York, First Second, 2008. Originally published separately as *Petit Vampire va a l'Ecole* in French by Guy Delcourt Productions France, in 1999; *Petit Vampire Fait du Kung-Fu!* by Guy Delcourt Productions, in 2000; and *Petit Vampire et la Societe Protectrice des Chiens* by Guy Delcourt Productions, in 2001. ISBN 978-1-59643-233-8, 1-59643-233-0. 92 p. (9 up). Graphic Novel.

These first three stories in the series, *Little Vampire Goes to School*, *Little Vampire Does Kung Fu*, and *Little Vampire and the Canine Defenders Club*, introduce readers to Little Vampire and to his best friend, a human boy named Michael. The prolific writer and artist Sfar combines some dark themes (including love, death, bullies, the plight of the orphan) with humor and childlike innocence. Through the interactions among the members of this charming and very likeable cast of characters, both human and ghoul, readers learn we are all more alike than different and discover the power of friendship. *Sfar's awards include 1998 Award for First Comic Book, René Goscinny Award, 2003 Oecumenic Jury Award and Polish Award, Award for Best Youth Album (7 to 8 years) at the Angoulême International Comics Festival, 2004 Best International Writer at the Max & Moritz Prizes, Germany 2006 Best U.S. Edition of Foreign Material at the Eisner Awards, and the 2007 Sproing Award for Best Foreign Translated Material–Norway. ae*

Author lives in Paris.

VAMPIRES, FRIENDSHIP, GRAPHIC NOVELS, FICTION

Siméon, Jean-Pierre. Translated by Claudia Zoe Bedrick. **This Is a Poem That Heals Fish**. Illustrated by Olivier Tallec. New York, Enchanted Lion Books, 2007. Originally published as *Ceci est un Poème qui Guérit les Poissons* in French by Rue du Monde Voisins-le-Bretonneux France, in 2005. ISBN 978-1-59270-067-7, 1-59270-067-5. 45 p. (4–8). Picture book.

When Arthur's fish is sick and dying of boredom, his mother advises him to give the fish a poem. Since Arthur doesn't know what a poem is, he asks his eccentric neighbors and family. The bicycle repairman's poem is "When you are in love and have the sky in your mouth" (n.p.). The baker's is left-over fresh bread. His grandma suggests that a poem "turns words around, upside down" (n.p.). Arthur offers the fish the answers he's received and saves his fish's life. Playful, bright paintings will inspire readers to view the world in a new way. *mjw*

Author and illustrator live in France.

POETRY, PETS–FISH, FICTION, FRANCE

Spillebeen, Geert. Translated by Terese Edelstein. **Kipling's Choice**. Boston, Houghton Mifflin, 2005. Originally published as *Kiplings Keuze* in Dutch by Averbode Belgium, in 2002. ISBN 978-0-618-43124-3, 0-618-43124-1. 147 p. (12 up). Novel.

See Belgium for description.

Trondheim, Lewis. Translated by E. Gauvin. **Kaput & Zösky**. Illustrated by Eric Cartier. New York, First Second, 2008. Originally published as *Kaput & Zosky: Les Zigouilleurs de L'infini* in French by Guy Delcourt Productions France, in 2002, and as *Kaput & Zosky: Les Flinguizeurs du Cosmos* in French by Guy Delcourt Productions France, in 2003. ISBN 978-1-59643-132-4, 1-59643-132-6. 76 p. (10 up). Graphic novels.

These thirteen whimsical stories introduce readers to the unlikely duo of inept alien space invaders Kaput & Zösky. Elements of satire combine with simple, silly, cartoon violence and sometimes scatological humor to create a quirky, often irreverent series of adventures in which these incompetent would-be overlords journey throughout the universe in search of planets to invade and conquer. Between most of these episodes are satirical, wordless, single-page cartoons featuring The Cosmonaut, a trigger-happy earthling in outer space. *American Library Association 2009 Quick Pick for Young Adults. ae*

Lewis Trondheim is the pseudonym of Laurent Chabosky. He lives in the south of France.

LIFE ON OTHER PLANETS, SCIENCE FICTION COMIC BOOKS, STRIPS, EXTRATERRESTRIAL BEINGS, FRENCH TRANSLATIONS INTO ENGLISH, GRAPHIC NOVELS, HUMOROUS FICTION

Tullet, Hervé. **Imagine**. Illustrated by the author. London, Harry N. Abrams Books/Tate Publishing, 2005. Originally published as *L'Imaginier* in French by Éditions du Seuil France, in 2005. ISBN 978-1-85437-656-5, 1-85437-656-X. n.p. (all ages). Toy book, Picture book.

Hervé Tullet's *Imagine* is a hard-to-describe book, but it will be a favorite for anyone who revels in Ed Emberley's work. At its core, *Imagine* is an inspiration to draw and explore—colors, textures, shapes, and sizes. Most images are silhouetted on graph paper, with the image color matching the red, blue, green, or other colored lines; some backgrounds have large-scale blocks, some minute. There are die cuts judiciously interspersed throughout. Topics range from animals to illness, tea time to "make a picture." *Imagine* beckons youngsters—no matter what skill level—to trace or draw original or reproduced depictions on plain or graph paper. *lmp*

Author lives in France.

CREATIVE ACTIVITIES, AMUSEMENTS, IMAGINATION, TOY AND MOVABLE BOOKS

Tullet, Hervé. **The Coloring Book**. Illustrated by the author. London, Harry N. Abrams Books/ Tate Publishing, 2008. Also published as *Livre de Coloriages* in French by Bayard Jeunesse France, in 2009. ISBN 978-1-85437-849-1, 1-85437-849-X. n.p. (all ages). Toy book, Picture book.

The Coloring Book offers scribbles, shapes, and scenes—with minimal text—so that color concepts come from the young artist. Tullet begins, "See what happens when you mix the colors" (n.p.). There is a closed scribble that encompasses six shapes labeled "Red," "Blue," "Yellow," with three adjacent "?" formations. Later pages ask the artist to imagine the city of tomorrow, or to "color the night" (n.p.). All images are black on white or the reverse, with cartoon, abstract, or naïve styles that are accessible to youngsters. *The Coloring Book* is an ode to visual literacy, to color, to imagination, and to inspiration. *lmp*

Author lives in France.

CREATIVE ACTIVITIES, AMUSEMENTS, IMAGINATION, TOY AND MOVABLE BOOKS

Tullet, Hervé. Translated by Isabelle Forissier & Rosie Thorp. **The Scribble Book**. Illustrated by the author. London, Harry N. Abrams Books/Tate Publishing, 2008. Originally published as *Á Toi de Gribouiller!* in French by Bayard Éditions Jeunesse France, in 2007. ISBN 978-1-85437-774-6, 1-85437-774-4. n.p. (all ages). Toy book, Picture book.

The Scribble Book does exactly that: encourages children to scribble. The complexity of the scribbling increases until the artist's work resembles writing, becomes shapes, reveals motion, and suggests complex patterns. "Scribble in some hair" (n.p.) demonstrates to the child that using different implements produces different looks: colored pencil, fine-tip ballpoint, and marker produce a variety of textures. Tullet grants youngsters enough latitude to practice scribbling. It is up to parents to teach their children when scribbling is appropriate—and when it's not! *lmp*

Author lives in France.

CREATIVE ACTIVITIES, AMUSEMENTS, IMAGINATION, TOY AND MOVABLE BOOKS

Valckx, Catharina. **Lizette's Green Sock**. Illustrated by the author. New York, Clarion Books, 2005. Originally published as *Chausette verte de Lisette* in French by l'École des Loisirs France, in 2002. ISBN 978-0-618-45298-9, 0-618-45298-2. 33 p. (4–8). Picture book.

Winsome Lizette, a bird in a polka-dot dress and blue kerchief, finds a green sock when out for a walk one day. She is teased by Tim and Tom, two bullying cats, who tell her that socks "come in pairs" (7). When her mouse friend Bert sees the now-clean sock, he wants to wear it as a cap. Tim and Tom find the matching sock but deliberately throw it in a pond. In the end, a fish has a "splendid sleeping bag" (33). Splashes of color inside brown outlines add interest to this delightful tale about Lizette and Bert's creativity, individuality, and friendship. *2006 USBBY-CBC Outstanding International Books List, 2005 Booklist Editors' Choice, 2005 Child Magazine Best Books of the Year, 2005 School Library Journal Best Books of the Year, 2006 Kansas State Reading Circle Recommendation, 2006 CCBC Choices, 2006 Bank Street Best Children's Books of the Year.* hc, mjw

Author lives in Amsterdam.

SOCKS, FRIENDSHIP, ANIMALS, FICTION

Vidal, Clara. Translated by Y. Maudet. **Like a Thorn**. New York, Random House/Delacorte Press, 2008. Originally published as *Mal à ma Mère* in French by Éditions La Découverte France, in 2005. ISBN 978-0-385-73564-3, 0-385-73564-2. 119 p. (14 up). Novel.

Mélie's mother has two personalities, rosy and dark. People see her mother's rosy side while Mélie sees both. Dark mother's behavior is bizarre and cruel. The gifts that Mélie receives from her mother are dolls without eyes or a much-desired violin without a bow. Mélie confides in her friend and her grandmother. Neither of them believes that Mélie's mother is abusive. When Mélie's grades and health suffer, the school suggests that she see a psychologist. Only when the psychologist blocks the mother from entering the room does the reader feel that Mélie might survive her childhood. *pwc*

Author lives in France.
MENTAL ILLNESS, MOTHERS AND DAUGHTERS, OBSESSIVE-COMPULSIVE
DISORDER, EMOTIONAL PROBLEMS, FAMILY PROBLEMS, FRANCE, FICTION

RELATED INFORMATION

Organizations

IBBY France
The French national section of IBBY is associated with the French National Centre for Children's Literature at the Bibliothèque nationale de France (BnF). In conjunction with the BnF, IBBY France regularly organizes seminars [the most recent were "European Encounters on Children's Literature" and "Children's Books and Reading in Mexico"] and collaborates with other nations at book fairs and conferences.

The French national section of IBBY publishes a series entitled, "Lire en V.O." [Read in Original Version]. It is meant to help librarians, teachers, and parents to choose the best books in a foreign language. Previously, IBBY France published a selection of books in Arabic in 2007, in Italian in 2009, and in Portuguese in 2010. There were also selections of books in Spanish, German, and English published in earlier years.

www.ibby.org/index.php?id=421

http://lajoieparleslivres.bnf.fr http://lajoieparleslivres.bnf.fr/masc/Default.asp?INSTANCE=JOIE

Book Fairs

Montreuil Book Fair
www.salon-livre-presse-jeunesse.net/accueil.html

Paris Book Fair

Awards

Literary Awards [Press Award for Young]
www.salon-livre-presse-jeunesse.net/slpj_interieur.html?rub=5

Le Prix du 1er album: Prize for a First Book (illustrator) in conjunction with the Association of Youth bookstores (ALSJ).
www.salon-livre-presse-jeunesse.net/slpj_interieur.html?rub=5

Prix Sorcières Award

The Baobab Book Award (Le Baobab de l'album). Given in partnership with *Le Monde*, the French Union of the library, and bookstores Youth Association. The award aims to highlight the French creation.
www.salon-livre-presse-jeunesse.net/slpj_interieur.html?rub=5

The Tam-Tam Children's Book [Les Tam-Tam du livre de jeunesse] (awards presented by young readers). The Tam-Tam are prizes of children's literature organized by the Book Fair and Youth Press in Seine-Saint-Denis and Bayard Jeunesse. These prizes are only awarded by a jury of children and youth from age eight.

GERMANY

Andres, Kristina. **Good Little Wolf**. Illustrated by the author. New York, NorthSouth Books, 2008. Originally published as *Ich bin ein Wolf* in German by NordSüd Verlag Switzerland, in 2008. ISBN 978-0-7358-2210-8, 0-7358-2210-7. 28 p. (3–6). Picture book.

Fanciful illustrations accompany simple first-person statements that attest to Wolf's goodness. Young readers will recognize that the wolf and his animal friends are all stuffed toys that Wolf's imagination has imbued with life. Andres's delicate ink and watercolor illustrations floating in white space capture the tender emotions that Wolf feels for his friends. *ss*

Author lives in Germany.

WOLVES, FANTASY

Barth-Grözinger, Inge. Translated by Anthea Bell. **Something Remains**. New York, Hyperion Books for Children, 2006. Originally published as *Etwas Bleibt* in German by Thienemann Verlag Germany, in 2004. ISBN 978-0-7868-3880-6, 0-7868-3880-9. 390 p. (12–14). Novel.

In the late 1930s, Germany was a nation of small towns where everyone knew each other. The Levi family prospered from their livestock business, and twelve-year-old Erich enjoyed a privileged lifestyle. When Hitler's Nazi Party assumed control, however, Erich's world fell apart. His father's business foundered; neighbors and friends spurned him. Erich was humiliated and bullied in school. This is not typical Holocaust fiction, however. Barth-Grözinger and her students researched the effects of Nazism on the Jewish

community in their town of Ellwangen, Germany, resulting in this book. Although some names have been changed, much of the book—including Erich Levi's story—is true. *2007 USBBY Outstanding International Books List. lmp*
   Author lives in Ellwangen, Germany.
   JEWS, GERMANY HISTORY 1933–1945, PREJUDICES, FRIENDSHIP, NAZIS, GERMANY, HISTORICAL FICTION

Bauer, Jutta. **Grandpa's Angel**. Illustrated by the author. Cambridge, MA, Candlewick Press, 2005. Originally published as *Opas Engel* in German by Carlsen Germany, in 2001. ISBN 978-0-7636-2743-0, 0-7636-2743-7. 43 p. (6–8). Picture book.
   Grandpa, who is hospitalized, loves to tell stories to his grandson. He talks about his life, good times, bad times, and mostly how lucky he has been. Although Grandpa does not know it, he is kept safe by an angel that has always accompanied him. When Grandpa passes on, the angel takes on a new job as companion to the grandson. *2002 Deutscher Jugendliteraturpreis nominee. pwc*
   Author lives in Hamburg, Germany.
   ANGELS, GRANDFATHERS, DEATH, GERMANY, FANTASY

Bauer, Sepp. Translated by Ben W. L. Sachtler. **The Christmas Rose**. Illustrated by Else Wenz-Viëtor. Watertown, MA, Charlesbridge, 2008. Originally published as *Die Christrose* in German by Lappan Verlag Germany, in 2006. ISBN 978-1-58089-232-2, 1-58089-232-9. 40 p. (8–12). Picture book.
   Fritz and Gretl's father is gravely ill. Saint Nikolaus advises the children to travel to the home of the Winter King, where they will find white winter roses with a fragrance that will cure their father. On the long and difficult journey, the children are assisted by kind animals and a giant. After receiving the rose and having it blessed by the Christ Child, they return home; the fragrance of the rose cures their father of his illness. German traditions are described in this old-fashioned book, originally published in 1920. *pwc*
   Author lived in Germany.
   VOYAGES AND TRAVELS, CHRISTMAS STORIES, GERMANY, FICTION

Berner, Rotraut Susanne. Translated by Neeltje Konings & Nick Elliot. **In the Town All Year 'Round**. Illustrated by the author. San Francisco, Chronicle Books, 2008. Originally published in four volumes as *Winter-Wimmelbuch, Frühlings-Wimmelbuch, Sommer-Wimmelbuch,* and *Herbst-Wimmelbuch* in German by Gerstenberg Verlag Germany, in 2003, 2004, 2005. ISBN 978-0-8118-6474-9, 0-8118-6474-X. 72 p. (4–8). Picture book.

A large cast of characters have a series of miniadventures through the seasons of the year in this almost wordless book featuring intricately detailed scenes of various places all around their town. There's a comfortably European feel to the book that invites children to "read" it again and again, following various characters in their activities throughout the year, noticing changes in the town with each season, making up stories to go along with the double-spread illustrations, or just enjoying the intricately detailed scenes in this oversized book. *2009 USBBY Outstanding International Books List. ca*
   Author lives in Munich, Germany.
   City and Town Life, Seasons, Year, Translated Books, Fiction

Berner, Rotraut Susanne. Translated by Shelley Tanaka. **Definitely Not for Little Ones: Some Very Grimm Fairy-Tale Comics**. Illustrated by the author. Toronto, Groundwood Books/House of Anansi Press, 2009. Originally published as *Rotraut Susanne Berners Märchen-Comics* in German by Jacoby & Stuart Germany, in 2008. ISBN 978-0-88899-957-3, 0-88899-957-7. 52 p. (9 up). Folk Tale Parodies, Graphic format.

   Sweet tales for young children these are not. There are bloody knives, lying, cheating, and stealing, all of which harkens back to the original Grimm's fairy tales. Although not all the tales in this book are well known, some are standards, like "Little Red Cap" and "Tom Thumb." Berner's attitude differentiates these retellings from other versions: her language and illustrations are irreverent and farcical, with a humor that is distinctly German. Happy endings include a postscript, "And they would still be alive today . . . if they hadn't died, that is" (n.p.). These updated versions of eight tales are quick reads that will appeal to a wide audience. *Rotraut Susanne Berner has won the German Youth Literature Prize on several occasions, the special German Youth Literature Prize for a body of work, and has been nominated three times for the Hans Christian Andersen Award. lmp*
   Author lives in Munich, Germany.
   Fairy Tales, Comic Books/Strips, Folklore, Germany

Bunge, Daniela. Translated by Kathryn Bishop. **Cherry Time**. Illustrated by the author. New York, Penguin/Minedition, 2007. Originally published as *Kirschenzeit mit Rubinella* in German by Minedition Germany, in 2007. ISBN 978-0-698-40057-3, 0-698-40057-7. 40 p. (4–8). Picture book.

   The child narrator in this delicate story is painfully shy. He notices a girl named Ruby sitting in a cherry tree and speaking to no one. With the help of Max, the fearless dog that he gets for his birthday, he befriends Ruby, and they spend the summer talking and enjoying cherries. Although Ruby's family moves away, they promise to be brave and hope that they will meet whenever it's cherry time. Double-page scenes of European cityscapes, unusual perspectives that emphasize the isolation of the shy boy, and the simple, quiet text encourage overcoming shyness and making friends. *mjw*

Author lives in Germany.

BASHFULNESS, COURAGE, FRIENDSHIP, FICTION

Chotjewitz, David. Translated by Doris Orgel. **Crazy Diamond**. New York, Simon & Schuster/Atheneum/Richard Jackson, 2008. Originally published in German by Carlsen Verlag Germany, in 2005. ISBN 978-1-4169-1176-0, 1-4169-1176-6. 252 p. (14 up). Novel.

Mira M., the hot, new, young pop star, has been found dead, floating in the aquarium in her producer's lavish apartment. Was she murdered, or was it suicide? This is a harsh, unromantic look at the music business and its effects on love, friendship, and musical integrity. It is told in CD-tracked chapters in which the stories of Mira (a refugee from the war in Croatia), Melody, Rosa, and Jackson (who stow away in a shipping container from Ghana), Kralle (their rescuer), and Zucka (the son of a music producer) intertwine as they all covet rock-star fame and fortune. *CCBC Choices. ae*

Author lives in Hamburg.

FAME, INTERPERSONAL RELATIONS, MUSICIANS, POPULAR MUSIC, DEATH, GERMANY, FICTION

Funke, Cornelia. Translated by Oliver Latsch. **The Wildest Brother**. Illustrated by Kerstin Meyer. New York, Scholastic/Chicken House, 2006. Originally published in German by Verlag Friedrich Oetinger Germany, in 2004; published as one story in A *Princess, A Pirate, and One Wild Brother* by Chicken House Great Britain, in 2003. ISBN 978-043982-862-8, 0-439828-62-7. n.p. (4–7). Picture book.

In his play, brave and fearless Ben gallantly protects his older sister Anna from a burglar, foxes, wolves, bears, a man-eating monster, and various other imaginary beasts. When darkness falls, however, Ben's lively imagination conjures up some scary thoughts, and he seeks his older sibling's protection from Night in her bed. The energetic, cartoon-style illustrations depict Ben's imaginative play and Anna's varied reactions. The inclusion in the illustrations of small guinea pigs watching and reacting to what is going on adds interest. *ca, hc*

Author is from Germany and now lives in the United States; illustrator lives in Germany.

COURAGE, BROTHERS AND SISTERS, FICTION

Funke, Cornelia. Translated by Anthea Bell. **Igraine the Brave**. Illustrated by the author. New York, Scholastic/Chicken House, 2007. Originally published as *Igraine Ohnefurcht* in German by Cecilie Dressler Verlag Germany, in 1998. Simultaneously published as *Igraine the Brave* in English by Chicken House Great Britain and Scholastic/Chicken House New York, in 2007. ISBN 978-0-439-90379-0, 0-439-90379-3. 224 p. (8–12). Novel.

Igraine, the daughter of magicians, has no interest in magic; she wants to be a knight. When their castle is besieged by Osmund the Greedy, an evil neighbor who wants to steal their Singing Books of Magic, it is up to Igraine to set things right—with the help of the Sorrowful Knight of the Mount of Tears. This is an engaging story for young fantasy fans with a cast of colorful characters (even their names are colorful). There's lots of humor mixed in with magic, which sometimes goes awry, and conflict between chivalrous and evil knights. *2008 USBBY Outstanding International Books List. ca*
Author is from Germany but currently lives in the United States.
KNIGHTS AND KNIGHTHOOD, MAGIC, FANTASY FICTION

Grossmann-Hensel, Katharina. Translated by Rachel Ward. **How Mommy Met Daddy**. Illustrated by the author. New York, NorthSouth Books, 2008. Originally published as *Wie Mama und Papa Verliebte wurden* in German by Annette Betz Verlag Germany, in 2006. ISBN 978-0-7358-2176-7, 0-7358-2176-3. 28 p. (4–8). Picture book.

A child narrator recounts the story of how his two very different parents, owners of neighboring stores, found love—by crashing into each other on the sidewalk. Although his father was neat and orderly and favored neutral colors and his mother was colorful and messy, each was drawn to the other. Stylized full-bleed paintings reflect the tastes of each parent, from their personal clothing to the décor of their stores, neither of which gets much business until they join forces to create one colorful, orderly, spectacular store. *ss*
Author was born in Germany but now lives in Paris.
PARENTS, FICTION

Janisch, Heinz. Translated by Belinda Cooper. **The Fantastic Adventures of Baron Munchausen**. Illustrated by Aljoscha Blau. New York, Enchanted Lion Books, 2010. Originally published as *Der Ritt auf dem Seepferd* in German by Aufbau Verlag GmbH Germany, in 2007. ISBN 978-1-59270-091-2, 1-59270-091-8. 30 p. (4–8). Picture book.

Janisch has us on the edge of our seats from the first page with these fantastical tales. The clever and resourceful baron carries sunshine in a sack to light up a dark forest, provides musical accompaniment to a pianist in the belly of a whale, and even tames a giant seahorse so he can ride about underneath the seas. Oh, to live in Munchausen's world! Janisch's playful writing is filled with a subtle, dry humor that makes this a book that adults are sure to enjoy as much as children. *Janisch was the Austrian nominee for the 2010 Hans Christian Andersen Award.* lvb

   Author lives in Vienna, Austria.

   IMAGINATION, FRIENDSHIP, VOYAGES AND TRAVELS, TALL TALES, HUMOROUS STORIES, GERMANY

Judge, Lita. **One Thousand Tracings: Healing the Wounds of World War II.** Illustrated by the author. New York, Hyperion Books for Children, 2007. ISBN 978-142310008-9, 1-423100-08-5. n.p. (8–12). Picture book.

   Two families—one in the United States and another in Germany—describe through their correspondence how difficult it is to return to "normal" after six years of war. The narrator's mother begins a campaign to send shoes to strangers who only weeks earlier had been the enemy. Letters about missing relatives, unemployment, but especially the scarcity of food, clothing, and even soap clearly reveal the aftereffects of war. Watercolor illustrations accompany photographs, shoe tracings, letters, and other memorabilia. An author's note explains the inspiration for this civilian relief effort. Candace Fleming's *Boxes for Katje* (Farrar, Straus and Giroux, 2003) provides information about other post–World War II assistance endeavors. lmp

   Author lives in the United States.

   WORLD WAR II (1939–1945), CIVILIAN RELIEF, UNITED STATES AND GERMANY, HISTORICAL FICTION

Könnecke, Ole. Translated by Nancy Seitz. **Anthony and the Girls.** Illustrated by the author. New York, Farrar, Straus and Giroux, 2006. Originally published as *Anton und die Mädchen* in German by Carl Hanser Verlag Germany, in 2004. ISBN 978-0-374-30376-1, 0-374-30376-2. 26 p. (4–8). Picture book.

   Cool Anthony wants to play in the sandbox with the girls. Even though he has a bucket, a shovel, and a really big car, the girls totally ignore him. He jumps high, lifts a branch, and slides headfirst down the slide. He still doesn't get a glance. Mad, he builds the biggest house in the world, which collapses. He cries. Only then do the girls notice him and give him a cookie. But then, along comes Luke with bigger, better toys. Spare, cartoon illustrations extend the simple text. *2007 USBBY Outstanding International Books List.* mjw

Author lives in Hamburg, Germany.

FRIENDSHIP, HUMOROUS STORIES, GERMAN TRANSLATIONS INTO ENGLISH, FICTION

McGowan, Keith. **The Witch's Guide to Cooking with Children**. Illustrated by Yoko Tanaka. New York, Henry Holt, 2009. ISBN 978-0-8050-8668-3, 0-8050-8668-4. 180 p. (9–12). Novel.

Sol and his younger sister Connie have moved to a new town. Because eleven-year-old Sol is a scientist and is logical, and brilliant, he realizes that the neighbor's dog is chewing an uncommon bone: a human femur. Thus, the mystery begins. The first chapter, written from Fay Holaderry—aka the witch's—point of view, sets the stage for a first-rate, high-spirited lampoon. "I love children. Eating them, that is" (1). This is a mystery that children—and parents—can really sink their teeth into. Hansel and Gretel redux—with a twist. *lmp*

Author lives in Austria, and illustrator lives in Thailand.

BROTHERS AND SISTERS, WITCHES, SELF-CONFIDENCE, INVENTORS, CHARACTERS IN LITERATURE, GERMANY, FICTION

Meyer, Kai. Translated by Elizabeth D. Crawford. **The Glass Word**. New York, Simon & Schuster/Margaret K. McElderry Books, 2008. Originally published as *Gläserne Wort* in German by Loewe Verlag Germany, in 2002. ISBN 978-0-689-87791-9, 0-689-87791-9. 282 p. (12 up). Novel.

See North Africa and the Middle East—Egypt for description.

Napp, Daniel. Translated by Hilary Schmitt-Thomas. **Professor Bumble and the Monster of the Deep**. Illustrated by the author. New York, Abrams Books for Young Readers, 2008. Originally published as *Dr. Brumm geht Baden* in German by Thienemann Verlag Germany, in 2006. ISBN 978-0-8109-9484-3, 0-8109-9484-4. 32 p. (4–8). Picture book.

Every Monday Professor Bumble the bear goes swimming with his goldfish friend Beluga. They arrive at the lake, and an otter tells Bumble that there is a monster in the lake. Bumble refuses to enter the water but watches the brave Beluga swimming in the lake. When Beluga disappears from sight, Bumble, with all sorts of safety equipment, dives into the water. When Beluga and the otter see Bumble surrounded by all the equipment, they believe him to be the monster. Everyone is frightened, and Bumble and Beluga retreat to the bathtub to enjoy a swim. *pwc*

Author lives in Germany.

FRIENDSHIP, BEARS, GOLDFISH, OTTERS, MONSTERS, FANTASY FICTION

Pausewang, Gudrun. Translated by Rachel Ward. **Traitor**. Minneapolis, MN, Lerner/Carolrhoda Books, 2006. Originally published as *Die Verräterin* in German by Ravensburger Buchverlag Germany, in 1995. ISBN 978-0-8225-6195-8, 0-8225-6195-6. 220 p. (12 up). Novel.

When we first meet Anna, she is a fifteen-year-old schoolgirl who detests the politics that permeate German life. Her brother lives for the day he can join the army. Their mother is grateful for the business war has brought to her inn. As the war drags on, Anna and her brother become more polarized. She cannot allow him to discover her secret—that she's hiding a Russian prisoner of war and bringing him food and clothing. Pausewang's suspenseful account of World War II offers multiple perspectives on the realities of German life during wartime and an emotionally charged, shocking ending. *2007 USBBY Outstanding International Books List. lmp*

Author lives in Germany.

WORLD WAR II (1939–1945), PRISONERS OF WAR, GERMANY, HISTORICAL FICTION

Pieńkowski, Jan. Translated by David Walser. **The Fairy Tales**. Illustrated by the author. New York, Penguin/Viking, 2006. Originally published in this form by Puffin Great Britain, in 2005; "Sleeping Beauty," "Snow White," "Hansel and Gretel," and "Cinderella" first published by William Heinemann and Gallery Five Great Britain, in 1977. ISBN 978-0-670-06189-1, 0-670-06189-1. 185 p. (4–8). Short Stories.

Translator David Walser and illustrator Jan Pieńkowski introduce these four tales—"Sleeping Beauty," "Snow White," "Hansel and Gretel," and "Cinderella"—by detailing their personal fascination with folk literature, followed by a brief history of Perrault and the Brothers Grimm. The first three are from an early, i.e., "grizzly" (vi) version by the Brothers Grimm (red-hot shoes and all), but "Cinderella" is drawn from Perrault's less vindictive version. What will mesmerize readers is the combination of Walser's language, in which he "preserve[s] the peculiar qualities of the original phrasing" (ix), and Pieńkowski's lacy silhouettes, delicate yet perfectly detailed with multihued marbled backgrounds. Everything else is a bonus. *2007 USBBY Outstanding International Books List. lmp*

The illustrator lives in London but was born in Poland and lived in Germany and Italy; the translator grew up speaking German, French, and English.

FAIRY TALES, FICTION, GERMAN, FRENCH

Pin, Isabel. Translated by Nancy Seitz. **When I Grow Up, I Will Win the Nobel Peace Prize**. Illustrated by the author. New York, Farrar, Straus and

Giroux, 2006. Originally published as *Wenn Ich Gross Bin, Werde Ich Nobel-preisträger* in German by Carl Hanser Verlag Germany, in 2005. ISBN 978-0-374-38313-8, 0-374-38313-8. 22 p. (4–8). Picture book.

A young narrator, who says he'll win the Nobel Peace Prize one day, tells of the great and heroic deeds he will accomplish when he grows up (including creating world peace, protecting the environment, and helping to save planet Earth, along with giving aid to people in need). The illustrations, however, show that the present-day behavior of this boy runs contrary to his lofty ambitions. Talk and action clearly differ until, at the end of the book, the boy takes a small first step toward working for his ideals. Includes a note on the Nobel Peace Prize. *2007 USBBY Outstanding International Books List, 2007 Notable Social Studies Trade Books for Young People. ca*

Author was born in France but now lives in Germany.

BEHAVIOR, NOBEL PRIZES, JUSTICE, FICTION

Pressler, Mirjam. Translated by Erik J. Macki. **Let Sleeping Dogs Lie**. Asheville, NC, Front Street, 2007. Originally published as *Zeit der Schlafenden Hunde* in German by Beltz & Gelberg Germany, in 2003. ISBN 978-1-932425-84-0, 1-932425-84-5. 207 p. (14 up). Novel.

After a mysterious prologue in which Johanna struggles with a moral dilemma raised during her recent school trip to Israel, her father learns that old Mr. Riemenschneider—his father—has killed himself—just as Johanna's grandmother did. Secretly, Johanna rages at her family. She knows she will have to confront her father now that her grandfather is gone. What effect will the truth have on her family? Can she rectify her family's transgressions? Pressler skillfully entwines past and present, scrutinizing Germany's most divisive contemporary issue—how to atone for Nazi horrors. *2008 USBBY Outstanding International Books List. lmp*

Author lives near Munich, Germany.

JEWISH HOLOCAUST (1939–1945), ECONOMIC ASPECTS, WORLD WAR II (1939–1945), CONFISCATIONS AND CONTRIBUTIONS, CLOTHING TRADE, ARYANIZATION, ANTISEMITISM GERMANY, INTERPERSONAL RELATIONS, GERMANY, FICTION

Rahlens, Holly-Jane. **Prince William, Maximilian Minsky, and Me**. Cambridge, MA, Candlewick Press, 2005. Originally published as *Prinz William, Maximilian Minsky und Ich* in German by Rowohlt-Taschenbuch-Verlag Germany, in 2002. ISBN 978-0-7636-2704-1, 0-7636-2704-6. 310 p. (12 up). Novel.

Nelly Sue Edelmeister is a skinny, thirteen-year-old, astronomy-loving nerd. She lives in Berlin with her overbearing Jewish American mother, her understanding Christian German father, and her wise substitute grandmother. She has a hopeless crush on Prince William, heir to the British throne, and she is determined to learn basketball so she can go with her school team to Great Britain and meet William. This well-crafted story, written in the first person, is filled with humor, emotion, and colorful characters and gives readers insight into being a Jewish teenager in contemporary Berlin. Includes a glossary of foreign terms. *Sydney Taylor Honor Book Award, Deutcher Jugendliteraturpreis. mjw*

Author lives in Berlin.

SELF-PERCEPTION, INTERPERSONAL RELATIONS, MOTHERS AND DAUGHTERS, FATHERS AND DAUGHTERS, JEWS, BERLIN, GERMANY, FICTION

Richter, Jutta. Translated by Anna Brailovsky. **The Cat, or, How I Lost Eternity**. Illustrated by Rotraut Susanne Berner. Minneapolis, MN, Milkweed Editions, 2007. Originally published as *Die Katze, Oder, Wie Ich Die Ewigkeit Verloren Habe* in German by Carl Hanser Verlag Germany, in 2006. ISBN 978-1-57131-676-9, 1-57131-676-0. 63 p. (9–12). Novella.

Eight-year-old Christine is late for school every day because a talking alley cat demands her attention, giving her much to think about as he tries to teach her to be spiteful and pitiless.

Much more than a simple fantasy tale, this thought-provoking fable forces the reader to think about larger themes of kindness, friendship, and what is important in life. Childlike yellow and black illustrations complement this fantastic, if philosophic story. *2008 Batchelder Honor Book, 2008 Notable Children's Books; the author has won the German Youth Literature Award, the Herman Hesse Prize for her body of work, and the Pied Piper's Prize of Hamelyn. djg*

Author lives in a castle in Germany and also in Italy.

SCHOOLS, CONDUCT OF LIFE, CATS, HUMAN-ANIMAL RELATIONSHIPS, GERMANY, FANTASY FICTION, NOVEL

Schmemann, Serge. **When the Wall Came Down: The Berlin Wall and the Fall of Soviet Communism**. Boston, Kingfisher, 2006. Originally published by Kingfisher Great Britain, in 2006. ISBN 978-0-7534-5994-2, 0-7534-5994-9. 127 p. (12 up). Nonfiction.

This compelling, first-person narrative recounts the events leading up to the building of the Berlin Wall in 1961 and its fall in 1989. Well-chosen articles and black-and-white and color photographs from the archives of the

New York Times bring the story to life. Maps, a time line of twentieth-century events, suggestions for further reading, and an index supplement the text. *NYPL Books for the Teen Age. The author received a Pulitzer Prize for his reporting of the reunification of Germany. lmp*

Serge Schmemann served as Bonn bureau chief for the New York Times *from 1987 to 1991. He currently lives in Paris.*

BERLIN WALL HISTORY (1961–1989), COMMUNISM–EASTERN EUROPE, 20TH CENTURY HISTORY, EAST GERMANY–POLITICS AND GOVERNMENT, GERMANY–HISTORY, UNIFICATION (1990), BERLIN, GERMANY, NONFICTION

Schröder, Monika. **The Dog in the Wood**. Honesdale, PA, Front Street, 2009. ISBN 978-1-59078-701-4, 1-59078-701-3. 163 p. (10–14). Novel.

The end of World War II brought confusion, deprivation, despair, and occupation to Nazi Germany. In an insignificant East German farming village, the days that led up to Hitler's demise were grueling for ten-year-old Fritz and his family. His grandfather—as head of the town's Nazi Party Farmer's Association—and Oma refused to flee as the Russians drew near. His mother, sister, and the hired hand, Lech, expected the Russians would bring liberation. No one expected what really transpired. Schröder's brutal honesty about postwar plunder, imprisonment, death, and despair is a perspective seldom found in children's books. *lmp*

Author was born in Germany but currently lives in New Delhi, India.

WORLD WAR II (1939–1945), RUSSIANS, POLITICAL PRISONERS, GERMANY, HISTORICAL FICTION

Sidjanski, Brigitte. Translated by Bernadette Watts. **The River**. Illustrated by the author. New York, Penguin/Minedition, 2008. Originally published as *Der Fluss* in German by Minedition Bargteheide Germany, in 2008. ISBN 978-0-698-40077-1, 0-698-40077-1. n.p. (4–8). Picture book.

The subtle, yet significant, interactions within the ecosystem are described in a lighthearted manner through the adventures of five pinecones. Their journeys are inspired by the course of the water that begins as a bubbling brook in the mountains and flows into a tumultuous sea. As the pinecones are swept along by the current of the water, each one discovers a suitable place to take root. Their homes include a beautiful countryside, a deep gorge, a green valley, a river bank, and a sandy seashore. *dgw*

Author lives near Zurich.

RIVERS, PINECONES, FICTION

Steffensmeier, Alexander. **Millie Waits for the Mail.** Illustrated by the author. New York, Walker Books, 2007. Originally published as *Lieselotte Lauert* in German by Patmos Verlag GmbH Germany, in 2006. ISBN 978-0-8027-9662-2, 0-8027-9662-1. 24 p. (4–8). Picture book.

Millie the cow stands patiently each morning as she is milked. Is she a perfectly contented cow? Perhaps not. Her real joy comes when the mail carrier delivers the mail and she is able to scare him off the farm. When her escapades result in the destruction of her own package as well as the mail carrier's delivery bicycle, Millie adds something new to her daily routine—helping to deliver the mail. The humorous, expressive illustrations transport readers into Millie's colorful world and detail her daily routine and fun. *2008 USBBY Outstanding International Books List.* ca

Author lives in Germany.

Cows, Letter Carriers, Fiction

Steinhöfel, Andreas. Translated by Alisa Jaffa. **The Center of the World.** New York, Delacorte Press, 2005. Originally published as *Die Mitte der Welt: Roman* in German by Carlsen Verlag GmbH Germany, in 1998. ISBN 978-0-385-72943-7, 0-385-72943-X. 467 p. (14 up). Novel.

Ostracized by the community for his single mother's behavior and his own reputation as one of "the witch's children," seventeen-year-old Phil grows up gay and lonely, disconnected even from his twin sister, until he falls in love with a schoolmate, who betrays him with his best friend. A rich concoction set in the German town where his mother fled, pregnant with her twins, this is slow going but rewarding. There is both homophobic violence and violence in the name of love. *2006 USBBY-CBC Outstanding International Books List, Buxtehuder Bulle Prize–Best YA Novel in Germany, shortlisted for the Deutscher Jugendliteraturpreis (German Children's Literature Prize).* kti

Author lives in Germany.

Coming of Age, Homosexuality, Families–Germany, Interpersonal Relations, Germany, Fiction

Thal, Lilli. Translated by John Brownjohn. **Mimus.** Toronto, Annick Press, 2005. Originally published as *Mimus* in German by Gerstenberg Germany, in 2003. ISBN 978-1-55037-925-9, 1-55037-925-9. 394 p. (12 up). Novel.

King Philip and King Theodo's kingdoms have battled for as long as Prince Florin can remember. So it is a joyous day when the sovereigns meet to sign the peace treaty. Instead, Philip and his men are flung into Theodo's dungeon. Twelve-year-old Florin is spared—only to be apprenticed to the king's fool, Mimus. Historical fiction readers will appreciate Thal's complex characterization, evocative setting, and meticulously detailed plot structure. Her descriptions of Florin's tower prison and his humiliation when labeled a soulless beast are so graphic that we shiver, starve, and suffer with the young prince. *Society of School Librarians International Honor Book Award, NYPL Books for the Teen Age, Bank Street College of Education Best Children's Books of the Year, School Library Journal's Best Books of the Year, YALSA Best Books for Young Adults. lmp*

    Author lives in Germany.

    GERMAN, SUSPENSE, ADVENTURE, DECEPTION, PRINCES, GOOD AND EVIL, HEROES, MIDDLE AGES, GERMANY, HISTORICAL FICTION

Weninger, Brigette. Translated by Kathryn Bishop. **28 Good Night Stories.** Illustrated by Eve Tharlet. New York, Penguin Group, 2008. Originally published as *28 Gute-Nacht Geschichten* in German by Minedition Bargteheide Germany, in 2006. ISBN 978-0-698-40081-8, 0-698-40081-X. 126 p. (3–5). Short Stories.

    An old bear is surprised by the lumbering manifestation of a delightful little guardian angel trainee who is sent to earth to whisper a special word to children and watch over them until the coming full moon. The old bear suggests to the angel that he should enliven his assignment by telling stories. The angel agrees, and he asks the bear to tell him a story. The bear consents only if the angel also agrees to tell a story. Thus begins the collection of twenty-eight bedtime stories of friendship, courage, and secrets told alternately by the bear and the angel. *dgw*

    Author lives in Austria.

    CHILDREN'S STORIES, SHORT STORIES

Wildner, Martina. Translated by James Skofield. **Shooting Stars Everywhere.** New York, Delacorte Press, 2006. Originally published as *Jede Menge Sternschnuppen* in German by Beltz & Gelberg Weinheim Germany, in 2003. ISBN 978-0-385-73250-5, 0-385-73250-3. 179 p. (12 up). Novel.

    Victor lives with his father, a taxi driver, in an urban apartment complex in Germany. The summer he turns thirteen, he is full of questions. Will his mom, a lawyer, remarry his dad? Will he ever learn to dive? Who is leaving sinister notes in his mailbox? Why won't the mysterious girl he meets at the community swimming pool and knows only as "D" take him home to meet her family? Victor's journal entries, fresh, funny, and honest, will resonate with confused adolescents who live well beyond the borders of his country. *mac*

Author lives in Germany.

MYSTERY AND DETECTIVE STORIES, DIARIES, INTERPERSONAL RELATIONS, FAMILY LIFE, GERMANY, FICTION

Winter, Jonah. **The Secret World of Hildegard**. Illustrated by Jeanette Winter. New York, Scholastic/Arthur A. Levine Books, 2007. ISBN 978-0-439-50739-4, 0-439-50739-1. n.p. (9–12). Biography.

Son and mother team Jonah and Jeanette Winter create a stunning biography of Hildegard, a remarkable woman who lived during the Middle Ages. As a child she had visions of an invisible world but never shared them, which led to headaches and bouts of confinement. Eventually, her parents sent her to a monastery, where after many years she heard God's voice urging her to share her visions. In finally doing so, she wrote scientific books and composed music. The simple text is extended by the rich illustrations on facing pages. Author's notes and a bibliography are provided. *NYPL Best Book for Reading and Sharing. nlh*

Author and illustrator live in the United States.

WOMEN MYSTICS, HILDEGARD VON BINGEN (1098–1179), GERMANY, BIOGRAPHY

Zusak, Markus. **The Book Thief**. New York, Random House/Alfred A. Knopf, 2006. Originally published by Pan Macmillan Australia, in 2005. ISBN 978-0-375-83100-3, 0-375-83100-2. 552 p. (14 up). Novel.

The setting is Nazi Germany, the protagonist is nine-year-old Liesel, and the narrator is Death. Liesel is travelling to a foster placement when she steals a book—*The Gravedigger's Handbook*—although she cannot read. Her foster father teaches her, and Liesel continues to steal, risking more with each book. Although Nazi prisoners footslog through the pages, Himmel (Heaven) Street appears undisturbed. No one knows of the hidden Jew in Liesel's basement. *The Book Thief* is a multilayered masterpiece of virtuoso character development, complex interwoven plots, and challenging themes that deserves to be read as more than just another Holocaust book. *2007 USBBY Outstanding International Books List, 2007 Michael L. Printz Honor for Excellence in Young Adult Literature, 2007 Notable Social Studies Trade Books for Young People. lmp*

Author lives in Australia.

BOOKS AND READING, STORYTELLING, DEATH, WORLD WAR (1939–1945),
JEWS–RESCUE, GERMANY–HISTORY (1933–1945), HISTORICAL FICTION

RELATED INFORMATION

Organizations

Arbeitskreis für Jugendliteratur [The Association for Children's and Youth Literature] (AKJ)

This is the umbrella State-sponsored organization for matters concerning youth publications. In its quarterly journal *JuLit* and in various other publications and topical book catalogues, the AKJ provides not only guidance and information but also acts as valuable selection and evaluation aids for the wide market of children's and youth literature. The AKJ, in collaboration with the German national section of IBBY, organizes national and international workshops and conferences to encourage interaction among those working on a daily basis in the field of children's and youth literature.

www.jugendliteratur.org/

German Book Office

The German Book Office New York, Inc. (GBO) serves as a bridge between the German and American publishing industries. Although not specific to works for children, their website includes links to sites about German authors, literary journals, and organizations.

www.newyork.gbo.org/en/

IBBY Germany

Since its founding in 1955, the **Arbeitskreis für Jugendliteratur** [The Association for Children's and Youth Literature] (AKJ) has been the German Section of the International Board on Books for Young People (IBBY).

www.ibby.org/index.php?id=422

Awards

The Goethe-Institut Kinder-und Jugendbücher website provides detailed information on virtually every aspect of Germany's children's literature. The German website is www.goethe.de/ins/cn/hon/prj/kij/pre/ghf/deindex.htm.

The translated website can be accessed at http://translate.google.com/translate?hl=en&sl=de&u=http://www.goethe.de/ins/cn/hon/prj/kij/pre/ghf/

deindex.htm&ei=tuAgTe_UCJmInAeiwvm1Dg&sa=X&oi=translate&ct=
result&resnum=6&ved=0CEkQ7gEwBQ&prev=/search%3Fq%3DGustav%
2BHeinemann%2BFriedenspreis%26hl%3Den%26client%3Dfirefox-a%26
hs%3DAOV%26rls%3Dorg.mozilla:en-US:official%26prmd%3Divns.

Buxtehuder Bulle Prize–Best YA Novel in Germany
www.buxtehuder-bulle.de/
Established in 1971, this award's mission is to "interest youth in active
and intensive reading, and at the same time to promote good youth books"
(www.buxtehuder-bulle.de/). Eligibility: Books that were first published in
German, including translations, during the past calendar year may participate in the competition. The target age groups are young adults, ages thirteen
or fourteen up.

Deutcher Jugendliteraturpreis
The AKJ is responsible for awarding the Deutscher Jugendliteraturpreis
(German Youth Literature Award), which has been awarded annually since
1956 in four categories: picture book, children's book, young adult book, and
nonfiction. Since 2003 an independent, young adult jury gives an award.
Furthermore, a special annual award for lifetime achievement is given alternately to a German author, German illustrator, or German translator. The
announcement and ceremony for these awards takes place in October at the
Frankfurt Book Fair.
www.djlp.jugendliteratur.org/

Gustav Heinemann Friedenspreis
The Gustav Heinemann Friedenspreis is considered the most important award for German language children's and youth literature after the
Deutsche Jugendliteraturpreis. It is awarded to books that encourage children
and young people to advocate for human rights, nonviolent forms of conflict
resolution, and peaceful coexistence.
www.goethe.de/ins/cn/hon/prj/kij/pre/ghf/deindex.htm

Herman Hesse Prize
www.hermann-hesse.de/eng/stiftung/framestiftung.shtml

Luchs Literaturpreis
The Luchs Award (translated Lynx) is a literary prize for children and
young people's books, sponsored jointly by the weekly newspaper *Die Zeit* and

Radio Bremen. The "Lynx of the Month" has been awarded since 1986 and the "Lynx of the Year" since 1997.

 http://de.wikipedia.org/wiki/Luchs_(Literaturpreis)

Collections

Institut fur Jugendbuchforschung/Institute for Youth Book Research

Collected here are historical and contemporary children's books, primarily German language. Johann Wolfgang Goethe-Universitat, Germany: www.uni-frankfurt.de/fb/fb10/jubufo/index.html (in German only).

Internationale Jugendbibliothek/International Youth Library

This is a noncirculating international collection of children's books. The International Youth Library is the largest library for international children's and youth literature in the world, consisting of 580,000 books in over 130 languages published within the past four hundred years. In addition, there are nearly thirty thousand titles of international secondary literature, approximately 250 professional periodicals, and forty thousand documents. About one thousand publishers from around the world send sample copies of their latest titles to the library each year. Ever since Jella Lepman established it in 1949, the IJB has been continuously expanded to an internationally recognized center for the world's children's and youth literature.

The IJB supports the work of IBBY and IBBY's international journal *Bookbird*. It sponsors the annual White Ravens List of the best international books submitted for the collection. It also assembles book and art exhibits, such as one that was on display at the IBBY Regional Conference in St. Charles, Illinois (October 2009), "An Imaginary Library: Children's Books that Don't Exist (Yet)," which featured seventy-two original works by children's book artists from thirty different countries. Other traveling exhibits have included "Hello, Dear Enemy," "Children between Worlds," and another featuring Canadian children's books.

The Internationale Jugendbibliothek is located in a five-hundred-year-old castle at Schloss Blutenburg, Munich, Germany. Information about the collection, travelling exhibits, and fellowships is available at the website www.ijb.de.

Picture Book Museum Burg Wissem in Troisdorf (near Cologne, Germany)

This museum offers a broad collection of picture-book illustrations, old and modern picture books, and artist books. The research library includes an extensive collection of *Little Red Riding Hood* texts.

 www.museum.troisdorf.de/bilderbuchmuseum/docs/we.html

Book Fairs

The Frankfurt Book Fair

The Frankfurt Book Fair is a meeting place for the industry's experts each year in October. This fair is the most important marketplace for books, media, rights, and licenses worldwide. The Frankfurt Book Fair attracts more than 7,300 exhibitors from one hundred countries, 299,000 visitors, and over ten thousand journalists from sixty-three countries.

www.buchmesse.de/en/fbf/

Leipzig Book Fair (held annually during March)

www.leipziger-messe.de/LeMMon/buch_web_eng.nsf

Online Resources

Litrix.de—German Literature Online

This website is a portal for the worldwide promotion of contemporary German literature, including children's and young adult books.

www.litrix.de/

GREAT BRITAIN

Adlington, L. J. **The Diary of Pelly D**. New York, HarperCollins/Greenwillow Books, 2005. Originally published by Hodder Children's Books Great Britain, in 2005. ISBN 978-0-06-076615-3, 0-06-076615-8. 282 p. (12 up). Novel.

In a postapocalyptic city on a colonized planet, fourteen-year-old Toni V works with a demolition crew to remove rubble in preparation for rebuilding City Five. When his drill strikes a sealed and battered water can, he discovers a package containing the diary of Pelly D, a flirtatious teen of privilege, beauty, and a compelling way of relating her life. Because scavenging is forbidden, Tony V reads the diary in stolen snatches of time after his days of backbreaking labor. As the diary unfolds, Pelly D's blithe acceptance of her life collapses when a mandated genetic profiling system determines her family to be of Galrezi heritage, the lowest clan. Adlington's dystopian world, with its class system, power, and genocide, will open to discussions of state-sponsored oppression and resistance. *2006 USBBY-CBC Outstanding International Books List, 2006 YALSA Best Books for Young Adults, 2006 CCBC Best-of-the-Year List. nlr*

Author has lived and worked in Japan and Spain. She now lives in Great Britain, where she has taught "hands-on" history lessons using artifacts such as war diaries.

WAR, REPRESSION, HOLOCAUST, CLASSISM, DIARIES, SCIENCE FICTION

Ahlberg, Allan. **The Children Who Smelled a Rat**. Illustrated by Katharine McEwen. Cambridge, MA, Candlewick Press, 2005. Originally published by Walker Books Great Britain, in 2005. ISBN 978-0-7636-2870-3, 0-7636-2870-0. 80 p. (9–14). Novel.

This fast-paced adventure begins with a mysterious package, baby Gary in a runaway shopping cart, and an oddly behaving teacher. Seemingly unrelated events come together in the surprise ending. The author and illustrator playfully use varied font, a slightly backward table of contents, tongue-in-cheek commentary, and talking cats and mice throughout this humorous story. *si*

Author lives in Great Britain.

PETS, TEACHERS, TRIPLETS, HUMOROUS STORIES

Ahlberg, Allan. **The Runaway Dinner**. Illustrated by Bruce Ingman. Cambridge, MA, Candlewick Press, 2006. Originally published by Walker Books Great Britain, in 2006. ISBN 978-0-7636-3142-0, 0-7636-3142-6. 40 p. (4–8). Picture book.

Banjo Cannon's very ordered life gets upset when his dinner sausage, Melvin, jumps off the plate, runs away, and is chased by the fork, knife, plate, table, chair, and a hungry little boy. The rest of Banjo's food, his parents, the cat, and a neighbor's dog join the pursuit, which ends with some mishaps and some narrow escapes for the runaway dinner. The tone of the story is chatty and conversational. The abundance of absurdities in the text (each of the peas, carrots, and French fries also has a name) and the action-packed acrylic illustrations, with animated food and other objects, add to the fun. *Ahlberg was a recipient of the 1986 Kurt Maschler Award with Janet Ahlberg. Ingman was awarded a UK National Art Library Illustrator's Award and the Mother Goose Award. ca, hc*

Author lives in Great Britain, and the illustrator lives in Great Britain and Ireland.

FOOD, HUMOROUS STORIES

Ahlberg, Allan. **Previously**. Illustrated by Bruce Ingman. Cambridge, MA, Candlewick Press, 2007. Originally published by Walker Books Great

Britain, in 2007. ISBN 978-0-7636-3542-8, 0-7636-3542-1. 29 p. (5–9). Picture book.

The adventures of nursery characters, including Goldilocks, the Frog Prince, and Cinderella, are told in reverse sequence and with all the stories linked together. Once you get into the rhythm of the sequence of events, you begin to anticipate what will happen next—that is, what happened previously. Ingman's illustrations detail the reverse sequence of each tale and provide visual links to the next one. The ending is particularly inventive as the characters are shown as the tiny babies that they were "once upon a time . . . previously" (n.p.). ca

Author lives in Great Britain, illustrator lives in Great Britain and Ireland.
CHARACTERS IN LITERATURE, FAIRY TALES, HUMOROUS STORIES

Ahlberg, Allan. **The Pencil**. Illustrated by Bruce Ingman. Cambridge, MA, Candlewick Press, 2008. Originally published by Walker Books Great Britain, in 2008. ISBN 978-0-7636-3894-8, 0-7636-3894-3. 45 p. (5–8). Picture book.

A lonely pencil draws a boy, a dog, a cat, a whole neighborhood, and then a paintbrush to make everything colorful. When the pencil draws an eraser, however, it begins to rub everyone and everything out. The pencil must come up with a plan to stop the eraser before it rubs him out, too. This is a clever, engaging story with cartoonlike illustrations, featuring the animated pencil, paintbrush, and eraser, that extend the sly humor of the text. The ending, which at first seems like it will be predictable, is inventive and surprising. ca

Author lives in Great Britain; illustrator lives in Great Britain and Ireland.
PENCILS, DRAWING, LONELINESS, HUMOROUS STORIES

Alborough, Jez. **Yes**. Illustrated by the author. Cambridge, MA, Candlewick Press, 2006. Originally published by Walker Books Great Britain, in 2006. ISBN 978-0-7636-3183-3, 0-7636-3183-3. n.p. (0–5). Picture book.

When it is "bath time," Bobo enthusiastically says "Yes," but when it is bedtime, Bobo responds with an emphatic "No." But after two friends, crocodile and elephant, splash and play with Bobo, he is soon yawning and is carried sleeping to his bed. The minimal text appears on selected pages in bubbles. The story is carried by the large double-spread illustrations rendered in gouache on board, which highlight the actions and facial expressions of the characters. This familiar bedtime routine is played out against

the blues, yellows, and greens of a river scene with trees and mountains in the background. *hc*
Author is from Great Britain.
CHIMPANZEES, BEDTIME, FICTION

Almond, David. **Clay**. New York, Random House/Delacorte Press, 2005. Originally published by Hodder Children's Books Great Britain, in 2005. ISBN 978-0-385-73171-3, 0-385-73171-X. 247 p. (14 up). Fiction.
Serving as altar boys at their Catholic church in the North of Great Britain, thirteen-year-old Davie and his friend Geordie's worst sins include stealing the altar wine and smoking cigarettes. Then, Father O'Mahoney asks Davie to be friends with Stephen, a gifted sculptor, who, expelled from the seminary, has come to live with his aunt, "Crazy Mary." Davie is drawn into helping Stephen make a clay monster that appears to come to life and addresses them as "Master." After his tormentor, the local town bully, is found dead, Davie grapples with the knowledge that he has been exposed to evil. *2007 USBBY Outstanding International Books List, 2007 YALSA Best Books for Young Adults. David Almond is the recipient of the 2010 Hans Christian Andersen Award. hc*
Author lives in Northumberland, Great Britain.
FRIENDSHIP, GANGS, BULLYING, SUPERNATURAL, HORROR, YOUNG ADULT FICTION, TEENAGE BOYS, GREAT BRITAIN

Almond, David. **Kate, the Cat and the Moon**. Illustrated by Stephen Lambert. New York, Random House, 2005. Originally published by Hodder Children's Books Great Britain, in 2004. ISBN 978-0-385-74691-5, 0-385-74691-1. n.p. (5–8). Picture book.
Late at night Kate wakes up to the meowing of a cat. Illustrations show Kate transforming herself into a cat as she joins the mysterious feline beneath the full moon. The pair climb a hill, where they meow and howl at the moon—which has become the face of a white cat. In a foldout page, the feline friends join the moon cat to fly through a sky full of dreams. The next morning when family members compare their dreams, Kate simply replies: "Meow." *David Almond won the 2010 Hans Christian Andersen Award. chs, nlr*
Author and illustrator live in Great Britain.
CATS, NIGHT, FICTION

Almond, David. **My Dad's a Birdman**. Illustrated by Polly Dunbar. Cambridge, MA, Candlewick Press, 2008. Originally published by Walker Books

Great Britain, in 2007. ISBN 978-0-7636-3667-8, 0-7636-3667-3. 115 p. (10 up). Novel.

David Almond's books are exemplars of multilayered texts. My *Dad's A Birdman*, Almond's first chapter book for younger audiences, is a good example. From an adult point of view, parents that squawk, eat worms and spiders, and wear wings are probably not sane. From an eight-year-old child's perspective, these behaviors may be understood simply as a way to heal a broken soul. In Almond's world, Lizzie intelligently takes over when her Dad assumes the aforementioned traits. Polly Dunbar's watercolor and collage illustrations, adorning virtually every page, increase the humor and pleasure of an already exuberant (albeit admittedly dark) fantasy. *2009 USBBY Outstanding International Books List, UKLA Children's Publishing Award. David Almond is the winner of the 2010 Hans Christian Andersen Award. He also has received the Whitbread Award and the Carnegie Medal. lmp*

Author lives in Northumberland, Great Britain.

FATHERS AND DAUGHTERS, NORTHERN GREAT BRITAIN, FLIGHT, GREAT BRITAIN, FANTASY FICTION

Almond, David. **Raven Summer**. New York, Delacorte Press, 2009. Originally published as *Jackdaw Summer* by Hodder Children's Books Great Britain, in 2008. ISBN 978-0-385-73806-4, 0-385-73806-4. 198 p. (12 up). Novel.

Andersen Award–winner David Almond's novels are never simple, and *Raven Summer* is no exception. Liam and Max discover a baby and a jar of cash. No one claims her, and the police have no leads. But Liam's mother decides to adopt her, and Liam's expectation of an endless summer of imaginary play in idyllic meadows cracks apart. Moral decisions loom larger than life, and the lads he has counted as his friends peel away like onionskin. Innocence battles adolescence, and when strangers enter the equation, innocence disappears. "There are savages everywhere, waiting their chance" (73). *David Almond is the winner of the 2010 Hans Christian Andersen Award. He also has received the Whitbread Award and the Carnegie Medal. lmp*

Author lives in Northumberland, Great Britain.

FOUNDLINGS, INTERPERSONAL RELATIONS, CONDUCT OF LIFE, SOLDIERS, FATE AND FATALISM, NORTHUMBERLAND, GREAT BRITAIN, FICTION

Almond, David. **The Boy Who Climbed into the Moon**. Illustrated by Polly Dunbar. Somerville, MA, Candlewick Press, 2010. Originally published by Walker Books Great Britain, in 2010. ISBN 978-0-7636-4217-4, 0-7636-4217-7. 120 p. (9–12). Illustrated Novel.

Paul lives in the basement of a high-rise building. He doesn't like school, and so, one day, he feigns sickness. When his parents allow him to stay home, he finds he is bored. The solution, of course, is to go to the top of his building and touch the sky. Paul naturally continues on to the moon so he can confirm his thesis that the moon is only a hole in the sky. As in *My Dad's a Birdman* (Almond, reviewed in this volume), Polly Dunbar's full-color, mainly double-page illustrations create an essential bridge between Almond's outrageously fantastic characters and his audience, thus enabling readers to suspend disbelief and enter into the author's wacky universe. *lmp*
Author lives in Great Britain.
ADVENTURE AND ADVENTURERS, BOYS, GREAT BRITAIN, FANTASY FICTION

Archer, Dosh & Mike Archer. **Looking after Little Ellie.** Illustrated by the authors. New York, Bloomsbury, 2005. Originally published by Bloomsbury Great Britain, in 2005. ISBN 978-1-58234-971-8, 1-58234-971-1. n.p. (0–5). Picture book.
Six mice agree to help out their friend by babysitting "Little Ellie," but they have a surprise when they find out that Ellie is not so little, but a baby elephant. The humor of the situation is reproduced in predominantly pastel illustrations with some inserted photographic images showing how the mice cope with feeding, changing a diaper full of realistic elephant dung, and with taking "Ellie" on an outing to the park. Short, one-line sentences tell what happens on each page. *hc*
Authors live in Great Britain.
SIZE, BABYSITTERS, BABIES, MICE, ELEPHANTS, FICTION

Avi. **The Traitors' Gate.** Illustrated by Karina Raude. New York, Simon & Schuster/Atheneum/A Richard Jackson Book, 2007. ISBN 978-0-689-85335-7, 0-689-85335-1. 353 p. (9–12). Novel.
Set in 1849 London, fourteen-year-old John Horatio Huffman tells about the misfortunes that befall his family when his father is arrested and sentenced for gambling debts. As he tries to help, John is caught up in a plot of intrigues and spies that involve his father's work in the Naval Ordinance Office and Scotland Yard. There are vivid descriptions of London with its chaotic, bustling streets and a full range of Dickensian characters. Avi's homage to Dickens includes descriptions of the villainous Sergeant Muldspoon's "Military Motivated Academy," a "sponge house," and the debtor's prison. *Among his numerous awards, Avi received the 2003 Newbery Award for* Crispin: The Cross of Lead. *hc*
Author lives in the United States but resided for a number of years in London.

Spy Stories, Poverty, Family Life, Mystery and Detective Stories, London–Great Britain History (1800–1950), Historical Fiction

Beaty, Andrea. **Iggy Peck, Architect**. Illustrated by David Roberts. New York, Harry N. Abrams Books, 2007. ISBN 978-0-8109-1106-2, 0-8109-1106-X. 32 p. (5–8). Picture book.

Iggy Peck had been building towers "since he was two" (n.p.). One night, he builds the "St. Louis Arch from pancakes and coconut pie" (n.p.). But in second grade, his teacher says architecture has "no place" in her classroom (n.p.). One day, Miss Greer takes the class on a hike. As they cross an old footbridge to an island, the bridge collapses, and they are stranded. Iggy rescues them with a bridge "dangling from shoestring suspension" (n.p.). The illustrations convey the whimsical humor of this rhyming story. Detailed drawings of buildings and bridges, some on graph paper, highlight Iggy's architectural ambitions. *David Roberts's awards include a 2006 Nestlé Gold for Mouse Noses on Toast.* hc

Author lives in the United States; illustrator lives in London.
Building, Schools, School Field trips, Stories in Rhyme

Bee, William. **And the Train Goes . . .** Illustrated by the author. Cambridge, MA, Candlewick Press, 2007. Originally published by Walker Books Great Britain, in 2007. ISBN 978-0-7636-3248-9, 0-7636-3248-1. 24 p. (2–5). Picture book.

As the station clock goes "Tick-tock, tickerty-tock . . ." (n.p.), a colorful train goes on its way down the tracks with a "Clickerty-click, clickerty-clack . . ." (n.p.), carrying carloads of passengers, all having something to say about the train ride. The text is simple but full of interesting-sounding words that are different from the sounds usually associated with the ticking of a clock, a moving train, noisy hens, and so on. The illustrations feature a string of intricately patterned and brightly colored cars on an old-fashioned train filled with equally detailed and colorful passengers. ca

Author/illustrator lives in Great Britain.
Railroad Trains, Fiction, Sounds

Bee, William. **Beware of the Frog**. Illustrated by the author. Cambridge, MA, Candlewick Press, 2008. Originally published by Walker Books Great Britain, in 2008. ISBN 978-0-7636-3920-4, 0-7636-3920-6. 40 p. (4–8). Picture book.

Mrs. Collywobbles, a sweet little old lady, has a pet frog that protects her from the horrible creatures that come out of the dark, scary woods by gobbling them up. When she gives the frog a thank-you kiss, however, she is transformed into a sweet little old lady frog and, none too pleased with this, gobbles him up. The rich, patterned language of the text reads aloud well. The illustrations, done in pen and ink then computer manipulated, contribute to the story's folktale flavor by exhibiting unwavering uniformity in Mrs. Collywobbles's house, the woods, and her personal appearance. *ca*

The author/illustrator lives in Great Britain.

FROGS, MONSTERS, OLD AGE, MAGIC, FICTION

Benjamin, Floella. **My Two Grannies**. Illustrated by Margaret Chamberlain. London, Frances Lincoln, 2008. Originally published by Frances Lincoln Great Britain, in 2007. ISBN 978-1-84507-643-6, 1-84507-643-5. n.p. (5–7). Picture book.

Alvina lives near her two grannies: Granny Vero who emigrated from Trinidad and Granny Rose who always lived in Great Britain. The two grannies offer to care for Alvina so her parents can take a vacation for their tenth anniversary. Cultural clashes—and a bit of jealousy—quickly intrude. Granny Vero suggests rice and peas with chicken and plantains. Granny Rose proposes a steak and kidney pie. Food is not the only debate: zoo or park? Dominoes or board game? "Anansi" or "Jack and the Beanstalk"? In the end, compromise diminishes all disagreements, so Alvina's week is a spectacular success—for everyone. *2009 USBBY Outstanding International Books List. lmp*

Author was born in Trinidad but lives in Dorset, Great Britain.

GRANDMOTHERS, RACIALLY MIXED CHILDREN, CULTURE CONFLICT, TRINIDAD AND TOBAGO, NORTHERN GREAT BRITAIN, PICTURE STORYBOOK

Bertagna, Julie. **Exodus**. New York, Walker Books, 2008. Originally published by Young Picador, an imprint of Pan Macmillan Great Britain, in 2002. ISBN 978-0-8027-9745-2, 0-8027-9745-8. 345 p. (14 up). Novel.

Because of global warming, Wing is almost submerged. Mara persuades her family and neighbors to leave their island for one of the "New World sky cities" (54). But, her family is drowned on the way. There is a boat refugee camp outside the city wall to keep newcomers out, but an urchin boy gets Mara beyond the wall, where she stays with the "Treenesters" who live under the city's towers. With the help of the "fox" she meets in cyberworld, who shuts down the city's communications, Mara rescues her friends and the city's slaves, then commandeers ships to sail to Greenland. The sequel, *Zenith*, was published in the United States in 2009. *2002 Whitbread Children's Book of the Year Award Shortlist. hc*

Author lives in Scotland.

SURVIVAL, VOYAGES AND TRAVELS, ALTRUISM, GLOBAL WARMING, FLOODS, SCIENCE FICTION

Blacker, Terence. **Boy2girl**. New York, Farrar, Straus and Giroux, 2005. Originally published by Macmillan Children's Great Britain, in 2004. ISBN 978-0-374-30926-8, 0-374-30926-4. 296 p. (12 up). Novel.

After the death of his mother, Sam travels from America to live with his cousin Matt and his family. Sam, Matt, Tyrone, and Jake (the "Sheds") decide to trick a group of female classmates (the "Bitches"), and Sam dresses like a girl and infiltrates their group. Sam enjoys playing this gender role more than his friends expect, and after several comical events, his secret is revealed. *si*

Author lives in Great Britain.

COUSINS, DEATH, SCHOOLS, FICTION

Brooks, Kevin. **The Road of the Dead**. New York, Scholastic/Chicken House, 2006. Originally puplished by Chicken House Great Britain, in 2005. ISBN 978-0-439-78623-2, 0-439-78623-1. 339 p. (14 up). Novel.

Two half-gypsy teenagers, Ruben and Cole, travel from their London home to the desolate Devon village of Lychcombe to discover the truth behind the brutal murder of their sister, Rachel, in a remote moorland field. Brooks's attention to descriptive details dramatically captures the moody atmosphere of the desolate moors and the depth of the brothers' anger and grief over their sister's death, as well as the strength of their close relationship. This is a suspenseful psychological thriller with a cast of well-defined characters, corruption, violence—and a touch of romance. *2007 Carnegie Medal Shortlist. ca, hc*

Author lives in Great Britain.

MURDER, BROTHERS, ROMANIES, GREAT BRITAIN, REALISTIC FICTION

Brooks, Kevin. **Being**. New York, Scholastic/Chicken House, 2007. Originally published by Penguin Great Britain, in 2007. ISBN 978-0-439-89973-4, 0-439-89973-7. 323 p. (14 up). Novel.

Sixteen-year-old Robert's routine endoscopy results are far from normal. He wakes from unconsciousness to find himself being operated on by a doctor who is being held at gunpoint by a man called Ryan. Robert escapes, opens up his wounds, and sees, for himself, his machinelike insides. Falsely accused of murder, Robert enlists the help of Eddi, who forges him a new identity and takes him to her house in Spain, but the mysterious Ryan stays on their trail. In this taut thriller, Robert, an orphan, struggles to understand who he

really is and what it really means to be human. *Kevin Brooks has been awarded YALSA Best Books for Young Adults in 2004 for* Lucas *and 2007 for* Road of the Dead, *2003 Branford Boase Award for Best First Novel (UK) for* Martyn Pig. Black Rabbit Summer *was nominated for the CILIP Carnegie Medal, 2009. hc*
  Author is from Great Britain.
  IDENTITY, ONTOLOGY, HUMAN DESIGN, SCIENCE FICTION

Browne, Anthony. **My Mom**. Illustrated by the author. New York, Farrar, Straus and Giroux, 2005. Originally published in Great Britain by Transworld/Doubleday, in 2005. ISBN 978-0-374-35098-7, 0-374-35098-1. n.p. (4–8). Picture book.

  Opening with an understated and frequently reiterated, "She's nice, my mom" (n.p.), Anthony Browne continues his series of companion books about the members of an unseen child's family—*My Dad* (2001) and *My Brother* (reviewed here). Mom is wrapped in flowers and hearts, but she's also tough when the going gets rough. The author Browne has produced great similes, "tough as a rhino" (n.p.), but the artist Browne provides the humor: the rhino sports a lovely bow on its tusk that matches mom's housecoat. Youngsters will enjoy creating their personal paean to mom using *My Mom* as a mentor text. *2006 USBBY-CBC Outstanding International Books List. Anthony Browne has won the Kate Greenaway Medal twice and was a recipient of the Hans Christian Andersen Award for his body of work. lmp*
  Author lives in Great Britain.
  MOTHERS, MOTHER AND CHILD, GREAT BRITAIN, FICTION, COMPANION BOOK TO MY BROTHER AND MY DAD

Browne, Anthony. **Silly Billy**. Illustrated by the author. Cambridge, MA, Candlewick Press, 2006. Originally published by Walker Books Great Britain, in 2006. ISBN 978-0-7636-3124-6, 0-7636-3124-8. 24 p. (5–8). Picture book.

  Worrying about everything keeps Billy awake until Grandma gives him some Guatemalan worry dolls to tell his worries to. Billy sleeps well—until he begins to worry about overburdening the tiny dolls with worries. His solution: crafting tiny worry dolls for the worry dolls. Color and layout are effectively used to create various moods in the surreal illustrations, which are filled with superb details, such as the change in the facial expressions of the worry dolls to frowns after Billy has transferred his worries to them and the labeling of each doll with its name. Includes a note on customs associated with Guatemalan worry dolls. *2007 Outstanding International Books List. Anthony Browne is the British Children's Laureate from 2009 to 2011. ca*

Author lives in Great Britain.
WORRY, DOLLS, FICTION

Browne, Anthony. **My Brother**. Illustrated by the author. New York, Farrar, Straus and Giroux, 2007. Originally published by Doubleday, an imprint of Random House Great Britain, in 2007. ISBN 978-0-374-35120-5, 0-374-35120-1. n.p. (2–6). Picture book.

Using a background of blue-lined writing paper, ubiquitous in elementary classrooms, a young boy lists all his sibling's amazing feats. The actual text is simple, "My brother is really COOL" (n.p.). What makes this book fascinating, and infinitely re-readable, are the arrows that lead from captions to specific "cool" aspects of the older brother. Browne has created a tribute to brotherly love that is a fitting companion to his other family books, *My Dad* (2001) and *My Mom* (reviewed here). *Anthony Browne is the recipient of the Hans Christian Andersen Award, the Kate Greenaway Award (twice), and is the British Children's Laureate for 2009 to 2011. lmp*

Author lives in Great Britain.
BROTHERS, REALISTIC FICTION, GREAT BRITAIN

Browne, Anthony. **Little Beauty**. Illustrated by the author. Somerville, MA, Candlewick Press, 2008. Originally published by Walker Books Great Britain, in 2008. ISBN 978-0-7636-3959-4, 0-7636-3959-1. 32 p. (4–8). Picture book.

When a very special gorilla (he's learned sign language) asks his keepers for a friend, they give him a kitten. The two do everything together. When the gorilla loses his temper and smashes the TV in their compound, however, the keepers fear for Beauty's safety. They plan to take her away, until she takes responsibility for the damage—using sign language. Visual references to "King Kong" and "Beauty and the Beast," the dramatic showcasing of the great size difference between the gorilla and Beauty, and Browne's signature stylistic touches make this a picture book that can be enjoyed by readers of all ages. *2009 USBBY Outstanding International Books List, Oppenheim Toy Portfolio Platinum Award Winner, Parents' Choice Award. Anthony Browne is a Hans Christian Andersen Medalist. ca*

Author lives in Great Britain.
GORILLA, CATS, SIGN LANGUAGE, HUMAN-ANIMAL COMMUNICATION, ZOOS, FICTION

Butterworth, Christine. **Sea Horse: The Shyest Fish in the Sea**. Illustrated by John Lawrence. Cambridge, MA, Candlewick Press, 2006. Originally published as *Seahorse* by Walker Books Great Britain, in 2006. ISBN 978-0-7636-2989-2, 0-7636-2989-8. 27 p. (3–7). Nonfiction.

A brief text covers the physical characteristics of the Barbour's sea horse (*Hippocampus barbouri*) and its food habits, movement, predators, and life cycle, including mating and the role of the male in carrying the eggs. Ten other species of sea horses are pictured and labeled with their common and scientific names on the endpapers. Using vinyl engravings, printed wood textures, and watercolor washes, Lawrence creates a detailed undersea setting. Back matter includes an index, brief notes about sea horses, and notes from the author and the illustrator about writing and illustrating the book. *2007 USBBY Outstanding International Books List*. ca

Author and illustrator live in Great Britain.

SEA HORSES, MARINE ANIMALS, NONFICTION TEXT

Cartwright, Reg. **What We Do**. Illustrated by the author. New York, Henry Holt, 2005. Originally published by Hutchinson Great Britain, in 2004. ISBN 978-0-8050-7671-4, 0-8050-7671-9. 24 p. (0–5). Picture book.

Each page features a different animal with a simple one-line sentence describing how each animal moves. The last words of sentences on facing pages rhyme. For example, "I'm a caterpillar. I creep" (n.p.) is followed by, "We are lambs and we leap" on the next facing page (n.p.). Colorful illustrations on glossy paper depict the animals in flattened perspective against flat backgrounds—some of which display a hint of natural habitat. The solid, somewhat abstract, figure of each animal is captured, akin to a photographic still, in the movement attributed to it in the accompanying words on the page. *hc*

Author lives in Great Britain.

ANIMAL LOCOMOTION, STORIES IN RHYME, ANIMAL LOCOMOTION, FICTION

Castle, Kate (with ballet direction by Anna du Boisson). **My First Ballet Book**. Illustrated by Richard Brown's photographs. Boston, Kingfisher, 2006. ISBN 978-0-7534-6026-9, 0-7534-6026-2. 64 p. (4–8). Nonfiction.

Including "What Is Ballet," "What to Wear," "Warming Up," "Ready to Perform," "Famous Ballets," and more, this guide captures the magic of dance. Accurate, detailed, specially commissioned color photographs show beginner and advanced dancers demonstrating barre work, turns, jumps, and pas de deux. Step-by-step instructions, helpful tips, and a glossary will help young dancers make the most of their ballet classes. Readers will also experience the thrill of dancing onstage and the wonder of watching a performance. *mjw*

Author is a former Royal Ballet dancer who lives in Great Britain.
PERFORMING ARTS, ENTERTAINMENT, DANCE, BALLET, NONFICTION

Chadda, Sarwat. **Devil's Kiss**. New York, Disney/Hyperion Books, 2009. ISBN 978-1-4231-1999-9, 1-4231-1999-1. 327 p. (14 up). Novel.

Fifteen-year-old Billi is not your normal, contemporary London teen. She lives in a darker part of the world, the first female member of the Knights Templar, now committed to waging the Bataille Tenebreuse, the Dark Battle, against supernatural powers that lust for human blood, flesh, and souls. Filled with werewolves, ghouls, and vampires led by the Angel of Death, Chadda's page-turner evokes images from Mid-East Asian religion and folklore. Fittingly enough, the story centers on the question of what are we willing to sacrifice for the greater good. The story of Abraham's sacrifice of Isaac lurks throughout. *jfc*

Author lives in Great Britain.
TEMPLARS, SUPERNATURAL, GOOD AND EVIL, LONDON, GREAT BRITAIN, FICTION

Chamberlain, Margaret. **Please Don't Tease Tootsie**. Illustrated by the author. New York, Penguin/Dutton Children's Books, 2008. Originally published by Hodder Children's Books Great Britain, in 2008. ISBN 978-0-525-47982-6, 0-525-47982-1. 29 p. (3–6). Picture book.

An unseen narrator offers a list of "don'ts" related to the treatment of all different kinds of pets. "Please don't tease Tootsie, or provoke Poochie" (n.p.), and so on. Then, in reverse order, the narrator tells just how each pet should be treated. This is a beautifully designed book: thick paper; uncluttered pages; a simple text in large print; backgrounds in bold, flat colors; and humorous illustrations featuring an array of pets clearly showing how they feel about their initial mistreatments and their pleasure when treated kindly. An engaging, be-kind-to-animals book for young children. *ca*

Author/illustrator lives in Great Britain.
PETS, KINDNESS, ANIMAL WELFARE, FICTION

Chichester Clark, Emma. **Melrose and Croc: A Christmas to Remember**. Illustrated by the author. New York, Walker Books, 2006. Originally published as *Melrose and Croc Together at Christmas* by HarperCollins Great Britain, in 2006. ISBN 978-0-8027-9597-7, 0-8027-9597-8. 32 p. (4–8). Picture book.

Croc, a little green crocodile, arrives too late to the city on Christmas Eve to visit Santa Claus at a department store. Melrose, a little yellow dog, is depressed, alone in the city, and not able to get into the holiday spirit by himself. The two crash into each other at a skating rink and quickly become friends in time for a magical Christmas. Sparkling, oversized watercolor illustrations bustle with Yuletide activity. *mjw*

Author lives in Great Britain.

FRIENDSHIP, LONELINESS, CHRISTMAS, CITY AND TOWN LIFE, DOGS, CROCODILES, FICTION

Child, Lauren. **Clarice Bean Spells Trouble**. Illustrated by the author. Cambridge, MA, Candlewick Press, 2005. Originally published by Orchard Books Great Britain, in 2004. ISBN 978-0-7636-2813-0, 0-7636-2813-1. 188 p. (8–11). Novel.

Clarice Bean Tuesday, an utter charmer and nonstop learner, prepares for a spelling bee, lands and loses a leading role in *The Sound of Music*, tries to please a wonderful new teacher, and is supportive of a friend with family problems. She is obsessed with her TV hero, Ruby Redfort, an eleven-year-old secret agent, and continually employs Ruby's rules to keep out of trouble and to help others. Random sketches, font changes, and made-up polysyllabic words add to the appeal of this "exceptionordinary" middle-grader. *Junior Library Guild Selection, CBC Choices, Chicago Public Library Best Books for Children and Teens. mjw*

Author lives in London.

FRIENDSHIP, AUTHORSHIP, SCHOOLS, FAMILY LIFE, HUMOROUS STORIES, FICTION

Child, Lauren. **But Excuse Me That Is My Book**. Illustrated by the author. New York, Penguin/Dial Books, 2006. Originally published by Puffin Great Britain, in 2005. ISBN 978-0-803-73096-0, 0-803-73096-9. 32 p. (4–8). Picture book.

Charlie's little sister, Lola, is dismayed when she discovers that her favorite library book, *Beetles, Bugs, and Butterflies*, has been checked out by another girl. Not quite understanding the concept of borrowing, Lola is not interested in another book. Charlie finally persuades her to try *Cheetahs and Chimpanzees*, and she ultimately decides that it is "probably the most best book in the whole wide world . . ." (n.p.). The photo and cartoon collage artwork is charming. Charlie and Lola also star in an animated television series on the Disney Channel. The text is based on the script written by Bridget Hurst and Carol Noble; illustrations are from the TV animation produced by Tiger Aspect (t.p. verso). *2006 School Library Journal Best Book. mjw*

Author lives in Great Britain.
BOOKS AND READING, BROTHERS AND SISTERS, LIBRARIES, FICTION

Church, Caroline Jayne. **Little Apple Goat**. Illustrated by the author. Grand Rapids, MI, Eerdmans Books for Young Readers, 2007. Originally published by Oxford University Press Great Britain, in 2007. ISBN 978-0-8028-5320-2, 0-8028-5320-X. n.p. (3–7). Picture book.

Little Apple Goat's favorite meal is fruit—apples, pears, cherries—whatever is available in the orchard. She eagerly anticipates her annual fall feast when ripe fruit drops to the ground. As she returns to the barn, she spits, then goes "Plippety, Plip! Plop!," thus disbursing the seeds she has consumed. When a severe storm destroys her orchard, Little Apple Goat is bereft. Soon, however, new trees appear, but readers must infer the new orchard's source. This simple tale of nature's regenerative cycles will entrance readers with its lively palette of watercolors and strong black-line and collage art. *lmp*
Author lives in Great Britain.
GOATS, ORCHARDS, FRUIT, DOMESTIC ANIMALS, FANTASY, GREAT BRITAIN

Church, Caroline Jayne. **Ping Pong Pig**. Illustrated by the author. New York, Holiday House, 2008. Originally published by Simon & Schuster Great Britain, in 2008. ISBN 978-0-8234-2176-3, 0-8234-2176-7. n.p. (4–8). Picture book.

Ping Pong Pig was too busy having fun to help the other animals on the farm. As a matter of fact, his bouncing and jumping caused everyone massive headaches. Ping Pong's unrestrained bouncing splashed mud on the freshly painted barn, shook apples from the tree, smashed the beehives, and knocked over the haystacks. What could the animals do to keep Ping Pong out of their way? *Ping Pong Pig* pairs nicely with other barnyard fantasies like *Click Clack Moo: Cows That Type* (Cronin 2000), or even *The Little Red Hen* (Galdone 1973). *lmp*
Author lives in Great Britain.
PIGS, DOMESTIC ANIMALS, BEHAVIOR, FLIGHT, FANTASY, GREAT BRITAIN

Church, Caroline Jayne. **One More Hug for Madison**. Illustrated by the author. New York, Scholastic/Orchard Books, 2010. Originally published as *One More Hug for Nutmeg* by Orchard Books Great Britain, in 2009. ISBN 978-0-545-16179-4, 0-545-16179-7. n.p. (0–4). Picture book.

Mommy calls out to her mouse daughter, "Time for bed, Madison" (n.p.). What follows initially is a parent's dream—Madison voluntarily stores her toys, washes her face, and brushes her teeth, then dons her pajamas. Bedtime quickly dissolves into one demand after another, until Mommy falls asleep as Madison whispers, "Just one last thing . . ." (n.p.). Collage, brush, and ink illustrations with nubby, pulp-paper backgrounds provide a tactile appearance that is perfectly suited to the age group. *lmp*

Author lives in Great Britain.

MOTHER AND CHILD, MICE, BEDTIME, FICTION

Clayton, Emma. **The Roar**. New York, Scholastic/Chicken House, 2009. Originally published by Chicken House Great Britain, in 2008. ISBN 978-0-439-92593-8, 0-439-92593-2. 481 p. (10 up). Novel.

In futuristic London, twins with supernaturally powerful eyes are manipulated by an evil leader who plots to use them to conquer the world. A compelling page-turner, this video game-style story conveys a strong environmental message and a warning about the use of excessive power. *2010 USBBY Outstanding International Books List.*

Author lives in Great Britain.

TWINS, KIDNAPPING, SCIENCE FICTION

Cole, Stephen. **Thieves Like Us**. New York, Bloomsbury, 2006. Originally published by Bloomsbury Great Britain, in 2006. ISBN 978-1-58234-653-3, 1-58234-653-4. 349 p. (14 up). Novel.

Nathaniel Coldhardt's children, four talented misfits, break seventeen-year-old Jonah Wish out of a Young Offender's Institution. They need his computer skills to help them crack a Spartan cipher code that will lead them to the substance, Amrita, said to grant eternal life (65). Jonah is swept up in one dangerous assignment after another in different locations, including a museum break-in in Cairo to steal an ancient jar. But the jar is shattered in a fight with acolytes of Coldhardt's rival. They are left with fragments that eventually lead them to Macedonia where, in an underground tomb, they find nightmarish secrets. *hc*

Author is from Great Britain.

ADVENTURE AND ADVENTURERS, INTERPERSONAL RELATIONS, FICTION, ADVENTURE STORIES

Collicutt, Paul. **This Rocket**. Illustrated by the author. New York, Farrar, Straus and Giroux, 2005. ISBN 978-0-374-37484-6, 0-374-37484-8. n.p. (4–8). Picture book.

Simple, one-sentence captions present basic concepts relating to rockets. Rockets zoom up or splash down, move fast or move slowly (n.p.). Sentences such as these can be used to teach opposites to younger children. Older children may find the factually detailed endpapers of interest. *si*

    Author lives in Great Britain.

    ROCKETS (AERONAUTICS)

Cooper, Helen. **A Pipkin of Pepper**. Illustrated by the author. New York, Farrar, Straus and Giroux, 2005. Originally published by Random House/ Doubleday Great Britain, in 2004. ISBN 978-0-374-35953-9, 0-374-35953-9. (4–8). Picture book.

    Cat, Squirrel, and Duck, from Cooper's Greenaway award-winning *Pumpkin Soup* (1999), are back and busy preparing their favorite pumpkin soup when they discover they are unfortunately out of salt. Duck, who has a habit of wandering off, insists on accompanying Cat and Squirrel on their shopping trip to the city. He promises to "hold on tight" and not get lost. But, when he spies a pepper shop and imagines peppered pumpkin soup, he forgets his friends. There follows a great flurry of searching by police dogs and fire dogs. All ends well: the trio is reunited and the soup is delicious. *Bank Street Best Children's Book of the Year, IRA-CBC Children's Choices. mjw*

    Author lives in Great Britain.

    DUCKS, CATS, SQUIRRELS, MISSING CHILDREN, CITY AND TOWN LIFE, FICTION

Cooper, Susan. **Victory**. New York, Simon & Schuster/Margaret K. McElderry Books, 2006. ISBN 978-1-4169-1477-8, 1-4169-1477-3. 196 p. (10–12). Novel.

    Told in alternating voices, this is the story of two young people: Sam Robbins living in 1803 and Molly Jennings living in the twenty-first century. Sam is a farm boy who is abducted and pressed into naval service. There is a war between Great Britain and France, and sailors are desperately needed. Sam is assigned to the HMS *Victory*, Admiral Nelson's flagship in the Battle of Trafalgar. Molly's mother has remarried an American after her husband—Molly's father—is killed in a plane accident. Cooper meticulously erects parallels between the two characters so that the dénouement is satisfying and credible. *Author won the Newbery Medal for* The Grey King *(1976) and Newbery Honor for* The Dark Is Rising *(1974). lmp*

    Author was born in Great Britain but lives in the United States.

    VICTORY (MAN OF WAR), SEA STORIES, GREAT BRITAIN NAVAL HISTORY–19TH CENTURY, HISTORICAL FICTION

Cousins, Lucy. **Maisy's Amazing Big Book of Words**. Illustrated by the author. Cambridge, MA, Candlewick Press, 2007. Originally published by Walker Books Great Britain, in 2007. ISBN 978-0-7636-0794-4, 0-7636-0794-0. 64 p. (0–5). Picture book.

Grouped into thematic categories such as getting dressed, on the farm, things that go, etc., more than three hundred basic vocabulary words are presented, each accompanied by a bright illustration. The two- to four-page groupings of words by themes make word study easy for children, parents, and preschool teachers. *nlh*

Author lives in Great Britain.

VOCABULARY, NONFICTION CONCEPT BOOK, LIFT-THE-FLAP BOOK

Cousins, Lucy. **Yummy: Eight Favorite Fairy Tales**. Illustrated by the author. Somerville, MA, Candlewick Press, 2009. Originally published as *Yummy: My Favourite Nursery Stories* by Walker Books Great Britain, in 2009. ISBN 978-0-7636-4474-1, 0-7636-4474-9. 121 p. (2–8). Anthology.

Yummy: Eight Favorite Fairy Tales is a perfect addition to folk tale collections, no matter how comprehensive. It includes the regulars—"Red Riding Hood," "Goldilocks," "Three Little Pigs," with two additional preschool favorites, "Henny Penny," and "Little Red Hen." Each abbreviated tale varies only slightly from older versions—Henny Penny's friends' names are Goosey Poosey and Ducky Daddles. What differentiates this from other folk tale collections is Cousins's inclusion of three frequently ignored tales: "The Enormous Turnip," "Three Billy Goats Gruff," and "The Musicians of Bremen." Oversized gouache illustrations, in Cousins's signature primary colors and naïve style, add unexpected humor to the text. *lmp*

Author lives in Great Britain.

FAIRYTALES

Cowell, Cressida. **That Rabbit Belongs to Emily Brown**. Illustrated by Neal Layton. New York, Hyperion Books for Children, 2007. Originally published by Orchard Books Great Britain, in 2006. ISBN 978-1-4231-0645-6, 1-4231-0645-8. 29 p. (3–6). Picture book.

Emily Brown is not giving her old gray rabbit, Stanley, to anyone, not even the queen. When bribery fails, the queen sends special commandos to steal Stanley while Emily is sleeping. In the morning Emily reclaims Stanley at the palace and teaches the queen how to make a brand-new teddy bear her own lovable toy. The text gives a matter-of-fact telling of this story of a child's extreme loyalty to a favorite toy, while the comic detailing of the mixed-media illustrations build on the fact that many aspects of the story are outrageously absurd. *ca*

    Author and illustrator live Great Britain.

    Toys, Rabbits, Play, Fiction

Crossley-Holland, Kevin. **Crossing to Paradise**. New York, Scholastic/Arthur A. Levine Books, 2008. Originally published as *Gatty's Tale* by Orion Children's Books Great Britain, in 2006. ISBN 978-0-545-05866-7, 0-545-05866-X. 339 p. (12 up). Novel.

    Crossing to Paradise, which tells the story of Gatty, a simple, medieval field girl, completes Crossley-Holland's "Arthur Trilogy." The hero of those books, Arthur de Caldecott, had been Gatty's companion before setting off to join the ill-fated Fourth Crusade. Returning without setting foot in the Holy Land, Arthur discovers that Gatty and Lady Gwyneth have left—for the Holy Land. When the group finally returns, Gatty and Lady Gwyneth have gained an understanding of Moorish culture and customs, and Lady Gwyneth has become an accomplished young woman, ready to assume her life as landowner and Arthur's wife. Crossley-Holland has again woven a rich tapestry of medieval life that can resonate with today's young readers. (n.b., The "Arthur Trilogy" was reviewed in *Crossing Boundaries with Children's Books*, p. 309). *2009 USBBY Outstanding International Books List. Kevin Crossley-Holland's awards include the Carnegie Medal and Guardian Children's Fiction Prize. mln*

    Author lives in Great Britain.

    Pilgrims and Pilgrimages, Self-actualization, Middle Ages, Adventure, Travel, Crusades, Italy, Jerusalem, Great Britain, Historical Fiction

Cutbill, Andy. **The Cow That Laid an Egg**. Illustrated by Russell Ayto. New York, HarperCollins, 2008. Originally published by HarperCollins Great Britain, in 2006. ISBN 978-0-06-137295-7, 0-06-137295-1. 29 p. (3–8). Picture book.

    The chickens hatch a plan to make Marjorie, a cow who's depressed because she's so ordinary, feel special. They paint black spots on an egg and put it under her. Marjorie awakes and discovers she's laid an egg! As Marjorie's fame grows, the other cows are jealous. They suspect the crafty chickens' involvement and demand that Marjorie prove the egg is hers—and she does. When the egg cracks open, out hops a chick that looks up at Marjorie and loudly Mooooooooos! The cartoonlike illustrations, done in collage, pen and ink, and watercolors, steal the show in this story of wacky barnyard fun. *ca*

Author and illustrator both live in Great Britain.
Cows, Chickens, Friendship, Humorous Stories, Fiction

Deacon, Alexis. **While You Are Sleeping**. Illustrated by the author. New York, Farrar, Straus and Giroux, 2006. Originally published by Hutchinson, an imprint of Random House Children's Books Great Britain, in 2006. ISBN 978-0-374-38330-5, 0-374-38330-8. n.p. (0–5). Picture book.

While a little girl sleeps, her favorite stuffed toys work hard all night to protect her. They check the room, squish bedbugs, and scare bad dreams away (n.p.). This gentle nighttime story is illustrated by the author with muted colors and several double-page spreads. *si*

Author lives in London.
Toys, Night, Sleep

Deary, Terry. **The Wicked History of the World: History with the Nasty Bits Left In!** Illustrated by Martin Brown. New York, Scholastic, 2006. Originally published as *Horrible Histories* by Scholastic Great Britain, in 2003. ISBN 978-0-439-87786-2, 0-439-87786-5. 93 p. (9–12). Illustrated Nonfiction.

Wacky humor and cartoon-style illustrations chronicle the disgusting-but-true details about foul-fighting, gruesome kings and queens, and the fifty most vicious villains of all time. Included are the horrible hunters from prehistory; the savage cities, terrible tombs, and rotten Rome of the Ancient World; beastly barbarians, nasty knights, and terrifying torture of the Middle Ages; the evil explorers and rowdy rebellions of the New World; and the cruel criminals and wicked wars of more modern times. A British to American glossary is provided. *mjw*

Author lives in Great Britain.
World History, Readers for New Literates, High-interest, Low Vocabulary, Illustrated Nonfiction Book

Delaney, Joseph. **The Last Apprentice: Revenge of the Witch**. New York, HarperCollins/Greenwillow Books, 2005. Originally published as *The Spook's Apprentice* by Random House/Bodley Head Great Britain, in 2004. ISBN 978-0-06-076618-4, 0-06-076618-2. 344 p. with 15 p. of illustrated glossary appended. (8–14). Novel.

At great peril, young Thomas Ward, the seventh son of a seventh son, takes over the work of Old Gregory, the village Spook, and begins the work of protecting ordinary folk from "ghouls, bogarts, and all manner of wicked beasties." Set in rural Great Britain in a time long ago, this scary tale is a real page-turner. The action continues in *Night of the Soul Stealer* (2007), *Attack of the Fiend* (2008), and *Clash of the Demons* (2009). *2006 USBBY-CBC Outstanding International Books List, 2006 Booklist Top 10 Fantasy Books for Youth. djg*

Author lives in Great Britain.

APPRENTICES, SUPERNATURAL, WITCHES, FICTION, NOVEL

Dewan, Ted. **One True Bear**. Illustrated by the author. New York, Walker Books, 2009. Originally published by Orchard Children's Books Great Britain, in 2009. ISBN 978-0-8027-8495-7, 0-8027-8495-X. n.p. (5–8). Picture book.

Darcy Brewster is a bear cub willing to test his stuffing against the world's most difficult boy, Damian. Many brave bears have failed in their attempts to tame Damian. Eventually, Darcy convinces the boy to play more gently when he explains that without arms, a bear can't hold him and banish bad dreams. Throughout, Damian pedals an ambulance, carries a medical kit, and stitches Darcy's injuries. As with *The Velveteen Rabbit*, Darcy is finally abandoned under the bed until an adult Damian returns with another special task for a very brave bear. An author's note indicates that additional drawings were contributed by children. *lmp*

Author lives in Great Britain.

TEDDY BEARS, HEROES, FICTION

Dickinson, John. **The Widow and the King**. New York, Random House/David Fickling Books, 2005. Originally published by David Fickling Books Great Britain, in 2005. ISBN 978-0-385-75084-4, 0-385-75084-6. 612 p. (14 up). Novel.

Raymonde Lackmere has stolen a book on witchcraft and now seeks a cup of power. He arrives at Ambrose's home in Tarceny and lets loose the "Heron Man," Ambrose's uncle, who, for three hundred years, has used "undercraft" to maintain his evil power. Ambrose, whose father was king of Tarceny, flees across the mountains to friends, but they are slain. Taken by Raymonde's father to the Widow Develin's castle, Ambrose narrowly escapes the massacre arranged by Raymonde. Gathering his own forces, and joined by Sophie, the widow's daughter, Ambrose hunts down his uncle and his "creatures" before being crowned king. This is the sequel to *The Cup of the World*. *hc*

Author lives in Great Britain.

FANTASY, ADVENTURE AND ADVENTURERS, WITCHCRAFT, YOUNG ADULT FICTION

Dickinson, Peter. **Angel Isle**. Illustrated by Ian P. Andrew. New York, Random House/Wendy Lamb Books, 2005. Originally published by MacMillan Children's Books Great Britain, in 2006. ISBN 978-0-385-74690-8, 0-385-74690-3. 500 p. (12 up). Novel.

Saranja, Maja, and Ribek have heard stories of their ancestors' fantastic journey to find the Ropemaker, who is the only person who can save their beloved valley from destruction. They begin a quest that mirrors the journey of those who have been dead for two hundred years. Along the way, this unlikely trio enlists the help of a talented young magician and an enemy spy, while discovering that each person they meet has unbounded potential as friend or foe. This sequel to Dickinson's award-winning book, *The Ropemaker*, intertwines a complex plot with intricate physics theory to create a four-dimensional world that is believable, yet profound. *2008 USBBY Outstanding International Books List.* nrr

Author lives in Great Britain.

Magic Young, Magicians, Young Adult, Fantasy Fiction

Dodd, Emma. **What Pet to Get?** Illustrated by the author. New York, Scholastic/Arthur A. Levine Books, 2008. Originally published by Templar Publishing Great Britain, in 2006. ISBN 978-0-545-03570-5, 0-545-03570-8. 32 p. (3–6). Picture book.

When Mom says he can have a pet, Jack suggests various animals—elephant, lion, polar bear, Tyrannosaurus Rex, giraffe, rhino, bison, crocodile, shark—and mother patiently explains why each would not be suitable. When Jack suggests a dog, Mother agrees to a little puppy. The surprise comes with the final foldout page showing that, instead of a small dog, Jack has chosen a gigantic shaggy beast named Fang. The cartoonlike illustrations are filled with each of the enormous exotic animals Jack suggests. They clearly and humorously show why each animal would not be an appropriate pet. ca

Author/illustrator lives in Great Britain.

Pets, Mothers and Sons, Humorous Stories, Fiction

Donaldson, Julia. **The Fish Who Cried Wolf**. Illustrated by Axel Scheffler. New York, Scholastic/Arthur A. Levine Books, 2008. Originally published as *Tiddler* by Alison Green Books Great Britain, in 2007. ISBN 978-0-439-92825-0, 0-439-92825-7. 40 p. (4–8). Picture book.

Little fish Tiddler has a big imagination. His teacher is annoyed by his stories explaining his tardiness. His classmates don't believe him either, except for Little Johnny Dory, who tells the stories to his granny. One day, Tiddler is swept up by a net and gets lost in the ocean. He overhears one of his stories and traces it from one sea creature to another until he is back home. The vibrant undersea illustrations and snappy rhyme are the creation of the team behind the award-winning *The Gruffalo* (1999). *mjw*

Author lives in Glasgow, Scotland; illustrator lives in London.

Fish, Storytelling, Stories in Rhyme, Fiction

Dowd, Siobhan. **The London Eye Mystery**. New York, Random House/ David Fickling Books, 2007. Originally published by David Fickling Books Great Britain, in 2007. ISBN 978-0-375-84976-3, 0-375-84976-9. 322 p. (10 up). Novel.

In this fast-paced thriller, Ted (whose brain runs on a "different operating system") and his sister Kat join forces to solve the mystery of what happened to their cousin Salim. Could he have just vanished into thin air aboard the London Eye? Their search for clues takes them across London as they race against time to save Salim. The unique voice of Ted as narrator gives the reader a glimpse into his way of thinking. He has Asperger's syndrome, and this difference enables him to solve the mystery, when even the police are stumped. *2009 USBBY Outstanding International Books List, Book Sense Children's Pick List Award 2008, School Library Journal Best Books of the Year Award 2008, Booklist Children's Editors' Choice Award 2008, Horn Book Fanfare Award 2008, Kirkus Reviews Best Children's Books Award, and the Book Links Lasting Connection Award 2008. ae*

Author was born in Ireland and lived in the United States and Great Britain. She died in 2007.

Asperger's Syndrome, Missing Children, Meteorology, Brothers and Sisters, Cousins, London (Great Britain), Fiction

Drake, Salamanda. **Dragonsdale: Book One**. Illustrated by Gilly Marklew. New York, Scholastic/Chicken House, 2007. Originally published by Chicken House Great Britain, in 2007. ISBN 978-0-439-87173-0, 0-439-87173-5. 269 p. (8–12). Novel.

Cara is not permitted to fly the dragons she loves. Her Dragonmaster father's protective ban stems from the death of Cara's mother in a dragon-flying accident. So Cara mucks out the stalls, cleans the tack, and nurtures Skydancer, her favorite dragon, as well as the other dragons on her father's training farm. When Skydancer's well-being is threatened by the spoiled and spiteful Hortense, Cara's obedience is tested. The fierce affection of the keeper for her charge is reminiscent of traditional horse stories, but this spirited series opener makes readers dragon experts as well. *nlr*

Author claims to be a sixteen-year-old girl who lives on the Isles of Bresel.
DRAGONS, COURAGE, FANTASY FICTION

Dunbar, Joyce. **Where's My Sock?** Illustrated by Sanja Rešcek. New York, Scholastic, 2006. Originally published by Chicken House Great Britain, in 2006. ISBN 978-0-439-74831-5, 0-439-74831-3. n.p. (4–8). Picture book.

Pippin the mouse can't find one of his yellow socks with clocks. Pippin and Tog look for the lost sock everywhere—in every drawer and in every basket—but no sock. They line up all the socks they have, and they eventually decide the sock must be hiding. Pippin and Tog give up and decide it is permissible to wear socks that don't match. They check their socks and realize Tog had on the missing sock all the time. *si*

Author lives in Great Britain.
SOCKS, LOST AND FOUND POSSESSIONS, MICE, CATS, FICTION

Dunbar, Polly. **Penguin.** Illustrated by the author. Cambridge, MA, Candlewick Press, 2007. Originally published by Walker Books Great Britain, in 2007. ISBN 978-0-7636-3404-9, 0-7636-3404-2. 32 p. (4–8). Picture book.

"Hello, Penguin" says Ben (n.p.). But "Penguin" does not speak no matter whether Ben tickles him, stands on his head, or tries to feed him to a "passing lion" (n.p.). The lion, however, eats Ben when Ben yells, "Say something!" at the top of his voice (n.p.), but a peck from his penguin's beak finally rescues him. Only then does Ben learn how his friend communicates—in pictures. This whimsical story is told in short sentences, while expressive cartoon-style illustrations in mixed media depict Ben's small figure in constant motion in opposition to his static penguin. *hc*

Author lives in Great Britain.
PENGUINS, HUMAN-ANIMAL COMMUNICATION, FRIENDSHIP, FICTION

Durant, Alan. **Burger Boy.** Illustrated by Mei Matsuoka. New York, Clarion Books, 2006. Originally published by Andersen Press Great Britain, in 2005. ISBN 978-0-618-71466-7, 0-618-71466-9. 29 p. (4–8). Picture book.

Just as his mother warned, picky eater Benny turns into a burger. The Burger Boy is chased around town by ten dogs, a herd of cows, and hungry boys. After his mother rescues Benny from Bigga Burgers, where the owner has put him on display, a diet of fruits and vegetables changes him back into a boy. Now, however, his love of vegetables has Benny in danger of becoming one. The language of this cautionary tale about being a picky eater is lively and the illustrations are full of humorous details, such as the round-headed

Benny in a black-and-orange sweater transitioning into a hamburger lathered in mustard. *ca*

Author lives in Great Britain; illustrator was born in Japan and now lives in Great Britain.

FOOD HABITS, HAMBURGERS, HUMOROUS STORIES, FICTION

Ellis, Andy. **When Lulu Went to the Zoo**. Illustrated by the author. Minneapolis, MN, Andersen Press USA/Lerner Group, 2010. Originally published by Andersen Press Great Britain, in 2008. ISBN 978-0-7613-5499-4, 0-7613-5499-9. 32 p. (4–9). Picture book.

Lulu is an animal rights activist, even if it's not in her vocabulary yet. Most children love the zoo, but Lulu just feels sad for animals that are confined in small cages and decides something must be done. She sneaks the animals back to her house. Life outside of small cages is good, but there's just not enough room in the bathtub when a polar bear wants to play in the bubbles, too. Luckily, the zookeepers listen to her idea for Lululand—a place where animals live and play in natural habitats with "oodles of space." *lvb*

Author lives in Great Britain.

STORIES IN RHYME, ZOO ANIMALS, FICTION

Fine, Anne. **The Return of the Killer Cat**. Illustrated by Steve Cox. New York, Farrar, Straus and Giroux, 2007. Originally published by the Penguin Group Great Britain, in 2003. ISBN 978-0-374-36248-5, 0-374-36248-3. 74 p. (7–10). Novel.

Tuffy thinks he will have a great week when the family is on vacation. But the vicar is not Tuffy's idea of a good cat-sitter. He refuses to open a new tin of cat food until Tuffy has finished the last one. Tuffy has to escape through the bathroom window after he has spent the night eating and "yowling" with the "gang." Escapade follows escapade until he falls into the hands of Melanie, who names him "Janet," dresses him up, and feeds him on tuna and cream until the gang intervenes. The black-and-white drawings add to the hilarity. Other Killer Cat books include *The Diary of a Killer Cat* (Farrar, Straus Giroux, 2006). *Anne Fine's awards include being named the 2001–2003 Children's Laureate of Great Britain. hc*

Author and illustrator are from Great Britain.

CATS, DIARIES, HUMOROUS STORIES

Fine, Anne. **Jamie and Angus Together**. Illustrated by Penny Dale. Cambridge, MA, Candlewick Press, 2007. Originally published by Walker Books

Great Britain, in 2007. ISBN 978-0-7636-3374-5, 0-7636-3374-7. 102 p. (4–8). Illustrated novel.

Jamie and his stuffed Highland bull, Angus, continue to share miniadventures in this sequel to *The Jamie and Angus Stories* (2002). In the six episodic chapters, Jamie encounters universal childhood situations: protecting his toy from manhandling visitors, creating tales, and imaginary play. "Something Different" will tickle every librarian who has ever shelved a book. Preschoolers can relate to Jamie's activities as the kinds of things they did when they, too, were "little." Dale's soft-pencil drawings add warmth to the charming stories in this transitional chapter book. *lmp, ca*

Author and illustrator live in Great Britain.

Toy Highland Bull, Friendship, Play, Great Britain, Fiction

French, Vivian. **The Daddy Goose Treasury**. Illustrated by Anna-Laura Cantone, Ross Collins, Joelle Dreidemy & Andrea Huseinovic. New York, Scholastic/Chicken House, 2006. Originally published as *The Daddy Goose Collection: Stories from Favourite Nursery Rhymes* by Chicken House Great Britain, in 2006. ISBN 978-0-439-79608-8, 0-439-79608-3. 93 p. (4–8). Illustrated book.

Daddy Goose tells twelve stories based on Mother Goose rhymes, including a tale about the way in which Humpty Dumpty was put back together again (Charlie Apricot, the helper in the royal kitchen, is an expert at using glue to mend plates broken by Cook when she gets angry) and another about how Old King Cole got more than he asked for when he called for his pipe (he gets Great Uncle Angus and his bagpipes). French's strong storytelling voice makes these funny, original tales great read-alouds. Using four illustrators (one Italian, one Scottish, one French, and one Croatian) makes this collection also a showcase of international artwork. *ca*

Vivian French lives in Scotland, as does Ross Collins; Anna-Laura Cantone lives in Italy, Joelle Dreidemy in France, and Andrea Huseinovic in Croatia.

Nursery Rhyme Adaptations, Humorous Stories, Mother Goose Characters, Fiction

Gaiman, Neil. **The Graveyard Book**. Illustrated by Dave McKean. New York, HarperCollins, 2008. Simultaneously published by Bloomsbury Great Britain. ISBN 978-0-06-053092-1, 0-06-053092-8. 312 p. (10 up). Novel.

In this unique supernatural fantasy novel, Neil Gaiman introduces the story of Nobody Owens, an orphan being raised by ghosts in a not-so-quiet graveyard. Nobody, or Bod for short, is the only living soul in the cemetery, but he is not alone. The protective ghosts that populate the graveyard do more than care for and educate Bod, they are also hiding the boy from the man who killed his family and is intent on finishing the job. The fast-paced plot, unusual characters, and clever dialogue will intrigue readers looking for a more unconventional mystery. Bod's indecision about his future and longing for acceptance and a place to belong provide a compelling story. *2009 USBBY Outstanding International Books List, Newbery Medal, Carnegie Medal in Literature, Hugo Award for Best Novel, Booktrust Teenage Prize, ALA Notable Children's Book, Horn Book Fanfare, Kirkus Reviews Best Children's Book, CCBC Choice, New York Public Library Stuff for the Teen Age, Dorothy Canfield Fisher Children's Book Award (Vermont), ALA Booklist Editors' Choice, ALA Best Book for Young Adults, New York Public Library's "One Hundred Titles for Reading and Sharing."* smv

Author was born in Great Britain but currently lives in Minnesota.

DEAD, SUPERNATURAL, CEMETERIES, ORPHANS, GREAT BRITAIN, FANTASY FICTION

Gardner, Sally. **I, Coriander**. New York, Penguin/Dial Books, 2005. Originally published by Orion Children's Books Great Britain, in 2005. ISBN 978-0-8037-3099-1, 0-8037-3099-3. 299 p. (12 up). Novel.

In a tale of both historical fiction and fairy fantasy, Coriander Hobie discovers she is caught between two worlds. The daughter of a London merchant in seventeenth-century Great Britain and a princess from the fairy world, Coriander never knew about her mother's fairy world until she receives a pair of silver shoes. When she puts them on, however, she gains the ability to travel between the two worlds. Unfortunately, both worlds hold trials for Coriander. Her London home has become a miserable prison, with a captive father and a wicked stepmother ever since the death of her mother. The fairy tale world, on the other hand, is ruled by an evil witch who turned a handsome prince into a fox and is determined to be in control. Although only a teenager, Coriander must find a way to save the people in both of her worlds and ultimately decide where she belongs. *2006 USBBY-CBC Outstanding International Books List, Nestlé Children's Book Prize Gold Award, shortlisted for the British Children's Book of the Year and the Stockton Children's Book of the Year, and longlisted for the Carnegie Medal.* smv

Author lives in London.

MAGIC, MOTHERS AND DAUGHTERS, FAIRIES, LONDON–GREAT BRITAIN HISTORY SEVENTEENTH-CENTURY, GREAT BRITAIN HISTORY COMMONWEALTH AND PROTECTORATE (1649–1660), GREAT BRITAIN, HISTORICAL FICTION FANTASY, NOVEL

Grant, K. M. **Blood Red Horse**. New York, Walker Books, 2005. Originally published by Puffin Great Britain, in 2004. ISBN 978-0-8027-8960-0, 0-8027-8960-9. 277 p. (10–12). Novel.

See Israel for description.

Gravett, Emily. **Wolves**. Illustrated by the author. New York, Simon & Schuster Books, 2006. Originally published by Macmillan Children's Books Great Britain, in 2005. ISBN 978-1-4169-1491-4, 1-4169-1491-9. 32 p. (4–8). Picture book.

Rabbit, a young bookworm bunny, selects *Wolves* during a trip to the library. He is so engrossed in his crimson cloth-covered volume that the lurking pack of wolves goes unnoticed until bunny reads about wolves' diet: "Wolves eat mainly meat . . . like beavers, voles, and . . ." (n.p.). The page turn reveals the missing word *rabbits* as well as a clawed and chewed red book cover. Gravett's illustrative humor counterbalances the serious, informative tone of the text. The final spread—including a library overdue notice and a bill collector's warning—allows for a nagging doubt that everyone did live "happily ever after" (n.p.). *2007 USBBY Outstanding International Books, Kate Greenaway Medal, Macmillan Prize, Nestlé Bronze Award, and the Boston Globe-Horn Book Honor Award. lmp*

Author lives in Great Britain.

WOLVES, RABBITS, BOOKS AND READING, HUMOROUS STORIES, FANTASY

Gravett, Emily. **Orange Pear Apple Bear**. Illustrated by the author. New York, Simon & Schuster Books, 2007. Originally published by Macmillan Children's Books Great Britain, in 2006. ISBN 978-1-4169-3999-3, 1-4169-3999-7. 32 p. (1–4). Picture book.

Dr. Seuss never created a book with only five words, but Emily Gravett manages it effortlessly. *Orange Pear Apple Bear* commences with a row of oranges, apples, and pears stretching from edge to edge of the front endpapers. Then, by repositioning words and using the distinct colors of each fruit, the bear (introduced in the title) transmogrifies into "orange bear" then "apple bear" and finally "pear bear." Gravett's characteristically straightforward watercolor cartooning provides a humorous introduction to color, shape, and food for toddlers. Going full circle, rinds and peels stretch from edge to edge on the final endpapers. *lmp*

Author lives in Great Britain.

BEARS, PLAYS ON WORDS, CONCEPT BOOK, GREAT BRITAIN

Gravett, Emily. **Monkey and Me**. Illustrated by the author. New York, Simon & Schuster Books, 2008. Originally published by Macmillan Children's Books Great Britain, in 2007. ISBN 978-1-4169-5457-6, 1-4169-5457-0. n.p. (2–6). Picture book.

In this perfect preschool book, a young girl and her stuffed monkey delight in mimicking all kinds of animals, such as marching penguins and stomping elephants. There is repetition—"Monkey and me / Monkey and me / Monkey and me / We went to see . . ."—followed by page turns that encourage prediction and finally, a surprise ending. Subdued watercolor and graphite illustrations provide clues about the animals that appear on the next page: monkey is stuffed inside "momma's" red-and-white-striped shirt, just as "real" Joeys hop with their "mommas" on the next page. Prepare to read this more than once, because once won't be enough! *Author won the Kate Greenaway Medal, Macmillan Prize, and the Nestlé Bronze Award for her book* Wolves. *lmp Author lives in Great Britain.*

MONKEYS, STUFFED ANIMALS—TOYS, ZOO ANIMALS, STORIES IN RHYME, ANIMALS, FICTION, GREAT BRITAIN

Gravett, Emily. **Little Mouse's Big Book of Fears**. Illustrated by the author. New York, Simon & Schuster Books, 2008. Originally published as *Emily Gravett's Big Book of Fears* by Macmillan Children's Books Great Britain, in 2007. ISBN 978-1-4169-5930-4, 1-4169-5930-0. n.p. (4–8). Picture book.

American librarians, parents, and teachers normally do not expect picture books to enumerate, illustrate, and define phobias for youngsters. Gravett turns all expectations upside down in this die-cut and nibbled, fold-out and flip-open simplification of ordinary—and extraordinary—fears. Using metafictive devices such as a newspaper interview with Mrs. Sabatier, the farmer's wife who cut off the tails of the three blind mice, the author effectively distances readers from their phobias. Furthermore, there are abundant opportunities for readers to laugh—at images, word play (whereamiophobia), and at themselves. The oil pencil and watercolor illustrations provide a topsy-turvy bricolage suitable to the subject. *Author won the Kate Greenaway Medal, Macmillan Prize, and the Nestlé Bronze Award for her book* Wolves. *lmp Author lives in Great Britain.*

TOY AND MOVABLE BOOKS, FEAR, MICE, FANTASY, GREAT BRITAIN

Gravett, Emily. **Spells**. Illustrated by the author. New York, Simon & Schuster Books, 2009. Originally published by Macmillan Children's Books

Great Britain, in 2008. ISBN 978-1416982-70-8, 1-41698-27-01. n.p. (4–8). Picture book.

With a wink of her eye and a split-page text, Emily Gravett uses every surface of this "Frog Prince" parody to challenge readers' imaginations. The opening double-page spreads depict an imaginative, albeit destructive, frog who flippantly tears pages from the spells book to create his fantasies. Suddenly he realizes that, with the proper spell, he can morph from frog to prince. Piecing together torn pages, he transforms into unusual creatures— a fabbit, a snewt—until he creates the necessary spell and shape-shifts into a handsome (but naked) prince. The beautiful princess's kiss precipitates a surprise ending, explained on the back endpapers. *lmp*

Author lives in Great Britain.

SPLIT-PAGE BOOKS, FROGS, MAGIC, FICTION, TOY & MOVABLE BOOKS, GREAT BRITAIN, FANTASY

Gravett, Emily. **The Odd Egg.** Illustrated by the author. New York, Simon & Schuster Books, 2009. Originally published by Macmillan Children's Books Great Britain, in 2008. ISBN 978-1-4169-6872-6, 1-4169-6872-5. n.p. (4–8). Picture book.

Everyone but duck has laid an egg. Disappointed, duck combs the neighborhood and returns with the perfect egg, whose muddy green splotches duplicate duck's own head feathers. Never mind that the egg is triple the size of Flamingo's. Duck incubates his mammoth embryo and watches as his friends' babies emerge as miniatures of their mamas. Comic watercolor illustrations, executed in subdued earth tones with crimson accents for parrot, flamingo, hen, and finch, conduct readers to the final surprise when duck's egg finally hatches. Small hands experience additional surprises as staggered interior pages unfold to reveal each fledgling greeted by its mama. *lmp*

Author lives in Great Britain.

EGGS, DUCKS, BIRDS, FANTASY FICTION

Gray, Kes. **Eat Your Peas.** Illustrated by Nick Sharratt. New York, Harry N. Abrams Books, 2006. Originally published by Bodley Head Children's Great Britain, in 2000. ISBN 978-0-8109-5974-3, 0-8109-5974-7. n.p. (4–8). Picture book.

Desperate to get her child to eat her peas, a mother puts forth one extravagant bribe followed by yet another and another—all seemingly to no avail. Finally, the child agrees to eat the much-hated vegetable—if her mother eats the brussels sprouts on her own plate. The battle of wills ends in a compromise as mother and daughter dive into bowls of ice cream instead of their veggies. This humorous story, the first title in the popular British Daisy series, will resonate with any child who has resisted a detested food. *Winner of Overall Prize in 2001 Children's Book Awards. mm*

Author lives in Great Britain.

MOTHERS AND DAUGHTERS, FOOD HABITS, REALISTIC FICTION

Grey, Mini. **Traction Man Is Here!** Illustrated by the author. New York, Random House/Alfred A. Knopf, 2005. Originally published by Jonathan Cape Great Britain, in 2005. ISBN 978-0-375-83191-1, 0-375-83191-6. n.p. (6–8). Picture book.

On Christmas, a little boy receives an action figure called Traction Man. Almost immediately Traction Man finds himself at the center of adventure and danger. With his adopted sidekick, a brave little scrubbing brush, Traction Man faces evil in all its many forms—pillows that hold farm animals captive, a poisonous dishcloth, a wicked spade that buries dollies. There seems to be no obstacle Traction Man cannot overcome—until he encounters Granny's gift—a knitted, green romper suit. This imaginative battle between good and evil will resonate with children who have created adventures for their own action figures. *2006 USBBY-CBC Outstanding International Books List. mm*

Author lives in Great Britain.

ACTION FIGURES, TOYS, BROOMS AND BRUSHES, FANTASY FICTION

Grey, Mini. **Traction Man Meets Turbodog.** Illustrated by the author. New York, Random House/Alfred A. Knopf/Borzoi, 2008. Originally published by Random House/Jonathan Cape Great Britain, in 2008. ISBN 978-0-375-85583-2, 0-375-85583-1. 30 p. (4–8). Picture book.

After a mud-spattered Scrubbing Brush is banished to the bin by Dad, action figure Traction Man, ineptly assisted by an annoying battery-powered robotic Turbodog, bravely ventures out to rescue his trusty sidekick. After a series of missteps, Scrubbing Brush is rescued from the "Dark and Terrible Underworld of the Bin" (n.p.), cleaned up, and ready to accompany Traction Man on their next dangerous exploration. Like *Traction Man Is Here!* (2005), this new adventure of Traction Man features zany, comic-book-style mixed-media illustrations and is filled with tongue-in-cheek humor. *2008–National Parenting Publications Awards (NAPPA), 2008–School Library Journal Best Book of the Year, 2008–Booklist Children's Editors' Choice, 2008–Horn Book Fanfare, 2008–Kirkus Reviews Best Children's Books, 2008–Bulletin Blue Ribbon Book, 2008–Book Links Lasting Connection, 2009–Gryphon Award Honor Book. ca*

Author lives in Great Britain.
ACTION FIGURES (TOYS), BROOMS AND BRUSHES, LOST AND FOUND POS-
SESSIONS, FICTION, SEQUEL TO *TRACTION MAN IS HERE!*

Gribbin, Mary & John R. Gribbin. **The Science of Philip Pullman's His**
Dark Materials. New York, Random House/Alfred A. Knopf, 2005. Originally published by Hodder Children's Books Great Britain, in 2003. ISBN
978-0-375-83144-7, 0-375-83144-4. 203 p. (14 up). Nonfiction.

In an introduction, Pullman explains that he tried to "get the science
right" for his "storytelling" (xvii). Clear explanations of the science underlying many of the phenomena encountered by Will and Lyra in Pullman's
trilogy are provided in this fascinating book, from the concept of parallel
worlds and "Dust" to the physics of light underlying the making of the *Amber*
Spyglass. Readers are introduced step-by-step to quantum physics, space-time,
string theory, and natural selection along with quotes from Pullman's texts.
2006 USBBY-CBC Outstanding International Books List. hc
    Authors live in Great Britain.
PULLMAN, PHILIP (1946–), HIS DARK MATERIALS, LITERATURE AND SCI-
ENCE, GREAT BRITAIN HISTORY 20TH CENTURY, ENGLISH HISTORY AND
CRITICISM, FANTASY FICTION CRITICISM

Grindley, Sally. **It's My School**. Illustrated by Margaret Chamberlain.
New York, Walker Books, 2006. Originally published by Bloomsbury Great
Britain, in 2005. ISBN 978-0-8027-8086-7, 0-8027-8086-5. 32 p. (4–7).
Picture book.

Her brother, Tom, will look after her, Alice's father tells her the night
before school. But Tom is not happy to have his little sister accompany him
and does not want to have anything to do with her when she runs excitedly
to him in the playground at lunchtime. However, Tom shows he can be the
protective big brother (and even gives her a kiss) when another boy has Alice's teddy bear. Lively, colorful illustrations (double-spread and full-page)
foreground characters and their emotions and imply a sense of continuous
motion as the children walk, run, and interact with each other. *Author won*
the 2004 Gold Nestlé Children's Book Prize. hc
    Author is from Great Britain.
FIRST DAY OF SCHOOL, BROTHERS AND SISTERS, SCHOOLS, REALISTIC
FICTION

Hannah, Jonny. **Hot Jazz Special**. Illustrated by the author. Cambridge,
MA, Candlewick Press, 2005. Originally published by Walker Books Great

Britain, in 2005. ISBN 978-0-7636-2308-1, 0-7636-2308-3. n.p. (8–14). Picture book.

Young Henry sweeps up at the Body and Soul Café, a jazz club where nine musicians and singers such as Louis Armstrong, Charlie Parker, and Billie Holiday perform. The language and colorful illustrations capture the rhythm and vibrancy of jazz as well as the time period, with phrases such as "dust the keys," "Mary Janes," "porkpie hat," and "hepcat." The author provides brief supplementary musician biographies at the end. *si*

Author lives in Great Britain.

JAZZ, FICTION

Hayes, Rosemary. **Mixing It**. London, Frances Lincoln, 2007. ISBN 978-1-84507-495-1, 1-84507-495-5. 185 p. (12 up). Novel.

Teenagers Fatimah and Steve are thrown together as the result of a deadly explosion orchestrated by Muslim terrorists. In the tragedy's aftermath, Fatimah is photographed rescuing Steve and endures repercussions in her Muslim community, while Steve struggles with his father's religious prejudices. *2008 USBBY Outstanding International Books List.*

Author lives in Great Britain.

BOMBINGS, VICTIMS OF TERRORISM, MUSLIM GIRLS, GREAT BRITAIN, FICTION

Hearn, Julie. **The Minister's Daughter**. New York, Simon & Schuster/Atheneum Books, 2005. Originally published as *The Merrybegot* by Oxford University Press Great Britain, in 2005. ISBN 978-0-689-87690-5, 0-689-87690-4. 363 p. (14 up). Novel.

Grace and Patience Madden, the minister's daughters, live in a small British village during the Puritan Revolution. Nell is the Cunning Woman's granddaughter and is learning the healing arts and midwifery from her grandmother. The devil, piskies, fairies, misunderstandings, and old superstitions influence the plot's outcome. Narrated in alternating chapters and voices, during alternating time periods (1692 and 1645) and locations (Great Britain and New Great Britain), *The Minister's Daughter* is a natural pairing with *The Crucible* (Miller 1953), Marc Aronson's nonfiction *Witch-Hunt: Mysteries of the Salem Witch Trials* (2003), or, at a lower reading level, *Beyond the Burning Time* (Lasky 1994). *2006 USBBY-CBC Outstanding International Books List, 2005 Aesop Accolades, ALA Best Books for Young Adults, Kirkus Editor's Choice. lmp*

Author lives in Great Britain.

MATTHEW HOPKINS (D. 1647), WITCHCRAFT TRIALS, FAIRIES, GREAT BRITAIN HISTORY CIVIL WAR, 1642–1649, SOMERSET (GREAT BRITAIN), SALEM (MA) HISTORY COLONIAL PERIOD, CA. 1600–1775, HISTORICAL FICTION

Heiligman, Deborah. **Charles and Emma: The Darwins' Leap of Faith**. New York, Henry Holt, 2009. ISBN 978-0-8050-8721-5, 0-8050-8721-4. 268 p. plus 8 p. of plates. (12 up). Nonfiction, Biography.

Charles and Emma: The Darwins' Leap of Faith invites readers into an exotic world, diametrically different from twenty-first-century lifestyles. Privileged by birth, both of the Darwins were expected to continue their families' tradition of a literate rural lifestyle, sustained by servants as they read, corresponded—by letter, not instant messaging—and leisurely walked or traveled the countryside. Charles was educated to the ministry before his life-altering voyage on *The Beagle*. Emma, his devoutly religious cousin, expected to remain unmarried. Their decision to wed was fraught with apprehension because of Charles's emerging theory of evolution. At its core, *Charles and Emma* is a love story that examines the lifestyle and religious beliefs of one of Great Britain's greatest scientists. *2009 National Book Award finalist, 2010 Printz Honor, first YALSA Excellence in Nonfiction Awards. lmp*

Author lives in New York.

CHARLES DARWIN (1809–1882), EMMA WEDGWOOD DARWIN (1808–1896), NATURALISTS, GREAT BRITAIN, BIOGRAPHY

Higgins, F. E. **The Eyeball Collector**. New York, Macmillan/Feiwel and Friends, 2009. Originally published by Macmillan Children's Books Great Britain, in 2009. ISBN 978-0-312-56681-4, 0-312-56681-6. 251 p. (10–14). Novel.

Young Hector decides to take revenge upon the man who caused his father's demise. Hector's passion for lepidopterology and his talent for posing and solving riddles prove the means by which he can pursue the perpetrator (whose own obsession for collecting glass eyes keeps him on the move). Hector enters a world where deception is the norm and seemingly the only way to change one's station in life. Readers of Higgins's previous books, *The Black Book of Secrets* and *The Bone Magician*, will recognize characters and places where and for whom the line between anonymity and notoriety is precarious. *2010 USBBY Outstanding International Books List. bef*

Author lives in Great Britain.

EYES, REVENGE, SUSPENSE, ORPHANS, EXTORTION, SCIENCE FICTION

Hinton, Nigel. **Time Bomb**. Berkeley, CA, Tricycle Press, 2006. Originally published by Penguin Group Great Britain, in 2005. ISBN 978-1-58246-186-1, 1-58246-186-4. 284 p. (11–14). Novel.

"I've never told this story to anyone because when I was twelve I swore an oath in blood that I would never tell it. But the friends I swore it with are dead . . ." (1). So begins *Time Bomb*, a riveting tale of four friends who discover an unexploded bomb in 1949. Narrated from an adult perspective, this suspenseful coming-of-age story details the traumatic incidents following the boys' discovery. *2007 USBBY Outstanding International Books List.*

Author lives in Great Britain.

CONDUCT OF LIFE, SECRETS, FRIENDSHIP, GREAT BRITAIN–HISTORY (1936–1952), HISTORICAL FICTION

Hooper, Mary. **Newes from the Dead**. New York, Roaring Brook Press, 2008. Originally published by Bodley Head Great Britain, in 2008. ISBN 978-1-59643-355-7, 1-59643-355-8. 263 p. (14 up). Novel.

Based loosely on actual events from Great Britain in the year 1650, this suspenseful novel is told through the alternating and parallel first-person narratives of Anne, a servant girl who has been falsely accused, convicted, and hanged for infanticide, and Robert Matthews, the young, stuttering medical student who is set to perform the autopsy on Anne when he notices that she may not yet be dead. Rich in period details from daily life and seventeenth-century medical practices, this is a thought-provoking and fairly creepy historical mystery. *2009 USBBY Outstanding International Book, Bank Street Best Children's Book of the Year, NYPL Stuff for the Teen Age, Capitol Choices Noteworthy Titles for Children and Teens, Texas TAYSHAS High School Reading List. ae*

Author lives in Oxfordshire, Great Britain, the same area Anne Green came from.

ANNE GREENE (B. 1628), DEATH, EXECUTIONS AND EXECUTIONERS, PREGNANCY, GREAT BRITAIN, HISTORICAL FICTION, BIOGRAPHICAL FICTION, NOVEL

Horáček, Petr. **Look Out, Suzy Goose**. Illustrated by the author. Cambridge, MA, Candlewick Press, 2008. ISBN 978-0-7636-3803-0, 0-7636-3803-X. n.p. (4–8). Picture book.

Silly Suzy Goose is back—perfect for lap time or preschool read-aloud. Each page offers opportunities for youngsters to participate with loud and soft onomatopoetic animal sounds. The hungry fox follows Suzy "Tiptoe,

Tiptoe" (n.p.); the wolf follows "Creep, Creep" (n.p.). Repetition combines with a predictably scary format to complete this splendid circle story of a silly goose who doesn't appreciate her flock's noise. Horáček's mixed-media illustrations—collage (reminiscent of Eric Carle's tissue papers), crayon, and thick brushstrokes—create a suitably deep, dark forest setting, scary enough to generate screams of pleasure followed closely by a chorused, "Again!" *lmp*

Author is originally from Prague but now lives in Great Britain.

Geese, Animals, Fantasy, Great Britain

Hornby, Nick. **Slam**. New York, G. P. Putnam's Sons, 2007. ISBN 978-0-399-25048-4, 0-399-25048-4. 309 p. (13 up). Novel.

Sam is a fifteen-year-old skateboarder who becomes a teenage parent with his ex-girlfriend, Alicia. He learns to cope with the challenges of raising a baby with a young girl whose family is less than welcoming. He attempts to understand what the future holds for him, always feeling uncertain about how he will handle being a father while still growing up himself. He turns to his hero, Tony Hawk, for advice. Sam's communication skills lack clarity, yet add humor to this serious novel. *2008 YALSA Best Books for Young Adults. The author's awards include the E. M. Forster Award of the American Academy of Arts and Letters.* dld, hc

Author lives in North London.

Teenage Fathers, Teenage Parents, Tony Hawk, Babies, Skate-boarding, Fiction, Great Britain

Horowitz, Anthony. **Raven's Gate**. New York, Scholastic, 2005. Originally published by Walker Books Great Britain, in 2005; based on an idea first published in 1983 as *The Devil's Doorbell*. ISBN 978-0-439-67995-4, 0-439-67995-8. 254 p. (14 up). Novel.

Feeling shackled by a town too small and a life too limited, fourteen-year-old Matt Freeman yields to the taunts of a streetwise punk and breaks into an electronics warehouse. The violent aftermath results in his sentencing to foster care in a curious Yorkshire village that harbors sinister secrets. There, Matt uncovers his destined role as a gatekeeper against the release of ancient evils through Raven's Gate, a portal in the town's abandoned nuclear plant. Threats surround Matt in the form of attacks by dinosaur skeletons, dark witchcraft, and the deaths of those who try to help. It's a heart-thumping contemporary thriller. *nlr*

Author lives in London.

Witches, Stone Circles, Supernatural, Foster Home Care, Identity, Yorkshire (Great Britain), Fantasy Fiction

Hughes, Shirley. **Rhymes for Annie Rose**. Illustrated by the author. Cambridge, MA, Candlewick Press, 2006. Originally published by Bodley Head Great Britain, in 1995. ISBN 978-0-7636-2940-3, 0-7636-2940-5. 48 p. (4–8). Poetry, Picture book.

Previously published in 1995, this collection of twenty-seven poems and lullabies stars Annie Rose and her brother Alfie. The simple rhymes depict everyday pleasures—coloring pictures, telling about cuddly stuffed animals, creating a playhouse under the table, splashing in the rain, and looking for rabbits' footprints in the snow. Realistic, double-page line and watercolor paintings display a messy warmth, wonderful domestic detail, and the siblings' joy, mischief, and affection. The fresh poems have a beat that children will love. *Shirley Hughes has won the Kate Greenaway Medal and the Eleanor Farjeon Award. mjw*
Author lives in London.
GREAT BRITAIN, POETRY

Hughes, Ted. **Collected Poems for Children**. Illustrated by Raymond Briggs. New York, Farrar, Straus and Giroux, 2007. Originally published by Faber and Faber Great Britain, in 2005. ISBN 978-0-374-31429-3, 0-374-31429-2. 259 p. (8 up). Illustrated Anthology.

This collection of over 250 poems provides a one-volume source of former poet laureate of Great Britain Ted Hughes's contribution to children's poetry. The full range of Hughes's creative genius is exemplified in poems that are playful, joyful, imaginative, and thoughtful. Poems for younger children from books such as *The Mermaid's Purse* (1991) and *The Cat and the Cuckoo* (1987) come first, followed by more complex poems from *What Is the Truth?* (1984) and *Season Songs* (1975) for older readers. Raymond Briggs has created many small, soft-pencil drawings to complement the subjects and moods of the poems. The volume is indexed by titles and by first lines. *ca*
Author lived in Great Britain; illustrator lives in Great Britain.
CHILDREN'S POETRY, ENGLISH

Hussey, Charmian. **The Valley of Secrets**. Illustrated by Christopher Crump. New York, Simon & Schuster Books, 2005. First published by Saint Piran Press Great Britain, in 2003. ISBN 978-0-689-87862-6, 0-689-87862-1. 382 p. (12 up). Novel.

See Brazil/Amazon River for description.

Ibbotson, Eva. **The Dragonfly Pool**. Illustrated by Kevin Hawkes. New York, Penguin/Dutton Children's Books, 2008. ISBN 978-0-52-542064-4, 0-52-542064-9. 377 p. (9–12). Novel.

Tally's first weeks at boarding school become bearable when she and a group of classmates are chosen to participate in a dance contest in Bergania—a country whose king refuses to cooperate with Hitler's latest demands. During the contest, the king is assassinated. Tally and her friends help the young prince of Bergania escape from the Nazi soldiers. Together, they discover each person's special talents and the value of lifelong compassion. This award-winning author interweaves a fantasy setting with historical fiction adventure. *2009 USBBY Outstanding International Books List. nrr*

Author was born in Vienna but lives in Great Britain.

Boarding Schools, Europe, World War II (1939–1945), Children, Boarding Schools, Great Britain, Historical Fiction

James, Charlie. **Billy the Fish**. Illustrated by Ned Jolliffe. New York, Bloomsbury, 2006. Originally published as *Fish* by Bloomsbury Great Britain, in 2006. ISBN 978-1-58234-732-5, 1-58234-732-8. 175 p. (7–10). Novel.

Ned Finn narrates how his six-year-old brother, Billy, can turn into a cod and then, back into a boy when he eats packs of their father's new "Super-Strong Fish Chips." This farcical fish tale includes Ned's droll comments about his parents and sister, Billy's narrow escapes while in cod form, and Ned's own ups and downs in the important school quiz competition. Ned also tells how he and his family foil the plots of "Donna Mezzweme" ("an industrial spy") to steal the fish food formula and whose exaggerated disguise as manager of the local aquarium resembles a nightmarish Hollywood starlet. *hc*

Author lives in Scotland.

Brothers, Fishes, Humorous Stories

Jeffers, Oliver. **The Way Back Home**. Illustrated by the author. New York, Penguin/Philomel Books, 2008. Originally published as *Lost and Found* by Collins Children's Books Great Britain, in 2004. ISBN 978-0-399-25074-3, 0-399-25074-3. 32 p. (4–8). Picture book.

A boy finds an airplane in his closet, flies to outer space, runs out of gas, and crash lands on the moon. There, he meets a Martian in a similar situation. They devise a rescue plan. The boy parachutes home for supplies and returns to the moon via a rope. Both spacecrafts are repaired, and the adventurers depart, wondering if they will meet again. Imaginative, comic mixed-media artwork extends this charming story of friendship. *mjw*

Author lives in Great Britain.

Space Flight, Extraterrestrial Beings, Cooperativeness, Space Flight Juvenile, Moon, Fantasy

Jones, Diana Wynne. **The Game**. New York, Penguin/Firebird, 2007. ISBN 978-0-14-240718-9, 0-14-240718-6. 179 p. (9–14). Novel.

As punishment for inadvertently entering an alternate, mythic universe, Hayley, a young, orphaned British girl, is banished from her grandparents' London home to a rambling, castlelike mansion in Ireland. There she meets a confusingly large group of cousins who draw her into a secret, forbidden game that takes place in "the mythosphere," a universe made up of stories. As she plays the game, Hayley discovers the true nature of her extraordinary family as well as her own considerable power, a power that she hopes will enable her to find her lost parents. *Author holds the 2007 World Fantasy Association Lifetime Achievement Award. mac*
Author died March 26, 2011.
GREEK MYTHOLOGY, COUSINS, FANTASY FICTION

Kennan, Ally. **Beast**. New York, Scholastic/Push, 2006. Originally published by Scholastic Great Britain, in 2006. ISBN 978-0-439-86549-4, 0-439-86549-2. 217 p. (14 up). Novel.

Seventeen-year-old Stephen has kept the "Beast" alive, despite the English weather, in a wire cage at the reservoir near his foster home with the Reynolds family. But "his boy" is now unmanageable. When he enlists the help of his deadbeat father, the killer crocodile escapes. Through Stephen's first-person narrative, a gripping story is told of how recapturing his former pet nearly costs him his life. Stephen also tells about his family relationships: the family that let Stephen down; his love for his dead brother; and his new relationship with sixteen-year-old teenager Carol Reynolds, who, surprisingly, becomes his ally. *2007 Carnegie Medal Shortlist, 2007 Branford Boase Award Shortlist. hc*
Author is from Great Britain.
CROCODILES, PROBLEM CHILDREN, FOSTER CHILDREN, TEENAGE BOYS, FAMILY RELATIONSHIPS, FICTION

Lawrence, Michael. **A Crack in the Line: Withern Rise, Book I**. New York, HarperCollins/Greenwillow Books, 2004. Originally published by Orchard Books Great Britain, in 2003. ISBN 978-0-06-072477-1, 0-06-072477-3. 323 p. (12 up). Novel.

The Withern Rise trilogy follows Naia and Alaric Underwood, teenagers identical in every aspect except gender, living in parallel realities clustered around a Victorian mansion built by their ancestors on the edge of the Ouse River in Great Britain. In *A Crack in the Line*, Alaric and Naia visited each other's realities, then accidentally and permanently switched places. *Small*

Eternities sent Alaric and Naia back to a Withern Rise of their grandfather's childhood, where a tragic accident left its mark on the family. Each section of *The Underwood See* begins with a continuing description of thirty-two-year-old Naia, forever marked by the switch in realities which only she remembers, driving home to Withern Rise to give birth to a baby. The events between these short sections take place in at least eight parallel realities and concern the divergent fates of several Alarics and his sets of parents. The writing is vivid and sure, but the splintering of characters prevents emotional engagement with them. The series's greatest strength is its precise and loving description of one small patch of land in Great Britain and the people who may have resided there. Sequels are *Small Eternities* (Greenwillow, 2005) and *The Underwood See* (Greenwillow, 2007). mac

    Author lives in Great Britain.

    Space and Time, Great Britain, Fantasy Fiction

Lee, Ingrid. **Dog Lost**. New York, Scholastic/Chicken House, 2008. Originally published by Chicken House Great Britain, in 2008. ISBN 978-0-545-08578-6, 0-545-08578-0. 197 p. (10–14). Novel.

    See Canada for description.

Lloyd, Sam. **Mr. Pusskins and Little Whiskers: Another Love Story**. Illustrated by the author. New York, Simon & Schuster/Atheneum, 2008. Originally published as *Mr. Pusskins and Little Whiskers* by Orchard Books, an imprint of Watts Great Britain, in 2007. ISBN 978-1-4169-5796-6, 1-4169-5796-0. n.p. (4–8). Picture book.

    Emily and Mr. Pusskins are perfectly happy singing love songs to each other—until Emily announces that she has "a fabulous surprise" for Mr. Pusskins. When Mr. Pusskins opens the box, he is not impressed. Little Whiskers seriously disrupts nap time, telly time, meal time, and play time. But when he bangs on the piano keys in the middle of the night, Emily blames Mr. Pusskins. This sequel to *Mr. Pusskins: A Love Story* (2007) may seem remarkably familiar to youngsters with a new baby in the family. lmp

    Author lives in Great Britain.

    Cats, Kittens, Fantasy, Great Britain

Lobel, Gillian. **Too Small for Honey Cake**. Illustrated by Sebastien Braun. Orlando, FL, Harcourt, 2006. Originally published by Orchard Books Great Britain, in 2005. ISBN 978-0-15-206097-8, 0-15-206097-9. n.p. (3–8). Picture book.

Little Fox struggles with the new changes Baby Fox brings to the family. Now Baby Fox sleeps in Little Fox's old crib, and Daddy Fox sings the same lullaby to the new baby. Simple text and a tightly written story portray children's typical emotions after the arrival of a new sibling. *si*

Author lives in Great Britain.

BABIES, PARENT AND CHILD, FOXES, FICTION

Lucas, David. **Nutmeg**. Illustrated by the author. New York, Random House/ Alfred A. Knopf, 2006. Originally published in Great Britain by Andersen Press Great Britain, in 2005. ISBN 978-0-375-83519-3, 0-375-83519-9. 24 p. (5–8). Picture book.

Tired of boring meals, Nutmeg uses the three wishes granted by a genie to ask for something different for supper, for breakfast, and for lunch. The magic spoon the genie gives Nutmeg stirs up not only a delicious supper but also the whole house, sending the occupants on a wild adventure that lands them on an island by breakfast time, where a delicious meal is set out for them on the beach, and leaving Nutmeg wondering what will be for lunch. The richly detailed illustrations depict the change of Nutmeg's world from drab to light and colorful in this wildly imaginative story. *ca*

Author/illustrator lives in London.

GENIES, MAGIC, SPOONS, FICTION

MacDonald, Margaret Read. **The Great Smelly, Slobbery, Small-Tooth Dog: A Folktale from Great Britain**. Illustrated by Julie Paschkis. Atlanta, GA, August House, 2007. ISBN 978-0-87483-808-4, 0-87483-808-4. 32 p. (8–12). Picture book.

Rich illustrations and simple text frame this traditional tale from Great Britain that features a great smelly, slobbery, small-tooth dog who rescues a rich man from thieves. Grateful for his help, the man offers to give him a treasure. However, the only treasure that the dog wants is the man's beautiful daughter. She agrees to fulfill her father's promise and goes to live with the dog in his castle. Eventually, she satisfies the tasks set for her, which enables the dog to become a handsome prince. *nlh*

Author and illustrator live in the United States.

DOGS, GREAT BRITAIN, FOLKLORE

Malley, Gemma. **The Declaration**. New York, Bloomsbury, 2007. Originally published by Bloomsbury Great Britain, in 2007. ISBN 978-1-59990-119-0, 1-59990-119-6. 300 p. (12 up). Novel.

In 2140, people can live forever as long as they do not procreate. If a child is born, it is considered a surplus, destined to spend life repaying its burden upon society. Fourteen-year-old Surplus Anna is content fulfilling this obligation until the day Peter arrives and challenges everything she knows. *2008 USBBY Outstanding International Books List.*

Author lives in Great Britain.

CHILDREN, AGING, IMMORTALITY, SCIENCE FICTION, GREAT BRITAIN, FICTION

Marriott, Zoë. **The Swan Kingdom**. Cambridge, MA, Candlewick Press, 2008. Originally published by Walker Books Great Britain, in 2007. ISBN 978-076363-48-10, 0-763634-81-6. 272 p. (11 up). Novel.

Alexandra, the only daughter of a king, cleverly outwits her new, evil stepmother, Zella, in this imaginative fantasy based on Hans Christian Andersen's "The Wild Swans." When Zella turns Alexandra's brothers into swans, she must learn how to use the special gifts she has inherited from her mother to save her family and the kingdom from the powerful and destructive Queen Zella. Marriott weaves magic, bravery, and romance together to create a richly detailed and totally engaging story. *2009 USBBY Outstanding International Books List. ca*

Author lives in Great Britain.

MAGIC, FANTASY FICTION

Matthews, L. S. **A Dog for Life**. New York, Random House/Delacorte Press, 2006. Originally published by Hodder Children's Books Great Britain, in 2006. ISBN 978-0-385-73366-3, 0-385-73366-6. 167 p. (10 up). Novel.

John Hawkins lives in northern Great Britain with his older brother, Tom, their mother, and their very special dog, Mouse, who can communicate with both brothers through thoughts. When Tom becomes seriously ill, Mouse can no longer live with the family, but John decides to run away with Mouse to search for his uncle in southern Great Britain. The journey becomes an adventure with stops along the way to stay with strangers, both kind and sinister. Readers interested in learning more about the "Gypsies" who befriend John and Mouse will want to read *A History of the Romani People* (Kyuchukov & Hancock) listed elsewhere in this book. *bal*

Author lives in Great Britain.

HUMAN-ANIMAL COMMUNICATION, RUNAWAYS, FRIENDSHIP, DOGS, GREAT BRITAIN, FICTION

McCartney, Paul & Philip Ardagh. **High in the Clouds**. Illustrated by Geoff Dunbar. New York, Penguin/Dutton Children's Books, 2005. Originally published by Faber and Faber Great Britain, in 2005. ISBN 978-0-525-47733-4, 0-525-47733-0. 96 p. (4–8). Picture book.

Wirral the Squirrel becomes homeless when his idyllic Woodland is destroyed by the evil Gretsch. He vows to find Animalia, a tropical island, where all animals live in freedom and without fear. When Wirral hears of Gretsch's plans to obliterate Animalia, he sets off with his friend Froggo to warn its residents. Bright, 3-D-quality cartoon illustrations and a fast-paced, present-tense narrative deliver an ever-timely message. Based on McCartney's animated film, *Tropical Island Hum*. mjw

Author lives in Great Britain.

ANIMALS, FANTASY FICTION

McCaughrean, Geraldine. **Not the End of the World**. New York, Harper-Collins/HarperTempest, 2005. Originally published by Oxford University Press Great Britain, in 2004. ISBN 978-0-06-076030-4, 0-06-076030-3. 244 p. (14 up). Novel.

In this imaginative retelling of Noah and the Ark, the unbearable conditions on the Ark are vividly described by Noah's daughter, Timna, who helps her brother, Japheth, rescue and hide the young boy, Kittim, and his baby sister. Timna, ready to sacrifice her life to save Kittim, is rescued by her mother, who helps Timna and Kittim escape by raft. In this thought-provoking book, readers are asked to think whether the dictatorial actions of Noah and his zealot son, Shem, are justified as Noah's wife expresses her views and animals and birds ruminate on their dark lives within the hold. *2006 USBBY-CBC Outstanding International Books List, 2004 Costa Children's Book Award (formerly the Whitbred Award)*. hc

Author lives in Great Britain.

NOAH (BIBLICAL FIGURE), OLD TESTAMENT–FICTION, FLOODS, BIBLE–HISTORY OF BIBLICAL EVENTS, NOAH'S ARK, FICTION

McGowan, Anthony. **Jack Tumor**. New York, Farrar, Straus and Giroux, 2009. Originally published as *Henry Tumour* by Doubleday Great Britain, in 2006. ISBN 978-0-374-32955-6, 0-374-32955-9. 292 p. (12 up). Novel.

The "voice" of fourteen-year-old Hector's brain tumor is an irreverent, pushy life coach named Jack—Jack Tumor. Alternating scenes of wild farce and sensitivity shot through with liberal doses of humor show Hector

emerging from his comfort zone to risk friendships, take on school bullies, and meet girls. *2010 USBBY Outstanding International Books List.*
   Author lives in Great Britain.
   TUMORS, SICK, SELF-ACTUALIZATION, SCHOOLS, FAMILIES, GREAT BRITAIN, FICTION

McKay, Hilary. **Permanent Rose.** New York, Simon & Schuster/Margaret K. McElderry Books, 2005. Originally published by Hodder Children's Books Great Britain, in 2005. ISBN 978-1-4169-0372-7, 1-4169-0372-0. 234 p. (10–14). Novel.
   Permanent Rose, set during a steamy British summer, carries over story lines from the first two books and adds insight to the Casson family history as Rose inadvertently discovers the identity of her adopted sister Saffy's father. The books in order of publication are: *Saffy's Angel* (2001), *Indigo's Star* (2003), *Permanent Rose* (2005), *Caddy Ever After* (2006), and *Forever Rose* (2007). *2006 USBBY-CBC Outstanding International Books List. djg*
   Author lives in Great Britain.
   SELF-CONFIDENCE, FRIENDSHIP, FATHERS, BROTHERS AND SISTERS, FAMILIES, GREAT BRITAIN, FICTION

McKay, Hilary. **Forever Rose.** New York, Simon & Schuster/Margaret K. McElderry Books, 2008. Originally published by Hodder Children's Books Great Britain, in 2007. ISBN 978-1-4169-5486-6, 1-4169-5486-4. 291 p. (10–14). Novel.
   All the Cassons are growing up and moving out, leaving Rose alone much of the time in this final book in a series that began with *Saffy's Angel* and *Indigo's Star* (previously reviewed in *Crossing Boundaries with Children's Books*). Readers will miss this quirky and lovable family and the gifted writing of the author, who "tells stories like some people paint pictures, sketching in the bare facts and then adding details as bright and alive as if they had just been picked from a new box of colors" (*Forever Rose,* pp. 10–11). In this book, Rose comes of age as she discovers the true meaning of friendship and family. *2009 USBBY Outstanding International Books List. djg*
   Author lives in Great Britain.
   CHRISTMAS, ECCENTRICS AND ECCENTRICITIES, FAMILY LIFE, GREAT BRITAIN, FICTION

McKee, David. **Elmer and Rose.** Illustrated by the author. Minneapolis, Lerner Group/Andersen Press USA, 2010. Originally published by Andersen Press Great Britain, in 2005. ISBN 978-0-7613-5493-2, 0-7613-5493-X. 32 p. (4–8). Picture book.

Elmer helps Rose, a lost elephant, find her way back to her herd. Rose is not a patchwork of colors or patterns like the elephants in Elmer's herd; she is solid pink, as is her entire herd. Although Elmer and Rose both think that elephants in colors different from their own look a little strange, they learn that being unique is about more than the color of one's skin. Books that celebrate diversity are important for children at all age levels, and McKee offers one here that is playful in the way it approaches the subject, avoiding heavy-handed didacticism. *David McKee won the Deutscher Jugendliteraturpreis in 1987.* lvb

Author lives in Great Britain.

ELEPHANTS, INDIVIDUALITY, BASHFULNESS, FICTION FOR CHILDREN

McKinley, Robin & Peter Dickinson. **Fire: Tales of Elemental Spirits**. New York, G. P. Putnam's Sons, 2009. ISBN 978-0-399-25289-1, 0-399-25289-4. 297 p. (10–14). Short Stories.

McKinley and Dickinson collaborate on five agreeably eerie fantasies that begin and end in fire. "Phoenix," set in modern Great Britain, expands the Egyptian myth as McKinley has done for other well-known folk tales. "Hellhound," possibly written as a salute to the authors' own hellhounds, features a dog of unearthly prowess and a cemetery haunted with evil zombies. A young boy is transformed into a powerful magician in "Salamander Man." "Fireworm" transports readers back to ancient times when men lived in caves and any threat to the clans' fires was a death sentence. "First Flight," an exquisite tale of dragons and boys, will leave readers begging for a sequel. lmp

Husband and wife authors live in Great Britain.

FIRE, MYTHICAL ANIMALS, FANTASY, SHORT STORIES

McNaughton, Colin. **When I Grow Up**. Illustrated by the author. Cambridge, MA, Candlewick Press, 2005. Originally published by Walker Books Great Britain, in 2005. ISBN 978-0-7636-2675-4, 0-7636-2675-9. 32 p. (3–6). Picture book.

Humorous "watercolor and pencil" illustrations present children acting out in a school "musical" what they would like to be when they "grow up." The skits, in rhyming verse, include wishes to be "king of the jungle," a poet, a pirate, performers in a band, "sweet shop" owners, soccer players, and "a mermaid," until the last scene in which a young boy in a frog suit freezes, stammers, and, then announces that he does not "wanna grow up!" (n.p.). Several illustrations are framed within sumptuous red stage curtains, reinforcing the effect of being present at a performance. *Author received the 1999 Emil Kurt Maschler Award and the 1996 Nestlé Smarties Award Gold Prize. hc*

Author is from Great Britain.

GROWTH, OCCUPATIONS, MUSICALS, SCHOOLS, STORIES IN RHYME, FICTION

McNaughton, Colin. **Once Upon an Ordinary School Day**. Illustrated by Satoshi Kitamura. New York, Farrar, Straus and Giroux, 2005. Originally published by Andersen Press Great Britain, in 2004. ISBN 978-0-374-35634-7, 0-374-35634-3. 32 p. (4–8). Picture book.

Once upon an ordinary school day, an ordinary boy woke from his ordinary dreams, got out of his ordinary bed, had an ordinary pee, and an ordinary bath . . . you get the picture with delightful, sepia-toned illustrations depicting the boy's bedroom, strewn with cricket bat, skateboard, and a cat pawing through school supplies and sneakers. But the school day takes a startling—and more colorful—turn when a new teacher, Mr. Gee, bounds into the classroom in his vibrant yellow suit carrying a Victrola. During the creative writing lesson, Mr. Gee plays music and inspires the students to use their imaginations. *2006 USBBY-CBC Outstanding International Books List, 2005 Bank Street School's Best Children's Books of the Year, 2005 Parents' Choice Award. djg*

Author lives in Great Britain.

SCHOOLS, TEACHERS, GREAT BRITAIN, FICTION

McQuinn, Anna & Rosalind Beardshaw. **Lola at the Library**. Illustrated by Rosalind Beardshaw. Watertown, MA, Charlesbridge, 2006. Originally published as *Layla Loves the Library* by Alanna Books Great Britain, in 2006. ISBN 978-1-58089-113-4, 1-58089-113-6. n.p. (4–8). Picture book.

On Tuesdays, Lola packs up her books and library card and goes to the library with her mother. At the library, she can talk to a friend, sing songs, listen to a story, and choose "any book she wants" (n.p.). Lola's day, from her library visit to her bedtime story, is illustrated in bright and colorful acrylic paintings. The choice of a perspective that enables a reader to see Lola and events from a child's point of view and the choice of text, printed in an easy-to-read font, make this paperback picture book appropriate for a shared reading experience. *hc*

Author and illustrator are from Great Britain.

LIBRARIES, BOOKS AND READING

Michael, Livi. **The Whispering Road**. New York, Penguin/G. P. Putnam's Sons, 2005. Originally published by Puffin Great Britain, in 2005. ISBN 978-0-399-24357-8, 0-399-24357-7. 326 p. (10 up). Novel.

In nineteenth-century Great Britain, Joe Sowerby looks after his strange little sister, Annie, at the workhouse and throughout their escape from an abusive farm placement until he leaves her with a circus to make his way to industrial Manchester. As Annie and Joe walk the Whispering Road, they are helped by a friendly tramp and a mysterious dog-woman. They are finally reunited thanks to a renegade printer working for better conditions for the poor. The book is a fast-paced Dickensian adventure with generous helpings of violence and old-time religion organized tidily into episodes just right for reading aloud. *2006 USBBY-CBC Outstanding International Books List, 2005 Nestlé Children's Book Prize Shortlist (9–11 years)*. kti, djg

   Author lives in Great Britain.

   ORPHANS, BROTHERS AND SISTERS, POVERTY, CHILD LABOR, CITY AND TOWN LIFE, SUPERNATURAL, MANCHESTER, GREAT BRITAIN–HISTORY–VICTORIA (1837–1901), HISTORICAL FICTION

Na, Il Sung. **A Book of Sleep**. Illustrated by the author. New York, Random House/Alfred A. Knopf, 2009. Originally published as *Zzzzz: A Book of Sleep* by Meadowside Children's Books Great Britain, in 2007. ISBN 978-0-375-86223-6, 0-375-86223-4. (0–4). Picture book.

The quiet, almost hypnotic text of this bedtime read-aloud is lovely and lyrical. But what makes this an extraordinary book, and one that toddlers will pick up even during the daytime, is the art. Layers of colors and textures provide interest: cut paper waves sport thick, azure gouache combed over a mottled aquamarine background, this against a slate blue sky—dominated by an enormous whale that occupies the double-page spread top to bottom, left to right. The dozing leviathan smiles benignly as it dreams sweet dreams—possibly of the hearts and flowers that tattoo its skin. In their playful, dreamy way, the computer-manipulated illustrations are reminiscent of Stephen Gammell's illustrations for *Will's Mammoth* (Martin, 1989). *2008 White Ravens, 2008 Shortlist for the British Book Design and Production Awards, 2010 Best Before Bed Read Aloud* (P&C Magazine). lmp

   Author was born in Korea but lives in Great Britain.

   ANIMALS, SLEEP BEHAVIOR IN ANIMALS, OWLS, FICTION

Naidoo, Beverley. **Web of Lies**. New York, HarperCollins/Amistad, 2006. Originally published by Penguin Group Great Britain, in 2004. ISBN 978-0-06-076077-9, 0-06-076077-X. 243 p. (10 up). Novel.

   See Africa/Nigeria for description.

Ness, Patrick. **The Knife of Never Letting Go: Chaos Walking Book 1**. Cambridge, MA, Candlewick Press, 2009. Originally published by Walker Books Great Britain, in 2008. ISBN 978-0-7636-3931-0, 0-7636-3931-1. 479 p. (14 up). Novel.

One month before he is to be a man, Todd walks into the swamp with his talking dog and encounters "Quiet" and Viola—events that lead to the uncovering of the truth about Prentisstown, a male community exiled more than a dozen years earlier for its crimes against humanity. Ness provides a dystopian vision of settlers whose solution to the planet's "Noise"—a constant streaming of information from men's thoughts but not women's—involves war and murder. In this taut thriller, Todd's guardians help him escape from Prentisstown, but Todd and Viola barely survive when they are pursued by the town's mad preacher and all-male army. *2009 USBBY Outstanding International Books List, 2009 Guardian Children's Fiction Prize; 2008 Booktrust Teenage Prize, Branford Boase Shortlist, 2009 Carnegie Medal Shortlist, ALA Best Books for Young Adults, Booklist Editors' Choice, Texas TAYSHAS List.* hc
Author was born in the United States but lives in Great Britain.
SOCIAL PROBLEMS, TELEPATHY, HUMAN-ANIMAL COMMUNICATION, SPACE COLONIES, SCIENCE FICTION

Ness, Patrick. **The Ask and the Answer: Chaos Walking Book 2**. Somerville, MA, Candlewick Press, 2009. Originally published by Walker Books Great Britain, in 2009. ISBN 978-0-7636-4490-1, 0-7636-4490-0. 519 p. (14 up). Novel.

In a futuristic colony on an unnamed planet, two factions seek to control the entire population. Todd, the unlikely hero readers met in *The Knife of Never Letting Go*, and Viola, only survivor of a space-scouting expedition, are in constant danger, pursued by ruthless Mayor Prentiss and his all-male army. The distaff group called "The Answer" seems to promise goodness and justice to Viola. Eventually, she realizes that their leader, Mistress Coyle, is even more ruthless, and she must act alone to free Todd. Their faith and trust in each other gives them the strength to act as the two opposing forces face off. *2010 USBBY Outstanding International Books List, 2009 Costa Children's Book Award (UK), Booklist Editors' Choice, Carnegie Medal Shortlist, Booklist Top SF/Fantasy Books for Youth, Publishers Weekly Best Books of the Year.* mln
Author lives in London.
COURAGE AND HEROISM, FRIENDSHIP, SURVIVAL STORIES, WAR, SPACE COLONIES, SOCIAL PROBLEMS, TELEPATHY, SCIENCE FICTION, BOOK TWO IN THE CHAOS WALKING SERIES

Nicholls, Sally. **Ways to Live Forever**. New York, Scholastic/Arthur A. Levine Books, 2008. Originally published by Scholastic Great Britain, in 2008. ISBN 978-0-545-06948-9, 0-545-06948-3. 224 p. (9–12). Novel.

Sam is eleven years old and is dying of leukemia. He has discovered his journal to be a place to preserve his thoughts, questions, pictures, stories, and, most importantly, a list of things he wants to do before dying. His writing gives the reader the perspective of a child facing the reality of death, but readers also discover through his eyes the different ways family members are coping with the situation. As those around him try to help him achieve his list of goals, readers also become a friend of—and mourn for—this fun-loving and genuine boy. This novel is realistic fiction at its best—full of emotion and sentiment but told from a very frank child's perspective. *2009 USBBY Outstanding International Book, 2008 Waterstone's Children's Book Prize, 2008 Glen Dimplex New Writers Award, 2008 New York Public Library Children's Books: 100 Titles for Reading and Sharing, Horn Book Fanfare Book, The Luchs Prize (Germany), 2009 ALA Notable Children's Book, 2009 NCTE Notable Children's Book for Language Arts. jm*
Author lives in Great Britain.
Leukemia, Authorship, Families, Death, Fiction, Novel

Ormerod, Jan. **When an Elephant Comes to School**. Illustrated by the author. New York, Scholastic/Orchard Books, 2005. Originally published by Frances Lincoln Great Britain, in 2004. ISBN 978-0-439-73967-2, 0-439-73967-5. (4–8). Picture book.

When an Elephant Comes to School is written as a "guide" to help children welcome an elephant into their classroom. Shy at first, the elephant soon gains confidence as the children invite him into their activities—painting, playing in the sand, helping with classroom tasks, and conducting science experiments. The pages of the text contain humorous, post-it style tips that may come in handy when making a newcomer to the class feel welcome. Ormerod's story does double duty: It provides comfort to jittery children facing their first day in a new school while simultaneously charming children with the tale of an endearing pachyderm. *mm*
Author lives in Great Britain.
First Day of School, Elephants, Fiction

Paver, Michelle. **Wolf Brother: Chronicles of Ancient Darkness**. New York, HarperCollins/Katherine Tegen Books, 2005. Originally published by Orion Children Books Great Britain, in 2004. ISBN 978-0-06-072825-0, 0-06-072825-6. 295 p. (9–12). Novel.

Because he had sworn an oath to his dying father, twelve-year-old Torak sets out for the Mountain of the World Spirit, learning more about his quest along the way, as he saves and nurtures a wolf cub who serves as his guide; acquires a companion and friend, Renn, a raven clan girl; and defies the demon bear in a far northern world six thousand years ago. The demon bear is the first of the Soul Eater challenges in this first in the six-volume Chronicle of Ancient Darkness series. *2006 USBBY-CBC Outstanding International Books List, 2005 Parents' Choice Gold Award. kti, nrr*

Author was born in Nyasaland (now Malawi), to a South African father and a Belgian mother. She and her family moved to Great Britain, where she lives now.

VOYAGES AND TRAVELS, PREHISTORIC PEOPLES, WOLVES, DEMONIAC POSSESSION, BEARS, FANTASY FICTION

Pratchett, Terry. **Wintersmith: A Tiffany Aching Adventure**. New York, HarperTempest, 2006. Originally published by Doubleday Great Britain, in 2006. ISBN 978-0-06-089031-5, 0-06-089031-2. 323 p. (10 up). Novel.

In this third book about the adventures of Tiffany Aching from the Discworld series, thirteen-year-old Tiffany, a young witch-in-training, unwittingly dances with the wrong person at the Dance of Seasons. Only Summer Lady can dance with Wintersmith to initiate the change of seasons. Tiffany's mistake brings a horrible, endless winter to the land. It takes Granny Weatherwax, the greatest witch in the world; the Wee Free Men, a clan of six-inch-high blue men; and her friend Roland to help Tiffany set things right. *2007 USBBY Outstanding International Books List. ca*

Author lives in Great Britain.

WINTER, WITCHES, FAIRIES, FANTASY FICTION

Pullman, Philip. **The Scarecrow and His Servant**. Illustrated by Peter Bailey. New York, Random House/Alfred A. Knopf, 2004. Originally published by Doubleday Great Britain, in 2004. ISBN 978-0-375-81531-7, 0-375-81531-7. 229 p. (8–10). Novel.

Jack is caught up in a series of fantastic adventures with an incorrigible Scarecrow when he agrees to become Scarecrow's servant. Scarecrow had been made by Mr. Pandolfo, who was fighting to save his lands from his rogue cousins, "the Buffalonis." But Scarecrow is stolen from his field and, then, miraculously comes alive when struck by lightning. Pursued by a lawyer for the Buffalino family, Scarecrow and Jack become embroiled with brigands, traveling players, and soldiers not realizing that hidden inside Scarecrow is the will that entitles him to inherit Mr. Pandolfo's Spring Valley. *2006 USBBY-CBC Outstanding International Books List, 2005 Nestlé Smarties Book*

Prize Silver Award, 2004 Carnegie Medal Shortlist, 2006 Children's Literature Assembly Notable Children's Book in the Language Arts. hc
   Author lives in Great Britain, and was a joint recipient of the 2005 Astrid Lindgren Memorial Award.
SCARECROWS, ORPHANS, ADVENTURE AND ADVENTURERS, FICTION

Ray, Jane. **The Apple-Pip Princess**. Illustrated by the author. Cambridge, MA, Candlewick Press, 2008. Originally published by Orchard Books Great Britain, in 2007. ISBN 978-0-7636-3747-7, 0-7636-3747-5. 32 p. (5–8). Picture book.
   The ruler of a kingdom turned barren and sad upon the death of the queen decides to select his successor by challenging each of his three daughters to do something to make him proud. The youngest plants an apple pip left to her by her mother, which sprouts and inspires others to plant seeds. The kingdom is magically renewed, and she is chosen. Ray writes with a strong storytelling voice; this original tale has the flavor of a folktale. The richly colored collage and watercolor illustrations, some of which are embellished with Ray's signature frames touched with gold, are stunning. *ca*
   Author/illustrator lives in Great Britain.
FAIRY TALES, PRINCESSES, KINGS, QUEENS, RULERS, APPLES, FICTION

Reeve, Philip. **Larklight, or, the Revenge of the White Spiders! Or, to Saturn's Rings and Back! A Rousing Tale of Dauntless Pluck in the Farthest Reaches of Space**. Illustrated by David Wyatt. New York, Bloomsbury, 2006. Originally published by Bloomsbury Great Britain, in 2006. ISBN 978-1-59990-020-9, 1-59990-020-3. 399 p. (8–10). Novel.
   In a fantastic Victorian Great Britain, it is up to Art and Myrtle Mumby, who live in Larklight, a rambling house traveling in an orbit beyond the moon, to save themselves and the British Empire (which includes outer space territories) from the attempts by crazy Dr. Ptarmigan to take over the universe. High adventure abounds as they are attacked by enormous, menacing spiders, left stranded on the moon, captured by a moth, rescued by a band of space pirates, and more. The Victorian tone is enhanced by the book's format, including the long, interest-catching title and descriptive chapter headings and Wyatt's intricately detailed black-and-white illustrations. Sequels are *Starcross: Larklight 2* and *Mothstorm: The Horror from Beyond Uranus Georgium Sidus!* 2007 Outstanding International Books List. *ca*
   Author and illustrator live in Great Britain.
BROTHERS AND SISTERS, SOLAR SYSTEM, OUTER SPACE, SCIENCE FICTION

Reeve, Philip. **A Darkling Plain: Hungry City Chronicles**. New York, HarperCollins/EOS, 2006. Originally published by Scholastic Great Britain, in 2006. ISBN 978-0-06-089055-1, 0-06-089055-X. 559 p. (10 up). Novel.

Reeve's highly imaginative science fiction adventure series *The Hungry City Chronicles*, which is set in a postapocalyptic future, comes to a conclusion with the creation of New London from the ruins of the once-mighty traction city. Now there is the promise of lasting peace between the Traction Cities and the airborne armies of the Green Storm of the stationary Anti-Tractionist cities. Treachery, sabotage, intrigue (and touches of humor) abound in the fourth book of this most satisfying series. *2008 USBBY Outstanding International Books List, 2006 Guardian's Children's Fiction Prize*. ca
Author lives in Great Britain.
NUCLEAR WEAPONS, CITY AND TOWN LIFE, STEAMPUNK, LONDON, GREAT BRITAIN, SCIENCE FICTION

Reeve, Philip. **Here Lies Arthur**. New York, Scholastic Press, 2008. Originally published by Scholastic Great Britain, in 2007. ISBN 978-0-545-09334-7, 0-545-09334-1. 339 p. (14 up). Novel.

Myrddin, Merlyn to readers of other Arthurian retellings, believes that his young friend Arthur—under the proper tutelage—could unite the warring factions of the British Isles. To do so, Myrddin uses sleight of hand, which he calls magic, skillful story-weaving (exaggeration), and a young orphan named Gwyna. During the years she serves Myrddin, Gwyna appears as the Lady of the Lake, a boy-warrior in training, and finally as a spy and handmaid to Arthur's wife, Gwenhwyfar. Reeve's tale suggests an alternative version of what might have happened and is probably more representative of the battles, deprivation, and treachery that a real Arthur might have experienced. *2009 Outstanding International Books List, 2007 Nestlé Children's Book Prize Shortlist, Booktrust Teenage Prize Shortlist*. lmp
Author lives in Great Britain.
KING ARTHUR, BARDS AND BARDISM, MAGIC, GREAT BRITAIN—HISTORY, ANGLO-SAXON PERIOD 449–1066, FANTASY FICTION

Riddell, Chris. **Ottoline and the Yellow Cat**. Illustrated by the author. New York, HarperCollins, 2007. Originally published by Macmillan Children's Books Great Britain, in 2007. ISBN 978-0-06-144879-9, 0-06-144879-6. 171 p. (8–10). Novel.

Ottoline's life is the embodiment of the old-fashioned orphan story. Her parents are not really dead—just off travelling—and they communicate via postcards bearing clairvoyant messages. She has oodles of money, people care for her every need, and a trusty sidekick named Mr. Munroe, who is "small, hairy, and from a bog in Norway" (2). Together they investigate the disappearance of pets and jewels from neighborhood residences. Chris Riddell, known principally as an illustrator, has served up a walloping good story—copiously illustrated—for readers willing to attempt more complex, but still short, chapter books. *2009 Outstanding International Books List. The author has won the Kate Greenaway Medal twice and the Nestlé Smarties Book Prize seven times. lmp*

Author was born in South Africa but has lived in Great Britain since he was a baby.

CRIME, CATS, DOGS, MYSTERY AND DETECTIVE STORIES, GIRLS, BURGLARY, FICTION

Robinson, Anthony & Annemarie Young. **Gervelie's Journey: A Refugee Diary**. Illustrated by June Allan. London, Frances Lincoln, 2008. ISBN 978-1-84507-652-8, 1-84507-652-4. 28 p. (8–10). Picture book.

See Africa/Congo for description.

Rose, Malcolm. **Framed!** Boston, Houghton Mifflin/Kingfisher, 2005. Originally published by Kingfisher Great Britain, in 2005. ISBN 978-0-7534-5971-3, 0-7534-5971-X. 223 p. (12 up). Novel.

In futuristic Birmingham, England, young Luke Harding has passed rigid examinations to become the youngest forensic investigator to graduate from his Authorities-controlled school set within a socially engineered community. His partner in detection is the mobile robot system, Malc, an acronym for a Mobile Aid to Law and Crime. Malc is capable of both instant and complex data collection and processing as well as deadpan literal comprehension. When three murders at the school appear to implicate Luke himself, he must use his own deductive skills and those of this technical sidekick to identify a killer who appears to be framing him. First book in the Traces series. *2006 USBBY-CBC Outstanding International Books List, American Library Association Quick Picks for Young Adults. nlr*

Author is a former lecturer in science who lives in Sheffield, Great Britain.

FORENSIC SCIENCES, MURDER, MYSTERY AND DETECTIVE STORIES, SCIENCE FICTION

Rosen, Michael. **Michael Rosen's Sad Book**. Illustrated by Quentin Blake. Cambridge, MA, Candlewick Press, 2005. Originally published by Walker

Books Great Britain, in 2004. ISBN 978-0-7636-2597-9, 0-7636-2597-3. n.p. (8 up). Picture book.

In this deeply personal picture book, Michael Rosen writes about feeling sad, particularly the deep sadness he feels over the death of his son. In simple, direct language, he describes the way sadness feels and how it affects him. He details the anger and anxiety he experiences and reveals the memories that offer him comfort. He also connects his own experiences with the sadness everyone feels from time to time. The emotional journey experienced in the author's ruminations and the illustrator's art is an honest, often lonely one, but it also includes glimmers of hope and even humor. It is a reassuring journey for readers of all ages who have known sadness in their lives. *2006 USBBY-CBC Outstanding International Books List, Exceptional Award for the Best Children's Illustrated Books of 2004 in the 4–11 Age Range from the English Association.* smv

Author and illustrator live in Great Britain.

SADNESS, EMOTIONS, FICTION

Rosen, Michael. **Totally Wonderful Miss Plumberry.** Illustrated by Chin-lun Lee. Cambridge, MA, Candlewick Press, 2006. Originally published by Walker Books Great Britain, in 2006. ISBN 978-0-7636-2744-7, 0-7636-2744-5. 32 p. (4–8). Picture book.

On this "wonderful day" (n.p.), Molly was taking a "crystal" to school that had been given to her by her grandmother, who lived a long way away. She runs into the classroom eager to share it with the other children, who crowd enthusiastically around until their attention is taken by Russell's stegosaurus. Now, the day is not so wonderful until Miss Plumberry realizes that Molly has something very special to share. Finely wrought watercolor and pencil drawings set the classroom scene in which a sad Molly is transformed back to happiness by a caring teacher with a great personality. *Michael Rosen's awards include the 1997 Eleanor Farjeon Award and Boston Globe Horn Book Honor Award.* hc

Author lives in Great Britain, and illustrator lives in Kaohsiung, Taiwan.

TEACHERS, CRYSTALS, SCHOOLS, FICTION

Rosenberry, Vera. **Vera's Baby Sister.** Illustrated by the author. New York, Henry Holt, 2005. ISBN 978-0-8050-7126-9, 0-8050-7126-1. 32 p. (4–7). Picture book.

Vera is *not* happy about Ruthie, her new baby sister: "That baby fills up the whole house . . . there is no room for me" (10). Grandfather distracts Vera by helping her build a backyard "bean tent." As the beans grow, Vera appreciates this secret place. In the fall she gathers seeds from the bean pods so she can create another bean tent in the spring. The last page shows Vera's reconciliation with Ruthie, who is now a toddler. It's spring, and Vera has created two bean tents side-by-side so the sisters can share this magic space. *chs*

Author/illustrator lives in Great Britain.

SIBLING RIVALRY, BABIES, GRANDFATHERS

Rosoff, Meg. **Just in Case**. New York, Random House/Wendy Lamb Books, 2006. Originally published by Penguin Great Britain, in 2006. ISBN 978-0-385-74678-6, 0-385-74678-4. 246 p. (14 up). Novel.

Fifteen-year-old David Case saves his baby brother from flying off the windowsill and is suddenly aware of the fragility of life. From then on, David takes on a new identity—Justin Case—in an attempt to avoid fate. But fate plays with Justin in this unique take on teenage angst: "I don't make deals, Justin. I deal" (90). He is nearly killed in an airport disaster and has a bittersweet relationship with a fashion photographer, Agnes, who uses him for her exhibits of "Doomed Youth." Helped by his friend, Peter, Justin is pulling himself back together when he unluckily contracts meningococcal meningitis. *2007 CILIP Carnegie Award, 2007 YALSA Best Books for Young Adults List. Meg Rosoff's awards include the Branford Boase Award, 2005, Guardian Children's Fiction Prize, 2004, Der Luchs des Jahres Book Prize, 2005, and Michael L. Printz Award, 2005. hc*

Author was born in the United States and lives in London.

FATE AND FATALISM, BROTHERS, GREAT BRITAIN, FICTION

Ross, Tony. **Say Please!** Illustrated by the author. La Jolla, CA, Kane/Miller Books, 2006. Originally published as *I Want My Dinner!* by Andersen Press Great Britain, in 1995. ISBN 978-1-933605-16-6, 1-933605-16-2. n.p. (3–6). Picture book.

A little "princess" keeps forgetting her manners, but even a princess must be polite. The "royalty" with whom she lives (the Queen and the General) gently assist the princess in remembering her manners. These lessons are well learned as evidenced by the little princess teaching an angry monster how to say "please" and "thank-you." This introduction to manners is written with such simple phrases that even prereaders will soon be reading along. This is the sixth Little Princess Book written by Tony Ross. *The author won the Dutch Silver Pencil Award for the first Little Princess book in the series. mm*

Author lives in Great Britain.

ETIQUETTE, MANNERS AND CUSTOMS, PRINCESSES, FANTASY FICTION

Rowling, J. K. **Harry Potter and the Deathly Hallows**. Illustrated by Mary GrandPré. Simultaneously published by Bloomsbury Great Britain, by Scholastic/Arthur A. Levine Books United States, by Raincoast Books Canada, and by Allen & Unwin Australia and New Zealand, in 2007. ISBN 978-0-545-01022-1, 0-545-01022-5. 759 p. (9 up). Novel.

Harry, aided by his loyal friends, his superior magical skills, and his deep personal integrity, sacrifices himself to defeat the Dark Lord. Loose ends are tied up and unanswered questions are addressed in this superbly wrought conclusion to the series. British elements add appeal to this international phenomenon. *2008 USBBY Outstanding International Books List, 2007 New York Times 100 Notable Books, New York Times Notable Children's Books, 2007 Publishers Weekly Best Books, 2008 ALA Best Books for Young Adults and Notable Children's Book, 2008 Colorado Blue Spruce Book Award.*

Author lives in Scotland.

Wizard, Magic, Coming of Age, Harry Potter (Fictitious Character), Schools, Hogwarts School of Witchcraft and Wizardry (Imaginary Organization), Great Britain, Fantasy Fiction

Sage, James. **Mr. Beast**. Illustrated by Russell Ayto. New York, Henry Holt, 2005. Originally published by HarperCollins Great Britain, in 2004. ISBN 978-0-8050-7730-8, 0-8050-7730-8. n.p. (4–8). Picture book.

When Charlie eats all the doughnuts his mother has made for Mr. Beast, Mr. Beast warns that he'll be coming to eat up Charlie during the night. The cartoon-style illustrations hint that, in spite of the grunting and thumping that goes on as Mr. Beast makes his way to Charlie's bedroom, the young boy is not afraid, which is just the way it should be, as it turns out Mr. Beast is Charlie's father. Ayto's illustrations include shadowy, menacing details, but the overall tone is playful and humorous, making this a good choice for young children who like scary-but-not-too-scary stories. *ca*

Author was born in the United States and now lives in Great Britain; the illustrator lives in Great Britain.

Monsters, Fathers and Sons, Fantasy

Schlitz, Laura Amy. **Good Masters! Sweet Ladies! Voices from a Medieval Village**. Illustrated by Robert Byrd. Cambridge, MA, Candlewick Press, 2007. ISBN 978-0-7636-1578-9, 0-7636-1578-1. 85 p. (10 up). Illustrated book.

This unusually informative and highly entertaining series of twenty-three monologues features adolescent residents of a thirteenth-century English manor. Each is written in verse; some are serious commentaries on medieval society, but others are humorous. "Lowdy, The Varlet's Child" bemoans the fleas that infest her and her father's hounds: "I'm used to the lice / Raising families in my hair. / I expect moths to nibble holes / In everything I wear. / I scrape away the maggots / When they crawl across the cheese. / I can get used to anything, / Except for the fleas!" (61). Interspersed are informative remarks on topics of particular interest, such as "Crusades," "Medieval Pilgrimage," "Jews in the Medieval Society," and "Falconry." *2008 Newbery Award. lmp*

Author lives in the United States.

MIDDLE AGES, MEDIEVAL GREAT BRITAIN, DRAMA, MONOLOGUES, CHILDREN'S PLAYS

Sedgwick, Marcus. **The Foreshadowing**. New York, Random House/Wendy Lamb Books, 2006. Originally published by Orion Children's Books Great Britain, in 2005. ISBN 978-0-385-74646-5, 0-385-74646-6. 293 p. (14 up). Novel.

The Foxes are a well-to-do British family: respected medical doctor, subservient mother, two sons at university, and seventeen-year old Alexandra. Tragically, Alexandra can envision the future—but only the imminent deaths of people she encounters. This becomes especially relevant when her brothers enlist in the British army at the outbreak of World War I. She foresees first her elder's, then younger brother's, deaths. Alexandra secretly departs for France in the guise of a volunteer nurse—hoping to safeguard her younger brother. *The Foreshadowing* can be paired with Iain Lawrence's *Lord of the Nutcracker Men* (2001) for a look at the sordid—and more primitive—aspects of war. *2007 USBBY Outstanding International Books List. lmp*

Author lives in Great Britain.

EXTRASENSORY PERCEPTION, NURSES, GREAT BRITAIN–HISTORY–GEORGE V, 1910–1936, WORLD WAR I (1914–1918), FRANCE, GREAT BRITAIN, FICTION

Skelton, Matthew. **Endymion Spring**. New York, Delacorte Press, 2006. Originally published by Puffin Great Britain, in 2006. ISBN 978-0-385-73380-9, 0-385-73380-1. 392 p. (10 up). Fiction.

Endymion Spring is a complex double fantasy that occurs concurrently in modern-day Oxford, England, and fifteenth century Mainz, Germany. Johannes Gutenberg, inventor of the modern printing press, and his apprentice, Endymion Spring, create a magical book that disappears then eventually resurfaces in Oxford. Only certain readers can see the book's print, and Blake Winters, who lives in Oxford with his sister and his mother, a visiting academic, is one. The plot turns dark when members of the Ex-Libris Society realize Blake has located the book they lust after. Mystery, historical fiction, contemporary fantasy adventure—*Endymion Spring* integrates each in a seamless plot that will keep readers turning pages. *2008 Red Maple Award (Canada)*. lmp

Author lives in Great Britain.

GUTENBERG, JOHANN (1397?–1468), BODLEIAN LIBRARY, DYSFUNCTIONAL FAMILIES, BOOKS AND READING, MAGIC, APPRENTICES, FAMILY PROBLEMS, MYSTERY AND DETECTIVE STORIES, GREAT BRITAIN, FANTASY, FICTION

Stewart, Joel. **Dexter Bexley and the Big Blue Beastie**. Illustrated by the author. New York, Holiday House, 2007. Originally published by Doubleday Great Britain, in 2007. ISBN 978-0-8234-2068-1, 0-8234-2068-X. 30 p. (4–8). Picture book.

Scheherazade has nothing on Dexter Bexley when it comes to delaying the inevitable. After literally running into a Big Blue Beastie who announces, "I'm big and I'm bored, . . . and you look small and tasty. I should probably eat you up" (n.p.), Dexter offers one alternative after another to prevent his death. The rotund, jaw-jutting, bowler-wearing Big Blue Beastie struggles to maintain his gruff demeanor, but his ultimate friendship with Dexter Bexley overcomes boredom and hunger. Stewart's humorous watercolor cartoons of Beastie and Dexter supply much of the story's meaning while keeping the tone light-hearted and never threatening. lmp

Author lives in London.

PLAY, MONSTERS, FRIENDSHIP, IMAGINATION, FANTASY, GREAT BRITAIN

Stewart, Paul & Chris Riddell. **Hugo Pepper: Far-Flung Adventures**. New York, Random House/David Fickling Books, 2007. Originally published by Random House/Doubleday Great Britain, in 2006. ISBN 978-0-385-75092-9, 0-385-75092-7. 272 p. (9–12). Novel.

Ten-year-old Hugo Pepper has been raised by kindly reindeer herders since being orphaned as an infant in the Frozen North, his parents eaten by polar bears. When Hugo inadvertently discovers an Aeronautical Snow Chariot, the very sled that had borne his parents northward, he sets off to find the story of his beginnings. Detailed ink drawings and silhouette insets provide the perfect accompaniment to a tongue-in-cheek telling that interweaves chapters of Hugo's search against a panoply of eccentric characters—including mermaids, pirates, inventors, lamplighters, and storytellers. There are also just-right doses of villainy, magic carpets, snow monsters, and hidden treasure. Third in a series. *2008 USBBY Outstanding International Books List; winner of 2006 Smarties Prize Silver Medal (6–8 Category)*. lmp

Authors live in Great Britain.

ADVENTURE AND ADVENTURERS, HUMOR, ORPHANS, TABLOID NEWSPAPERS, NEWSPAPERS, YETI, STORYTELLERS, FANTASY, FICTION

Taylor, Eleanor. **Beep, Beep, Let's Go!** Illustrated by the author. New York, Bloomsbury, 2005. Originally published by Bloomsbury Great Britain, in 2005. ISBN 978-1-58234-973-2, 1-58234-973-8. 32 p. (4–7). Picture book.

Time to head to the beach! Animals aplenty pile into a motley collection of vehicles—cars, bikes, motor scooters, buses, trucks, and bikes—to make the trip. Action continues once the animals arrive—spreading towels, buying snacks, building sand castles, splashing water. The brightly colored double-page spreads become increasingly busy as more and more vehicles crowd the road for the drive to the beach. The accompanying text is a celebration of sound—beep, beep, chugga, chugga, toot, toot. This simple story will strike a responsive chord in any child who has anticipated a trip to the seashore. *mm*

Author lives in London.

SEASHORE, ANIMALS, FANTASY FICTION

Thompson, Kate. **Highway Robbery.** Illustrated by Jonny Duddle & Robert Dress. New York, HarperCollins/Greenwillow Books, 2009. Originally published by Bodley Head Great Britain, in 2008. ISBN 978-0-06-173034-4, 0-06-173034-3. 118 p. (10 up). Novel.

"Hold the mare for me, lad. And when I come back, I'll give you a golden guinea" (11). The beggar boy was bewitched. And for a guttersnipe without shoes or bread, a golden guinea was a fortune. However, the arrival of hard-riding soldiers who forcefully enlist him as bait to catch Dick Turpin—the Highwayman—causes our cold and hungry young hero great pangs of conscience. Should he warn Turpin? Escape with the horse, Black Bess? Or aid the king's army? This is an artfully drawn metanarrative that affirms new readers' intelligence and concludes with a wink of the eye at the storyteller's clever conceit. *2009 Children's Books Ireland (CBI) Judges Special Recognition Award. lmp*

Author lives in Ireland.

BRIGANDS AND ROBBERS, RICHARD TURPIN (1706–1739), HORSES, ADVENTURE AND ADVENTURERS, GREAT BRITAIN HISTORY 18TH CENTURY, HISTORICAL FICTION

Tierney, Fiona. **Lion's Lunch?** Illustrated by Margaret Chamberlain. New York, Scholastic/Chicken House, 2010. Originally published by Chicken

House Great Britain, in 2010. ISBN 978-0-545-17691-0, 0-545-17691-3. n.p. (4–8). Picture book.

While walking in her local jungle, Sarah happens into a "great big angry lion!" (n.p.). He tells her that no one walks in the jungle—or sings—then lists the ways animals move and communicate. It seems that the only thing Sarah is good for is LUNCH. She objects, so Lion allows her to draw a picture of him, but he challenges the image he sees. When the other animals agree that he really is a "great big angry lion!," he decides to change. Although the book is marginally didactic, young readers will enjoy the rhythmic, onomatopoetic language. *lmp*

Author lives in Dublin, Ireland; illustrator lives in Great Britain.

Lion, Animals, Jungles, Drawing, Fantasy Fiction

Turnbull, Ann. **Forged in the Fire**. Cambridge, MA, Candlewick Press, 2007. Originally published by Walker Books Great Britain, in 2006. ISBN 978-0-7636-3144-4, 0-7636-3144-2. 320 p. (12 up). Novel.

In this sequel to *No Shame, No Fear*, Susanna and Will must endure separation while he works in London to earn enough money for their marriage. The people of London are not sympathetic to Will's Quaker beliefs. He endures imprisonment and barely survives the plague. After being reunited, Will and Susanna face the challenge of starting a new life in the midst of political turmoil. The book culminates with the people of London fleeing the historic blaze that leveled much of the city in 1666. The story is written in the Quaker language style of the 1600s. *2008 USBBY Outstanding International Books List, NYPL Books for the Teen Age. nrr*

Author lives in Great Britain.

Plague–Great Britain, Quakers, Fires–Great Britain, Great Britain–History–Charles II (1660–1685), Love Stories, Fiction, Sequel to No Shame, No Fear (2004)

Umansky, Kaye. **The Silver Spoon of Solomon Snow**. Cambridge, MA, Candlewick Press, 2005. Originally published by Puffin Great Britain, in 2004. ISBN 978-0-7636-2792-8, 0-7636-2792-5. 289 p. (8–12). Novel.

Through Dickensian allusions, including tumbledown cottages, characters with aptronymic names, and surprising turns of fortune, Umansky tells a tongue-in-cheek Victorian tale of Solomon Snow, abandoned on the doorstep of a poor village couple—with a silver spoon in his mouth. When Solomon eventually sets off to solve the mystery of his identity, he is aided by two sharp-witted girls, one a budding writer, the other a circus sideshow runaway. Together with some plucky Oliver Twist–type orphans, the main characters provide a melodramatic romp (announced with chapter division placards) while also managing to convey some of the bleakness of nineteenth-century cities. *nlr*

Author lives in London.

FOUNDLINGS, FRIENDSHIP, IDENTITY, 19TH CENTURY GREAT BRITAIN, HISTORICAL FICTION

Umansky, Kaye. **Clover Twig and the Magical Cottage**. Illustrated by Johanna Wright. New York, Roaring Brook Press, 2009. Originally published as *Clover Twig and the Incredible Flying Cottage* by Bloomsbury Great Britain, in 2008. ISBN 978-1-59643-507-0, 1-59643-507-0. 304 p. (9 up). Novel.

Sensible, orderly Clover Twig not only cleans up the mess in Mrs. Eckles's magical cottage in the woods but also manages to return it to its proper place after Mrs. Eckles's grasping sister-witch Mesmeranza sneakily spirits it away and lands Clover in the dungeons of Castle Coldiron. Focused alternately on Clover and Wilf (her hapless helper), then on Mesmeranza, this is a satisfying story. It is also a good introduction for upper elementary school students to the mixture of magic and humor they will find later in works by Terry Pratchett and Diana Wynne Jones. *2010 USBBY Outstanding International Books List. kti*

Author lives in London.

WITCHES, HOUSEHOLD EMPLOYEES, DWELLINGS, SISTERS, MAGIC, FANTASY FICTION

Updale, Eleanor. **Montmorency on the Rocks: Doctor, Aristocrat, Murderer?** New York, Scholastic/Orchard Books, 2005. Originally published by Scholastic Great Britain, in 2004. ISBN 978-0-439-60676-9, 0-439-60676-4. 362 p. (10 up). Novel.

After a successful stint as international spies, Montmorency and Lord George Fox-Selwyn return to Victorian London, where Lord George is determined to enlist Dr. Robert Farcett to help cure Montmorency's drug addiction, but in the process the three become involved with a mysterious rash of baby deaths on a remote Scottish island. This delightful sequel to the earlier *Montmorency: Thief, Liar, Gentleman?* stands alone and offers an excellent introduction to this clever, likeable burglar and his friends. Sequels include *Montmorency and the Assassins: Book 3* (2006) and *Montmorency's Revenge: Book 4* (2007). *2006 USBBY-CBC Outstanding International Books List. kti*

Author lives in Great Britain.

BRIGANDS AND ROBBERS, ROBBERS AND OUTLAWS, IDENTITY, LONDON, GREAT BRITAIN–HISTORY (1800–1950), GREAT BRITAIN–HISTORY–VICTORIA (1837–1901), MYSTERY, FICTION

Valentine, Jenny. **Me, the Missing, and the Dead**. New York, HarperTeen, 2008. Originally published as *Finding Violet Park* by HarperCollins Great Britain, in 2007. ISBN 978-0-06-085068-5, 0-06-085068-X. 201 p. (14 up). Novel.

Lucas Swain is almost sixteen when he first "meets" Violet Park. He doesn't know her name at first because technically it's her ashes he chances upon—she's been dead for at least eighteen months. He follows leads and "hears" Violet's voice, until he's convinced there *is* a connection between the urn he's discovered and his father's mysterious disappearance five years ago. First-time author Jenny Valentine has written a cleverly crafted mystery that will keep readers guessing until the final page turn. *2009 William C. Morris YA Debut Honor Award, ALA Best Book for Young Adults, Texas Library Association TAYSHAS High School Reading List. lmp*
    Author lives in Great Britain.
FATHERS, MISSING PERSONS, DEATH, SINGLE-PARENT FAMILIES, COMING OF AGE, LONDON (GREAT BRITAIN), FICTION

Valentine, Jenny. **Broken Soup**. New York, HarperCollins, 2009. Originally published by HarperCollins Great Britain, in 2008. ISBN 978-0-06-085071-5, 0-06-085071-X. 216 p. (14 up). Novel.

Fifteen-year-old Rowan relates the story of her family's collapse following the unexpected death of her older brother two years earlier. Strong characterizations, unusual plot turns, and thoughtful explorations of love, grief, and responsibility characterize this life-affirming tale. *2010 USBBY Outstanding International Books List.*
    Author lives in Great Britain.
FAMILY PROBLEMS, FAMILIES, GRIEF, LONDON, GREAT BRITAIN, FICTION

Walsh, Melanie. **10 Things I Can Do to Help My World: Fun and Easy Eco-Tips**. Illustrated by the author. Cambridge, MA, Candlewick Press, 2008. Originally published by Walker Books Great Britain, in 2008. ISBN 978-0-7636-41443, 0-7636-4144-8. 32 p. (3–7). Picture book.

Bold graphics and minimal text introduce young children to ten "eco-tips," such as remembering to turn off the light when you leave a room. With each tip, there is a one-sentence explanation as to why this is important. For example, "Turning off lights and using more efficient light bulbs saves valuable energy" (n.p.). This is a good introduction for young children on becoming environmentally conscious and living an eco-friendly life. It may also encourage them to put some of the tips into action in their classrooms, schools, homes, and neighborhoods. *ca*

The author/illustrator lives in Great Britain.

ENVIRONMENT, WASTE MINIMIZATION, NONFICTION

Ward, Helen. **Little Moon Dog**. Illustrated by Wayne Anderson. New York, Penguin/Dutton Children's Books, 2007. Originally published as *Moon Dog* by Templar Publishing Great Britain, in 2005. ISBN 978-0-525-47727-3, 0-525-47727-6. 332 p. (4–6). Picture book.

The Man in the Moon and Little Moon Dog live together in their peaceful lunar home, but every summer, fairies disrupt the quiet. Over time, the fairies grow tired of Little Moon Dog's company and move on to other things, leaving a very sad and lonely puppy. All the while, the Man in the Moon misses his canine companion and searches until he finds his friend. Anderson's desolate lunar landscape, appropriately reclusive moon man, bouncy puppy, and delicately drawn mischievous fairies provide a charming complement to Ward's lilting language. *nlh, lmp*

Author lives in Great Britain.

FAIRIES, MOON, FRIENDSHIP, FICTION

Whitford, Rebecca. **Little Yoga: A Toddler's First Book of Yoga**. Illustrated by Martina Selway. New York, Henry Holt, 2005. Simultaneously published by Random House/Hutchinson Children's Books Great Britain. ISBN 978-0-8050-7879-4, 0-8050-7879-7. n.p. (4–8). Picture book.

Children are introduced to a series of simple yoga poses. Each spread features a child demonstrating a particular pose, while the opposing page presents the animal the pose reflects. For example, on one page the viewer sees a child spreading his arms and the opposite page features a flying butterfly. Children will delight in copying the movements of different animals, all the while bending, stretching, breathing, balancing, and doing relaxation movements. To aide parents and caregivers in working with their children, the author includes practice tips, explanations of the poses, and photos of actual children practicing the poses. *Sleepy Little Yoga* (reviewed here) is a sequel. *mm*

Author and illustrator live in Great Britain.

HATHA YOGA FOR CHILDREN, NONFICTION BOOKS

Whitford, Rebecca. **Sleepy Little Yoga**. Illustrated by Martina Selway. New York, Henry Holt, 2007. Simultaneously published by Random House/ Hutchinson Children's Books Great Britain. ISBN 978-0-8050-8193-0, 0-8050-8193-3. n.p. (1–4). Picture book.

Sleepy Little Yoga features a simple yoga sequence designed to help toddlers and young children relax before a nap or bedtime. Each yoga pose is described as an animal movement, and the accompanying double-page spread shows both a child and the animal doing the move. For example, on one spread the illustrator features a child and a rabbit "flopping down like a tired bunny" (n.p.). This engaging presentation invites young children to try each pose. At the end of the book adults will find practice tips, an explanation of each pose, and photographs of young children practicing them. *mm*
    Author and illustrator live in Great Britain.
    Hatha Yoga for Children, Nonfiction Books

Wilkins, Rose. **So Super Stylish**. New York, Dial Books, 2006. Originally published by Macmillan Children's Books Great Britain, in 2005. ISBN 978-0-8037-3064-9, 0-8037-3064-0. 280 p. (14 up). Novel.

    In this tongue-in-cheek look at the celebrity world, sixteen-year-old Octavia tells how she has left her private school, attended by the offspring of celebrities, to attend the local public school in London, where she is trying to keep "a low profile" and catch up on her academic studies (5). But her intentions and her relationship with her new boyfriend are complicated by her mother, an actress, who is making tabloid news over her romance with an American television executive, and by India Withers, an ambitious young actress who is using Octavia's new school and family to advance her own career. *hc*
    Author is from Great Britain.
    Fame–Celebrities, Stepfamilies, Dating, Schools, Teenage Girls, London, Fiction

Williams, Marcia. **Archie's War: My Scrapbook of the First World War, 1914–1918**. Illustrated by the author. Cambridge, MA, Candlewick Press, 2007. Originally published by Walker Books Great Britain, in 2007. ISBN 978-0-7636-3532-9, 0-7636-3532-4. 45 p. (9–12). Picture book.

    Archie is ten years old when his Uncle Colin gives him his scrapbook. Shortly afterward, World War I erupts and Archie uses it to reflect on news from the front. The fictional narrator also includes his own illustrations and reproductions of postcards, letters, flyers, and more. Through Archie's scrapbook, readers get a glimpse of the impact of the war on British families, from enduring air raids and food shortages to anxiously awaiting letters from soldiers at the front. The endpapers echo the scrapbook theme. Included is a short glossary of terms. *Bank Street College Best Children's Book of the Year, Notable Social Studies Trade Books for Young People*. nlh

Author lives in Great Britain.

DIARIES, WORLD WAR I (1914–1918), LONDON GREAT BRITAIN HISTORY 20TH CENTURY, HISTORICAL FICTION

Willis, Jeanne. **Misery Moo**. Illustrated by Tony Ross. New York, Henry Holt, 2005. Originally published by Andersen Press Great Britain, in 2003. ISBN 978-0-8050-7672-1, 0-8050-7672-7. 32 p. (4–8). Picture book.

A cow with an Eeyore outlook, who sits on her bottom, udder akimbo, can't help but evoke laughter, even in the face of her self-proclaimed misery. Misery Moo despairs over rain and birthdays, sameness, winter, and even holidays. Ultimately, her doleful stance weighs too heavily on her friend, the cheery lamb. Lamby Poo's optimism is stretched past its limits as she tries to be convincing about silver linings and glasses half full. So it's up to Misery Moo to decide that being a friend means making someone else happy. And the "biggest, sunniest [funniest] smiles" (n.p.) are a starting point. nlr

Author and illustrator live in Great Britain.

SADNESS, HAPPINESS, FRIENDSHIP, COWS, SHEEP, FANTASY

Willis, Jeanne. **Delilah D. at the Library**. Illustrated by Rosie Reeve. New York, Clarion Books, 2007. Originally published as *Delilah Darling Is in the Library* by Puffin Great Britain, in 2006. ISBN 978-0-618-78195-9, 0-618-78195-1. 32 p. (3–6). Picture book.

Deliah D. loves books and has an over-the-top imagination. As she tells Library Anne, in Faraway Land where she is queen, the library is a special place. They have lots of books, but they also give away free cupcakes, patrons use a trapeze to reach books on the high shelves, a beautiful princess reads to the children, and there are no rules against running, shouting, and singing. The illustrations for this celebration of both the imagination and books are warm and exuberant. Young children will probably agree that Deliah D.'s Faraway Land library sounds inviting, even if Library Anne doesn't. ca

Author and illustrator both live in Great Britain.

BOOKS, LIBRARIES, IMAGINATION, HUMOROUS STORIES, FICTION

Wilson, Jacqueline. **The Illustrated Mum**. New York, Delacorte Press, 2005. Originally published by Doubleday Great Britain, in 1999. ISBN 978-0-385-73237-6, 0-385-73237-6. 282 p. (11 up). Novel.

Eleven-year-old Dol lives in a constant state of impermanence and unpredictability with an adolescent sister, Star, and a mentally unstable mother, Marigold. She therefore loves the idea of her mum's tattoos lasting forever. Marigold has accumulated a body full of them to record the most joyous moments and to celebrate the most special people in her life. It's a fix for her, though; she inks when she's manic but drinks when she's low. Pretending can be a fun and protective form of escape from this "yo-yo" (233) for Dol, until a crisis forces her to have to "suss out what's real" (168). *2006 USBBY-CBC Outstanding International Books List. bef*

Author has written over seventy award-winning books for young readers of all ages. She lives in Great Britain in a small house crammed with fifteen thousand books.

Mothers and Daughters, Manic-Depressive Illness, Single-Parent Families, Tattooing, Great Britain, Fiction

Wilson, Jacqueline. **Candyfloss**. Illustrated by Nick Sharratt. New York, Roaring Book Press, 2007. Originally published by Doubleday Great Britain, in 2006. ISBN 978-1-59643-241-3, 1-59643-241-1. 339 p. (9–12). Novel.

Floss has decided to stay in London to help her amusingly creative, inept father run his failing, greasy spoon café rather than move to Australia with her mom, prosperous stepfather, and new brother. At school, she loses her superficial, snob friends, but she makes friends with smart, sensitive Susan. After several tough trials, Floss's father finally puts the divorce behind him, meets cotton-candy maker and fortune-teller Rose, and the three make a plan for the future. Each chapter opens with comic-book sketches that preview the action. "Floss's Glossary" helps readers with unfamiliar British terms. *2008 USBBY Outstanding International Books List. mjw*

Author was the 2005–2007 British Children's Laureate. She lives in Great Britain.

Divorce, Fathers and Daughters, Friendship, Schools, Great Britain, Fiction

Winterson, Jeanette. **Tanglewreck**. New York, Bloomsbury, 2006. Originally published by Bloomsbury Great Britain, in 2006. ISBN 978-1582349190, 1582349193. 416 p. (9–12). Novel.

Eleven-year-old Silver of Tanglewreck Mansion lost her family and the Timekeeper (clock) in a Time Tornado. Wicked Abel Darkwater and evil Regalia Mason scheme to possess the Timekeeper and become rulers of the

Universe; however, they are thwarted by Gabriel and other Throwbacks who save Silver and Time. *2007 USBBY Outstanding International Books List.*
Author lives in Great Britain.
TIME, TIME TRAVEL, SPACE AND TIME, CLOCKS AND WATCHES, FICTION

Wooding, Chris. **Poison.** New York, Scholastic/Orchard Books, 2005. Originally published by Scholastic Great Britain, in 2003. ISBN 978-0-439-75570-2, 0-439-75570-0. 273 p. (12 up). Novel.
Poison is a dark and disturbing fantasy novel with a compelling protagonist on a coming-of-age quest. Raised in the isolated village of Gull, Poison, a dark-haired, violet-eyed sixteen-year-old, refuses to accept the life for which she was raised. When her beloved baby sister Azalea is kidnapped and a changeling left in her place, Poison leaves the Realm of Man for the Realm of Phaeries in order to confront the Phaerie Lord and bring her sister home. As she makes her way, Poison and the devoted friends she makes on her journey must confront a variety of strange and dangerous creatures and challenge the powerful Lord Aelthar, who helps Poison find her own destiny along the way. *2006 USBBY-CBC Outstanding International Books List, LCC Children's Book of the Year Award, and Dracula Society for Best Gothic Novel of 2004. smv*
Author lives in Great Britain.
FAIRIES, STORYTELLING, FANTASY FICTION

Wormell, Christopher. **Ferocious Wild Beasts!** Illustrated by the author. New York, Random House/Alfred A. Knopf, 2009. Originally published by Jonathan Cape Great Britain, in 2009. ISBN 978-0-375-86091-1, 0-375-86091-6. n.p. (5–8). Picture book.
Ferocious Wild Beasts! is a perfect read-aloud rendition of a familiar tale, reminiscent of Roald Dahl's *The Minpins.* Jack has been warned never to venture into the forest where ferocious wild beasts lurk. The amusing twist is that the ferocious beasts—lion, bear, wolf, python, crocodile, elephant—are more frightened than the boy, who forecasts an increasingly horrific doom. Watercolor illustrations are suitably eerie, evocative of the imaginings of any Jack whose mother has warned of unimaginable horrors. In the final scene, Jack reluctantly accompanies his mother while attesting, "I didn't see any ferocious wild beasts" (n.p.). *lmp*
Author lives in London.
ANIMALS, HUMOROUS STORIES, FICTION

RELATED INFORMATION

Organizations

IBBY UK

IBBY UK looks forward to hosting the 2012 IBBY Congress in London: *Crossing Boundaries: Translations and Migrations*, from August 23–26, 2012. More information is available at www.ibbycongress2012.org.uk.

www.ibby.org/index.php?id=462

www.ibby.org.uk/

Awards

Booktrust Prizes

www.booktrust.org.uk/Prizes-and-awards

Booktrust is an independent charity dedicated to encouraging people of all ages and cultures to engage with books and is responsible for a number of successful national reading promotions, sponsored book prizes, and creative reading projects aimed at encouraging readers to discover and enjoy books. These include:

- **Blue Peter Awards**

  The goal of the Blue Peter Book Awards is to guide children toward high-quality literature, encouraging them to read and establish a love of reading for life. Blue Peter Awards are chosen in three categories: (1) Favorite Story, (2) Most Fun Story with Pictures, and (3) Best Book with Facts.

  www.booktrustchildrensbooks.org.uk/Prizes-and-awards/Blue-Peter
  -Book-Awards

- **Booktrust Best New Illustrators Award**

  The Booktrust Best New Illustrators Award celebrates the best rising talent in the field of children's illustration today. First awarded in 2008, the prize is given to ten emerging illustrators whose work demonstrates remarkable creative flair, artistic skill, and boundless imagination. The second award will be announced in March 2011. No information is available on the frequency or future status of the award.

  www.booktrustchildrensbooks.org.uk/show/feature/Picture%20
  Books/Best-New-Illustrators-Award-2011

- **Booktrust Early Years Award**

  The Early Years Award honors books that are dynamic and creative in words, design, and illustration, encouraging a sustained passion for books in each child. There are three categories: (1) The Best Book for babies under one year old, (2) The Best Picture Book for children up to five years old, and (3) Best Emerging Illustrator for children up to five years old.

www.booktrustchildrensbooks.org.uk/Prizes-and-awards/Booktrust -Early-Years-Awards

- **The Booktrust Teenage Prize**
The Booktrust Teenage Prize, originated in 2002, is a national book prize that recognizes and celebrates the best in contemporary writing for teenagers. The jury is composed of adults and young adults. The award is administered and publicized by The Reading Agency, Booktrust, and UK libraries. For the purpose of the prize, "teenage" encompasses young adults between the ages of twelve and sixteen.

www.booktrust.org.uk/Prizes-and-awards/Booktrust-Teenage-Prize

- **Branford Boase Award**
The Branford Boase Award was established to honor the most promising new writers and their editors, as well as to reward excellence in writing and in publishing. The award is made annually to the most promising book for children seven years old and up by a first-time novelist.

www.branfordboaseaward.org.uk/

- **The Children's Laureate**
The role of Children's Laureate celebrates the outstanding achievement of an author or illustrator of children's books. The appointment of a Children's Laureate acknowledges the importance of exceptional children's authors in creating the readers of tomorrow. This program began in 1999 and is awarded biennially. The current laureate is author and illustrator Anthony Browne (2009–2011). Previous Children's Laureates have been Michael Rosen (2007–2009), Jacqueline Wilson (2005–2007), Michael Morpurgo (2003–2005), Anne Fine (2001–2003), and Quentin Blake (1999–2001).

www.childrenslaureate.org.uk

- **CILIP Carnegie Medal and Kate Greenaway Medal**
The Carnegie Medal is awarded by children's librarians to the writer of the most outstanding book for children and young people. www.carnegiegreenaway.org.uk/home/index.php

The Kate Greenaway Medal is awarded by children's librarians to the illustrator of the most outstanding book for children and young people.

www.carnegiegreenaway.org.uk/home/index.php

- **Costa Book Awards** (Formerly known as the **Whitbread Award**)
  The Costa Book Awards began in 1971 as the Whitbread Literary Awards. From 1985 to 2006, they were known as the Whitbread Book Awards. In 2006 Costa Coffee assumed sponsorship. These awards honor the most enjoyable books in five categories: (1) First Novel, (2) Novel, (3) Biography, (4) Poetry, and (5) Children's Book. The books must have been published in the previous year by writers based in the UK and Ireland.
  www.costabookawards.com/
- **Eleanor Farjeon Award**
  In memory of the children's author, Eleanor Farjeon, the Children's Book Circle (CBC) recognizes an outstanding contribution to the world of children's books by an individual or organization.
  www.childrensbookcircle.org.uk/farjeon.asp
- **Guardian Children's Fiction Prize**
  The Guardian Children's Fiction Prize or Guardian Award is a prominent award for works of children's literature by British or Commonwealth authors, published in the UK during the preceding year. The award has been given annually since 1967.
  www.guardian.co.uk/books/guardianchildrensfictionprize
- **Macmillan Prize**
  The Macmillan Prize, funded by Macmillan Children's Books, was established in 1985 in order to stimulate new work from young illustrators in art school and to help launch their professional careers.
  www.panmacmillan.com/Help/displayPage.asp?PageTitle=Aspiring %20authors%20and%20illustrators%20FAQ
- **The Red House Children's Book Award**
  The Red House Children's Book Award is the only British award voted on entirely by children.
  www.redhousechildrensbookaward.co.uk/
- **Roald Dahl Funny Prize**
  The Roald Dahl Funny Prize was initiated in 2008 by Michael Rosen as part of his Children's Laureateship. It is the first prize of its kind, founded to honor books that simply make children laugh. There are two categories: Funniest Book for Children Aged Six and Under and Funniest Book for Children Aged Seven to Fourteen.
  www.booktrustchildrensbooks.org.uk/Prizes-and-awards/Roald -Dahl-Funny-Prize
- **The Stockton** [Borough Council] **Children's Book of the Year**
  www.stockton.gov.uk/citizenservices/leisureandents/libraries/child andyouth/scby/

- **UK National Art Library Illustrator's Award**
  The Victoria & Albert (V&A) Illustration Awards are sponsored by
  the Enid Linder Foundation to encourage and recognize creativity.
     www.vam.ac.uk/activ_events/events/illustration_awards/
- **Waterstone's Children's Book Prize**
  The Waterstone's Children's Book Prize is a distinguished award in the
  world of kids' books. The award highlights the passion of booksellers
  (Waterstone's is a bookstore in Great Britain) in championing emerg-
  ing talent in the world of kids' books.
     www.waterstones.com/waterstonesweb/navigate.do?pPageID=1185

Discontinued Awards

British Children's Book of the Year

All references lead to defunct websites. This seems to have been folded
into other awards, possibly Booktrust awards.

Emil Kurt Maschler Award

The Emil Kurt Maschler Award was established in 1982 by Kurt Maschler
and was awarded annually until 1999, when it was discontinued. www.book
awards.bizland.com/kurt_maschler_award_for_children.htm

Mother Goose Award

The Mother Goose Award was an annual British award, presented by Books
for Children, to the best new illustrator. Established in 1979, the award was last
given in 1999. For a list of award winners, go to the Children's Literature Web
Guide site at http://people.ucalgary.ca/~dkbrown/mothergoose.html.

Nestlé Smarties Award was discontinued in 2008 by mutual agreement
between Booktrust and Nestlé.

Collections

Roehampton University: Children's Literature Collection

This is a specialist collection that is housed in the Learning Resources
Centre. It exists to support children's literature studies at Roehampton and the
work of the National Centre for Research in Children's Literature (NCRCL).

As well as reference books and journals, the Collection houses a large
number of children's books of historical interest, mainly from the nineteenth
and early twentieth centuries.
   http://core.roehampton.ac.uk/digital/chlitindex.htm

Museums and Other Sites to Visit

Bateman's

Bateman's is the seventeenth-century home of Rudyard Kipling and his family. Located in East Sussex, the rooms and grounds are open to the public.
www.nationaltrust.org.uk/main/w-batemans

Great Maytham Hall

The gardens at Great Maytham Hall, near Rolvenden, Kent, are famous for providing the inspiration for *The Secret Garden* by Frances Hodgson Burnett.

The Manor, Hemingford Gray (Green Knowe)

The Manor is the house that inspired Lucy Boston's *Green Knowe* books.
www.greenknowe.co.uk/

Oxford

The place where C. S. Lewis wrote the Narnia stories, Lewis Carroll met Alice in Wonderland, and Philip Pullman created his Northern Lights trilogy. Christ Church, a college of the University of Oxford, was used as a setting for parts of the Harry Potter films. A Story Museum is being built in Oxford to celebrate these and other local children's authors.
www.visitoxford.org/

The Roald Dahl Museum and Story Centre

The Roald Dahl Museum and Story Centre is a small museum situated in the village where Roald Dahl lived and wrote.
www.roalddahlmuseum.org/

Seven Stories: The Centre for Children's Books

Seven Stories: The Centre for Children's Books is a museum in Newcastle upon Tyne dedicated to the art of British children's books.
www.sevenstories.org.uk

Online Resources

Storybook England

Storybook England is an interactive website where you can find out more about children's books set in England.
www.storybookengland.com/

Additional Resources Available through Booktrust UK

www.booktrustchildrensbooks.org.uk/

- **Booked Up**
  Booked Up is a national program whose goal is to give a free book to every child starting secondary school in England. The program is run by the national charity, Booktrust.
  www.bookedup.org.uk
- **Bookstart**
  Bookstart is a national program that works through local organizations to give a free pack of books to young children, with guidance materials for parents and caregivers.
  www.bookstart.org.uk
- **Booktime**
  Booktime encourages reading for pleasure and provides ideas and research on reading with children.
  www.booktime.org.uk
- **Children's Book Week**
  Children's Book Week is celebrated annually during October. For book suggestions and ideas for planning your own celebrations, go to www .childrensbookweek.org.uk.

Other Programs Supported by or Available through the Booktrust Website

- Big Picture
  www.bigpicture.org.uk
- Bookbite
  www.bookbite.org.uk
- Bookmark: Books and Disability
  www.bookmark.org.uk
- Everybody Writes
  www.everybodywrites.org.uk
- Letter Box Club
  www.letterboxclub.org.uk

GREECE

Couloumbis, Audrey & Akila Couloumbis. **War Games: A Novel Based on a True Story**. New York, Random House Children's Books, 2009. ISBN 978-0-375-85628-0, 0-375-85628-5. 232 p. (10–12). Novel.

Petros and Zola lounge in the shade, arguing about their skill with a sling-shot. Stavros, their cousin, joins their competition, but the bird he shoots is a swallow—and to kill a swallow is definitely bad luck. Early on, the authors establish themes (bad luck), foreshadow events (accidents with a slingshot), and skillfully build tension as Nazi sightings and skirmishes move closer. Finally, soldiers march into town and the German commandant seizes Petro and Zola's family home. Akila and Audrey Couloumbis narrate a rousing adventure and account of World War II that seldom is examined in American children's books. *2009 Horn Book Fanfare, 2010 NCSS/CBC Notable Children's Trade Books in the Field of Social Studies.* lmp

Akila Couloumbis was raised in Greece, and he based this book on his wartime memories. Newbery Honor winner Audrey Couloumbis is married to Akila. They live in the United States.

WORLD WAR II (1939–1945), UNDERGROUND MOVEMENTS–GREECE, BROTHERS, COUSINS, GREECE–HISTORY–OCCUPATION (1941–1944), FICTIONALIZED AUTOBIOGRAPHY

Deary, Terry. **The Fire Thief**. Boston, Kingfisher, 2005. ISBN 978-0-7534-5818-1, 0-7534-5818-7. 253 p. (10–14). Novel.

An initially undisclosed narrator with a sassy attitude sets his story of the Greek Titan, Prometheus, both in Greece at the dawn of time and in the mid-nineteenth century town of Eden City. In chapters that alternate across sites, Prometheus attempts to escape the wrath of Zeus by accepting the god's challenge to find one good man that "makes all the other creeping creatures worth saving" (36). Traveling forward in time, "Theus" must dodge Zeus's Avenging Fury as well as navigate a Dickensian cast of scoundrels, actors, and thieves—including a young orphan named Jim. The author packs the story with allusions, asides, and acerbic wit. Sequels are *Flight of the Fire Thief* (Kingfisher, 2006) and *The Fire Thief Fights Back* (Kingfisher, 2007). nlr

Author, who lives in Great Britain, has written two more books to complete the Fire Thief trilogy.

PROMETHEUS (GREEK DEITY), TIME TRAVEL, ADVENTURE, FANTASY

RELATED INFORMATION

Greek Section of IBBY

The Greek IBBY national section is part of the Circle of Greek Children's Books, a nonprofit, nongovernmental cultural association. Individuals within the Greek Children's Literature movement had been in contact with IBBY since 1958 but did not officially become members until 1969.

www.ibby.org/index.php?id=424

www.greekibby.gr

Awards

The Greek IBBY national section biennially nominates in three categories for the IBBY Honor List: Translation, Illustration, and Writing. They also submit nominations for the **Hans Christian Andersen Award**, the **Astrid Lindgren Award** and, until it was disbanded, the **Janusz Korczak Award**.

Penelope Delta Award, given for an author's body of work and named in honor of the first Greek author for children, may have been discontinued after the 2007 award was presented.

Annual awards presented by the Circle of Greek Children's Book/Greek Section of IBBY include the following awards: (1) Books for Younger Children, (2) Books for Intermediate Readers, (3) Books for Older Children and Young Adults, and (4) an award for Illustrations.

www.greekibby.gr/english.html

HUNGARY

Cheng, Andrea. **The Lace Dowry**. Asheville, NC, Front Street, 2005. ISBN 978-1-93242-520-8, 1-93242-520-9. 113 p. (10 up). Novel.

Every family preserves traditions, but Juli cannot understand her mother's insistence on buying her a lace tablecloth for her dowry. After all, it is 1933 and Budapest is a modern, up-to-date city. The other twelve-year-old girls in her class mock her family's old-fashioned ways by singing kissing songs and asking whom she is going to marry. The tension between mother and daughter, between an idolized country life and reality, and the bullying that goes on behind teachers' backs are contemporary topics that will resonate with readers, even though they know little about lace or Hungary. *lmp*

The author, whose parents fled Hungary during World War II, live in the United States.

Friendship, Sex Role, Lace Makers, Hungary–History (1918–1945), Historical Fiction

Cheng, Andrea. **The Bear Makers**. Asheville, NC, Front Street, 2008. ISBN 978-1-59078-518-8, 1-59078-518-5. 117 p. (9–12). Novel.

The post–World War II era is one that is not well documented in children's books. That is one reason *The Bear Makers* is especially interesting. Bella and Kata return from hiding when the war ends. Their parents had sent them to the country because being Jewish and Hungarian was extremely dangerous. Now the danger lies with the Hungarian Worker's Party, the official arm of the Communist Party. Kata's brother fears for his future until he finds a way to escape to the West. Cheng's story is based on one told by her grandmother, who was the original Bear Maker. *lmp*

Author lives in the United States.

Family Life, Hungary–History 1945–1989, Hungary, Historical Fiction

Marillier, Juliet. **Wildwood Dancing**. New York, Random House/Alfred A. Knopf, 2007. Originally published by Pan Macmillan Australia, in 2006. ISBN 978-0-375-83364-9, 0-375-83364-1. 407 p. (12 up). Novel.

See Transylvania for description.

RELATED INFORMATION

Organizations

IBBY Hungary

The IBBY Hungary website is not available in English, but a pdf of Hungarian books presented at the 2006 Bologna Book Fair can be downloaded.
www.ibby.hu/im/bologna2006_konyvek.pdf
www.ibby.org/index.php?id=425
www.ibby.hu/

ICELAND

Erlingsson, Friðrik. **Benjamin Dove**. New York, NorthSouth Books, 2007. Originally published as *Benjamín Dúfa* in Icelandic by Vaka-Helgafell Reykjavík Iceland, in 1992. First published in English by Meadowside Children's Books Great Britain, in 2006. ISBN 978-0-7358-2150-7, 0-7358-2150-X. 206 p. (11–14). Novel.

Benjamin, Jeff, and Manny are a few of the many children who play on "the Ground," a playground of sorts in a blue-collar neighborhood. Inspired by a newcomer, Roland, who claims to be a descendant of a Scottish king, the boys pretend they are knights. They call themselves the Order of the Red Dragon. When fighting injustice, they take on a bully who has terrorized their neighborhood. There are unexpected tragic consequences. The boys strive to correct the situation, and eventually the community joins in their crusade. *2008 USBBY Outstanding International Books List, International Board on Books for Young People (IBBY) Honor List, The Icelandic Children's Book Award, and the Reykjavik City Children's Book Award. pwc*
Author lives in Iceland.
Boys, Friendship, Games, Self-confidence, Coming of Age, Iceland, Fiction

RELATED INFORMATION

Icelandic Section of IBBY
www.ibby.org/index.php?id=426
www.ibby.is/ http://www.ibby.is/english.htm

Awards

These awards are presented by the Icelandic Section of IBBY:
Sögusteinninn, an honor prize to an active Icelandic writer who has made an important contribution to Icelandic children's literature.
Vorvindar (Spring Winds), three recognitions awarded each year for a contribution to children's culture in Iceland, a newcomer to children's literature, and/or a great contribution to children's literature.
In addition, the Icelandic section of IBBY nominates books, authors, translators, and illustrators for the IBBY Honor List and the Hans Christian Andersen awards.

IRELAND

Andrekson, Judy. **Little Squire: The Jumping Pony**. Illustrated by David Parkins. Toronto, Tundra Books, 2007. ISBN 978-0-88776-770-8, 0-88776-770-2. 67 p. (8–11). Chapter book.

One of a series of *True Horse Stories* by Judy Andrekson, *Little Squire: The Jumping Pony*, is a short chapter book about Little Squire, a pony born in the 1930s, and his trainer and friend, Mickey Walsh, the man who oversaw the horse's care and life. Together the two would bring excitement and joy to the horse world and show how important the bond is between man and animal. *ak*

Author lives in Alberta, Canada.

LITTLE SQUIRE (HORSE), SHOW JUMPERS, CONNEMARA PONY, IRELAND, UNITED STATES, BIOGRAPHY

Brennan, Herbie. **Ruler of the Realm**. New York, Bloomsbury, 2006. Originally published by Bloomsbury Great Britain, in 2006. ISBN 978-1-58234-881-0, 1-58234-881-2. 429 p. (14 up). Novel.

When her treacherous uncle Lord Hairstreak proposes a negotiated truce between the Faeries of the Light and the Faeries of the Night, Queen Blue suspects his motives. While on a mission to discover the truth, the queen is kidnapped by servants of Beleth—"King of Hell." Blue nearly succumbs to Beleth's plans to make her his consort, but her brother Pyrgus, her trusted advisors, and human friend, Henry, eventually fathom and foil the dark plots that were meant to destroy the Faery Realm. *The Faerie Wars Chronicles: Book Three*. Sequel to *The Purple Emperor*. *hc*.

Author is from Ireland.

FAIRIES, WAR, SUPERNATURAL, FANTASY, FICTION

Dowd, Siobhan. **Bog Child**. New York, Random House/David Fickling Books, 2008. Originally published by David Fickling Books Great Britain, in 2008. ISBN 978-0-385-75169-8, 0-385-75169-9. 321 p. (12 up). Novel.

Fergus McCann and his uncle regularly cross the border between the South, where they live, and Northern Ireland to illegally cut peat. Early one morning, Fergus discovers a perfectly preserved child buried in the bog. Archeologists arrive, one with her teenage daughter in tow. At the same time, Joe McCann, member of the provisional IRA, joins the hunger strike at Long Kesh prison. Fergus cannot fathom why his brother joined the IRA—and resists even though he's being pressured to do so. Dowd has skillfully woven multiple plots into one mesmerizing tale of love, discovery, pain, and sacrifice. Other Young Adult books by Siobhan Dowd include *A Swift Pure Cry* (2007) and *Solace of the Road* (2009). *2009 USBBY Outstanding International Books List, 2009 CILIP Carnegie Medal, 2008 Publishers Weekly Best Children's Book of the Year, 2008 Kirkus Reviews Best Young Adult Books*. *lmp*

Author was born in Ireland and lived in the United States and Great Britain. In 2007, she died of breast cancer.

Political Prisoners, Political Violence, Terrorism, Bog Bodies, Family Life, Ireland 20th Century History, Ireland, Fiction

Ó Flatharta, Antoine. **Hurry and the Monarch**. Illustrated by Meilo So. New York, Random House/Alfred A. Knopf, 2005. ISBN 978-0-375-83003-7, 0-375-83003-0. 32 p. (5–9). Picture book.

See Mexico for description.

Parkinson, Siobhán. **Something Invisible**. New Milford, CT, Roaring Brook Press, 2006. Originally published by Puffin Great Britain, in 2006. ISBN 978-1-59643-123-2, 1-59643-123-7. 156 p. (11–14). Novel.

Jake was clueless about his mother's weight gain. "He felt stupid . . . not to notice . . . [but] there are other things to think about . . . football and fish and stuff" (14). Daisy's birth revolutionizes Jake's world—and not just because he's no longer an only child. Because of Daisy he's met Stella and her boisterous family. But of all the events that occur in the time following Daisy's arrival, it's the horrendous accident that Jake thinks he caused that reunites Jake and Stella. Parkinson's poetic prose wings off the page into readers' hearts, where it builds a nest—one that is feather light and painfully heavy. *2007 USBBY Outstanding International Books List. Siobhán Parkinson won the Bisto Book of the Year Award, Ireland's prestigious award for children's literature. lmp*

Author lives in Ireland.

Friendship, Families, Death

Scott, Michael. **The Alchemyst: Secrets of the Immortal Nicholas Flamel Book 1**. New York, Random House/Delacorte Press, 2007. ISBN 978-0-385-73357-1, 0-385-73357-7. 375 p. (12 up). Novel.

Michael Scott's six-part epic fantasy, *The Secrets of the Immortal Nicholas Flamel*, features Josh and Sophie, fifteen-year-old twins, who find themselves entwined in an otherworldly adventure. In Book 1, the twins learn of a reference to themselves in an ancient prophecy, of Nicholas and his wife Perenelle's immortality, and of the Flamels' impending death unless the three missing pages of the Codex can be found. Based on a legend about the real Nicholas Flamel, fourteenth-century alchemist who reportedly discovered the secret of immortality, the book is a fast-paced fantasy steeped in world mythology and packed with high action. *2008 Texas Lone Star Award, 2007 Winner Book Sense Children's Pick List. nlr, ebf*

Author lives in Dublin, Ireland.

Nicolas Flamel (d. 1418), Niccolò Machiavelli (1469–1527), John Dee (1527–1608), Alchemists, Magic, Supernatural, Great Britain, Brothers and Sisters–Twins, Paris, France, San Francisco, CA, Fantasy Fiction

Scott, Michael. **The Magician: Secrets of the Immortal Nicholas Flamel Book 2**. New York, Random House/Delacorte Press, 2008. ISBN 978-0-385-73358-8, 0-385-73358-5. 496 p. (12 up). Novel.

The Magician in Book 2 of the series refers to Dr. John Dee, who is in pursuit of the twins, as well as Nicholas and Perenelle Flamel. Sophie and Josh continue their quest for the missing Codex in Paris, where they are aided by Joan of Arc and other allies. John Dee is joined by the powerful Niccoló Machiavelli. A battle ensues among Flamel, the twins, and their allies and all the monsters and evil beings unleashed by John Dee. Time is running out to rescue Perenelle and find the Codex. *ebf*

Author lives in Dublin, Ireland.

Nicolas Flamel (d. 1418), Niccolò Machiavelli (1469–1527), John Dee (1527–1608), Alchemists, Magic, Supernatural, Great Britain, Brothers and Sisters–Twins, Paris, France, Fantasy Fiction

Scott, Michael. **The Sorceress: Secrets of the Immortal Nicholas Flamel Book 3**. New York, Random House/Delacorte Press, 2009. ISBN 978-0-385-73529-2, 0-385-73529-4. 488 p. (12 up). Novel.

Having found the twins of legend and destroyed Paris in Book 2, Nicholas Flamel and Sophie and Josh Newman escape to London. However, Dr. John Dee has marshaled the Dark Elders' British allies, who are there to greet the trio. Flamel is not without resources, specifically Palamedes, Gilgamesh, and Will Shakespeare. Chapters—and viewpoints—alternate among Perenelle, imprisoned in Alcatraz; Machiavelli in Paris; and Josh with his twin and Flamel in Great Britain. *The Sorceress* is the third book in the series *The Secrets of the Immortal Nicholas Flamel*. *lmp*

Author lives in Ireland.

Nicolas Flamel (d. 1418), Niccolò Machiavelli (1469–1527), John Dee (1527–1608), Alchemists, Magic, Supernatural, Brothers and Sisters, Twins, Alcatraz Island, Great Britain, Fantasy Fiction

Scott, Michael. **The Necromancer: Secrets of the Immortal Nicholas Flamel Book 4**. New York, Random House/Delacorte Press, 2010. ISBN 978-0-385-73531-5, 0-385-73531-6. 403 p. (12 up). Novel.

Sophie and Josh have become highly suspicious of Nicholas Flamel's motivations—is he using them as he used other twins throughout history? Will they meet the same barbarous death as their predecessors? These doubts allow John Dee to convince Josh to join forces with him. Dee's plan is to set loose the Archons and take over the world. Only Josh can be transformed into the ultimate tool—a Necromancer—to achieve what Dee cannot: he can raise the Mother of the Gods from the dead. The final cliffhanger will leave you wondering, can Sophie save her twin—and the world? *lmp*

Author lives in Dublin, Ireland.

Nicolas Flamel (d. 1418), Niccolò Machiavelli (1469–1527), John Dee (1527–1608), Alchemists, Magic, Supernatural, Great Britain, Brothers and Sisters–Twins, London, Great Britain, Fantasy Fiction

Spillebeen, Geert. Translated by Terese Edelstein. **Age 14**. Boston, Houghton Mifflin Harcourt, 2009. Originally published as *Age 14* in Dutch by Averbode The Netherlands, in 2000. ISBN 978-0-547-05342-4, 0-547-05342-8. 216 p. (14 up). Novel.

Not having much interest or success in school, and never satisfying his father's expectations, twelve-year-old Patrick Condon flees his erratic job on the docks in Ballybricken, Ireland, for an idealized army life. A not-so-scrupulous recruiter simply winks when Patrick adopts his brother John's identity and age—seventeen—to enlist. When war is declared, Patrick again lies about his age and identity so that he can be sent into action. Based on factual material and two years of research, Spillebeen relates the story of the youngest casualty of World War I. Patrick's grave in Flanders Field is simply marked, "Age 14." *lmp*

Author lives in Belgium.

World War I (1914–1918), Soldiers, False Enlistment, False Identity, Ireland (1910–1921), Historical Fiction

Thompson, Kate. **The New Policeman**. New York, HarperCollins/Greenwillow Books, 2007. Originally published by Random House/Bodley Head Great Britain, in 2005. ISBN 978-0-06-117427-8, 0-06-117427-0. 448 p. (14 up). Novel.

This fantasy tale deftly interweaves Irish folklore and traditional music with a contemporary quest for more time. Time has been passing more and more quickly, and it is up to JJ to stop time's spilling into Tír na nÓg (The Land of Eternal Youth) before it spells disaster for everyone. Along the way he may help to answer some other questions as well, like who is that odd new policeman anyway, and where do all those socks go? *2008 USBBY Outstanding*

International Books List, 2005 Guardian Children's Book Prize, Costa (Whitbread) Children's Book Award, 2005 Dublin Airport Authority Children's Book of the Year Award, ALA Notable Children's Book, Publishers Weekly Best Book, ALA Best Book for Young Adults, ALA Best of the Best Books for Young Adults, Texas Library Association TAYSHAS High School Reading List. ae
    Author lives in Ireland.
SPACE AND TIME, FAIRIES, MUSIC, IRELAND, FANTASY FICTION, NOVEL

Thompson, Kate. **Creature of the Night**. New York, Roaring Brook Press, 2009. Originally published by Bodley Head Great Britain, in 2008. ISBN 978-1-59643-511-7, 1-59643-511-9. 250 p. (14 up). Novel.

This is a realistic coming-of-age story infused with a layer of underlying faerie magic. Bobby wants to leave his family's new home in the countryside and go back to Dublin and his thieving, drinking gang of friends. It is not quite that simple, though, and Bobby slowly begins to change and grow with the guidance of his new neighbors. Unanswered questions remain concerning the history of his family's new home, and Bobby tries to uncover the magical truth surrounding the mysterious and possibly murderous events of the past. *2010 USBBY Outstanding International Books List, CCBC Choices. ae*
    Author lives on the west coast of Ireland.
JUVENILE DELINQUENTS, IRELAND–DUBLIN, IRELAND COUNTRY LIFE, MURDER, FICTION

Waddell, Martin. **Sleep Tight, Little Bear!** Illustrated by Barbara Firth. Cambridge, MA, Candlewick Press, 2005. Originally published by Walker Books Great Britain, in 2005. ISBN 978-0-7636-2439-2, 0-7636-2439-X. 32 p. (4–8). Picture book.

Little Bear discovers a new little-bear-size cave. He sets up house there, furnishes it with all the important things, and plans to spend the night. Then, Little Bear wonders if Big Bear misses him, and he returns to the old Bear Cave to be read to and cuddled to sleep. *Sleep Tight, Little Bear*, the fifth adventure of Little Bear and his caretaker, reveals the tension between independence and protection. Soft, expressive watercolors add appeal and atmosphere. In an accompanying DVD, Waddell reads the story and explains the significance of a parent and child sharing books. The *Little Bear* series has sold over seven million copies worldwide. *Oppenheim Toy Portfolio Platinum Award Winner, CBC Children's Choices. Waddell is the 2004 Hans Christian Andersen Medal Winner. Barbara Firth won the Kate Greenaway Medal and Smarties Book Prize for an earlier Little Bear book. mjw*
    Author lives in Northern Ireland. Illustrator lives in Great Britain.
BEARS, LONELINESS, SELF-RELIANCE, FICTION, DVD–VIDEO DISCS

RELATED INFORMATION

Organizations

Children's Books Ireland

Children's Books Ireland is the national children's book organization of Ireland. It was formed in 1996 through the merger of the Children's Literature Association of Ireland and the Irish Children's Book Trust.

www.childrensbooksireland.ie/

IBBY Ireland

www.ibby.org/index.php?id=429

IBBY Ireland's informative website provides a wealth of information on members and activities.

www.ibbyireland.ie/

Awards

Bisto Book of the Year Award Winner 2010

The Bisto Book of the Year Awards, in partnership with CBI, are the leading annual Children's Book Awards in Ireland. The awards are made annually by Children's Books Ireland and Bisto Foods to authors and illustrators born or resident in Ireland. The shortlist for the awards is announced annually in March, and the winners are announced in May. The award is open to books written in Irish or English. There are a total of six awards: (1) Bisto Book of the Year Award, (2) Eilis Dillon Award for a first children's book, (3) Bisto Honour Award for Writing, (4) Bisto Honor Award for Illustration, (5) Special Judges Award, and (6) Children's Choice Award. More information about criteria is available at www.childrensbooksireland.ie/index.php?option=com_content&task=view&id=81&Itemid=191.

Dublin Airport Authority Children's Book of the Year Award

There are two categories for the Dublin Airport Authority Children's Book of the Year Award: the junior category for readers aged eight and under and the senior category for children in the nine-plus age group.

www.irishbookawards.ie/AwardDetails.aspx

Glen Dimplex New Writers Award

The Glen Dimplex New Writers Awards were provided by the Glen Dimplex group in association with the Irish Writers Centre. The annual awards offered support and exposure for emerging writers in a wide range of genres, including children's books. Unfortunately, no information is available either at the Irish Writers Centre, www.writerscentre.ie/, or through the Dimplex websites.

Professional Resources

Coghlan, Susanna, Mary Fitzpatrick, & Lucy O'Dea (Eds.). **Changing Faces—Changing Places: A Guide to Multicultural Books for Children.** Dublin, IBBY Ireland, 2001. ISBN 978-0-954135201, 0-954135202. 64 p.

Changing Faces—Changing Places is the first guide to multicultural books for children to be produced specifically for Ireland. This guide contains a number of articles with an Irish perspective on multiculturalism as well as reviews of dual-language picture books, folk tales, reference books, and general fiction.

Multiculturalism, Ireland, Bibliography

Morris, Liz & Susanna Coghlan (Eds.). **Cross-Currents: A Guide to Multicultural Books for Young People.** Dublin, IBBY Ireland, 2005. ISBN 978-0-954135218, 0-954135210. 96 p.

Cross-Currents is a guide to the role that books can play in promoting respect for human and cultural diversity. It includes reviews of almost 180 books for toddlers through to teenagers, covering picture books, fiction for all ages, dual-language books, poetry, folktales, mythology, and nonfiction. There are articles about development and intercultural education and extensive listings of relevant resource organizations and publishers. Supplements an earlier volume, *Changing Faces—Changing Places*.

Multiculturalism, Bibliography, Book Reviews

ITALY

Avi. **Murder at Midnight.** New York, Scholastic, 2009. ISBN 978-0-545-08090-3, 0-545-08090-8. 272 p. (10–12). Novel.

Fabrizio is an unschooled orphan when the city of Pergamontio, Italy, binds him to Mangus the Magician as an indentured servant. Mangus is a crotchety old man who insists that Fabrizio does no magic—only illusions. This is an important distinction in Pergamontio because the king has declared magic—and magicians—illegal, a crime punishable by death. When hundreds of fliers advocating the overthrow of King Claudio appear in Pergamontio, Mangus and Fabrizio are accused of magic because the writing on each of the papers is identical. Avi imbues this mystery with the ignorance and superstition of the Dark Ages while introducing a new invention—Gutenberg's printing press. *Avi is the recipient of the Newbery Award and two Newbery Honor Awards. lmp*

Author lives in the United States.

Magicians, Orphans, Mystery, Renaissance Italy, Fiction

Baccalario, Pierdomenico. Translated by Leah D. Janeczko. **Ring of Fire.** Illustrated by Iacopo Bruno. New York, Random House, 2009. Originally published as *L'Anello di Fuoco* in Italian by Edizion Piemme Italy, in 2006. ISBN 978-0-375-85895-6, 0-375-85895-4. 293 p. (9–12). Novel, Mystery.

By sheer coincidence, four teenagers—from Italy, France, the United States, and China—find themselves the focus of a chase involving ancient maps, mysteries, and the constellations, culminating in a desperate attempt to piece together the clues that lie in modern-day Rome. By design, there are certain things that are supposed to occur when the four come together, but when the Parisian is abducted, it becomes clear that the plan has gone awry. The matters of who to trust—or not—including oneself, and of cosmic purpose define this first book in the *Century Quartet* series. Book 2, *Star of Stone,* was released in fall 2010. *bef*

Author lives in Italy.

Good and Evil, Rome, Italy, Mystery, Fiction

Bontempelli, Massimo. Translated by Estelle Gilson. **The Chess Set in the Mirror.** Philadelphia, PA, Paul Dry Books, 2007. Originally published as *La Scacchiera Davanti allo Specchio* in Italian by R. Bemporad & Figlio Italy, in 1922, then reprinted by Sellerio Palermo, in 1981/1990. ISBN 978-1-58988-031-3, 1-58988-031-5. 114 p. (9–12). Novel.

Locked in a room as punishment, a ten-year-old boy discovers a world on the other side of a large mirror. Objects and people that have at any time been reflected in the mirror are in this new world. The boy meets the craftsman who made the mirror, a burglar who at one time broke into the house; his grandmother whom he has never met; and a large, living chess set. Once inside the mirror he wonders if he will ever be able to return to his own world. *pwc*

Author (1878–1960) was an Italian poet, novelist, and dramatist.

Mirrors, Chess, Italy, Fantasy Fiction

Cali, Davide. **Piano, Piano**. Illustrated by Eric Héliot. Watertown, MA, Charlesbridge, 2007. Originally published as *Piano, Piano* in French by Editions Sarbacane France, in 2005. ISBN 978-1-58089-191-2, 1-58089-191-8. 28 p. (6–8). Picture book.

Marcolino's mother wants him to be a grand pianist, and so he practices his scales even though he hates it. He'd much rather be a grand formula-one racer, a grand pirate, or a grand flying acrobat. Marcolino's grandfather rescues him by providing old photographs of his mother, which reveal she was not the grand pianist she claimed to be. Marcolino then takes up the tuba, an instrument he prefers. Offbeat cartoon and collage illustrations are full of movement and goofy details. *2008 USBBY Outstanding International Books, Bologna Ragazzi Special Mention, Bank Street College of Education's Best Books of the Year. mjw*

Author lives in Genoa, Italy; illustrator lives in Rouen, France.
PIANO INSTRUCTION AND STUDY, MOTHERS AND SONS, GRANDFATHERS, FICTION

Chessa, Francesca. **Holly's Red Boots**. Illustrated by the author. New York, Holiday House, 2008. Originally published by Gullane Children's Books, an imprint of Alligator Books Great Britain, in 2008. ISBN 978-0-8234-2158-9, 0-8234-2158-9. n.p. (2–6). Picture book.

According to her mom, Holly must wear boots—not slippers or a sombrero—when she goes out into the falling snow. What follows is a search worthy of a pirate's treasure. Preschool audiences will enjoy the interactive nature of spotting and naming all the red objects Holly uncovers. When she finally realizes her dinosaur has "borrowed" her boots, Holly confronts a new challenge. Which boot fits which foot? She eventually emerges, only to discover that the snow has melted. All ends well as Holly and mom splash in puddles—both wearing their boots. Chessa's art is vibrantly alive, adding a topsy-turvy playfulness and naiveté to the text. *lmp*

Author lives in Italy.
BOOTS, COLOR RED, CATS, SNOW, CONCEPT BOOK

De Mari, Silvana. Translated by Shaun Whiteside. **The Last Dragon**. New York, Hyperion Books for Children/Miramax Books, 2006. Originally published as *L'Ultimo Elfo* in Italian by Adriano Salani Italy, in 2004. ISBN 978-0-7868-3636-9, 0-7868-3636-9. 361 p. (10 up). Novel.

The world had succumbed to darkness, floods, and wickedness. Elves had vanished, except for a newborn, sent to safety before the deluge inundated his village. There was a prophecy, however, that foretold a better future:

"When the last dragon and the last elf / break the circle . . . the sun of a new summer / will shine in the sky" (51). Locating the last dragon becomes the quest of a ragtag band: a hunter, a woman, a dog, and the last elf—Yorshkrunsquarkljolnerstrink, Yorsh to his friends. *The Last Dragon* is a magical tale that will mesmerize readers with its innocence and imagery. *2007 Batchelder Honor, ALA Notable Children's Book, A Kirkus Reviews Best Childrens Book of 2006, A Book Sense Autumn 2006 Children's Pick, 2011 Nutmeg Teen Book Award Nominee. lmp*

Author lives in Italy.

DRAGONS, ELVES, FANTASY, FICTION

Ferri, Giuliano. Translated by Charise Myngheer. **Little Tad Grows Up**. Illustrated by the author. New York, Penguin Group, 2007. Originally published as *Paul Quappe* in German by Minedition/Michael Neugebauer Germany, in 2007. ISBN 978-0-698-40060-3, 0-698-40060-7. 32 p. (4–8). Picture book.

Little Tadpole sees no good in growing legs. He would rather swim and play with the other tadpoles. Aunt Salamander, Cousin Newt, an old prawn, and older frogs tell him to be patient and that he will learn what to do with his legs. Still, he does not want to grow up. When a sneaky water snake almost catches him, his legs react naturally, and he springs out of the pond to safety. He discovers an amazing new world outside the water. Soft blue and green underwater scenes further depict Tad's transformation. *mjw*

Author lives in Italy.

TADPOLES, GROWTH, SELF-PERCEPTION, FICTION

Gavin, Jamila. **The Blood Stone**. New York, Farrar, Straus and Giroux, 2005. Originally published by Egmont Great Britain, in 2003. ISBN 978-0-374-30846-9, 0-374-30846-2. 340 p. (11 up). Novel.

See India for description.

Guarnaccia, Steven. **The Three Little Pigs: An Architectural Tale**. Illustrated by the author. New York, Abrams Books for Young Readers, 2010. Originally published as *I Tre Porcellini* in Italian by Maurizio Corraini Editore Italy, in 2009. ISBN 978-0-8109-8941-2, 0-8109-8941-7. n.p. (4–8). Picture book.

Illustration elements take Guarnaccia's thoroughly modern retelling to an entirely new level—one in which three pigs live surrounded by, and in, masterpieces of design. They live together in a version of Frank Lloyd Wright's Fallingwater House, sit on Frank Gehry chairs, and even have a garden greenhouse shaped like I. M. Pei's Louvre pyramid. These are three little piggies with an eye for design! The endpapers provide illustrations of all of the architectural and industrial designs featured throughout the book, accompanied by labels providing the names of the pieces, their designers, countries of origin, and date of design. *lvb*

Author lives in the United States.

PIGS, FOLKLORE, FAIRY TALES, ARCHITECTS, DESIGN

Hoffman, Mary. **Stravaganza: City of Flowers**. New York, Bloomsbury, 2005. Originally published by Bloomsbury Great Britain, in 2005. ISBN 978-1-58234-887-2, 1-58234-887-1. 488 p. (14 up). Novel.

Sky Meadows has been taking care of his sick mother, but when he arrives home to find a "small blue glass bottle" on the doorstep, his life changes (29). It is a "talisman" that enables him to "stravagate" back and forth to a city named Giglia, which bears resemblance to sixteenth-century Florence. In his double life, Sky joins up with Nicholas, formerly Prince Falco of Giglia, and Georgia (who both attend his school in Great Britain) to help Brother Sulien and other "Stravagante" save the lives of friends caught in the murderous feuds between the di Chimici and the Nucci families. Sequel to *Stravaganza: City of Masks* and *Stravaganza: City of Stars*. *hc*

Author is from Great Britain.

SPACE AND TIME, RENAISSANCE ITALY, ADVENTURE AND ADVENTURERS, FICTION

Hoffman, Mary. **The Falconer's Knot: A Story of Friars, Flirtation, and Foul Play**. New York, Bloomsbury, 2007. Originally published by Bloomsbury Great Britain, in 2007. ISBN 978-1-59990-056-8, 1-59990-056-4. 304 p. (12 up). Novel.

Nobleman Silvano is accused of murder and given sanctuary in a friary. Lacking a dowry, beautiful Chiara is placed in a nearby convent by her brother. Simple plot? Never! There are twists and turns that involve machinations and mayhem, conspiracy, detection, and murder most foul. And all of this in a fascinating Italian Renaissance setting. *The Falconer's Knot* is a witty, well-plotted introduction to the mystery genre that will appeal to both boys and girls. *2008 USBBY Outstanding International Books List, Booklist Editor's Choice, NYPL Books for the Teen Age, Texas TAYSHAS Reading List. lmp*

Author lives in Great Britain.

RELIGIOUS LIFE, LOVE STORIES, MURDER, RENAISSANCE ITALY, MYSTERY AND DETECTIVE STORIES, ITALY HISTORY 1268–1492, HISTORICAL FICTION, MYSTERY FICTION

Masini, Beatrice. **Here Comes the Bride**. Illustrated by Anna Laura Cantone. Toronto, Tundra Books, 2010. Originally published as *Una Sposa Buffa, Buffisima, Bellisima* in Italian by Edizioni Arka Italy, in 2002. ISBN 978-0-88776-898-9, 0-88776-898-9. 32 p. (4–7). Picture book.

Filomena isn't simply a seamstress; she is a visionary of bridal couture, the one who brings to life brides' hopes for the most beautiful dresses ever made. But Filomena's own bridal gown is still just a dream because Rusty, the mechanic next door, has yet to work up the courage to propose to her. As she waits, she dreams in visions of lace and embroidery. In fact, she works herself into such a frenzy that when Rusty finally does propose, the dress she's creating for her wedding day is the only thing that matters. Realizing her mistake, she decides that being with Rusty is more important than finery and frippery. *2001 White Ravens Award nominee, 2003 Andersen Award Best Picture Book. lvb*

Author and illustrator live in Milan, Italy.

WOMEN DRESSMAKERS, BRIDES, WEDDING COSTUME, FICTION

Montanari, Eva. **My First**. Illustrated by the author. Boston, Houghton Mifflin, 2007. Originally published as *Il mio Primo* in Italian by Kite Edizioni Italy, in 2004. ISBN 978-0-618-64644-9, 0-618-64644-2. n.p. (0–5). Picture book.

Alice anxiously awaits the birthday present she believes will be a doll. But on her birthday, to her dismay, the present is not a doll. It is a book. Alice is disappointed, and her mother must console her. She tells Alice that the book will stay with her for life, telling her stories. Alice learns to appreciate the delightful experiences that evolve from the book. Even though Alice is reluctant to disclose the gift to her friends, eventually they find out, but they, too, discover its wonders. *dgw*

Author lives in Rimini, Italy.

DOLLS, GIFTS, BOOKS AND READING, FICTION

Morpurgo, Michael. **The Mozart Question**. Illustrated by Michael Foreman. Cambridge, MA, Candlewick Press, 2008. Originally published by Walker Books Great Britain, in 2007. ISBN 978-0-7636-3552-7, 0-7636-3552-9. 66 p. (8–12). Novel.

A young journalist's interview with a world-famous violinist reveals his family's secret story of World War II and the Holocaust and the power of music to transform and heal. Paolo Levi won't perform Mozart because it was poisoned for him when he was forced to play it in a concentration camp. Many years later, though, it reunited his family. The subdued watercolors of beautiful Venice canals and dark death camps enrich this multilayered narration. *Author was 2003–2005 British Children's Laureate. mjw*

Author and illustrator live in Great Britain.

VENICE, ITALY, JEWISH HOLOCAUST (1939–1945), VIOLIN, HISTORICAL FICTION

Napoli, Donna Jo. **Fire in the Hills**. New York, Penguin/Dutton Children's Books, 2006. ISBN 978-0-525-47751-8, 0-525-47751-9. 215 p. (10–12). Novel.

Roberto, kidnapped at thirteen from a Venice movie theater, returns to Italy after a year's imprisonment in a German forced-labor camp. He struggles from Sicily to Naples, Rome, and northward, attempting to reach Venice. During his journey, Roberto matures into a man who learns he must take an active role to free Italy from Hitler's grasp. This sequel to *Stones in Water* (Dutton 1997) provides seldom-mentioned information about Italy's partisan resistance efforts against the Nazis and Fascists. Much of the information about Roberto and other partigiani is based on experiences of the author's Italian friends. *lmp*

Author lives in the United States and Italy.

WORLD WAR II (1939–1945), UNDERGROUND MOVEMENTS–ITALY, FICTION, SURVIVAL, ITALY HISTORY, GERMAN OCCUPATION (1943–1945), FICTION

RELATED INFORMATION

Organizations

IBBY Italy

Formed from the collaboration of libraries, universities, publishers, the Bologna Book Fair, and a number of organizations, IBBY Italy has five major objectives: promote, defend, stimulate, encourage, and support cooperation and international understanding through books for children and teens.

www.ibby.org/index.php?id=431

www.bibliotecasalaborsa.it/ragazzi/ibby/

Book Fairs

Bologna Children's Book Fair

According to their website, "The Bologna Children's Book Fair is the most important international event dedicated to the children's publishing and multimedia industry" (www.bookfair.bolognafiere.it/en/info/). It has been held for almost fifty years and regularly attracts 1,300 exhibitors from more than sixty-five nations.

In even-numbered years, IBBY announces the winners of the Hans Christian Andersen Award at Bologna. Other IBBY business conducted at Bologna includes the IBBY Executive Committee Meetings and special presentations at the IBBY stand. These may include information about the IBBY Honour List, the Outstanding Books for Young People with Disabilities, the International Children's Book Day, future IBBY Congresses, and IBBY's journal, *Bookbird*.

www.bookfair.bolognafiere.it/en/

Torino Book Fair [Salone Internazionale del Libro Torino]
This international book exposition is held annually in May.
www.salonelibro.it/

Awards

Bologna Children's Bookfair—Fundación SM International Award for Illustration

In 2009, the Bologna Children's Book Fair and the SM Foundation initiated the Bologna Children's Book Fair—SM Foundation International Award for Illustration. The winner is selected from exhibitors in the Bologna Children's Book Fair Illustrators Exhibition.

Bologna Ragazzi Award

Presented annually at the Bologna Children's Book Fair, this award promotes the best books in terms of graphic and editorial design. In 2010, along with Fiction, Nonfiction, and New Horizons categories, a new category called Opera Prima, honoring the works of new authors and illustrators, was introduced.

www.bookfair.bolognafiere.it/en/boragazziaward/

KAZAKHSTAN

Shulevitz, Uri. **How I Learned Geography**. Illustrated by the author. New York, Farrar, Straus and Giroux, 2008. ISBN 978-0-374-33499-4, 0-374-33499-4. n.p. (8–10). Picture book.

Uri Shulevitz storytells this memoir using his remarkable artistic talent—and few words. The spare text focuses all senses on the illustrations, the heart of the story. Color establishes the mood: shades of reds, grays, blacks, and browns reflect the bombing of Poland. The dismal Kazakhstan room is awash in Shulevitz's blue pallet, so prevalent in *Toddlecreek Post Office* (1992). When his father buys a wall map rather than bread, Uri fumes. But the colors and exotic lands transport him, as only imagination can, out of his dispossession into a world he continues to illustrate almost seventy years later. Childhood artifacts conclude the memoir. *2009 Caldecott Honor Award; author has won the Caldecott Medal and two additional Caldecott Honor Awards; ALA Notable Children's Books, Indie Next Kids' List Great Read, Bank Street Best Children's Book of the Year, CCBC Choice, NYPL Book for Reading and Sharing, Parents' Choice Honor Books, Charlotte Zolotow Award / Honor Book, NCSS-CBC Notable Trade Book in the Field of Social Studies, Booklinks Lasting Connection, Booklist Editors' Choice, Publishers Weekly Best Children's Books of the Year, School Library Journal Best Books of the Year, Capitol Choices Noteworthy Titles for Children and Teens, Michigan Great Lakes Great Books Award Master List.* lmp

Author was born in Warsaw, Poland, moved to Kazakhstan during World War II, then France and Israel, but now lives in New York.

Shulevitz, Uri (1935–), Childhood and Youth, Refugees, Maps, Geography, Imagination, Fictionalized Memoir, Poland, Kazakhstan

NETHERLANDS

Alma, Ann. **Brave Deeds: How One Family Saved Many from the Nazis.** Toronto, Groundwood Books, 2008. ISBN 978-0-88899-791-3, 0-88899-791-4. 95 p. (9–14). Creative nonfiction.

Using a fictional narrator, Alma tells the true story of the Braal family, Frans and Mies, who as members of the Dutch resistance movement hid scores of children and adults in their secluded house on a coastal island and fed hundreds of others. The story spans the nine months leading to the end of the war, combining moving scenes of everyday life with suspenseful passages of near discovery. Photographs of the Braals and others mentioned in the story, along with artifacts such as ration books and ID cards and a map of Europe, underscore the story's basis in reality; historical notes provide background information on Hitler's invasion of the Netherlands and the Dutch resistance. *2010 Golden Oak Award nominee, Chocolate Lily Award nominee,*

2009 Silver Birch Award Honour Book, Resource Links' 2008 List of Best Canadian Nonfiction Books, Bank Street College Best Children's Books List. ss
    Author lives in British Columbia.
    BRAAL FAMILY, WORLD WAR II (1939–1945), JEWS, RESCUE, NETHERLANDS, UNDERGROUND MOVEMENTS NETHERLANDS, RIGHTEOUS GENTILES IN THE HOLOCAUST, NETHERLANDS, BIOGRAPHY

Cate, Marijke ten. **Where Is My Sock?** Illustrated by the author. Honesdale, PA, Boyds Mills Press/Lemniscaat, 2010. Originally published as *Waar is Mijn Sok?* in Dutch by Lemniscaat The Netherlands, in 2009. ISBN 978-1-59078-808-0, 1-59078-808-7. n.p. (2–6). Picture book.
    Marijke ten Cate asks the universal question, "Where is my sock?" and the response is a rollicking game of hide-and-seek. A young boy quite seriously undertakes dressing himself (apparently a new skill) as the world around him devolves into total chaos. With assistance from a monkey, snake, alligator, parrot, goat, several babies, and various friends, he manages to unearth his garments so he and his friends can go outside to play. Limited vocabulary— "Where is My . . .?" enables toddlers to "read" the book to caregivers. Add in backgrounds that are color-coded to the missing garb for an engaging participatory experience. *lmp*
    Author lives in the Netherlands.
    CLOTHING AND DRESS, THE NETHERLANDS, TRANSLATIONS INTO ENGLISH

Dijkstra, Lida. **Cute.** Illustrated by Marije Tolman. Honesdale, PA, Boyds Mills Press/Lemniscaat, 2007. Originally published as *Schattig* in Dutch by Lemniscaat The Netherlands, in 2006. ISBN 978-1-59078-505-8, 1-59078-505-3. 28 p. (5–8). Picture book.
    Toby the rabbit dislikes being fuzzy and cute. To transform himself into "cool," Toby adds dark glasses, pierces his ear, tattoos his arm, and buys a noisy motorcycle. When he meets Tara, she is not impressed with Toby. Toby quickly discards his tough look and discovers that Tara likes cute and fuzzy. Together they raise their twelve mischievous baby rabbits. Ink-and-watercolor illustrations highlight Toby's amusing activities. *pwc, mjw*
    Author and illustrator live in the Netherlands.
    RABBITS, THE NETHERLANDS, FANTASY FICTION

Gerritsen, Paula. **Nuts.** Illustrated by the author. Asheville, NC, Front Street, 2006. Originally published as *Noten* in Dutch by Lemniscaat The Netherlands, in 2005. ISBN 978-1-932425-66-6, 1-932425-66-7. 24 p. (3–6). Picture book.

On an autumn day, Mouse makes the treacherous journey from her burrow to collect nuts from a far-off tree only to find that all the nuts have been blown away by an ongoing storm. Upon returning home she is greeted by a special surprise: the wind has blown a large store of nuts to her burrow. The mixed-media illustrations, done in warm fall colors, feature little grey Mouse dressed in a bright red coat and long, yellow neck scarf stalwartly proceeding as heavy winds make her unable to hear Gull, Hare, and Sheep's warnings of impending danger. *ca*

Author/illustrator lives in the Netherlands.

Mice, Storms, Nuts, Autumn, Fiction

Heide, Iris van der. **A Strange Day**. Illustrated by Marijke ten Cate. Honesdale, PA, Boyds Mills Press/Lemniscaat, 2007. Originally published as *Een Rare Dag* in Dutch by Lemniscaat The Netherlands, in 2006. ISBN 978-1-932425-94-9, 1-932425-94-2. 24 p. (4–8). Picture book.

One windy day, Jack is disappointed that he didn't receive a letter from the judges of a drawing contest. He mutters and wanders through his neighborhood, unaware that he has stopped a runaway baby carriage, rescued a bird's egg, and saved a dog from a bicycle collision. Meanwhile, the detailed illustrations reveal a second story of the mailman courageously chasing the flyaway letter so he can deliver it to Jack. Clueless, Jack returns home to the good news that he has won and to a crowd gathered to honor him and his heroic deeds. Funny visuals reflect the Dutch setting. *2008 USBBY Outstanding International Books List. mjw*

Author and illustrator live in the Netherlands.

Heroes, Postal Service, Contests and Talent Shows, Boys

Hof, Marjolijn. Translated by Johanna Henrica Prins & Johanna W. Prins. **Against the Odds**. Toronto, Groundwood Books, 2009. Originally published as *Een Kleine Kans* in Dutch by Querido The Netherlands, in 2006. ISBN 978-0-88899-935-1, 0-88899-935-6. 124 p. (10–12). Novel.

Kiki's father is a doctor who often travels to countries at war to provide medical assistance. When he is declared missing, Kiki's mother tries to comfort her by telling her it is against the odds that her father is dead because most children have a living father. Kiki wonders if she could adjust the odds further if her pet dog were to die. Kiki knows no one with both a deceased father and pet. A stranger saves Kiki from making a tragic mistake, and she is relieved when her father finally returns home. *2010 USBBY Outstanding International Books List, Winner of the Golden Owl Juvenile Literature Prize, the Golden Owl Young Reader's Prize, and the Golden Slate Pencil. pwc*

Author lives in Krommenie, the Netherlands.
FEAR IN CHILDREN, PETS, TRANSLATED BOOKS, FICTION

Jongman, Mariken. Translated by Wanda Boeke. **Rits**. Asheville, NC, Front Street, 2008. Originally published as *Rits* in Dutch by Lemniscaat The Netherlands, in 2005. ISBN 978-1-59078-545-4, 1-59078-545-2. 236 p. (10 up). Novel.

Rits is living with his Uncle Corry while his father travels with a girlfriend and his mother is in a rest home. Trying to make the best of a confusing situation, Rits begins to cook for his unemployed, unkempt uncle. As they try to work out their lives together, Uncle Corry begins to care. When Rits's father arrives to take him home, Uncle Corry tells Rits that he is always welcome to come back. There is an uncertainty about Rits's future, but the reader does know that no matter what happens he will be a survivor. *pwc*
Author lives in the Netherlands.
UNCLES, DYSFUNCTIONAL FAMILIES, FRIENDSHIP, EMOTIONAL PROBLEMS, THE NETHERLANDS, FICTION

Kromhout, Rindert. Translated by Marianne Martens. **Little Donkey and the Birthday Present**. Illustrated by Annemarie van Haeringen. New York, NorthSouth Books, 2007. Originally published as *Kleine Ezel en Jarige Jakkie* in Dutch by Leopold The Netherlands, in 2001. ISBN 978-0-7358-2132-3, 0-7358-2132-1. 24 p. (3–6). Picture book.

Little Donkey decides he'd like to keep the kite bought for his friend Jackie Yak's birthday present, but Mama insists he must stick with the original plan. Happily, his friend shares and Little Donkey learns that he will soon have a birthday. Observant children will see the wrapped kite tucked behind a chest and know that Little Donkey, too, will soon have a kite. The simple but expressive illustrations, done in black ink, watercolor, and paper collage (the kite presents are covered in brown wrapping paper), are on a creamy white background. *ca*
Author and illustrator both live in the Netherlands.
DONKEYS, YAKS, BIRTHDAYS, GIFTS, FICTION

Kuijer, Guus. Translated by John Nieuwenhuizen. **The Book of Everything: A Novel**. New York, Scholastic/Arthur A. Levine Books, 2006. Originally published as *Boek van Alle Dingen* in Dutch by Querido The Netherlands, in 2004. ISBN 978-0-439-74918-3, 0-439-74918-2. 112 p. (12 up). Novel.

In the post–World War II years of Amsterdam, Thomas, a young lad whose goal in life is to be happy, lives with a Bible-quoting father who is abusive toward his family and blames it on religion. However, as the story unfolds, readers learn along with Thomas that it is his fear that is behind his cowardice. Thomas keeps a journal, *The Book of Everything*, and in it he records his imaginative observations and experiences, his changing beliefs, and even his talks with Jesus. With themes of fear, the search for happiness, and hope, this short novel invites deeper thinking for older readers, but it tells a story with simplicity and humor that appeals to all. *2007 USBBY Outstanding International Books List, Golden Owl (the Flemish equivalent of the Newbery), Golden Pencil (the Dutch equivalent of the Newbery), 2006 Book Sense Summer Pick, The Washington Post's Ten Best Books for Children. jm*

Author lives in the Netherlands.

Family Problems, Christian Life, Dysfunctional Families, Amsterdam, The Netherlands, Novel, Fiction

Lieshout, Elle van & Erik van Os. **The Wish**. Illustrated by Paula Gerritsen. Honesdale, PA, Front Street/Lemniscaat, 2007. Originally published as *De Wens* in Dutch by Lemniscaat The Netherlands, in 2006. ISBN 978-1-932425-91-8, 1-932425-91-8. 32 p. (4–8). Picture book.

Lila, who lives far from the rest of the world with her cat and a distant neighbor with a red tractor, sows sunflowers, picks beans, and makes applesauce. During winter, when her food runs out, she wishes on a star and gets enough flour to make bread. She never wishes for extravagant feasts or finery. The night before her birthday, she wishes for, and gets, two cakes and a red tractor with a chauffeur. The final watercolor spread shows Lila and the neighboring farmer tearing through the sunflowers on the tractor, revealing the hidden love story. *mjw*

Authors and illustrator live in the Netherlands.

Wishes, Solitude, Fantasy Fiction

Metselaar, Menno & Ruud van der Rol. Translated by Arnold Pomerans. **Anne Frank: Her Life in Words and Pictures from the Archives of the Anne Frank House**. New York, Roaring Brook Press/Flash Point, 2009. Originally published as *Het verhaal van Anne Frank* in Dutch by Anne Frank Stichting The Netherlands, in 2004. ISBN 978-1-59643-546-9, 1-59643-546-1. 215 p. (8 up). Biography.

Most students read *The Diary of Anne Frank* (1947) by the time they enter high school, which often is too young to comprehend her experiences. *Anne Frank: Her Life in Words and Pictures* is the perfect supplement to contextualize her *Diary*. Primarily illustrated with black-and-white photographs, remarkably sharp considering their age, this photobiography animates Anne and her family before their sequestration, during their time in the attic, and relates the return of Anne's diary after her ultimate death. Actual pages with her writing, more photos, and an occasional sketch provide visual, concrete details of Anne Frank's life and confinement. *2010 USBBY Outstanding International Books List, 2010 Sydney Taylor Honor Book for Older Readers. lmp*

Authors live in the Netherlands.

Anne Frank (1929–1945), Jews, Holocaust (1939–1945), Amsterdam, The Netherlands, Biography

Ommen, Sylvia van. **The Surprise**. Illustrated by the author. Asheville, NC, Front Street, 2007. Originally published as *Der Verrassing* in Dutch by Lemniscaat The Netherlands, in 2004. ISBN 978-1-932425-85-7, 1-932425-85-3. 28 p. (3–6). Wordless Picture book.

In this crafty wordless book, a very fluffy Sheep weighs herself on a scale. She eyes herself in the mirror, measures the depth of her wool, and sets off on her motor scooter to the store. She purchases red dye and returns home to dye her fleece. Sheep carefully shears her wool, spins it into yarn, and starts to knit. The final illustrations show Sheep presenting her friend Giraffe with a gift of a red sweater. In return, Sheep receives a kiss. Bright, humorous, uncluttered paintings bring Sheep's surprise to life. *pwc, mjw*

Author lives in the Netherlands.

Sheep, Art, Clothing and Dress, Friendship, Stories without Words, Fantasy

Peet, Mal. **Tamar: A Novel of Espionage, Passion, and Betrayal**. Cambridge, MA, Candlewick Press, 2007. Originally published by Walker Books Great Britain, in 2005. ISBN 978-0-7636-3488-9, 0-7636-3488-3. 420 p. (14 up). Novel.

Tamar is a sophisticated, well-plotted, and beautifully written coming-of-age mystery combining secrecy and survival with love and war. When her beloved grandfather dies and leaves fifteen-year-old Tamar a box containing a series of cryptic clues and coded messages, she begins to uncover the secrets of the past, both her grandfather's and her own. The action alternates between the Resistance in the Netherlands during World War II and modern-day Great Britain, deftly interweaving the tales of two people named Tamar. This is a story of passion, espionage, and betrayal, both past and present. *2008 USBBY Outstanding International Books List, 2005 Carnegie Medal Winner. ae*

Author lives in Great Britain.

GRANDFATHERS, GUILT, WORLD WAR II (1939–1945), UNDERGROUND MOVEMENTS, GERMAN OCCUPATION, GREAT BRITAIN, THE NETHERLANDS, FICTION

Poole, Josephine. **Anne Frank**. Illustrated by Angela Barrett. New York, Random House/Alfred A. Knopf, 2005. Originally published by Hutchinson Great Britain, in 2005. ISBN 978-0-375-83242-0, 0-375-83242-4. 32 p. (9–14). Picture book.

Beginning with an extract from her diary, the story of Anne Frank's life is told in the context of Nazi Germany, from the time she is born until she and her family go into hiding in Amsterdam and then are arrested. Life in the crowded annex is recounted as Anne writes her "most private thoughts" into her diary (n.p.). Detailed, realistic illustrations capture the mood and tone of the text and convey dark times in subtle, somber colors. One dramatic full-page illustration shows Anne being led away by Nazis, with her face looking directly outward toward readers. A chronology is provided. *hc*
Author and illustrator live in Great Britain.

FRANK, ANNE (1929–1945), PICTORIAL WORKS, JEWISH CHILDREN IN THE HOLOCAUST–AMSTERDAM (1939–1945), THE NETHERLANDS, BIOGRAPHY

Post, Hans. Translated by Nancy Forest-Flier. **Creepy Crawlies**. Illustrated by Irene Goede. Asheville, NC, Front Street/Lemniscaat, 2006. Originally published as *Kriebelpoten* in Dutch by Lemniscaat The Netherlands, in 2005. ISBN 978-1-932425-65-9, 1-932425-65-9. 24 p. (4–8). Picture book.

A simple story of a cat's exploration inside and outside a house is paired with side notes on the more than fifty animals she encounters. Each double spread includes a brief narrative, an illustration showing the cat in a particular area (bedroom, terrace, garden, and so on), and five short notes providing close-up portraits and details on the animals seen. Some of the animals, such as the mouse and cockroaches shown amid garbage from an overturned pail in the kitchen, truly fit the "creepy crawlie" designation; most are simply animals found in a traditional European setting. *Creepy Crawlies* invites children to explore the natural world around them. *ca*
Author and illustrator live in The Netherlands.
CATS, ANIMALS

Post, Hans & Kees Heij. **Sparrows**. Illustrated by Irene Goede. Honesdale, PA, Boyds Mills Press Lemniscaat, 2008. Originally published as *Mus* in Dutch by Lemniscaat The Netherlands, in 2006. ISBN 978-1-59078-570-6, 1-59078-570-3. n.p. (2–6). Nonfiction.

The life of the common house sparrow—from hatching to munching to fledging—is presented in language suitable for kindergarten and primary-age children. Post and Heij have sterling credentials for writing nonfiction books, and Goede illustrates the birds' year so that their coloring, behaviors, and habitats are easily distinguished from other birds. An addendum provides information about the sparrow's arrival in North America around 1850 as well as other interesting facts. Imported, translated nonfiction—such as *Sparrows*—is rare and, except for the fact that house sparrows are so pervasive, we could say this book is a rare bird. lmp

Authors and illustrator live in the Netherlands.

ENGLISH SPARROWS, NONFICTION

Rinck, Maranke. **I Feel a Foot!** Illustrated by Martijn van der Linden. Honesdale, PA, Boyds Mills Press/Lemniscaat, 2008. Originally published as *Ik Voel een Voet!* in Dutch by Lemniscaat The Netherlands, in 2008. ISBN 978-1-59078-638-3, 1-59078-638-6. 32 p. (4–8). Picture book.

Different animals (turtle, bird, bat, octopus, and goat) try to discover what is rustling in the dark near their hammock. Each animal examines just one part of the intruder and believes that it is an oversized version of itself. Just as they conclude that the huge beast is a Tur-Bat-Octo-Bird-Goat, it trumpets and they know it's an elephant. They invite the elephant to join them in their hammock, and all is well until they hear another sound. The stunning illustrations for this original retelling of an old folktale feature boldly colored and patterned animals on a midnight black background. *2009 USBBY Outstanding International Books List. ca*

Author and illustrator live in the Netherlands.

ANIMALS, IMAGINATION, FICTION

Schubert, Ingrid & Dieter Schubert. **Elephant Soup.** Illustrated by the authors. Honesdale, PA, Boyds Mills Press/Lemniscaat, 2010. Originally published as *Olifantensoep* in Dutch by Lemniscaat The Netherlands, in 2008. ISBN 978-1-59078-807-3, 1-59078-807-9. n.p. (4–8). Picture book.

Mouse is down in the dumps. He sends out an SOS and hoists an enormous pot over his head. Only one thing can help—elephant soup. As mouse makes this pronouncement (wryly grinning), his friends march across the double-page spread bearing soup ingredients (slightly gnawed). All goes well until they attempt to cover the boiling elephant (slightly wilted) with a lid— and she careens from the pot. The penultimate spread features a scowling elephant, tail and tush uncomfortably pinked, with a no-longer-sad mouse (slightly abashed) explaining future plans. The representational watercolor illustrations drolly capture the absurdity of each spread. *The Schuberts and their books have received many awards, including the Golden Brush Award, a Dutch prize for best-illustrated book.* lmp

Authors were born in Germany but live in Amsterdam.

MICE, ELEPHANTS, THE NETHERLANDS, HUMOROUS FICTION

Spillebeen, Geert. Translated by Terese Edelstein. **Age 14**. Boston, Houghton Mifflin Harcourt, 2009. Originally published as *Age 14* in Dutch by Averbode The Netherlands, in 2000. ISBN 978-0-547-05342-4, 0-547-05342-8. 216 p. (14 up). Novel.

See Ireland for description.

Stein, Mathilde. **Brave Ben**. Illustrated by Mies Van Hout. Asheville, NC, Front Street, 2006. Originally published as *Bang Mannetje* in Dutch by Lemniscaat The Netherlands, in 2005. ISBN 978-1-932425-64-2, 1-932425-64-0. n.p. (3–6). Picture book.

Scaredy-cat Ben turns to the Yellow Pages under "Help for Cowards." The next day as he travels through the dark forest to keep his appointment with "Magic Tree," Ben encounters wild and weird creatures, including a dragon, an enormous spider, an ugly witch, and skeletons, all of which he greets politely. Upon reaching the magic tree and asking for help on being less afraid, Ben is informed that he's already taken care of the problem on his journey. Ben happily returns home as Brave Ben. Van Hout's illustrations for this story about magically finding bravery through one's own actions feature cartoonlike characters against colorful painted backgrounds. ca

Author and illustrator live in the Netherlands.

EMOTIONS, FEAR, COURAGE, FICTION

Stein, Mathilde. **Monstersong**. Illustrated by Gerdien van der Linden. Asheville, NC, Front Street, 2007. Originally published as *Het Monsterlied* in Dutch by Lemniscaat The Netherlands, in 2006. ISBN 978-1-932425-90-1, 1-932425-90-X. 26 p. (4–6). Picture book.

Little pig can't sleep because there is a monster pestering him. Mom pulls a small, green monster from under the bed. She tucks him in bed with her startled child, saying, "There's plenty of room in your bed." After several more monsters are added to the bed, little pig convinces the monsters that they would be much more comfortable in his mother's larger bed. pwc

Author lives in the Netherlands.

MONSTERS, STORIES IN RHYME, FANTASY

Stein, Mathilde. **The Child Cruncher**. Illustrated by Mies van Hout. Honesdale, PA, Boys Mills Press Lemniscaat, 2007. Originally published as *De Kindereter* in Dutch by Lemniscaat The Netherlands, in 2007. ISBN 978-1-59078-635-2, 1-59078-635-1. 24 p. (4–8). Picture book.

A young girl yearning for excitement and adventure is kidnapped by a large, hairy villain. As she is carted away, her distracted father tells her to have fun. Her hope is that she will have many adventures. Unfortunately the girl discovers that the villain is just an ordinary child cruncher, and he only wants to eat her. She escapes. When she returns home her father, not realizing she has been on a hair-raising adventure, offers to read her a book. She agrees—then adds, ". . . but nothing too frightening." *pwc*

Author lives in the Netherlands.

Adventures and Adventurers, Imagination, Fathers and Daughters, The Netherlands, Fantasy Fiction

Stoffels, Karlijn. Translated by Laura Watkinson. **Heartsinger**. New York, Scholastic/Arthur A. Levine Books, 2009. Originally published as *Koningsdochter, Zeemanslief* in Dutch by Em Querido's Uitgeverij B.V. The Netherlands, in 2005. ISBN 978-0-545-06929-8, 0-545-06929-7. 134 p. (14 up). Novel.

Mee is a child with sad, dark eyes who never smiles. His parents are deaf and have never heard Mee's beautiful singing. His songs comfort people. He is hired to sing by people who are in need of consolation. He sings to the sick, at funerals, and after disasters. Mitou was born on the same day as Mee. She plays an accordion, dresses in brightly colored clothes, and is known as the finest merrymaker in the land. She seeks out Mee, who is uncomfortable with Mitou's cheerfulness. When Mitou travels on without Mee, he realizes his great loss and begins a journey to find her. *pwc*

Author lives in the Netherlands.

Love, Loss, Voyages and Travels, Singing, Storytellers, Musicians, Fantasy Fiction

Straaten, Harmen van. Translated by MaryChris Bradley. **For Me?** Illustrated by the author. New York, NorthSouth Books, 2007. Originally published as *Eendje voor jou* in Dutch by Leopold The Netherlands, in 2007. ISBN 978-0-7358-2163-7, 0-7358-2163-1. 32 p. (3–6). Picture book.

Duck, Toad, Otter, and Hedgehog each receive an envelope with a rose and a picture of an enormous red heart. Puzzled by the anonymous gifts, the friends try to figure out who the sender might be. In the middle of their detective work, their new neighbor—a shy mole—admits to sending the gifts. The animals enjoyed receiving the roses but are more pleased that they have a new friend. *pwc*

Author lives in the Netherlands.

LETTERS, FRIENDSHIP, ANIMALS, FANTASY FICTION

Tolman, Marije & Ronald Tolman. **The Tree House**. Illustrated by the authors. Honesdale, PA, Boyds Mills Press/Lemniscaat, 2010. Originally published as *De Boomhut* in Dutch by Lemniscaat The Netherlands, in 2009. ISBN 978-1-59078-806-6, 1-59078-806-0. n.p. (3 up). Wordless Picture book.

The Tree House rises from the ocean as a polar bear, swimming through frigid waters, moves in and makes herself comfortable. More creatures arrive as the sea subsides. Seasons change until fall returns and all migrate—except the polar and brown bears. Winter returns to complete the cycle. In this wordless picture book, Marije Tolman's pastel backgrounds and watercolor drawings over her father's etchings of *The Tree House* manage to remain static yet vary with each season. Imagination, friendship, Noah's Ark, global ecology, the creation, or the potential of books—whatever the theme—*The Tree House* is a visual smorgasbord for all ages. *2010 Winner of the Bologna Ragazzi Award–Fiction. lmp*

Authors, who are father and daughter, live in the Netherlands.

TREE HOUSES, BEARS, ANIMALS, THE NETHERLANDS, WORDLESS FANTASY

Van Rossum, Heleen. **Will You Carry Me?** Illustrated by Peter Van Harmelen. La Jolla, CA, Kane/Miller Books, 2005. Originally published as *Wil Je Me Dragen?* in Dutch by Zirkoon Uitgevers The Netherlands, in 2004. ISBN 978-1-929132-74-4, 1-929132-74-3. n.p. (2–4). Picture books.

Tired from a day at the park, Thomas stretches out his arms and begs his mother to carry him home, but this very clever mother convinces her son that, if he is too tired to walk, they should try getting home other ways. Together Thomas and his mother hop, fly, jump, swim, and laugh their way home. The pastel shades that dominate the illustrations are in perfect keeping with the lighthearted mood of the story. The illustrations feature urban scenes in a decidedly European city. *mm*

Author was born in the Netherlands but has lived in Great Britain and the United States; the illustrator lives in Amsterdam.

TODDLERS, MOTHER AND CHILD, FATIGUE, HUMAN LOCOMOTION, DUTCH TRANSLATIONS INTO ENGLISH, FICTION

Vries, Anke de. **Raf**. Illustrated by Charlotte Dematons. Honesdale, PA, Boyds Mills Press/Lemniscaat, 2009. Originally published as *Raf* in Dutch by Lemniscaat The Netherlands, in 2008. ISBN 978-1-59078-749-6, 1-59078-749-8. n.p. (3–5). Picture book.

"Ben and Raf are always together" (n.p.), except for the desolate, dark day that Raf disappears. It snows all day, but without Raf, Ben refuses to play. When the mailbox clatters the next morning, Ben receives the first in a series of postcards from his missing stuffed giraffe: "I have been found! I am traveling through Africa . . . the sun burns my head. I am as brown as chocolate" (n.p.). Raf reports meeting flamingos, elephants, monkeys, and giraffes. Vacation over, he arrives in time for Ben's birthday—a changed giraffe. Dematons's illustrations invite conversation about color, mood, dreadlocks, and Raf's wonder-filled vacation. *The author has been awarded the Silver Pen (the Dutch National Book Award).* lmp

　Author lives in the Hague and France; illustrator lives in the Netherlands.

Loneliness, Stuffed Animals, Toys, Fiction

Westera, Marleen. Translated by Nancy Forest. **Sheep and Goat**. Illustrated by Sylvia Van Ommen. Asheville, NC, Front Street, 2006. Originally published as *Schaap en Geit* in Dutch by Lemniscaat The Netherlands, in 2004. ISBN 978-1-932425-81-9, 1-932425-81-0. 99 p. (6–8). Illustrated Short Stories.

　Ten short stories tell about the small dilemmas of Sheep and Goat, who live a seemingly lonely and boring life together in a meadow on a farm. Although they are opposites in personality and are at odds from time to time, they are true friends. Simple black-and-white drawings featuring the pair add to the warmth and gentle humor of this short chapter book that works equally well as a read-aloud or read-alone choice. ca

　Author and illustrator live in the Netherlands.

Sheep, Goats, Friendship, Humorous Short Stories, Fiction

Wigersma, Tanneke. **Baby Brother**. Illustrated by Nynke Mare Talsma. Asheville, NC, Front Street, 2005. Originally published as *Broertje* in Dutch by Lemniscaat The Netherlands, in 2005. ISBN 978-1-932425-55-0, 1-932425-55-1. 24 p. (3–6). Picture book.

　Mia writes to her grandmother about the recent strange changes in the appearance and behavior of her cat, Stripe. At the end of the letter Mia reports that Stripe has given birth to five cute kittens—and adds, seemingly as an afterthought, that she also has a new baby brother. In the text, Mia's focus

is clearly on the cat, while the pen-and-ink and watercolor illustrations also depict Mia's mom's pregnancy and the birth of Mia's baby brother. *ca*
Author and illustrator live in the Netherlands.
SIBLINGS, BABIES, BROTHERS AND SISTERS, CATS, LETTERS, FICTION

RELATED INFORMATION

Organizations

Collective Promotion for the Dutch Book (CPNB) [Stichting Collectieve Propaganda van het Nederlandse Boek]

The CPNB was organized by professional publishing and bookselling bodies, the Nederlandse Boekverkopersbond (Dutch Booksellers Federation) and the Groep Algemene Uitgevers (Trade Publishing Group). During the ten days of Children's Book Week in March, the organization distributes a free copy of a specially commissioned children's book to everyone who purchases books from a bookseller. Approximately 750,000 books are distributed each year. For more information, visit
http://web.cpnb.nl/cpnb/index.vm?template=english.

IBBY—Nederland

The Netherlands national section produces numerous publications each year, including *Literature without Age*, which appears three times a year in the form of a booklet of about 160 pages. They sponsor the Jenny Smelik/IBBY Prize to a book that contributes to a better understanding between different ethnic groups in society. There are symposiums and meetings and a researchers' working group. This is an extremely active IBBY national section.
www.ibby.org/index.php?id=442
www.duijx.net/ibby/

Awards

Information on children's book awards for the Netherlands is available at http://web.cpnb.nl/cpnb/campagne.vm?sp=100&hp=73. (Complete information is provided in Dutch only.)

The Gouden Griffel (Golden Pen)

This is an important award given to authors of children's or teenager's literature in the Netherlands. Only novels written in Dutch are eligible for the Gouden Griffel. Since 1971, it has been awarded each year during the

Dutch Children's Books Week, by the Stichting Collectieve Propaganda van het Nederlandse Boek (see information in Organizations) for the best children's books written in the past year. This replaces the earlier Children's Book of the Year Award. Since 1970, Griffels have been awarded in several categories:

Gouden Penseel (Golden Paintbrush) is awarded to the best-illustrated children's books.

Gouden Zoen (Golden Kiss), since 1997, awarded to the best books for teenagers.

Silver Griffels (the runner-up awards) may go to translated works.

Silver Penseel (the runner-up awards)

Silver Zoen (the runner-up awards): http://web.cpnb.nl/cpnb/home.vm, http://www.kinderboekenweek.nl/.

A list of award winners in English and much of the information listed above is available through Wikipedia at http://en.wikipedia.org/wiki/Gouden_Griffel.

Constantijn Huygens Prize

The Constantijn Huygens Prize is awarded for an author's entire body of work.

http://www.nlpvf.nl/children/

Gouden Uil (Golden Owl)

The Golden Owl prize is awarded every year to the best new Dutch-language book and children's book.

www.nlpvf.nl/news/award/

The Jenny Smelik / IBBY Prize

This prize is awarded biennially to writers and illustrators of children's and youth literature that contribute to a better understanding between different ethnic groups in society.

http://duijx.net/ibby/?page_id=8

Key Colours

The Key Colours is an international award for picture book concepts—aimed at children from ages two to seven. It was formerly called the Prix Hasselt. In 2010, there were 323 works from twenty-three different countries submitted. The winner receives a monetary prize as well as publication by Clavis Publishing House.

www.keycolours.com/

Nienke van Hichtum Prize
The biennial Nienke van Hichtum Prize for children's and youth literature was named after a well-known Frisian Dutch children's author.
www.leesplein.nl/LL_plein.php?hm=8&sm=3&id=11

Theo Thijssen Prize
Awarded in a three-year cycle for the complete body of an author's
writings.
http://www.nlpvf.nl/children/

Collections

Centrale Catalogus Kinderboeken (Central Catalogue of Children's Books)
Searchable catalog and other resources. The home page can be accessed
in English at www.kb.nl.

Kinderboekenmuseum (Children's Book Museum). This is an attractive and
seemingly informative site about children's literature at the Nation Library.
www.kinderboekenmuseum.nl/ (Dutch only)

Koninklijke Bibliotheek (National Library)
www.kb.nl or http://www.letmus.nl

Letterkundigmuseum. Appears to be a gateway to information about children's and young adult book sites at the National Library as well as important
authors and cartooning pages.
www.letterkundigmuseum.nl/ (Dutch only)

Print and Online Resources

Linders, Joke & Marita de Sterck (with an introduction by Aidan Chambers). Translated by Jan Michael & Rina Vergano. **Behind the Story: Children's Book Authors in Flanders and the Netherlands**. Published under
the auspices of the Ministerie van de Vlaamse Gemeenschap Administratie
Cultuur, 1996. ISBN 978-90-803223-1-8, 90-803223-1-8. 239 p.
    This second book about Dutch and Flemish children's authors is the suc-
cessor to *Nice to Meet You* (1993). An overview of the literature of the Low
Countries is followed by biographical information about prominent children's
book authors and illustrators, a listing of the awards, and selected institutions,

organizations, and periodicals. A list of translators from the Dutch language and publishing houses in Flanders and the Netherlands is appended.

CHILDREN'S LITERATURE, DUTCH LITERATURE 20TH CENTURY—HISTORY AND CRITICISM, FLEMISH LITERATURE 20TH CENTURY—HISTORY AND CRITICISM, CHILDREN'S BOOKS AND READING—NETHERLANDS, CHILDREN BOOKS AND READING—FLANDERS

NORWAY

Bringsværd, Tor Åge. Translated by James Anderson. **Ruffen: The Sea Serpent Who Couldn't Swim**. Illustrated by Thore Hansen. San Francisco, CA, Mackenzie Smiles, 2008. Originally published as *Ruffen: Sjøromen Son Ikke Kunne Svømme* in Norwegian by Den Norske Bokkluben Norway, in 1972. ISBN 978-0-97903479-4, 0-97903479-5. 63 p. (4–8). Picture book.

When Ruffen, a very small sea serpent who is afraid of the water, rescues an octopus entrapped in some rocks, the octopus agrees to give him swimming lessons. Ruffen becomes an excellent swimmer and also a hero when he pulls a ship lost in a hurricane to safety in New York Harbor. Awarded a gold medal for his heroism, Ruffen begins the long swim home, happily singing his favorite song. The intricately detailed pen-and-ink illustrations, touched with color, feature an island full of sea serpents, each of which sparkles with personality. Includes words and music to "Ruffen's Song." *ca*

Author and illustrator live in Norway.

SEA MONSTERS, HEROISM, FICTION

Gaiman, Neil. **Odd and the Frost Giants**. Illustrated by Brett Helquist. New York, HarperCollins, 2009. Originally published by Bloomsbury Great Britain, in 2008. ISBN 978-0-06-167173-9, 0-06-167173-8. 117 p. (8–14). Novella.

Odd and the Frost Giants introduces three major gods of Norse Mythology—Odin, Thor, and Loki—and a twelve-year-old boy named Odd. In Gaiman's signature chatty style, readers learn that Odd is a lucky name, but the boy Odd is not so lucky. His father has died, and Odd has crushed his leg and foot and is crippled. As in the best folktales, Odd escapes his cruel stepfather and meets the three gods who are trapped in animal form. How Odd tricks the Frost Giant and releases his companions from their animal prisons makes for a rousing introduction to Norse storytelling. *2010 USBBY*

Outstanding International Books List. Odd and the Frost Giants *was written for World Book Day in Great Britain. lmp*

    Author was born in Great Britain but now lives in Minnesota.

    Loki (Norse Deity), Thor (Norse Deity), Odin (Norse Deity), Giants, Mythology, Norse Heroes, Fiction

Hagerup, Klaus. Translated by Tara Chace. **Markus + Diana**. Asheville, NC, Front Street, 2006. Originally published as *Markus og Diana: Lyset fra Sirius* in Norwegian by Aschehoug Norway, in 1994. ISBN 978-1-932425-59-8, 1-932425-59-4. 188 p. (10 up). Novel.

    Timid, Norwegian sixth-grader Markus Simonsen writes outlandish letters to celebrities, pretending to be someone else in hopes of adding to his autograph collection. He writes to the beautiful actress Diana Mortensen, claiming to be a thirty-six-year-old, mountain-climbing millionaire. They exchange letters, and she decides to come to Norway to meet him. With the help of his intelligent and fearless sidekick friend Sigmund, he works up a scheme for the encounter. Scenes are hilarious, charming, and creative in this story, which was first published in 1997 and is part of a popular series written by the Norwegian author. *2007 USBBY Outstanding International Books List. mjw*

    Author lives in Norway.

    Self-esteem, Actors and Actresses, Friendship, Imagination, Norway, Fiction

Hole, Stian. Translated by Don Bartlett. **Garmann's Summer**. Illustrated by the author. Grand Rapids, MI, Eerdmans Books for Young Readers, 2008. Originally published as *Garmanns Sommer* in Norwegian by J. W. Cappelens Forlag Norway, in 2006. ISBN 978-0-8028-5339-4, 0-8028-5339-0. 40 p. (6–10). Picture book.

    Summer is over, and six-year-old Garmann will be starting school. He is scared. He asks his three elderly aunts if they are ever afraid. The aunts admit to a fear of having to eventually use a walker and a fear of icy pavements. His parents share their fears with Garmann. His father tells him "I think everyone is scared of something" (n.p.). This unique story ends with Garmann gazing out of the window, still wondering what school will be like. Hole's exploration of childhood emotion is expressed visually in intriguing mixed-media collages. *2009 USBBY Outstanding International Books List, 2007 Bologna Ragazzi Award, 2009 Nordic Association of School Librarians Children's Literature Prize, 2009 ALA Batchelder Honor Book, 2009 NYPL and the Ezra Jack Keats Foundation New Writer Award, 2009 CCBC Choices, 2010 IBBY Honour List. lmp, ca*

The author lives in Norway.

Aunts, Fear, First Day of School, Family Life, Change, Norwegian Translations into English, Fiction

Hole, Stian. Translated by Don Bartlett. **Garmann's Street**. Illustrated by the author. Grand Rapids, MI, Eerdmans Books for Young Readers, 2010. Originally published as *Garmanns Gate* in Norwegian by J. W. Cappelens Forlag Norway, in 2008. ISBN 978-0-8028-5357-8, 0-8028-5357-9. n.p. (6–10). Picture book.

Norwegian author/illustrator Stian Hole continues the story of the peculiar boy featured in *Garmann's Summer*. New challenges torment Garmann, who has overcome his school phobia. Roy, the street's alpha boy, taunts Garmann into lighting a match that starts a flash fire in the dry grass. Instead of running, as Roy does, Garmann fights the fire and gains the reputedly evil "Stamp Man's" respect. Philosophical in tone with themes that are thought provoking and intriguing, *Garmann's Street* hints at concepts but respects readers' intelligence by allowing the ideas to remain abstract. The mixed-media collage illustrations are suitably ambiguous, surreal, and engrossing. *lmp*

The author lives in Norway.

Friendship, Bullies, Peer Pressure, Norwegian Fiction, Translations into English, Fiction, Sequel to Garmann's Summer, which was a 2009 Batchelder Honor Book

RELATED INFORMATION

Organizations

IBBY Norway

IBBY Norway was founded in 1956. It is an independent organization that promotes information about literature for children and young people.
www.ibby.org/index.php?id=444
www.ibby.no

Norwegian Institute of Children's Books (NBI)

The NBI is home to the country's most comprehensive collection of Norwegian and international academic literature on the subject of children and young peoples' books. www.barnebokinstituttet.no/en/info/main_page_the_ norwegian_institute_of_childrens_books

Awards

IBBY Norway has its own prize, called Askeladden, which was first awarded in 1981. This prize can be awarded to authors, illustrators, critics, scholars, or institutions for efforts in promoting literature for children.

Collections

IBBY Documentation Centre of Books for Disabled Young People
www.ibby.org/index.php?id=271

To read more about the history of the Centre in an article by Tordis Ørjasæter that appeared in the journal *IBBY Norway–50 Years!*, please go to www.ibby.no/index.php?id=116.

Professional and Online Resources

IBBY Norway arranges annual seminars on children's and young people's literature in more than twenty-five cities all over the country. These seminars offer an overview of the previous year's books published in Norwegian.

Barnebokforum

The IBBY Norway magazine *Barnebokforum* is published quarterly with information about these seminars, reviews of current books, and other news. More information is available at the IBBY Norway website at www.ibby.no.

Nordic Journal of Childlit Aesthetics (BLFT)

BLFT is a new peer-reviewed journal that publishes in the Nordic languages and English.

www.childlitaesthetics.net/index.php/blft/ (Norwegian only)

For English information, see www.barnebokinstituttet.no/en/info/main_ page_the_norwegian_institute_of_childrens_books

Yearbook: Children's and Young Adult Literature

The *Yearbook* was first published in 1998 by Det Norske Samlaget. The Norwegian Institute of Children's Books produces it. The yearbook includes articles, research criticism, author interviews, and essays. In addition, the yearbook includes statistics, bibliographies, and an overview of literary prize winners.

www.barnebokinstituttet.no/en/info/main_page_the_norwegian_institute_ of_childrens_books

POLAND

Greif, Jean-Jacques. Translated by the author. **The Fighter**. New York, Bloomsbury, 2006. Originally published as *Le Ring de la Mort* in French by l'École des Loisirs France, in 1998. ISBN 978-1-58234-891-9, 1-58234-891-X. 211 p. (12 up). Novel.

Moshe Wisniak was born weak, with legs powerless to flee Warsaw's anti-Semitic bullies. So he learned to fight and think and defend himself. A move to Paris transformed him to Maurice, and coaching honed his skills as a boxer. The Nazis sentenced him to Auschwitz, but boxing kept him alive. The SS guards recognized his athletic prowess almost immediately and pitted Maurice against a Muselman, a dying inmate, but Maurice refused to play their game. As a result, he was mercilessly pummeled but learned to survive. *The Fighter's* first-person narrative voice brings immediacy to this factually based Holocaust novel. *2007 USBBY Outstanding International Books List, CCBC Choices, NYPL Books for the Teen Age, and School Library Journal Best Book of the Year, the French award for best YA novel in 2000—five French awards altogether.* lmp
Author lives in Paris.

Holocaust, Jewish (1939–1945), Concentration Camps, Auschwitz, Jews, Historical Fiction

Philip, Neil. **The Pirate Princess and Other Fairy Tales**. Illustrated by Mark Weber. New York, Scholastic/Arthur A. Levine Books, 2005. ISBN 978-0-590-10855-3, 0-590-10855-7. 96 p. (10 up). Short Stories.

Seven tales told by the famous Jewish storyteller Reb Nachman of Bratslav are made accessible to readers. Seemingly similar to traditional fairy tales, these all have a spiritual underpinning based on Kabalistic beliefs. An introduction, background notes, and an extensive bibliography are included in this handsome book. *2006 USBBY-CBC Outstanding International Books List.*
Author lives in Great Britain.

Hasidic Rabbi Nachman of Bratslav, Jewish Legends, Fairy Tales, Short Stories, Jewish Folklore, Metaphorical Tales

RELATED INFORMATION

IBBY Poland
The Polish section of IBBY was established in 1974. Each year the section organizes two awards: the Book of the Year contest and an annual medal for lifetime achievements to outstanding Polish authors and illustrators.

The activities of the Polish section of IBBY are financed by the Ministry of Culture and additional sponsors. The section is an important source of information about Polish children's books, both in Poland and around the world.

www.ibby.org/index.php?id=448
www.ibby.pl

Awards

The following awards are all functions of IBBY Poland.

Book of the Year Award
This award is presented by IBBY Poland to an author, illustrator, and to librarians or other individuals for book promotion.

www.ibby.pl/index.php?option=com_content&view=article&id=52&Itemid=60&lang=en

Dong's Award (Polish only)

Polish Section of IBBY Medal (Polish only)

Book Fairs

Books for Children & Young People Fair
April 3–6, 2011, at the Poznan International Fair Grounds, Poznan Poland.
www.targiksiazki.pl/en/

ROMANIA

Marillier, Juliet. **Wildwood Dancing**. New York, Random House/Alfred A. Knopf, 2007. Originally published by Pan Macmillan Australia, in 2006. ISBN 978-0-375-83364-9, 0-375-83364-1. 407 p. (12 up). Novel.

See Transylvania for description.

RELATED INFORMATION

Organizations

IBBY Romania

Activities sponsored by the IBBY National Section of Romania are

Gaudeamus: The School Book Fair (September)
The International Hall of Books for Young Children: The Mysterious Island—IBBY (November 2004). The primary purpose was to make the public more aware of IBBY as well as to celebrate the Jules Verne Centenary (a UNESCO event).

The Joys of Reading

The Joys of Reading, a reading incentive program, began with a study in Bucharest during the 2004–2005 school year. The participants were 2,600 children between ten and fiteen years. The findings suggested that for "68% of children the concept of leisure [reading] is . . . nonexistent" (IBBY Romania website, Joy of Reading, ¶2).

Two other IBBY Romania sponsored events are called **Anderseniada—Books for Children Olympics** and **The Book Worms Club**.

www.ibby.org/index.php?id=450

www.uer.ro/

For a translation of the web pages, go to http://translate.google.com/ translate?hl=en&sl=ro&u=http://www.uer.ro/&ei=AQkhTYPhHcGfnwed _em8Dg&sa=X&oi=translate&ct=result&resnum=1&ved=0CB4Q7gEw AA&prev=/search%3Fq%3Dhttp://www.uer.ro/%26hl%3Den%26client %3Dfirefox-a%26hs%3DEPD%26rls%3Dorg.mozilla:en-US:official%26 prmd%3Divns

RUSSIA

Andrekson, Judy. **Miskeen: The Dancing Horse**. Illustrated by David Parkins. Toronto, Tundra Books, 2007. ISBN 978-0-88776-771-5, 0-88776-771-0. 82 p. (8–11). Chapter book.
See Bahrain for description.

Holub, Josef. Translated by Michael Hofmann. **An Innocent Soldier**. New York, Scholastic/Arthur A. Levine Books, 2005. Originally published as *Der*

Russlander in German by Verlag Friedrich Oetinger Germany, in 2002. ISBN 978-0-439-62772-6, 0-439-62772-9. 231 p. (12–14). Novel.

Adam Feuchter, an orphaned farmhand, finds himself conscripted into Napoleon's Grand Armée and swept up in the French emperor's invasion of Russia. After enduring merciless bullying by a cruel sergeant, Adam is employed by a young lieutenant, the well-born Konrad Klara. At first master and servant, these two innocent soldiers depend on each other to survive exhaustion, exposure, starvation, and illness as they retreat from Moscow during the Russian winter. Adam tells his story in first person, present tense, in a voice alternately humorous, ironic, and stoic, leaving the reader to ponder the futility of a disastrous war conceived by an arrogant leader. *2006 USBBY-CBC Outstanding International Books List. Arthur A. Levine won the 2006 Batchelder Award for this book. The author has won many awards, including the Peter Hartling Prize for Children's Literature and the prestigious Zurich Children's Book Prize. mac*

Author was born in Bohemia, part of the Czech Republic. He currently lives in Germany.

NAPOLEONIC WARS (1800–1815), CAMPAIGNS, RUSSIA, HISTORICAL FICTION

Romanova, Yelena. **The Perfect Friend**. Illustrated by Boris Kulikov. New York, Farrar, Straus and Giroux/Frances Foster Books, 2005. ISBN 978-0-374-35821-1, 0-374-35821-4. 32 p. (4–7). Picture book.

Archie the hound looks forward to the surprise he has been promised by his human family. Will it be the friend he has always wanted? When his owners bring home Max, the new baby, Archie finds himself being ignored. Finally, his extended family attempts to make up for months of neglect with a series of misguided activities. Still longing for a companion, Archie realizes that Max has gotten old enough to be "the perfect friend" (31). Full-color illustrations with a surreal twist add a humorous, bizarre dimension to the story. *Children's Magazine Best Books of the Year; Parents' Choice Award Winner. chs*

Author and illustrator were born and raised in Russia and now live in Brooklyn, New York.

BABIES, DOGS, FRIENDSHIP, FICTION

Wolff, Ferida & Harriet May Savitz. **The Story Blanket**. Illustrated by Elena Odriozola. Atlanta, GA, Peachtree, 2008. Originally published by Andersen Press Great Britain, in 2008. ISBN 978-1-56145-466-2, 1-56145-466-4. 24 p. (4–8). Picture book.

Babba Zarrah is not only the village storyteller but also a keen observer of her neighbors' needs. Bit by bit, she borrows yarn from her story blanket to knit socks, scarves, mittens, and shawls for the needy villagers. When they discover who has knit these secret gifts, they surprise her with yarn for a new story blanket. Spanish illustrator Elena Odriozola's abstract watercolor illustrations are airy and whimsical and will have readers examining each item closely to see how it is related to the original blanket. *lmp*

Authors live in the United States; illustrator lives in Spain.

SHARING, FRIENDSHIP, FICTION, RUSSIA

RELATED INFORMATION

IBBY Russia

There are two branches of IBBY: Board on Books for Young People of Russia, which is located in Moscow (c/o Russian Cultural Foundation) and the Russian Section of IBBY—St. Petersburg Branch, located in the Central Children's Library. The Russian national section of IBBY has quite a long history, under the leadership of Sergey Mikhalkov. The St. Petersburg Branch came into existence in 1998. The two branches are heavily invested in joint presentations and exhibits with other European nations.

www.ibby.org/index.php?id=451

www.rbby.ru/

Collections

Alexander Pushkin Library Children's Collection

The St. Petersburg Library and the St. Petersburg section of IBBY are housed in this nineteenth-century building. It includes a "playing room for children from 3 to 8 years old," and the rare book division houses approximately three thousand rare children's books and the Pushkiniana collection. There is also a description of the Children's American Corner.

www.pushkinlib.spb.ru/eng/sectionibby.html

SCOTLAND

Donaldson, Julia. **The Giants and the Joneses**. Illustrated by Greg Swearingen. New York, Henry Holt, 2005. Originally published by Egmont Great Britain, in 2004. ISBN 978-0-8050-7805-3, 0-8050-7805-3. 215 p. (8–10). Novel.

Intrigued by the fairy tale about the "iggly plop" who climbed up the "bimplestonk" to the kingdom of Groil high in the clouds, Jumbeelia, an eight-year-old giantess, climbs down a beanstalk and collects three children, whom she plays with as tiny toys. Play turns dangerous at the hands of Jumbeelia's brother, and the three human siblings must band together to plan their escape and their successful return home. Groilish-English dictionaries are included to help with the translation of the language spoken by the giants of Groil. *Author won the Smarties Book Prize for her book* The Gruffalo. nrz

Author lives in Scotland; the illustrator lives in the United States.

GIANTS, BROTHERS AND SISTERS, FANTASY FICTION

Donaldson, Julia. **Running on the Cracks**. New York, Henry Holt, 2009. Originally published by Egmont Great Britain, in 2009. ISBN 978-0-8050-9054-3, 0-8050-9054-1. 218 p. (12 up). Novel.

In her first young adult novel, Julia Donaldson (winner of the Smarties Prize for *The Gruffalo*) paints a vivid picture of life on the lam. Leo's fear, uncertainty, hunger, and exhaustion are palpable and compounded by her innocence. She is running away from an abusive uncle, cousins who taunt her, and the loneliness of losing everyone she's ever cherished. She's running toward a new country, a new identity, and a family she never knew existed. However, since the newspaper headlines announced "Orchestra Orphan Missing" (along with her photo), reward seekers—and her uncle—have been closing in. Everyone wants her—except the grandfather she's never met. *2010 USBBY Outstanding International Books List.* lmp

Author lives in Glasgow, Scotland.

RUNAWAY TEENAGERS, ORPHANS, SEXUAL ABUSE, CHINESE, RACIALLY MIXED PEOPLE, GLASGOW, SCOTLAND, FICTION

Yolen, Jane & Robert J. Harris. **The Rogues**. New York, Penguin/Philomel Books, 2007. ISBN 978-0-399-23898-7, 0-399-23898-0. 277 p. (12 up). Novel.

The Scottish Highlands were ruled for generations by trust, family bonds, love of the land, and the honor of the local laird. When death took the laird of Glendoun, Thomas McRoy, his half brother, inherited the lands. Looking to make a profit from poor soil, Thomas leased the land to the English for their sheep and forcefully evicted the tenant farmers. Roddy Macallan, young and romantically inclined, refuses to leave when his family's cottage burns. Instead, he joins forces with Alan Dunbar, dubbed "The Rogue," to stymie the laird and his minions. The Highland Clearances, which took place during the eighteenth century, remain one of the most dishonorable periods in

Scottish history. *The Rogues* is the fourth book in Yolen and Harris's *Stuart Quartet: Queen's Own Fool* (2000), *Girl in a Cage* (2002), and *Prince across the Water* (2004). lmp

Yolen lives in the United States and Scotland; Harris lives in Scotland.

ADVENTURE AND ADVENTURERS, SCOTLAND HISTORY 18TH CENTURY, HISTORICAL FICTION

OUTER HEBRIDES

Frost, Helen. **The Braid**. New York, Farrar, Straus and Giroux/Frances Foster Books, 2006. ISBN 978-0-374-30962-6, 0-374-30962-0. 95 p. (12 up). Novel in Verse.

"You / me / sisters / always" (7). In 1850, Sarah and Jeannie's family are evicted from their home in the Outer Hebrides and forced to emigrate to Canada. But Sarah decides to stay behind with their grandmother on Mingulay and makes a braid of Jeannie's hair and her own so that each will carry with them a symbol of their love. Similarly, Frost's masterfully written tale of the Highland Clearances braids together the sisters' stories of their different lives heard in alternating narrative poems interspersed with short "praise poems." The settings of Mingulay and Cape Breton together with historical details, relevant to each context, are beautifully rendered in this novel in verse. *2007 YALSA Best Books for Young Adults, The Lion and Unicorn Award for Excellence in North American Poetry, 2007 NCSS-CSC Notable Trade Book in the Field of Social Studies, 2007 Notable Book in Historical Fiction, 2007 Notable Children's Book in the Language Arts List.* hc

Author lives in the United States.

SISTERS, FAMILY, ISLANDS, EMIGRATION AND IMMIGRATION, MINGULAY (SCOTLAND), CAPE BRETON ISLAND (N.S.), SCOTLAND, CANADA, HISTORICAL FICTION 1841–1867

SLOVENIA

Prap, Lila. **Why?** Illustrated by the author. La Jolla, CA, Kane/Miller Books, 2005. Originally published as *Zakaj?* in Slovenian by Mladinska knjiga Zalozba

Slovenia, in 2003. ISBN 978-1-929132-80-8, 1-929132-80-8. 32 p. (5–8). Picture book.

Arranged in a question-and-answer format, *Why?* explores facts about animals with a humor that is spot-on for the early elementary crowd. Double spreads pose a question, such as "Why do kangaroos have pouches?" Surrounding the framed oil pastel drawings, Prap offers humorous (and serious) possibilities. The title page, however, informs readers that some answers may be silly, but the real, scientific answer is starred. The accurate response for the kangaroo, for example, explains that the pouches are where the joeys—baby kangaroos—stay safe and drink their mothers' milk. Prap's vibrant illustration and lively page layout make for a delightfully playful introduction to zoology. *Prap is a Hans Christian Andersen Medal nominee. lvb*
Author/illustrator lives in Slovenia.
ANIMALS, ZOOLOGY, NONFICTION

Prap, Lila. **Animals Speak**. Illustrated by the author. New York, NorthSouth Books, 2006. Originally published as *Animals' International Dictionary* in Slovenian by Mladinska Knjiga Zalozba Slovenia, in 2004. ISBN 978-0-7358-2058-6, 0-7358-2058-9. 32 p. (3–7). Picture book.

In this fascinating book, sounds are provided for fourteen different animals in forty-one languages so that one learns, for example, that in Estonian a pig says "RUIK" while in Swahili, it says "ROK" (n.p.). Each double spread presents a colorful, stylized representation of an animal accompanied by the English word for its sound and how that sound is written in four other languages. Sounds are identified in columns of forty-one national flags and animal noises, each headed by one of fourteen animal pictures. These columns introduce and conclude the book, since they appear on the endpapers. *Lila Prap was a 2006 nominee for the Hans Christian Andersen Illustrator Award and the 2007 Astrid Lindgren Award nominee. hc*
Lila Prap (pseudonym for Lilijana Praprotnik Zupancic) is from Slovenia.
ANIMAL SOUNDS, NONFICTION BOOK

Prap, Lila. **Once Upon . . . 1001 Stories**. Illustrated by the author. La Jolla, CA, Kane/Miller Books, 2006. Originally published as *Tisoc in Ena Pravljica* in Slovenian by Mladinska knjiga Zalozba Slovenia, in 2005. ISBN 978-1-929132-92-8, 1-929132-92-1. 32 p. (5–10). Picture book.

Fairy tales may never be the same! Prap has created a choose-your-adventure collection of familiar tales that become absurdly unfamiliar as the reader decides which story option on each page sounds like the path she would like the story to take. An adventure through once-upon-a-time can twist and turn in ways that comically weave together a frog prince, three bears, a wicked

witch, a big bad wolf, and a myriad of other fairy tale favorites. Readers will be actively engaged in co-constructing the story from the very first page to the happily-ever-after. *Prap is a Hans Christian Andersen Medal nominee. lvb Author/illustrator lives in Slovenia.*
TRADITIONAL LITERATURE, FAIRY TALES, FANTASY

Prap, Lila. **Animal Lullabies**. Illustrated by the author. New York, North-South Books, 2006. Originally published as *Živalske Uspavanke* in Slovenian by Mladinska Knjiga Slovenia, in 2000. ISBN 978-0-7358-2097-5, 0-7358-2097-X. 30 p. (3–5). Picture book.

All of the fourteen animals presented have their own distinct lullaby. Most of the lullabies describe animals preparing to bed down, although the owls are preparing for a time of fun. Elephant has broken his bed by jumping on it. The baby mice nibble the moon until it is out of sight. These short, soothing poems are perfect read-alouds that will lull little ones to sleep. *Lila Prap was Slovenia's nominee for the 2006 Hans Christian Andersen Award for illustration and was a 2007 Astrid Lindgren Award nominee. pwc Author, whose actual name is Lilijana Praprotnik Zupancic, lives in Slovenia.*
LULLABIES, ANIMALS, STORIES IN RHYME, SLOVENIA, POETRY

Prap, Lila. **Daddies**. Illustrated by the author. New York, NorthSouth Books, 2007. Originally published as *Mojacka* in Slovenian by Mladinska Knjiga Slovenia, in 2007. ISBN 978-0-7358-2140-8, 0-7358-2140-2. 32 p. (3–5). Picture book.

Not yet ready for bed, a young boy tries to extend his playtime by suggesting that he and his dad pretend to be animals. Father and son become a dozen different animals, eventually pretending to be bears snuggling up for a winter's snooze. *Lila Prap was Slovenia's 2006 Hans Christian Andersen Award Nominee. pwc Author, whose actual name is Lilijana Praprotnik Zupancic, lives in Slovenia.*
FATHERS AND SONS, ANIMALS, BEDTIME, SLOVENIA, STORIES IN RHYME

RELATED INFORMATION

IBBY Slovenia

Shortly after the formation of the independent state of Slovenia, the Slovene section of IBBY was established in 1992. Many of the founding members were involved in the former National Section of Yugoslavia.

www.ibby.org/index.php?id=453

www.ibby.si/ (Slovenian only)

SPAIN

Carranza, Maite. Translated by Noël Baca Castex. **War of the Witches**. New York, Bloomsbury, 2008. Originally published as *La Guerra de las Brujas: El Clan de la Loba* in Spanish by Edebé Spain, in 2005. ISBN 978-1-59990-102-2, 1-59990-102-1. 341 p. (14 up). Novel.

Anaíd wakes up one morning to find that her mother has vanished. Soon relatives begin to arrive. Among much secrecy, Anaíd learns that her mother is a very powerful witch, one who was prophesied to end the war between the Omar and Odish witch clans. She also learns that many of her mother's past actions were simply to protect Anaíd from the witches. As Anaíd journeys to find her mother, she discovers that she also possesses great powers. *Author has received the Edebé Children's Literature Prize. pwc*

Author lives in Spain.

WITCHES, COMING OF AGE, MISSING PERSONS, SPAIN, FICTION

Lindo, Elvira. Translated by Joanne Moriarty. **Manolito Four-Eyes**. Illustrated by Emilio Urberuaga. Tarrytown, NY, Marshall Cavendish, 2008. Originally published as *Manolito Gafotas* in Spanish by Grupo Santillana de Ediciones Spain, in 1994. ISBN 978-0-7614-5303-1, 0-7614-5303-2. 144 p. (9–11). Novel.

Manolito likes his nickname, Four-Eyes, as only the cool kids have nicknames. He lives in a blue-collar suburb of Madrid with his parents, his grandfather, and his younger brother, "the Bozo" (7). His entertaining misadventures often involve his eccentric grandfather, whom Manolito describes as a "whole lotta cool" (7). Urberuaga's illustrations are a perfect match for these amusing tales. Two sequels are available: *Manolito Four-Eyes: The Second Volume of the Great Encyclopedia of My Life* and *Manolito Four-Eyes: The Third Volume of the Great Encyclopedia of My Life*. *Author has received Spain's National Children's Book Award. pwc*

Author lives in Spain.

FAMILY LIFE, GRANDFATHERS, SCHOOLS, SPAIN, FICTION

O'Callaghan, Elena. Translated from the Catalan. **What's Going On?** Illustrated by África Fanlo. La Jolla, CA, Kane/Miller Books, 2008. Originally published as *S'han Tornat Bojos!* in Catalan by la Galera SAU Editorial Spain, in 2006. ISBN 978-1-933605-65-4. 32 p. (5–8). Picture book.

A little boy notices that something strange is happening at home. Dad accidentally brushed his teeth with hair gel. Mom mistook bug spray for her hairspray. And, horror of horrors, bedtime stories are now short! What's going on? Double-page before-and-after spreads show how life at home used to be (neat and quiet) and how it is now (messy and chaotic). The only one who isn't acting strangely is the new little baby sister. The book focuses not on sibling rivalry but on a cozy look into how one family's life changed after a welcome new addition to the family. *pwc, lvb*

Author and illustrator live in Spain.

FAMILY, SIBLINGS, NEW BABY, FICTION

Prats, Joan de Déu. Translated by Roser Ruiz. **Sebastian's Roller Skates**. Illustrated by Francesc Rovira. La Jolla, CA, Kane/Miller Books, 2005. Originally published as *Patins del Sebastià* in Spanish by Hospital Sant Joan de Déu Spain (*Los patines de Sebastián* in Catalan by Círculo de Lectores in La Galera), in 2003. ISBN 978-1-929132-81-2, 1-929132-81-6. 32 p. (5–8). Picture book.

Sebastian is painfully shy: he doesn't talk to his neighbors, he doesn't talk in school, he doesn't even tell the barber that he hates it when his haircut ends up looking like a billiard ball. All this begins to change when Sebastian serendipitously finds a pair of old roller skates left in the park. Slowly, cautiously, he teaches himself to skate, and the newfound confidence gives him the courage to start talking to everyone who has been patiently waiting to hear what he has to say. In fact, he even befriends the shy girl in his class and offers to teach her to skate, too. *2006 USBBY-CBC Outstanding International Books List. lvb*

Author lives in Catalonia, Spain.

ROLLER SKATING, BASHFULNESS, FICTION

Rodríguez, Rachel. **Building on Nature: The Life of Antoni Gaudí**. Illustrated by Julie Paschkis. New York, Henry Holt, 2009. ISBN 978-0-8050-8745-1, 0-8050-8745-1. 32 p. (6–8). Nonfiction.

Antoni Gaudí was born in mid-nineteenth-century Spain. He spent a sickly childhood observing his father and mother at their forge. As he grew, he recognized a connection between nature and architecture—a vision he infused into each project he undertook. From pomegranate-inspired endpapers to rooms wrapped by forest- and olive-green tendrils, Paschkis's illustrations complement Rodríguez's text and enflame readers' imaginations. The gouache portrayals present Gaudí's architecture; "they sparkle and glitter and whisper with joy" (n.p.). This colorful and lyrical biography concludes with a detailed author's note, websites, and selected bibliography. *IRA Children's Book Award, CCBC Choice. lmp*

Author's family is from Spain, but she lives in the United States. The illustrator lives in the United States.

Antoni Gaudí (1852–1926), Architects, Spain, Picture Book, Biography

RELATED INFORMATION

Organizations

Amigo del Libro Infantil y Juvenil (Friends of Children's and Youth Books)
This Association was established in 1981 to support the goals advocated by IBBY.

www.amigosdelibro.com/web/principal2.htm

IBBY Spain
The Spanish section of IBBY is known as OEPLI (Spanish Organization for Children and Young People's Literature) and began in 1982. Some of its major projects are the International Children's Book Fair and the coordination of the Prize Lazarillo to the best unpublished literary or illustrated works for children and young people.

www.oepli.org/pag/cas/lazarillo.php

IBBY Spain was the host of the 2010 IBBY World Congress in Santiago de Compostela, "The Strength of Minorities," www.ibbycompostela2010.org/. It was also the sponsor of 2010 International Children's Book Day.

www.ibby.org/index.php?id=1005
www.ibby.org/index.php?id=455
www.oepli.org/

There are four branches of OEPLI (Spanish Organization for Children and Young People's Literature), the Spanish National Section of IBBY:

Basque Branch of Spanish IBBY: www.galtzagorri.org/
Castilian Branch of Spanish IBBY: www.oepli.org
Catalán Branch of Spanish IBBY: www.clijcat.cat/
Galician Branch of Spanish IBBY: www.galix.org/

Awards

EDEBÉ Award for Children's and Young Adult Literature
In 2010, the EDEBÉ Award attracted a total of 260 original entries, 157 in the young adult and 103 in the children's categories. Of these works, 57

are in Catalan, 180 in Spanish, 8 in Euskera, and 15 in Galician. The entries must be written in one of the official Spanish languages but are not limited to Spain; numerous works have been submitted from the United States and Latin America. In addition to a large cash prize, the two winning works are published in the four official languages of the Spanish State by Grupo Edebé: Catalan, Spanish, Euskera, and Galician, and in Braille. The novels will be in bookstores as of the month of March.

www.edebe.com/foreign_rights/edebe_awards.asp

Prize Lazarillo

This is the oldest literary prize in Spain for children's literature. There are two awards presented each year: writing and illustration. The categories—children's books and young adult books—alternate years.

www.oepli.org/pag/cas/lazarillo.php

Collections

Centro Internacional del Libro Infantil y Juvenil (International Centre for Children's and Young Adult's Books)

Founded in 1985, the CILJ took an innovative approach toward libraries for children's books, analytical tools for literature and illustration, and projects for engaging families and children with literacy. It has become a model especially for the Spanish-speaking countries.

www.fundaciongsr.es/centros
www.fundaciongsr.es/wfuns/

Book Fairs

Liber Feria Internacional del Libro (Barcelona)

www.ifema.es/web/ferias/liber/default.html

SWEDEN

Anderson, Lena. Translated by Joan Sandin. **Hedgehog, Pig, and the Sweet Little Friend.** Illustrated by the author. New York, R&S Books, 2007. Originally published as *Kotten, Grisen och Lilla Vännen* in Swedish by Rabén & Sjögren Sweden, in 2006. ISBN 978-91-29-66742-4, 91-29-66742-9. 26 p. (3–6). Picture book.

As Hedgehog and her friend Pig enjoy some soup and a chat, a lost, teary-eyed piglet appears at the door. The next day Pig reunites the piglet, Fia, with her mother, a baker. Pig is rewarded with one hundred sweet rolls but, more importantly, he has discovered that Fia is the sweet he loves best. The softly colored, detailed illustrations are lovely to look at. Each character has a distinct personality, and their emotions are expressed clearly. The English translation is smooth considering it is written in rhyme; the story reads aloud well. *ca*

The author/illustrator lives in Sweden.

HEDGEHOGS, PIGS, LOST CHILDREN, SWEDEN

Bergström, Gunilla. Translated by Elisabeth Kallick Dyssegaard. **Very Tricky, Alfie Atkins.** Illustrated by the author. New York, Farrar, Straus and Giroux/R&S Books, 2005. Originally published as *Aja Baja Alfons Åberg* in Swedish by Rabén & Sjögren Sweden, in 1972. ISBN 978-91-29-66152-1, 91-29-66152-8. 27 p. (4–7). Picture book.

While Daddy is distracted with his newspaper, Alfie takes advantage and asks permission to use Daddy's toolbox. However, Daddy has one firm rule: "You may not use the saw" (10). Alfie builds a helicopter that "flies" him over the jungle. When Alfie lands, he yells for Daddy to help him escape from a dangerous lion. He tells Daddy he's stuck and needs to use the saw to escape the lion. Instead of letting Alfie saw himself out, Daddy joins him on his adventure and together they "fly for a long, long time" (23). Both father and son enjoy time spent in imaginary play. *2006 Svenska Akademiens Schullströmska Award for Children's and Youth Literature. chs*

Author lives in Sweden.

TOOLS, FATHERS AND SONS, BUILDING, IMAGINATION, FICTION

Bergström, Gunilla. Translated by Elisabeth Kallick Dyssegaard. **Good Night, Alfie Atkins.** Illustrated by the author. New York, Farrar, Straus and Giroux/R&S Books, 2005. Originally published as *God natt, Alfons Åberg* in Swedish by Rabén & Sjören Sweden, in 1972. ISBN 978-91-29661-54-5, 9-12966-15-44. 26 p. (4–7). Picture book.

Four-year-old Alfie Atkins does not want to go to sleep. He gives his daddy many excuses to stay up later, such as reading a story, brushing his teeth, and wanting his teddy bear. Finally, it's exhausted Daddy who falls asleep on the living room floor. Alfie tucks a blanket around him and goes to sleep at last. Cartoon-style mixed-media illustrations create a homey setting. *2006 Svenska Akademiens Schullströmska Award for Children's and Youth Literature. chs*

Author lives in Sweden.
FATHERS AND SONS, BEDTIME, TRANSLATED WORKS, FICTION

Eriksson, Eva. Translated by Elisabeth Kallick Dyssegaard. **A Crash Course for Molly**. Illustrated by the author. New York, R&S Books, 2005. Originally published as *Malla cyklar* in Swedish by Rabén & Sjören Sweden, in 2005. ISBN 978-91-29-66156-9, 91-29-66156-0. 32 p. (4–7). Picture book.
In this companion book to *Molly Goes Shopping*, Molly (a pig) has learned to ride her bike. However, when she's on a bike ride with her grandma, she concentrates so hard on not hitting objects that she runs right into them. A friendly driving instructor gives her a lesson on looking straight down the road, not at objects she's trying to avoid. Full-color illustrations help convey the book's subtle humor. *2005 Notable Children's Book. Eriksson was a 2004 Hans Christian Andersen Award nominee. chs*
Author/illustrator lives in Sweden.
BICYCLES, GRANDPARENT AND CHILD, FANTASY FICTION

Kruusval, Catarina. Translated by Joan Sandin. **Franny's Friends**. Illustrated by the author. New York, Farrar, Straus and Giroux, 2008. Originally published as *Fia Och Djuren* in Swedish by Eriksson & Lindgren, in 2007. ISBN 978-91-29-66836-0, 91-29-66836-0. n.p. (4–8). Picture book.
Franny has a large circle of friends—all stuffed. Early one morning, Franny awakens, announcing to everyone, "We're going on an outing" (n.p.). Each of the seven animals is named, so as she dresses them, she calls them by name, a pattern that repeats on almost every page. Through her watercolor illustrations, executed in calming pastel hues, Kruusval imbues Franny and her critters with obvious personality. Anger, remorse, excitement, sadness, and finally joy play on even the tiniest faces as the picnickers face a parent's worst fear: missing children. All is well as the happy party marches home—bandages and all. *pwc, lmp*
Author lives in Sweden.
PICNICKING, LOST CHILDREN, MISSING CHILDREN, SWEDEN

Kruusval, Catarina. Translated by Joan Sandin. **Ellen's Apple Tree**. Illustrated by the author. New York, Farrar, Straus and Giroux, 2008. Originally published as *Ellens Äppelträd* in Swedish by Rabén & Sjögren Sweden, in 2006. ISBN 978-91-29-66905-3, 91-29-66905-7. n.p. (4–8). Picture book.
Ellen lives in a small house with a yard all around it. Together with her friend Ollie, Ellen enjoys her playhouse and sandbox and a rock dubbed

Ellen's small mountain. But Ellen and Ollie's favorite place is the apple tree in the middle of the yard. From the moment readers open this book, they will be intrigued by Kruusval's detailed watercolor illustrations of life in Ellen's community, how the apple tree changes with the seasons, and the process of planting a new tree "just like the old tree" (n.p.). The children's impatience and curiosity will feel familiar to most readers. *2009 USBBY Outstanding International Books List. lmp*

Author lives in Sweden.

TREES, PLAY, FICTION, SWEDEN

Landström, Lena. Translated by Joan Sandin. **Four Hens and a Rooster.** Illustrated by Olof Landström. New York, Farrar, Straus and Giroux, 2005. Originally published as *Fyra Honor Och en Tupp* in Swedish by Rabén & Sjögren Sweden, in 2004. ISBN 978-91-29-66336-5, 91-29-66336-9. 28 p. (7–11). Picture book.

Roosters are known for being pushy and aggressive, and the small rooster in this story is no exception. He bullies the hens until he has more space and more food than the others. The hens find that a kind request for change is totally ineffective, so they begin a self-help program to improve their self-esteem and assert their rights. This feminist barnyard story will be useful in schools where bullying is a problem. Some subtle yet plucky humor will be noted primarily by older children and adults. *Washington Post Best Book of the Year. nrz*

Author lives in Sweden and is one of Sweden's best-known children's book authors.

HENS, ROOSTERS, SELF-ESTEEM, BULLIES, FAIRNESS, SWEDEN, FANTASY FICTION

Landström, Lena. Translated by Joan Sandin. **Boo and Baa Have Company.** Illustrated by Olof Landström. New York, R&S Books, 2006. Orginally published as *Bu och Bä får besök* in Swedish by Rabén & Sjögren Sweden, in 2006. ISBN 978-9129665468, 9129665469. n.p. (3–6). Picture book.

Sheep Boo and Baa are raking leaves when they discover a cat in the branches of a tree. Unable to coax the cat out of the tree using a board to the window of their room, Boo tries a ladder rescue only to become stranded in the same tree. While Boo waits to be rescued, the cat navigates the board and is now safe in the house. When Boo is rescued, the cat returns to the tree. All ends well as the final illustration reveals Boo and Baa asleep in their beds with the cat tucked under the rug in their room. This is the seventh book about Boo and Baa. *pwc*

Author and illustrator live in Sweden.
SHEEP, CATS, HUMOROUS STORIES, SWEDEN, FANTASY

Lindenbaum, Pija. Translated by Elisabeth Kallick Dyssegaard. **When Owen's Mom Breathed Fire**. Illustrated by the author. New York, R&S Books, 2006. Originally published as *När Åkes mamma glömde bort* in Swedish by Rabén & Sjögren Sweden, in 2005. ISBN 978-91-29-66548-2, 91-29-66548-5. 24 p. (4–8). Picture book.

One morning Owen discovers that his much-harried mother has turned into a dragon. Dragon Mom licks the dishes clean, eats beetles, and loves to breathe fire. The doctor cannot find a remedy for Mom, so they visit Grandma. Grandma calmly tells Owen, "It'll probably wear off in a few days" (n.p.). The next morning Owen's mom is back in her human form—the only difference is she is a much more relaxed mom. *pwc*

Author, who was named 1993 Illustrator of the Year at the Children's Book Fair in Bologna, lives in Sweden.
CHILDREN'S DREAMS, DRAGONS, FANTASY FICTION, SWEDEN

Lindenbaum, Pija. Translated by Elisabeth Kallick Dyssegaard. **Mini Mia and Her Darling Uncle**. Illustrated by the author. New York, R&S Books, 2007. Originally published as *Lill-Zlatan och Morbror Raring* in Swedish by Rabén & Sjögren Sweden, in 2006. ISBN 978-91-29-66734-9, 91-29-66734-8. 40 p. (4–8). Picture book.

Mini Mia adores her Uncle Tommy, who knows how to keep her happy. He dyes her hair different colors, jumps on both feet, and enjoys the opera and people watching. When Tommy's boyfriend, Fergus, enters the picture, Mia does not want to share their special relationship. Mia reacts by pouring sugar on Fergus's sneakers and soaking the toilet paper. Then she learns they both have a passion for playing soccer. The last page shows the two men arm-in-arm with a smiling, spunky Mia between them. Comic illustrations, complete with wild patterns and retro furniture, enhance the lighthearted text. *mjw*

Author lives in Sweden.
FAMILY, UNCLES, FICTION, JEALOUSY, GAY/LESBIAN IDENTITY, FICTION

Lindgren, Barbro. Translated by Elisabeth Kallick Dyssegaard. **Oink, Oink, Benny**. Illustrated by Olof Landström. New York, Farrar, Straus and Giroux/R&S Books, 2008. Originally published as *Nöff nöff Benny* in Swedish by Rabén & Sjögren Sweden, in 2007. ISBN 978-91-29-66855-1, 91-29-66855-7. n.p. (0–5). Picture book.

Benny and his pacifier-sucking, comfort-object-toting baby brother are bored. Mom's final words as they run out in the sunshine—"Stay away from the mudhole"—quickly dissipate when they spot their best friend, Klara. Everyone enjoys a game of chase until "mean old Rafe" pushes Benny's little brother into the water. Klara rescues and cuddles him on her lap, so jealous Benny "accidentally" falls in, too. It is not until they are walking home that they realize how angry Mom will be. Olof Landström's humorous watercolor illustrations contribute additional meaning to this tale of two dirty pigs. *pwc, lmp*

Author lives in Sweden.

BROTHERS, PLAY, OBEDIENCE, PIGS (SWINE), FANTASY, SWEDEN

Mankell, Henning. Translated by Laurie Thompson. **A Bridge to the Stars**. New York, Random House/Delacorte Press, 2007. Originally published as *Hunden Som Sprang Mot en Stjärna* in Swedish by Rabén & Sjögren, in 1990. ISBN 978-0-385-73495-0, 0-385-73495-6. 164 p. (10 up). Novel.

He woke with a start, scraped ice from the wintry window, and saw the dog—fearful and sniffing the air—then running as if for a distant star. Bullied and virtually friendless, Joel Gustafson escapes into his imagination by searching nightly for that dog in his insubstantial, northern Swedish village. He creates a secret society and invites Ture, new to town, to join. Their midnight reconnaissance forays take a cruel turn when Ture usurps power from Joel. Readers viscerally comprehend the constant loneliness and isolation that eleven-year-old Joel experiences. The translator uses strong language as emphasis in one angry scene. *lmp*

Author lives in Sweden and Mozambique.

FATHERS AND SONS, SINGLE-PARENT FAMILIES, SELF-ACTUALIZATION, SECRET SOCIETIES, HISTORICAL FICTION, SWEDEN

Mankell, Henning. Translated by Laurie Thompson. **Shadows in the Twilight**. New York, Random House/Delacorte Press, 2008. Originally published as *Skuggorna vaxer i skymningen* in Swedish by Rabén & Sjögren Sweden, in 1991. ISBN 978-0-385-73496-7, 0-385-73496-4. 199 p. (12 up). Novel.

In this companion book to *A Bridge to the Stars*, twelve-year-old Joel is run over by a bus. Somehow he survives without a scratch. People repeatedly call it a miracle, and so Joel decides it must be. He feels that he has to repay the miracle by performing a good deed, so Joel chooses to play matchmaker to a woman who is disfigured. When his good deed does not turn out as planned, Joel puts together a scheme to repair hurt feelings. Mankell's companion

novels about Joel and his father are *A Bridge to the Stars*, *When the Snow Fell*, and *Journey to the End of the World*. pwc
Author lives in Sweden and Africa. He writes for adults and children.
TRAFFIC ACCIDENTS, MIRACLES, FATHERS AND SONS, SINGLE-PARENT FAMILIES, SECRET SOCIETIES, SWEDEN — 20TH CENTURY, FICTION

Näslund, Görel Kristina. Translated by Laaren Brown. **Our Apple Tree.** Illustrated by Kristina Digman. New Milford, CT, Roaring Brook Press, 2005. Originally published as *Lilla Appelboken* in Swedish by Rabén & Sjögren Sweden, in 2002. ISBN 978-1-59643-052-5, 1-59643-052-4. 26 p. (3–6). Nonfiction book.

A pair of tiny elfin narrators, who live in an apple tree, explain the life cycle of the apple tree, mention some apple art projects, talk about some of the ways apples are served, hold an apple party for their friends in the fall, and declare that "Everyone likes apples" (n.p.). Everyone even includes a personified worm shown in a cutaway section of an apple. A recipe for Apple Crisp is included. Digman's intricately detailed paintings show seasonal changes and make this simple introduction to apples just right for young children. *2006 USBBY-CBC Outstanding International Books List. ca*
Author and illustrator live in Sweden.
APPLES, LIFE CYCLES FOR CHILDREN, NONFICTION BOOK

Nilsson, Per. Translated by Tara Chace. **You & You & You.** Asheville, NC, Front Street, 2005. Originally published as *Du & Du & Du* in Swedish by Rabén & Sjögren Sweden, in 1998. ISBN 978-1-932425-19-2, 1-932425-19-5. 301 p. (14 up). Novel.

Three protagonists. Three interwoven stories, interspersed with magical realism. Three variations on a motif. Anon mentally and emotionally isolates himself from the taunts of his classmates. He knows the purse he has found will lead him to the perfect soulmate. Nils believes his life will be transformed when he understands the meaning of death. Zarah recognizes she is gorgeous and her boyfriend is enticing, even if abusive. In the end, each of the protagonists recognizes reality—not in the clouds or in the grave or in an idealized pretend world—and finds unfamiliar but lovely new friendships. There is explicit sex in this book that is intended for older readers. *2006 USBBY-CBC Outstanding International Books List. lmp*
Author lives in Sölvesborg, Sweden.
FRIENDSHIP, FAMILY LIFE, SCHOOLS, LOVE, SWEDEN, FICTION

Thor, Annika. Translated by Linda Schenck. **A Faraway Island**. New York, Random House/Delacorte Press, 2009. Originally published as *En ö I Havet* in Swedish by Bonnier Carlsen Sweden, in 1996. ISBN 978-0-385-73617-6, 0-385-73617-7. 247 p. (8–12). Novel.

In 1939, two young sisters disembark from a train in a strange land. They have arrived in Sweden and are about to meet their new "families." Stephie and Nellie are among a trainload of Jewish children who have been spirited out of Austria to the relative safety of Sweden. The transition is difficult—new language, food, customs, religion—especially with no friends and an all-consuming concern for their parents' safety. *A Faraway Island*, the recipient of the 2010 Batchelder Award for translation, is the first of four books about the Steiner sisters and their life in Sweden during World War II. *2010 US-BBY Outstanding International Books List, 2010 Mildred L. Batchelder Award, 2010 Sydney Taylor Honor Award. lmp*

Author lives in Sweden.

WORLD WAR II (1939–1945), REFUGEES, SISTERS, JEWS, SWEDEN, FICTION

Wahl, Mats. Translated by Katarina E. Tucker. **The Invisible**. New York, Farrar, Straus and Giroux, 2007. Originally published as *Den Osynlige* in Swedish by Brombergs Sweden, in 2000. ISBN 978-0-374-33609-7, 0-374-33609-1. 186 p. (12 up). Novel.

In the middle of a windy spring in northern Sweden, "so-normal" fifteen-year-old Hilmer suffers a horrific act of brutality, presumably motivated by the anti-immigrant sentiments and neo-Nazi sympathies of a few of his classmates. One of them, in fact, believes that by burying "the problem," it disappears. While Detective Fors investigates the case, Hilmer remains determined to defy invisibility in the wake of his own burial. *2008 USBBY Outstanding International Books List, NYPL Books for the Teen Age. bef*

Author lives in Sweden.

GHOSTS, MURDER, CRIMINAL INVESTIGATION, SWEDEN, FANTASY, FICTION

RELATED INFORMATION

Organizations

IBBY Sweden

The Swedish section of IBBY, established in 1956, was called Internationella Ungdomsboksrådet, IUR (International Youth Book Council). The

Swedish Comics Committee, established in 1953 under the auspices of the Women's International League for Peace and Freedom, had a similar goal of promoting good literature for children and young people. The Comics Committee and IUR joined together in 1967 under the name of Children and Youth Book Council, today IBBY Sweden.

www.ibby.org/index.php?id=456

www.ibby.se

Awards

The Gulliver Prize

The Gulliver Prize, established in 1969, is awarded annually by IBBY Sweden. It is presented to a person "who by work of critical, theoretical or practical character has significantly contributed to advanc[ing] understanding of child and youth literature."

http://ibby.se/priser/tidigare-gulliver-pristagare/

Peter Pan Award

The Peter Pan Award is a literary prize that is awarded annually to a translated children's or young adult book. The prize was established in 2000 by IBBY Sweden and Book Fair. http://sv.wikipedia.org/wiki/Peter_Pan-priset

Svenska Akademiens Schullströmska Award for Children's and Youth Literature

The Schullströmska Prize is a literary prize awarded biennially since 2002 to a prominent writer of children's or young adult books. The prize is awarded by the Swedish Academy.

http://sv.wikipedia.org/wiki/Svenska_Akademien

SWITZERLAND

Damjan, Mischa. **The Clown Said No!** Illustrated by Gian Casty. New York, Penguin/Minedition, 2007. Originally published as *Der Clown Sagte Nein* in German by Nord-Süd Verlag Switzerland, in 1962. ISBN 978-0-698-40063-4, 0-698-40063-1. 32 p. (4–8). Picture book.

The author was the cofounder of the Swiss publisher Nord-Süd Verlag in 1962, and this was the very first book published by the company. It is the story of a clown, a donkey, and four other rebelling circus performers who are tired of doing their tricks. They create their own circus for children and poets and find true happiness. The dazzling illustrations are reminiscent of glass painting. *mjw*

Author, whose real name was Dimitrÿe Sidjanski-Hanhart, is deceased.

CIRCUS, CLOWNS, ANIMALS, INDIVIDUALITY, FICTION

Hächler, Bruno. Translated by Friederike Rave. **Anna's Wish**. Illustrated by the author. New York, NorthSouth Books, 2008. Originally published as *Anna's Wunsch* in German by Nord-Süd Verlag Switzerland, in 2008. ISBN 978-0-7358-2207-8, 0-7358-2207-7. 28 p. (3–6). Picture book.

A subtle theme of climate change runs through this story of a town that hasn't seen snow in a generation. Rave's illustrations realistically capture scenes of everyday life in Anna's European neighborhood as people walk their dogs, do their errands, and prepare for the winter holidays. Anna unearths the old sled in the basement and imagines what it would be like to ride it. As if in answer to her wish, snow magically begins to fall. *ss*

Author lives in Switzerland.

CLIMATE CHANGE, SNOW, FICTION

RELATED INFORMATION

Organizations

French-Swiss Branch of IBBY (Lausanne)
Jeunesse et Médias Arole
www.jm-arole.ch/

IBBY Switzerland
The Swiss national section of IBBY is composed of several different organizations and branches. Since 2002, it includes the Swiss Institute for Child and Youth Media (SIKJM) and Jeunesse et Médias Arole. Their main goal is to promote literature for children and young people.
www.ibby.org/index.php?id=457

Swiss Section of IBBY (Zurich)

Schweizerisches Institut für Kinder-und Jugendmedien (SIKJM)

www.sikjm.ch

Awards

Prix Suisse Jeunesse et Médias

The winners of the Award Enfantaisie are selected by children who choose from a predetermined selection of books. It recognizes children's books in the following categories: picture books for seven- to ten-year-olds and novels for eleven- to thirteen-year-olds.

www.isjm.ch/isjm.html

Book Fairs

Salon international du livre et de la presse de Genève (Die Internationale Genfer Messe für Buch und Presse) (International Fair for Books and Press)

The Geneva Book Fair has been in existence since 1987. It is the largest event of its kind in Switzerland. It is generally held at the end of April.

www.salondulivre.ch/en/

Collections

The Swiss Institute for Child and Youth Media

The Swiss Institute for Child and Youth Media has a library containing some fifty thousand items. These include the picture book collections of Elisabeth Waldmann and Bettina Hürlimann and the Johanna Spyri Archive as well as primary and secondary literature going back as far as 1750.

www.sikjm.ch/

Publications

Jugendliteratur. Zeitschrift des Schweizerischen Bundes für Jugendliteratur

Swiss quarterly published by the Swiss Children's Literature Institute. It contains short articles on Swiss and international children's literature, media, and reading.

TRANSYLVANIA

Marillier, Juliet. **Wildwood Dancing**. New York, Random House/Alfred A. Knopf, 2007. Originally published by Pan Macmillan Australia, in 2006. ISBN 978-0-375-83364-9, 0-375-83364-1. 407 p. (12 up). Novel.

High on a forested mountain in Transylvania, practical sixteen-year-old Jenica and her four sisters live with their merchant father in the mouldering castle of Piscul Dracului. For nine years on each full moon, Jenica and her sisters have stolen away through a portal they discovered in their bedchamber to dance through the night in the Other Kingdom, a place of magical creatures and faerie folk. But when Jenica's older sister falls in love on a moonlit night with a silent man who may be one of the Night People, a drinker of blood, the sisters' idyll is threatened. Steeped in folktales of dancing princesses and enchanted frogs, the story nonetheless evokes a solid sense of place through the author's attention to Romanian foods, traditions, and even a pronunciation guide for names and terms. A sequel, *Cybele's Secret* (2008), follows the fourth sister. *2008 USBBY Outstanding International Books List, 2006 Winner of the Aurealis Award for Best Fantasy Novel, 2009 Winner of the Beehive Book Award (Utah), 2007 Bank Street College of Education Best Children's Books of the Year, 2007 YALSA Best Book for Young Adults. nlr*
    Author is a native New Zealander who lives in Australia.
    Sisters, Magic, Enchantment, Romance, Fantasy Fiction

UKRAINE

Philip, Neil. **The Pirate Princess and Other Fairy Tales**. Illustrated by Mark Weber. New York, Scholastic/Arthur A. Levine Books, 2005. ISBN 978-0-590-10855-3, 0-590-10855-7. 96 p. (10 up). Short Stories.
    See Poland for description.

Sedgwick, Marcus. **My Swordhand Is Singing**. New York, Random House/ Wendy Lamb Books, 2006. Originally published by Orion Children's Books Great Britain, in 2006. ISBN 978-0-375-84689-2, 0-375-84689-1. 205 p. (14 up). Novel.

Shunned by villagers wherever they have lived, Tomas and Peter seem to have found grudging acceptance in the small Eastern European settlement of Chust. Another woodcutter has been found dead in the forest, which generates more call for Peter's sled of logs. But, as St. Andrew's Eve draws nearer, more bodies are found and Chust folks bar their shutters, fearing the return of the Shadow Queen. Sedgwick thoroughly documents the vampire tradition of seventeenth-century eastern Europe, where this story is set. Steeped in fantasy and interwoven with Romani—Gypsy—folklore, *My Swordhand Is Singing* will captivate fans of gothic historical fiction. *2007 Booktrust Teenage Prize. lmp*

The author lives in Great Britain.

SUPERNATURAL, MURDER, FATHERS AND SONS, VAMPIRES, ROMANIES, VILLAGES, SUPERSTITION, EASTERN EUROPE, HISTORY SEVENTEENTH-CENTURY, FANTASY FICTION [Note: Chust is a city with a long history that has existed under the flags of many nations. Today, it is part of Ukraine, but Chust has also been ruled by Hungary, Russia, Transylvania, and Romania.]

RELATED INFORMATION

Organizations

Ukrainian Section of IBBY

The Ukranian IBBY website is translated into English and is enjoyable to browse. There is an author/illustrator feature and information about one of the two sponsor organizations, the Central Library for Children in Dnepropetrovsk. The Children's Reading Association (CRA) is the second IBBY Ukraine sponsor.

www.ibby.org/index.php?id=461

www.childlib.dp.ua (translated website: www.childlib.dp.ua/ibby_eng.php)

WALES

Dyer, Heather. **The Girl with the Broken Wing**. Illustrated by Peter Bailey. New York, Scholastic/Chicken House, 2005. Originally published by Chicken House Great Britain, in 2005. ISBN 978-0-439-74827-8, 0-439-74827-5. 147 p. (9–12). Novel.

In this witty Welsh novel, a girl crashes onto a skylight and startles twins James and Amanda out of bed. This girl, whose name is Hilary and who just happens to have wings, has decided to stay for an unspecified period of time with the siblings' family. Many humorous moments ensue as this "guardian angel" experiences daily life at school and on family outings. *2006 USBBY-CBC Outstanding International Books List, one of Richard and Judy's "Best Children's Books Ever" in 2007, Ottakar's Book of the Month, October.*

Author was born in Scotland, spent most of her childhood in Wales, and also has lived in Canada in a cabin by a lake.

ANGELS, TWINS, BEDTIME, FICTION

Nimmo, Jenny. **The Snow Spider**. New York, Scholastic/Orchard Books, 2006. Originally published by Methuen Children's Books Great Britain, in 1986. ISBN 978-0-439-84675-2, 0-439-84675-7. 146 p. (8–12). Novel.

Imagine discovering you were a magician! Gwyn makes such a discovery on his ninth birthday after his grandmother Nain gives him five peculiar gifts that, when thrown into the wind, return to him as magnificent creations from another world. The first gift, a metal brooch, returns to him as a snowflake that changes into a spider. Nain says the spider will give Gwyn his heart's desire. Knowing he wants nothing more than to see his sister, Bethan, who disappeared five years before, he learns to battle good and evil in his quest to repair his fractured family. *1986 Smarties Prize. dld*

Author lives in Wales.

MAGIC, FATHERS AND SONS, WALES, FICTION

UNSPECIFIED EUROPEAN SETTING

RELATED INFORMATION

Additional IBBY National Sections

IBBY Albania
  Activities

- 1993–present: A literary, artistic, and informative magazine, *Sirena e vogël* (*Little Mermaid*) for children eight to twelve years old. The magazine reaches children all over Albania.
- 1997–1998: *Sirena e vogël*, a full-color artistic literary magazine for children four to eight years old.

- 1997–1998: *Bota ime* (*My World*), an informative, sociocultural magazine for teenagers.
- 1999: Two anthologies of Balkan literature with selected tales and short stories from IBBY sections in the region.

www.ibby.org/index.php?id=403

Children's Cultural Centre in Tirana

www.soschildrensvillages.org.uk/sponsor-a-child/europe/albania/child
-sponsorship-background-from-tirana-albania

IBBY Croatia

IBBY Croatia is a nonprofit organization supported by the Zagreb city government and the Croatian Ministry of Culture. It is part of the Zagreb city network of twenty-five public libraries.

www.ibby.org/index.php?id=413
www.kgz.hr

IBBY Cyprus

www.ibby.org/index.php?id=415
www.cybby.org

IBBY Estonia

The Estonian section of IBBY was first founded in 1993 and reestablished in 2003.

www.ibby.org/index.php?id=419
www.eltk.ee

Awards

Tallinn Illustrations Triennial Exhibit and Contest

"The Power of Pictures," a contest and exhibition for children's book illustrators from the Baltic Sea region (Estonia, Latvia, Lithuania, Germany, Russia, Poland, Finland, Norway, and Denmark).

Tower of Babel Honor Diploma

The Estonian section of IBBY administers the annual Tower of Babel Honor Diploma, which is given to a foreign author for an outstanding children's book published in a foreign language and translated into Estonian.

www.ibby.org/index.php?id=531

Collections

National Library of Estonia
www.nlib.ee/en

The Finnish Institute for Children's Literature
The Finnish Institute for Children's Literature (SNI), established in 1978, is a documentation, information, and research center. The institute's three full-time experts provide information to teachers, university students, and members of the general public. The institute serves as a connecting link for organizations, researchers, and individuals active in the field.
www.tampere.fi/kirjasto/sni/sneinfo.htm

IBBY Finland
The Finnish section of IBBY was founded in 1957 and went under the name Suomen nuortenkirjaneuvosto (The Finnish Board of Children's Books) until 2003, when its name was changed to IBBY Finland.
www.ibbyfinland.fi/

Awards

Nordic Council's Literature Prize
It is unclear if children's books are eligible for this award.
www.norden.org/en/nordic-council/the-nordic-council-prizes/literature
-prize

The Finlandia Prize
The Finlandia Prize, the most prestigious literary award in Finland, is awarded annually to the author of the best Finnish novel, children's book, and nonfiction book. www.booksfromfinland.fi/tags/finlandia-prize/

IBBY Latvia
The Latvian section of IBBY is implementing the White Wolf Books project in association with the Children's Literature Centre of the National Library of Latvia, Writers' Union of Latvia, a number of regional libraries, institutions of higher education, museums, theatres, and major Latvian media outlets.
www.ibby.org/index.php?id=436

Awards

Jānis Baltvilks Prize
Since 2005, the Jānis Baltvilks Prize has been awarded as an international sign of appreciation awarded to children's writers from the Baltic Sea countries. For more information, go to the IBBY website at www.ibby.org/index .php?id=436.

IBBY Lithuania
www.ibby.org/index.php?id=438

IBBY Moldova
The Moldovian section of IBBY was founded in 1996 at the Ion Creanga National Children's Library. The membership includes about sixty collective members: libraries, publishing houses, professional associations of writers and illustrators, and educational organizations.
www.ibby.org/index.php?id=441

Awards

The jury of the International Children's Book Fair in Chisinau awards the following prizes: Best Children's Book of the Year, Book—Sympathy of Children, Best Science Book for Children, Best Collection for Children, Best Graphic Presentation of a Book, Best Translation of Books for Children and other prizes.
www.ibby.org/index.php?id=441

Book Fairs

Children's Book Fair in Chisinau
This fair has been in existence since 1997.
www.ibby.org/index.php?id=441

IBBY Slovakia
The membership of the Slovak IBBY section includes those interested in artistic and cultural activities intended for children and young people, their development, and promotion. Its members are mostly writers, illustrators, teachers, librarians, and workers of other types of cultural institutions.
www.ibby.org/index.php?id=452
www.bibiana.sk

Awards

Ludmila Podjavorinska Plaque
This is a prize awarded for distinguished service promoting Slovak children's literature abroad.

L'udovít Fulla Award

The Most Beautiful and Best Children's Books of Spring, Summer, Autumn, and Winter in Slovakia
This is a competition to assess the most successful illustration and literary production for children and young people published in Slovakia during the previous year.

The Triple Rose Award (Trojruza)
These are the two most prestigious tokens of appreciation that can be awarded to authors of stories and illustrations for children and young people in Slovakia.

Book Fairs

Belgrade's International Book Fair
This is the site of the well-known exhibition of BIB award-winning illustrators.

www.bibiana.sk/index.php?id=51&L=2&no_cache=1&tx_ttnews[tt_news]=138&tx_ttnews[backPid]=1

Collections

The Bibiana Library
IBBY Slovakia's Secretariat is housed at the headquarters for Bibiana, International House of Art for Children, in Bratislava. In the Bibiana Library, the IBBY Slovakia has archived the IBBY Honour List, making this international collection available for study purposes.

The Bibiana website is partially in English, which allows access to the extensive information about the library's digital collections of award-winning illustrations. There is also a photo gallery, the Biennial of Animation (BAB), and an opportunity to view Golden Apple award winners through the Biennial of Illustration.

www.bibiana.sk

Professional Resources

***Bibiana*—Revue of Arts for Children and Young People (the official publication of SKBBY)**

Bibiana is the only magazine in Slovakia to regularly revue and evaluate the artistic and literary production for children and young people (literature, fine arts, radio, television, film, theatre production, etc.). The revue includes articles, studies, papers, essays, book reviews, polemics, and interviews with the most prominent authors in the field.

CHAPTER TEN

Global and Multinational Books

Malay Children

Adams, Simon. **The Kingfisher Atlas of the Medieval World**. Illustrated by Kevin W. Maddison. Boston, Kingfisher, 2007. Originally published by Kingfisher Great Britain, in 2006. ISBN 978-07534-5946-1, 0-75345946-9. 44 p. (4–8). Nonfiction.

This attractive, large-format atlas begins with a world map on which there are picture symbols relating to a "medieval civilization, kingdom, culture, or race of people" covered in subsequent pages (pp. 4–5). The following maps covering the different continents and civilizations are colorful, detail important events for each geographic place of importance, and include time lines. Interspersed are pages of text replete with illustrations. Examples of topics are "The Arab World: Islamic Culture," "Medieval India," "Medieval Europe: Castles and Villages," "African Kingdoms," and "Central America: The Aztecs." An index is provided. *chs*

Author lives in Great Britain.

MEDIEVAL CIVILIZATION, MIDDLE AGES

Amnesty International. **We Are All Born Free: The Universal Declaration of Human Rights in Pictures**. London, Frances Lincoln Children's Books, 2008. Originally published by Frances Lincoln Children's Books Great Britain, in 2008. ISBN 978-1-84507-650-4, 1-84507-650-8. 64 p. (8–12). Nonfiction.

The Universal Declaration of Human Rights, signed on December 10, 1948, in Paris, declares the rights of all people. In *We Are All Born Free*, published to coincide with the sixtieth anniversary of the Declaration, each of the thirty articles of the Declaration has been simplified for young readers and is illustrated by an internationally renowned artist. The back matter includes a simplified version of the Declaration by Amnesty International; a "Now meet the artist!" section that identifies the illustrator of each article and provides brief biographical information and a photograph; and brief notes on the work of Amnesty International. *2009 USBBY Outstanding International Books List. ca*

Illustrators live in different countries around the globe.

HUMAN RIGHTS, NONFICTION

Bednar, Sylvie. Translated by Gita Daneshjoo. **Flags of the World**. Illustrated by the author. New York, Abrams Books for Young Readers, 2009. Originally published as *Les Drapeaux du Monde Expliqués aux Enfants* in French by Éditions de la Martinière France, in 2008. ISBN 978-0-8109-8010-5, 0-8109-8010-X. 187 p. (8–12). Nonfiction.

A flag does more than identify a country; it represents the history and cultural beliefs of the citizens of that country. *Flags of the World* features the flags of all the countries of the world (organized into five groups: Europe, the Americas, Oceania, Africa, and Asia), explains the colors and symbols of the flags, and provides basic facts (continent, capital, currency, official language, area, and highest point) and brief notes of interest about each of the countries. Each country's flag is featured in full color, and there is a

world map on the endpapers. Includes an index. *2010 USBBY Outstanding International Books List. ca*
  Author lives in France.
  FLAGS, NONFICTION

Chin-Lee, Cynthia. **Akira to Zoltán: Twenty-Six Men Who Changed the World**. Illustrated by Megan Halsey & Sean Addy. Watertown, MA, Charlesbridge, 2006. ISBN 978-1-57091-579-6, 1-57091-579-2. 32 p. (8 up). Picture book.
  Celebrated in this picture book for older grades are men from different countries and backgrounds who, in their various fields, have changed the world through peaceful means. A full page is devoted to providing basic information on how each man has made a contribution for change and has helped others, whether, for example, through filmmaking (Akira Kurowasa), sports (Greg Louganis, Pelé), arts (Langston Hughes, Rudolph Nureyev), sciences (Ivan Pavlov, Jacques-Yves Cousteau), or social and political activism (Badshah Khan, Cesar Chavez). An accompanying illustration in "mixed media" represents each man embedded in a design that symbolizes his work. A companion book, *Amelia to Zora: Twenty-Six Women Who Changed the World* (Charlesbridge, 2005), also received the Notable Social Studies Trade Books for Young People. A bibliography is included. *2006 Notable Social Studies Trade Books for Young People. hc*
  Author lives in the United States.
  HEROES, MEN, BIOGRAPHY

Cole, Heidi & Nancy Vogl. **Am I a Color Too?** Illustrated by Gerald Purnell. Bellevue, WA, Illumination Arts, 2005. ISBN 978-0-9740190-5-5, 0-9740190-5-4. n.p. (4–9). Picture book.
  Authors Heidi Cole and Nancy Vogl's narrator, young Tyler, ponders the question "Am I a Color Too?" as he looks at the world and sees more than color. He wonders where he fits in the whole scheme of things with a mother that people call "white" and a father that people call "black." In the end, he answers his own question with great clarity and innocence. The beautiful, thought-provoking illustrations are a perfect complement to the text. *Benjamin Franklin Award for Best Multicultural Book, the Christopher Award for Best Book for Young People, and the Wanda Gág Award for Outstanding Read-Aloud Book. ak*
  The authors and illustrator live in the United States.
  SKIN COLOR, RACIALLY MIXED PEOPLE, FICTION

Crebbin, June (Ed.). **Horse Tales**. Illustrated by Inga Moore. Cambridge, MA, Candlewick Press, 2005. Originally published by Walker Books Great Britain, in 2005. ISBN 978-0-7636-2657-0, 0-7636-2657-0. 148 p. (8–14). Short Stories.

A lovely anthology of fourteen stories arranged into categories: "Difficult Horses," "Dream Horses," "From the Horse's Mouth," "Horses in Danger," and "Horses to the Rescue." Included are short excerpts from classics, *Black Beauty* and *Misty of Chincoteague* and other books, such as Michael Morpurgo's *War Horse*, Peter Dickinson's *Merlin Dreams*, and K. M. Peyton's story of a pit pony, *Pony in the Dark*. Other selections include retold stories from folktale and romance sources plus an American Indian story, "Mud Pony." New short stories include "Bucephalus" and Crebbin's "The Gift Horse." A glorious full-page watercolor illustration accompanies each story. hc

Compiler is from England.

HORSES, CHILDREN'S STORIES, AMERICAN, ENGLISH, SHORT STORIES

D'Harcourt, Claire. **Masterpieces Up Close: Western Painting from the 14th to 20th Centuries**. San Francisco, CA, Chronicle Books, 2006. Originally published as *Chefs d'Oeuvre à la Loupe* in French by Éditions du Seuil France, in 2004. ISBN 978-0-8118-5403-0, 0-8118-5403-5. 63 p. (9–14). Nonfiction Illustrated book.

D'Harcourt invites young viewers to explore masterworks by stating, "the fame of many art masterpieces has worn them out" (front matter). Readers encounter works of art by one groundbreaking artist arranged chronologically on each spread. These are surrounded by five to ten thumbnail closeups; a description of the technique, innovation, detail, or symbolism; and questions about perspective, time, or interpretation for readers to consider. D'Harcourt also provides narrative synopses of the paintings to further highlight subject and contextual information. Concise artist biographies are on lift-the-flap picture maps at the back of the book. Oversized trim proportions and high-resolution reproductions allow for close scrutiny. *2007 USBBY Outstanding International Books List. bef*

Author lives in France.

PAINTING THEMES AND MOTIVES, PAINTING APPRECIATION, NONFICTION

Filipović, Zlata & Melanie Challenger (Eds.). **Stolen Voices: Young People's War Diaries, from World War I to Iraq**. New York, Penguin Group, 2006. ISBN 978-0-14-303871-9, 0-14-303871-0. 293 p. (plus 23 pages of front matter). (12 up). Nonfiction, Autobiography, Anthology.

These fourteen diary entries, some published for the first time, trace what it has been like growing up in the middle of war. Diarists are from across the globe, including Russia, Germany, Sinapore, Palestine, and Israel, among others. Readers view the brutality, horrors, and injustice of war through the eyes of innocent young people, most of whom did not survive. In the words of editor Melanie Challenger: "These diaries are the fingerprints of flesh, the traces of those hands that dared to hold a pen in wartime" (xxiii). *chs*

Zlata Filipović grew up in Sarajevo and now lives in Ireland. Melanie Challenger divides her time between Penzance, Cornwall, and New York.

CHILDREN AND WAR, YOUTH DIARIES, WAR DIARIES, NONFICTION, AUTOBIOGRAPHY

Freedman, Russell. **Who Was First? Discovering the Americas**. New York, Clarion Books, 2007. ISBN 978-0-618-66391-0, 0-618-66391-6. 88 p. (10 up). Nonfiction.

Freedman probes the accounts of the past and inaugurates recent archeological findings that reveal the astounding history of the Americas that began approximately fifty thousand years before the arrival of Columbus. Evidence is presented that reveals the advanced culture of ancient civilizations whose dwellings included wooden framed houses with kitchen saunas and apartment buildings. Botanical gardens, zoos, European-influenced spearheads, and African features carved into sculptures all contribute to the rich and exciting history of the Americas. *dgw*

Author lives in the United States.

EXPLORERS–AMERICA, AMERICA–DISCOVERY AND EXPLORATION, PRE-COLUMBIAN, BIOGRAPHY

Gifford, Clive. **The Kingfisher Soccer Encyclopedia**. Boston, Kingfisher, 2006. ISBN 978-0-7534-5928-7, 0-7534-5928-0. 144 p. (8 up). Illustrated book.

This attractive and comprehensive guide to the worldwide game of soccer includes information about key players, key teams and clubs, and competitions. Other topics include: soccer skills and tactics, what it is like to be a soccer player, and some of the problems that accompany a sport that is "big business" (102). The text is amply illustrated with color photographs and computer imagery. A reference section is included with facts and figures about U.S. soccer. *hc*

Author is from England.

SOCCER, ENCYCLOPEDIAS

The Global Fund for Children. **Global Babies**. Illustrated by photographs. Watertown, MA, Charlesbridge, 2007. ISBN 978-1-58089-174-5, 1-58089-174-8. 16 p. (0–4). Board book.

This sixteen-page board book is colorful, sturdy, and full of bright-eyed, inquisitive infants. Each photograph is distinctive and keyed to that page's concept: "Wherever they live" —countries are labeled. "Wherever they go" features a baby from Mali on her mother's back. From Afghanistan to South Africa, from Bhutan to Rwanda, *Global Babies* radiate love. *lmp*

The Global Fund donates part of this book's sales to support innovative community-based organizations that serve the world's most vulnerable children and youth.

INFANTS, CROSS-CULTURAL STUDIES, BOARD BOOKS

Greenberg, Jan (Ed.). **Side by Side: New Poems Inspired by Art from around the World**. New York, Harry N. Abrams Books, 2008. ISBN 978-0-8109-9471-3, 0-8109-9471-2. 88 p. (12 up). Poetry.

This global poetry anthology explores the connections between a work of art and a poet's response to it. Samplings from world art history inspire poems from thirty-three countries, in languages such as Spanish, Turkish, Vietnamese, Russian, Navajo, and more. An English translation accompanies the original language of each poem. A world map and biographies of the poets, artists, and translators as well as notes about each artist's medium are included. *mjw*

Editor lives in the United States.

CHILDREN'S POETRY, ART, TRANSLATIONS INTO ENGLISH

Greenfield, Eloise. **When the Horses Ride By: Children in the Times of War**. Illustrated by Jan Spivey Gilchrist. New York, Lee & Low Books, 2006. ISBN 978-1-58430-249-0, 1-58430-249-6. n.p. (7–11). Poetry.

Dedicated to the courageous children of the world, Greenfield's poems of children's puzzlements about conflict across time and around the world are illustrated with stunning collage. For the opening, "I Think I Know," a poem about how wars begin, Gilchrist juxtaposes faces of innocent children with insets of battlements, warriors, and fighter jets. Each spread matches the geography and history of the subject—whether line drawings of Chinese workers or textured paintings of Egyptian warriors. In the poignant "Wherever We Are," children speak of simple needs: "Wherever we are, / we search for a place / to be unafraid. / Wherever we are" (n.p.). *IRA Notable Books for a Global Society, CCBC Choices. nlr*

Author and illustrator live in the United States.

CHILDREN AND WAR, AMERICAN CHILDREN'S POETRY, POETRY

Kerley, Barbara. **You and Me Together: Moms, Dads, and Kids around the World**. Illustrated by photographs from around the world. Washington, DC, National Geographic, 2005. ISBN 978-0-7922-8297-6, 0-7922-8297-3. n.p. (6–10). Nonfiction.

You and Me Together is all about images: children and parents eating and cooking, dancing and praying. It celebrates everyday pursuits from Australia to Suriname to Iceland that demonstrate simple acts of parental love. Barbara Kerley's lyrical text offers rhythmic and comforting images—a perfect bedtime read-aloud. A world map, on which each picture's location is pinpointed and identified, introduces the back matter. The same double-page spread features a thumbnail of each photo, photographic credits, location, and a detailed explanation of the pictured activity. "A Note on the World's Children" by Marian Wright Edelman provides an inspirational conclusion. *ALA Notable Book. lmp*

Author lives in the United States.

PARENT AND CHILD, WORLD, NONFICTION, CONCEPT BOOKS

Kerley, Barbara. **A Little Peace**. Illustrated by photographs from around the world. Washington, DC, National Geographic, 2007. ISBN 978-1-4263-0086-8, 1-4263-0086-7. n.p. (6–10). Nonfiction.

"All it takes is / One hand / One smile / A single voice . . ." (n.p.). Adults and children share equally in this summons to create "a little peace" (n.p.). The book's message, that peace is possible through cooperation and understanding, appears only through the photos, which subtly draw attention to our shared commonalities and prevent the book from becoming didactic. Back matter includes a world map that pinpoints all locations. Thumbnails of photos, credits, locations, and a detailed explanation of each pictured activity help identify how citizens of the world come together to create peace. *Notable Social Studies Trade Book for Young People, Chicago Public Library Best of the Best. lmp*

Author lives in the United States.

PEACE, WORLD, NONFICTION, CONCEPT BOOKS

Kerley, Barbara. **One World, One Day**. Illustrated by photographs from around the world. Washington, DC, National Geographic, 2009. ISBN 978-1-4263-0460-6, 1-4263-0460-9. 56 p. (6–10). Nonfiction.

As with the previous three books in this series, the author's crisp, poetic text is immeasurably extended by stunning photographs of children partaking in routine activities. Homework, chores, meals, games, and family rituals appear in various cultural depictions. Kerley ends with an explanation of the "spirit behind these books" (42)—her time in Nepal as a Peace Corps volunteer. Thumbnails of each photo, photographic credits, location, and a detailed explanation of the pictured activity introduce the back matter. Additionally, there is a world map, on which each picture's location is pinpointed and identified. *lmp*

Author lives in the United States.

CHILDREN, SOCIAL LIFE AND CUSTOMS, WORLD, NONFICTION, CONCEPT BOOKS

Kyuchukov, Hristo & Ian F. Hancock. **A History of the Romani People**. Honesdale, PA, Boyds Mills Press, 2005. ISBN 978-1-56397-962-0, 1-56397-962-4. 32 p. (7–12). Picture book.

The two authors, both of Romani heritage, collaborated on this book to provide a brief historical overview of the Romani people (often called Gypsies by outsiders). They trace the origins of Romanies from India around AD 900–1100 to the present day. Each two-page spread features a different subtopic, including names and language, traditions and religion, courtship and marriage, family and children, transportation, occupations, traditional law, and hardships. Photographs with captions, including photos of the authors' families, enrich the basic text. A map depicts the locations of Romani populations around the world, and an index and list of photo credits are provided. *bal*

Kyuchukov is a leading figure in the advancement of human rights for Romani children. He works at the Institute for Educational Policy in Budapest, Hungary. He has also taught in Bulgaria. Ian Hancock is director of the Romani Archives and Documentation Center at the University of Texas at Austin. He was Ambassador for the Romani people to the United Nations, and in 1998 was appointed by President Clinton as the sole Romani member of the U.S. Holocaust Memorial Council.

ROMANI HISTORY, ROMANI SOCIAL LIFE AND CUSTOMS, PHOTO-ESSAY, NONFICTION

Park, Linda Sue & Julia Durango. **Yum! Yuck! A Foldout Book of People Sounds**. Illustrated by Sue Ramá. Watertown, MA, Charlesbridge, 2005. ISBN 978-1-57091-659-5, 1-57091-659-4. n.p. (4–8). Picture book.

In this multilingual guessing game, the authors present "people sounds" from languages around the world. For example, on one double-page spread, readers learn how to say "Yikes" in Yoruba, Spanish, Polish, and Japanese. The facial expressions of the children in the illustrations help readers guess the English word even before opening the accompanying foldout, which presents the English version. As a bonus, observant readers discover a story told through the foldouts: a little dog creates turmoil and excitement as it travels along a street—evoking a wide variety of people sounds in a host of different locations. *ALA Notable Book.* mm

Author and illustrator live in the United States.

Grammar, Interjections, Exclamations, Languages, Nonfiction Books, Toy and Movable Books

Prelutsky, Jack. **Me I Am!** Illustrated by Christine Davenier. New York, Farrar, Straus and Giroux/Melanie Kroupa, 2007. ISBN 978-0-374-34902-8, 0-374-34902-9. 32 p. (4–8). Picture book.

Colorful and lively illustrations punctuate the simple, positive lines of this picture book poem celebrating individuality. The focus is on each individual's uniqueness. The full text of the poem is on the final page. nlh

Author lives in the United States, and the illustrator lives in France.

Children's Poetry, Self-concept, Individuality

Reynolds, Jan. **Celebrate! Connections among Cultures.** Illustrated by the author's photographs. New York, Lee & Low Books, 2006. ISBN 978-1-58430-253-7, 1-58430-253-4. 32 p. (6–12). Nonfiction.

An informative photo essay that highlights the celebrations of various world cultures, including those of the Inuit, Balinese, Yanomani, Taureg, Sami, Aborigines, Tibetans, and Sherpas. Traditional music, food, dance, dress, and facial decorations for each of the cultures are compared with customs in the United States. Photographs highlight the many similarities that connect cultures around the world. Resources at the end include a map pinpointing the geographic region for each group as well as additional sources for further research. *Best of the Best Books–Chicago Public Library, 2007 Bank Street College Children's Book of the Year (Outstanding Merit). All seven books in the author's* Vanishing Cultures *series have been recognized as Notable Social Studies Trade Books for Young People.* nlh

The author lives in the United States.

Holidays, Festivals, Fasts and Feasts, Nonfiction

Ruurs, Margriet. **My Librarian Is a Camel: How Books Are Brought to Children around the World.** Honesdale, PA, Boyds Mills Press, 2005. ISBN 978-1-59078-093-0, 1-59078-093-0. 30 p. (8 up). Picture book.

In rural Zimbabwe, a new "donkey-driven electro-communications cart" brings "solar-powered TV and VCR" to children (30–31), while in Kenya camels deliver books to people in the desert. In this fascinating book, Ruurs documents ways in which librarians reach out to children in specific communities in thirteen countries focusing, especially, on the use of mobile libraries, whether these are buses, boats, or elephants. Color photographs and a box with a map, flag, and geographic information accompany the main text for each country, which includes details about specific programs that extend library services beyond traditional library walls. *1996 International Reading Association Notable Book for a Global Society. hc*

Author lives in Canada.

TRAVELING LIBRARIES, LIBRARIANS, NONFICTION BOOKS

Strauss, Rochelle. **One Well: The Story of Water on Earth**. Illustrated by Rosemary Woods. Toronto, Kids Can Press, 2007. ISBN 978-1-55337-954-6, 1-55337-954-3. 32 p. (8 up). Nonfiction.

Humanity shares one global well, the earth's water. This visually stunning nonfiction book points out that the amount of water on Earth has not changed, but the population has dramatically increased. Beautifully illustrated spreads provide facts about our water sources, plants, animals, access and demand for water, pollution and recycling, and conservation. A pictograph detailing access to the global well is particularly compelling, with its comparison of average daily water use per person: fifty-five buckets in North America compared to one bucket in Ethiopia. Endnotes focus readers on the water crisis and offer ways to become involved. *2008 CBC Notable Social Studies Trade Books for Young People, Society of School Librarians International Book Award. nlh*

Author lives in Canada, illustrator lives in England.

WATER, USE, CONSERVATION, NONFICTION

Thong, Roseanne. **Wish: Wishing Traditions around the World**. Illustrated by Elisa Kleven. San Francisco, CA, Chronicle Books, 2008. ISBN 978-0-8118-5716-1, 0-8118-5716-6. 36 p. (4–8). Picture book.

Perfectly articulated in verse for young audiences but expanded in prose for older readers and adults, *Wish* transports children to other lands in a whirlwind of excitement. Will blowing dandelion fluff or throwing combs and flowers into the sea make wishes come true? Kleven's collage and painted illustrations promise excitement and celebration and a feast of details to pore over. Maps and lucky symbols hidden throughout will intrigue all age groups. Included are traditions from fifteen nations, including Iran, Brazil, Guatemala, Japan, Mexico, Russia, and Thailand. Based on the author's research. *lmp*

Author lived in Hong Kong for many years, but now she and illustrator live at opposite ends of California.
WISHES, PICTURE BOOK, INFORMATIONAL TEXT

Williams, Marcia. **Hooray for Inventors!** Illustrated by the author. Cambridge, MA, Candlewick Press, 2005. Originally published as *Three Cheers for Inventors!* by Walker Books Great Britain, in 2005. ISBN 978-0-7636-2760-7, 0-7636-2760-7. 36 p. (8 up). Picture book.

In comic-strip format, Williams introduces facts about selected inventors from different times and different parts of the world, beginning with Johannes Gutenberg and the invention of moveable type and ending with a potpourri of her favorite inventors who invented such items as the paper clip and the baby stroller. The amount of information varies from two pages of facts for major inventors such as James Watt, George Stephenson, and Thomas Edison to clips of information about inventors of "Useful Things" (18) and women inventors. There is, in addition, a nice double-page spread devoted to the Wrights' "flying invention" (26–27). *hc*
Author is from England.
INVENTORS–WORLD, BIOGRAPHY

RELATED INFORMATION

Online Resources

International Children's Digital Library
http://en.childrenslibrary.org/
The ICDL is a public library for the world, and the collection reflects diverse cultures, perspectives, and historical periods. The mission of the ICDL is to select, collect, digitize, and organize children's materials in their original languages and to create appropriate technologies for access and use by children three to thirteen years old. The creators of the site caution "some materials may not be appropriate for sensitive readers." Books are organized by age groups three to six, six to nine, and ten to thirteen and are categorized by genre and length. Books in twenty-seven languages are digitized. The International Children's Digital Library is a project of the University of Maryland.

International Children's Literature
http://reading.indiana.edu/ieo/bibs/intlchlit.html

The materials listed here are intended to provide an introduction to children's literature portraying people and cultures from around the world. They were assembled from the World Wide Web, ERIC database, and a variety of other bibliographic resources. Be advised: many of the links are not current. The database of articles can be valuable.

International Research Society for Children's Literature

www.irscl.com/

The foundations of the IRSCL were laid at the Frankfurt Colloquium of 1969, which was organized by the members of the Institut fur Jugendbuchforschung of the Goethe University in Frankfurt, Germany. Members of the Frankfurt Institute proposed that an international organization support and promote research in the field of literature for children and young people.

Words without Borders: The Online Magazine of International Literature

www.wordswithoutborders.org

Words without Borders undertakes to promote international communication through translation of the world's best writing—selected and translated by a distinguished group of writers, translators, and publishing professionals—and publishing and promoting these works (or excerpts) on the web. *Words without Borders* also serves as an advocacy organization for literature in translation, producing events that feature the work of foreign writers and connecting these writers to universities and to print and broadcast media. The first issue devoted to Children's Literature was in November/December 2004. Look for another piece in the January issue. The back issues will be kept in perpetuity. Readers may search the site under the category "children's literature."

Print Resources

Bookbird: A Journal of International Children's Literature (ISSN 0006 7377)

This refereed journal is published quarterly by IBBY. It covers many facets of international children's literature and includes news from IBBY and IBBY national sections. The editors, Sylvia Vardell and Catherine Kurkjian, work in cooperation with an international Editorial Review Board, guest reviewers, and correspondents who are nominated by IBBY national sections. The editorial office is supported by Central Connecticut State University in New Britain, Connecticut, in the United States. *Bookbird*'s goal is to communicate new ideas to the whole community of readers interested in children's books.

Bookbird includes news of IBBY projects and events that are highlighted in the Focus IBBY column. Other regular features include coverage of children's literature studies and children's literature awards around the world. *Bookbird* also pays special attention to reading promotion projects worldwide.

Recently, there has been an effort to translate *Bookbird* articles by IBBY national sections into their local languages, which are then posted online. *Bookbird* also presents a special biennial Hans Christian Andersen issue that celebrates the two winners and all of the other authors and illustrators who were nominated for the Hans Christian Andersen Awards.

The White Ravens: An annual selection of international children's and youth literature by the Internationale Jugendbibliothek in Munich. Additional print materials are also available from the International Youth Library.

For more information, contact Internationale Jugendbibliothek, Schloss Blutenburg, D - 81247 München, telefon: ++49 | 89 | 89 12 11- 0, fax: ++49 | 89 | 811 75 53, e-mail: info@ijb.de, and the website www.ijb.de.

IBBY publications are available at www.ibby.org/index.php?id=publications &no_cache=1

- IBBY-Asahi Reading Promotion Award
- IBBY Documentation Centre of Books for Disabled Young People (catalogs available for 2009, 2007, 2005, 2002)
- IBBY Honour List
- International Children's Book Day
- Stories from across the Globe
- Hans Christian Andersen Awards 1956–2002
- Jubilee Congress Proceedings: A Worldwide Challenge: 50 Years of IBBY
- From Basel: To Those Who Bring Books and Children Together

Books

A Bridge of Children's Books
Jella Lepman's inspiring autobiography. Originally published as *Die Kinderbuchbrücke* in 1964. Available from IBBY or USBBY (www.usbby.org).

Peace Story
Written and illustrated by international children's authors and illustrators commissioned for the Nambook-10, the Nami Island Children's Book Festival, Korea. ISBN: 978-89-91591-46-2 (77800). For ordering information, please

contact Lee Kye-young, Nami Books Korea, 2nd Floor, Gallery Sang Building, 157 Insa-dong, Johgno-gu, Seoul 110-290 Republic of Korea, phone: +82-2-318-6262; fax: +82-2-318-6263; e-mail: wnpub@chol.com.

Under the Spell of the Moon

In honor of IBBY, and to support its future work, many of the world's greatest illustrators for children—both famous and relatively unknown—have donated a work of art based on a text of their choice drawn from their childhood and culture. The result is a book that celebrates art created for children from around the world. IBBY will receive 15 percent of every book sold. Published by Groundwood Books, Toronto. English and original language, hardback, full color, ISBN: 0-88899-559-8. Available from www.amazon.com.

Additional Books: Professional Resources

Alabado, Ceres S. C. Multimedia Multicultural Children's Literature in the Philippines: A Historical Perspective. Quezon City, Philippines: New Day Publishers, 2001.

Bologna Annual 2009. Bologna, Italy/New York: Bologna Children's Book Fair/Penguin/Minedition, 2009.

Bologna Annual 2008. Bologna, Italy/New York: Bologna Children's Book Fair/Penguin/Minedition, 2008.

Bologna Annual 2006. Bologna, Italy/New York: Bologna Children's Book Fair/Penguin/Minedition, 2007.

Bologna Annual 2005. Bologna, Italy/New York: Bologna Children's Book Fair/Penguin/Minedition, 2005.

Botelho, Maria José, and Masha Kabakow Rudman. Critical Multicultural Analysis of Children's Literature: Mirrors, Windows, and Doors. Language, Culture, and Teaching. New York: Routledge, 2009.

Brett, Clive, and Lynne Randle. The Global Dimension: Multicultural Fiction for Children and Young People 3 to 16 Years. Glenfield, Leicestershire (England): Leicestershire County Council Library Services for Education Community Services, 2004.

Cai, Mingshui. Multicultural Literature for Children and Young Adults: Reflections on Critical Issues. Contributions to the Study of World Literature No. 116. Westport, CT: Greenwood Press, 2002.

Coghlan, Susanna, Mary Fitzpatrick, and Lucy O'Dea. Changing Faces—Changing Places: A Guide to Multicultural Books for Children. Dublin, Ireland: IBBY Ireland, 2001.

East, Kathy, and Rebecca L. Thomas. *Across Cultures: A Guide to Multicultural Literature for Children*. Children's and Young Adult Literature Reference Series. Westport, CT: Libraries Unlimited, 2007.

Fox, Dana L., and Kathy Gnagey Short. *Stories Matter: The Complexity of Cultural Authenticity in Children's Literature*. Urbana, IL: National Council of Teachers of English, 2003.

Freeman, Evelyn B., and Barbara A. Lehman. *Global Perspectives in Children's Literature*. Boston, MA: Allyn and Bacon, 2001.

Gates, Pamela S., and Dianne L. Hall Mark. *Cultural Journeys: Multicultural Literature for Elementary and Middle School Students*. Lanham, MD: Rowman & Littlefield, 2010.

Gilton, Donna L. *Multicultural and Ethnic Children's Literature in the United States*. Lanham, MD: Scarecrow Press, 2007.

Gopalakrishnan, Ambika. *Multicultural Children's Literature: A Critical Issues Approach*. Thousand Oaks, CA: Sage Publications, 2011.

Kohl, Herbert R. *Should We Burn Babar? Essays on Children's Literature and the Power of Stories*. New York: New Press, 2007.

Kuharets, Olga R., and Ethnic and Multicultural Information Exchange Round Table. *Venture into Cultures: A Resource Book of Multicultural Materials and Programs*. 2nd ed. Chicago: American Library Association, 2001.

Lathey, Gillian. *The Translation of Children's Literature: A Reader*. Topics in Translation. Clevedon, England: Multilingual Matters, 2006.

Lathey, Gillian. *The Role of Translators in Children's Literature: Invisible Storytellers*. Children's Literature and Culture. New York: Routledge, 2010.

Lehman, Barbara A., Evelyn B. Freeman, and Patricia L. Scharer. *Reading Globally, K–8: Connecting Students to the World through Literature*. Thousand Oaks, CA: Corwin, 2010.

Morris, Liz, and Susanna Coghlan. *Cross-Currents: A Guide to Multicultural Books for Young People*. Dublin, Ireland: IBBY Ireland, 2005.

Norton, Donna E. *Multicultural Children's Literature: Through the Eyes of Many Children*. 3rd ed. Boston: Allyn & Bacon/Pearson, 2009.

Mpesha, Nyambura. *African Children's Literature: A Bibliography*. Bloomington, IN: Author House, 2007.

Peterson, Shelly, David Booth, and Carol Jupiter. *Books, Media, & the Internet: Children's Literature for Today's Classroom*. Winnipeg, Canada: Portage & Main Press, 2009.

Pinsent, Pat. *No Child Is an Island: The Case for Children's Literature in Translation*. NCRCL Papers. Lichfield, England: Pied Piper, 2006.

Robles de Melendez, Wilma J., and Verna Beck. *Teaching Young Children in Multicultural Classrooms: Issues, Concepts, and Strategies*. 2nd ed. Clifton Park, NY: Thomson Delmar Learning, 2007.

Smolen, Lynn Atkinson, and Ruth A. Oswald. *Multicultural Literature and Response: Affirming Diverse Voices*. Santa Barbara, CA: Libraries Unlimited, 2011.

Steiner, Stanley F. *Promoting a Global Community through Multicultural Children's Literature*. Englewood, CO: Libraries Unlimited, 2001.

Taylor, Gail Singleton, KaaVonia Hinton, and Lisa Moore. *Teaching Multicultural Literature to Help Children Understand Ethnic Diversity: Essays and Experiences*. Lewiston, NY: Edwin Mellen Press, 2008.

Valdez, Alora J. *Learning in Living Color: Using Literature to Incorporate Multicultural Education into the Secondary Curriculum*. Boston: Allyn & Bacon, 2009.

van Coillie, Jan, and Walter Verschueren. *Children's Literature in Translation: Challenges and Strategies*. Manchester, UK/Kinderhook, NY: St. Jerome Publishing, 2006.

York, Sherry. *Ethnic Book Awards: A Directory of Multicultural Literature for Young Readers*. Worthington, OH: Linworth Publishing, 2005.

PART III

RESOURCES

CHAPTER ELEVEN

Children's Book Awards with an International Focus

INTERNATIONAL AWARDS

Astrid Lindgren Memorial Award

The Astrid Lindgren Memorial Award (ALMA) was established by the Swedish government in 2002 upon the death of Sweden's most honored children's book author. The annual prize of SEK 5 million (equivalent to approximately $777,000 or €566,500) may be awarded to authors, illustrators, storytellers, and individuals or organizations active in reading promotion whose work reflects the spirit of Astrid Lindgren. The aim of the award is to increase interest in children's and young people's literature, to indicate that reading by children and young adults is extremely important, and to inspire those involved in this field. It is administered by the Swedish Arts Council.

Website: www.alma.se, and for a list of winners, see www.alma.se/en/Award-winners/Links/.

Award Winners
2011   Shaun Tan
2010   Kitty Crowther (Illustrator, Belgium)
2009   Tamer Institute (The Tamer Institute for Community Education in Ramallah is an independent organization that carries out reading promotion work for children and young people in the West Bank and Gaza.)
2008   Sonya Hartnett (Author, Australia)

2007   Banco del Libro (Nonprofit institution headquartered in Caracas, Venezuela.)
2006   Katherine Paterson (Author, United States)
2005   Ryôji Arai (Illustrator, Japan)
2005   Philip Pullman (Author, Great Britain)
2004   Lygia Bojunga (Author, Brazil)
2003   Christine Nöstlinger (Author, Austria)
2003   Maurice Sendak (Illustrator, United States)

Hans Christian Andersen Award

This international award, frequently called the "Little Nobel Prize," is sponsored by the International Board on Books for Young People, is given biennially to a living author, and, since 1966, has been given to a living illustrator whose complete works have made a lasting contribution to children's literature.

Website: For the latest news about the Hans Christian Andersen Award, please go to www.ibby.org/index.php?id=273, and for a list of all winners, please go to www.ibby.org/index.php?id=308.

2010   Author: David Almond (UK)
        Illustrator: Jutta Bauer (Germany)
2008   Author: Jürg Schubiger (Switzerland)
        Illustrator: Roberto Innocenti (Italy)
2006   Author: Margaret Mahy (New Zealand)
        Illustrator: Wolf Erlbruch (Germany)
2004   Author: Martin Waddell (Ireland)
        Illustrator: Max Velthuijs (Netherlands)
2002   Author: Aiden Chambers (UK)
        Illustrator: Quentin Blake (UK)
2000   Author: Ana Maria Machado (Brazil)
        Illustrator: Anthony Browne (UK)
1998   Author: Katherine Paterson (USA)
        Illustrator: Tomi Ungerer (France)
1996   Author: Uri Orlev (Israel)
        Illustrator: Klaus Eniskat (Germany)
1994   Author: Michio Mado (Japan)
        Illustrator: Jörg Müller (Switzerland)
1992   Author: Virginia Hamilton (USA)
        Illustrator: Kveta Pacovská (Czechoslovakia)
1990   Author: Tormod Haugen (Norway)

Illustrator: Lisbeth Zwerger (Austria)
1988   Author: Annie M. G. Schmidt (Netherlands)
        Illustrator: Dusan Kállay (Czechoslovakia)
1986   Author: Patricia Wrightson (Australia)
        Illustrator: Robert Ingpen (Australia)
1984   Author: Christine Nöstlinger (Austria)
        Illustrator: Mitsumasa Anno (Japan)
1982   Author: Lygia Bojunga Nunes (Brazil)
        Illustrator: Zbigniew Rychlicki (Poland)
1980   Author: Bohumil Riha (Czechoslovakia)
        Illustrator: Suekichi Akaba (Japan)
1978   Author: Paula Fox (USA)
        Illustrator: Svend Otto S. (Denmark)
1976   Author: Cecil Bödker (Denmark)
        Illustrator: Tatjana Mawrina (USSR)
1974   Author: Maria Gripe (Sweden)
        Illustrator: Farshid Mesghali (Iran)
1972   Author: Scott O'Dell (USA)
        Illustrator: Ib Spang Olsen (Denmark)
1970   Author: Gianni Rodari (Italy)
        Illustrator: Maurice Sendak (USA)
1968   Authors: James Krüss (Germany) and José Maria Sanchez-Silva
        (Spain)
        Illustrator: Jirí Trnka (Czechoslovakia)
1966   Author: Tove Jansson (Finland)
        Illustrator: Alois Carigiet (Switzerland)
1964   Author: René Guillot (France)
1962   Author: Meindert DeJong (USA)
1960   Author: Erich Kästner (Germany)
1958   Author: Astrid Lindgren (Sweden)
1956   Author: Eleanor Farjeon (UK)

The Biennale of Illustrations Brataslava (BIB)

The Biennial of Illustrations Bratislava (BIB) is an international competition and exhibit of original book illustrations for children and youth. The BIB and its associated international organizations, the International Board on Books for Young People (IBBY), UNESCO, and international artists' organizations, support the multilateral development of original art for children's and young adult books. The BIB exhibit takes place in Bratislava, the Slovak Republic.

Website: www.bibiana.sk/index.php?id=1&L=2

The Bologna Book Fair Ragazzi Awards

Promoted by the Bologna Children's Book Fair, this initiative rewards the best books in terms of graphic and editorial design. Awards are presented in the traditional fiction and nonfiction categories. New Horizons is a *special recognition reserved for the publishing industry in the Arab countries, Latin America, Asia, and Africa*. In 2010, an additional bracket was established called Opera Prima, devoted to the works of new authors and illustrators. Its goal was to acknowledge publishers' efforts to develop new talent. Examples of the awards are presented on the award website.

Website: www.bookfair.bolognafiere.it/en/boragazziaward/

Janusz Korczak Literary

Every two years from 1979 to 1987, then again from 1990 to 2000, the Polish national section of IBBY awarded the Janusz Korczak Literary International Prizes. The award was again suspended in 2000 because of lack of funds. There have been no Janusz Korczak Literary Awards since then.

Noma Concours for Children's Picture Book Illustrations

The Noma Concours for Picture Book Illustrations was given to illustrators in Asia, Africa, Arab States, Oceania, Latin America, and the Caribbean to encourage them to show their works more widely. The biennial award was organized by the Asia/Pacific Cultural Centre for UNESCO (ACCU), supported by the Noma International Book Development Fund from 1978 to 2008. The purposes of this prize were

- to discover up-and-coming illustrators, graphic designers, and artists in Asia (except Japan), the Pacific, Africa, Arab States, and Latin America and the Caribbean,
- to provide an opportunity to present their works,
- to offer incentives for their creative activities.

The Noma Concours for Picture Book Illustrations concluded its history at the 16th Concours in 2008.

Website: www.accu.or.jp/noma/english/e_index.html

Tehran International Biennal of Illustrations (Crystal Pen Award)

No accessible website found.

UNESCO Prize for Children's Literature in the Service of Tolerance

The United Nations Educational, Scientific, and Cultural Organization established this prize to carry the message of the United Nations Year for Tolerance beyond 1995. The prize was awarded every two years in recognition of works for the young that best embodied the concepts and ideals of tolerance and peace and promoted mutual understanding based on respect for other peoples and cultures. There were two categories: books for children under thirteen and those for thirteen- to eighteen-year-olds. The author of the prize-winning book in each category received a cash award of U.S. $8,000 donated by the Fundación Santa María / Ediciones S.M. of Spain. This award was abolished in 2004.

White Ravens List

The International Youth Library (Internationale Jugendbibliothek)
International Youth Library
Schloss Blutenburg
81247 Munich, Germany
Telephone: ++49 | 89 | 89 12 11- 0
Fax: ++49 | 89 | 811 75 53
E-Mail: info@ijb.de
Website: www.ijb.de/

Each year, the language specialists at the International Youth Library select recently published books that they consider especially noteworthy. This "premium label" is given to books of international interest that deserve a wider reception on account of their universal theme or their exceptional and often innovative artistic and literary style and design.

White Ravens lists can be accessed online through the OPAC Online Catalog: https://ijboz1.bib-bvb.de/webOPACClient.ijbsis/start.do?Login=woijb.

INTERNATIONAL AWARDS: UNITED STATES

Jane Addams Children's Book Awards

The Jane Addams Children's Book Awards are given annually to children's picture books and longer books published the preceding year that effectively promote the cause of peace, social justice, world community, and the equality of the sexes and races as well as meeting conventional standards for excellence. The awards have been presented annually since 1953 by the Women's International League for Peace and Freedom and the Jane Addams Peace

Association. Beginning in 1993, a picture book category was created. Honor books may be chosen in each category. Website: www.janeaddamspeace.org/

Earlier lists of the Jane Addams Children's Book Award and Honor Books can be downloaded as PDF files at www.janeaddamspeace.org/jacba/history .shtml. An annotated bibliography (PDF download) of the 2004–2010 books can be accessed at the same URL.

2010
Award Book for Older Readers
Marching for Freedom: Walk Together, Children, and Don't You Grow Weary, written by Elizabeth Partridge. Viking Children's Books, an imprint of Penguin Young Readers Group, 2009.
Honor Books
Almost Astronauts: 13 Women Who Dared to Dream, written by Tanya Lee Stone. Candlewick Press, 2009.

Claudette Colvin, written by Phillip Hoose. Melanie Kroupa Books/Farrar, Straus and Giroux, an imprint of Macmillan Children's Publishing Group, 2009.
Award Book for Younger Readers, Picture Book Category
Nasreen's Secret School: A True Story from Afghanistan, written and illustrated by Jeanette Winter. Beach Lane Books, an imprint of Simon & Schuster Children's Publishing, 2009.
Honor Books
Sojourner Truth's Step-Stomp Stride, written by Andrea Davis Pinkney and Brian Pinkney. Illustrated by Brian Pinkney. Jump at the Sun Books/ Hyperion, an imprint of Disney Publishing, 2009.

You and Me and Home Sweet Home, written by George Ella Lyon and Stephanie Anderson. Richard Jackson Books/Atheneum Books for Young Readers, an imprint of Simon & Schuster Children's Publishing, 2009.

2009
Award Book for Older Readers
The Surrender Tree: Poems of Cuba's Struggle for Freedom, written by Margarita Engle. Henry Holt Books for Young Readers, an imprint of Macmillan Children's Publishing Group, 2008.
Honor Books
The Shepherd's Granddaughter, written by Anne Laurel Carter. House of Anansi Press, an imprint of Groundwood Books, 2008.

Ain't Nothing But a Man: My Quest to Find the Real John Henry, written by Scott Nelson and Marc Aronson. National Geographic, 2008.

Award Book for Younger Readers, Picture Book Category

Planting the Trees of Kenya: The Story of Wangari Maathai, written and illustrated by Claire A. Nivola. Frances Foster Books/Farrar, Straus and Giroux, an imprint of Macmillan Children's Publishing Group, 2008.

Honor Books

The Storyteller's Candle / La velita de los cuentos, written by Lucía González. Illustrated by Lulu Delacre. Children's Book Press, 2008.

Silent Music: A Story of Baghdad, written and illustrated by James Rumford. Neal Porter Books/Roaring Brook Press, an imprint of Macmillan Children's Publishing Group, 2008.

2008

Award Book for Older Readers

We Are One: The Story of Bayard Rustin, written by Larry Dane Brimner. Boyds Mills Press, 2007.

Honor Books

Rickshaw Girl, written by Mitali Perkins. Illustrated by Jamie Hogan. Charlesbridge, 2007.

Elijah of Buxton, written by Christopher Paul Curtis. Scholastic Press, an imprint of Scholastic, Inc., 2007.

Birmingham, 1963, written by Carole Boston Weatherford. Wordsong, an imprint of Boyds Mills Press, 2007.

Award Book for Younger Readers, Picture Book Category

The Escape of Oney Judge: Martha Washington's Slave Finds Freedom, written and illustrated by Emily Arnold McCully. Farrar, Straus and Giroux, 2007

Honor Book

One Thousand Tracings: Healing the Wounds of World War II, written and illustrated by Lita Judge. Hyperion Books for Children, 2007.

2007

Award Book for Older Readers

Weedflower, written by Cynthia Kadohata. Atheneum Books for Young Readers, an imprint of Simon & Schuster, 2006.

Honor Books

Freedom Walkers, written by Russell Freedman. Holiday House, 2006.

Counting on Grace, written by Elizabeth Winthrop. Wendy Lamb Books, an imprint of Random House, 2006.

Award Book for Younger Readers, Picture Book Category
A Place Where Sunflowers Grow, written by Amy Lee-Tai. Illustrated by
Felicia Hoshino. Children's Book Press, 2007.

Honor Books
Night Boat to Freedom, written by Margot Theis Raven. Illustrated by E. B.
Lewis. Melanie Kroupa Books, an imprint of Farrar, Straus and Giroux,
2006.
Crossing Bok Chitto: A Choctaw Tale of Friendship & Freedom, retold by
Tim Tingle. Illustrated by Jeanne Rorex Bridges. Cinco Puntos Press,
2006.

2006
Award Book for Older Readers
Let Me Play: The Story of Title IX, the Law That Changed the Future of
Girls in America, written by Karen Blumenthal. Atheneum Books, an
imprint of Simon and Schuster, 2005.

Honor Books
The Crazy Man, written by Pamela Porter. House of Anansi Press, an imprint of Groundwood Books, 2005.
Sweetgrass Basket, written by Marlene Carvell. Dutton Children's Books,
a division of Penguin Young Readers Group, 2005.

Award Book for Younger Readers, Picture Book Category
Delivering Justice: W. W. Law and the Fight for Civil Rights, written by Jim
Haskins. Illustrated by Benny Andrews. Candlewick Press, 2005.

Honor Book
Poems to Dream Together = Poemas Para Soñar Juntos, written by Francisco
X. Alarcón. Illustrated by Paula Barragán. Lee and Low Books, 2005.

2005
Award Book for Older Readers
With Courage and Cloth: Winning the Fight for a Woman's Right to Vote,
written by Ann Bausum. National Geographic Society, 2004.

Honor Book
The Heaven Shop, written by Deborah Ellis. Groundwood Books, an imprint of Fitzhenry & Whiteside, 2004.

Award Book for Younger Readers, Picture Book Category
Sélavi, That Is Life: A Haitian Story of Hope, written and illustrated by
Youme Landowne, Cinco Puntos Press, 2004.

Honor Books
Hot Day on Abbott Avenue, written by Karen English. Illustrated by Javaka
Steptoe. Clarion Books, 2004.

Henry and the Kite Dragon, written by Bruce Edward Hall. Illustrated by William Low. Philomel Books, an imprint of Penguin Young Readers Group, 2004.

Sequoyah: The Cherokee Man Who Gave His People Writing, written and illustrated by James Rumford. Translated into Cherokee by Anna Sixkiller Huckaby. Houghton Mifflin Books for Children, 2004.

Mildred L. Batchelder Award

This award, sponsored by the American Library Association's Association for Library Services to Children, is given to the American publisher of a children's book considered to be the most outstanding book originally published in a country other than the United States in a language other than English, and subsequently translated and published in the United States during the previous year. The purpose of the award is to encourage American publishers to seek out superior children's books from other countries and to promote communication among the peoples of the world. Before 1979, there was a lapse of two years between the original publication date and the award date; to convert to the new system, two awards were announced in 1979, one for 1978 and one for 1979. Beginning in 1994, honor recipients were also selected.

2010   **Delacorte Press, an imprint of Random House Children's Books**, for *A Faraway Island*, written by Annika Thor (2009), translated from Swedish by Linda Schenck.
   Honor books
   Farrar, Straus and Giroux, for *Eidi*, written by Bodil Bredsdorff (2009), translated from Danish by Kathryn Mahaffy.
   Enchanted Lion Books, for *Big Wolf and Little Wolf*, written by Nadine Brun-Cosme (2009), translated from French by Claudia Bedrick, illustrated by Olivier Tallec.
   Arthur A. Levine Books, an imprint of Scholastic, for *Moribito II: Guardian of the Darkness*, written by Nahoko Uehashi (2009), translated from Japanese by Cathy Hirano, illustrated by Yuko Shimizu.

2009   **Arthur A. Levine Books, an imprint of Scholastic**, for *Moribito: Guardian of the Spirit*, written by Nahoko Uehashi (2008), translated from Japanese by Cathy Hirano.
   Honor books
   Eerdmans Books for Young Readers, an imprint of Wm. B. Eerdmans, for *Garmann's Summer*, written by Stian Hole (2008), translated from Norwegian by Don Bartlett.

Amulet Books, an imprint of Harry N. Abrams, for *Tiger Moon,* written by Antonia Michaelis (2008), translated from German by Anthea Bell.

2008   **VIZ Media,** for *Brave Story,* written by Miyuki Miyabe (2007), translated from Japanese by Alexander O. Smith.

Honor books

Milkweed Editions, for *The Cat: Or, How I Lost Eternity,* written by Jutta Richter (2007), translated from German by Anna Brailovsky.

Phaidon Press, for *Nicholas and the Gang,* written by René Goscinny (2007), translated from French by Anthea Bell.

2007   **Delacorte Press,** for *The Pull of the Ocean,* written by Jean-Claude Mourlevat (2006), translated from French by Y. Maudet.

Honor books

Delacorte Press, for *The Killer's Tears,* written by Anne-Laure Bondoux (2006), translated from French by Y. Maudet.

Hyperion/Miramax, for *The Last Dragon,* written by Silvana De Mari (2006), translated from Italian by Shaun Whiteside.

2006   **Arthur A. Levine Books,** for *An Innocent Soldier,* written by Josef Holub (2005), translated from German by Michael Hofmann.

Honor books

Phaidon Press, for *Nicholas,* written by René Goscinny (2005), translated from French by Anthea Bell, illustrated by Jean-Jacques Sempé.

Bloomsbury Children's Books, for *When I Was a Soldier,* written by Valérie Zenatti (2005), translated from French by Adriana Hunter.

2005   **Delacorte Press/Random House Children's Books,** for *The Shadows of Ghadames,* written by Joëlle Stolz (2004), translated from French by Catherine Temerson.

Honor books

Farrar, Straus and Giroux, for *The Crow-Girl: The Children of Crow Cove,* written by Bodil Bredsdorff (2004), translated from Danish by Faith Ingwersen.

Richard Jackson Books/Simon & Schuster's Atheneum, for *Daniel Half Human and the Good Nazi,* written by David Chotjewitz (2004), translated from German by Doris Orgel.

2004   **Walter Lorraine Books/Houghton Mifflin,** for *Run, Boy, Run,* written by Uri Orlev (2003), translated from Hebrew by Hillel Halkin.

Honor book

    Chronicle Books, for *The Man Who Went to the Far Side of the Moon: The Story of Apollo 11 Astronaut Michael Collins*, written by Bea Uusma Schyffert (2003), translated from Swedish by Emi Guner.

2003   **Chicken House/Scholastic Publishing**, for *The Thief Lord*, written by Cornelia Funke (2002), translated from German by Oliver Latsch.

Honor book

    David R. Godine, for *Henrietta and the Golden Eggs*, written by Hanna Johansen (2002), translated from German by John Barrett, illustrated by Käthi Bhend.

2002   **Cricket Books/Carus Publishing**, *How I Became an American*, written by Karin Gündisch (2001), translated from German by James Skofield.

Honor book

    Viking Press, for *A Book of Coupons*, written by Susie Morgenstern (2001), translated from French by Gill Rosner, illustrated by Serge Bloch.

2001   **Arthur A. Levine/Scholastic Press**, for *Samir and Yonatan*, written by Daniella Carmi (2000), translated from Hebrew by Yael Lotan.

Honor book

    David R. Godine, for *Ultimate Game*, written by Christian Lehmann (2000), translated from French by William Rodarmor.

2000   **Walker Books**, for *The Baboon King*, written by Anton Quintana (1999), translated from Dutch by John Nieuwenhuizen.

Honor books

    Farrar, Straus and Giroux, for *Collector of Moments*, written by Quint Buchholz (1999), translated from German by Peter F. Neumeyer.

    R & S Books, for *Vendela in Venice*, written by Cristina Björk (1999), translated from Swedish by Patricia Crampton, illustrated by Inga-Karin Eriksson.

    Front Street, for *Asphalt Angels*, written by Ineke Holtwijk (1999), translated from Dutch by Wanda Boeke.

1999   **Dial**, for *Thanks to My Mother*, written by Schoschana Rabinovici (1998), translated from German by James Skofield.

Honor book

    Viking, for *Secret Letters from 0 to 10*, by Susie Morgenstern (1998), translated from French by Gill Rosner.

1998 **Henry Holt**, for *The Robber and Me*, written by Josef Holub (1997), edited by Mark Aronson and translated from German by Elizabeth D. Crawford.

    Honor books

        Scholastic Press, for *Hostages to War: A True Story*, written by Tatjana Wassiljewa (1997), translated from the German by Anna Trenter.

        Viking, for *Nero Corleone: A Cat's Story*, written by Elke Heidenrich (1997), translated from German by Doris Orgel.

1997 **Farrar, Straus and Giroux**, for *The Friends*, written by Kazumi Yumoto (1996), translated from Japanese by Cathy Hirano.

1996 **Houghton Mifflin**, for *The Lady with the Hat*, written by Uri Orlev (1995), translated from Hebrew by Hillel Halkin.

    Honor books

        Henry Holt, for *Damned Strong Love: The True Story of Willi G. and Stepan K.*, written by Lutz Van Dijk (1995), translated from German by Elizabeth D. Crawford.

        Walker, for *Star of Fear, Star of Hope*, written by Jo Hoestlandt (1995), translated from French by Mark Polizzotti.

1995 **E. P. Dutton**, for *The Boys from St. Petri*, written by Bjarne Reuter (1994), translated from the Danish by Anthea Bell.

    Honor book

        Lothrop, Lee & Shepard, for *Sister Shako and Kolo, the Goat: Memories of My Childhood in Turkey*, written by Vedat Dalokay (1994), translated from Turkish by Güner Ener.

1994 **Farrar, Straus and Giroux**, for *The Apprentice*, written by Pilar Molina Llorente (1993), translated from Spanish by Robin Longshaw. Illustrated by Juan Ramón Alonso Díaz-Toledo.

    Honor books

        Farrar, Straus and Giroux, for *The Princess in the Kitchen Garden*, written by Annemie and Margriet Heymans (1993), translated from Dutch by Johanna H. Prins and Johanna W. Prins.

        Viking, for *Anne Frank: Beyond the Diary: A Photographic Remembrance*, written by Ruud van der Rol and Rian Verhoeven, in association with the Anne Frank House (1993), translated from Dutch by Tony Langham and Plym Peters.

1993 No award given.

1992 **Houghton Mifflin**, for *The Man from the Other Side*, written by Uri Orlev (1991), translated from Hebrew by Hillel Halkin.

1991 **E. P. Dutton**, for *A Hand Full of Stars*, written by Rafik Schami (1990), translated from German by Rika Lesser.

1990 **E. P. Dutton**, for *Buster's World*, written by Bjarne Reuter (1989), translated from Danish by Anthea Bell.

1989 **Lothrop, Lee & Shepard**, for *Crutches*, written by Peter Härtling (1988), translated from German by Elizabeth D. Crawford.

1988 **McElderry Books**, for *If You Didn't Have Me*, written by Ulf Nilsson (1987), translated from Swedish by Lone Thygesen Blecher and George Blecher. Illustrated by Eva Eriksson.

1987 **Lothrop, Lee & Shepard**, for *No Hero for the Kaiser*, written by Rudolf Frank (1986), translated from German by Patricia Crampton.

1986 **Creative Education**, for *Rose Blanche*, written by Christophe Gallaz and Roberto Innocenti (1985), translated from Italian by Martha Coventry and Richard Craglia. Illustrated by Roberto Innocenti.

1985 **Houghton Mifflin**, for *The Island on Bird Street*, written by Uri Orlev (1984), translated from Hebrew by Hillel Halkin.

1984 **Viking Press**, for *Ronia, the Robber's Daughter*, written by Astrid Lindgren (1983), translated from Swedish by Patricia Crampton.

1983 **Lothrop, Lee & Shepard**, for *Hiroshima No Pika*, written by Toshi Maruki (1892), translated from Japanese through Kurita-Bando Literacy Agency.

1982 **Bradbury Press**, for *The Battle Horse*, written by Harry Kullman (1981), translated from Swedish by George Blecher and Lone Thygesen Blecher.

1981 **William Morrow**, for *The Winter When Time Was Frozen*, written by Els Pelgrom (1980), translated from Dutch by Maryka and Raphael Rudnik.

1980 **E. P. Dutton**, for *The Sound of the Dragon's Feet*, written by Alki Zei, translated from Greek by Edward Fenton.

1979 Two awards given:
    Franklin Watts, for *Konrad*, written by Christine Nöstlinger (1977), translated from German (Austrian) by Anthea Bell, illustrated by Carol Nicklaus.
    Harcourt Brace Jovanovich, for *Rabbit Island*, written by Jörg Steiner (1978), translated from German by Ann Conrad Lammers, illustrated by Jörg Müller.

1978 No award given.

1977 **Atheneum**, for *The Leopard*, written by Cecil Bødker (1975), translated from Danish by Gunnar Poulsen.

1976   **Henry Z. Walck,** for *The Cat and the Mouse Who Shared a House*, written by Ruth Hürlimann, translated from German by Anthea Bell.

1975   **Crown,** for *An Old Tale Carved Out of Stone*, written by Aleksander M. Linevskii (1973), translated from Russian by Maria Polushkin.

1974   **E. P. Dutton,** for *Petros' War*, written by Aliki Zei (1972), translated from Greek by Edward Fenton.

1973   **William Morrow,** for *Puldga*, written by Siny Rose Van Iterson, translated from Dutch by Alexander and Alison Gode.

1972   **Holt, Rinehart & Winston,** for *Friedrich*, written by Hans Peter Richter (1970), translated from German by Edite Kroll.

1971   **Pantheon Books,** for *In the Land of Ur: The Discovery of Ancient Mesopotamia*, written by Hans Baumann, translated from German by Stella Humphries, illustrated by Hans Peter Renn.

1970   **Holt, Rinehart & Winston,** for *Wildcat under Glass*, written by Aliki Zei (1968), translated from Greek by Edward Fenton.

1969   **Charles Scribner's Sons,** for *Don't Take Teddy*, written by Babbis Friis-Baastad (1967), translated from Norwegian by Lise Sømme McKinnon.

1968   **Alfred A. Knopf,** for *The Little Man*, written by Erich Kästner, translated from German by James Kirkup. Illustrated by Rick Schreiter.

Notable Books for Global Society

In 1995, the Children's Literature and Reading Special Interest Group of the International Reading Association formed the Notable Books for a Global Society (NBGS) Committee. This committee undertook to identify outstanding trade books that it felt would help promote understanding across lines of culture, race, sexual orientation, values, and ethnicity.

Subsequently, they annually publish a list of twenty-five outstanding trade books for enhancing student understanding of people and cultures throughout the world. Winning titles include fiction, nonfiction, and poetry written for students in grades K–12. A brief history of the Notable Books for a Global Society, the selection criteria, and the selected books from 2005 through the current list are posted at http://mysite.verizon.net/vzeeioxu/id14.html.

USSBY Outstanding International Books List

Since 2006, USBBY has selected an annual list of Outstanding International Books for children and young adults. The selection committee is charged with choosing international books that are deemed the most outstanding of those published during the previous calendar year. For the purposes of this honor list, the term *international book* is used to describe a book published or distributed in the United States that originated or was first published in a country other than the United States.

The Outstanding International Books List is announced each year at the American Library Association's midwinter meetings. A commemorative bookmark, listing all the books, their origin, and approximate grade levels, is available at that time. The annotated book list is published each year in the February issue of *School Library Journal*. We have attempted to review each book on the five Outstanding International Books lists from 2006–2010 in this volume. Resources related to the Outstanding International Books List can be accessed at www.usbby.org/outstanding_international_books_list.htm.

2010 USBBY Outstanding International Books List

First Published	Book (by Author)	Level
Australia	Herrick, Steven. *Cold Skin*. Front Street/ Boyds Mills.	Gr 9 Up
Australia	Lawrence, L. S. *Escape by Sea*. Holiday House.	Gr 6–8
Australia	Meehan, Kierin. *Hannah's Winter*. Kane/ Miller.	Gr 6–8
Australia	Millard, Glenda. *The Naming of Tishkin Silk*. Illus. by Patrice Barton. Farrar, Straus and Giroux.	Gr 3–5
Australia	Tan, Shaun. *Tales from Outer Suburbia*. Arthur A. Levine/Scholastic.	Gr 6–8
Canada	Argueta, Jorge. *Sopa de Frijoles: Un Poema para Cocinar = Bean Soup: A Cooking Poem*. Illus. by Rafael Yockteng. Groundwood.	Gr K–2
Canada	Ellis, Deborah. *Children of War: Voices of Iraqi Refugees*. Groundwood.	Gr 6–8
Canada	Gingras, Charlotte. *Pieces of Me*. Trans. by Susan Ouriou. Kids Can.	Gr 9 Up
Canada	Khan, Rukhsana. *Wanting Mor*. Groundwood.	Gr 6–8
Canada	Larsen, Andrew. *The Imaginary Garden*. Illus. by Irene Luxbacher. Kids Can.	Gr K–2

Canada	Mordecai, Martin. *Blue Mountain Trouble*. Arthur A. Levine/Scholastic.	Gr 6–8
Canada	Roberts, Ken. *Thumb and the Bad Guys*. Illus. by Leanne Franson. Groundwood.	Gr 3–5
Canada	Slade, Arthur. *Jolted: Newton Starker's Rules for Survival*. Wendy Lamb/Random House.	Gr 6–8
Canada	Teevee, Ningeokuluk. *Alego*. Trans. by Nina Manning-Toonoo. Groundwood.	Gr K–2
Denmark	Bredsdorff, Bodil. *Eidi*. Trans. by Kathryn Mahaffy. Farrar, Straus and Giroux.	Gr 3–5
France	Bednar, Sylvie. *Flags of the World*. Trans. by Gita Daneshjoo. Abrams.	Gr 3–5
France	Cali, Davide. *The Enemy: A Book about Peace*. Illus. by Serge Bloch. Random House	Gr 3–5
France	Combres, Élisabeth. *Broken Memory: A Novel of Rwanda*. Trans. by Shelley Tanaka. Groundwood.	Gr 9 Up
France	Mourlevat, Jean-Claude. *Winter's End*. Trans. by Anthea Bell. Candlewick.	Gr 9 Up
France	Sellier, Marie. *What the Rat Told Me: A Legend of the Chinese Zodiac*. Illus. by Catherine Louis. Calligraphy and chop marks by Wang Fei. NorthSouth.	Gr K–2
Great Britain	Almond, David. *Raven Summer*. Delacorte/Random House.	Gr 9 Up
Great Britain	Clayton, Emma. *The Roar*. Chicken House/Scholastic.	Gr 6–8
Great Britain	Donaldson, Julia. *Running on the Cracks*. Henry Holt.	Gr 6–8
Great Britain	Gaiman, Neil. *Odd and the Frost Giants*. Illus. by Brett Helquist. Harper/HarperCollins.	Gr 3–5
Great Britain	Higgins, F. E. *The Eyeball Collector*. Feiwel & Friends.	Gr 9 Up
Great Britain	Mahy, Margaret. *Bubble Trouble*. Illus. by Polly Dunbar. Clarion.	Gr 9 Up
Great Britain	McGowan, Anthony. *Jack Tumor*. Farrar, Straus and Giroux.	Gr 6–8
Great Britain	Michael, Jan. *City Boy*. Clarion.	Gr 6–8

Great Britain	Ness, Patrick. *The Ask and the Answer* (Chaos Walking Series). Candlewick.	Gr 9 Up
Great Britain	Pellegrino, Marge. *Journey of Dreams*. Frances Lincoln.	Gr 6–8
Great Britain	Thompson, Kate. *Creature of the Night*. Roaring Brook.	Gr 9 Up
Great Britain	Umansky, Kaye. *Clover Twig and the Magical Cottage*. Illus. by Johanna Wright. Roaring Brook.	Gr 3–5
Great Britain	Valentine, Jenny. *Broken Soup*. HarperTeen/ HarperCollins.	Gr 9 Up
India	Nayar, Nandini. *What Should I Make?* Illus. by Proiti Roy. Tricycle.	Gr K–2
Japan	Baasansuren, Bolormaa. *My Little Round House*. Adapted by Helen Mixter. Groundwood.	Gr K–2
Japan	Uehashi, Nahoko. *Moribito II: Guardian of the Darkness*. Trans. by Cathy Hirano. Illus. by Yuko Shimizu. Arthur A. Levine/Scholastic.	Gr 6–8
The Netherlands	Hof, Marjolijn. *Against the Odds*. Trans. by Johanna H. Prins and Johanna W. Prins. Groundwood.	Gr 3–5
The Netherlands	Metselaar, Menno & Ruud van der Rol. *Anne Frank: Her Life in Words and Pictures*. Trans. by Arnold J. Pomerans. Roaring Brook.	Gr 6–8
New Zealand	Mahy, Margaret. *The Magician of Hoad*. Margaret K. McElderry/Simon & Schuster.	Gr 9 Up
Sweden	Thor, Annika. *A Faraway Island*. Trans. by Linda Schenck. Delacorte/Random House.	Gr 6–8
Switzerland	Kilaka, John. *The Amazing Tree*. NorthSouth.	Gr K–2

2009 USBBY Outstanding International Books List

Australia	Goodman, Alison. *Eon: Dragoneye Reborn*. Viking.	Gr 6–8
Australia	Graham, Bob. *How to Heal a Broken Wing*. Illus. by author. Candlewick.	Gr K–2

Australia	Greenwood, Mark. *The Donkey of Gallipoli: A True Story of Courage in World War I.* Illus. by Frané Lessac. Candlewick.	Gr 3–5
Canada	Campbell, Nicola I. *Shin-chi's Canoe.* Illus. by Kim LaFave. Groundwood.	Gr 3–5
Canada	Carter, Anne Laurel. *The Shepherd's Granddaughter.* Groundwood.	Gr 6–8
Canada	Ibbitson, John. *The Landing.* Kids Can.	Gr 9 Up
Canada	Jocelyn, Marthe. *Would You.* Random/ Wendy Lamb Books.	Gr 9 Up
Canada	Milway, Katie Smith. *One Hen: How One Small Loan Made a Big Difference.* Illus. by Eugenie Fernandes. Kids Can.	Gr 3–5
Canada	Skrypuch, Marsha Forchuk. *Daughter of War.* Fitzhenry & Whiteside.	Gr 9 Up
Canada	Wynne-Jones, Tim. *Rex Zero, King of Nothing.* Farrar/Melanie Kroupa Books.	Gr 6–8
Germany	Berner, Rotraut Susanne. *In the Town All Year 'Round.* Trans. by Neeltje Konings and Nick Elliot. Illus. by author. Chronicle.	Gr K–2
Germany	Michaelis, Antonia. *Tiger Moon.* Trans. by Anthea Bell. Abrams/Amulet.	Gr 9 Up
Great Britain	Almond, David. *My Dad's a Birdman.* Illus. by Polly Dunbar. Candlewick.	Gr 3–5
Great Britain	Amnesty International. *We Are All Born Free: The Universal Declaration of Human Rights in Pictures.* Illus. Frances Lincoln.	Gr 3–5
Great Britain	Benjamin, Floella. *My Two Grannies.* Illus. by Margaret Chamberlain. Frances Lincoln.	Gr K–2
Great Britain	Browne, Anthony. *My Mom.* Illus. by author. Candlewick.	Gr K–2
Great Britain	Crossley-Holland, Kevin. *Crossing to Paradise.* Scholastic/Arthur A. Levine Books.	Gr 6–8
Great Britain	Doherty, Berlie. *The Girl Who Saw Lions.* Roaring Brook/A Neal Porter Book.	Gr 6–8
Great Britain	Dowd, Siobhan. *Bog Child.* Random/David Fickling Books.	Gr 9 Up

Great Britain	Dowd, Siobhan. *The London Eye Mystery.* Random/David Fickling Books.	Gr 6–8
Great Britain	Gaiman, Neil. *The Graveyard Book.* Illus. by Dave McKean. HarperCollins.	Gr 6–8
Great Britain	Grey, Mini. *Traction Man Is Here!* Illus. by author. Knopf/Borzoi.	Gr K–2
Great Britain	Hooper, Mary. *Newes from the Dead.* Roaring Brook.	Gr 9 Up
Great Britain	Ibbotson, Eva. *The Dragonfly Pool.* Illus. by Kevin Hawkes. Dutton.	Gr 6–8
Great Britain	Laird, Elizabeth. *A Fistful of Pearls and Other Tales from Iraq.* Illus. by Shelley Fowles. Frances Lincoln.	Gr 3–5
Great Britain	Lee, Ingrid. *Dog Lost.* Scholastic/Chicken House.	Gr 3–5
Great Britain	Marriott, Zoë. *The Swan Kingdom.* Candlewick.	Gr 6–8
Great Britain	McKay, Hilary. *Forever Rose.* Simon & Schuster/Margaret K. McElderry Books.	Gr 6–8
Great Britain	Ness, Patrick. *The Knife of Never Letting Go* (Chaos Walking Series, Book.1). Candlewick.	Gr 9 Up
Great Britain	Nicholls, Sally. *Ways to Live Forever.* Scholastic/Arthur A. Levine Books.	Gr 6–8
Great Britain	Pratchett, Terry. *Nation.* HarperCollins.	Gr 6–8
Great Britain	Reeve, Philip. *Here Lies Arthur.* Scholastic.	Gr 9 Up
Great Britain	Riddell, Chris. *Ottoline and the Yellow Cat.* Illus. by author. HarperCollins.	Gr 3–5
Great Britain	Robinson, Anthony & Annemarie Young. *Gervelie's Journey: A Refugee Diary.* Illus. by June Allan. Frances Lincoln.	Gr 3–5
Great Britain	Taylor, Sean. *The Great Snake: Stories from the Amazon.* Illus. by Fernando Vilela. Frances Lincoln.	Gr 3–5
India	Ravishankar, Anushka. *Elephants Never Forget!* Illus. by Christiane Pieper. Houghton Mifflin.	Gr K–2
Japan	Nakagawa, Chihiro. *Who Made This Cake?* Trans. by the author. Illus. by Junji Koyose. Front Street.	Gr K–2

Japan	Uehashi, Nahoko. *Moribito: Guardian of the Spirit.* Trans. by Cathy Hirano. Illus. by Yuko Shimizu. Scholastic/Arthur A. Levine Books.	Gr 6–8
The Netherlands	Rinck, Maranke. *I Feel a Foot!* Illus. by Martijn van der Linden. Boyds Mills/Lemniscaat.	Gr K–2
Norway	Hole, Stian. *Garmann's Summer.* Trans. by Don Bartlett. Illus. by author. Eerdmans.	Gr K–2
South Korea	Choung, Eun-hee. *Minji's Salon.* Illus. by author. Kane/Miller.	Gr K–2
Sweden	Kruusval, Catarina, *Ellen's Apple Tree.* Trans. by Joan Sandin. Illus. by author. R & S.	Gr K–2

2008 USBBY Outstanding International Books List

Australia	Bateson, Catherine. *Being Bee.* Holiday House.	Gr 3–5
Australia	Clarke, Judith. *One Whole and Perfect Day.* Front Street.	Gr 9 Up
Australia	Herrick, Steven. *The Wolf.* Front Street.	Gr 9 Up
Australia	Lofthouse, Liz. *Ziba Came on a Boat.* Illus. by Robert Ingpen. Kane/Miller.	Gr 3–5
Australia	Marillier, Juliet. *Wildwood Dancing.* Knopf.	Gr 9 Up
Australia	Marsden, John. *While I Live* (The Ellie Chronicles). Scholastic.	Gr 9 Up
Australia	Tan, Shaun. *The Arrival.* Illus. by author. Scholastic/Arthur A. Levine Books.	Gr 6–8
Canada	Amado, Elisa. *Tricycle.* Illus. by Alfonso Ruano. Groundwood.	Gr K–2
Canada	Brooks, Martha. *Mistik Lake.* Farrar/Melanie Kroupa Books.	Gr 9 Up
Canada	Debon, Nicolas. *The Strongest Man in the World: Louis Cyr.* Illus. by author. Groundwood.	Gr 3–5
Canada	Diakité, Baba Wagué. *Mee-An and the Magic Serpent: A Folktale from Mali.* Illus. by author. Groundwood.	Gr 3–5
Canada	Ellis, Deborah. *Sacred Leaf* (The Cocalero Novels). Groundwood.	Gr 6–8

Canada	Rivera, Raquel. *Arctic Adventures: Tales from the Lives of Inuit Artists*. Illus. by Jirina Marton. Groundwood.	Gr 3–5
Canada	Wynne-Jones, Tim. *Rex Zero and the End of the World*. Farrar/Melanie Kroupa Books.	Gr 6–8
France	Cali, Davide. *Piano, Piano*. Trans. by Randi Rivers. Illus. by Éric Heliot. Charlesbridge.	Gr K–2
France	Lacombe, Benjamin. *Cherry and Olive*. Trans. by Silvia Levy. Illus. by author. Walker.	Gr K–2
France	Sellier, Marie. *Legend of the Chinese Dragon*. Trans. by Sibylle Kazeroid. Illus. by Catherine Louis. Calligraphy and chop marks by Wang Fei. NorthSouth.	Gr 3–5
Germany	Funke, Cornelia. *Igraine the Brave*. Trans. by Anthea Bell. Illus. by author. Scholastic/Chicken House.	Gr 3–5
Germany	Pressler, Mirjam. *Let Sleeping Dogs Lie*. Trans. by Erik J. Macki. Front Street.	Gr 9 Up
Germany	Steffensmeier, Alexander. *Millie Waits for the Mail*. Trans. from German. Illus. by author. Walker.	Gr K–2
Great Britain	Beake, Lesley. *Home Now*. Illus. by Karin Littlewood. Charlesbridge.	Gr K–2
Great Britain	Daly, Niki. *Pretty Salma: A Little Red Riding Hood Story from Africa*. Clarion.	Gr K–2
Great Britain	Dickinson, Peter. *Angel Isle*. Illus. by Ian Andrew. Random/Wendy Lamb Books.	Gr 9 Up
Great Britain	Gravett, Emily. *Meerkat Mail*. Illus. by author. Simon & Schuster.	Gr K–2
Great Britain	Hayes, Rosemary. *Mixing It*. Frances Lincoln.	Gr 6–8
Great Britain	Hoffman, Mary. *The Falconer's Knot: A Story of Friars, Flirtation and Foul Play*. Bloomsbury.	Gr 9 Up
Great Britain	Malley, Gemma. *The Declaration*. Bloomsbury.	Gr 9 Up
Great Britain	Peet, Mal. *Tamar*. Candlewick.	Gr 9 Up
Great Britain	Reeve, Philip. *A Darkling Plain* (The Hungry City Chronicles). HarperCollins/Eos.	Gr 6–8

Great Britain	Rowling, J. K. *Harry Potter and the Deathly Hallows*. Illus. by Mary GrandPré. Scholastic/Arthur A. Levine Books.	Gr 6–8
Great Britain	Stewart, Paul & Chris Ridell. *Hugo Pepper* (Far-Flung Adventures). Illus. by Chris Ridell. Random/David Fickling Books.	Gr 3–5
Great Britain	Thompson, Kate. *The New Policeman*. HarperCollins/Greenwillow.	Gr 6–8
Great Britain	Toksvig, Sandi. *Hitler's Canary*. Roaring Brook/A Deborah Brodie Book.	Gr 6–8
Great Britain	Turnbull, Ann. *Forged in the Fire*. Candlewick.	Gr 9 Up
Great Britain	Wilson, Jacqueline. *Candyfloss*. Illus. by Nick Sharratt. Deborah Brodie/Roaring Brook.	Gr 3–5
Iceland	Erlings, Friðrik. *Benjamin Dove*. NorthSouth.	Gr 6–8
Korea	Bae, Hyun-Joo. *New Clothes for New Year's Day*. Illus. by author. Kane/Miller.	Gr K–2
Korea	Kwon, Yoon-duck. *My Cat Copies Me*. Illus. by author. Kane/Miller.	Gr K–2
The Netherlands	Van der Heide, Iris. *A Strange Day*. Trans. from Dutch. Illus. by Marijke ten Cate. Boyds Mills/Lemniscaat.	Gr K–2
Sweden	Wahl, Mats. *The Invisible*. Trans. by Katarina E. Tucker. Farrar.	Gr 9 Up

2007 USBBY Outstanding International Books List

Australia	Hartnett, Sonya. *Surrender*. Candlewick.	Gr 9 Up
Australia	Herrick, Steven. *By the River*. Boyds Mills.	Gr 9 Up
Australia	Kelleher, Victor. *Dogboy*. Boyds Mills.	Gr 9 Up
Australia	Lanagan, Margo. *White Time*. HarperCollins.	Gr 9 Up
Australia	Zusak, Markus. *The Book Thief*. Knopf.	Gr 9 Up
Denmark	Rasmussen, Halfdan. *The Ladder*. Trans. by Marilyn Nelson. Illus. by Pierre Pratt. Candlewick.	Gr K–2
France	Bondoux, Anne-Laure. *The Killer's Tears*. Trans. by Y. Maudet. Delacorte.	Gr 9 Up
France	D'Harcourt, Claire. *Masterpieces Up Close: Western Painting from the 14th to 20th Centuries*. Trans. by Shoshanna Kirk. Chronicle.	Gr 6–8

France	Faller, Régis. *The Adventures of Polo.* Illus. by author. Roaring Brook/A Neal Porter Book.	Gr K–2
France	Greif, Jean-Jacques. *The Fighter.* Trans. by author. Bloomsbury.	Gr 9 Up
France	Ichikawa, Satomi. *My Father's Shop.* Illus. by author. Kane/Miller.	Gr K–2
Germany	Barth-Grözinger, Inge. *Something Remains.* Trans. by Anthea Bell. Hyperion.	Gr 6–8
Germany	Jansen, Hanna. *Over a Thousand Hills I Walk with You.* Trans. by Elizabeth D. Crawford. Lerner.	Gr 9 Up
Germany	Pausewang, Gudrun. *Traitor.* Trans. by Rachel Ward. Lerner.	Gr 9 Up
Germany	Pin, Isabel. *When I Grow Up, I Will Win the Nobel Peace Prize.* Trans. by Nancy Seitz. Illus. by author. Farrar.	Gr 3–5
Great Britain	Almond, David. *Clay.* Delacorte.	Gr 9 Up
Great Britain	Browne, Anthony. *Silly Billy.* Illus. by author. Candlewick.	Gr K–2
Great Britain	Butterworth, Chris. *Sea Horse: The Shyest Fish in the Sea.* Illus. by John Lawrence. Candlewick.	Gr K–2
Great Britain	Foreman, Michael. *Mia's Story: A Sketchbook of Hopes and Dreams.* Illus. by author. Candlewick.	Gr 3–5
Great Britain	Gravett, Emily. *Wolves.* Illus. by author. Simon & Schuster.	Gr K–2
Great Britain	Henderson, Kathy. *Lugalbanda: The Boy Who Got Caught Up in a War.* Illus. by Jane Ray. Candlewick.	Gr 3–5
Great Britain	Hinton, Nigel. *Time Bomb.* Tricycle.	Gr 6–8
Great Britain	Laird, Elizabeth, with Sonia Nimr. *A Little Piece of Ground.* Haymarket.	Gr 9 Up
Great Britain	Mahy, Margaret. *Down the Back of the Chair.* Illus. by Polly Dunbar. Clarion.	Gr K–2
Great Britain	Naidoo, Beverley. *Web of Lies.* HarperCollins/Amistad.	Gr 6–8
Great Britain	Pienkowski, Jan. *The Fairy Tales.* Trans. by David Walser. Illus. by the author. Viking.	Gr 3–5

Great Britain	Pratchett, Terry. *Wintersmith* (A Tiffany Aching Adventure). HarperTempest.	Gr 6–8
Great Britain	Reeve, Philip. *Larklight: A Rousing Tale of Dauntless Pluck in the Farthest Reaches of Space*. Illus. by David Wyatt. Bloomsbury.	Gr 3–5
Great Britain	Sedgwick, Marcus. *The Foreshadowing*. Random/Wendy Lamb Books.	Gr 9 Up
Great Britain	Winterson, Jeanette. *Tanglewreck*. Bloomsbury.	Gr 6–8
India	Rao, Sandhya. *My Mother's Sari*. Illus. by Nina Sabnani. NorthSouth.	Gr K–2
India	Singh, Vandana. *Younguncle Comes to Town*. Illus. by B. M. Kamath. Viking.	Gr 3–5
Ireland	Parkinson, Siobhán. *Something Invisible*. Roaring Brook.	Gr 6–8
Malaysia	Lat. *Kampung Boy*. Illus. by author. Roaring Brook/First Second.	Gr 6–8
The Netherlands	Kuijer, Guus. *The Book of Everything*. Trans. by John Nieuwenhuizen. Scholastic/Arthur A. Levine Books.	Gr 6–8
Norway	Hagerup, Klaus. *Markus and Diana*. Trans. by Tara Chace. Boyds Mills.	Gr 6–8
South Africa	Daly, Niki. *Happy Birthday, Jamela!* Illus. by author. Farrar, Straus & Giroux.	Gr K–2
Thailand	Vejjajiva, Jane. *The Happiness of Kati*. Trans. by author & Prudence Borthwick. Simon & Schuster/Atheneum.	Gr 6–8
Vietnam	Ha, Song. *Indebted as Lord Chom/No Nhu Chua Chom: The Legend of the Forbidden Street*. Trans. by William Smith. Illus. by Ly Thu Ha. East West Discovery.	Gr 3–5

2006 USBBY Outstanding International Books List

Australia	Clarke, Judith. *Kalpana's Dream*. Front Street.	Gr 6–8
Australia	Laguna, Sofie. *Surviving Aunt Marsha*. Scholastic.	Gr 3–5
Australia	Lanagan, Margo. *Black Juice*. HarperCollins/Eos.	Gr 9 Up

Australia	Ormerod, Jan. *Lizzie Nonsense: A Story of Pioneer Days.* Illus. by author. Clarion.	Gr K–2
Australia	Zusak, Markus. *I Am the Messenger.* Knopf.	Gr 9 Up
Belgium	Spillebeen, Geert. *Kipling's Choice.* Trans. by Terese Edelstein. Houghton Mifflin.	Gr 9 Up
Canada	Haworth-Attard, Barbara. *Theories of Relativity.* Holt.	Gr 9 Up
Canada	Wynne-Jones, Tim. *A Thief in the House of Memory.* Farrar/Melanie Kroupa Books.	Gr 9 Up
France	Ma, Yan. *The Diary of Ma Yan: The Struggles and Hopes of a Chinese Schoolgirl.* Trans. by Lisa Appignanesi and He Yanping. HarperCollins.	Gr 6–8
France	Morgenstern, Susie. *It Happened at School: Two Tales.* Trans. by Gillian Rosner. Illus. by Serge Bloch. Viking.	Gr 3–5
France	Valckx, Catharina. *Lizette's Green Sock.* Illus. by author. Clarion.	Gr K–2
France	Zenatti, Valérie. *When I Was a Soldier.* Trans. by Adriana Hunter. Bloomsbury.	Gr 9 Up
Germany	Holub, Josef. *An Innocent Soldier.* Trans. by Michael Hofmann. Scholastic/Arthur A. Levine Books.	Gr 6–8
Germany	Steinhöfel, Andreas. *The Center of the World.* Trans. by Alisa Jaffa. Delacorte.	Gr 9 Up
Great Britain	Adlington, L. J. *The Diary of Pelly D.* HarperCollins/ Greenwillow.	Gr 6–8
Great Britain	Browne, Anthony. *My Mom.* Illus. by author. Farrar.	Gr K–2
Great Britain	Daly, Niki. *Ruby Sings the Blues.* Illus. by author. Bloomsbury.	Gr K–2
Great Britain	Delaney, Joseph. *Revenge of the Witch* (The Last Apprentice Series, Book #1). HarperCollins/Greenwillow.	Gr 6–8
Great Britain	Dyer, Heather. *The Girl with the Broken Wing.* Illus. by Peter Bailey. Scholastic/ Chicken House.	Gr 3–5
Great Britain	Gardner, Sally. *I, Coriander.* Dial.	Gr 6–8
Great Britain	Grant, K. M. *Blood Red Horse* (The de Granville Trilogy Book #1). Walker.	Gr 6–8

Great Britain	Grey, Mini. *Traction Man Is Here!* Illus. by author. Knopf/Borzoi.	Gr K–2
Great Britain	Gribbin, Mary & John Gribbin. *The Science of Philip Pullman's His Dark Materials.* Illus. by Tony Fleetwood. Knopf.	Gr 9 Up
Great Britain	Hearn, Julie. *The Minister's Daughter.* Simon & Schuster/Atheneum.	Gr 9 Up
Great Britain	Hussey, Charmian. *The Valley of Secrets.* Illus. by Christopher Crump. Simon & Schuster.	Gr 6–8
Great Britain	McCaughrean, Geraldine. *Not the End of the World.* HarperTempest.	Gr 9 Up
Great Britain	McKay, Hilary. *Permanent Rose.* Simon & Schuster/Margaret K. McElderry Books.	Gr 6–8
Great Britain	McNaughton, Colin. *Once Upon an Ordinary School Day.* Illus. by Satoshi Kitamura. Farrar.	Gr K–2
Great Britain	Michael, Livi. *The Whispering Road.* Putnam.	Gr 6–8
Great Britain	Paver, Michelle. *Wolf Brother* (The Chronicles of Ancient Darkness Series, Book #1). HarperCollins.	Gr 6–8
Great Britain	Philip, Neil. *The Pirate Princess: And Other Fairy Tales.* Illus. by Mark Weber. Scholastic/Arthur A. Levine Books.	Gr 3–5
Great Britain	Pullman, Philip. *The Scarecrow and His Servant.* Illus. by Peter Bailey. Knopf.	Gr 3–5
Great Britain	Rose, Malcolm. *Framed!* (Traces Series). Kingfisher.	Gr 6–8
Great Britain	Rosen, Michael. *Michael Rosen's Sad Book.* Illus. by Quentin Blake. Candlewick.	Gr 3–5
Great Britain	Updale, Eleanor. *Montmorency on the Rocks: Doctor, Aristocrat, Murderer?* Illus. by Nick Hardcastle. Scholastic/Orchard.	Gr 6–8
Great Britain	Wilson, Jacqueline. *The Illustrated Mum.* Delacorte.	Gr 6–8
Great Britain	Wooding, Chris. *Poison.* Scholastic/Orchard.	Gr 6–8
India	Heydlauff, Lisa. *Going to School in India.* photos by Nitin Upadhye. Charlesbridge.	Gr 3–5
Spain	Gallego García, Laura. *The Legend of the Wandering King.* Trans. by Dan Bellm. Scholastic/Arthur A. Levine Books.	Gr 6–8

Spain	Prats, Joan de Déu. *Sebastian's Roller Skates*. Trans. by Laaren Brown. Illus. by Francesc Rovira. Kane/Miller.	Gr K–2
Sweden	Näslund, Görel Kristina. *Our Apple Tree*. Illus. by Kristina Digman. Roaring Brook.	Gr K–2
Sweden	Nilsson, Per. *You & You & You*. Trans. by Tara Chace. Front Street.	Gr 9 Up

Links to the School Library Journal Articles

2010: *Crisscrossing the Globe: A World of International Books for Young People* by Elizabeth Poe. *School Library Journal*, v. 56, n. 2 (Feb. 2010), pp. 42–45. www.schoollibraryjournal.com/article/CA6716600.html

2009: *World Class: The Latest Outstanding International Books List Offers Tales That Speak to Every Student* by Carolyn Angus. *School Library Journal*, v. 55, n. 2 (Feb. 2009), pp. 36–39. www.schoollibraryjournal.com/article/CA6632971.html

2008: *A World of Stories: 2008 Outstanding International Books* by Carolyn Angus. *School Library Journal*, v. 54, n. 2 (Feb. 2008), pp. 44–47. www.schoollibraryjournal.com/article/CA6527345.html?q=USBBY

2007: *Book Your Trip Now: The Outstanding International Booklist Is Just the Ticket to Take Readers to Some Faraway Places* by Kathleen Isaacs. *School Library Journal*, v. 53, n. 2 (Feb. 2007), pp. 44–48. www.schoollibraryjournal.com/article/CA6410489.html?q=outstanding+international

2006: *It's a Big World After All: Books Are the Best Way to Open Kids' Minds* by Kathleen Isaacs. *School Library Journal*, v. 52, n. 2 (Feb. 2006), pp. 40–44. www.schoollibraryjournal.com/article/CA6302985.html?industryid=47054 &q=outstanding+international+books

CHAPTER TWELVE

Organizations and Research Collections

While numerous organizations work on behalf of international literacy and children's literature, these are the most closely associated with USBBY in North America. The research collections listed here are located primarily in the United States; however, several are international but searchable in English. The final list includes virtual libraries and research collections.

United States Board on Books for Young People (USBBY)
United States Board on Books for Young People (USBBY)
c/o Center for Teaching through Children's Books
National Louis University
5202 Old Orchard Road, Suite 300
Skokie, IL 60077, USA
Phone: 1-224-233-2030
E-mail: Secretariat@usbby.org
Website: www.usbby.org

USBBY Executive Secretary
V. Ellis Vance
5503 N. El Adobe Drive
Fresno, CA 93711-2363 USA
Phone: 1-559-351-6119
E-mail: Executive.Secretary@usbby.org

USBBY PATRONS

American Library Association
50 E Huron Street, Chicago, IL 60611-2795
Phone: 1-800-545-2433 ext. 5037
Fax: 1-312-280-5033
E-mail: ala@ala.org
Website: www.ala.org

The Children's Book Council
54 West 39th Street, 14th Floor
New York, NY 10018
Phone: 1-212-966-1990
Fax: 212-966-2073
E-mail: cbc.info@cbcbooks.org
Website: www.cbcbooks.org

International Reading Association
800 Barksdale Road
P.O. Box 8139
Newark, DE 19714-8139
Phone—United States and Canada: 1-800-336-7323
Phone—Outside the United States and Canada: 1-302-731-1600
Fax: 1-302-731-1057
E-mail: pubinfo@reading.org
Website: www.reading.org

National Council of Teachers of English
1111 W. Kenyon Road
Urbana, IL 61801-1096
Phone: 1-217-328-3870 or 1-877-369-6283
Fax: 1-217-328-9645
E-mail: https://secure.ncte.org/forms/contactus
Website: www.ncte.org

INTERNATIONAL ORGANIZATIONS

International Board on Books for Young People (IBBY)
IBBY Secretariat
Nonnenweg 12, Postfach
CH-4003 Basel, Switzerland
Phone: [int. + 4161] 272 29 17
Fax: [int.+ 4161] 272 27 57
E-mail: ibby@ibby.org
Website: www.ibby.org

International Research Society for Children's Literature (IRSCL)
International Research Society for Children's Literature
Clare Bradford, President IRSCL
Deakin University
Arts Faculty
221 Burwood Highway
Burwood, Victoria 3125 Australia
Phone: +61 3 9244 6487
Fax: +61 3 9244 6755
E-mail: clarex@deakin.edu.au
Website: www.irscl.com/

The International Federation of Library Associations and Institutions
IFLA Headquarters
Prins Willem-Alexanderhof 5
2595 BE The Hague Netherlands
Postal Address
P.O. Box 95312
2509 CH The Hague Netherlands
Phone: +31 70 3140884
Fax: +31 70 3834827
E-mail: ifla@ifla.org
Website: www.ifla.org

INTERNATIONAL RESEARCH COLLECTIONS

IBBY Documentation Centre of Books for Disabled Young People
Director: Heidi Cortner Boiesen
Baerum Municipality
Haug School and Resource Centre
Haugtunveien 3
N-1304 Sandvika Norway
Phone: [int. +47] 67 16 40 00
Fax: [int. +47] 67 16 40 01
E-mail: heidicbo@online.no
Website: www.haug.skole.no
Website: www.ibby.org/index.php?id=271
   The Centre offers information, consultation, and documentation services for organizations, research workers, teachers, students, librarians, publishers, authors, illustrators, policy makers, and the media who work with young people with special needs.

International Library of Children's Literature (ILCL)
Zhejiang Normal University
Zhejiang (China)
Website: www.chchc.cn/ [Translation not available]
   Formally unveiled on May 25, 2007, ILCL is the only international and largest children's literature library on the Chinese mainland. ILCL serves mainly to facilitate children's literature study through a public lending system.

The International Library of Children's Literature
12-49 Ueno Park
Taito-ku Tokyo
110-0007 Japan
Phone: +81-3-3827-2053
Phone Guide: +81-3-3827-2069
Fax: +81-3-3827-2043
E-mail: webinfo@ndl.go.jp
Website: www.kodomo.go.jp/english/
   The ILCL provides internationally linked library services for children's literature and related materials published in Japan and in other countries.

International Institute for Children's Literature, Osaka (Japan)
Osaka Prefectural Central Library
1-2-1, Aramoto-kita, Higashi

Osaka-shi, 577-0011, JAPAN
Phone: +81-6-6876-8800
E-mail: kokusai@iiclo.or.jp
Website: www.iiclo.or.jp/f_english/index.html

Founded by Mr. Shin Torigoe in 1979. Makes available a research collection of Japanese children's books and books from other countries, provides reference services, sponsors lectures and events, and publishes an annual bulletin and newsletter.

International Youth Library (Internationale Jugendbibliothek München)
Schloss Blutenburg
D-81247 Munich, Germany
Phone: ++49 89 89 12 11- 0
Fax: ++49 89 811 75 53
E-mail: info@ijb.de
Website: www.ijb.de

The International Youth Library is the largest library for international children's and youth literature in the world. Ever since it was opened in 1949 by Jella Lepman, the ILY has been continuously expanded to an internationally recognized center for the world's children's and youth literature. The White Ravens collection resides here.

Osborne Collection of Early Children's Books
Toronto Public Library
4th Floor, Lillian H. Smith Branch
239 College Street
Toronto, ON M5T 1R5 Canada
Phone: 416-393-7753
Website(s): www.torontopubliclibrary.ca/osborne/
www.torontopubliclibrary.ca/books-video-music/specialized-collections/childrens-literature.jsp
Leslie McGrath, Curator

The Osborne Collection encompasses the development of English children's literature from the fourteenth century through the end of the Edwardian period (1910). Highlights include Florence Nightingale's childhood library, Queen Mary's children's books, and the Pettingell Collection of periodicals and penny dreadfuls.

Roehampton University
National Centre for Research in Children's Literature (NCRCL)
Erasmus House
Roehampton Lane
London
SW15 5PU

Phone: 020 8392 3000 (UK)

+44 20 8392 3000 (International)

Website: www.roehampton.ac.uk/researchcentres/ncrcl/

   Promoting critical debate and inquiry in the field of children's literature through excellence in teaching and research.

Seven Stories (Great Britain)

Ouseburn Valley

Newcastle upon Tyne

NE1 2PQ

Phone: 0845 271 0777 ext. 715.

E-mail: info@sevenstories.org.uk

Website: www.sevenstories.org.uk/

   Seven Stories' focus goes beyond the finished product to include all that goes into the making of a book—roughs, drafts, dummy books, correspondence, and other papers. The Seven Stories collection includes about thirty thousand books and original artwork and manuscripts by around eighty authors and illustrators, including Philip Pullman, Robert Westall, Edward Ardizzone, and Judith Ker.

Swiss Institute for Children's and Youth Media

Schweizerisches Institut für Kinder- und Jugendmedien SIKJM

Zeltweg 11

CH-8032 Zürich

Phone: +41 43 268 39 00

Fax: +41 43 268 39 09

E-mail: info@sikjm.ch

Website: www.euread.com/organisations/details/the_swiss_institute_for_
childrens_youth_and_media/

   The main activities of the Swiss Institute for Children's and Youth Media (SIKJM) are research and documentation in the field of children's and youth media and reading promotion.

University of British Columbia Library: Rare Books and Special Collections
Arkley Collection of Historical Children's Literature

UBC Library

1961 East Mall

Vancouver, B.C.

Canada V6T 1Z1

Phone: 604-822-6375

Fax: 604-822-3893
Katherine Kalsbeek, curator
E-mail: katherine.kalsbeek@ubc.ca
Website: www.library.ubc.ca/spcoll/

The collection contains British and North American children's books from the late eighteenth century to 1939. The collection is particularly strong in material by and about Lewis Carroll. Some unique items include Canadian "firsts," early editions of classics, and works of important illustrators.

RESEARCH COLLECTIONS: UNITED STATES

Alice M. Jordan (1870–1960) Collection
www.bpl.org/research/special/collections.htm#jordan

Foreign language material from eighty countries is represented.

American Antiquarian Society: A National Research Library of American History, Literature, & Culture through 1876
Worcester, Massachusetts
Laura E. Wasowicz, Curator of Children's Literature
Phone: 508-471-2146
E-mail: lwasowicz@mwa.org
Website: www.americanantiquarian.org/children.htm

Resource for studies in the fields of the history of childhood, child discipline, and the education of children; the history of reading; and the history of publishing, printing, and the graphic arts. Children's books, 1654–1900.

Boston Public Library in Copley Square
The Central Library comprises two buildings, the Johnson Building and the McKim Building
700 Boylston Street
Boston, MA 02116
Phone: (617) 859-2225

Burton Historical Collection
Rare Books Collection
Detroit Public Library
Main Library, 1st Floor
Detroit, MI
Phone: (313) 481-1401

Coordinator for Special Collections
Mark Bowden
E-mail: mbowden@detroitpubliclibrary.org
Website: www.detroit.lib.mi.us/burton/burton_index.htm

This collection houses over thirteen thousand volumes dating from the sixteenth through the twentieth centuries. Of note are the Kate Greenaway Collection, the Walter Crane Collection, Samuel Clemens Collection, and the Laura Ingalls Wilder Collection. There are also examples of early book formats for children: battledores, chapbooks, and hornbooks.

Children's Literature Collections and Special Collections
www.bpl.org/research/special/collections.htm

Drawings for Children's Books
www.bpl.org/research/special/collections.htm#drawings

A collection of original drawings for children's books by Arthur Rackham, Kate Greenaway, Robert McCloskey, C. W. Anderson, Judith Gwyn Brown, Barbara Cooney, Doris and George Hauman, Fritz Kredel, Elizabeth MacKinsty, Katherine Milhous, Henry C. Pitz, and others.

Free Library of Philadelphia Early American Children's Books Collection
Website: http://libwww.library.phila.gov/collections/collectionDetail.cfm?id=5

This historical collection ranges in date from 1682 through the second half of the nineteenth century and encompasses the full spectrum of books produced for children. A particular focus is children's books produced in the frontier settlements of the United States.

Free Library of Philadelphia
Illustrated Children's Books
1901 Vine Street
Philadelphia, PA 19103
Children's Department
Ground Floor
Phone: 215-686-5369
Website: http://libwww.library.phila.gov/collections/collectionDetail.cfm?id=4

Works illustrated by those listed in Bertha E. Mahony's Illustrators of Children's Books, 1744–1945, *and subsequent volumes form the foundation of this collection. Other illustrators are included based on their importance to the world of children's book illustration. In all, the collection contains more than thirty thousand books.*

Juvenile Collection
www.bpl.org/research/special/collections.htm#juvenile
Includes two "Donatus leaves" from the popular Latin schoolboy grammar originating in Holland in the middle of the fifteenth century.

Library of Congress
Young Readers Center
Thomas Jefferson Building
Room LJ G31 (ground floor)
10 First Street S.E.
Washington, DC 20540
Phone: (202) 707-1950
Website: www.read.gov/yrc/

The Morgan Library & Museum
Reading Room (Research Services)
Phone: (212) 590-0315
Fax: (212) 768-5615
E-mail: readingroom@themorgan.org
Website: www.themorgan.org/
Anna Lou Ashby, Andrew W. Mellon Curator of Printed Books
Research materials range from original manuscripts (Perrault, Saint Exupéry, de Brunhoff) to strong holdings in American, English, and European printed materials from the eighteenth to the early twentieth century. Includes printed games and the Arthur Houghton collection of Lewis Carroll.

Paul (1909–1996) and Ethel L. (1918–1997) Heins Collection
www.bpl.org/research/special/collections.htm#heins
This collection contains 4,500 children's books used by the former Horn Book Magazine *editors in their work as critics, teachers, and reviewers of children's literature.*

Rare Book and Special Collections Division
Children's Literature Center
101 Independence Avenue SE
Thomas Jefferson Building, LJ 129
Washington, DC 20540-4620
Phone: (202) 707-5535
Fax: (202) 707-4632
Website: www.loc.gov/rr/child/

The Center houses a reference and a showcase collection of illustrated children's books. Visitors and their school-age children are welcome to the Center to see the smallest children's book in the world and other rare and special items on display.

Sarah Ware Bassett (b. 1872) Library
www.bpl.org/research/special/collections.htm#bassett

UNIVERSITY-BASED COLLECTIONS

California State University
Arne Nixon Center for the Study of Children's Literature
5200 N. Barton Avenue
Henry Madden Library
3rd Floor South 3204
Fresno, CA 93740-8014
Phone: 559-278-8116
Website: www.arnenixoncenter.org/
Angelica Carpenter, Curator

This research center of children's and young adult literature has 38,000 books, periodicals, manuscripts, and illustrations dating from 1865 to current publications. Multicultural and foreign language books, especially Nordic and Finnish language books, reflecting Arne Nixon's heritage, are included.

Carthage College
Hedberg Library
2001 Alford Park Drive
Kenosha, WI 53140
Phone: 262-551-8500
E-mail: jstewig@carthage.edu
John Warren Stewig, Director
Website: www.carthage.edu/childrens-literature/

The Center for Children's Literature houses a collection of more than twenty-five thousand children's trade books.

Emporia State University
May Massee Collection
1200 Commercial Street
Emporia, KS 66801

William Allen White Library
Campus Box 4051
Phone: (620) 341-5207
Fax: (620) 341-6208
Website: www.emporia.edu/libsv/maymassee.htm
Heather A. Wade, University Archivist

The collection houses materials associated with the books published under May Massee's direction, allowing users to follow a book's creation from drafts and sketches to a finished product and even into foreign-language translation. It is possible to search the collection online.

Florida State University Libraries
The John Mackay Shaw Childhood in Poetry Collection
Special Collections
Tallahassee, FL
Website: www.fsu.edu/%7Especcoll/shaw.htm

The Shaw Childhood in Poetry Collection contains more than twenty-five thousand volumes primarily of English and American poetry from the mid-eighteenth through the early twentieth centuries. In addition to works by both major and minor poets, there are many illustrated editions and hundreds of gift books and juvenile periodicals.

Indiana University
Lilly Library's Collection of Children's Materials
1200 East Seventh Street
Bloomington, IN 47405-5500
Phone: 812-855-2452
Fax: 812-855-3143
E-mail: liblilly@indiana.edu
Website: www.indiana.edu/~liblilly/overview/lit_child.shtml

The emphasis of the collection is on English-language books of the eighteenth and nineteenth centuries, but it also includes a large number of twentieth-century books and representative works in French and German. There are Newbery and Marshall imprints and original art by children's book illustrators, including Kate Greenaway, Walter Crane, Randolph Caldecott, and Ernest Shepard.

Kansas State University Libraries
Richard L. D. & Marjorie J. Morse Department of Special Collections
506 Hale Library
Manhattan, KS 66506

E-mail: rcadams@ksu.edu
Website: www.lib.ksu.edu/depts/spec
Roger C. Adams, Associate Professor

The Morse Department of Special Collections includes Dr. Seuss ephemera and first editions, radical children's literature, Louisa May Alcott, the David J. Williams III L. Frank Baum Collection, and the David J. Williams III Science Fiction, Fantasy, & Horror Collection. Some international materials are available, but they are not a focus.

National Louis University
Center for Teaching through Children's Books
5202 Old Orchard Road, Suite 300
Skokie, IL 60077
Phone: 224-233-2288
E-mail: ctcb@nl.edu
Website: http://nl.edu/library/ctcb/ctcb.cfm
Junko Yokota, Gail Bush, Directors

The Center for Teaching through Children's Books is dedicated to excellence in teaching with quality literature for children and adolescents. It considers multicultural and international literature a core resource for learning about the world.

Princeton University Library
Cotsen Children's Library
1 Washington Road
Princeton, NJ 08544
Phone: (609) 258-1148
Fax: (609) 258-2324
E-mail: aimmel@princeton.edu
Website: www.princeton.edu/cotsen/
Andrea Immel, Curator

Major historical collection has rare illustrated children's books, manuscripts, original artwork, prints, and educational toys from the fifteenth century to the present in over thirty languages.

University of Arizona, College of Education
World of Words (WOW) International Collection of Children's and Adolescent Literature
1430 East Second Street
Tucson, AZ 85721
Phone/Fax: (520) 621-9340

E-mail: wow@email.arizona.edu
Website: http://wowlit.org/

Worlds of Words website has many useful resources for building bridges between cultures. These resources include multiple strategies for locating and evaluating culturally authentic international children's and adolescent literature as well as ways of engaging students with these books in classrooms and libraries.

University of California, Berkeley
Children's Literature Collection
Education and Psychology Library
2600 Tolman Hall #6000
Berkeley, CA 94720
Phone: 510-642-2475
Website: www.lib.berkeley.edu/EDP/children.html

The Children's Literature Collection of the UCB Education Psychology Library is a selective, academic collection with an emphasis on K–3 grades, primarily illustrated and picture books, some with no text at all.

University of Connecticut Libraries
Northeast Children's Literature Collection
Thomas J. Dodd Research Center
405 Babbidge Road, Unit 1205
Storrs, CT 06269-1205
Phone: 860-486-4500
Fax: 860-486-4521
Website: http://nclc.uconn.edu/
Terri J. Goldich, Curator

The collection acquires, preserves, and makes accessible works of historical and artistic significance in the field of children's literature. The thirty-six-thousand-item cataloged collection includes books, manuscripts, illustrations, correspondence, and artifacts of ninety authors and illustrators.

University of Florida
Baldwin Library of Historical Children's Literature
Gainesville, FL 32611
Phone: 352-392-3261
Rita Smith, Curator
Website for the Baldwin Library of Historical Children's Literature: http://web.uflib.ufl.edu/SPEC/baldwin/baldwin.html
Website for the Baldwin Digital Collection: http://ufdc.ufl.edu/?c=juv

The Baldwin Library contains more than ten thousand volumes published in Great Britain and the United States from the early 1700s through the 1990s. Its holdings of more than eight hundred early American imprints is the second largest such collection in the United States. A great strength of the collection is the many English and American editions of the same work. The Baldwin Digital Collection includes full versions of thousands of texts from the collection, and it's growing daily.

University of Illinois at Urbana-Champaign
School (S)-Collection
Education and Social Science Library
1408 W. Gregory Drive
Urbana, IL 61801
Phone: 217-333-2290
Website(s): www.library.illinois.edu/edx/index.html
www.library.illinois.edu/edx/s-about.htm

The School (S)-Collection consists of more than 100,000 cataloged volumes of primarily American and British children's and young adult literature in a total collection of over 140,000 volumes. Volumes date from 1800 to the present, and over three thousand new books are added annually.

Additional collections at the University of Illinois include:

- **The Center for Children's Books, University of Illinois**
  http://ccb.lis.illinois.edu/
- **Curriculum Collection**
  www.library.illinois.edu/edx/specialcollections/curriculum/index.html
- **Rare Book and Manuscript Library**
  www.library.uiuc.edu/rbx

University of Maryland
Gordon W. Prange Children's Book Collection
4200 Hornbake Library North
College Park, MD 20742
Phone: 301-405-9348
Fax: 301-314-2447
E-mail: prangebunko@umd.edu
Website: http://lib.umd.edu/prange/index.jsp
Eiko Sakaguchi, Curator

The Gordon W. Prange Collection contains more than eight thousand children's books published in Japan between 1945 and 1949 that were originally file copies of the Civil Censorship Detachment during the Allied Occupation of Japan. The collection is currently being digitized, and books are added to the Prange Digital Children's Book Collection, http://digital.lib.umd.edu/prange.jsp, *on a regular basis.*

University of Michigan
Children's Literature Collection

7th Floor, Hatcher Graduate Library
913 S. University Avenue
Ann Arbor, MI 48109-1190
Phone: 734-764-9377
Fax: 734-764-9368
E-mail: special.collections@umich.edu
Website: www.lib.umich.edu/spec-coll/

Core collection supplemented by specialized collections: Hubbard Imaginary Voyages Collection (3,500 titles, editions, translations, adaptations, and spin-offs of Robinson Crusoe *and* Gulliver's Travels*); Lee Walp Family Juvenile Book Collection (6,000+ titles of picture books as well as archives featuring correspondence and artworks); William A. Gosling Pop-up and Moveable Book Collection (2,700+ titles); Janice Dohm Collection (3,500+ titles emphasizing fairy tales and English works); Chalat Family Arthur Rackham Collection (first and limited editions); and G. A. Henty collection (400+ volumes).*

University of Minnesota
Kerlan Collection

Children's Literature Research Collections
Room 113, Elmer L. Andersen Library
222 21st Avenue South
Minneapolis, MN 55455
Phone: (612) 624-4576
E-Mail: clrc@umn.edu
Website: http://special.lib.umn.edu/clrc/kerlan/index.php
Karen Nelson Hoyle, Curator

The Kerlan Collection at the University of Minnesota is one of the world's great children's literature research collections. It presently contains more than 100,000 children's books as well as original manuscripts, artwork, galleys, and color proofs for more than twelve thousand children's books. The Collection includes books that are significant in the history of children's literature, award books, classics, and representative books from Great Britain, Australia, Denmark, Japan, the Netherlands, Germany, and others.

University of North Carolina at Chapel Hill
The Susan Steinfirst Picture Book Collection
Children's Collection of the School of Information and Library Science
216 Lenoir Drive
100 Manning Hall
Chapel Hill, NC 27599-3360
Phone: (919) 962-8366
Fax: (919) 962-8071
E-mail: info@ils.unc.edu
Website: http://sils.unc.edu/itrc/library/index.html
Rebecca B. Vargha, Librarian

The Susan Steinfirst Picture Book Collection is part of the twelve thousand volume juvenile collection located in the School of Information and Library Science. This collection is the only juvenile collection on the campus of the University of North Carolina at Chapel Hill and contains primarily award-winning and recommended titles, including picture books (2,700 volumes), fiction (5,600), graphic novels (300) and nonfiction works (3,000). One highlight is a noncirculating juvenile historical collection (400 volumes), with the majority of the materials published from 1839 through 1920.

University of Pittsburgh
The Elizabeth Nesbitt Room
Information Sciences Building, Room 305
Pittsburgh, PA
Phone: (412) 624-4710
Website: www.library.pitt.edu/libraries/is/nesbitt.html

The Elizabeth Nesbitt Room is located at the University of Pittsburgh and houses several special collections related to the history of children and their books and media. The volumes in this collection include more than twelve thousand books and magazine titles of interest dating from the 1600s through today.

University of South Carolina
Rare Books and Special Collections
Thomas Cooper Library
University of South Carolina
Columbia, SC
E-mail: makalaj@sc.edu
Website(s): www.sc.edu/library/spcoll/rarebook.html
www.sc.edu/library/spcoll/rarebooks_childrensLiterature.html
Jeffrey Makala, Assistant Special Collections Librarian

Rare Books and Special Collections at Thomas Cooper Library houses three major special collections of children's literature: The Augusta Baker Collection of African American Children's Literature and Folklore (1,500+ volumes) dating from the 1930s to the present; the Historical Children's Literature Collection (4,000+ volumes) dating from the mid-seventeenth to the mid-twentieth centuries; and the William Savage Historical Textbook Collection, of primarily American schoolbooks dating from the 1780s to the 1980s (5,000+ volumes).

University of Southern Mississippi
de Grummond Children's Literature Collection
Box 5148
Hattiesburg, MS 39406
Phone: (601) 266-4349
Website: www.lib.usm.edu/~degrum/
Ellen Ruffin, Curator

The de Grummond Children's Literature Collection is one of North America's leading research centers in the field of children's literature. The main focus is on American and British children's literature, historical and contemporary. The Collection holds the original manuscripts and illustrations of more than 1,200 authors and illustrators as well as 100,000+ published books dating from 1530 to the present.

University of Wisconsin, Madison
Cooperative Children's Book Center
4290 Helen C. White Hall
600 North Park Street
Madison, WI 53706
Phone: (608) 263-3720
Fax: (608) 262-4933
E-mail: ccbcinfo
Website: www.education.wisc.edu/ccbc/
Kathleen T. Horning, Director

An examination and research collection that focuses on twentieth-century American children's and young adult literature. CCBC also includes an extensive collection of multicultural literature published for children and teens in the twentieth century. Lists of outstanding international books, by age and continent, are included in the CCBC Bibliographies and Booklists: Global Reading: Selected Literature for Children and Teens Set in Other Countries.

www.education.wisc.edu/ccbc/books/detailListBooks.asp?idBookLists=280

DIGITAL COLLECTIONS

ALA-Association for Library Services to Children (ALSC) Special Collections in Children's Literature Wikiography

Website: http://wikis.ala.org/alsc/index.php/special_collections_in_children%27s_literature_wikiography

The objective of this wiki is to provide an easily accessible bibliography that identifies collections that are of use to scholarly researchers studying children and their literature. Members only.

International Children's Digital Library

University of Maryland
4105 Hornbake Building, South Wing
College Park, MD 20742
Phone: +1 800-997-ICDL in North America
Fax: +1 617-848-9600 outside North America
Website: http://en.childrenslibrary.org/

The ICDL Foundation's goal is to build a collection of books that represents outstanding historical and contemporary books from throughout the world. Ultimately, the Foundation aspires to have every culture and language represented so that every child can know and appreciate the riches of children's literature from the world community.

Project Gutenberg

Project Gutenberg is the place where you can download over 33,000 previously published books that are out of copyright in the United States. These books are downloaded as e-books for most formats.

Website: www.gutenberg.org

Rosetta Project

Children's Books Online
P.O. Box 808
Searsport, ME 04974
Website: www.childrensbooksonline.org/index.htm

The Rosetta Project is designed to be an online library for all the world's children, and we hope that people from around the world will join us in this effort.

CHAPTER THIRTEEN

Publishers

The North American Publishers listed here have an international focus or consistently include international titles on their publishing lists. A more comprehensive list of names and addresses of children's book publishers can be obtained from the Children's Book Council (www.cbcbooks.org). The addresses below are current at the time of publication but are subject to change. For updated information, consult the current edition of Books in Print or Literary Marketplace, available in most libraries, or visit the Children's Book Council website.

Barefoot Books
2067 Massachusetts Avenue
Cambridge, MA 02140
Phone: (617) 576-0660
Fax: (617) 576-0660
Website: www.barefoot-books.com
E-mail: online form
The U.S. counterpart of a British company, Barefoot Books brings together crafted children's books, CDs, games, puppets, puzzles, and gifts that celebrate enduring values and inspire creativity (from book and website).

Bloomsbury Publishing
175 Fifth Avenue
New York, NY 10010
Phone: (212) 982-2837
Fax: (212) 780-0115
Website: http://www.bloomsburykids.com
E-mail: info@bloomsburyusa.com

Bloomsbury Children's Books USA, a division of Bloomsbury USA, was launched in 2002 as a general-interest publisher of children's books for readers of all ages. In 2005 Bloomsbury acquired the adult and children's divisions of Walker and Company, which was founded over fifty years ago. For Walker Books for Young Readers, check out BloomsburyKids.com.

Boyds Mills Press
815 Church Street
Honesdale, PA 18431
Phone: (570) 253-1164, toll free 1-800-490-5111
Website: www.frontstreetbooks.com
Website: www.boydsmillspress.com
E-mail: contact@boydsmillspress.com

"We believe in and are committed to publishing and exposing young readers to the best literature available in other countries, cultures, and languages. We believe in new voices. Finally, we believe books should be beautiful to look at and to hold" (www.boydsmillspress.com/about-us, ¶ 8).

Candlewick Press
99 Dover Street
Somerville, MA 02144
Phone: (617) 661-0565
Fax: (617) 661-0565
Website: www.candlewick.com
E-mail: salesinfo@candlewick.com

Candlewick Press publishes outstanding children's books for readers of all ages. It is one of the largest independent publishing companies, not just in the United States, but in the world.

Charlesbridge Publishing
85 Main Street
Watertown, MA 02472
Phone: (800) 225-3214 or (617) 926-0329

Fax: (800) 926-5775
Website: www.charlesbridge.com
E-mail: books@charlesbridge.com

As a publisher of the Global Fund for Children books, Charlesbridge introduces the cultures of the world to children.

Chicken House
2 Palmer Street
Frome, Somerset
BA11 1D5
United Kingdom
Phone: +44 (0) 1373 454488
Fax: +44 (0) 1373 454499
Website: www.doublecluck.com
E-mail: chickenhouse@doublecluck.com

An independent children's book publishing company in the United Kingdom with an enthusiasm for developing new writers, artists, and ideas that have worldwide popularity making an impact on an international scale. Chicken House became part of the Scholastic group in 2005.

The Creative Company
P.O. Box 227, Mankato, MN 56002
Phone: (800) 445-6209
Fax: (507) 388-2746
Website: http://www.thecreativecompany.us/
E-mail: info@thecreativecompany.us

This division of Creative Education regularly publishes a number of high-quality international picture books, primarily from France and Germany.

David R. Godine, Publisher
9 Hamilton Place
Boston, MA 02108-4715
Phone: (617) 451-9600
Fax: (617) 350-0250
Website: www.godine.com
E-mail: info@godine.com

A small publishing house that offers original fiction and nonfiction of the highest rank, rediscovered masterworks, translations of outstanding world literature, poetry, art, photography, and beautifully designed books for children.

DK Publishing
375 Hudson Street
New York, NY 10014
Phone: (646) 674-4047
Website: www.dk.com

    DK, the U.S. sister company of Dorling Kindersley, England, specializes in beautifully photographed informational books in a variety of formats for all ages, many originating in England. DK also produces companion CD-ROMs and videos.

Egmont USA
443 Park Avenue South, Suite 806
New York, NY 10016
Phone: (212) 685-0102
Website: http://www.egmontusa.com/
E-mail: egmontusa@egmont.com

    Egmont USA is part of the Egmont Group, one of Scandinavia's leading media groups, with activities in more than thirty countries.

Farrar, Straus and Giroux
175 Fifth Avenue
New York, NY 10010
Phone: (212) 741-6900
Website: http://us.macmillan.com/FSGYoungReaders.aspx
E-mail: childrens.publicity@fsgbooks.com.

    As a result of an earlier translation and distribution agreement with the largest Swedish publisher of children's books, Rabén and Sjögren (R&S), Farrar, Straus and Giroux publishes a number of translated Swedish picture books every year. Farrar, Straus and Giroux also publishes translated fiction for young adults. Since becoming part of the Macmillan Group, R&S is no longer listed on FSG's website.

Front Street Books
    Front Street Books has been disbanded. Stephen Roxburgh, founder of Front Street, is now involved with namelos, a consortium of independent publishing professionals with experience in editing, design, art direction, subsidiary rights, sales, and marketing. In 2004 Front Street was acquired by Boyds Mills Press, where Roxburgh was publisher until September 2008.
    namelos website: http://services.namelos.com/index.html
    E-mail: info@namelos.com

Groundwood Books
110 Spadina Avenue, Suite 801
Toronto, ON, Canada M5V 2K4
Phone: (416) 363-4343, toll free (800) 788-3123
Fax: (416) 363-1017
Website: www.groundwoodbooks.com
E-mail: online form
   Groundwood, a Canadian company, also has a Latino imprint, Libros Tigrillo, dedicated to books from Spanish-speaking people living in this hemisphere.

Harry N. Abrams, Inc.
Abrams Books for Young Readers
115 West 18th Street, 6th Floor
New York, NY 10011
Phone: (212) 206-7715
Fax: (212) 519-1210
Website: www.abramsbooks.com
E-mail: abrams@abramsbooks.com
   Publisher of illustrated books on the subjects of art, architecture, photography, graphic design, interior design, comic arts and graphic novels, sports, and general interest.

Houghton Mifflin Harcourt Children's Book Group
Clarion Books
215 Park Avenue South
New York, NY 10003
Phone: (212) 420-5800
Fax: (212) 420-5850
Website: www.houghtonmifflinbooks.com/hmcochild/
Clarion website: www.houghtonmifflinbooks.com/clarion/
E-mail: online form
   The late Dorothy Briley, a tireless promoter of internationalism, brought many authors and illustrators of note to this list.

Kane/Miller Book Publishers
4901 Morena Boulevard, Suite 213
San Diego, CA 92117
Website: http://www.kanemiller.com
E-mail: info@kanemiller.com

This small press specializes in children's picture books from around the world, both in translation and from English-language countries.

Kids Can Press
Canada
25 Dockside Drive
Toronto ON
Canada M5A 0B5
Phone: (416) 479-7000
Fax: (416) 960-5437
United States
2250 Military Road
Tonawanda, NY 14150
Website: www.kidscanpress.com/us/

Lee & Low Books
95 Madison Avenue, Suite 1205
New York, NY 10016
Phone: (212) 779-4400
Fax: (212) 683-1894
Website: www.leeandlow.com/
E-mail: general@leeandlow.com

Lee & Low is an independent children's book publisher focusing on diversity. It is the company's mission to meet the need for stories that all children can identify with and enjoy.

Lerner Publishing Group
1251 Washington Avenue N
Minneapolis, MN 55401
Phone: (800) 328-4929
Fax: (800) 332-1132
Website: www.lernerbooks.com
E-mail: custserve@lernerbooks.com
Andersen Press USA
Website: www.lernerbooks.com/About-Lerner/Pages/Andersen-Press-USA.aspx

Distributed by Lerner Publishing Group, the Andersen Press USA imprint brings some of the most well-known and best-loved children's books that have been published in the United Kingdom to American readers.

Margaret K. McElderry Books, an imprint of Simon & Schuster
1230 Avenue of the Americas
New York, NY 10020
Phone: (212) 698-7200
Fax: (212) 698-2793
Website: www.simonandschuster.com
E-mail: online form
    Margaret K. McElderry, children's book publisher and editor, is recognized for her leadership in bringing international children's books to the United States.

Mondo Publishing
980 Avenue of the Americas
New York, NY 10018
Phone: (888) 88-MONDO
Fax: (888) 532-4492
Website: www.mondopub.com
E-mail: info@mondopub.com
    Mondo's eclectic list contains selections from Australia, Canada, and New Zealand as well as an excellent series of folktales from around the world.

NorthSouth Books
350 Seventh Avenue, Suite 1400
New York, NY 10001-5013
Phone: (212) 706-4545
Fax: (212) 268-5951
Website: http://northsouth.com
E-mail: info@northsouth.com
    NorthSouth Books is the English-language imprint of Nord-SüdVerlag, the Swiss children's books publisher. The company emphasizes high-quality multinational copublications featuring lesser-known authors and illustrators and regularly reissues older international titles.

Star Bright Books, Inc.
30-19 48th Avenue
Long Island City, NY 11101
Phone: (718) 784-9112
Fax: (718) 784-9012
Website: www.starbrightbooks.com
E-mail: info@starbrightbooks.com

This small press publishes a few original titles and other books from around the world.

Tundra Books of Northern New York

P.O. Box 1030
Plattsburgh, NY 12901
Tundra Books in Canada
75 Sherbourne Street, 5th Floor
Toronto, Ontario
M5A 2P9
Phone: (416) 598-4786, toll free 1-800-788-1074
Website: http://www.tundrabooks.com/
E-mail: Tundra@mcclelland.com

A Canadian-owned and managed company with a New York State address, Tundra specializes in French-English bilingual, Canadian, and Native American books for children and exceptional picture book art.

SMALL PRESSES THAT PUBLISH
MULTICULTURAL BOOKS FOR
CHILDREN AND YOUNG ADULTS

African Presses

Africa World Press

541 West Ingham Avenue, Suite B
Trenton, NJ 08607
Phone: (609) 695-3200
Website: www.africaworldpressbooks.com/servlet/StoreFront

Asian Presses

Asian American Curriculum Projects

(formerly JACP)
529 East Third Avenue
San Mateo, CA 94401
Phone: (800) 874-2242 or (650) 375-8286
Website: www.asianamericanbooks.com/

Asian American Curriculum Projects also distributes Asian and Asian American books from small and large presses.

Bess Press
3565 Harding Avenue
Honolulu, HI 96816
Phone: (808) 734-7159
Website: www.besspress.com/

China Books
360 Swift Avenue, Suite 48
South San Francisco, CA 94080
Phone: (800) 818-2017
Website: www.chinabooks.com/

Immedium
P.O. Box 31846
San Francisco, CA 94131
Phone: (415) 452-8546
Website: www.immedium.com/

Many Cultures Publishing
San Francisco Study Center
1095 Market Street, Suite 602
San Francisco, CA 94103
Phone: (888) 281-3757 or (415) 626-1650
Website: www.studycenter.org/

Master Communications
4480 Lake Forest Drive, Suite 302
Cincinnati, OH 45242-3726
Phone: (513) 563-3100, 1-800-765-5885
Website: www.master-comm.com/
    Distributes Asian and Asian American books and related products. Six different presses represented, including Asia for Kids.
    Website: www.afk.com/

Polychrome Publishing Corp.
4509 N. Francisco
Chicago, IL 60625-3808
Phone: (773) 478-4455
Website: www.polychromebooks.com/

Shen's Books
1547 Palos Verdes Mall #291
Walnut Creek, CA 94957
Phone: (800) 456-6660
Phone: (925) 262-8108
Toll-Free Fax: (888) 269-9092
Fax: (925) 415-6136
Website: www.shens.com/

Stone Bridge Press
P.O. Box 8208
Berkeley, CA 94707
Phone: (800) 947-7271
Website: www.stonebridge.com/default.asp
E-mail: sbpedit@stonebridge.com

Latino Presses

BOPO Bilingual Books
P.O. Box 6696
Columbia, MD 21045-6696
Website: www.bopobooks.com/index.htm
E-mail: publisher@bopobooks.com

Latin American Literary Review Press
P.O. Box 17660
Pittsburgh, PA 15235
Phone: (412) 824-7903
Fax: (412) 351-0770
Website: www.lalrp.org/index.htm
E-mail: editor@lalrp.org, lalrp.editor@gmail.com

Pinata Books/Arte Publico
University of Houston
452 Cullen Performance Hall
Houston, TX 77204
Phone: (800) 663-2783
Website: www.latinoteca.com/arte-publico-press/

OTHER SMALL PRESSES AND
MAINSTREAM PUBLISHERS COMMITTED TO
PUBLISHING MULTICULTURAL LITERATURE

Annick Press
15 Patricia Avenue
Toronto, Ontario
M2M 1H9 Canada
Phone: (416) 221-4802
Vancouver Office
119 West Pender Street, Suite 205
Vancouver, BC V6B 1S5
Website: www.annickpress.com/

Children's Book Press
965 Mission Street, Suite 425
San Francisco, CA 94103
Phone: (866) 935-2665 or (415) 543-2665
Website: www.childrensbookpress.org/

Enchanted Lion Books
20 Jay Street
Studio M-18
Brooklyn, NY 11231
Phone: (646) 785-9272
Website: www.enchantedlionbooks.com/index.html

Fifth House
Website: www.fifthhousepublishers.ca/
Fifth House is an imprint of Fitzhenry & Whiteside Ltd.
195 Allstate Parkway
Markham, Ontario
L3R 4T8 Canada
Website: www.fitzhenry.ca/fifthhouse.aspx

Frances Lincoln Publishers
4 Torriano Mews, Torriano Avenue
London NW5 2RZ
England

Phone: 020 7284 4009
Fax: 020 7485 0490
Website: www.franceslincoln.com/

Lollipop Power/Carolina Wren

120 Morris Street
Durham, NC 27701
Phone: (919) 560-2738
Website: carolinawrenpress.org/

Minedition—Michael Neugebauer Publishing

Website: www.minedition.com/
    The headquarters for Michael Neugebauer Publishing Ltd. is located in Hong Kong. The publishing headquarters for the German-speaking countries is located in North Germany with distribution through the Egmont Publishing Group in Cologne. Minedition France, established in 2007, is based in Paris, and Minedition rights and licenses are handled from the Zurich, Switzerland, office.

Open Hand Publishing

P.O. Box 20207
Greensboro, NC 27420
Phone: (336) 292-8585
Website: www.openhand.com/

Second Story Press

20 Maud Street, Suite 401
Toronto, Ontario
M5V 2M5 Canada
Phone: (416) 537-7850
Fax: (416) 537-0588
Website: http://secondstorypress.ca/
E-mail: info@secondstorypress.ca

CHAPTER FOURTEEN

Sources for Foreign-Language and Bilingual Books

The following distributors and publishers are sources for children's books in other languages, most often imported from other countries but in some cases written and published in the United States to serve distinct language communities. These sources can be useful in finding books that have not been published in the United States as well as in locating the original language edition of a book published in translation or other books by the same author or illustrator.

Since the last edition, online booksellers have flourished. It is now possible to go to any of Amazon's (for example) international websites and order books. If you know the title of the book you wish to locate, book resellers such as ABE Books (www.abebooks.com) can be a less expensive alternative. AbeBooks International has (virtual) locations in the United Kingdom, Germany, France, Italy, Spain, Australia, New Zealand, and Canada.

This list was originally compiled by the Children's Services Division of the San Francisco Public Library and is reproduced with the permission of Grace W. Ruth, Children's Materials Selection Specialist. It has been edited and updated for this edition.

Abril Armenian Bookstore & Publishing (Armenian)
415 E. Broadway, # 102
Glendale, CA 91205-1029
Phone: (818) 243-4112
Website: www.AbrilBooks.com

Arabic Book Outlet (Arabic)
P.O. Box 312
Don Mills, Ontario
M3C 2S7 Canada
Phone: (647) 273-3738
E-mail: sales@arabicbookoutlet.ca
Website: www.arabicbookoutlet.ca

Arkipelago Philippine Arts Books Crafts (Filipino/Tagalog)
1010 Mission Street @ the Bayanihan Community Center
San Francisco, CA 94103
Phone: (415) 553-8185
Fax: (415) 553-8176
E-mail: arkpelagobooks@yahoo.com
Website: www.arkipelagobooks.com

Atlantico Books (Portuguese)
2117 Broadway, Suite 6539
Astoria, New York 11106
USA
Phone: (718) 880-9024
Fax: (718) 726-5007
E-mail: form
Website: www.atlanticobooks.com/

Balkatha (Indic Languages)
13042 Essex Lane
Cerritos, CA 90703
Phone: (562) 865-4633
Fax: (562) 403-0432
Website: www.balkatha.com/
(Web is not operable)

Bilingual Publications Company (Spanish)
270 Lafayette Street, Suite 705
New York, NY 10012
Phone: (212) 431-3500
Fax: (212) 431-3567
Contact: Linda Goodman: Approval Plan
E-mail: lindagoodman@juno.com

Casalini Libri (Italian)
Via Benedetto da Maiano, 3
50014 Fiesole Fl
Italy
Phone: ++39 055 50 18 1
Fax: ++39 055 50 18 201
E-mail: info@casalini.it
Website: www.casalini.it

Children's Book Press (Chinese, Korean, Spanish, Tagalog, Vietnamese)
965 Mission Street, Suite 425
San Francisco, CA 94103
Phone: (866) 935-2665 or (415) 543-2665
Fax: (415) 543-3394
E-mail: sales@childrensbookpress.org
Website: www.childrensbookpress.org

Cypress Book (US) Company, Inc. (Chinese from People's Republic, using simplified characters)
360 Swift Avenue, Units #42 & #48
South San Francisco, CA 94080
Phone: (650) 872-7718
Fax: (650) 872-7808
E-mail: info@cypressbook.com
Website: www.cypressbook.com

Daya Imports & Exports, Inc. (Gujarati, Hindi, Tamil, Urdu—Books in Indic languages from India)
5863 Leslie Street, Suite 205
Toronto, Ontario, Canada M2H 1J8

Vancouver:
6540 East Hasting Street, Suite 334
Burnaby, BC, Canada V5B 4Z5
Phone: None Listed
E-mail: kris@daya.com
Website: www.daya.com/urdu.htm

Eastwind Books & Arts, Inc. (Chinese from People's Republic, Hong Kong)
1435A Stockton Street
San Francisco, CA 94133

Phone: (415) 772-5888
Fax: (415) 772-5885
E-mail: contact@eastwindbooks.com
Website: www.eastwindbooks.com/

923 Westwood Boulevard
Los Angeles, CA 90024
Phone: (310) 824-4888
Fax: (310) 824-4838
E-mail: info_la@eastwindbooks.com
Website: www.eastwindbooks.com

European Book Company (French, German)
925 Larkin Street
San Francisco, CA 94109
Phone: (877) 746-3666 or (415) 474-0626
Fax: (415) 474-0630
E-mail: info@european.com
Website: www.europeanbook.com/hyper.html

Far Eastern Books (Arabic, Bengali, Greek, Gujarati, Hindi, Punjabi, Tamil, Urdu, Vietnamese)
250 Cochrane Drive, Suite 14
Markham, Ontario
Canada L3R 8E5
Phone: (USA and Canada): (800) 291-8886
Phone: (905) 477-2900
Fax: (905) 479-2988
E-mail: books@fareasternbooks.com
Website: https://fareasternbooks.com/

Globus: A Slavic Bookstore (Russian)
332 Balboa Street
San Francisco, CA 94118
Phone/Fax: (415) 668-4723
E-mail: globusbook@sbcglobal.net
Website: www.globusbooks.com

Gozlan's Sefer Israel (Hebrew)
28 West 27th Street, Suite 402
New York, NY 10001

Phone: (212) 725-5890, toll free (outside NY) 1-877-733-7019
Fax: (212) 689-6534
E-mail: online form
Website: www.seferisrael.com

Harrassowitz KG, Otto (German)
Booksellers & Subscription Agents
65174 Wiesbaden
Germany
Phone: +49-(0)611-530 0
Fax: +49-(0)611-530 560
E-mail: service@harrassowitz
Website: www.harrassowitz.de

Hrvatska Knjiga
Croatian Bookshop (Croatian)
22 Spencer Street
Fairfield N.S.W. 2165
Australia
Phone: (02) 9728 6207
Fax: (02) 9755 0281
E-mail: Crobook@bigpond.com
Website: www.hrvatskaknjiga.com.au/

Irish Books & Media (Irish Gaelic)
1433 Franklin Avenue
Minneapolis, MN 55402
Phone: (612) 871-3505
Website: www.irishbook.com

Jeong-Eum-Sa Imports (Korean)
3921 Wilshire Boulevard, Suite 501
Los Angeles, CA 90010
Phone: (213) 738-9140
Fax: (213) 738-9141

Ketabsara Persian Bookstore & Publishers (Farsi)
Phone: (888) 538-2272
Website: www.ketabsara.com

Kinokuniya Bookstores of America Company, Ltd. (Japanese)
1581 Webster Street #285
San Francisco, CA 94115
Phone: (415) 567-7625
Fax: (415) 567-4109

525 South Weller Street
Seattle, WA 98104
Phone: (206) 587-2477
Websites: www.kinokuniya.com (in Japanese)
www.uwajimayavillage.com/marchants/kinokuniya/index.htm (in English, Seattle location)

Language Lizard
P.O. Box 421
Basking Ridge, NJ 07920
Phone: (888) 554-9273 or (732) 784-2889 (outside United States)
Fax: (908) 613-3639
E-mail: Info@languagelizard.com
Website: www.languagelizard.com/
   Dual-language books, CDs, and posters are offered in over forty languages, including both popular and less commonly taught languages. Albanian, Arabic, Bengali, Bulgarian, Chinese–Simplified, Chinese–Simplified+Pinyin, Chinese–Traditional, Croatian, Czech, English, Farsi, French, German, Greek, Gujarati, Haitian-Creole, Hebrew, Hindi, Hmong, Hungarian, Irish, Italian, Japanese, Khmer, Korean, Kurdish, Lithuanian, Malay, Malayalam, Multilingual, Nepali, Panjabi, Patois, Polish, Portuguese, Romanian, Russian, Scottish Gaelic, Serbo-Croatian, Shona, Slovakian, Somali, Spanish, Swahili, Tagalog, Tamil, Thai, Turkish, Twi, Urdu, Vietnamese, Welsh, Yoruba

Lectorum Publications, Inc.
A subsidiary of Scholastic, Inc.
E-mail: Lectorum@scholastic.com
Website: www.lectorum.com/eng/index.htm
   Other Scholastic subsidiaries can be located at www.scholastic.com/aboutscholastic/international/.

Mandarin Language & Cultural Center (Chinese from Taiwan)
1630 Oakland Road, Suite, A207
San Jose, CA 95131

Other campuses are available:
Phone: (408) 441-9114
Fax: (408) 441-9116
E-mail: micc@mandarinschool.org

Many Cultures Publishing/Study Center (multicultural curriculum materials, bilingual Southeast Asian folktales–Cambodian, Laotian, Tagalog, Vietnamese)
1095 Market Street, Suite 601
San Francisco, CA 94103
Phone: (415) 626-1650 / (888) 281-3757
Fax: (415) 626-7276
E-mail: heidi@studycenter.org
Website: www.studycenter.org

Multi-Cultural Books and Videos (Arabic, Chinese, French, Indic, Korean, Persian, Russian, Spanish, bilingual)
30007 John R Road
Madison Heights, MI 48071
USA
Phone: (248) 559-2676 / (800) 567-2220
Fax: (800) 208-0976

1594 Caille Avenue
Belle River, Ontario NOR 1AO
Canada
Phone: (519) 727-4155
Fax: (519) 727-4199, toll free (800) 567-2220
E-mail: service@multiculbv.com
Website: http://multiculturalbooksandvideos.com

Pacific Books & Art (Chinese, Hong Kong)
524 A Clement Street
San Francisco, CA 94118
Phone: (415) 751-2238

Pan Asian Publications, Inc. (Chinese, Hmong, Japanese, Khmer, Korean, Lao, Russian, Spanish, Vietnamese)
U.S. Office
29564 Union City Boulevard
Union City, CA 94587

Phone: (800) 909-8088
Fax: (510) 475-1489
E-mail: sales@panap.com
Website: www.panap.com

Polonia Bookstore, Inc. (Polish)
4738 N. Milwaukee Avenue
Chicago, IL 60630
Phone: (773) 481-6968 or (866) 210-6451
Fax: (773) 481-6972
E-mail: books@polonia.com
Website: www.polonia.com

Rainbow Book Company
500 East Main Street
Lake Zurich, IL 60047
Phone: (800) 255-0965 or (847) 726-9930
Fax: (847) 726-9935
E-mail: sales@rainbowbookcompany.com
Website: www.rainbowbookcompany.com
   Distributor and publisher representative. It appears the only non-English books are Spanish.

Shen's Books (Asian Languages)
1547 Palos Verdes Mall #291
Walnut Creek, CA 94597
Phone: (800) 456-6660 / (925) 262-8108
Fax: (888) 269-9092 / (925) 415-6136
E-mail: info@shens.com
Website: www.shens.com

Siam Book Center
5178 Hollywood Boulevard
Los Angeles, CA 90027
Phone: (323) 665-4236 / (323) 665-4237
Fax: (323) 665-0521
E-mail: service@siambookcenter.com
Website: www.siambookcenter.com

SinoAmerican Books & Arts (Chinese from Taiwan, books, videos)
751 Jackson Street
San Francisco, CA 94133
Phone: (415) 421-3345
Website: www.sinoamericanbooks.com/

South Pacific Books, Ltd. (Maori, Samoan, Tongan, etc.)
P.O. Box 3533
Auckland, New Zealand
Phone: (649) 838-3821
Fax: (649) 838-3822
E-mail: sales@southpacificbooks.co.nz
Website: www.southpacificbooks.co.nz

Szwede Slavic Books (Czech, Polish, Russian)
1629 Main Street
Redwood City, CA 94063
P.O. Box 1214
Palo Alto, CA 94302
Phone: (650) 780-0966 / (650) 851-0748
Fax: (650) 780-0967
E-mail: slavicbooks@szwedeslavicbooks.com

Tatak Pilipino (Tagalog)
1660 Hillhurst Avenue
Los Angeles, CA 90027
Phone: (323) 953-8660 / (800) 828-2577
Other stores: San Diego, CA; Daly City, CA
Fax: (323) 953-1878
E-mail: koleksyon@tatak.com
Website: www.koleksyon.com (click on PHILBOOKS)

Toan Thu Bookstore (Vietnamese, mail order, A-V materials also)
2115 Pedro Avenue
Milpitas, CA 95035
Phone: (408) 945-7959
Fax: (408) 942-660
Hours: By appointment
Payments accepted: Cash

The Toan Thu Bookstore is a home-based bookstore in Milpitas. It offers Vietnamese books, cassettes, CDs, and videos for customers. Toan Thu does not offer shipping or delivery services.

V & W Cultural Company (Chinese)
18850 Norwalk Boulevard
Artesia, CA 90701-5973
Phone: (562) 865-8882
Fax: (562) 865-5542
(Mail order only, good source for Chinese-speaking materials)

GERMAN (PRIMARILY—BUT SOME CARRY OTHER LANGUAGES) BOOKSTORES IN NORTH AMERICA

Bookstores in North America that sell German titles, listed alphabetically by store name. A web link is indicated for those stores that have one.

ABC Kinderladen
2411 NE 14th
Renton, WA 98056
Phone: (866) 357-5953
Website: www.abckinderladen.com

Adler's Foreign Books Inc.
915 Foster Street
Evanston, IL 60201-3199
Phone: (847) 864-0664
Fax: (847) 864-0804
Website: www.afb-adlers.com

Continental Book Company (Spanish, French, German, Italian, Latin, Arabic, Chinese)
6425 Washington Street, #7
Denver, CO 80229
Phone: (303) 289-1761
Fax: (800) 279-1764
Eastern Division
80-21 Myrtle Avenue
Glendale, NY 11385
Website: www.continentalbook.com

Der Buchwurm
Bücher und Musik direkt aus Deutschland
P.O. Box 1532
Lombard, IL 60148-8532, USA
Phone: (630) 495-3440
Fax: (630) 519-3139
E-mail: info@buchwurm.com
Website: www.buchwurm.com

Die Bücherstube
P.O. Box 700
Pelion, SC 29123
Phone: 1-888-BUECHER (283-2437) toll free in United States/Canada
Fax: (803) 894-5307
E-mail: info@buecherstube.com
Website: www.buecherstube.com/

Europa Bookstore
832 N. State Street
Chicago, IL 60610
Phone: (312) 335-9677
Fax: (312) 335-9679
Part of Schoenhof's Bookstores: www.schoenhofs.com/aboutus.asp
Review: www.centerstagechicago.com/literature/bookstores/europa-books.html

Europa at Princeton
The Princeton University Store
36 University Place
Princeton, NJ 08540
Phone: (609) 921-0633
Fax: (609) 924-9651
E-mail: inquire@pucc.princeton.edu

Galda + Leuchter International Booksellers
Galda Library Services, Inc.
520 University Avenue
Madison, WI 53703
Phone: +1 608-250-2344
Fax: +1 608-251-6510
E-mail: contact@galda.com
Website: www.galda.com/
Also located in Germany. See website.

Gerold Buch & Co.
Gerold and Schweitzer International
35-23 Utopia Parkway
Flushing, NY 11358
Phone: (718) 358-4741
Fax: (718) 358-3688
Will order any available Austrian or German book.

GLP German Language Publications, Inc.
153 South Dean Street
Englewood Cliffs, NJ 07631
Phone: (201) 871-1010
Fax: (201) 871-0870
E-mail: 75557.105@compuserve.com
Website: www.glpnews.com
NOTE: German newspaper/magazine subscriptions only. No books.

I.B.D. International Book Distributors
P.O. Box 467
214 Hudson Street
Kinderhook, NY 12106
Phone: (518) 758-1411
Fax: (518) 758-1959
E-mail: lankhof@aol.com

IBIS International Book Import Service, Inc.
161 Main Street
P.O. Box 8188
Lynchburg, TN 37352-8188
Phone: (800) 277-4247 (8:00 a.m. to 6:00 p.m. Central, Monday–Friday)
Fax: (931) 759-7555
E-mail: IBIS@IBIService.com
Web: www.ibiservice.com/

John Voigts, Bookseller
P.O. Box 9572
Springfield, IL 62791
Phone: (217) 698-1040
Fax: (217) 698-1040
E-mail: jvoigts@compuserve.com

New Mastodon Books and Fine Art
5820 Wilshire Boulevard #101
Los Angeles, CA 90036
Phone: (323) 525-1948
Fax: (323) 525-0266
E-mail: newmastodon@earthlink.net
Website: www.paperview.com

Schoenhof's Foreign Books
76 A Mount Auburn Street
Cambridge, MA 02138
Phone: (617) 547-8855
E-mail: weborders@schoenhofs.com
Website: www.schoenhofs.com

Author/Translator/Illustrator Index

Title Index

Subject Index

About the Editor

Linda M. Pavonetti is an associate professor of reading and language arts at Oakland University in Rochester, Michigan, where she teaches graduate and undergraduate courses in children's and young adult literature and qualitative research methodology. Dr. Pavonetti is vice president of the executive committee for the International Board on Books for Young People (IBBY) and past president of the United States Board on Books for Young People.

She edited *Children's Literature Remembered: Issues, Trends, and Favorite Books* (2004) and has contributed chapters to a number of other books in addition to articles in academic journals. She is a former co-editor of the *Michigan Reading Journal*, editor of the professional books column for the *Journal of Children's Literature*, and the children's book column editor for the *Michigan Reading Journal*.